Stalingrad

The Death of the German Sixth Army on the Volga, 1942-1943

Volume 1

The Bloody Fall

Colonel French L. MacLean
United States Army, (Ret.)

Schiffer

Schiffer Publishing Ltd

4880 Lower Valley Road • Atglen, PA 19310

Generalfeldmarschall Friedrich Paulus, Commander of the Sixth Army.

Book Design by John P. Cheek

Library of Congress Control Number: 2013937205

Printed in China.
ISBN: 978-0-7643-4343-8

We are interested in hearing from authors with book ideas on related topics.

Published by Schiffer Publishing Ltd.
4880 Lower Valley Road
Atglen, PA 19310
Phone: (610) 593-1777
FAX: (610) 593-2002
E-mail: Info@schifferbooks.com.
Visit our web site at: www.schifferbooks.com
Please write for a free catalog.
This book may be purchased from the publisher.
Please include $5.00 postage.
Try your bookstore first.

In Europe, Schiffer books are distributed by:
Bushwood Books
6 Marksbury Avenue
Kew Gardens
Surrey TW9 4JF
England
Phone: 44 (0) 20 8392-8585
FAX: 44 (0) 20 8392-9876
E-mail: Info@bushwoodbooks.co.uk.

CONTENTS

Dedication 4
Introduction 6
August, 1942 24
September, 1942 86
October, 1942 214

Dedication

This book is dedicated to the almost one million soldiers and civilians who died as a direct result of the battle at Stalingrad.

This work also is dedicated to the Stalingrad "Grognards," historians and general enthusiasts around the world. From the shores of Australia to the ambiance of Charleston, South Carolina, they study and dissect the battle fought on the Volga so many years ago with the detail and professionalism reminiscent of the old German Army General Staff. Here are just a few of the perhaps thousands of those who refight the battle in their sleep each night.

David M. Glantz and Jonathan M. House – The authors of the Stalingrad Trilogy have been superb authors for a number of years. Never has a 900-page volume seemed so light to hold when you are paging through the pre-eminent sources for the Soviet story of the battle. How they translated such a difficult language for thousands and thousands of pagers remains a marvel. Dave Glantz deserves a Pulitzer Prize for lifetime achievement in our understanding of the Soviet perspective of the Eastern Front.

Jason D. Mark – If the Glantz/House team is the Tchaikovsky of the Soviet side of the battle, then certainly Jason Mark is the Johann Sebastian Bach of the German recollections of the battle. Specializing in first-person accounts, with particular expertise concerning the 24th *Panzer* Division and the Battle for the Barrikady Gun Factory, Jason's accurate descriptions, photographs and maps supersede all adequate descriptions of excellence.

John Calvin – Some researchers view their efforts as a labor of love and this must be the case with John, who operates *World War II Aerial Photos and Maps* (john@wwii-photos-maps.com). The site has almost everything: digitized copies of maps, still photos, and aerial photographs copied primarily from originals in the U.S. National Archives, the U.S. Library of Congress, and donations from fellow researchers. It includes aerial photographs of Stalingrad and the 1942 *Lage Ost* situation maps. There are also collections of German and Russian daily reports and situation maps and many other types of maps. Many of the photos of German generals in this book came from the National Archives through John's web site, as did all of the ***Lage Ost*** maps.

Florian *Freiherr* von und zu Aufsess – This German author is somewhat hard to contact, but at any rate, he published ***Die Anlagenbände zu den Kriegstagebüchern der 6. Armee***, a collection of the Sixth Army's daily operation reports. This three-volume set is outstanding, although getting more difficult to find.

John Hill – war game designer extraordinaire, he invented the popular Avalon Hill ***Squad Leader*** and turned his attention to creating the ***Battle for Stalingrad***. It is a classic and remains popular even after the advent of computer games.

Manfred Kehrig – German historian, who wrote ***Stalingrad: Analyse und Dokumentation einer Schlacht***, a seminal work that showed that getting down to the details was imperative if one was to understand the complex Stalingrad campaign.

Congratulations to all, from a Stalingrad neophyte.

Finally, this book is dedicated to the millions and millions of family members who waited up to a decade after the battle to find out if their loved ones survived the fight and the ensuing incarceration in dreadful prisoner of war camps. About 95% of these parents, spouses, children, and siblings ultimately received the dismal communication that they would never see their son, grandson, husband, fiancé, brother, father or uncle again.

• • •

I would also like to take this opportunity to praise the best editor I have ever known, Bob Biondi. For those of you contemplating writing a book, after a while you begin to know in your sleep every page of the draft and what you are trying to say in every paragraph.

Your editor at the publisher does not know your book to the level that you do – they have not been "living" your book for the last two or three years, and sometimes longer.

Bob is different. For the last nine books before this one, he has been more like a partner. He can sense what I am trying to write. He knows where to put that exact photo to make all the difference in a chapter. Famed Prussian military theorist Carl Clausewitz termed this ability "Fingerspitzengefühl." This German term literally means "finger tips feeling." Clausewitz meant a military intuitive flair or instinct and great situational awareness. We would probably be more comfortable describing it as maintaining, with great accuracy in attention, to detail an ever-changing operational and tactical situation by maintaining a mental map of the battlefield.

I would submit that some editors in their own domain now demonstrate their own "Fingerspitzengefühl." For these talented people, "Fingerspitzengefühl" is cognitively related to the possession of multiple intelligences (not multiple personalities!), pertinent to visual and spatial data processing. Few people are born with it; most people are not. Bob Biondi has it.

Bob, you're simply the best.

Introduction

Nowhere in the laws of nature or the tenets of biology is a military army listed as a living organism. It is not a mammal, a fish, a bird or a plant. It has no traditional DNA to examine under powerful analytical devices. Scientists would tell us that since a military army is never alive it could never die. They are wrong.

A military army does have a unique "DNA" of a sort. We cannot find it under the magnification of the world's most powerful electron microscope, but rather in documents, known as, tables of organization. It is important at this moment to reinforce the point that we are not talking in this introduction or the entire book for that matter, about the German Army as a whole – although that would be an interesting parallel study. The military army that is the subject of this work is the level of a ground-combat field command that is higher than a corps and lower than an army group. In our particular case, we are discussing the German Sixth Army, a subordinate organization of Army Group B. The German Sixth Army in World War II was born on October 10, 1939; it died on February 2, 1943 at Stalingrad.

The "parents" of a military army are the armies that have come before it and the leadership that decides to create it. Military armies are different from one another; there are no identical twins, even though on paper they may look the same. Military armies of the same nation may even look the same in formation or from the air when in battle. That is because soldiers wear uniforms and often use the same equipment: the same tanks; the same trucks; the same artillery pieces and so forth.

Therefore, from a theoretical sense, military armies may look the same. They may have the same type and numbers of soldiers, weapons and equipment listed required them to accomplish their missions. This description is termed the authorized strength of a military army. Most military army commanders can only wish that their armies were at authorized strength; almost none are at that level, even at the moment that they are born. Some pieces of equipment and some soldiers are never assigned; those that are assigned are sometimes not operational due to maintenance problems in the case of things and due to illness, injury and death when it comes to personnel. In other cases, a military army does have the total number of – say artillery – pieces of equipment that it is authorized, but some of those pieces are substitutes of lesser capability. On paper this is just, for example, a simple number change – perhaps substituting a 3.7cm anti-tank gun for a 5cm anti-tank gun; for soldiers in an open field outside of Stalingrad against charging Soviet T-34/76 tanks that nomenclature modification will become lethal – for the anti-tank gunners rather than their intended targets. The same is true concerning personnel. If there are not enough majors or lieutenant colonels to staff all the positions in a military army that are authorized officers of these grades, the leadership may decide to substitute captains in their place. It may be a one-for-one exchange of bodies, but it is not an equal substitution of experience or talent.

An army exists in three domains: the physical, the cybernetic and the moral. The physical domain consists of all the pieces of equipment mentioned above – and many other thousands of types of tangible material – and all the soldiers that pull the triggers, drive the trucks, load the supplies, and emplace the communication lines and so forth. These soldiers can be quite many, often several hundred thousand. In zoological terms, the physical domain of an army consists of the legs, paws, bones, skin and teeth of an army. The legs of an army – the legs of the soldiers in that army and the horses and motor vehicles assigned – help the army move. Obviously, it is more complicated than that, made doubly so because the subordinate units of an army can move at different rates of speed. The artillery, assault guns (***Sturmgeschützen***) and tanks (***Panzer***) are an army's claws – they kill from a distance – immobilizing an enemy so the army can go around it, or paralyzing an enemy so the army can close with it for further mayhem. The infantry (nicknamed ***Landser***) and the combat engineers (***Pioniere***) are the army's teeth. They rip and slash from a very close range, with submachineguns, grenades, flamethrowers, bayonets and even entrenching tools swung as medieval battle-axes, seeking to tear the throat out of an

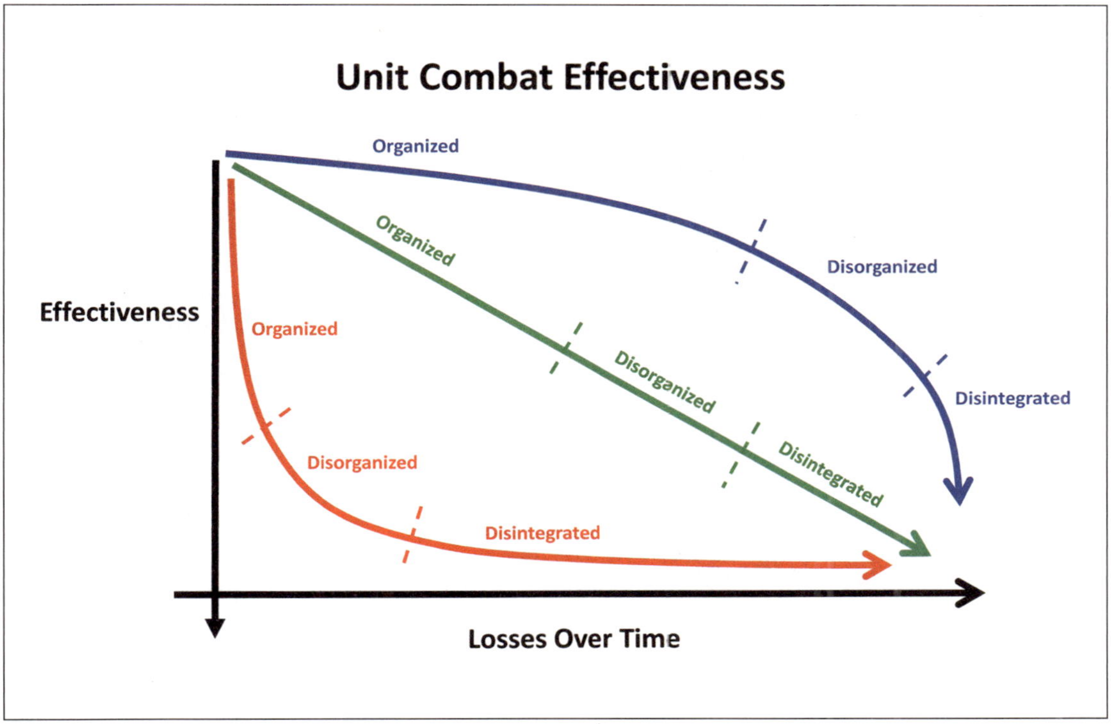

Unit Combat Effectiveness. The path shows how losses over time will affect a unit; the curve downwards for an elite unit is in blue, a regular unit in green and a "brittle" unit in red. A unit high in "Fighting Power" – and the Sixth Army began the war in this status – will remain organized, despite losses over time, longer than many other units. On the other hand, a "brittle" unit can sometimes experience just a few losses and disintegrate quickly.

enemy force. Above this frenzied beast are its friends, birds of prey that swoop from the sky to help blind, cripple and destroy those enemies that would kill it.

The cybernetic component of an army is its collective wisdom and its ability to communicate instructions to its hundreds of thousands of moving parts. Zoologically it is the brain, spinal cord and nervous system of an army (Non-commissioned officers are often termed the "backbone" of an army.) Although the wisdom of the army commander plays a role, the cybernetic domain is much larger than one person is, no matter how gifted that commander may be. Every leader in an army brings a level of inherent intelligence, military training and previous combat experience to the table. Multiplying those three factors together will give the officer or non-commissioned officer a mental ability to perform the mission, while protecting the lives and health of as many soldiers as possible.

That mental ability is constantly challenged, because while the nature of war (violence, fear, friction and uncertainty) is constant, the character and conduct of war is constantly evolving. Because what works today in battle may not work tomorrow, every leader in the army must constantly be "sniffing the wind," to determine how the characteristics of combat are changing and how that leader must adapt to those changes.

The cybernetic component does not consist solely of people. Radios, telephones and even the signal whistles of infantry and combat engineer sergeants play an important role in transmitting the intent of one to the ears of many. If the transmitter of a message is using a codebook, and the intended recipient of that message does not have that same codebook, the message will not be understood. In today's warfare, computers play a huge role in the cybernetic domain; at Stalingrad, exhausted staff officers completed that function, using stubby lead pencils writing on dirty sheets of notebook paper.

The last – but in many ways the most important – component of an army is the moral domain, the fighting spirit of an army. It is also the most difficult to measure; one often talks in terms of

Captured German generals outside hut, early February 1943. Note the gaunt appearance of the officers; these men are psychologically disoriented; their ability to fight has disintegrated. (Left, with mountain cap) is ***Generalleutnant*** Werner Sanne of the 100th ***Jäger*** Division; Sanne died on September 26, 1952 at the Soviet Krasnopol Prison Camp. (Left center, with fur hat) is ***Generalleutnant*** Arno von Lenski of the 24th ***Panzer*** Division; von Lenski was held in the Soviet Krasnogorsk Prison Camp, before being transferred to the Suzdal Prison Camp; he was released from captivity on August 17, 1949. (Center, standing highest with "crusher" hat) is ***Generaloberst*** Karl Strecker of the XI Corps; Strecker; he was released from captivity on October 9, 1955. (Right center, with overseas cap) is ***Generalmajor*** Erich Magnus of the 389th Infantry Division; he was released from captivity on October 6, 1955.

bravery, cohesion, discipline and initiative. Every soldier in an army, from the lowliest private to the commander, has a psychological outlook on how the fighting is progressing; that outlook is shaped by that soldier's own level of bravery, cohesion, discipline and initiative. Some zoologists might say that this is the heart of the army; others would couch it in terms of "fight or flight." That psychological viewpoint can change over weeks and months; in very stressful situations, it can also change in mere minutes. In almost every failed offensive, there comes a moment when – except for the extreme heroes – every attacking infantryman or combat engineer says quietly to himself: "I cannot, I will not, go any further." It happened at Culloden (when Clan MacLean and other Highlanders – armed with Scottish Claymore swords – charged the volleys of musket fire and the artillery grape shot of the British Army), at Waterloo, at Pickett's Charge at Gettysburg, at the Somme in World War I and at Stalingrad. Moreover, it will happen again in the future until every living, breathing soldier is replaced by a robot.

In modern history, at least from the time of Napoleon, armies have used decorations and medals to not only reward outstanding military bravery and achievement, but also to encourage similar behavior in other soldiers. In the German military, the highest series of decorations in World War II was that of the Knight's Cross, with follow-on awards of the Oak Leaves and subsequently the Swords. Higher still was the award of Diamonds to the Knight's Cross. All of the Knight's Cross series of awards required final approval by Adolf Hitler. During the Stalingrad campaign, some 120 Knight's Crosses, ten Oak Leaves and one Swords decoration were awarded to officers and men in the Sixth Army. It is hard to measure the effect on morale of these various decorations. Given the degree in society to which these decorations were esteemed, it probably was of some value, but in the hell of Stalingrad, medals only go so far.

Historian Martin van Creveld, in his seminal work, ***Fighting Power: German and U.S. Army Performance, 1939-1945***, combined the

Captured German generals in a snowy field, early February 1943. (Left, with peaked cap and monocle, facing right) is ***Generalleutnant*** Carl Rodenburg of the 76th Infantry Division; he was released from captivity on January 10, 1955. (Center left, with "crusher" hat, facing left) is ***Generalmajor*** Martin Lattmann of the 14th ***Panzer*** Division; he was released from captivity in 1948. (Center, in mountain cap) is ***Generalleutnant*** Werner Sanne of the 100th ***Jäger*** Division. (Right, with crusher hat, facing left) is ***Generaloberst*** Karl Strecker of the XI Corps. Many German generals, captured at Stalingrad, later agreed to assist the Soviets by renouncing the National Socialist régime in Germany.

cybernetic and moral components in World War II in this manner:

> "The mental, intellectual and organizational foundations; its manifestations, in one combination or another, are discipline and cohesion, morale and initiative, courage and toughness, the willingness to fight and the readiness, if necessary, to die."

Van Creveld defined this combination as "Fighting Power" – the sum total of the mental qualities that make armies fight. This study has specifically added "military training" and "previous combat experience" to van Creveld's definition (although van Creveld talked in detail about both later in his study.) The professor, who was generally contemplating the German Army as a whole, advanced his theory by postulating that an army's worth as a military instrument was equal to the quality and quantity of its equipment multiplied by its "Fighting Power." In addition, he illustrated in a counter-intuitive sense that armies that were strong and well equipped sometimes disintegrated at the first shock of combat.

Despite the violence of modern combat, most armies do not really die. In a victorious war, an army ends its days remaining on the nation's ground combat table of organization, often in a reduced size. When a victorious army does inactivate, it does so with pomp and ceremony as its colors are cased one final time and for the next several decades, old men meet annually to discuss the days of their youth in that army, often with much gaiety and exaggeration. In final defeat, most armies disband – abandoning their equipment, the soldiers then drift home, dispose of their uniforms and attempt to resume their civilian life of family and work. While the title of army may be gone, most of the officers and men of that army survive. Sometimes the old men of these defeated armies also meet from time to time, but theirs is a more somber gathering, mostly to remember fallen comrades. Over the years, these old men then close their gatherings with a song, be that "Dixie" or "Ich hatt' einen Kameraden."

Most defeated armies have an avenue of escape, where the enemy may overrun and destroy some subordinate units, but the bulk of the army survives to fight another day. However, when a defeated army has no means of rescue or retreat, the result can be a disaster. Moreover, when the victorious enemy is an ideological or racial opponent, the outcome can become sickeningly horrible.

A military army dies in three arenas: the physical domain, the cybernetic domain and the moral domain. The problem is – how do we measure that demise? In the physical domain, it is sometimes possible to start with a known numerical strength of an army in personnel and equipment and subtract combat losses, as they occur. If a subordinate unit is authorized ten tanks and it loses two, it must be at 80% strength. Every intelligence officer in every army knows how to "do the math." However, the problem is that not all equipment losses are catastrophic kills; many combat vehicles can be recovered and repaired – perhaps not to their original capability, but at least to be able to shoot, move and communicate. Not every soldier

Grave of Generalfeldmarschall Friedrich Paulus. Grave is located in Section 9 at the Baden-Baden city cemetery. After he was released from Soviet captivity in 1953, Paulus served as the civilian chief of the East German Military History Research Institute, but he was never allowed to return home.

shot will die. While some are seriously wounded and evacuated – never to fight again – others are treated and return to their units in weeks or months, or even in hours for lesser wounds ("walking wounded".) Replacements often move to the front from the homeland to substitute for those killed or seriously wounded. Even with these caveats, measuring the decline in manpower and equipment can be done in accurate terms.

This brings us to a discussion of the end of an army, in this case the German Sixth Army at Stalingrad in 1942/1943. We can use aggregate German Army casualty figures in assessing the wounded of the Sixth Army. According to the German Army Medical Service, at about the time of Stalingrad – throughout the entire German field force – of every 100 casualties, 24% were killed in action, while 76% were wounded in action (30% seriously wounded and 46% lightly wounded.) Massive direct hits (***Volltreffer***) on a soldier accounted for 15.23% of those killed in action, but just 0.45% of those seriously wounded and 0.17% of those; in other words, not much could be done for the recipient. Head (***Kopf***) wounds accounted for 42.61% of those killed in action, 16.66% of those seriously wounded and 16.49% of those lightly wounded in action. Wounds to the chest (***Brust***) comprised 22.11% of those killed in action, 11.28% of those seriously wounded in action and 3% of those lightly wounded in action. Stomach and lower abdomen (***Bauch***) wounds produced 7.95% of those killed, 7.69% of those seriously wounded and 0.79% of those lightly wounded. Back (***Rücken***) wounds accounted for 4.11% of the killed in action, 10.45% of the seriously wounded in action and 9.06% of the lightly wounded in action. Throat (***Hals***) wounds weighed in at 3.36% of the killed in action, 2.92% of the seriously wounded in action and 2.82% of the lightly wounded in action. Leg (***Beine***) wounds led to 3.04% killed in action (such as severance of a femoral artery), 22.53% seriously wounded in action (damage of bone, nerves or tendons) and 29.90% lightly wounded in action (flesh wounds). Arm (***Arme***) wounds caused only 0.64% of those killed in action, 22.53% severely wounded in action and 37.77% lightly wounded in action.

A German Army study in July 1942, just before the Stalingrad campaign began, showed that of those wounds examined by medics, the most frequent were: lower leg (***Unterschenkel***) at 28.3%, lower arm (***Unterarm***) at 16.5%, upper leg (***Oberschenkel***)

Gravestone of the Paulus family. Paulus died in Dresden, East Germany on February 1, 1957 a year after developing motor neuron disease. His wife had died in 1949. His son, ***Hauptmann*** Friedrich Paulus, died at Ponte Rotto, Italy on February 29, 1944.

at 10.1% and face (***Gesicht***) with 8%. Other studies showed that enemy shrapnel of all types (artillery, tank fire, mortar, grenade, rocket and bomb) produced 58.7% of the wounds to German soldiers, while infantry fire (rifle, sub-machinegun and machinegun) caused 35.7% of the wounds.

Illness and disease played a role as well. Jaundice (Hepatitis A) was rampant among Sixth Army forces at Stalingrad; tuberculosis appeared as well. After several months in deplorable conditions, epidemic typhus reared its lethal ugly head. Aggregate German field force figures for 1942 – 1943, included 1,187,498 wounded and 3,103,199 sick. This indicates that for every wounded casualty caused by enemy action, there were 2.61 times as many who suffered from illness and disease. Jaundice could lead to sepsis; early in the campaign, patients with severe jaundice went back to Germany, but this proved almost impossible after the Soviet encirclement in November 1942. Typhus could – and did – kill; it would be at its worst in the prisoner of war camps. The bacterium that causes the disease, found on lice, infested a vast majority of German soldiers, if their letters home are any indication.

The Sixth Army daily reports summarized frostbite injuries, but only Grade 2 and Grade 3, not Grade 1. Any level of frostbite would have reduced the combat efficiency of the soldier, but we have nothing to measure that for German troops during the campaign. We do have aggregate German Army statistics that show that during the winter of 1942 – 1943 there were 25,969 frostbite casualties. Of these, 68% were Grade 1, 17% were Grade 2 and 15% were Grade 3. The mean winter temperature at Stalingrad was 17.9° F. There would be no respite from frostbite that year. Added to the misery was a lack of proper winter clothing. For example, through late October 1942, only 57% of the soldiers had heavy winter overcoats. Winter uniforms finally reached the rear of the army group by November 21, 1942, but much of the shipment had not reached the front when snow first fell. Soldiers could get over Grade 1 pain, but Grade 2 caused severe blisters, while Grade 3 detroyed blood vessels.

Those yardsticks can measure the deterioration in the physical domain; the decline in the cybernetic domain is more difficult to measure. Radios and communication's equipment were certainly lost or irreparable during the campaign, but effective command is much more than that. We can begin by assuming that as losses to combat leaders mounted in Stalingrad, many of the replacements for these veteran officers and non-commissioned officers would have possessed less combat experience. Major Generals (***Generalleutnant***) led divisions at the beginning of the campaign, while later, as losses mounted, brigadier generals (***Generalmajor***) and even colonels (***Oberst***) commanded the same units. In the case of the ***Luftwaffe***'s 9th ***Flak*** Division, the final commander, days before the fall of the pocket, was a lieutenant colonel!

The decline in the cybernetic arena is better measured in three terms describing the efficiency of a military unit: organized, disorganized, and disintegrated. At the start of a campaign, an army – and the Sixth Army was no exception – is in an organized state. Commanders can quickly formulate battle plans; staffs swiftly and accurately transmit those plans to subordinate units, which conduct limited rehearsals to practice the more-intricate schemes of maneuver. Because the German Army operated under a system of mission-oriented orders, German units were able to respond quickly to changing situations. Mission-oriented orders (***Auftragstaktik***) expressed the will (intent) of the commander in a clear way. The object of the mission, the course of action, mission constraints (such as limited time) were to be clear and definite without restricting the freedom of action of subordinates more than necessary, so they could use their own initiative and knowledge of the local situation to get the task done. Most of the restraints that were imposed occurred only where they were essential for coordination with other commands (So, for example, a unit's flank would not be hanging open because the adjacent unit took all his forces somewhere else.) The German term for this degree of operational maneuver was ***Bewegungskrieg*** (Movement War) and when successful, it resulted in tens of thousands of enemy prisoners of war and hundreds of miles of seized territory.

However, as losses mount over time, effectiveness of an army goes down and starts to drop towards disorganization. Units are unable to accomplish their missions in a timely manner. Exhaustion, injury and illness begin to rob decision-makers of their ability to make quick, correct decisions. Maneuvers start to take longer. Staff officers start to submit routine reports late to higher headquarters; some reports never arrive. All these symptoms lead to higher casualties that speed up the disorganization into a spiral. In the chart at the beginning of this section, this path shows the curve downwards for an elite unit in blue, a regular unit in green and a "brittle" unit in red.

A unit high in "Fighting Power" – and the Sixth Army began the war in this status – will remain organized, despite losses over time, longer than many other units. On the other hand, a "brittle" unit can sometimes experience just a few losses and collapse rather quickly.

However, it gets worse. At some point, the disorganization leads into disintegration. Subordinates begin to disobey orders; units retreat under pressure, despite orders to the contrary. More and more soldiers become "missing in action." When operations are going well, missing in action often means that a soldier's body could not be found after death; when a unit is disintegrating, missing in action also indicates that more and more soldiers are surrendering to the enemy. Events showing disintegration are shown in **Bold Red** in this study. An army that can no longer feed or provide medical support to its own wounded is in the disintegration phase of its existence.

Problems with food and medicine did not come as a surprise to German Army logisticians. The German Sixth Army at Stalingrad started from a position of logistical disadvantage. No supply or troop train ever travelled directly from Germany to Stalingrad for the simple reason that it was impossible to do so. In the 19th century, Imperial Russian railway engineers chose a gauge (the distance between the two steel rails) broader than standard gauge used throughout Europe. Because of this break-of-gauge, trains and rolling stock could not travel from the Polish border to the east and freight and passengers had to be trans-loaded to Russian trains – a time-consuming process, fraught with loss, breakage and theft. Aware of this potential problem, the German Army formed railroad engineer units that slowly converted Russian-gauge rail to European standard. However, by mid-October 1942 this conversion had not reached Stalingrad. The two closest points to Stalingrad that would support European-gauge traffic were the Tinguta Rail Station, about 20 miles south of Stalingrad and the Tschir Rail Station, south of Kalach and 40 miles to the west of Stalingrad. From these two end-points, cargo had to be trans-loaded to a Russian-gauge train or hauled by motorized trucks or horse-drawn transport. In the case of replacement soldiers, they often walked to the city from these two terminals. Transferring goods from one train to another was a huge task. Every month, 104 supply trains arrived in the army group area, along with 60,000 farm animals that would be consumed as food.

The final area in which an army dies is the moral domain. In many respects, this parallels a decline in the cybernetic domain. Morale starts to decline. Instances of senior officers becoming intoxicated on duty or even committing suicide increases. Courts-martial increase, as more and more soldiers disobey orders. In the last week of the battle, German authorities inside the Stalingrad encirclement, for example, issued and carried out 364 death sentences for reported acts of cowardice or disobedience. In this study, personal letters from soldiers of the Sixth Army to their loved ones at home have been examined for indicators of morale. Without looking at the envelope, one can read the letter and accurately determine when the letter was written. Contents of letters invariably changed during the first third of the Stalingrad campaign (when the Sixth Army was ascendant), the middle third of the fighting (when the issue was in doubt) or the final third of the campaign, as the end of the army approached closer every day.

Finally an army dies. The dead and dying remain on the battlefield to rot, while the survivors are herded to prisoner of war camps to face an uncertain future. For the survivors of the Sixth Army, this meant up to twelve years' incarceration and less than a five percent chance of ever returning home. A post-battle chapter will examine these camps and in one of the appendices, the reader will find a historical certificate of death, where we will determine the strategic, operational and tactical causes of this death.

† † †

It may seem that the above discussion of wounds and frostbite may seem to be too detailed, but this study had to resort to great fidelity due to several conclusions that became apparent after a two-year preparation and research process. There are two stunning inferences that one can make in processing campaign situational information concerning the Sixth Army at Stalingrad. First, the units in the Sixth Army, based on the various morning and other reports found in the War Diaries (***Kriegstagebuch***) of the Sixth Army were frequently late in reporting combat and casualty information to the army headquarters. In addition, in many instances, they did not submit reports at all over periods of several days. This study, based on the frequency of these reporting failures, has concluded that on any given day the commander of the Sixth Army, Friedrich Paulus, did not know exactly how many casualties his command had suffered. To be sure, he knew of the magnitude of the losses, but concerning the details, he was let down by his subordinates in the reporting arena. The effect of this situation on this study is that differing casualty figures for the same unit often had to be weighed and reconciled and the best "estimate" presented in this work.

The second astonishing conclusion that this study made was concerning unit locations: not all unit maps, Sixth Army maps, ***Lage Ost*** German Army High Command maps and post-war unit history maps were consistent in their depiction of Sixth Army division locations on each day. As with casualty figures, the study was forced to evaluate the discrepancies, generally selecting period information from primary sources instead of post-war interpretations. While it can be expected that in the severe confusion of fighting inside the destroyed ruins of the city of Stalingrad mistakes would occur, often the exact dates of when divisions on the flanks of the Sixth Army were relieved of their defensive sector and began moving toward Stalingrad varied. Perhaps the largest discrepancy concerned the 76th Infantry Division. Many post-war general studies of the battle indicate that this unit fought inside the city of Stalingrad as a complete division, but wartime maps show it never came near the city, except perhaps for a few disorganized remnants that fled into the city confines in the final two or three days, after all organized defense had evaporated. One is left with the question of how detailed a picture of unit locations Friedrich Paulus had of his command on many days.

† † †

The format of the study is that of a day-by-day presentation. Light data (moon, sunrise and sunset) and weather data are presented first. Various subordinate corps are listed in numerical order, with the divisions listed under each corps. The German Army frequently changed task organization, so the reader should not note with alarm that a division is assigned to one corps on one day, a second corps for the next couple of days and even a third corps within the same week. The study has attempted to describe what each division was doing, where it was located and how many losses it suffered for the day. Only a few subordinate units (regiments, battalions and detachments) are mentioned: this is an operational-level study, not a tactical. The strategic level of war is generally thought of as army groups and higher-level commands; armies and corps comprise the operational level of war, divisions and below are the tactical level of war. There are numerous tactical-level books about Stalingrad and this author felt no desire to compete against them. The study also includes portions of the Fourth ***Panzer*** Army that fought very close to Stalingrad – and many of these units were later reassigned to the Sixth Army. The decision, of which subordinate Fourth ***Panzer*** Army units to include, was purely subjective and consisted primarily of the IV Corps and the XXXXVIII ***Panzer*** Corps..

Left at this point, this study might have been too antiseptic, valuable for hard-core Stalingrad researchers and "Grognards," but not interesting enough for other, less detail-driven readers. To present a human-interest side, I decided to include for as many days possible a remembrance/death card (***Sterbebild***) for a soldier who died in the Sixth Army during the Stalingrad campaign. Josef Stalin, for whom the city was named, reportedly said during the war, "The death of one man is a tragedy; the death of millions is a statistic." While the exact origin of the quotation has been called into serious doubt, its validity remains true; reading the personal details of each of the soldiers listed on the death cards drives home the point that the death of the Sixth Army was a crushing blow throughout Germany in hundreds of thousands of homes. The study includes many letters home from soldiers in the 71st Infantry Division, 79th Infantry Division, 94th Infantry Division, 100th ***Jäger*** Division and 371st Infantry Division. This cross-section of the Sixth Army reflects how the individual soldier survived in the midst of lice, poor rations, an implacable enemy and a hopelessly cold winter.

While the end date of the campaign – February 2, 1943 – is obvious, a start date proved more elusive to determine. Several could have been selected. ***Case Blue***, the attack east toward Stalingrad and the Caucasus began June 28, 1942. August 23, 1942 marked the date that the 16th ***Panzer*** Division of the Sixth Army dashed to the Volga River just north of Stalingrad; either date could have been logical. This study selected August 15, 1942 – the date that Sixth Army units reached the portion of the Don River north of Kalach. This segment of the Don River was the final natural barrier west of Stalingrad. Breaching that, it would be only a matter of time until German forces reached the Volga. What they did after they reached the river was a different story. To the Sixth Army it was one more river to conquer. What Paulus and his generals did not realize was that the Volga River was horribly mis-named. As events would prove, a more-appropriate moniker would have been "Phlegethon" – the name of the river of blood that boils men's souls, found in the Seventh Circle of Hell in ***Dante's Inferno***.

† † †

As to the city of Stalingrad, it was much more than another large industrial Russian city. Founded in 1589, Stalingrad was initially named Tsaritsyn – The City of the Czar. It was not until 1925 until it became the namesake of Joseph Stalin. Established as a frontier post to defend the southern Russian border, Tsaritsyn's location at the confluence of the north-to-south flowing Volga River and the smaller Tsaritsa River – that flowed west to east at the bottom of steep embankments – led to a transition as a trading settlement. Life remained low-key until about 1800. The town's population then was only 3,000 but that would increase to almost 85,000 a century later. Russian engineers constructed the first railroad into the city in 1862. The city began to blossom. Tsaritsyn acquired a theater in 1872. The year 1913 was a banner one; engineers built the first street car line and installed electric lights in the city's center. During the Russian Civil War, heavy fighting occurred at the city as the White Army, opponents of the Communists (Red Army) conducted several assaults on the city. Joseph Stalin played a key role in the Red defenses in those early days of the revolution, which resulted in the name change on April 10, 1925. By 1939, the population had swelled to 446,000.

Built on the west bank of the Volga, by 1939 the city had formed into a long, but relatively narrow, urban sprawl from the Mokraya Mechetka River in the north to Krasnoarmeyskaya in the south – a third of a mile to three miles wide, by almost 40 miles long. The western bank of the Volga was not a gradual sandy shoreline but a rocky, steep escarpment that was almost impassable to vehicles.

The parallel Volga River had a width at Stalingrad of two-thirds to one and one-quarter miles; its depth was 16 to 78 feet. The largest river in Russia, and for that matter all of Europe in terms of length, the Volga carried large amounts of water traffic from the industrial areas (moved to the Ural Mountains after the German invasion) to the oil fields by the Caspian Sea. As a transportation center, Stalingrad saw the movement of 30,000,000 tons of goods per year, including almost 9,000,000 tons of oil. There were no bridges across the Volga at or near Stalingrad. However, for German operational planners, Stalingrad was not so much a city as a potential long, fortified bridgehead on the western side of the Volga River, from which the enemy could launch an attack into the flank of any German force moving south, such as Army Group A in its drive to the Caucuses and Soviet oilfields.

Dividing the city into sectors were several rivers flowing west to east into the Volga. South of the village of Rynok was the river in the steep-sided ravine of the Skuchaya Mechetka. Between Spartakovka and the Dzerzhinsky Tractor Factory flowed the Mokraya Mechetka River. Much further to the south, the Tsaritsa River emptied into the Volga roughly midway between the two rail stations. In the south, ran the El'shanka River, through the southern suburb of the same name.

Stalingrad was a city of factories and some of the heaviest fighting in the campaign took place at these locations. In the north of the city was the huge Dzerzhinsky Tractor Factory – named after Felix Edmundovich Dzerzhinsky, a Communist revolutionary and first director of the Bolshevik secret police, the ***Cheka***. Prior to the war, this industrial giant of some 210,200 square meters, also known as the Stalingrad Tractor Factory, produced 25% of all large farm tractors in the Soviet Union, making it one of the three largest in the country. Each month, the plant's 20,000 workers produced 3,200 tractors. Plowshares had given way to swords, however, and by the beginning of 1942, Dzerzhinsky was producing 250 T-34/76 tanks per month, more than twice the number of tanks authorized for an entire German ***panzer*** division during the period of the campaign. The major structures included Hall 1 (Iron Foundry), Hall 2 (Assembly), Hall 3 (Repair), Hall 4 (Laboratory and Design Engineering), Hall 5 (Motor Test), Hall 6 (Fuel Storage), Hall 7 (Electrical Engineering), Hall 8 (Administration) and Hall 9 (Workshops). Eminent historian Robert M. Citino has liked the Dzerzhinsky Tractor Factory to the massive Ford River Rouge Complex in Dearborn, Michigan.

About 2,500 meters to the south of Dzerzhinsky was the Barrikady Gun Factory, a steelworks that – now that war had engulfed the motherland – was producing 100 medium and heavy-caliber artillery pieces. Overall production of steel in the Soviet Union was eight to nine million tons per year; Stalingrad steel mills produced one million tons of that total. There were at least 51 buildings in the Barrikady Gun Factory, which totaled 173,100 square meters in area. The major structures included Hall 1 (Siemans-Martin Electrofurnace), Hall 2 (Gun Construction), Hall 3 (Gun Tube Thermal Processing), Hall 4 (Assembly), Hall 5 (three adjacent buildings of foundries), Hall 6 (seven buildings of manufacturing stations) and Hall 7 (Assistant Power Plant and Oil Heating.)

About 2,000 meters south of the Barrikady loomed the massive Krasny Oktyabr Steel Factory (Red October Steel Factory) which totaled 243,300 square meters. Established on April 30, 1897, the electric-powered steel works employed 12,000 workers. In addition to producing steel for tank construction, the annual output was enough to produce 60,000 pieces of artillery (that were constructed elsewhere.) The major structures included Hall 1 (Siemans-Martin Electrofurnace), Hall 2 (Fuel Storage), Hall 3 (Fabrication), Hall 4 (Rolling Mills), Hall 5 (Wire Production), Hall 6 (Fabrication), Hall 7 (Projectile Works), Hall 8 (Iron Foundry), Hall 9 (Administration) and Hall 10 (Workshops.)

Each of these three giant factories had their own workers' settlements nearby that made for a quick, easy transportation for the workers to their place of labor. Stalingrad also had a plethora of smaller industries. The Nail Factory (a small warehouse) was on Gogol Street northeast of the southern railway station. It was also about 600 meters from the Volga River. Near the Nail Factory was the Stalgres Power Station; it provided electrical power for the entire city. Close by were the main post office and the city water works. These three structures were only 350 meters from the river. An industrial alcohol factory was located 1,000 meters west of Stalingrad Rail Station Nr.1. The Meat Factory lay northwest of the Lazur Chemical Works.

Stalingrad also owned one of the most important oil refineries in the country. It was located near the Volga River, beginning 750 meters south of the Lazur Chemical Works and stretching from almost 2,500 meters. The Lazur Chemical Works was a series of about 20 yellow-brick buildings around which circled a railway track; this area measured about 750 meters by 750 meters. From the air, the oblong area looked like a tennis racquet, which is what the Germans began calling the district. Another major factory was Explosive Works Nr.91. Producing high explosives, it was staffed by 8,000 workers.

The city had two major railway stations; Stalingrad Rail Station Nr.1, also known as the Central Rail Station, was located in Stalingrad's center, some 900 meters from the Volga. Stalingrad Rail Station Nr.2 was found in southern Stalingrad; 750 meters to the southeast was river. From the latter, lay the important Stalingrad-Tinguta-Kotelnikovo-Rostov rail line. The distance between the two railway stations was 3,500 meters. Stalingrad also had two small airports; a very small one was located at Stalingradskii (runway 400 meters long by 60 meters wide), while a larger aerodrome was located at Gumrak, west of the city. The Grain Elevator, only 250 meters from Stalingrad Rail Station Nr.2 in southern Stalingrad, was a massive structure measuring about 120 feet tall, 180 feet long and 50 feet wide. The elevator was 550 meters from the river; closer to the Volga was the Canning Factory.

Downtown Stalingrad had several squares; the largest and southernmost was Red Square, with its Gorki Theater and Univermag department store. The southeast edge of the square was very close to the river, separated only by a rail line. Slightly to the north, was The 9th of January Square. Adjacent to this square was the NKVD headquarters. To the northwest of this location was the Mamayev Kurgan, an ancient grassy burial mound, shown on topographical maps as Hill 102. It dominated observation of the city; to defend the hill, the Russians built several strong defensive lines of trenches, barbed-wire obstacles and minefields.

It would be a bloody fight all around. In the whole of the Stalingrad Campaign, the Red Army suffered 1,100,000 casualties – a full 485,751 were killed in action or those who shortly afterward died of their wounds. These bloody losses, combined with the casualties experienced by the Germans, led to Stalingrad assuming a strategic importance that would ensure that the loser of the battle would have its national will seriously questioned by its populace.

† † †

Stalingrad would become the perfect storm that would lead to the death of an army. Led by Adolf Hitler, who insisted that his forces fight to the last man and bullet, the Sixth Army became enticed by an objective that continued to be just past their grasp. Believing that Stalingrad would be theirs "if only" one more attack against the urban rubble was mounted, the Sixth Army did not see that it was in a situation, where if something did go wrong, it would not "see" impending doom until it was too late. That something was the massive Soviet attack that broke through both flanks of the Sixth Army in mid-November in such a violent manner and to such a great operational depth that any hope of relieving the surrounded pocket from the outside in such horrible winter conditions was probably illusionary. Soon after the encirclement, Hitler had based his decision to keep Sixth Army at Stalingrad on two assumptions: that sufficient ground forces to conduct a successful relief operation could be assembled and that the Sixth Army could be sustained as a viable fighting force by air supply until the relief was accomplished. Both assumptions proved faulty.

Thus, defeat was in order for the Sixth Army, but it would not end there. Adolf Hitler had insisted that this would be a fight between the supermen of Aryan Germany against the sub-humans of Slavic Russia. In this fight, according to Nazi ideology, the sub-humans had no right to live. Given the polar ideological differences of Fascism and Communism, combined with this racial antagonism, when the Red Army did gain the upper hand and isolate the German forces around Stalingrad in November 1942, the situation guaranteed that the Sixth Army would not only be defeated, but that it and most of its soldiers were headed for annihilation.

Sources, Introduction: ***L. Anissimov, A. Aleshin and O. Anisimova, "Hydrological basins in the Volgograd urban area: waste storage, catchment and water contamination," presented at the Proceedings of the International Conference, Hefei/Anhui, China, 22-31 March 2004; Antony Beevor, Stalingrad: The Fateful Siege: 1942-1943, London: Penguin Books, 1998, 394; Robert M. Citino, Death of the Wehrmacht: The German Campaigns of 1942, Lawrence, Kansas: University Press of Kansas, 2077, 15, 249, 251, 252, 253; Alan Clark, Barbarossa: The Russian-German Conflict, 1941-45, New York: William Morrow and Company, 1965, 240; Martin van Creveld, Fighting Power: German and U.S. Army Performance, 1939-1945, London: Arms and Armour Press, 1983, entire book; John Erickson, The Road to Stalingrad, New York: Harper & Row, 1975, 387; Hubert Fischer, Der deutsche Sanitätsdienst, 1921-1945, Organisation, Dokumente und persönliche Erfahrungen, Band 4, Teil C: Der Sanitätsdienst der Wehrmacht im 2. Weltkrieg, Osnabrück, FRG: Biblio Verlag, 1985, 3192-3196; Joel S.A. Haywood, Stopped at Stalingrad: The Luftwaffe and Hitler's Defeat in the East, 1942-1943, Lawrence, Kansas: University of Kansas Press, 1998, 251; Manfred Kehrig, Stalingrad: Analyse und Dokumentation einer Schlacht, Stuttgart, FRG: Deutsche Verlags-Anstalt, 1976, 74-76, 81; Robert J. Kershaw, War Without Garlands: Operation Barbarossa, 1941/42, New York: Sarpedon, 2000, 176; Jason Mark, Island of Fire: The Battle for the Barrikady Gun Factory in Stalingrad, November 1942 – February 1943, Sydney, Australia: Leaping Horsemen Books, 2006, fold-out map; Janusz Piekalkiewicz, Stalingrad: Anatomie einer Schlacht, München, BRD: Wilhelm Heyne Verlag, 1977, 15-18, 150 and 151; Georg Tessin, Verbände und Truppen der deutschen Wehrmacht und Waffen-SS im Zweiten Weltkrieg 1939-1945, Dritter Band: Die Landstreitkräfte 6-14, Osnabrück, FRG, 1974, 1.***

Northern Stalingrad

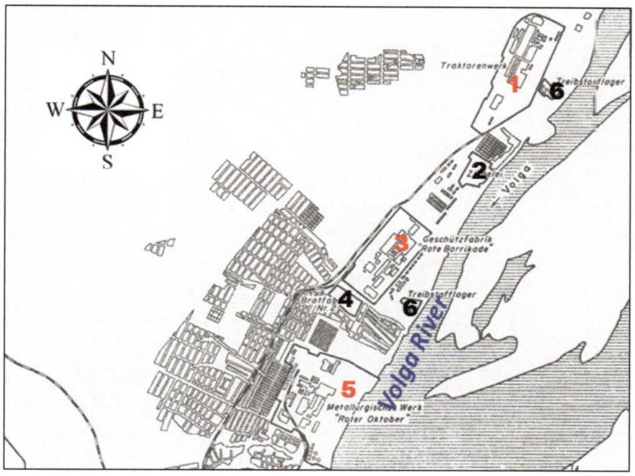

1. Dzerzhinsky Tractor Factory
2. Brick Works
3. Barrikady Gun Factory
4. Bread Factory Nr. 2
5. Krasny Oktybr Steel Factory
6. Fuel Yards

Central Stalingrad

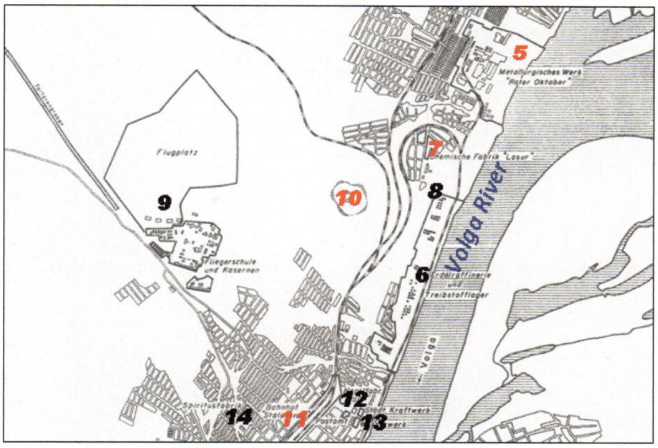

5. Krasny Oktybr Steel Factory
6. Fuel Yards
7. Lazur Chemical Plant
8. "Tennis Racquet"
9. Soviet Flying School
10. Hill 102 – Mamayev Kurgan
11. Stalingrad Rail Station Nr. 1 – Central Rail Station
12. Nail Factory
13. Power Station
14. Alcohol Factory

Southern Stalingrad

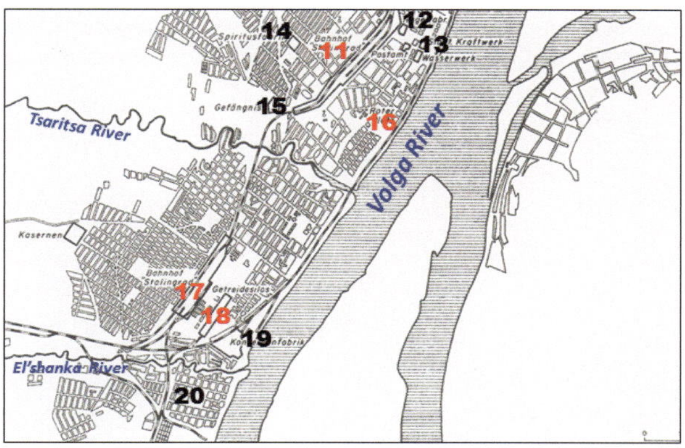

11. Stalingrad Rail Station Nr. 1 – Central Rail Station
12. Nail Factory
13. Power Station
14. Alcohol Factory
15. Prison
16. Red Square
17. Stalingrad Rail Station Nr. 2
18. Grain Elevator
19. Canning Factory
20. El'shanka Suburb

Soviet map of Stalingrad area. City is at the lower right. The scale is 1:100,000. The Germans used Soviet maps to supplement their own by adding checkpoint numbers. The terrain west of the city was open, rolling, with little vegetation.

German 1942 map of Stalingrad city. This map, produced in June 1942, took a basic Soviet map and removed all place names, written in Russian. The scale is 1:20,000. The Germans then divided the city into 28 districts (Roman Numerals), such as "Fabrikstadt" (Factory City), and denoting 76 key features.

***Luftwaffe* aerial photo of Central Stalingrad.** The photo was taken on August 23, 1942, before massive bombing raids began to destroy the city. Area inside the red rectangle is the Krasny Oktyabr Steel Factory; inside the yellow rectangle is the Barrikady Gun Factory. The curved railroad line in the bottom right corner is part of the "Tennis Racquet."

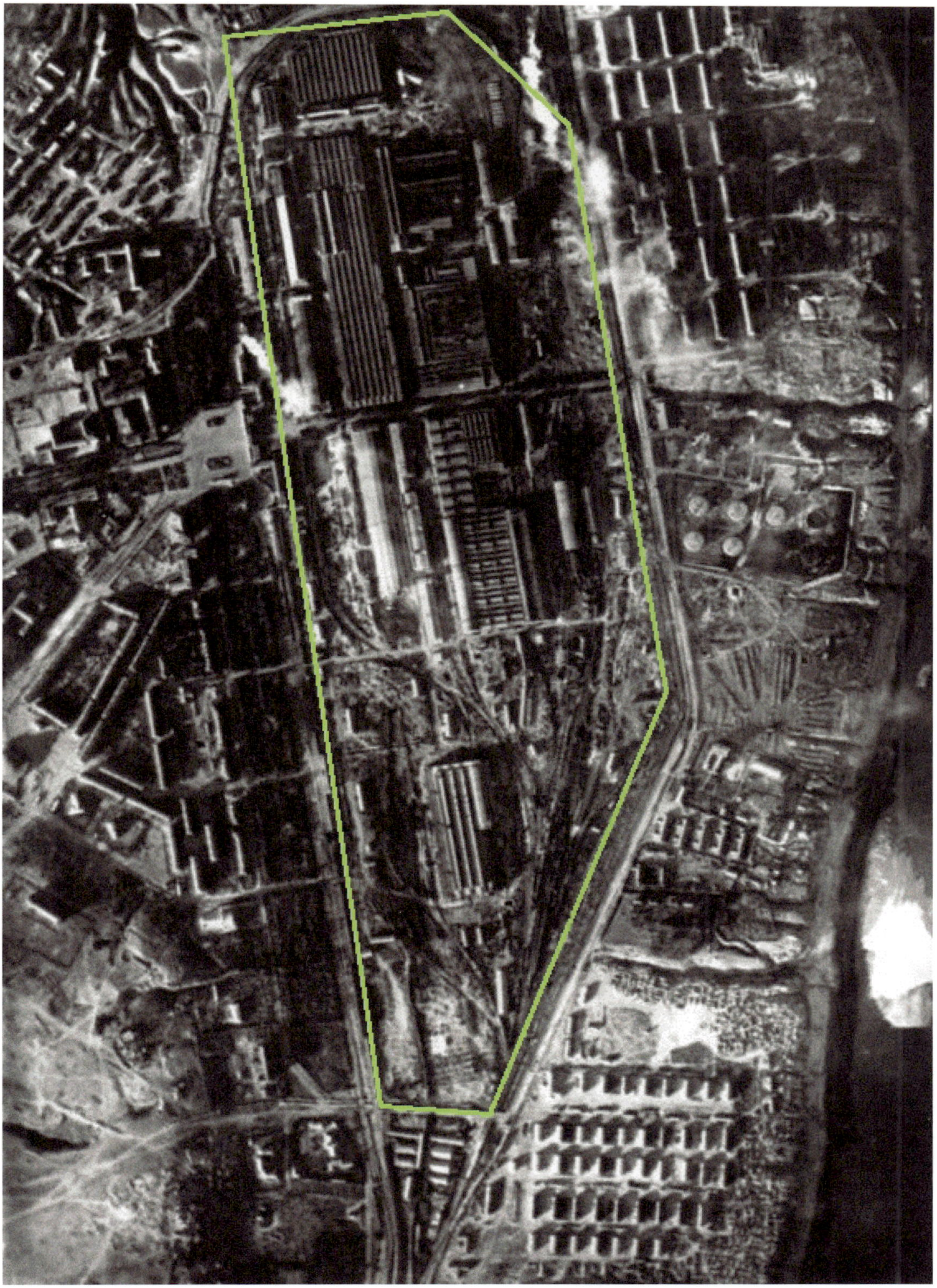

***Luftwaffe* aerial photo of Northern Stalingrad.** The area inside the green border is the Dzerzhinsky Tractor Factory.

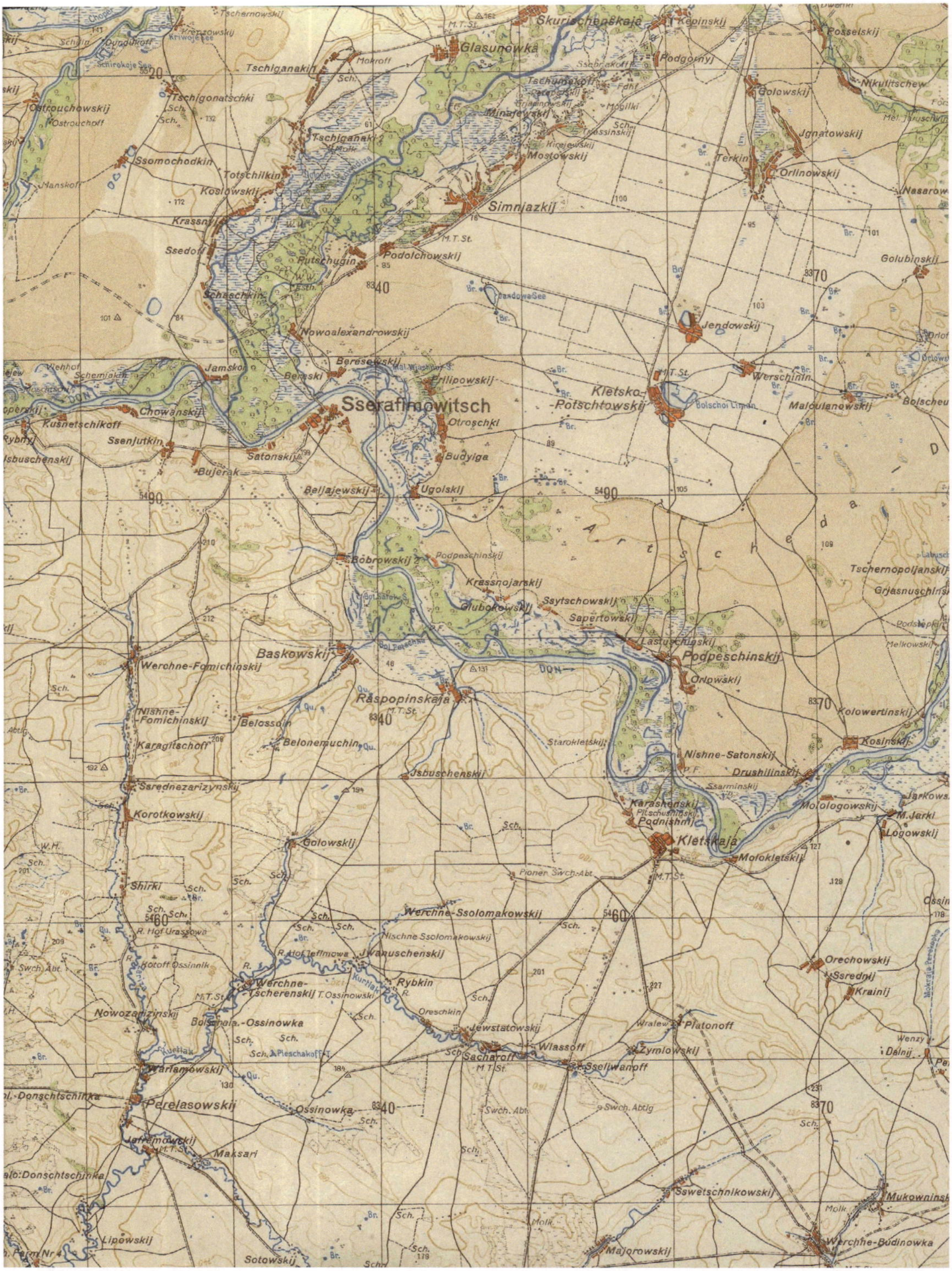

German map of Don River from Serafimovich to Kletskiy. The Don was a formidable barrier but Soviet units slowly established bridgeheads south of the river against Romanian and weaker German units during much of the fighting in the city. In November 1942, the Soviets would exploit those positions.

German map of Don River from Perekopskaya to Chlebnyj. By the time of the Soviet offensive, the Red Army was already on the south side of the Don River in 80% of this sector – a great advantage.

AUGUST, 1942

August 15, 1942
Weather: very windy, clear then stormy, changing cloudiness, 72° F, dusty visibility, cool at night
Sunrise: 4:54 a.m.; **Sunset:** 7:18 p.m.
Moon: Waxing Crescent; 12% illumination

Sixth Army – ***General der Panzertruppe*** Friedrich Paulus was the army commander; ***Generalmajor*** Arthur Schmidt was the chief of staff and ***Oberst*** Hans Eichlepp served as the operations officer. The army went over to the offensive at 4:30 a.m. against the Soviet 4th Tank Army in the small loop of the Don River. The headquarters was located at Ajaburkin.

VIII Corps – ***General der Artillerie*** Walter Heitz was the corps commander; ***Oberst*** Bernhard Steinmetz was the chief of staff and ***Major*** Hans Schwanbeck served as the operations officer. The 244th ***Sturmgeschütz*** Detachment was assigned to the corps. The corps suffered the following officer casualties: 11 killed in action; 17 wounded in action.

305th Infantry Division – The division attacked northeast in zone from Ventsy against the 205th Rifle Division. The division reported 300 casualties. To the northwest was the 100th ***Jäger*** Division; to the southeast was the 389th Infantry Division. ***Generalmajor*** Kurt Oppenländer served as division commander. The division was authorized 17,734 men, including 8,000 infantrymen and 779 combat engineers; also authorized were 36 medium anti-tank guns, 20 light guns (7.5cm), 36 medium howitzers (10.5cm), 18 heavy howitzers (15cm) and 4,842 horses.

384th Infantry Division – The division attacked northeast in zone against the 184th Rifle Division, seizing Hill 161.2, Hill 199.6 and Hill 186.5. The division lost three officers and 52 NCOs/enlisted killed in action; two officers and 278 NCOs/enlisted were wounded in action; 11 NCOs/enlisted were listed as missing in action. To the northwest was the 389th Infantry Division; to the southeast was the 295th Infantry Division. ***Generalleutnant*** Eccard ***Freiherr*** von Gablenz served as division commander. The division was authorized 17,734 men, including 8,000 infantrymen and 779 combat engineers; also authorized were 36 medium anti-tank guns, 20 light guns (7.5cm), 36 medium howitzers (10.5cm), 18 heavy howitzers (15cm) and 4,842 horses.

389th Infantry Division – The division attacked northeast in zone against the 192nd Rifle Division. The division reported that losses were "bloody" and totaled roughly 100. To the northwest was the 305th Infantry Division; to the south was the 384th Infantry Division. The division headquarters was located at Verkhne-Golubaja. ***Generalleutnant*** Erwin Jaenecke served as division commander. The division was authorized 17,734 men, including 8,000 infantrymen and 779 combat engineers; also authorized were 36 medium anti-tank guns, 20 light guns (7.5cm), 36 medium howitzers (10.5cm) and 18 heavy howitzers (15cm) and 4,842 horses.

XI Corps – ***General der Infanterie*** Karl Strecker was the corps commander; ***Oberst*** Helmuth Groscurth was the chief of staff and ***Major*** Wolf Zabel served as the operations officer. The 521st ***Panzerjäger*** Detachment was assigned to the corps. The corps suffered the following officer casualties: four killed in action; 18 wounded in action.

100th Jäger Division – The division attacked northeast in zone south of Kletskiy. The division suffered three officers and 52 NCOs/enlisted killed in action; nine officers and 253 NCOs/enlisted were wounded in action; 11 NCOs/enlisted were reported missing in action. To the northwest was the 376th Infantry Division; to the southeast was the 305th Infantry Division. ***Generalleutnant*** Werner Sanne served as division commander. The division was authorized 14,500 men, including 6,800 infantrymen and 779 combat engineers; also authorized were 48 medium anti-tank guns, 12 light guns (7.5cm), 36 medium howitzers (10.5cm), 12 heavy howitzers (15cm) and 3,300 horses.

376th Infantry Division – The division attacked northeast in zone south of Kletskiy. The division lost three officers and 50 NCOs/enlisted killed in action; ten officers and 196 NCOs/enlisted were wounded in action. To the northwest was the 113th Infantry Division; to the southeast was the 100th ***Jäger*** Division. ***Generalmajor*** Alexander Edler von Daniels served as division commander. The division was authorized 17,734 men, including 8,000 infantrymen and 779 combat engineers; also authorized were 36 medium anti-tank guns, 20 light guns (7.5cm), 36 medium howitzers (10.5cm), 18 heavy howitzers (15cm) and 4,842 horses.

XIV *Panzer* Corps – ***General der Infanterie*** Gustav von Wietersheim was the corps commander; ***Oberst*** Eberhard Thunert was the chief of staff and ***Major*** Hermann Richard Schmoll served as the operations officer. The corps suffered the following officer casualties: one killed in action.

3rd Infantry Division (Motorized) – Initially, the division was in an assembly area west of the 389th Infantry Division. The division attacked eastward in zone and penetrated forward enemy defenses. The division suffered two men killed in action. ***Generalmajor*** Helmuth Schlömer served as division commander. The division was authorized 16,400 men, including 7,100 infantrymen and 779 combat engineers; also authorized were 63 medium anti-tank guns, eight 8.8cm ***flak*** guns, 20 light guns (7.5cm), 36 medium howitzers (10.5cm), 12 heavy howitzers (15cm), 77 ***panzer***s (20 Mark II tanks, 42 Mark III tanks and 15 Mark IV tanks) and 2,800 motor transport vehicles.

16th Panzer Division – The division attacked east in zone, broke through enemy defenses south of Blizhniaia-Perekopka and reached Trekhostrovskaya on the Don River. The division reported one officer killed in action and 20 NCOs and enlisted killed in action; two officers were wounded in action as were 77 enlisted. ***Generalleutnant*** Hans Valentin Hube served as division commander. The division was authorized 15,600 men, including 5,500 infantrymen and 779 combat engineers; also authorized were 75 medium anti-tank guns, 18 light guns (7.5cm), 36 medium howitzers (10.5cm), 16 heavy howitzers (15cm), 165 armored fighting vehicles (including 22 Mark II tanks, 87 Mark III tanks and 26 Mark IV tanks) and 2,800 motor transport vehicles.

60th Infantry Division (Motorized) – The division attacked east in zone, broke through enemy defenses and reached the Don River south of Sirotinskaya. ***Generalmajor*** Otto Kohlermann served as division commander. The division was authorized 16,400 men, including 7,100 infantrymen and 779 combat engineers; also authorized were 63 medium anti-tank guns, 20 light guns (7.5cm), eight 8.8cm ***flak*** guns, 36 medium howitzers (10.5cm), 12 heavy howitzers (15cm), 77 ***panzer***s (20 Mark II tanks, 42 Mark III tanks and 15 Mark IV tanks) and 2,800 motor transport vehicles.

XVII Corps – ***General der Infanterie*** Karl-Adolf Hollidt was the corps commander; ***Oberst*** Hans Doerr was the chief of staff and ***Major*** Heinrich Schäfer served as the operations officer. The corps suffered the following officer casualties: three killed in action; three wounded in action; two missing in action.

22nd Panzer Division – The division occupied an assembly area west of the front line at Evstratovskiy and then advanced to the Don River. To the west was the 79th Infantry Division; to the east was the 113th Infantry Division. ***Generalmajor*** Wilhelm von Apell served as division commander. The division was authorized 15,600 men, including 5,500 infantrymen and 779 combat engineers; also authorized were 75 medium anti-tank guns, 18 light guns (7.5cm), 36 medium howitzers (10.5cm), 16 heavy howitzers (15cm), 165 armored fighting vehicles (including 22 Mark II tanks, 87 Mark III tanks and 26 Mark IV tanks) and 2,800 motor transport vehicles.

79th Infantry Division – The division defended in sector, along the Don River at Serafimovich, against the 96th Rifle Division. The division reported two officers and seven NCOs/enlisted killed in action; 31 NCOs/enlisted were wounded in action; one officer and five NCOs/enlisted were listed missing in action. The division's 226th Infantry Regiment submitted a separate report of two officers and 68 NCO/enlisted casualties. To the east was the 22nd ***Panzer*** Division; to the west was the XXXV Corps of the Italian Eighth Army. ***Generalmajor*** Richard von Schwerin served as division commander. The division was authorized 15,273 men, including 8,000 infantrymen and 779 combat engineers; also authorized were 36 medium anti-tank guns, 20 light guns (7.5cm), 36 medium howitzers (10.5cm), 18 heavy howitzers (15cm) and 4,854 horses.

113th Infantry Division – The division occupied an assembly area west of the front line east of Evstratovskiy and then advanced north to the Don River. The division lost 15 NCOs/enlisted wounded in action. To the east was the 376th Infantry Division; to the west was the 22nd ***Panzer*** Division. ***Generalleutnant*** Hans-Heinrich Sixt von Arnim served as division commander. The division was authorized 17,734 men, including 8,000 infantrymen and 779 combat engineers; also authorized were 36 medium anti-tank guns, 20 light guns (7.5cm), 36 medium howitzers (10.5cm), 18 heavy howitzers (15cm) and 4,842 horses.

XXIV *Panzer* Corps – ***Generalleutnant*** Willibald ***Freiherr*** von Langermann und Erlenkamp was the corps commander; ***Oberst*** Otto Heidkämper was the chief of staff and ***Major*** Kurt Sengpiel served as the operations officer. The corps suffered the following officer casualties: two killed in action; six wounded in action.

76th Infantry Division – The division attacked northwest in zone, destroyed the 18th Rifle Division and seized Akimovskii on the Don River. The division suffered one officer killed in action and seven officers wounded in action; 12 NCO/enlisted were killed in action and 90 wounded in action. To the north was the 295th Infantry Division; to the south was the 44th Infantry Division. ***Generalmajor*** Carl Rodenburg served as division commander. The division was authorized 15,273 men, including 8,000 infantrymen and 779 combat engineers; also authorized were 36 medium anti-tank guns, 20 light guns (7.5cm), 36 medium howitzers (10.5cm), 18 heavy howitzers (15cm) and 4,854 horses.

295th Infantry Division – The division attacked northwest in zone, destroyed the 18th Rifle Division and seized Akimovskii on the Don River. To the north was the 384th Infantry Division; to the south was the 76th Infantry Division. ***Oberst*** Dr. Otto Korfes served as division commander. The division was authorized 17,734 men, including 8,000 infantrymen and 779 combat engineers; also authorized were 36 medium anti-tank guns, 20 light guns (7.5cm), 36 medium howitzers (10.5cm) and 18 heavy howitzers (15cm) and 4,842 horses.

LI Corps – ***General der Artillerie*** Walter von Seydlitz-Kurzbach was the corps commander; ***Oberst*** Hans Clausius was the chief of staff and ***Major*** Leo Sprenger served as the operations officer. The corps suffered the following officer casualties: one wounded in action.

44th Infantry Division – The division defended in sector along the Don River from Malogolubinskiy to Kumovka against the 131st Rifle Division. The division lost four enlisted men killed in action and two wounded in action. To the north was the 76th Infantry Division; to the south was the 71st Infantry Division. ***Generalmajor*** Heinrich Deboi served as division commander. The division was authorized 17,734 men, including 8,000 infantrymen and 779 combat engineers; also authorized were 36 medium anti-tank guns, 20 light guns (7.5cm), 36 medium howitzers (10.5cm), 18 heavy howitzers (15cm) and 4,842 horses.

71st Infantry Division – The division defended in sector along the Don River from Kumovka southward against the 20th Motorized Rifle Brigade. The division lost one NCO killed in action, and one officer and nine NCOs/enlisted wounded in action. To the north was the 44th Infantry Division; to the south was the Fourth ***Panzer*** Army. ***Generalmajor*** Alexander von Hartmann served as division commander. The division was authorized 15,273 men, including 8,000 infantrymen and 779 combat engineers; also authorized were 75 medium anti-tank guns, 26 light guns (7.5cm), 36 medium howitzers (10.5cm), 12 heavy howitzers (15cm) and 4,854 horses.

Sixth Army Reserve

24th Panzer Division – The division moved southward to join Fourth ***Panzer*** Army. ***Generalmajor*** Bruno ***Ritter*** von Hauenschild served as division commander. The division was authorized 15,600 men, including 5,500 infantrymen and 779 combat engineers; also authorized were 75 medium anti-tank guns, 18 light guns (7.5cm), 36 medium howitzers (10.5cm), 16 heavy howitzers (15cm), 165 armored fighting vehicles (including 22 Mark II tanks, 87 Mark III tanks and 26 Mark IV tanks) and 2,800 motor transport vehicles.

297th Infantry Division – The division moved southward to join Fourth ***Panzer*** Army. ***Generalleutnant*** Max Pfeffer served as division commander. The division was authorized 17,734 men, including 8,000 infantrymen and 779 combat engineers; also authorized were 36 medium anti-tank guns, 20 light howitzers (7.5cm), 36 medium howitzers (10.5cm), 18 heavy howitzers (15cm) and 4,842 horses.

Sources, August 15, 1942: *Oberkommando des Heeres, Lage Ost: Stand: 15.8.42, Eastern Front Situation Map, National Archives Identifier: 559733, Record Group 242 – National Archives Collection of Foreign Records Seized, 1675-1958, National Archives, College Park, Maryland; Ia, Armeeoberkommando 6, "Morgen Meldung" and assorted reports, Kriegstagebuch 13, 16 August 1942, as found in Microfilm Series, T-312, Records of German Field Commands, Armies, Roll 1682, National Archives and Records Service, College Park, Maryland; 22nd Panzer Division, Kriegstagebuch 2, 15 August 1942, as found in Microfilm Series T-315, Roll 784, National Archives and Records Service, College Park, Maryland; 76th Infantry Division, Kriegstagebuch, 15 August 1942, as found in Microfilm Series T-315, Roll 1090, National Archives and Records Service, College Park, Maryland; 384th Infantry Division, Kriegstagebuch, 15 August 1942, as found in Microfilm Series T-315, Roll 2188, National Archives and Records Service, College Park, Maryland; Die 71. Infanterie-Division, 1939-1945: Gefechts- und Erlebnisberichte aus Kämpfen der "Gluckhaften Division" von Verdun bis Stalingrad, vom Monte Cassino bis zum Plattensee, Eggolsheim, FRG: Edition Dörfler, 1973, 462-463; Gerhard Dieckhoff, Die 3.Division, Göttingen, FRG: Eric Börries Druck und Verlag 1960, 169; James F. Dunnigan, War in the East: The Russo-German Conflict, 1941-45, Strategy & Tactics Staff Study Nr.1, New York: Simulations Publications Incorporated, 1977, 141-146; John Erickson, The Road to Stalingrad, New York: Harper & Row, 1975, 369; David M. Glantz, & Jonathan M. House, To the Gates of Stalingrad: Soviet-German Combat Operations, April-August 1942, (The Stalingrad Trilogy, Volume 1), Lawrence, Kansas: University Press of Kansas, 2009, 309-313; Friedrich Wilhelm Hauck, Eine Deutsche Division in Russland und Italian: 305. Infanterie-Division, 1941-1945, Dorheim, FRG: Podzun Verlag, 1975, 62; Jochen Löser, Bittere Pflicht: Kampf und Untergang der 76. Berlin-Brandenburgischen Infanterie-Division, Osnabrück, FRG: Biblio Verlag, 1986, 179; Kurt Mehner, Die Geheimen Tagesberichte der Deutschen Wehrmachtführung im Zweiten Weltkrieg 1939 – 1945, Band 5: 1. Juni 1942 – 30. November 1942, Osnabrück, Germany: Biblio Verlag, 1991, 313-332.*

Maria, Mutter Gottes, Mutter der Barmherzigkeit, bitte für uns und für alle die im Frieden des Herrn verschieden sind.

Andenken im Gebete an
Georg Graf,
Soldat in einem Inf.-Rgt.,
gefallen am 15. August 1942
im Osten (Rußland)
im 32. Lebensjahre.

O weine nicht! Ich bin dir nicht geſtorben,
Ein ewig ſelig Leben ging mir auf.
O ſähſt du ihn, den Kranz, den ich erworben.
Es hemmte gleich ſich Deiner Tränen Lauf.
Hier wohnt der Friede, leuchtet ew'ges Licht.
O weine nicht!

O weine nicht! Sieh, wie die Jahre ſchwinden!
Auch Dich trägt bald ein Engel zu mir her,
Du wirſt mich ſelig unter Sel'gen finden,
Und ewig trennt uns dann kein Sterben mehr.
Drum hebe fromm zu Gott Dein Angeſicht
Und weine nicht!

Vater unſer. Ave Maria.

Carl Mayr, Amberg

Soldat Georg Graf was born in Poppenricht near Amberg, Bavaria on November 29, 1911. An infantryman, he was killed in action on August 15, 1942, about four miles northeast of Orekovskij, probably assigned to the 376th Infantry Division. His name is listed in the remembrance book at the German Military Cemetery at Rossoschka, 23 miles northwest from the city center of currently named Volgograd.

Alexander Edler von Daniels, Commander of the 76th Infantry Division.

Wir können Dir nicht Blumen bieten,
Dein Grab liegt gar ſo fern und weit,
Du ſchlummerſt ſanft in ſtillem Frieden,
Befreit von namenloſem Leid.
Dein Grab in einem fernen Land
Iſt uns wohl eine ſchwere Pein,
Doch nimm das Wort zum Unterpfand,
Dein Grab ſoll nicht verlaſſen ſein;
All' Abend, wenn die Glocken ſingen,
Zieht liebend unſer Geiſt dorthin
Und ſtreut Dir betend Andachtsblumen
Aufs Heldengrab mit frommem Sinn.

Jeſus! Maria! Joſef!

Zum frommen Andenken
an unſern lieben, unvergeßlichen Sohn, unſern guten Bruder, Vetter und Neffen

Andreas Wollenweber

Kanonier in einem Art.-Regt.

Er war geboren am 14. Auguſt 1922 zu Kötterichen und ſtarb am 25. Auguſt 1942 in einem Feldlazarett an den Folgen einer ſchweren Verwundung, die er am 15. Auguſt im Oſten erlitten hat.

Auf dem Heldenfriedhof in Werchnaja-Buſinowka wurde er zur letzten Ruhe gebettet. Nun ruht er fern von uns in ſowjet-ruſſiſcher Erde, aber in unſern Herzen wird er weiter leben. Wer ihn gekannt, wird unſern großen Schmerz ermeſſen können. Wiederſehen war ſeine und unſere einzige Hoffnung.

Wir bitten um ein ſtilles Gebet für den lieben Verſtorbenen, auf daß er ruhe im ewigen Frieden!

Kötterichen, im September 1942.

In tiefem Schmerz:
Seine Eltern, Geſchwiſter
und die übrigen Anverwandten.

Das erſte Seelenamt iſt am Donnerstag, den 24. Sept. 1942, in der Pfarrkirche zu Uersfeld.

***Kanonier* Andreas Wollenweber** was born in Kötterichen in the Eifel region of the Rhineland-Palatinate. Assigned to an artillery regiment, he was seriously wounded in action on August 15, 1942, and rushed to a field hospital. He died at the 2/542 Field Hospital at Verkhne-Businovka on August 25, 1942. He is buried at the German Military Cemetery at Rossoschka in Block 12, Row 12 in Grave 447.

August 16, 1942

Weather: hot, dry, sunny, bright, clear, 90° F, 61° F at night, very dusty visibility, light rain at night

Sunrise: 4:55 a.m.; **Sunset:** 7:17 p.m.

Moon: Waxing Crescent; 19% illumination

Sixth Army – The aim of the army was to clear all enemy forces from west of the Don River bend. The army headquarters was located at Dobrinka.

VIII Corps – The aim of the corps was to reach the Don River and establish bridgeheads over it. The corps suffered the following officer casualties: three killed in action; 12 wounded in action.

305th Infantry Division – The division attacked in zone east to the Don River and seized Sirotinskaya against the 4th Guards Rifle Division. To the northwest was the 100th ***Jäger*** Division. To the southeast was the 60th Infantry Division (Motorized.)

384th Infantry Division – The division attacked in zone east to the Don River against the 22nd Motorized Rifle Brigade. To the north was the 389th Infantry Division; to the south was the 76th Infantry Division. During the fighting, two regiments of the division seized a bridgehead over the Don River at Akimov. The 855th Heavy Artillery Detachment was assigned to support the division, as was one battery of the 244th ***Sturmgeschütz*** Detachment. The division headquarters was located at Kissljakow. The division lost 20 NCOs/enlisted killed in action; two officers and 83 NCOs/enlisted were wounded in action.

389th Infantry Division – The division attacked in zone east to the Don River against the 37th Guards Rifle Division. To the north was the 3rd Infantry Division (Motorized); to the south was the 384th Infantry Division.

XI Corps – The aim of the corps was to clear enemy forces from the upper Don River bend at Kremenskaya. The corps headquarters was located at Sredne.

100th Jäger Division – The division attacked in zone east toward the Don River against the 205th Rifle Division. The division suffered 12 NCOs/enlisted men killed in action and 124 NCOs/enlisted wounded in action. To the northwest was the 376th Infantry Division; to the southeast was the 305th Infantry Division.

376th Infantry Division – The division attacked northeast in zone and seized Kremenskaya against the 343rd Rifle Division. The division reported six NCOs/enlisted men killed in action and five NCOs/enlisted men wounded in action. To the west was the 113th Infantry Division; to the southeast was the 100th ***Jäger*** Division.

XIV *Panzer* Corps – The aim of the corps was to attack east to the Don River and be prepared to cross. The corps suffered the following officer casualties: one killed in action; six wounded in action.

3rd Infantry Division (Motorized) – The division attacked in zone east, smashing the 39th Guards Rifle Division against the Don River. To the west was the 60th Infantry Division (Motorized); to the south was the 389th Infantry Division.

16th Panzer Division – The division attacked throughout its zone against multiple enemy formations, seizing Hill 132.4 and Nizhne-Akatov; at the end of the day it received an order to withdraw west to an assembly area for rest and refit. The division reported (late) that it had 25 NCOs/enlisted killed in action and 62 NCOs/enlisted wounded in action.

60th Infantry Division (Motorized) – The division attacked in zone east, smashing the 37th Guards Rifle Division against the Don River. To the northwest was the 305th Infantry Division; to the east was the 3rd Infantry Division (Motorized.)

XVII Corps – The aim of the corps was to clear all enemy forces from south of the Don River and protect the northwest flank of the army. The corps suffered the following officer casualties: one killed in action; two wounded in action.

22nd Panzer Division – The division withdrew from the Don River to an assembly area west of the front line at Evstratovskiy.

79th Infantry Division – The division defended in sector, along the Don River at Serafimovich, against the attacking 76th Rifle Division and the 124th Rifle Division. To the southeast was the 113th Infantry Division. To the west was the 2nd Italian Infantry Division of the XXXV Corps of the Italian Eighth Army. Part of the Italian "Celere" Division fought in the division sector.

113th Infantry Division – The division defended in sector along the Don River near Raspopinskaya against the 63rd Rifle Division and the 278th Rifle Division. The division estimated its casualties at 15 wounded in action. To the northwest was the 79th Infantry Division; to the east was the 376th Infantry Division.

XXIV *Panzer* Corps – The aim of the corps was to clear all enemy forces from west of the Don River.

295th Infantry Division – The division attacked in zone east to the Don River and seized footholds on the east bank against the 131st Rifle Division. The division reported 170 total casualties. To the north was the 389th Infantry Division; to the south was the 384th Infantry Division.

LI Corps – The aim of the corps was to advance to the Don River and protect the southern flank of the army. The corps headquarters was located at Jewlampijewskij. The 733rd Heavy Artillery Detachment and the 245th ***Sturmgeschütz*** Detachment were assigned to the corps. The corps suffered the following officer casualties: two killed in action; nine wounded in action.

44th Infantry Division – The division defended in sector along the Don River against the 131st Rifle Division and prepared to withdraw to an assembly area to the west. The division reported one NCO/enlisted killed in action and three NCOs/enlisted wounded in action. To the north was the 76th Infantry Division; to the south was the 71st Infantry Division.

71st Infantry Division – The division defended in sector along the Don River against the 20th Motorized Rifle Brigade. The division suffered two NCOs/enlisted killed in action and eight NCOs/enlisted wounded in action. To the north was the 44th Infantry Division; to the south was an open flank.

76th Infantry Division – All elements of the division reached the Don River and seized footholds across the river on the east bank against the 98th Rifle Division. The division lost 14 NCOs/enlisted killed in action, 83 NCOs/enlisted wounded in action and two men were missing in action. To the north was the 384th Infantry Division; to the southwest was the 44th Infantry Division.

Sixth Army Reserve

24th Panzer Division – The division moved southward to join Fourth ***Panzer*** Army.

297th Infantry Division – The division moved southward to join Fourth ***Panzer*** Army.

Sources, August 16, 1942: ***Oberkommando des Heeres, Lage Ost: Stand: 16.8.42, Eastern Front Situation Map, National Archives Identifier: 559733, Record Group 242 – National Archives Collection of Foreign Records Seized, 1675-1958, National Archives, College Park, Maryland; Ia, Armeeoberkommando 6, "Morgen Meldung" and assorted reports, Kriegstagebuch 13, 17 August 1942, as found in Microfilm Series, T-312, Records of German Field Commands, Armies, Roll 1682, National Archives and Records Service, College Park, Maryland; 22nd Panzer Division, Kriegstagebuch 2, 16 August 1942, as found in Microfilm Series T-315, Roll 784, National Archives and Records Service, College Park, Maryland; 76th Infantry Division, Kriegstagebuch, 16 August 1942, as found in Microfilm Series T-315, Roll 1090, National Archives and Records Service, College Park, Maryland; 384th Infantry Division, Kriegstagebuch, 16 August 1942, as found in Microfilm Series T-315, Roll 2188, National Archives and Records Service, College Park, Maryland; David M. Glantz, & Jonathan M. House, To the Gates of Stalingrad: Soviet-German Combat Operations, April-August 1942, (The Stalingrad Trilogy, Volume 1), Lawrence, Kansas: University Press of Kansas, 2009, 313-317, 384; Jochen Löser, Bittere Pflicht: Kampf und Untergang der 76. Berlin-Brandenburgischen Infanterie-Division, Osnabrück, FRG: Biblio Verlag, 1986, 179, 185, 187 and 189; Wolfgang Werthen, Geschichte der 16. Panzer-Division 1939-1945, Friedberg, FRG: Podzun-Pallas-Verlag, 1958, 105; Vom Donez zum Don: Erfahrungsbericht der 384. I.D. vom 17. 5. – 5. 9.1942, Traditionsverbandes der 384. I. D., 1984.***

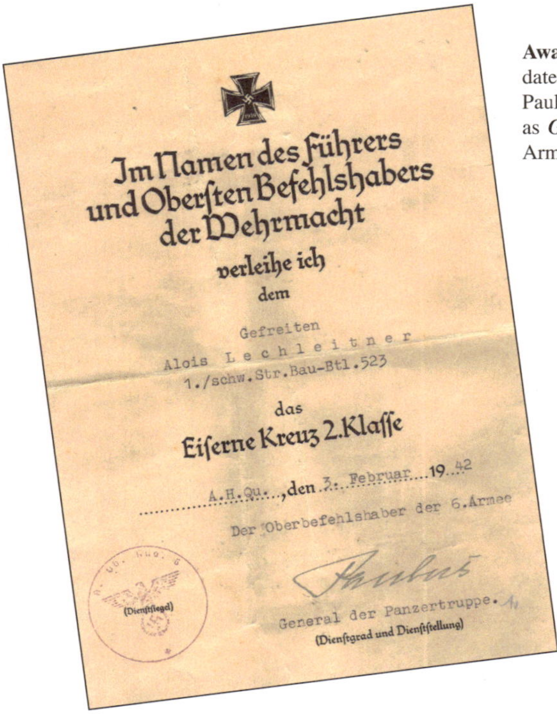

Im Namen des Führers
und Obersten Befehlshabers
der Wehrmacht
verleihe ich
dem
Gefreiten
Alois Lechleitner
1./schw.Str.Bau-Btl.523
das
Eiserne Kreuz 2.Klasse

A.H.Qu., den 3. Februar 1942

Der Oberbefehlshaber der 6.Armee

(Dienstsiegel)

Paulus

General der Panzertruppe.
(Dienstgrad und Dienststellung)

Award Document for Iron Cross 2nd Class. Document, dated February 3, 1942, is signed by ***General der Panzertruppe*** Paulus. The 523rd Heavy Street Construction Battalion, as well as ***Gefreiter*** Alois Lechleitner, was transferred from the Sixth Army before the command reached Stalingrad.

Generalfeldmarschall **Walter von Reichenau.** He commanded the Sixth Army before Friedrich Paulus.

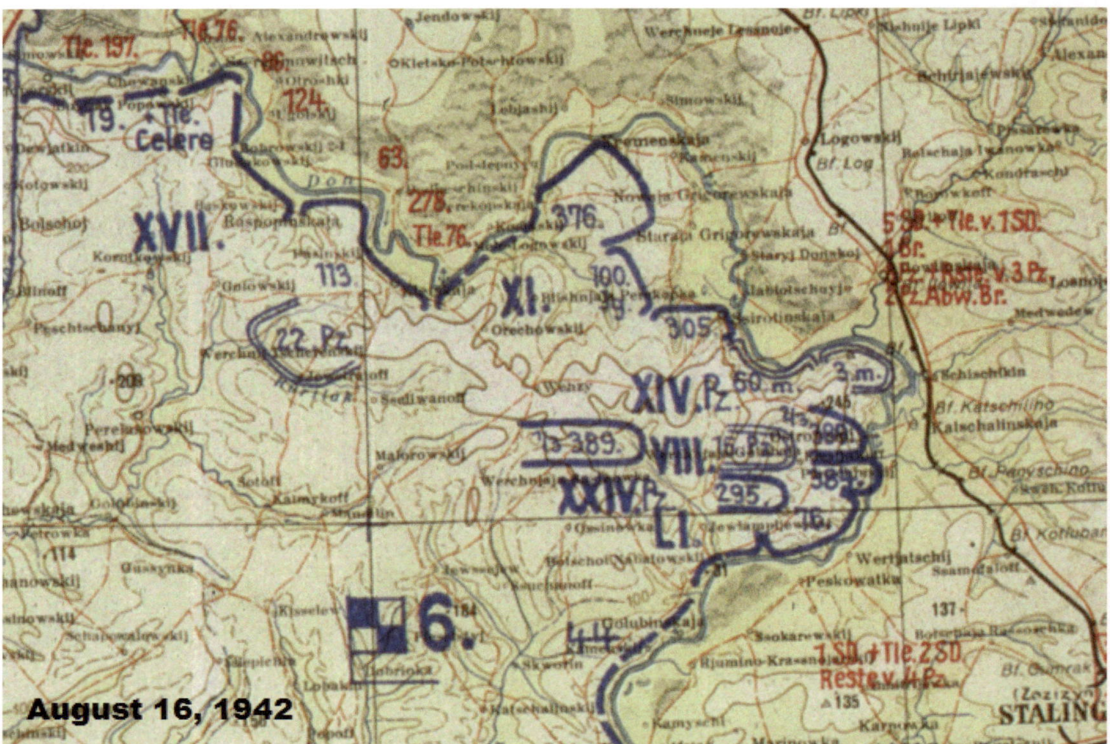

August 17, 1942
Weather: hot, dry, bright, sunny, clear, 91° F, cool at night, good road conditions
Sunrise: 4:56 a.m.; **Sunset:** 7:15 p.m.
Moon: Waxing Crescent; 29% illumination

Sixth Army – The army headquarters was located at Dobrinka.

VIII Corps – The 2nd ***Werfer*** Regiment was assigned to support the corps. The corps suffered the following officer casualties: two killed in action; 16 wounded in action.

305th Infantry Division – The division attacked in zone toward the Don River against the 4th Guards Rifle Division. The division lost four NCOs and 17 enlisted men killed in action; six officers and 102 NCOs/enlisted were wounded in action. To the northwest was the 100th ***Jäger*** Division; to the southeast was the 60th Infantry Division (Motorized.) Two-thirds of the division occupied an assembly area to the south in preparation for future combat.

384th Infantry Division – The division attacked and seized Verkhne-Gniloj and then defended in sector along the Don River against the 18th Rifle Division. The division suffered 45 NCOs/enlisted killed in action; two officers and 139 NCOs/enlisted were wounded in action; six men were reported missing in action. To the north was the 389th Infantry Division; to the south was the 76th Infantry Division. The division's nine infantry battalions had an aggregate Combat/Fighting Strength of 49%.

389th Infantry Division – The division defended in sector along the Don River against the 39th Guards Rifle Division. The division lost three officers killed in action and three wounded in action; the unit also had 45 other casualties to NCOs/enlisted. To the north was the 3rd Infantry Division (Motorized); to the south was the 384th Infantry Division. The division headquarters was located at Kissljakov. The division's nine infantry battalions had an aggregate Combat/Fighting Strength of 40%.

XI Corps – The aim of the corps was to continue to clear enemy forces from the upper Don River bend at Kremenskaya. The corps headquarters was located at Sredne. The 521st ***Panzerjäger*** Detachment and the 177th ***Sturmgeschütz*** Detachment were assigned to the corps. The corps suffered the following officer casualties: two killed in action; seven wounded in action.

22nd Panzer Division – The division occupied an assembly area behind the front at Evstratovskiy.

44th Infantry Division – The division defended in sector along the Don River against the 399th Rifle Division and then moved to an assembly area. To the northeast was the 295th Infantry Division; to the south was the 71st Infantry Division. The division's nine infantry battalions had an aggregate Combat/Fighting Strength of 53%.

100th Jäger Division – The division attacked in zone along the northern loop of the Don River toward Starogrigor'evskaya against the 40th Guards Rifle Division. The division suffered one officer and 15 NCOs/enlisted killed in action, two officers and 112 NCOs/enlisted wounded in action and nine NCOs/enlisted missing in action. To the southeast was the 305th Infantry Division; to the northwest was the 376th Infantry Division. The division's four ***jäger*** battalions had an aggregate Combat/Fighting Strength of 28%. The attached Croatian infantry battalion had an aggregate Combat/Fighting Strength of 70%.

376th Infantry Division – The division continued to attack in zone to the Don River and then defended in sector south of the Don River from Perekopka-Perekopskaya-Novogrigor'evskaia against the 321st Rifle Division and the 38th Guards Rifle Division. The division lost one officer killed in action and 33 NCOs/enlisted wounded in action; the separated 672nd Infantry Regiment reported 50-60 casualties. To the west was the 113th Infantry Division; to the southeast was the 100th ***Jäger***

Division. The division's nine infantry battalions had an aggregate Combat/Fighting Strength of 31%.

XIV *Panzer* Corps – The corps suffered the following officer casualties: two killed in action; two wounded in action.

3rd Infantry Division (Motorized) – The division defended in sector along the Don River against the 192nd Rifle Division, receiving orders to be prepared to move to an assembly area for rest and refit operations. The division suffered two NCOs/enlisted killed in action and nine NCOs/enlisted wounded in action. The division's four motorized infantry battalions had an aggregate Combat/Fighting Strength of 62%.

16th Panzer Division – The division conducted rest and refit operations behind the front line in an assembly area, but casualty figures indicate that they ran into several bypassed enemy units. The division reported one officer killed in action and three NCOs/enlisted killed in action; 29 NCOs/enlisted were wounded in action. The division's four ***panzer*** grenadier battalions had an aggregate Combat/Fighting Strength of 68%.

60th Infantry Division (Motorized) – The division defended in sector along the Don River against the 4th Guards Rifle Division, receiving orders to be prepared to move to the rear to an assembly area for rest and refit operations. The division reported one officer and nine NCOs/enlisted killed in action; 30 NCOs/enlisted were wounded in action. The division's six motorized infantry battalions had an aggregate Combat/Fighting Strength of 60%.

XVII Corps

79th Infantry Division – The division defended in sector along the Don River against two enemy attacks by the 304th Rifle Division. The division reported 43 NCOs/enlisted killed in action and 95 NCOs/enlisted wounded in action; one officer and 55 NCOs/enlisted were reported missing in action. To the west was the 2nd Italian Infantry Division of the XXXV Corps of the Italian Eighth Army. To the southeast was the 113th Infantry Division. The division's nine infantry battalions had an aggregate Combat/Fighting Strength of 34%.

113th Infantry Division – The division defended in sector, along the Don River near Raspopinskaya, against the 278th Rifle Division and the 63rd Rifle Division. The division suffered 45 casualties along with two men reported missing in action. To the northwest was the 79th Infantry Division; to the east was the 376th ***Jäger*** Division. The division's six infantry battalions had an aggregate Combat/Fighting Strength of 43%.

XXIV *Panzer* Corps

71st Infantry Division – The division defended in sector along the Don River against the 20th Motorized Rifle Brigade. One NCO/enlisted was killed in action and four NCOs/enlisted were wounded in action. To the north was the 44th Infantry Division; to the south was an open flank. The division's nine infantry battalions had an aggregate Combat/Fighting Strength of 31%.

LI Corps – The 45th Pioneer Battalion was assigned to the corps. The corps suffered the following officer casualties: one killed in action; two wounded in action.

76th Infantry Division – The division defended in sector along the Don River against the 98th Rifle Division. The division suffered two men killed in action; one officer, two NCOs and 21 enlisted were wounded in action. To the north was the 384th Infantry Division; to the south was the 295th Infantry Division. The division's nine infantry battalions had an aggregate Combat/Fighting Strength of 42%.

295th Infantry Division – The division defended in sector along the Don River against the 40th Tank Brigade. The division amended its previous day's report; for the two day period of August 16 and 17 the unit suffered two officers killed in action, two NCOs killed in action and 19 enlisted men killed in action; nine officers were wounded in action as were 25 NCOs and 90 enlisted; one enlisted man was reported missing in action. To the north was the 76th Infantry Division; to the south was the 44th Infantry Division. The division's seven infantry battalions had an aggregate Combat/Fighting Strength of 65%.

Sources, August 17, 1942: ***Oberkommando des Heeres, Lage Ost: Stand: 17.8.42, Eastern Front Situation Map, National Archives Identifier: 559733, Record Group 242 – National Archives Collection of Foreign Records Seized, 1675-1958, National Archives, College Park, Maryland; Ia, Armeeoberkommando 6, "Morgen Meldung" and assorted reports, Kriegstagebuch 13, 18 August 1942, as found in Microfilm Series, T-312, Records of German Field Commands, Armies, Roll 1682, National Archives and Records Service, College***

Park, Maryland; 22nd Panzer Division, Kriegstagebuch 2, 17 August 1942, as found in Microfilm Series T-315, Roll 784, National Archives and Records Service, College Park, Maryland; 79th Infantry Division, Kriegstagebuch, 17 August 1942, as found in Microfilm Series T-315, Roll 1108, National Archives and Records Service, College Park, Maryland; 384th Infantry Division, Kriegstagebuch, 17 August 1942, as found in Microfilm Series T-315, Roll 2188, National Archives and Records Service, College Park, Maryland; David M. Glantz, & Jonathan M. House, To the Gates of Stalingrad: Soviet-German Combat Operations, April-August 1942, (The Stalingrad Trilogy, Volume 1), Lawrence, Kansas: University Press of Kansas, 2009, 314-330, 384, 391; Jochen Löser, Bittere Pflicht: Kampf und Untergang der 76. Berlin-Brandenburgischen Infanterie-Division, Osnabrück, FRG: Biblio Verlag, 1986, 188.

German rear echelon troops encampment at Zymlov near Kletskaya. The wagon on the left is the "goulash cannon" that cooked hot meals. Soldiers are living in 2-3-man tents; the photo appears to have been taken in August or September 1942.

Walter von Reichenau. A complex man, he was a Nazi supporter and anti-Semite, yet he helped conceal the Jewish boyfriend of his sister in law. He suffered a cerebral hemorrhage in Russia; during the medical evacuation flight to Germany, he suffered a heart attack and died on January 17, 1942.

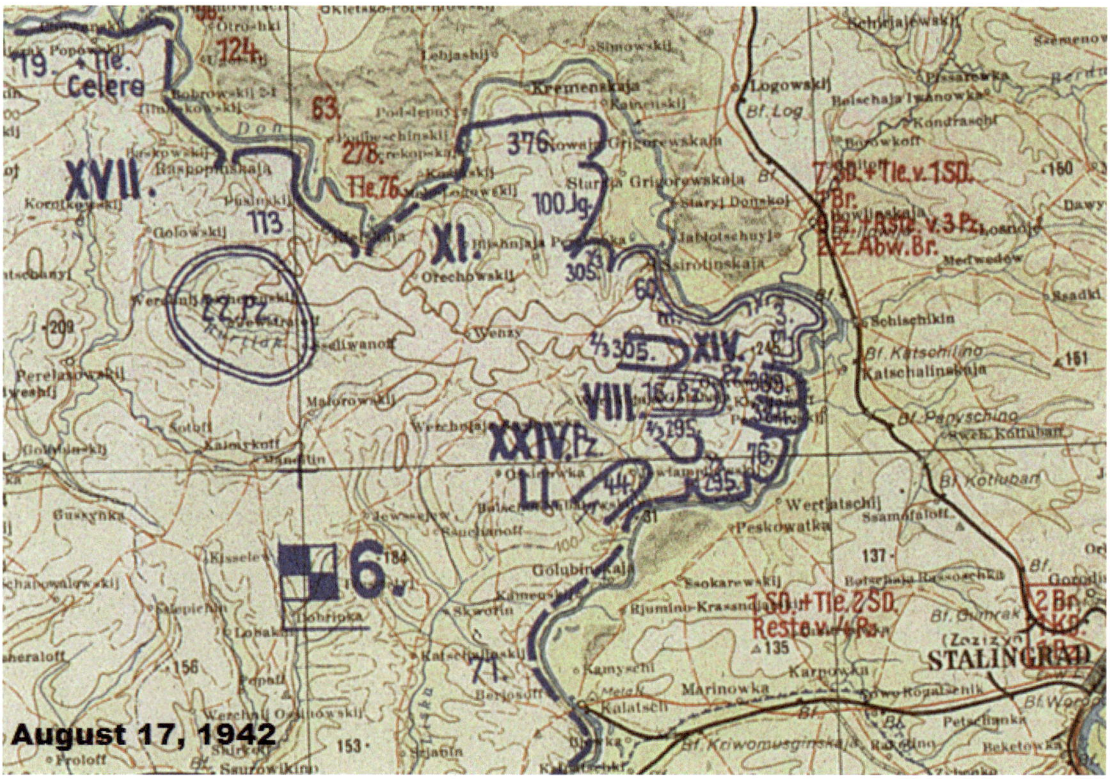

August 18, 1942
Weather: east wind, overcast, light rain showers, 68° F, 54° F and rain at night
Sunrise: 4:58 a.m.; **Sunset:** 7:13 p.m.
Moon: Waxing Crescent; 39% illumination

Sixth Army – The army headquarters was located at Dobrinka.

VIII Corps – The 2nd Heavy ***Werfer*** Regiment and the 754th Pioneer Battalion were assigned to the corps. The corps suffered the following officer casualties: one killed in action; 12 wounded in action.

305th Infantry Division – The division defended in sector near the Don River. To the north was the 100th ***Jäger*** Infantry Division; to the southeast was the 60th Infantry Division (Motorized.) Two-thirds of the division occupied an assembly area west of the front lines.

384th Infantry Division – The division expanded its bridgehead across the Don River near Verkhne-Gnilovskii against the 39th Guards Rifle Division. The division lost one officer and 64 NCOs/enlisted killed in action; seven officers and 204 NCOs/enlisted were wounded in action; 12 men were reported missing in action. To the north was the 389th Infantry Division; to the south was the 76th Infantry Division.

389th Infantry Division – The division expanded its bridgehead across the Don River near Nizhne-Akatov against the 214th Rifle Division. To the north was the 3rd Infantry Division (Motorized); to the south was the 384th Infantry Division.

XI Corps – The corps suffered the following officer casualties: four killed in action; six wounded in action.

22nd Panzer Division – The division moved northeast and counter-attacked a Soviet penetration across the Don River southwest of Logowskii; it then defended in sector against the 76th Rifle Division. To the west was the 113th Infantry Division; to the northeast was the 376th Infantry Division. The division headquarters was located at Orekhov.

100th Jäger Division – The division attacked along the northern loop of the Don River near Perekopka against the 40th Guards Rifle Division. The division suffered 29 NCOs/enlisted killed in action; six officers and 76 NCOs/enlisted were wounded in action; seven NCO/enlisted were reported missing in action. To the southeast was part of the 305th Infantry Division; to the northwest was the 376th Infantry Division.

376th Infantry Division – The division defended in sector south of the Don River, from Perekopka-Perekopskaya-Novogrigor'evskaia, against the 98th Rifle Division. To the southwest was 22nd ***Panzer*** Division; to the southeast was the 100th ***Jäger*** Division.

XIV *Panzer* Corps – The corps suffered the following officer casualties: one killed in action; one wounded in action. Corps troops suffered three enlisted men killed in action; one officer and 18 enlisted were wounded in action.

3rd Infantry Division (Motorized) – The division defended in sector along the Don River. To the west was the 60th Infantry Division (Motorized); to the south was the 389th Infantry Division.

16th Panzer Division – The division conducted rest and refit operations west of the front line in an assembly area.

60th Infantry Division (Motorized) – The division defended in sector along the Don River. To the west was part of the 305th Infantry Division; to the east was the 3rd Infantry Division (Motorized.)

XVII Corps – Corps troops reported one officer and 27 NCO/enlisted killed in action; five officers and 82 NCO/enlisted were wounded in action; one officer and 30 NCO/enlisted were missing in action. The corps suffered the following officer casualties: nine wounded in action; one missing in action.

79th Infantry Division – The division defended in sector along the Don River against the 304th Rifle Division and the 96th Rifle Division. To the west was the 2nd Italian Infantry Division of the XXXV Corps of the Italian Eighth Army; to the southeast was the 113th Infantry Division.

113th Infantry Division – The division defended in sector along the Don River near Raspopinskaya against the 63rd Rifle Division and the 278th Rifle Division. To the northwest was the 79th Infantry Division; to the east was the 22nd *Panzer* Division.

XXIV *Panzer* Corps – The corps reported that two enlisted men were killed in action and six wounded in action.

71st Infantry Division – The division defended in sector along the Don River against the 399th Rifle Division. To the north was the 295th Infantry Division; to the south was an open flank.

LI Corps – The aim of the corps was to prepare to cross the Don River in force. The corps suffered the following officer casualties: one killed in action; six wounded in action. The corps reserve was the 604th Engineer Regimental Staff (Motorized), the 672nd Pioneer Battalion and the 655th Bridge Construction Battalion.

44th Infantry Division – The division occupied an assembly area west of the Don River.

76th Infantry Division – The division expanded its bridgehead across the Don River near Perepol'nyi against the 98th Rifle Division. The division suffered six men killed in action and 15 men wounded in action. To the north was the 384th Infantry Division; to the southwest was the 295th Infantry Division. The division was reinforced by the 413th Engineer Regimental Staff, the 60th Pioneer Battalion (Motorized), the 652nd Pioneer Battalion and the 912th Assault Boat Commando.

295th Infantry Division – The division expanded its bridgehead across the Don River near Peskovatka against the 87th Rifle Division. To the north was the 76th Infantry Division; to the southwest was the 71st Infantry Division. The division was reinforced by the 605th Engineer Regimental Staff (Motorized), the 41st Pioneer Battalion (Motorized) and the 45th Pioneer Battalion (Motorized.)

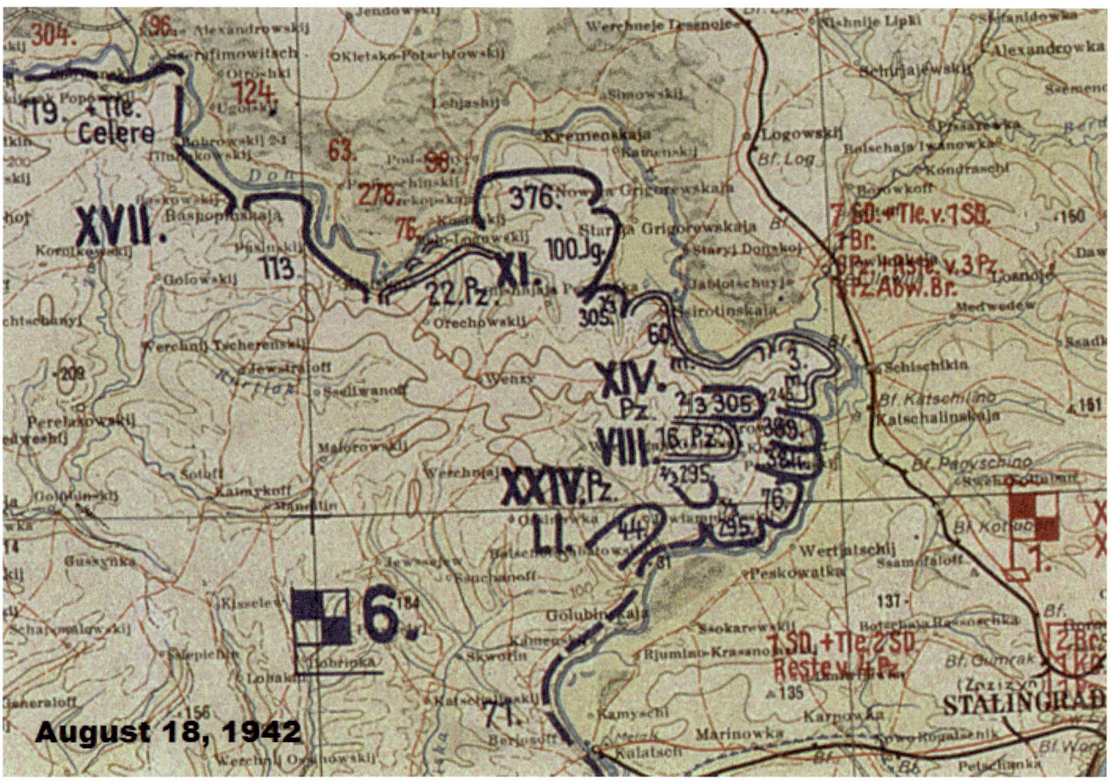

Sources, August 18, 1942: ***Oberkommando des Heeres, Lage Ost: Stand: 18.8.42, Eastern Front Situation Map, National Archives Identifier: 559733, Record Group 242 – National Archives Collection of Foreign Records Seized, 1675-1958, National Archives, College Park, Maryland; Ia, Armeeoberkommando 6, "Morgen Meldung" and assorted reports, Kriegstagebuch 13, 19 August 1942, as found in Microfilm Series, T-312, Records of German Field Commands, Armies, Roll 1682, National Archives and Records Service, College Park, Maryland; 22nd Panzer Division, Kriegstagebuch 2, 18 August 1942, as found in Microfilm Series T-315, Roll 784, National Archives and Records Service, College Park, Maryland; 384th Infantry Division, Kriegstagebuch, 18 August 1942, as found in Microfilm Series T-315, Roll 2188, National Archives and Records Service, College Park, Maryland; David M. Glantz, & Jonathan M. House, To the Gates of Stalingrad: Soviet-German Combat Operations, April-August 1942, (The Stalingrad Trilogy, Volume 1), Lawrence, Kansas: University Press of Kansas, 2009, 317-330, 384, 391; Friedrich Wilhelm Hauck, Eine Deutsche Division in Russland und Italian: 305. Infanterie-Division, 1941-1945, Dorheim, FRG: Podzun Verlag, 1975, 62; Jochen Löser, Bittere Pflicht: Kampf und Untergang der 76. Berlin-Brandenburgischen Infanterie-Division, Osnabrück, FRG: Biblio Verlag, 1986, 193-194; Kurt Mehner, Die Geheimen Tagesberichte der Deutschen Wehrmachtführung im Zweiten Weltkrieg 1939-1945, Band 5: 1. Juni 1942 – 30. November 1942, Osnabrück, Germany: Biblio Verlag, 1991, 150.***

Soldat **Karl Hofstetter** was born on June 14, 1922 in Gutau, near Linz, Austria. He was killed in action at Perekopka on August 18, 1942, very likely assigned to the 100th ***Jäger*** Division. His name is listed in the remembrance book at the German Military Cemetery at Rossoschka.

Schütze **Franz Wolkenstein** was born in Borotitz, Moravia on September 30, 1923. Assigned to an infantry regiment, probably in the 113th Infantry Division, he was killed in action at Raspopinskaya on August 18, 1923. He was buried at this location, although his remains have never been found.

Letter from *Unteroffizier* Johannes "Hannes" Weichs, near Abganerovo, to a cousin on August 18, 1942. The soldier was assigned to the 9th Battery in the 4th Battalion of the 371st Artillery Regiment in the 371st Infantry Division. In his letter, he writes:

> "Thank you for the nice book and letter I got from you yesterday. It was stamped July 16 and got here after four weeks in transit. I hope you are well and I can tell you that I am OK too. We are in new positions now, east of the Don [River] and making good headway. The talk is that part of our division has reached the Volga [River.] But right now, the fighting is inside the city and we hope for a speedy capture.
>
> When this happens, I am sure it will knock the Russians over; they cannot escape much further east. There is not much activity going on in my section here; we are engaged in a few artillery duels trying to get into better positions. We are to the north; it's a hot day today and only at night will we have a bit of relief. In the daytime, we have a special seat to see our ***Luftwaffe*** over the city. They flew 20 attacks yesterday; added to that is the artillery fire and you can imagine the good show we have.
>
> How are things at home? Do people think that the war will be over this year? Well, let's hope so. Most of us have been here in Russia since June 1941 and have not been home yet. Those who were in France in 1940 have already had home leave. But honestly, who wants to go home from here? The end is near and everybody wants to be present when resistance collapses; the Russians have no air left to breathe. The weather is still good and let winter wait a while. I have received mail from Hans Henges; he is up north in Finland. There, winter will come soon. Otto Cerberitus is in Africa; he was recently awarded the Iron Cross 1st Class, pinned on by General Rommel himself in Tobruk. Well, I must close now; my guard duty starts at 2:00 p.m."

August 19, 1942
Weather: changing cloudiness, increasing clouds after noon, light wind, 73° F, 54° F at night, good road conditions
Sunrise: 4:59 a.m.; **Sunset:** 7:11 p.m.
Moon: First Quarter; 50% illumination

Sixth Army – ***General der Panzertruppe*** Friedrich Paulus issued the order for the Sixth Army attack on Stalingrad, beginning August 21, 1942. The army headquarters moved east to Ossinowskij. Bombers and dive-bombers from the ***Luftwaffe***'s VIII Air Corps pounded the east side of the Don River in large-scale attacks.

VIII Corps – The corps suffered the following officer casualties: two killed in action; 11 wounded in action; one accidental death; one missing in action.

305th Infantry Division – The division relieved the 3rd Infantry Division (Motorized) and defended in sector along the Don River against the 37th Guards Rifle Division. The division reported two men wounded in action. To the northwest was the 60th Infantry Division (Motorized); to the south was the 389th Infantry Division. The division transferred the 578th Infantry Regiment to the 384th Infantry Division for operations. One third of the division defended in sector between the 100th ***Jäger*** Division and the 60th Infantry Division (Motorized.)

384th Infantry Division – The division expanded its bridgehead across the Don River near Verkhne-Gnilovskii against the 84th Rifle Division. The division suffered one officer and 63 NCOs/enlisted killed in action; five officers and 202 NCOs/enlisted were wounded in action; 17 men were reported missing in action. To the north was the 389th Infantry Division; to the south was the 76th Infantry Division. The 578th Infantry Regiment was assigned to the division.

389th Infantry Division – The division expanded its bridgehead across the Don River near Nizhne-Akatov against the 22nd Motorized Rifle Brigade. To the north was the 305th Infantry Division; to the south was the 384th Infantry Division.

XI Corps – The 521st ***Panzerjäger*** Detachment was assigned to the corps. The corps suffered the following officer casualties: one killed in action; one wounded in action. The corps headquarters was located at Orekovskij.

22nd Panzer Division – The division defended along the Don River against the 76th Rifle Division and the 343rd Rifle Division. The division lost one officer and eight NCO/enlisted killed in action; 59 NCO/enlisted were wounded in action; two NCOs/enlisted were missing in action. To the west was the 113th Infantry Division; to the northeast was the 376th Infantry Division. The ***panzer*** regiment was detached to 376th Infantry Division.

44th Infantry Division – The division occupied an assembly area west of the Don River.

100th Jäger Division – The division attacked along the northern loop of the Don River near Perekopka against the 40th Guards Rifle Division. The division suffered one officer and 11 NCO/enlisted killed in action; one officer and 59 NCO/enlisted were wounded in action. To the north was the 376th Infantry Division; to the south was part of the 305th Infantry Division.

376th Infantry Division – The division defended in sector against the 321st Rifle Regiment and the 88th Rifle Regiment south of the Don River, from Perekopka-Perekopskaya-Novogrigor'evskaia. The division reported one officer killed in action and 11 NCO/enlisted wounded in action; ten NCO/enlisted were missing in action. To the southwest was the 22nd ***Panzer*** Division; to the southeast was the 100th ***Jäger*** Division. The division headquarters was located at Orekovskij.

XIV *Panzer* Corps – The corps suffered the following officer casualties: one killed in action; one wounded in action.

3rd Infantry Division (Motorized) – The division occupied an assembly area south of the Don River behind the front. The division suffered three men killed in action and 11 men wounded in action. To the northwest was the 60th Infantry Division (Motorized); to the southeast was the 389th Infantry Division.

16th Panzer Division – The division conducted rest and refit operations behind the front line in an assembly area.

60th Infantry Division (Motorized) – The division defended in sector along the Don River. To the west was part of the 305th Infantry Division; to the east was the remainder of the 305th Infantry Division.

XVII Corps

79th Infantry Division – The division defended in sector along the Don River against the 304th Rifle Division and the 96th Rifle Division. The division suffered four NCO/enlisted killed in action, 17 NCO/enlisted wounded in action and 4 NCO/enlisted missing in action. To the west was the 2nd Italian Infantry Division of the XXXV Corps of the Italian Eighth Army; to the south was the 113th Infantry Division.

113th Infantry Division – The division defended in sector along the Don River near Raspopinskaya against the 63rd Rifle Division and the 278th Rifle Division. The division sustained one man killed in action and seven NCO/enlisted wounded in action. To the northwest was the 79th Infantry Division; to the east was the 22nd ***Panzer*** Division.

XXIV *Panzer* Corps

71st Infantry Division – The division defended in sector along the Don River against the 399th Rifle Division and the 131st Rifle Division. The division lost two men killed in action and 13 men wounded in action. To the north was the 295th Infantry Division; to the south was an open flank.

LI Corps – The 244th ***Sturmgeschütz*** Detachment was assigned to the corps. The corps suffered the following officer casualties: one killed in action; seven wounded in action.

76th Infantry Division – The division expanded its bridgehead across the Don River near Perepol’nyi against the 98th Rifle Division. The division lost three NCOs/enlisted wounded in action. To the north was the 384th Infantry Division; to the south was the 295th Infantry Division.

295th Infantry Division – The division expanded its bridgehead across the Don River near Peskovatka against the 87th Rifle Division. To the north was the 76th Infantry Division; to the southwest was the 71st Infantry Division.

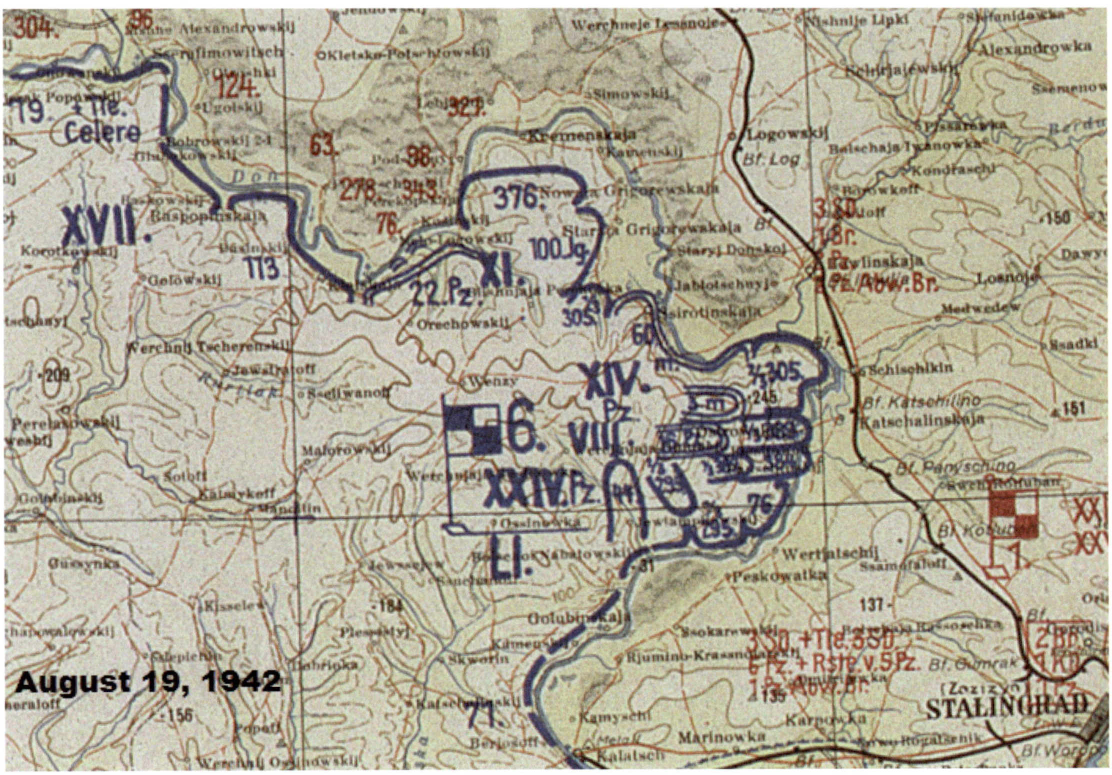

Sources, August 19, 1942: *Oberkommando des Heeres, Lage Ost: Stand: 19.8.42, Eastern Front Situation Map, National Archives Identifier: 559733, Record Group 242 – National Archives Collection of Foreign Records Seized, 1675-1958, National Archives, College Park, Maryland; Ia, Armeeoberkommando 6, "Morgen Meldung" and assorted reports, Kriegstagebuch 13, 20 August 1942, as found in Microfilm Series, T-312, Records of German Field Commands, Armies, Roll 1682, National Archives and Records Service, College Park, Maryland; 22nd Panzer Division, Kriegstagebuch 2, 19 August 1942, as found in Microfilm Series T-315, Roll 784, National Archives and Records Service, College Park, Maryland; 384th Infantry Division, Kriegstagebuch, 19 August 1942, as found in Microfilm Series T-315, Roll 2188, National Archives and Records Service, College Park, Maryland; David M. Glantz, & Jonathan M. House, To the Gates of Stalingrad: Soviet-German Combat Operations, April-August 1942, (The Stalingrad Trilogy, Volume 1), Lawrence, Kansas: University Press of Kansas, 2009, 317-330, 384, 391; Friedrich Wilhelm Hauck, Eine Deutsche Division in Russland und Italian: 305. Infanterie-Division, 1941-1945, Dorheim, FRG: Podzun Verlag, 1975, 65; Jochen Löser, Bittere Pflicht: Kampf und Untergang der 76. Berlin-Brandenburgischen Infanterie-Division, Osnabrück, FRG: Biblio Verlag, 1986, 191.*

Nur eine kleine Weile und wir werden uns wiedersehn.

Zur Erinnerung im Gebete
an den tapferen Krieger
Jäger in einem Gebirgsjäger-Regt.
Karl Mayrhofer
Bauerssohn
vom Hauergute in Nieder-Zirking
welcher am 19. August 1942 im Südabschnitt der Ostfront im Alter von 20 Jahren für Führer, Volk und Vaterland gefallen ist.

O, ihr lieben Eltern und Schwestern mein,
Ich kehre nicht mehr zu euch heim,
Im Heldentod fürs Vaterland
Umschlang mich eurer Liebe Band.
Mein letzter Gedanke, mein letzter Blick,
Er kehrte noch zu euch zurück.
Lebt wohl!
Möge euer Schmerz vergehn,
Im Himmel dort auf Wiedersehn.

Besteller: Maria Zeller, Ried in der Riedmark. — L-0278 3526-42

Jäger* Karl Mayrhofer** was born on September 30, 1922 in Rieder-Zirking, Austria. The son of a farmer, and assigned to a mountain infantry regiment in the 100th ***Jäger Division, he died of his wounds on August 19, 1942 at the 2/542 Field Hospital near Verkhne-Businovka. He is buried at the German Military Cemetery at Rossoschka in Block 12, Row 13 in Grave 514.

August 20, 1942
Weather: cloudy, dry, warm, good flying weather, strong northeastern wind, 77° F, 54° F at night
Sunrise: 5:01 a.m.; **Sunset:** 7:09 p.m.
Moon: Waxing Gibbous; 62% illumination

Sixth Army – The army repelled ten large attacks aimed at reducing the bridgehead over the Don River. The army headquarters was located at Ossinowskij. Fighters from the ***Luftwaffe***'s VIII Air Corps defended the airspace over the forward German units on the Don River.

VIII Corps – The 652nd Pioneer Battalion was assigned to the corps. The corps suffered the following officer casualties: 16 wounded in action. The corps reported 38 medium and 16 heavy anti-tank guns as operational.

305th Infantry Division – The division defended in sector, assuming responsibility for the old sector of the 3rd Infantry Division (Motorized.) The division lost two NCOs/enlisted wounded in action. To the west was the 60th Infantry Division (Motorized); to the south was the 389th Infantry Division.

384th Infantry Division – The division expanded its bridgehead across the Don River near Verkhne-Gnilovskii, repelled an enemy attack and prepared for the offensive. The division lost one officer and 81 NCOs/enlisted killed in action; four officers and 257 NCOs/enlisted were wounded in action; 19 men were reported missing in action. To the north was the 389th Infantry Division; to the south was the 76th Infantry Division.

389th Infantry Division – The division expanded its bridgehead across the Don River near Nizhne-Akatov, repelled an enemy attack and prepared for the offensive. To the north was the 305th Infantry Division; to the south was the 384th Infantry Division.

XI Corps – The corps headquarters was located at Orekovskij.

22nd Panzer Division – The division defended in sector along the Don River against the 76th Rifle Division and the 343rd Rifle Division. To the west was the 113th Infantry Division; to the northeast was the 376th Infantry Division.

44th Infantry Division – The division began to assume responsibility for the 60th Infantry Division (Motorized) sector.

100th Jäger Division – The division defended in sector near Perekopka and prepared for the offensive against the 40th Guards Rifle Division. To the north was the 376th Infantry Division; to the south was part of the 305th Infantry Division.

376th Infantry Division – The division conducted defended in sector south of the Don River from Perekopka-Perekopskaya-Novogrigor'evskaia against the 343rd Rifle Division and the 321st Rifle Division. The division prepared for the offensive. To the west was the 22nd ***Panzer*** Division; to the southeast was the 100th ***Jäger*** Division. The division headquarters was located at Orekovskij.

XIV *Panzer* Corps – The corps suffered the following officer casualties: one wounded in action.

3rd Infantry Division (Motorized) – The division conducted rest and refit operations in an assembly area to the rear of the front and prepared for the offensive.

16th Panzer Division – The division conducted rest and refit operations behind the front line in an assembly area and prepared for the offensive.

60th Infantry Division (Motorized) – The division defended in sector along the Don River. To the west was part of the 305th Infantry Division; to the east was the rest of the 305th Infantry Division. The division began to transfer its sector to the 44th Infantry Division.

XVII Corps – The corps suffered the following officer casualties: two wounded in action.

79th Infantry Division – The division defended in sector along the Don River near Serafimovich, repelling the 304th Rifle Division. The division lost four NCOs/enlisted killed in action; 17 NCOs/enlisted were wounded in action; 17 men were reported missing in action. To the west was the 2nd Italian Infantry Division of the XXXV Corps of the Italian Eighth Army; to the southeast was the 113th Infantry Division.

113th Infantry Division – The division defended in sector along the Don River near Raspopinskaya, repelling an enemy attack across the Don and prepared for the offensive. The division lost one NCO/enlisted killed in action; seven NCOs/enlisted were wounded in action. To the northwest was the 79th Infantry Division; to the east was the 22nd ***Panzer*** Division.

XXIV *Panzer* Corps

71st Infantry Division – The division defended in sector along the Don River against the 399th Rifle Division and the 131st Rifle Division. To the north was the 295th Infantry Division; to the south was an open flank.

LI Corps – The corps suffered the following officer casualties: one killed in action.

76th Infantry Division – The division expanded its bridgehead across the Don River near Perepol'nyi against the 98th Rifle Division. To the north was the 384th Infantry Division; to the south was the 295th Infantry Division.

295th Infantry Division – The division expanded its bridgehead across the Don River near Peskovatka against the 87th Rifle Division. To the north was the 76th Infantry Division; to the southwest was the 71st Infantry Division.

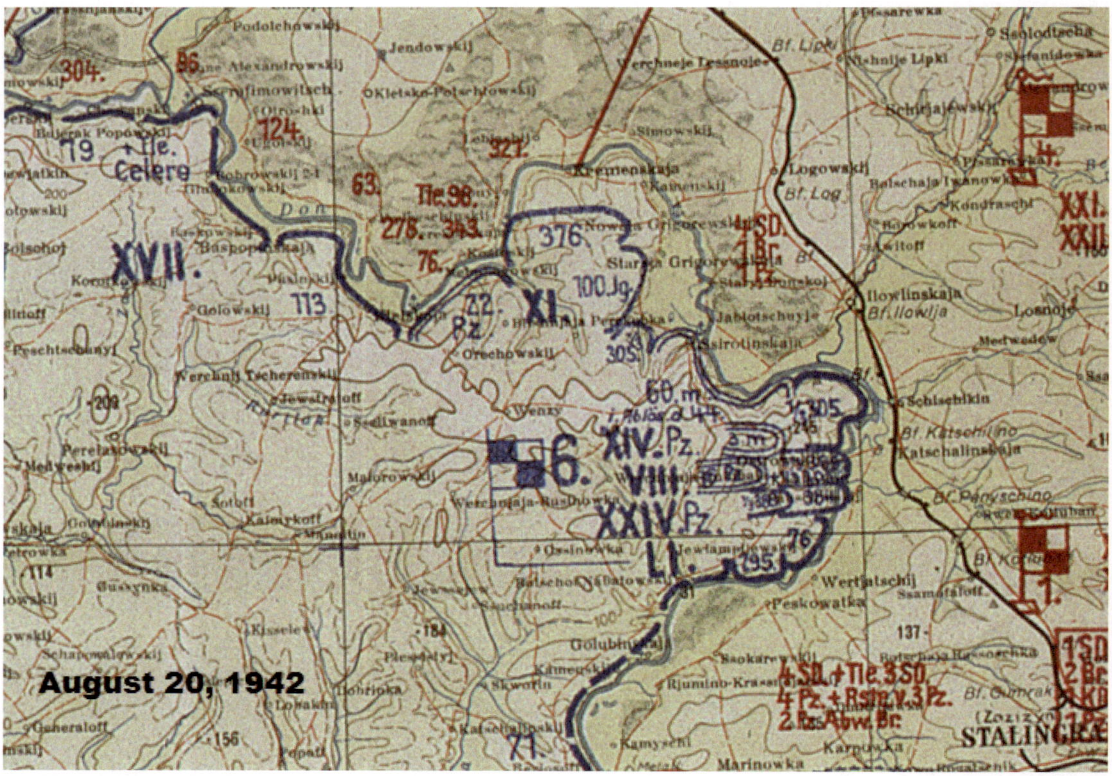

Sources, August 20, 1942: *Oberkommando des Heeres, Lage Ost: Stand: 20.8.42, Eastern Front Situation Map, National Archives Identifier: 559733, Record Group 242 – National Archives Collection of Foreign Records Seized, 1675-1958, National Archives, College Park, Maryland; Ia, Armeeoberkommando 6, "Morgen Meldung" and assorted reports, Kriegstagebuch 13, 21 August 1942, as found in Microfilm Series, T-312, Records of German Field Commands, Armies, Roll 1682, National Archives and Records Service, College Park, Maryland; 22nd Panzer Division, Kriegstagebuch 2, 20 August 1942, as found in Microfilm Series T-315, Roll 784, National Archives and Records Service, College Park, Maryland; 384th Infantry Division, Kriegstagebuch, 20 August 1942, as found in Microfilm Series T-315, Roll 2188, National Archives and Records Service, College Park, Maryland; David M. Glantz, & Jonathan M. House, To the Gates of Stalingrad: Soviet-German Combat Operations, April-August 1942, (The Stalingrad Trilogy, Volume 1), Lawrence, Kansas: University Press of Kansas, 2009, 321-330, 384, 391; Percy E. Schramm, Editor, Kriegstagebuch des Oberkommandos der Wehrmacht, 1942, Band II – Band III, München, BRD: Bernhard & Graefe Verlag, 1982, Band II, 619.*

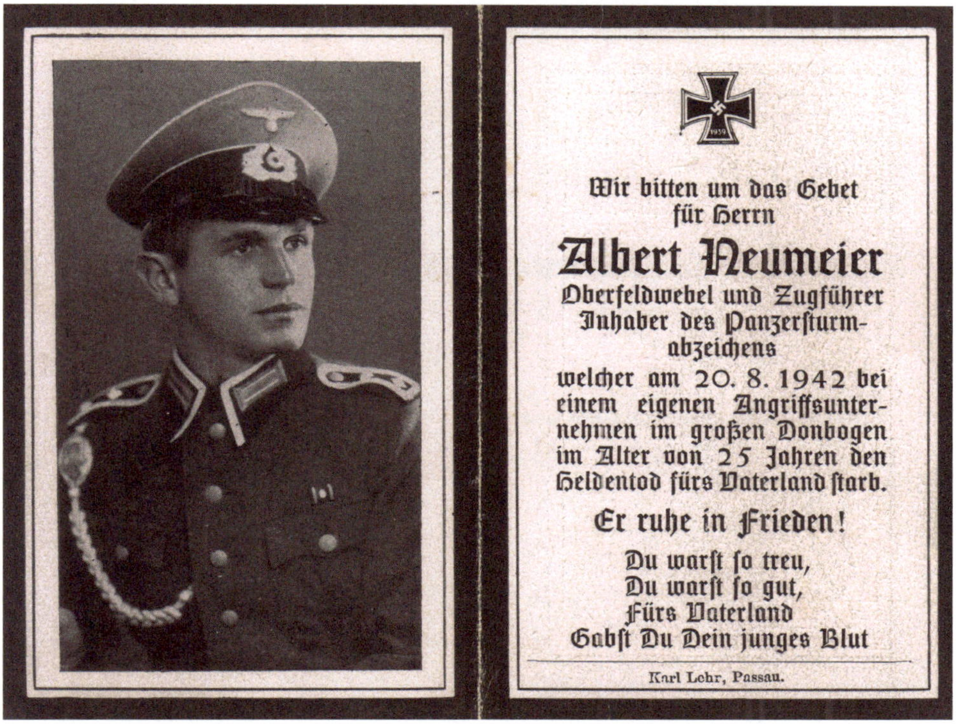

Oberfeldwebel **Albert Neumeier** was born in Haselbach in the Straubing-Bogen region of Bavaria on September 17, 1917. An infantryman, he was killed in action about two miles east of Melo-Kletskiy on August 20, 1942. The winner of the Panzer Assault Badge, he was almost certainly in the 22nd *Panzer* Division. His name is listed in the remembrance book at the German Military Cemetery at Rossoschka.

Zum Andenken

an SA.-Mann

Josef Aschenberger

Gefreiter und erster MG.-Schütze in einem Infanterieregiment

Inhaber des Verwundeten-Abzeichens

Bauerssohn vom Pauschenberger-gute in Schönberg, Lohnsburg

welcher am 20. August 1942 im Kampfe gegen den Bolschewismus für seinen Führer und seine geliebte Heimat im 21. Lebensjahre den Heldentod fand.

Banges Hoffen, banges Sehnen
Trieb mich stets der Heimat zu;
Doch des Schöpfers Wille wollte,
Daß ich fern von Euch, ihr Lieben,
Gebettet ward in kühler Grabesruh'.

Reiberstorfer, Lohnsburg. 3536—42

Gefreiter **Josef Aschenberger** was born in Pauschenberg near Schönberg in Upper Austria in 1921. The son of a farmer, he was a machine-gunner in an infantry regiment and had previously received a Black Wound Badge. He was killed on August 20, 1942, but further details of his death are unknown.

Frommes Gebets-Andenken

an unseren lieben, unvergeßlichen Gatten, Vater, Sohn und Bruder

Fritz Höppl

Bauer in Wolfing

Unteroffizier in einem Inf.-Reg.

welcher am 20. August 1942 im 27. Lebensjahre bei den schweren Kämpfen an der Ostfront den Heldentod fand.

Trauernd als verlass'ne Waisen
Stehen nun am Hause wir
Und von blaßgehärmter Wange
Fließt die Träne schwer zu dir.
Ach, so oft, so sehnlich suchet
Dich der Kinder treuer Blick,
O, du bist so schnell entschwunden,
Vater, unseres Lebens Glück.
O Eltern, klaget Gott nicht an,
Er hat es so gefügt,
Was Gott tut, das ist wohlgetan,
Wenn's auch recht bitter drückt.
Ich bitt' euch alle, schließt mich ein
In's Herz und in's Gebet
Und laßt mich nie vergessen sein,
Wenn ihr zur Kirche geht.

Innviertler Verlagsgesellschaft Braunau a. I.

Unteroffizier **Fritz Höppl** was born in Wolfing/Tarsdorf, Upper Austria on July 10, 1915. A farmer, who was married and was a father, he was killed in the Nizhne-Akatov bridgehead over the Don River on August 20, 1942. He was assigned to the 389th Infantry Division.

August 21, 1942
Weather: overcast, dry, windy, 79° F, 50° F at night, good road conditions
Sunrise: 5:02 a.m.; **Sunset:** 7:07 p.m.
Moon: Waxing Gibbous; 73% illumination

Sixth Army – The army headquarters was located at Ossinowskij.

VIII Corps – The 244th ***Sturmgeschütz*** Detachment was assigned to the corps. The corps suffered the following officer casualties: five killed in action; 11 wounded in action.

305th Infantry Division – The division defended in sector along the Don River against the 37th Guards Rifle Division. The division reported 70 NCOs/enlisted killed in action and 80 NCOs/enlisted wounded in action. To the west was the 44th Infantry Division; to the south was the 389th Infantry Division.

384th Infantry Division – The division expanded its bridgehead across the Don River near Verkhne-Gnilovskii against the 39th Guards Rifle Division. The division suffered one officer and 45 NCOs/enlisted killed in action; one officer and 162 NCOs/enlisted were wounded in action; 12 men were reported missing in action. To the north was the 389th Infantry Division; to the south was the 76th Infantry Division.

389th Infantry Division – The division expanded its bridgehead across the Don River near Nizhne-Akatov against the 22nd Motorized Rifle Brigade. To the north was the 305th Infantry Division; to the south was the 384th Infantry Division.

XI Corps – The corps suffered the following officer casualties: two killed in action; five wounded in action.

44th Infantry Division – The division defended in sector along the Don River near Sirotinskaya against the 4th Guards Rifle Division. To the east was the 305th Infantry Division; to the northwest was the 100th ***Jäger*** Division.

100th Jäger Division – The division defended in sector along the Don River against the 40th Guards Rifle Division and prepared to move from the Don River bend west to assume defensive positions west Sirotinskaya. The division suffered 12 NCOs/enlisted killed in action and one officer, 40 NCO/enlisted wounded in action. To the southeast was the 44th Infantry Division; to the north was the 376th Infantry Division.

376th Infantry Division – The division defended in sector south of the Don River from Perekopka-Perekopskaya-Novogrigor'evskaia against the 321st Rifle Division and the 98th Rifle Division. The division reported one officer and 20 NCOs/enlisted were killed in action; three officers and 21 NCOs/enlisted were wounded in action; nine NCOs/enlisted were missing in action. To the southwest was the 22nd ***Panzer*** Division; to the southeast was the 100th ***Jäger*** Division.

XIV *Panzer* Corps – The corps suffered the following officer casualties: four killed in action; three wounded in action.

3rd Infantry Division (Motorized) – The division prepared to move from its assembly area east to cross the Don River and prepare for the attack in bridgeheads on the east side of the river.

16th Panzer Division – The division prepared to move from its assembly area east to cross the Don River and prepare for the attack in bridgeheads on the east side of the river.

60th Infantry Division (Motorized) – The division moved to an assembly area and prepared for the attack in bridgeheads on the east side of the river.

XVII Corps

79th Infantry Division – The division defended in sector along the Don River near Serafimovich, as enemy pressure mounted from the 304th Rifle Division and the 96th Rifle Division. The division lost 22 NCOs/enlisted killed in action; one officer and 22 NCOs/enlisted were wounded in action; three NCOs/enlisted were missing in action. To the west was the 2nd Italian Infantry Division of the XXXV Corps of the Italian Eighth Army; to the southeast was the 113th Infantry Division.

113th Infantry Division – The division defended in sector along the Don River near Raspopinskaya and prepared for the offensive. The division reported one NCO/enlisted killed in action, four NCOs/enlisted were wounded in action; two men were reported missing in action. To the northwest was the 79th Infantry Division; to the northeast were elements of the 22nd ***Panzer*** Division.

XXIV *Panzer* Corps

71st Infantry Division – The division defended in sector along the Don River against the 399th Rifle Division and the 31st Rifle Division. The division reported two NCOs/enlisted killed in action and four NCOs/enlisted wounded in action. To the north was the 295th Infantry Division; to the south was an open flank.

LI Corps – The 912th Assault Boat Commando was assigned to the corps. The corps suffered the following officer casualties: six killed in action; 20 wounded in action. The corps troops suffered the following officer casualties: one killed in action; two wounded in action.

76th Infantry Division – The division crossed the Don River in force and established a bridgehead near Peskovatka-Vertyachiy, repelling a large enemy armored attack. The division lost one officer and 36 NCOs/enlisted

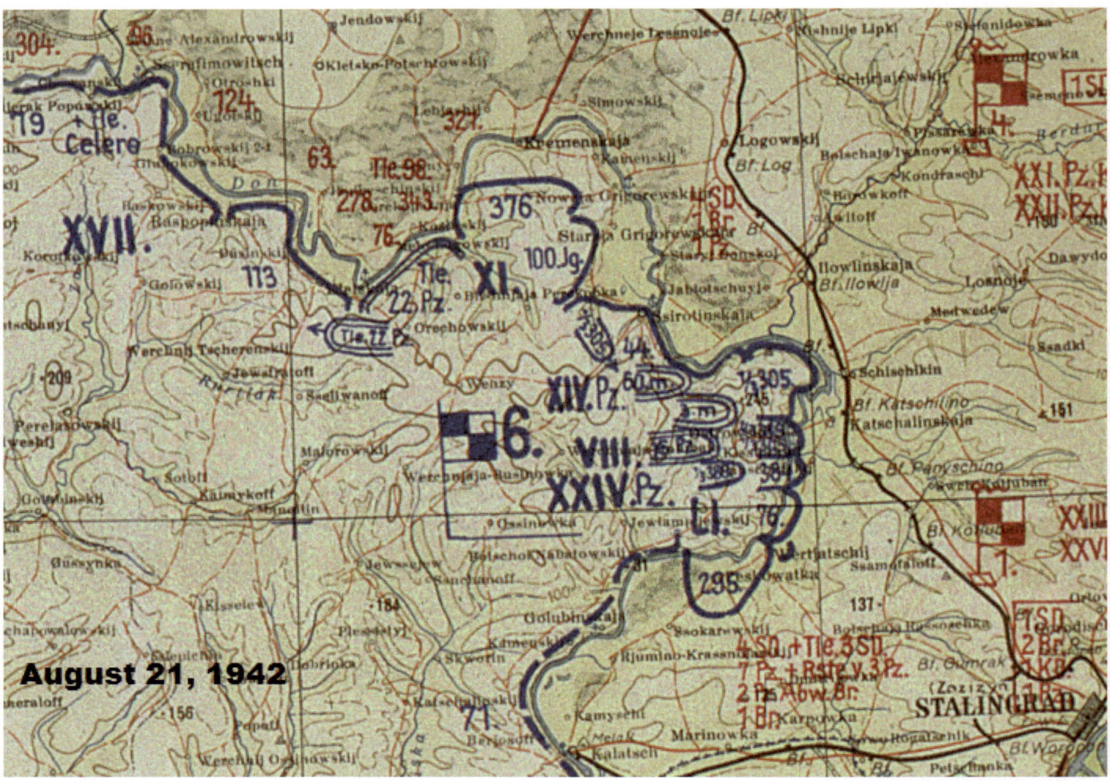

August 21, 1942

killed in action; eight officers and 198 NCOs/enlisted were wounded in action.

295th Infantry Division – The division crossed the Don River in force and established a bridgehead east of Peskovatka against the 137th Tank Brigade. The division reported three officers and 20 NCOs/enlisted were killed in action; four officers and 91 NCOs/enlisted were wounded in action; three men were reported missing in action; three men drowned. To the north was the 76th Infantry Division; to the south was the 71st Infantry Division.

Sixth Army Reserve

22nd Panzer Division – The ***panzer*** regiment of the division moved northeast between the 376th Infantry Division and the 100th ***Jäger*** Division and attacked the 38th Guards Rifle Division just south of the Don River, seizing Hill 199.1. Part of the division defended in sector. A third portion of the division moved west toward the XVII Corps. The division lost seven NCOs/enlisted killed in action and 41 NCO/enlisted wounded in action. To the northeast was the 376th Infantry Division; to the west was the 113th Infantry Division.

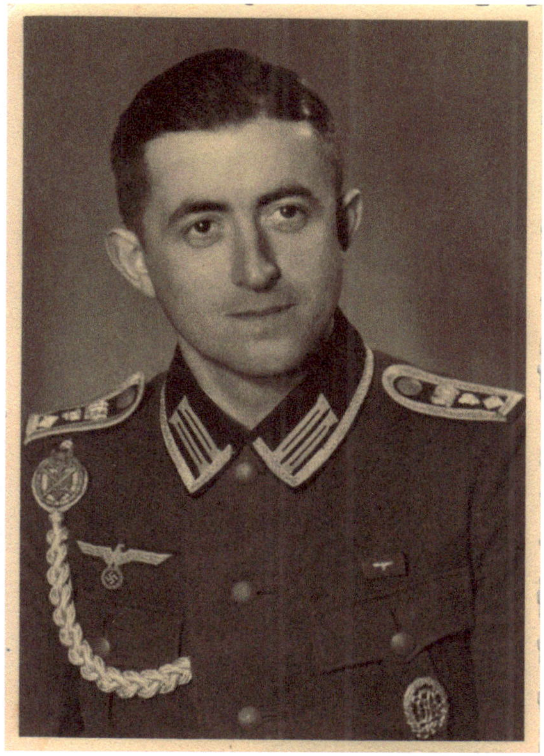

Feldwebel **Hellmuth Meyenburg** was born on July 8, 1911 in Arendsee near Salzwedel in Saxony-Anhalt. Assigned to the 76th Infantry Division, he was killed in action on August 21, 1942 near Vertyachiy, near the Don River. The location of his remains is unknown.

Sources, August 21, 1942: ***Oberkommando des Heeres, Lage Ost: Stand: 21.8.42, Eastern Front Situation Map, National Archives Identifier: 559733, Record Group 242 – National Archives Collection of Foreign Records Seized, 1675-1958, National Archives, College Park, Maryland; Ia, Armeeoberkommando 6, "Morgen Meldung" and assorted reports, Kriegstagebuch 13, 22 August 1942, as found in Microfilm Series, T-312, Records of German Field Commands, Armies, Roll 1682, National Archives and Records Service, College Park, Maryland; 22nd Panzer Division, Kriegstagebuch 2, 21 August 1942, as found in Microfilm Series T-315, Roll 784, National Archives and Records Service, College Park, Maryland; 79th Infantry Division, Kriegstagebuch, 21 August 1942, as found in Microfilm Series T-315, Roll 1108, National Archives and Records Service, College Park, Maryland; 384th Infantry Division, Kriegstagebuch, 21 August 1942, as found in Microfilm Series T-315, Roll 2188, National Archives and Records Service, College Park, Maryland; David M. Glantz, & Jonathan M. House, To the Gates of Stalingrad: Soviet-German Combat Operations, April-August 1942, (The Stalingrad Trilogy, Volume 1), Lawrence, Kansas: University Press of Kansas, 2009, 321-333, 384-386, 391; Janusz Piekalkiewicz, Stalingrad: Anatomie einer Schlacht, München, BRD: Wilhelm Heyne Verlag, 1977, 97.***

August 22, 1942
Weather: sunny, mostly hotter, 72° F, 46° F at night
Sunrise: 5:03 a.m.; **Sunset:** 7:05 p.m.
Moon: Waxing Gibbous; 81% illumination

Sixth Army – The army headquarters was located at Ossinowskij.

VIII Corps – The corps headquarters was located at Rodionov. The 2nd ***Werfer*** Regiment was assigned to the corps. The corps suffered the following officer casualties: three killed in action; 14 wounded in action.

305th Infantry Division – The division defended in sector along the Don River against the 37th Guards Rifle Division. To the west was the 44th Infantry Division; to the south was the 389th Infantry Division.

384th Infantry Division – The division defended the bridgehead east of Nizhne-Akatov against the 39th Guards Rifle Division. The division lost 26 NCOs/enlisted killed in action; four officers and 104 NCOs/enlisted were wounded in action; five men were reported missing in action. To the north was the 389th Infantry Division; to the south was the 76th Infantry Division.

389th Infantry Division – The division defended the bridgehead east of Nizhne-Akatov against the 22nd Motorized Rifle Brigade. To the north was the 305th Infantry Division; to the south was the 384th Infantry Division.

XI Corps – The corps suffered the following officer casualties: seven killed in action; 13 wounded in action. The corps headquarters was located at Ossinskij.

44th Infantry Division – The division defended in sector Kurchajessowskij-Kamyshinskiy-Hill 171.0-Hill 180.9-Sirotinskaya-Khmelevskoy, against the 40th Guards Rifle Division. The division headquarters was located in Verkhne-Golubaja. The division reported three officers and 27 NCOs/enlisted killed in action; five officers and 124 NCOs/enlisted were wounded in action. To the east was the 305th Infantry Division; to the northwest was the 100th ***Jäger*** Division.

100th Jäger Division – The division defended in sector west of Starogrigor'evskaya against the 41st Guards Rifle Division, the 38th Guards Rifle Division, the 40th Guards Rifle Division and the 182nd Rifle Division. The division suffered 26 NCOs/enlisted killed in action; one officer and 68 NCOs/enlisted were wounded in action. To the southeast was the 44th Infantry Division; to the northwest was the 376th Infantry Division.

376th Infantry Division – The division defended in sector against the 41st Guards Rifle Division, the 38th Guards Rifle Division, the 205th Rifle Division and the 321st Rifle Division. The division lost three officers, six NCOs and 17 enlisted men killed in action; 23 NCOs and 139 enlisted men were wounded in action; seven NCOs and 46 enlisted men were missing in action. To the southwest was an assortment of battle groups; to the southeast was the 100th ***Jäger*** Division.

XIV *Panzer* Corps – The 616th Heavy Artillery Detachment was assigned to the corps. The corps suffered the following officer casualties: two wounded in action; one missing in action.

3rd Infantry Division (Motorized) – The division crossed over the Don River in the 76th Infantry Division zone and prepared to attack out of the bridgehead east of the river.

16th Panzer Division – The division crossed the 140-meter long pontoon bridge over the Don River in the 295th Infantry Division zone and prepared to attack out of the bridgehead east of the river.

60th Infantry Division (Motorized) – The division prepared to cross over the Don River and attack out of its bridgehead east of the river.

XVII Corps – The corps suffered the following officer casualties: two wounded in action.

79th Infantry Division – The division defended in sector along the Don River near Serafimovich, as enemy pressure continued by the 304th Rifle Division, 86th Rifle Division and the 124th Rifle Division. The division lost 19 NCOs/enlisted killed in action; two officers and 72 NCO/enlisted were wounded in action. To the west was the 2nd Italian Infantry Division of the XXXV Corps of the Italian Eighth Army. To the southeast was the 113th Infantry Division. The division headquarters was located at Verkhne-Fomichinskii.

113th Infantry Division – The division defended in sector along the Don River against the 63rd Rifle Division and the 278th Rifle Division. The division reported six NCOs/enlisted men wounded in action. To the northwest was the 79th Infantry Division; to the east was an assortment of battle groups.

XXIV *Panzer* Corps – The corps suffered the following officer casualties: one wounded in action.

71st Infantry Division – The division defended in sector along the Don River against the 399th Rifle Division and the 131st Rifle Division. The division suffered four NCOs/enlisted wounded in action. To the north was the 295th Infantry Division; to the south was an open front.

LI Corps – The corps suffered the following officer casualties: six killed in action; 13 wounded in action.

76th Infantry Division – The division expanded its bridgehead over the Don River north of Vertyachiy against the 98th Rifle Division. To the north was the 384th Infantry Division; to the south was the 295th Infantry Division.

295th Infantry Division – The division defended in the Don River bridgehead south of Vertyachiy against the 87th Rifle Division and the 137th Tank Brigade, expanding its bridgehead to the southwest. The division suffered 44 NCOs/enlisted wounded in action. To the north was the 76th Infantry Division; to the south was the 71st Infantry Division.

Sixth Army Reserve

22nd Panzer Division – The division moved northwest to the XI Corps sector; the ***panzer*** regiment moved to Perilasowskij. Part of the division defended in sector along the Don River. The division reported four NCOs/enlisted killed in action and seven NCOs/enlisted wounded in action. To the northeast was the 376th Infantry Division; to the west was the 113th Infantry Division.

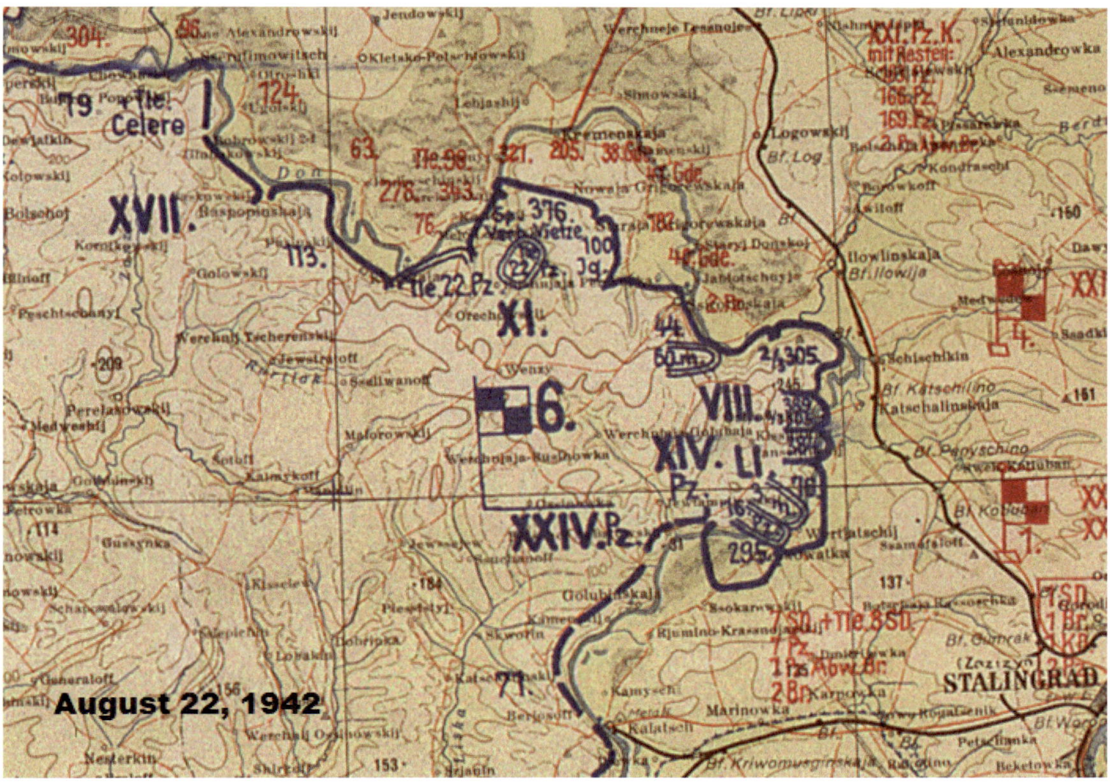

Sources, August 22, 1942: *Oberkommando des Heeres, Lage Ost: Stand: 22.8.42, Eastern Front Situation Map, National Archives Identifier: 559733, Record Group 242 – National Archives Collection of Foreign Records Seized, 1675-1958, National Archives, College Park, Maryland; Ia, Armeeoberkommando 6, "Morgen Meldung" and assorted reports, Kriegstagebuch 13, 23 August 1942, as found in Microfilm Series, T-312, Records of German Field Commands, Armies, Roll 1682, National Archives and Records Service, College Park, Maryland; 22nd Panzer Division, Kriegstagebuch 2, 22 August 1942, as found in Microfilm Series T-315, Roll 784, National Archives and Records Service, College Park, Maryland; 384th Infantry Division, Kriegstagebuch, 22 August 1942, as found in Microfilm Series T-315, Roll 2188, National Archives and Records Service, College Park, Maryland; David M. Glantz, & Jonathan M. House, To the Gates of Stalingrad: Soviet-German Combat Operations, April-August 1942, (The Stalingrad Trilogy, Volume 1), Lawrence, Kansas: University Press of Kansas, 2009, 329-337, 384-386, 389-393; Hans Neidhardt, Mit Tanne und Eichenlaub: Kriegschronik der 100. Jäger Division vormals 100. leichte Infanterie Division, Graz, Austria: Leopold Stocker Verlag, 1981, 203; Anton Schimak, Karl Lamprecht & Friedrich Dettmer, Die 44. Infanterie Division: Tagebuch der Hoch- und Deutschmeister, Wien: Verlag Austria Press, 169, 233 and Map: Marschweg der 44. Infanterie Division im Russland.*

Zur frommen Erinnerung im Gebete an

Franz Wagner

Notargehilfe aus Mkt. Eisenstein
Schütze in einem Inf.-Rgt.

welcher am 22. Aug. 1942 im Osten im Blütenalter von 19¼ Jahren sein hoffnungsvolles Leben für Führer und Vaterland hingab.

Den Heldentod bin ich gestorben,
Hab' mir den besten Teil erworben.
In Gottes Hand liegt jede Gab',
Ich ruh, in Rußlands kühlem Grab.
Die Kugel hat mich gut getroffen,
Doch Kriegern steht der Himmel offen.
Eltern und ihr Lieben mein
Schließet in euer Gebet mich ein,
Vergeßet eueren Franz doch nicht,
Der in Feindesland begraben liegt.
Der Wille Gottes ist gescheh'n,
Im Himmel werden wir uns wiederseh'n !

0562

Reiter **Franz Wagner**, a notary assistant, was born on March 27, 1923 in Markt Eisenstein in what was then the Sudentenland. Assigned to an infantry regiment in the 44th Infantry Division, he was killed in action on August 22, 1942 at Bol'shaya Kamyschinskij. The division lost 30 men killed in action that day. He is probably buried at Block 19 as part of the unknowns in the Rossoschka German Military Cemetery.

Schütze **Gottfried Jebinger** was born in Eden near Diersbach in Upper Austria on April 20, 1922. Assigned to the 100th *Jäger* Division, he was killed in action at Perekopka on August 22, 1942. The division suffered 26 men killed in action that day.

Christliches Andenken
an unseren lieben Sohn und Bruder
Schütze
in einem Gebirgsjäger-Regt.

Gottfried Jebinger

Hausbesitzersfohn v. Kollerhaufe
in Eden, Pfarre Diersbach

welcher am 22. August 1942 bei den Kämpfen in Rußland im 21. Lebensjahre den Heldentod erlitten hat. Er gab sein junges Leben, getreu seinem Eide, für die geliebte Heimat, Führer, Volk und Vaterland. Er wurde unter militärischen Ehren in Perekopke begraben.

Lebet wohl, geliebte Eltern,
Lebet wohl, Geschwister mein.
Laßt das Klagen, laßt das Weinen,
Denkt, ich fiel ja nicht allein.
Du teure Mutter, guter Vater,
Denkt mit dem Gebet an mich.
Der, ums Vaterland zu retten,
Starb als Held, für Ehr und Pflicht.

Zu b.ziehen durch: Reisinger, Diersbach
N/0504

August 23, 1942
Weather: sunny, windy, clear, 82° F, 43° F at night
Sunrise: 5:05 a.m.; **Sunset:** 7:04 p.m.
Moon: Waxing Gibbous; 90% illumination

Sixth Army – The aim of the army was to advance a corps to the Volga River. Bombers and dive-bombers from the ***Luftwaffe***'s VIII Air Corps pounded Stalingrad in large-scale attacks. The army headquarters was located at Ossinowskij.

VIII Corps – The aim of the corps was to secure a stable bridgehead to enable the XIV ***Panzer*** Corps to pass forward and attack east. The corps headquarters was located at Rodionov. The corps suffered the following officer casualties: nine wounded in action; two missing in action.

305th Infantry Division – The division defended in sector near the Don River against the 37th Guards Rifle Division and the 39th Guards Rifle Division. The division suffered four enlisted men killed in action, two enlisted wounded in action and two enlisted missing in action. To the west was the 44th Infantry Division; to the south was the 389th Infantry Division. The division had one infantry regiment detached to the 389th Infantry Division.

384th Infantry Division – The division expanded its bridgehead east of Nizhne-Akatov, reaching Hill 87.0 and Hill 73.2. The division repelled a combined attack of the 35th Guards Rifle Division and the 214th Rifle Division. The division reported one officer and nine NCOs/enlisted killed in action; six officers and 111 NCOs/enlisted were wounded in action; 15 NCOs/enlisted were reported missing in action. To the north was the 389th Infantry Division; to the south was the 76th Infantry Division.

389th Infantry Division – The division defended the bridgehead east of Nizhne-Akatov against the 32nd Motorized Rifle Brigade. To the north was the 305th Infantry Division; to the south was the 384th Infantry Division. The division lost between 70 and 80 casualties. The division had one infantry regiment attached from the 305th Infantry Division.

XI Corps – The corps suffered the following officer casualties: one killed in action; four wounded in action. The corps headquarters was located at Ossinskij.

44th Infantry Division – The division defended in the sector Kurchajessowskij-Kamyshinskiy-Hill 171.0-Hill 180.9-Sirotinskaya-Khmelevskoy, against the 40th Guards Rifle Division. The division lost eight NCOs/enlisted killed in action; 41 NCOs/enlisted were wounded in action; one NCO/enlisted was reported missing in action. The division headquarters was located at Verkhne-Golubaja. To the east was the 305th Infantry Division; to the northwest was the 100th ***Jäger*** Division.

100th Jäger Division – The division defended in sector along the Don River west of Starogrigor'evskaya, slowly giving ground to an enemy attack by the 41st Guards Rifle Division. The division suffered 12 NCOs/enlisted killed in action; five officers and 81 NCOs/enlisted were wounded in action; one NCO/enlisted was reported missing in action. To the southeast was the 44th Infantry Division; to the northwest was the 376th Infantry Division.

376th Infantry Division – The division defended in sector along the Don River near Perekopskaya, slowly giving ground to the 38th Guards Rifle Division. The division reported six NCOs/enlisted killed in action; two NCOs/enlisted were missing in action. To the southwest was an assortment of battle groups; to the east was the 100th ***Jäger*** Division.

XIV *Panzer* Corps – The corps attacked on a five-mile-wide corridor for 38 miles to the Volga River, north of Stalingrad. The corps suffered the following officer casualties: two killed in action; seven wounded in action.

3rd Infantry Division (Motorized) – The division attacked east out of the bridgehead and followed the 16th ***Panzer*** Division toward the Volga River. The division lost ten NCOs/enlisted killed in action; one officer and 29 NCOs/enlisted were wounded in action; one man was reported missing in action.

16th Panzer Division – The division attacked at 4:30 a.m. and broke through enemy positions of the 87th Rifle Division east of the Don River, crossed the Tartar Ditch, crossed the Frolov-Stalingrad railroad, reached Rynok and pushed lead elements to the Volga River at Spartakovka by 4:30 p.m.

60th Infantry Division (Motorized) – The division attacked east out of the bridgehead, following the 3rd Infantry Division (Motorized), reaching Baburkin. Late in the day, enemy forces from the 35th Guards Rifle Division and the 169th Tank Brigade penetrated the division's hedgehog positions.

XVII Corps – The corps suffered the following officer casualties: two wounded in action.

79th Infantry Division – The division defended in sector along the Don River near Serafimovich as enemy pressure continued from the 304th Rifle Division. The division reported eight NCOs/enlisted killed in action; one officer and 26 NCOs/enlisted were wounded in action. To the west was the 2nd Italian Infantry Division of the XXXV Corps of the Italian Eighth Army; to the southeast was the 113th Infantry Division. The division headquarters was located at Verkhne-Fomichinskii.

113th Infantry Division – The division defended in sector along the Don River against the 278th Rifle Division. The division reported nine NCOs/enlisted wounded in action. To the northwest was the 79th Infantry Division; to the east was an assortment of battle groups.

XXIV *Panzer* Corps

71st Infantry Division – The division defended in sector along the Don River against the 399th Rifle Division and the 131st Rifle Division. To the north was the 295th Infantry Division; to the south was an open flank. The division detached an infantry regiment to the 295th Infantry Division.

LI Corps – The 101st Heavy Artillery Detachment was assigned to the corps. The corps suffered the following officer casualties: eight killed in action; one wounded in action; three missing in action.

76th Infantry Division – The division attacked east from the bridgehead over the Don River against the 87th Rifle Division, reaching almost to Malaia Rossoschka. The division lost one officer and five NCOs/enlisted killed in action; two officers and 14 NCOs/enlisted were wounded in action.

295th Infantry Division – The division attacked south from the bridgehead over the Don River near Peskovatka and almost reaching Dmitriyevka against the 1251st Anti–Tank Regiment. The division suffered 34 casualties. The division received the attachment of an infantry regiment from the 71st Infantry Division. To the northeast was the 76th Infantry Division; to the west was the 71st Infantry Division.

Sixth Army Reserve

22nd Panzer Division – The division moved northwest to the XI Corps sector. Part of the division defended in sector against the 76th Rifle Division. The division suffered seven NCOs/enlisted wounded in action. To the west was the 113th Infantry Division; to the northeast was the 376th Infantry Division.

Sources, August 23, 1942: ***Oberkommando des Heeres, Lage Ost: Stand: 23.8.42, Eastern Front Situation Map, National Archives Identifier: 559733, Record Group 242 – National Archives Collection of Foreign Records Seized, 1675-1958, National Archives, College Park, Maryland; Ia, Armeeoberkommando 6, "Morgen Meldung" and assorted reports, Kriegstagebuch 13, 24 August 1942, as found in Microfilm Series, T-312, Records of German Field Commands, Armies, Roll 1682, National Archives and Records Service, College Park, Maryland; 22nd Panzer Division, Kriegstagebuch 2, 23 August 1942, as found in Microfilm Series T-315, Roll 784, National Archives and Records Service, College Park, Maryland; 384th Infantry Division, Kriegstagebuch, 23 August 1942, as found in Microfilm Series T-315, Roll 2188, National Archives and Records Service, College Park, Maryland; John Erickson, The Road to Stalingrad, New York: Harper & Row, 1975, 369; David M. Glantz, & Jonathan M. House, To the Gates of Stalingrad: Soviet-German Combat Operations, April-August 1942, (The Stalingrad Trilogy, Volume 1), Lawrence, Kansas: University Press of Kansas, 2009, 331-342, 348, 384-386, 389-393; Jochen Löser, Bittere Pflicht: Kampf und Untergang der 76. Berlin-Brandenburgischen Infanterie-Division, Osnabrück, FRG: Biblio Verlag, 1986, 207; Anton Schimak, Karl Lamprecht & Friedrich Dettmer, Die 44. Infanterie Division: Tagebuch der Hoch- und Deutschmeister, Wien: Verlag Austria Press, 169, 233 and Map: Marschweg der 44. Infanterie Division im Russland; Vom Donez zum Don: Erfahrungsbericht der 384. I. D. vom 17. 5. – 5. 9.1942, Traditionsverbandes der 384. I. D., 1984.***

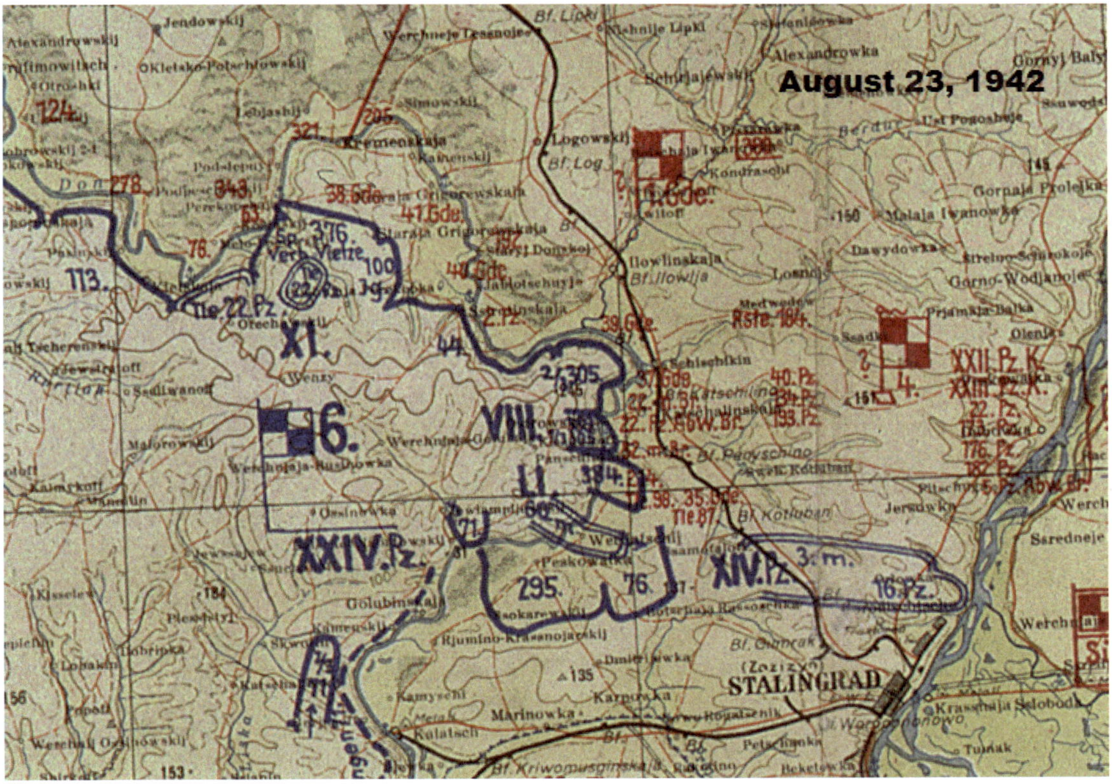

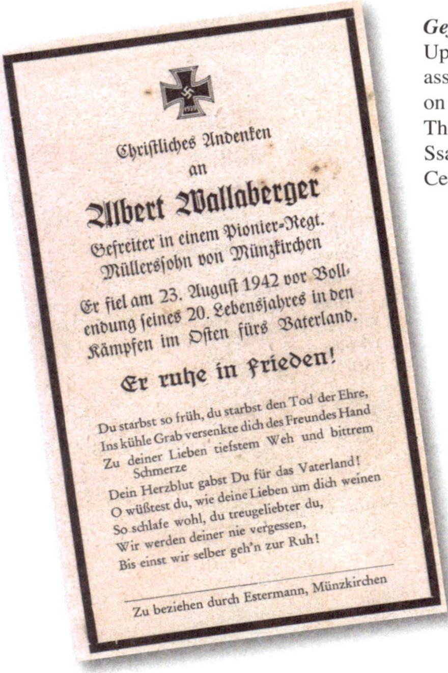

Christliches Andenken
an
Albert Wallaberger
Gefreiter in einem Pionier-Regt.
Müllerssohn von Münzkirchen
Er fiel am 23. August 1942 vor Vollendung seines 20. Lebensjahres in den Kämpfen im Osten fürs Vaterland.

Er ruhe in Frieden!

Du starbst so früh, du starbst den Tod der Ehre,
Ins kühle Grab versenkte dich des Freundes Hand
Zu deiner Lieben tiefstem Weh und bittrem Schmerze
Dein Herzblut gabst Du für das Vaterland!
O wüßtest du, wie deine Lieben um dich weinen
So schlafe wohl, du treugeliebter du,
Wir werden deiner nie vergessen,
Bis einst wir selber geh'n zur Ruh!

Zu beziehen durch Estermann, Münzkirchen

***Gefreiter* Albert Wallaberger** was born in Münzberger, Upper Austria on September 22, 1922. An engineer, probably assigned to the 297th Infantry Division, he was killed in action on August 23, 1942, one month before his twentieth birthday. The son of a miller, he was killed near Station 74 along the Ssaisk-Stalingrad rail line. He is buried at the German Military Cemetery at Rossoschka in Block 30, Row 23 and Grave 801.

***Gefreiter* Albert Wallaberger**

August 24, 1942
Weather: dry, 30% cloud cover, 73° F, 43° F at night, good road conditions
Sunrise: 5:06 a.m.; **Sunset:** 7:02 p.m.
Moon: Waxing Gibbous; 96% illumination

Sixth Army – The aim of the army was to secure the attack corridor of the XIV ***Panzer*** Corps and push supplies forward to the corps. Bombers and dive-bombers from the ***Luftwaffe***'s VIII Air Corps pounded Spartakovka in large-scale attacks. The army headquarters was located at Ossinowskij.

VIII Corps – The corps suffered the following officer casualties: six killed in action; seven wounded in action.

305th Infantry Division – The division defended in sector near the Don River against the 4th Guards Rifle Division. To the west was the 44th Infantry Division; to the south was the 389th Infantry Division. One infantry regiment was detached to the 389th Infantry Division. The division's nine infantry battalions had an aggregate Combat/Fighting Strength of 36%.

384th Infantry Division – The division repulsed enemy attacks supported by tanks at Kisslov against the 214th Rifle Division, five miles south of Pan'shino. To the north was the 389th Infantry Division; to the south was the 76th Infantry Division. The division lost four officers and 31 NCOs/enlisted killed in action; seven officers and 148 NCOs/enlisted were wounded in action; three men were reported missing in action. The division reported the following battle strengths for its three infantry regiments: 534th Infantry Regiment – ten officers and 538 NCOs/enlisted; 535th Infantry Regiment – 22 officers and 576 NCOs/enlisted; and 536th Infantry Regiment – one officer and 160 NCOs/enlisted. The division's nine infantry battalions had an aggregate Combat/Fighting Strength of 30%.

389th Infantry Division – The division defended its positions east of the Don River against the 98th Rifle Division. To the north was the 305th Infantry Division; to the south was the 384th Infantry Division. The division's nine infantry battalions had an aggregate Combat/Fighting Strength of 32%. The division was reinforced with an infantry regiment detached from the 305th Infantry Division.

XI Corps – The corps suffered the following officer casualties: three killed in action; five wounded in action.

22nd Panzer Division – The division served as the reserve for the XI Corps sector, operating against the 63rd Rifle Division east of Kletskiy, repulsing the enemy attack. Part of the division defended in sector south of the Don River against the 76th Rifle Division. The division's three ***panzer*** grenadier battalions had an aggregate Combat/Fighting Strength of 48%.

44th Infantry Division – The division defended in the sector Kurchajessowskij-Kamyshinskiy-Hill 171.0-Hill 180.9-Sirotinskaya-Khmelevskoy, against the 40th Guards Rifle Division. The division headquarters was located at Verkhne-Golubaja. To the southeast was the 305th Infantry Division; to the northwest was the 100th ***Jäger*** Division. The division's nine infantry battalions had an aggregate Combat/Fighting Strength of 60%.

100th Jäger Division – The division defended in sector along the Don River west of Starogrigor'evskaya, slowly giving ground to the enemy attack by the 41st Guards Rifle Division. To the east was the 44th Infantry Division; to the west was the 376th Infantry Division. The division's three ***jäger*** battalions had an aggregate Combat/Fighting Strength of 44%, while the Croatian infantry battalion had a Combat/Fighting Strength of 70%.

376th Infantry Division – The division defended in sector along the Don River near Perekopskaya, slowly giving ground to the 38th Guards Rifle Division. To the west was an assortment of battle groups; to the east was the 100th ***Jäger*** Division. The division's eight infantry battalions had an aggregate Combat/Fighting Strength of 28%.

XIV *Panzer* Corps – The corps suffered the following officer casualties: three killed in action; five wounded in action.

3rd Infantry Division (Motorized) – The division conducted hedgehog defenses in the corridor centered on Kuz'michi to the north and Konnaia Station to the south. The division lost three officers and 33 NCOs/enlisted killed in action; 85 NCOs/enlisted were wounded in action; four men were reported missing in action. To the east was the 16th ***Panzer*** Division; to the west was the 60th Infantry Division (Motorized.) The division's four motorized infantry battalions had an aggregate Combat/Fighting Strength of 58%.

16th Panzer Division – The division attacked and seized the Mokraya Mechetka River Mouth and the landing site for the rail ferry just north of the Dzerzhinsky Tractor Factory. Forming hedgehog defenses, the division's southern line was Hill 135.4-Hill 144.2-Hill 147.6. The division's positions along the Volga River ran from Akatovka-Vinnovka-Lataschanka. To the west was the 3rd Infantry Division (Motorized.) The division's four ***panzer*** grenadier battalions had an aggregate Combat/Fighting Strength of 64%.

60th Infantry Division (Motorized) – The division moved east in the corridor to Nadezhda. The 35th Guards Rifle Division and the 169th Tank Brigade recaptured Malaia Rossoschka. To the east was the 3rd Infantry Division (Motorized); to the west was the 76th Infantry Division. The division's six motorized infantry battalions had an aggregate Combat/Fighting Strength of 58%.

XVII Corps

79th Infantry Division – The division defended in sector along the Don River near Serafimovich as enemy pressure continued from the 304th Rifle Division. The division lost seven NCOs/enlisted killed in action; 27 NCOs/enlisted were wounded in action; one NCO/enlisted was missing in action. To the west was the 2nd Italian Infantry Division of the XXXV Corps of the Italian Eighth Army; to the southeast was the 113th Infantry Division. The division headquarters was located at Verkhne-Fomichinskii. The division's nine infantry battalions had an aggregate Combat/Fighting Strength of 50%.

113th Infantry Division – The division defended in sector along the Don River. To the northwest was the 79th Infantry Division; to the east was an assortment of battle groups. The division's six infantry battalions had an aggregate Combat/Fighting Strength of 56%.

Italian Celere Motorized Division – Elements of the division transferred from the corps to the Italian Eighth Army.

XXIV *Panzer* Corps

71st Infantry Division – The division conducted defensive/security operations along the Don River against the 399th Rifle Division. One infantry regiment moved across the river to the 295th Infantry Division area. To the northeast was the 295th Infantry Division; to the south was an open flank. The division's nine infantry battalions had an aggregate Combat/Fighting Strength of 36%.

LI Corps – The corps suffered the following officer casualties: three killed in action; 17 wounded in action.

76th Infantry Division – The division continued to attack east in zone against the 134th Tank Brigade, reaching Zapadnovka. To the north was the 384th Infantry Division; to the south was the 295th Infantry Division. The division's nine infantry battalions had an aggregate Combat/Fighting Strength of 52%.

295th Infantry Division – The division, augmented by one infantry regiment from the 71st Infantry Division, continued the attack in zone southeast to Dmitriyevka, seizing the village of Sokarevka against the 87th Rifle Division and the 35th Guards Rifle Division. To the northeast was the 76th Infantry Division; to the southwest was the 71st Infantry Division. The division's seven infantry battalions had an aggregate Combat/Fighting Strength of 65%.

Sources, August 24, 1942: *Oberkommando des Heeres, Lage Ost: Stand: 24.8.42, Eastern Front Situation Map, National Archives Identifier: 559733, Record Group 242 – National Archives Collection of Foreign Records Seized, 1675-1958, National Archives, College Park, Maryland; Ia, Armeeoberkommando 6, "Morgen Meldung" and assorted reports, Kriegstagebuch 13, 25 August 1942, as found in Microfilm Series, T-312, Records of German Field Commands, Armies, Roll 1682, National Archives and Records Service, College Park, Maryland; 22nd Panzer Division, Kriegstagebuch 2, 24 August 1942, as found in Microfilm Series T-315, Roll 784, National Archives and Records Service, College Park, Maryland; 79th Infantry Division, Kriegstagebuch, 24 August 1942, as found in Microfilm Series T-315, Roll 1108, National Archives and Records Service, College Park, Maryland; 384th Infantry Division, Kriegstagebuch, 24 August 1942, as found in Microfilm Series T-315, Roll 2188, National Archives and Records Service, College Park, Maryland; Paul Carell, Stalingrad: The Defeat of the German Sixth Army, Atglen, Pennsylvania: Schiffer Publishing, 1993, 127; David M. Glantz, & Jonathan M. House, To the Gates of Stalingrad: Soviet-German Combat Operations, April-August 1942, (The Stalingrad Trilogy, Volume 1), Lawrence, Kansas: University Press of Kansas, 2009, 340-351, 384-386, 389-393; Anton Schimak, Karl Lamprecht & Friedrich Dettmer, Die 44. Infanterie Division: Tagebuch der Hoch- und Deutschmeister, Wien: Verlag Austria Press, 169, 233 and Map: Marschweg der 44. Infanterie Division im Russland.*

Zum Andenken
an unseren lieben, unvergeßlichen
Sohn und Bruder

Josef Aigner

Hofbauerssohn in Weng
Gefreiter eines Infanterie=Regimentes und Träger des EK. 2. Kl. und des Infanterie=Sturmabzeichens in Silber

welcher am 24. August 1942 im im 22. Lebensjahre in soldatischer Pflichterfüllung im Osten den Heldentod fand.

Eltern, Geschwister und Freunde mein,
So gern schrieb ich aus der Ferne heim,
Doch heut' ist's zum letztenmal,
Daß ich Euch grüße tausendmal.
Und sage Dank für jede Gab',
Die ich von Euch empfangen hab'.
Habe an Euch die letzte Bitt':
Vergeßt ja im Gebet mich nicht.
Nur keine Träne, keine Klag',
Der liebe Gott, der mir das Leben gab,
Rief mich so früh ins Heldengrab.
Auf meiner Brust sah man das Zeichen glänzen,
Das nur von Ruhm und Heldentaten spricht
Und ich werde in des Himmels Auen
Im Lorbeerkranz Euch wiederschauen.

Innviertler Verlagsgesellschaft Braunau.

Gefreiter **Josef Aigner**, a farmer's son, was born in Weng near Braunau am Inn in Upper Austria on November 14, 1920. Assigned to an infantry regiment, he had previously been awarded the Iron Cross 2nd Class and the Infantry Assault Badge; he was most likely assigned to the 371st Infantry Division, then in the Fourth ***Panzer*** Army. He was killed in action on August 24, 1942 at the Abganerowa Rail Station.

Jäger **Ernst Lehner** was born in Leppersdorf near Linz in Austria on December 23, 1922. Assigned to an infantry regiment in the 100th ***Jäger*** Division, he was killed in action at Perekopka on August 24, 1942.

Christliches Andenken
an Gefreiten in einem Inf.-Regt.

Ernst Lehner

welcher am 24. August 1942 an der Ostfront im 20. Lebensjahre den Heldentod fand.

August 25, 1942
Weather: clear, 75° F, 43° F at night
Sunrise: 5:08 a.m.; **Sunset:** 7:00 p.m.
Moon: Waxing Gibbous; 99% illumination

Sixth Army – Army units penetrated to both sides of Dmitriyevka. Bombers and dive-bombers from the ***Luftwaffe***'s VIII Air Corps pounded Stalingrad in large-scale attacks. The army headquarters was located at Ossinowskij. ***General der Panzertruppe*** Friedrich Paulus was suffering from dysentery.

VIII Corps – The corps suffered the following officer casualties: two killed in action; seven wounded in action. The 244th ***Sturmgeschütz*** Detachment was assigned to the corps.

305th Infantry Division – The division defended in sector near the Don River against the 39th Guards Rifle Division. The division lost six enlisted men killed in action and 15 enlisted wounded in action. To the northwest was the 44th Infantry Division; to the south was the 389th Infantry Division. One infantry regiment was detached to the 389th Infantry Division.

384th Infantry Division – The division defended in sector north of Vertiachii against the 214th Rifle Division. The division lost two officers and 30 enlisted men killed in action; three officers and 123 enlisted were wounded in action; 22 men were reported missing in action. To the north was the 389th Infantry Division; to the south was the 76th Infantry Division.

389th Infantry Division – The division defended in sector east of the Don River outside Pan'shino against the 32nd Motorized Rifle Brigade. The division suffered six NCOs/enlisted killed in action; 15 NCOs/enlisted were wounded in action. The division was reinforced by one infantry regiment from the 305th Infantry Division. To the north was the 305th Infantry Division; to the south was the 384th Infantry Division. The division reported 12 5cm and four 7.5cm anti-tank guns as operational.

XI Corps – The corps suffered the following officer casualties: four wounded in action.

22nd Panzer Division – The division defended as the reserve for the XI Corps sector. Part of the division defended in sector south of the Don River against the 76th Rifle Division. To the northwest was the 113th Infantry Division; to the northeast was the 376th Infantry Division.

44th Infantry Division – The division defended in the sector Kurchajessowskij-Kamyshinskiy-Hill 171.0-Hill 180.9-Sirotinskaya-Khmelevskoy, against the 40th Guards Rifle Division. The division headquarters was located at Verkhne-Golubaja. To the east was the 305th Infantry Division; to the northwest was the 100th ***Jäger*** Division.

100th Jäger Division – The division defended in sector along the Don River west of Starogrigor'evskaya against the 38th Guards Rifle Division, slowly giving ground to the enemy attack. To the southeast was the 44th Infantry Division; to the west was the 376th Infantry Division.

376th Infantry Division – The division defended in sector along the Don River near Perekopskaya, slowly giving ground to the enemy attack by the 41st Guards Rifle Division. To the west was an assortment of battle groups; to the east was the 100th ***Jäger*** Division.

XIV *Panzer* Corps – The corps suffered the following officer casualties: one killed in action; seven wounded in action.

3rd Infantry Division (Motorized) – The division conducted hedgehog defenses in the corridor centered on Kuz'michi to the north and Konnaia Station to the south, repelling several enemy attacks from the south. The division lost six NCOs/enlisted killed in action; 40 NCOs/enlisted were wounded in action; three men were reported missing in action. To the east was the 16th ***Panzer*** Division; to the west was the 60th Infantry Division (Motorized.)

16th Panzer Division – The division conducted hedgehog defenses and repelled an attack on the western edge of Spartakovka. To the west was the 3rd Infantry Division (Motorized.)

60th Infantry Division (Motorized) – The division conducted hedgehog defenses in the corridor. To the east was the 3rd Infantry Division (Motorized.) To the west was the 76th Infantry Division.

XVII Corps – The corps suffered the following officer casualties: one killed in action; four wounded in action.

79th Infantry Division – The division defended in sector along the Don River near Serafimovich as enemy pressure continued from the 304th Rifle Division; the 5th Guards Cavalry Division and the 6th Guards Cavalry Division split the division's boundary with the 2nd Italian Infantry Division. The division lost one officer and 17 NCOs/enlisted killed in action; two officers and 60 NCOs/enlisted were wounded in action; ten NCOs/enlisted were reported missing in action. To the west was the 2nd Italian Infantry Division of the XXXV Corps of the Italian Eighth Army; to the southeast was the 113th Infantry Division. The division headquarters was located at Verkhne-Fomichinskii.

113th Infantry Division – The division defended in sector along the Don River. To the northwest was the 79th Infantry Division; to the east was an assortment of battle groups.

LI Corps – The 45th Pioneer Battalion was assigned to the corps. The corps suffered the following officer casualties: one killed in action; four wounded in action.

71st Infantry Division – The division attacked east across the Don River north of Kalach against the 399th Rifle Division. The division suffered 32 NCOs/enlisted killed in action; four officers and 153 NCOs/enlisted were wounded in action. To the northeast was the 295th Infantry Division; to the south was an open flank. One infantry regiment continued to be detached to the 295th Infantry Division.

76th Infantry Division – The division continued to attack east in zone against the 134th Tank Brigade. The division lost one NCO/enlisted killed in action; 17 NCOs/enlisted were wounded in action. To the north was the 384th Infantry Division; to the south was the 295th Infantry Division; to the east was the 60th Infantry Division (Motorized.)

295th Infantry Division – The division continued the attack east to Nizhne-Alexejewskij against the 87th Rifle Division, while one regiment attacked southwest to clear the east bank of the Don River. The division reported (late) that six NCOs/enlisted were killed in action and 24 NCOs/enlisted were wounded in action. To the northeast was the 76th Infantry Division; to the southwest was the 71st Infantry Division.

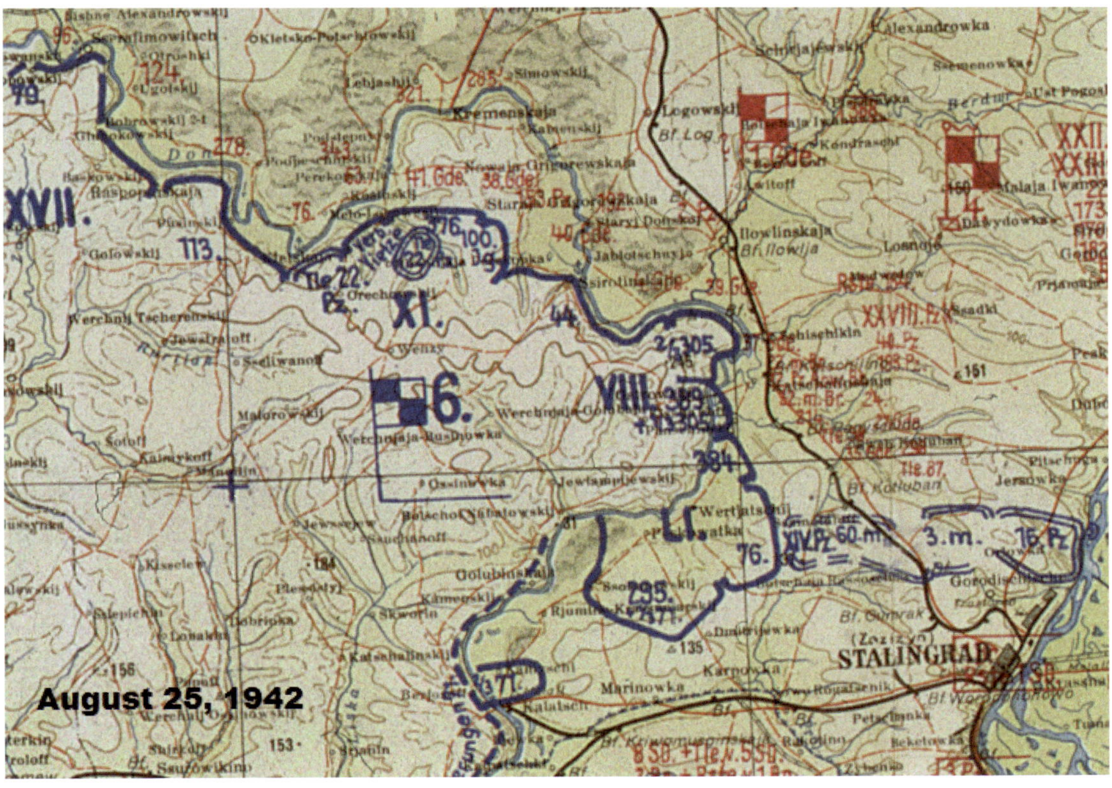

Sources, August 25, 1942: *Oberkommando des Heeres, Lage Ost: Stand: 25.8.42, Eastern Front Situation Map, National Archives Identifier: 559733, Record Group 242 – National Archives Collection of Foreign Records Seized, 1675-1958, National Archives, College Park, Maryland; Ia, Armeeoberkommando 6, "Morgen Meldung" and assorted reports, Kriegstagebuch 13, 26 August 1942, as found in Microfilm Series, T-312, Records of German Field Commands, Armies, Roll 1682, National Archives and Records Service, College Park, Maryland; 79th Infantry Division, Kriegstagebuch, 25 August 1942, as found in Microfilm Series T-315, Roll 1108, National Archives and Records Service, College Park, Maryland; 384th Infantry Division, Kriegstagebuch, 25 August 1942, as found in Microfilm Series T-315, Roll 2188, National Archives and Records Service, College Park, Maryland; Antony Beevor, Stalingrad: The Fateful Siege: 1942-1943, London: Penguin Books, 1998, 110; David M. Glantz, & Jonathan M. House, To the Gates of Stalingrad: Soviet-German Combat Operations, April-August 1942, (The Stalingrad Trilogy, Volume 1), Lawrence, Kansas: University Press of Kansas, 2009, 344-360, 384-386, 389-393; Anton Schimak, Karl Lamprecht & Friedrich Dettmer, Die 44. Infanterie Division: Tagebuch der Hoch- und Deutschmeister, Wien: Verlag Austria Press, 169, 233 and Map: Marschweg der 44. Infanterie Division im Russland; Percy E. Schramm, Editor, Kriegstagebuch des Oberkommandos der Wehrmacht, 1942, Band II – Band III, München, BRD: Bernhard & Graefe Verlag, 1982, Band II, 639.*

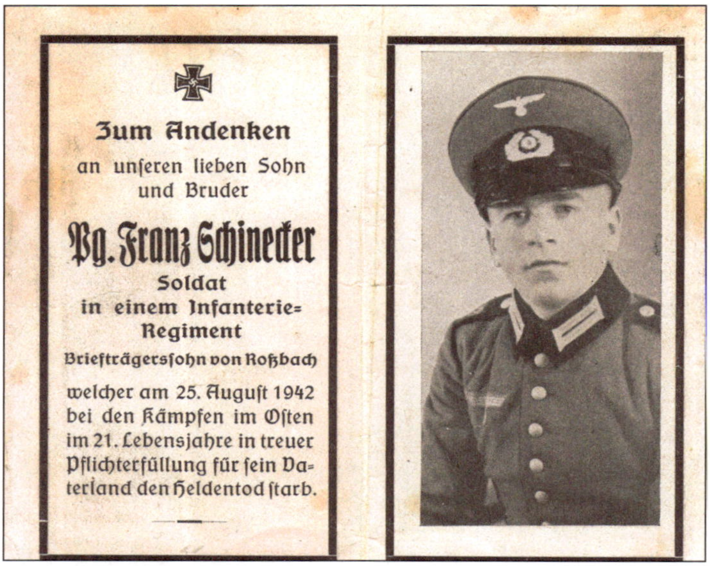

Reiter **Franz Schinecker,** a Nazi Party member, was the son of a mailman. Born at Sankt Laurenz, Austria on January 17, 1922, he served in an infantry regiment before he was killed in action at Bol'shaya Kamyschinskij on August 25, 1942. His name is listed in the remembrance book at the German Military Cemetery at Rossoschka; he was probably assigned to the 44th Infantry Division.

Feldwebel **Xaver Schwinghammer** was born in Oberschmiddorf near Dirnach in Bavaria. His father was a farmer and the ***Bürgermeister*** (Mayor) of the small village. Schwinghammer fought in the campaigns in Poland, France and Russia; he had previously won the Iron Cross 2nd Class and was a platoon leader in an infantry regiment. ***Feldwebel*** Schwinghammer was killed in action on August 25, 1942 in Orekovskij, probably assigned to the 376th Infantry Division. His name is listed in the remembrance book at the German Military Cemetery at Rossoschka.

August 26, 1942
Weather: sunny, bright, 79° F, 46° F at night
Sunrise: 5:09 a.m.; **Sunset:** 6:58 p.m.
Moon: Full Moon; 100% illumination

Sixth Army – The army headquarters was located at Ossinowskij. ***General der Panzertruppe*** Friedrich Paulus received the Knight's Cross.

VIII Corps – The 53rd ***Werfer*** Regiment was assigned to support the corps. The corps suffered the following officer casualties: two killed in action; 14 wounded in action.

305th Infantry Division – The division defended in sector near the Don River against the 39th Guards Rifle Division. The division lost ten enlisted men killed in action; 25 enlisted were wounded in action and two enlisted were missing in action. To the west was the 44th Infantry Division; to the south was the 389th Infantry Division. One infantry regiment was detached to the 389th Infantry Division.

384th Infantry Division – The division defended in sector northwest of Vertiachii, repelling shock groups from the 4th Tank Army. The division reported two officers and 26 NCOs/enlisted killed in action; two officers and 101 NCOs/enlisted were wounded in action. To the north was the 389th Infantry Division; to the southeast was the 76th Infantry Division.

389th Infantry Division – The division defended its positions east of the Don River outside Pan'shino, repelling several enemy attacks by the 39th Guards Rifle Division. The division lost one enlisted man killed in action and 26 enlisted wounded in action. To the north was the 305th Infantry Division; to the south was the 384th Infantry Division.

XI Corps – The corps suffered the following officer casualties: one killed in action; eight wounded in action; one accidental death.

22nd Panzer Division – The division defended in sector between the 113th Infantry Division to the northwest and the 376th Infantry Division to the northeast, as the reserve for the XI Corps sector. Part of the division moved west toward the XVII Corps. The division lost NCOs/enlisted killed in action; two officers and 14 NCOs/enlisted were wounded in action.

44th Infantry Division – The division defended in sector Kurchajessowskij-Kamyshinskiy-Hill 171.0-Hill 180.9-Sirotinskaya-Khmelevskoy, against the 40th Guards Rifle Division. The division headquarters was located at Verkhne-Golubaja. The division reported five NCOs/enlisted killed in action; one officer and 34 NCOs/enlisted were wounded in action. To the east was the 305th Infantry Division; to the northwest was the 100th ***Jäger*** Division.

100th Jäger Division – The division defended in sector along the Don River west of Starogrigor'evskaya, slowly giving ground to the enemy attack from the northeast. The division lost 23 NCOs/enlisted killed in action; 98 NCOs/enlisted were wounded in action; 30 NCOs/enlisted were missing in action. To the southeast was the 44th Infantry Division; to the west was the 376th Infantry Division.

376th Infantry Division – The division defended in sector along the Don River near Perekopskaya, slowly giving ground to the enemy attack from the north by the 41st Guards Rifle Division. To the southwest was an assortment of battle groups; to the east was the 100th ***Jäger*** Division.

XIV *Panzer* Corps – The corps requested to withdraw from the corridor due to supply difficulties and mounting casualties, but the army commander denied the request. The corps suffered the following officer casualties: six killed in action; 12 wounded in action.

3rd Infantry Division (Motorized) – The division conducted hedgehog defenses in the corridor centered on Kuz'michi to the north and

Konnaia Station to the south, repelling attacks by the 4th Tank Corps and the 16th Tank Corps. The division reported (late) that for the period of August 24 through August 26 it had 22 killed in action, 133 wounded in action and ten missing in action. To the east was the 16th ***Panzer*** Division; to the west was the 60th Infantry Division (Motorized.)

16th Panzer Division – The division repelled attacks by elements of the 2nd Tank Corps and 23rd Tank Corps north of the Mokraya Mechetka River. The division reported (late) that for the period August 23 through August 26 it suffered four officers and 56 NCOs/enlisted killed in action; 15 officers and 278 NCOs/enlisted were wounded in action; five soldiers were reported missing in action. To the west was the 3rd Infantry Division (Motorized.)

60th Infantry Division (Motorized) – The division conducted hedgehog defenses in the corridor, repelling attacks by the 4th Tank Corps and the 16th Tank Corps. The division lost one officer and 15 NCOs/enlisted killed in action; 50 NCOs/enlisted were wounded in action. To the east was the 3rd Infantry Division (Motorized); to the west was the 76th Infantry Division.

XVII Corps

79th Infantry Division – The division was forced to withdraw from its defensive positions along the Don River near Serafimovich and moved southward due to heavy pressure from the 304th Rifle Division and the 14th Guards Rifle Division. The division suffered four NCOs/enlisted killed in action; one officer and 18 NCOs/enlisted were wounded in action. One infantry regiment moved southwest. To the west was the 2nd Italian Infantry Division of the XXXV Corps of the Italian Eighth Army; to the southeast was the 113th Infantry Division. The division headquarters was located at Karagichev.

113th Infantry Division – The division defended in sector along the Don River. The division reported one enlisted man wounded in action. To the northwest was the 79th Infantry Division; to the east was an assortment of battle groups.

LI Corps – The corps suffered the following officer casualties: two killed in action; seven wounded in action.

71st Infantry Division – The division attacked east across the Don River three miles north of Kalach, turning the flank of the 399th Rifle Division and reaching Illarionowskij. The division suffered two officers and 116 NCOs/enlisted as casualties. To the northeast was the 295th Infantry Division; to the south was an open flank. One infantry regiment was detached to the 295th Infantry Division.

76th Infantry Division – The division continued to attack southeast, driving back the 35th Guards Rifle Division and the 196th Rifle Division. The division reported five enlisted killed in action and 65 NCOs/enlisted wounded in action. To the northwest was the 384th Infantry Division; to the southwest was the 295th Infantry Division; to the east was the 60th Infantry Division (Motorized.)

295th Infantry Division – The division repelled shock groups from the 62nd Army and simultaneously attacked southeast, driving back the 169th Tank Brigade. The division lost one officer and 17 NCOs/enlisted killed in action; four officers and 132 NCOs/enlisted were wounded in action. The division was reinforced with one infantry regiment from the 71st Infantry Division. To the north was the 76th Infantry Division; to the southwest was the 71st Infantry Division.

Sources, August 26, 1942: ***Oberkommando des Heeres, Lage Ost: Stand: 26.8.42, Eastern Front Situation Map, National Archives Identifier: 559733, Record Group 242 – National Archives Collection of Foreign Records Seized, 1675-1958, National Archives, College Park, Maryland; Ia, Armeeoberkommando 6, "Morgen Meldung" and assorted reports, Kriegstagebuch 13, 27 August 1942, as found in Microfilm Series, T-312, Records of German Field Commands, Armies, Roll 1682, National Archives and Records Service, College Park, Maryland; 22nd Panzer Division, Kriegstagebuch 2, 26 August 1942, as found in Microfilm Series T-315, Roll 784, National Archives and Records Service, College Park, Maryland; 79th Infantry Division, Kriegstagebuch, 26 August 1942, as found in Microfilm Series T-315, Roll 1108, National Archives and Records Service, College Park, Maryland; 384th Infantry Division, Kriegstagebuch, 26 August 1942, as found in Microfilm Series T-315, Roll 2188, National Archives and Records Service, College Park, Maryland; David M. Glantz, & Jonathan M. House, To the Gates of Stalingrad: Soviet-German Combat Operations, April-August 1942, (The Stalingrad Trilogy, Volume 1), Lawrence, Kansas: University Press of Kansas, 2009, 345, 351- 363, 384-386, 389-393; Janusz Piekalkiewicz, Stalingrad: Anatomie einer Schlacht, München, BRD: Wilhelm Heyne Verlag, 1977, 113; Anton Schimak, Karl Lamprecht & Friedrich Dettmer, Die 44. Infanterie Division: Tagebuch der Hoch- und Deutschmeister, Wien: Verlag Austria Press, 169, 233 and Map: Marschweg der 44. Infanterie Division im Russland.***

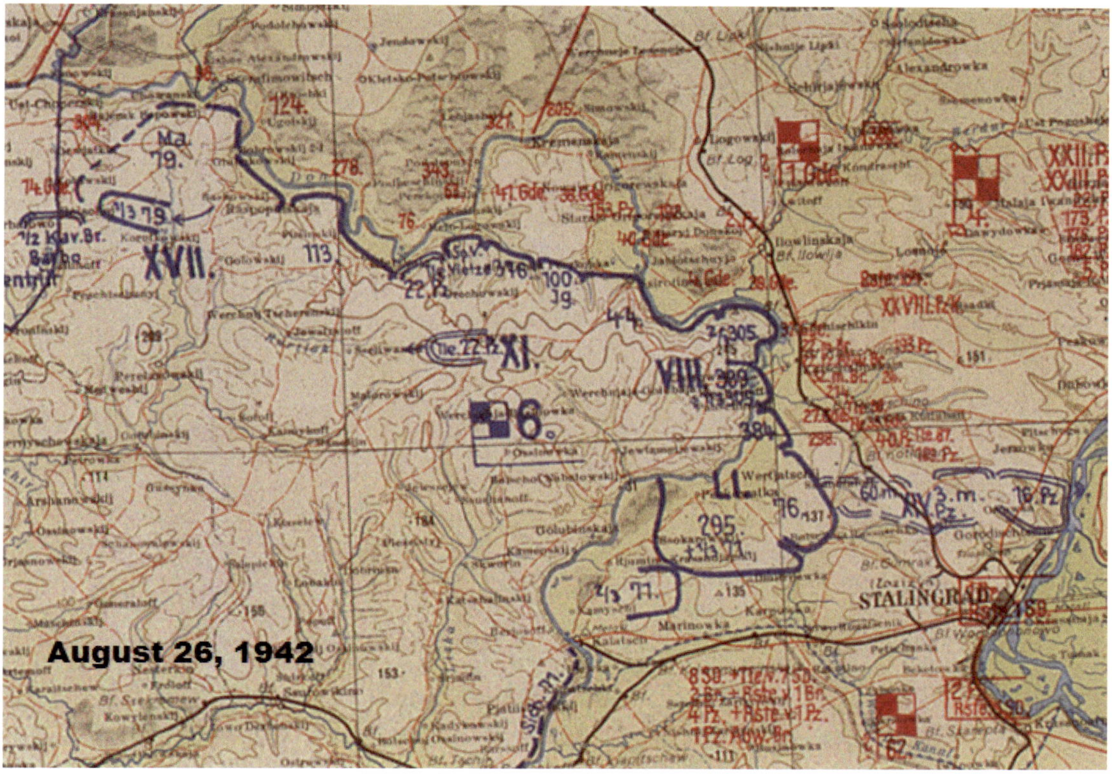

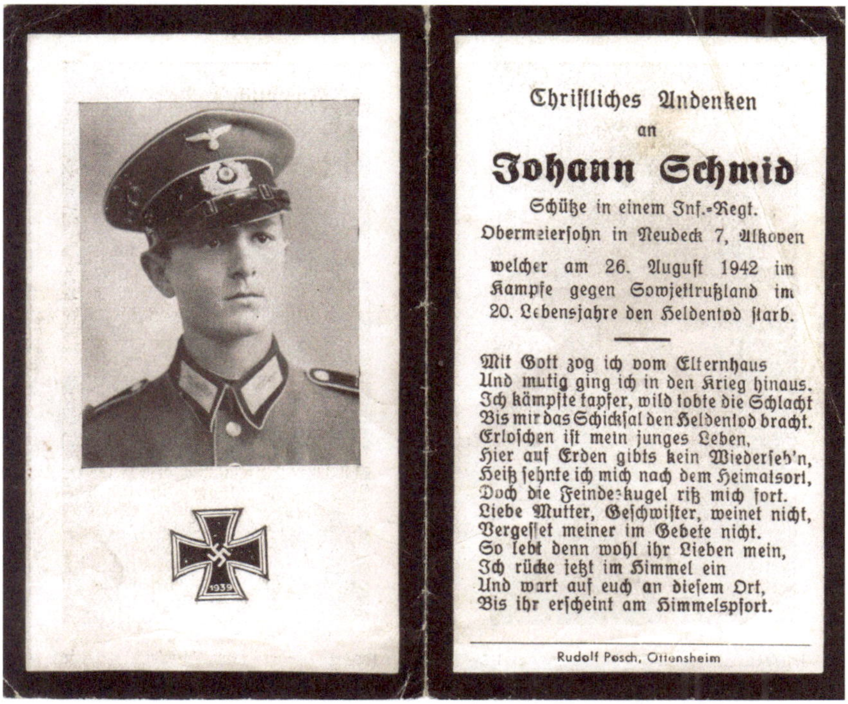
Christliches Andenken
an
Johann Schmid
Schütze in einem Inf.-Regt.
Obermeiersohn in Neudeck 7, Alkoven
welcher am 26. August 1942 im Kampfe gegen Sowjetrußland im 20. Lebensjahre den Heldentod starb.

Mit Gott zog ich vom Elternhaus
Und mutig ging ich in den Krieg hinaus.
Ich kämpfte tapfer, wild tobte die Schlacht
Bis mir das Schicksal den Heldentod bracht.
Erloschen ist mein junges Leben,
Hier auf Erden gibts kein Wiederseh'n,
Heiß sehnte ich mich nach dem Heimatsort,
Doch die Feindeskugel riß mich fort.
Liebe Mutter, Geschwister, weinet nicht,
Vergesset meiner im Gebete nicht.
So lebt denn wohl ihr Lieben mein,
Ich rücke jetzt im Himmel ein
Und wart auf euch an diesem Ort,
Bis ihr erscheint am Himmelspfort.

Rudolf Posch, Ottensheim

Schütze **Johann Schmid** was born in Neudeck/Alkoven, near Passau, in Bavaria on May 31, 1923. Assigned to an infantry regiment in the 113th Infantry Division, the 19-year-old was killed in action on August 26, 1942 near Raspopinskaja. His gravesite is unknown.

August 27, 1942
Weather: warm, no clouds, windy, 77° F, 43° F at night, dusty visibility, good road conditions
Sunrise: 5:10 a.m.; **Sunset:** 6:56 p.m.
Moon: Waxing Gibbous; 98% illumination

Sixth Army – Dive-bombers from the ***Luftwaffe***'s VIII Air Corps pounded Rynok. The army headquarters was located at Ossinowskij.

VIII Corps – The corps suffered the following officer casualties: one killed in action; one wounded in action.

305th Infantry Division – The division defended in sector near the Don River against the 39th Guards Rifle Division. One infantry regiment was detached to the 389th Infantry Division. The division reported two NCOs/enlisted killed in action; one NCO and five enlisted men were wounded in action. To the west was the 44th Infantry Division; to the south was the 389th Infantry Division.

384th Infantry Division – The division defended in sector northwest of Vertiachii against the 298th Rifle Division. The division lost five NCOs/enlisted killed in action; one officer and 33 NCOs/enlisted were wounded in action. To the northwest was the 389th Infantry Division; to the southeast was the 76th Infantry Division.

389th Infantry Division – The division defended its positions east of the Don River outside Pan'shino against the 214th Rifle Division. The division suffered one NCO/enlisted killed in action and 11 NCOs/enlisted wounded in action. The division was reinforced with one infantry regiment from the 305th Infantry Division. To the north was the 305th Infantry Division; to the south was the 384th Infantry Division.

XI Corps

22nd Panzer Division – The division occupied an assembly area between the 113th Infantry Division to the west and the 376th Infantry Division to the east, while other elements moved westward to assist the 79th Infantry Division. The division lost six NCOs/enlisted killed in action; one officer and 21 NCOs/enlisted were wounded in action.

44th Infantry Division – The division defended in sector Kurchajessowskij-Kamyshinskiy-Hill 171.0-Hill 180.9-Sirotinskaya-Khmelevskoy, against the 40th Guards Rifle Division and the 38th Guards Rifle Division. The division suffered one officer and 15 NCOs/enlisted killed in action; one officer and 48 NCOs/enlisted were wounded in action; one enlisted was missing in action. The division headquarters was located at Verkhne-Golubaja. To the east was the 305th Infantry Division; to the northwest was the 100th ***Jäger*** Division.

100th Jäger Division – The division reformed a new defensive line near Blizhniaia-Perekopka and repelled several attacks from the northwest from the 41st Guards Rifle Division. The division reported two NCOs/enlisted killed in action; one officer and 19 NCOs/enlisted were wounded in action and three NCOs/enlisted were posted missing in action. To the southeast was the 44th Infantry Division; to the west was the 376th Infantry Division.

376th Infantry Division – The division reformed a new defensive line southwest of Perekopka. To the west was an assortment of battle groups; to the east was the 100th ***Jäger*** Division.

XIV *Panzer* Corps – The corps suffered the following officer casualties: six killed in action; eight wounded in action; one missing in action.

3rd Infantry Division (Motorized) – The division conducted hedgehog defenses in the corridor centered on Kuz'michi to the north and Konnaia Station to the south, as ammunition supplies reached critical levels. The division lost three officers and 34 NCOs/enlisted killed in action; three officers and 86 NCOs/enlisted were wounded in action. To the east was the 16th ***Panzer*** Division; to the west was the 60th Infantry Division (Motorized.)

16th Panzer Division – The division continued to hold terrain just north of Stalingrad; enemy artillery barrages blocked contact with the 3rd Infantry Division (Motorized) to the west. In the afternoon, the division attacked Rynok.

60th Infantry Division (Motorized) – The division conducted hedgehog defenses in the corridor, as ammunition supplies reached critical levels. To the east was the 3rd Infantry Division (Motorized); to the west was the 76th Infantry Division.

XVII Corps – The corps suffered the following officer casualties: one killed in action; one wounded in action.

79th Infantry Division – The division halted the enemy advance south of Serafimovich and attacks by the 3rd Guards Cavalry Corps and the 304th Rifle Division. The division lost four NCOs/enlisted killed in action; one officer and 34 NCOs/enlisted were wounded in action; one officer and nine NCOs/enlisted were reported missing in action. To the west was the 2nd Italian Infantry Division of the XXXV Corps of the Italian Eighth Army; to the southeast was the 113th Infantry Division. The division headquarters was located at Karagichev.

113th Infantry Division – The division defended in sector along the Don River against the 278th Rifle Division and the 76th Rifle Division. The division reported five men killed in action and eight men wounded in action. To the northwest was the 79th Infantry Division; to the east was an assortment of battle groups.

LI Corps – The corps suffered the following officer casualties: one killed in action; nine wounded in action.

71st Infantry Division – The division continued to attack east, northeast of Kalach, almost encircling the 399th Rifle Division. The infantry regiment returned from the 295th Infantry Division. To the north was the 295th Infantry Division; to the southeast was the Fourth ***Panzer*** Army.

76th Infantry Division – The division continued to attack east and shifted to the northeast to ease pressure along the corridor. The division

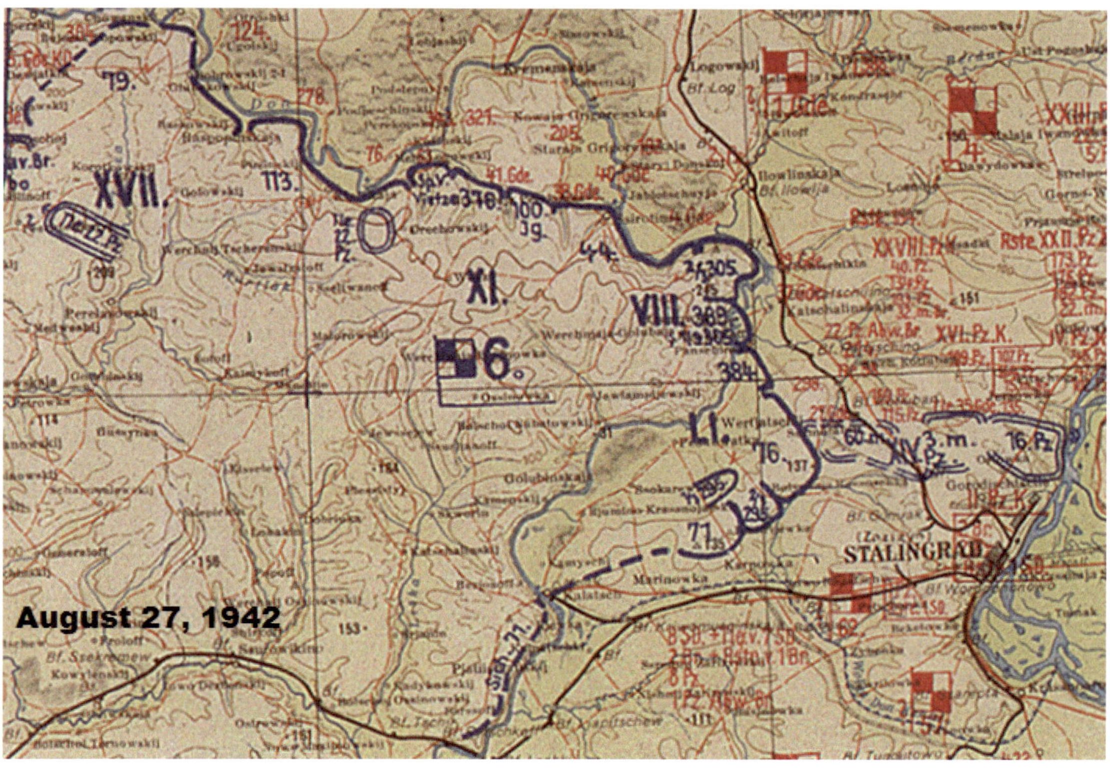

reported two NCO/enlisted wounded in action. To the northwest was the 384th Infantry Division; to the southwest was the 295th Infantry Division; to the east was the 60th Infantry Division (Motorized.)

295th Infantry Division – The division continued to attack east, approaching within mortar range of the Kalach-Stalingrad railroad; it then moved northeast to assist in reducing pressure against the corridor. One infantry regiment occupied an assembly area northwest of Dmitriyevka. The division lost one man killed in action and 20 NCOs/enlisted wounded in action. To the north was the 76th Infantry Division; to the south was the 71st Infantry Division.

✝

Christliches Andenken an Obergefreiten

Erich Böcksteiner

welcher am 27. August 1942 im 26. Lebensjahre an der Ostfront vor Stalingrad für das Vaterland den Heldentod erlitten hat

Im schönsten Alter in der vollsten Kraft
Hat der Krieg dich dahingerafft.
Und wenn uns auch bricht das blutende Herz,
Wir müssen ertragen den bitteren Schmerz.
Und schweift zu dir auch tränenschwer der Blick
Du kehrst zu uns doch nimmer zurück.
Geliebter Sohn und Bruder
Ruh' nun still in Frieden
Ewig beweint von deinen Lieben.

Verlag Karl Hebsacker Leonfelden.

Obergefreiter **Erich Böcksteiner** was born on February 10, 1917 at Burgfried in the Steiermark region of Austria. Most likely a member of the 16th ***Panzer*** Division, he was killed in action on August 27, 1942 three miles west of Jersovka and was buried at Orlovka.

Reinen Herzens ging ich in den Kampf und rein habe ich meinen Lebenslauf vollendet.

Ich habe den guten Kampf gekämpft, den Lauf vollendet, den Glauben bewahrt, nun liegt die Krone der Gerechtigkeit für mich bereit. (Paulus 2. Thim.)

Zum Gedenken im Gebete an

Walter Oppitz

Leutnant in einem Artillerie-Regiment, Abiturient der Handelsakademie, Kaufmannssohn aus Andorf.

Er fand als Führer eines Verbindungskommandos im Nordteil des großen Donbogens, nordwestl. Stalingrad, in treuester Pflichterfüllung im 22. Lebensjahre den Heldentod und liegt in Ossinkij bei Kremenskaja am Don in Rußland begraben.

✝

Du hast ihn uns geliehen, o Herr, und er war unser Glück. Du hast ihn zurückgefordert und wir geben ihn Dir ohne Murren, aber das Herz voller Wehmut. (Hl. Hieronymus)

Leutnant **Walter Oppitz** was born in Schärding, Austria on May 18, 1921. The son of a businessman, he passed his ***Abitur*** examination and was studying for a higher degree in business. ***Leutnant*** Oppitz served in an artillery survey unit in the 4th Battalion of the 376th Artillery Regiment in the 376th Infantry Division. He was killed in action at Ossinskij on August 27, 1942. His name is listed in the remembrance book at the German Military Cemetery at Rossoschka. It is also listed at the war memorial in Andorf, Austria.

Sources, August 27, 1942: ***Oberkommando des Heeres, Lage Ost: Stand: 27.8.42, Eastern Front Situation Map, National Archives Identifier: 559733, Record Group 242 – National Archives Collection of Foreign Records Seized, 1675-1958, National Archives, College Park, Maryland; Ia, Armeeoberkommando 6, "Morgen Meldung" and assorted reports, Kriegstagebuch 13, 28 August 1942, as found in Microfilm Series, T-312, Records of German Field Commands, Armies, Roll 1682, National Archives and Records Service, College Park, Maryland; 22nd Panzer Division, Kriegstagebuch 2, 27 August 1942, as found in Microfilm Series T-315, Roll 784, National Archives and Records Service, College Park, Maryland; 384th Infantry Division, Kriegstagebuch, 27 August 1942, as found in Microfilm Series T-315, Roll 2188, National Archives and Records Service, College Park, Maryland; David M. Glantz, & Jonathan M. House, To the Gates of Stalingrad: Soviet-German Combat Operations, April-August 1942, (The Stalingrad Trilogy, Volume 1), Lawrence, Kansas: University Press of Kansas, 2009, 361-362, 386-393; Anton Schimak, Karl Lamprecht & Friedrich Dettmer, Die 44. Infanterie Division: Tagebuch der Hoch- und Deutschmeister, Wien: Verlag Austria Press, 169, 233 and Map: Marschweg der 44. Infanterie Division im Russland; Wolfgang Werthen, Geschichte der 16. Panzer-Division 1939-1945, Friedberg, FRG: Podzun-Pallas-Verlag, 1958, 109.***

Letter from *Oberjäger* "Erich" to his parents on August 27, 1942. Erich was assigned to the 3rd Company, 100th Combat Engineer Battalion in the 100th ***Jäger*** Division. In his letter, he writes:

"Yesterday I got your letter dated May 22 and thank you very much. I hope you are all well at home. I myself have a slight wound, but nothing to be worried about. Last Monday [August 24], we were detailed to an obstacle-clearing detail. Six of us left our position to remove a barbed-wire barricade. It was 10:00 p.m., but the moon was shining. Someone in our own guard post about 100 meters to our left got nervous and let loose a star [illumination] shell.

Naturally, this woke the Russians up 500 meters in front of us. All hell broke loose with enemy machineguns and we all dropped for cover. No one was hurt but then came the crawl back to our own lines of about 150 meters and the Russians opened up with mortars. One mortar round exploded near me and some small shrapnel went into my left foot. It went through my boot and made a small hole; blood came out and I could not walk naturally, as the Russians would have seen us standing up.

Two of my comrades put a rope around my arms and in that way they were able to pull me into our cover. Once in the bunker, we found that one of my toes was smashed. A corpsman bandaged me and gave me an injection. I cannot get to the rear now because of enemy observation planes. Maybe tonight I will be taken [to the rear.] So please do not worry. You could please though send me some new socks; all the others are gone now.

I need nothing else right now. I hope I will stay for a few days in the rear area and have more time to write. Josef Primels has sent me a card from Romania and it looks like he loves it there. Let me send all my greetings."

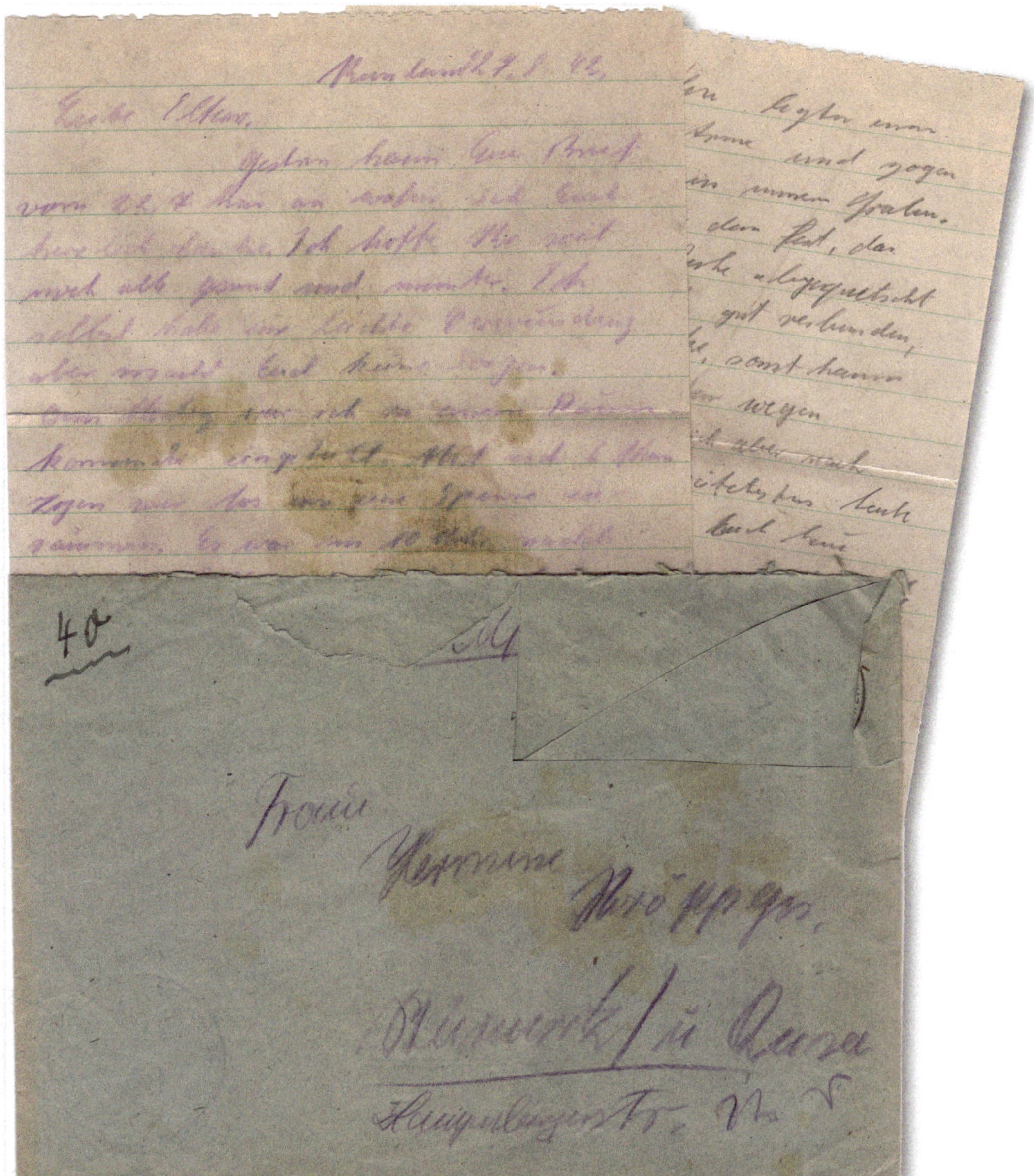

August 28, 1942
Weather: sunny, bright, warm, 57° F, 39° F at night, dusty visibility, good road conditions
Sunrise: 5:12 a.m.; **Sunset:** 6:54 p.m.
Moon: Waxing Gibbous; 93% illumination

Sixth Army – The army headquarters was located at Ossinowskij.

VIII Corps

305th Infantry Division – The division defended in sector near the Don River against the 39th Guards Rifle Division. The division suffered two NCOs/enlisted killed in action; 12 NCOs/enlisted were wounded in action. One infantry regiment was detached to the 389th Infantry Division. To the west was the 44th Infantry Division; to the south was the 389th Infantry Division.

384th Infantry Division – The division defended in sector northwest of Vertiachii against the 298th Rifle Division. The division reported one officer and six NCOs/enlisted wounded in action; two men were reported missing in action and three men injured in an accident. To the northwest was the 389th Infantry Division; to the southeast was the 76th Infantry Division.

389th Infantry Division – The division defended its positions east of the Don River outside Pan'shino against the 27th Guards Rifle Division. The division lost one NCO/enlisted killed in action; eight NCOs/enlisted were wounded in action. To the north was the 305th Infantry Division; to the south was the 384th Infantry Division.

XI Corps – The 521st ***Panzerjäger*** Detachment was assigned to the corps. The corps suffered the following officer casualties: nine wounded in action; two missing in action.

22nd Panzer Division – The division shifted westward to support German defenses on the west flank of the 79th Infantry Division. The division headquarters was located at Verchne-Tscherenrkij.

44th Infantry Division – The division defended in the sector Kurchajessowskij-Kamyshinskiy-Hill 171.0-Hill 180.9-Sirotinskaya-Khmelevskoy, against the 40th Guards Rifle Division. The division lost 24 NCOs/enlisted killed in action; six officers and 58 NCOs/enlisted were wounded in action; four NCOs/enlisted were missing in action. The division headquarters was located at Verkhne-Golubaja. To the east was the 305th Infantry Division; to the northwest was the 100th ***Jäger*** Division.

100th Jäger Division – The division defended in sector near Blizhniaia-Perekopka, repelling an attack from the north by the 41st Guards Rifle Division. The division reported 12 NCOs/enlisted killed in action; 67 NCOs/enlisted were wounded in action; one officer and seven NCOs/enlisted were missing in action. To the southeast was the 44th Infantry Division; to the northwest was the 376th Infantry Division.

376th Infantry Division – The division defended in sector southwest of Perekopka, repelling an armored attack from the north and the 321st Rifle Division. The division suffered four NCOs/enlisted killed in action and 18 NCOs/enlisted wounded in action. To the west was an assortment of battle groups; to the east was the 100th ***Jäger*** Division.

XIV *Panzer* Corps – The aim of the corps was to defend its corridor until supplies and reinforcements could arrive. The corps suffered the following officer casualties: nine killed in action; ten wounded in action.

3rd Infantry Division (Motorized) – The division conducted hedgehog defenses in the corridor centered on Kuz'michi to the north against the 35th Guards Rifle Division and Konnaia Station to the south, as ammunition supplies remained at critical levels. The division lost 12 NCOs/enlisted killed in action; one officer and 55 NCOs/enlisted were wounded in action; one man was reported missing in action. To the east was the 16th ***Panzer*** Division; to the west was the 60th Infantry Division (Motorized.)

16th Panzer Division – The division continued to hold terrain just north of Stalingrad;

enemy artillery barrages blocked contact with the 3rd Infantry Division (Motorized.)

60th Infantry Division (Motorized) – The division conducted hedgehog defenses in the corridor, as ammunition supplies remained at critical levels. To the east was the 3rd Infantry Division (Motorized); to the west was the 76th Infantry Division.

XVII Corps – The corps suffered the following officer casualties: three killed in action; four wounded in action.

79th Infantry Division – The division defended in sector from Bol'shoy-Verkhne-Kalmykovskii-Verkhne-Fomichinskii-Baskowskij against the 304th Rifle Division. The division suffered three officers and 21 NCOs/enlisted killed in action; four officers and 125 NCOs/enlisted were wounded in action. The division headquarters was located at Karagichev. To the west was the XXXV Corps of the Italian Eighth Army; to the southeast was the 113th Infantry Division.

113th Infantry Division – The division defended in sector along the Don River. The division lost one enlisted man killed in action; 13 NCOs/enlisted were wounded in action; ten NCOs/enlisted were reported missing in action. To the northwest was the 79th Infantry Division; to the southeast was an assortment of battle groups.

LI Corps – The aim of the corps was to keep open a resupply route for the XIV ***Panzer*** Corps. The corps suffered the following officer casualties: two killed in action; three wounded in action.

71st Infantry Division – The division continued to attack in zone east toward the Rossoschka River, while a regiment penetrated Kalach against the 131st Rifle Division. The division lost one officer and seven NCOs/enlisted killed in action; 40 NCOs/enlisted were wounded in action. To the northeast was the 295th Infantry Division; to the southeast was the Fourth ***Panzer*** Army.

76th Infantry Division – The division defended in sector against the 298th Rifle Division. The division reported 20 NCOs/enlisted wounded in action. To the northwest was the 384th Infantry Division; to the southwest was the 295th Infantry Division; to the east was the 60th Infantry Division (Motorized.)

295th Infantry Division – The division defended in sector. To the northeast was the 76th Infantry Division; to the southwest was the 71st Infantry Division.

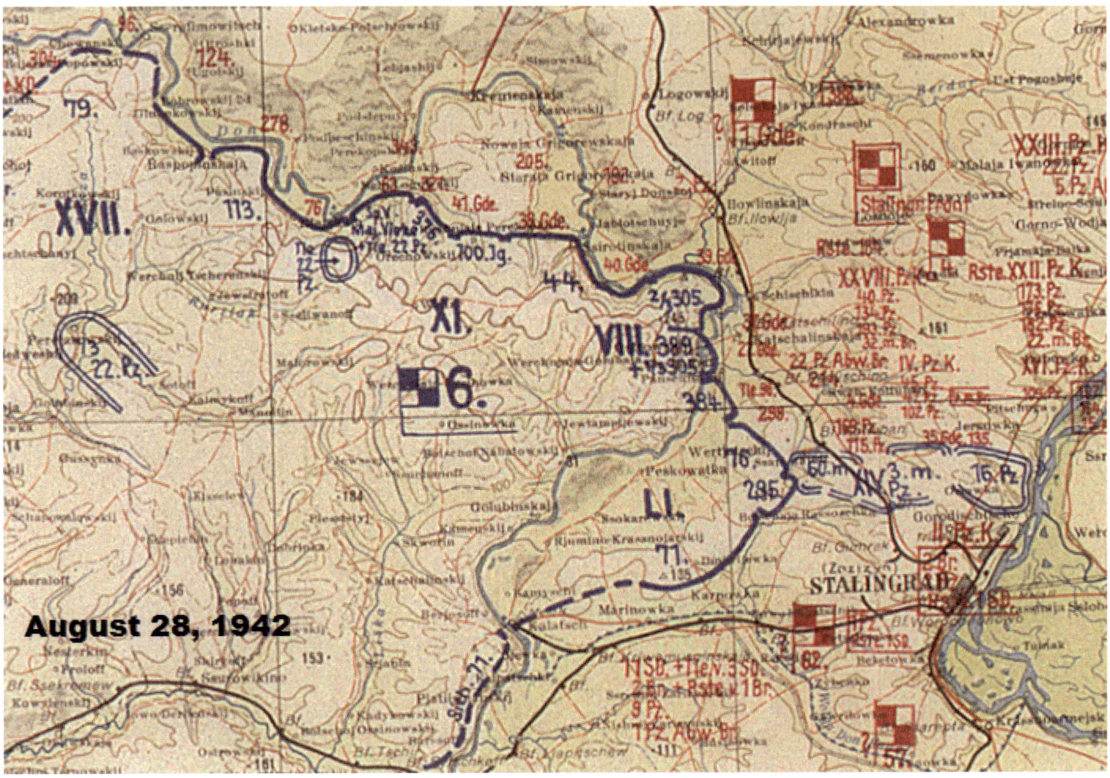

Sources, August 28, 1942: ***Oberkommando des Heeres, Lage Ost: Stand: 28.8.42, Eastern Front Situation Map, National Archives Identifier: 559733, Record Group 242 – National Archives Collection of Foreign Records Seized, 1675-1958, National Archives, College Park, Maryland; Ia, Armeeoberkommando 6, "Morgen Meldung" and assorted reports, Kriegstagebuch 13, 29 August 1942, as found in Microfilm Series, T-312, Records of German Field Commands, Armies, Roll 1682, National Archives and Records Service, College Park, Maryland; 79th Infantry Division, Kriegstagebuch, 28 August 1942, as found in Microfilm Series T-315, Roll 1108, National Archives and Records Service, College Park, Maryland; 384th Infantry Division, Kriegstagebuch, 28 August 1942, as found in Microfilm Series T-315, Roll 2188, National Archives and Records Service, College Park, Maryland; David M. Glantz, & Jonathan M. House, To the Gates of Stalingrad: Soviet-German Combat Operations, April-August 1942, (The Stalingrad Trilogy, Volume 1), Lawrence, Kansas: University Press of Kansas, 2009, 362-363, 386-393; Kurt Mehner, Die Geheimen Tagesberichte der Deutschen Wehrmachtführung im Zweiten Weltkrieg 1939-1945, Band 5: 1. Juni 1942 – 30. November 1942, Osnabrück, Germany: Biblio Verlag, 1991, 163; Anton Schimak, Karl Lamprecht & Friedrich Dettmer, Die 44. Infanterie Division: Tagebuch der Hoch- und Deutschmeister, Wien: Verlag Austria Press, 169, 233 and Map: Marschweg der 44. Infanterie Division im Russland.***

Dead bodies at a Soviet entrenchment in front of Stalingrad.

August 29, 1942
Weather: overcast, light clouds, rainy all day, 73° F, 39° F at night, some bad road conditions, trenches filled with water
Sunrise: 5:13 a.m.; **Sunset:** 6:52 p.m.
Moon: Waxing Gibbous; 87% illumination

Sixth Army – The army headquarters was located at Ossinowskij.

VIII Corps – The 754th Pioneer Battalion was assigned to the corps. The corps suffered the following officer casualties: two killed in action; one wounded in action.

305th Infantry Division – The division defended in sector near the Don River against the 39th Guards Rifle Division. The division suffered three NCOs/enlisted killed in action and six NCOs/enlisted wounded in action. The infantry regiment returned from the 389th Infantry Division. To the west was the 44th Infantry Division; to the south was the 389th Infantry Division.

384th Infantry Division – The division defended in sector northwest of Vertiachii against the 298th Rifle Division. The division lost one NCO/enlisted killed in action; four NCOs/enlisted were wounded in action. To the north was the 389th Infantry Division; to the southeast was the 76th Infantry Division.

389th Infantry Division – The division defended its positions east of the Don River outside Pan'shino against the 27th Guards Rifle Division. The division lost two officers and five NCOs/enlisted killed in action. To the north was the 305th Infantry Division; to the south was the 384th Infantry Division.

XI Corps – The corps suffered the following officer casualties: three killed in action; seven wounded in action; one missing in action.

22nd Panzer Division – The division, interspersed with the 79th Infantry Division, defended in sector against the 304th Rifle Division and the 96th Rifle Division south of Serafimovich. Part of the division remained in an assembly area in the XI Corps sector. The division reported one NCO/enlisted killed in action and seven NCOs/enlisted wounded in action.

44th Infantry Division – The division defended in sector Kurchajessowskij-Kamyshinskiy-Hill 171.0-Hill 180.9-Sirotinskaya-Khmelevskoy, against the 40th Guards Rifle Division and the 4th Guards Rifle Division. The division suffered two officers and 24 NCOs/enlisted killed in action; four officers and 107 NCOs/enlisted were wounded in action; one officer and 25 NCOs/enlisted were missing in action. The division headquarters was located in Verkhne-Golubaja. To the east was the 305th Infantry Division; to the northwest was the 100th ***Jäger*** Division.

100th Jäger Division – The division defended in sector near Blizhniaia-Perekopka against the 23rd Rifle Division and the 38th Guards Rifle Division. The division lost five NCOs/enlisted killed in action; one officer and 34 NCOs/enlisted were wounded in action; one NCO/enlisted was missing in action. To the east was the 44th Infantry Division; to the west was the 376th Infantry Division. The division headquarters was located in Perekopskoi.

376th Infantry Division – The division defended in sector southwest of Perekopka against the 321st Rifle Division and the 41st Guards Rifle Division. The division reported four NCOs/enlisted wounded in action. To the west was an assortment of battle groups; to the east was the 100th ***Jäger*** Division. The division headquarters was located in Ventsy.

XIV *Panzer* Corps – The corps suffered the following officer casualties: one killed in action; four wounded in action.

3rd Infantry Division (Motorized) – The division conducted hedgehog defenses in the corridor centered on Kuz'michi to the north and Konnaia Station to the south, repelling several enemy attacks from the south. The division lost six NCOs/enlisted killed in action; 40 NCOs/enlisted were wounded in action. To the east was the 16th ***Panzer*** Division; to the west was the 60th Infantry Division (Motorized.)

16th Panzer Division – The division continued to hold terrain just north of Stalingrad; enemy artillery barrages blocked contact with the 3rd Infantry Division (Motorized.)

60th Infantry Division (Motorized) – The division conducted hedgehog defenses in the corridor. To the east was the 3rd Infantry Division (Motorized); to the west were the 76th Infantry Division and the 295th Infantry Division.

XVII Corps – The corps suffered the following officer casualties: two killed in action; five wounded in action.

79th Infantry Division – The division defended in sector from Bol'shoy-Verkhne-Kalmykovskii-Verkhne-Fomichinskii-Baskowskij against the 124th Rifle Division and the 96th Rifle Division. The division reported losing approximately 120 killed and wounded. The division headquarters was located at Karagichev. To the west was the XXXV Corps of the Italian Eighth Army; to the southeast was the 113th Infantry Division.

113th Infantry Division – The division defended in sector along the Don River against the 76th Rifle Division and the 278th Rifle Division. The division lost one officer and two NCOs/enlisted killed in action; 25 NCOs/enlisted were wounded in action. To the northwest was the 79th Infantry Division; to the east was an assortment of battle groups.

LI Corps – The corps suffered the following officer casualties: eight wounded in action.

71st Infantry Division – The division continued to attack east from Dmitriyevka and reached the Rossoschka River north and south of Malaia Rossoschka; one regiment continued to sweep through Kalach with very small losses. The division reported seven NCOs/enlisted killed in action and 28 NCOs/enlisted wounded in action (this report could have been a restatement from the previous day's losses.) To the northeast was the 295th Infantry Division; to the south was an open flank.

76th Infantry Division – The division defended in sector against the 298th Rifle Division. The division suffered 47 men killed in action; 145 were wounded in action; four were missing in action. To the northwest was the 384th Infantry Division; to the southwest was the 295th Infantry Division; to the east was the 60th Infantry Division (Motorized.)

295th Infantry Division – The division defended its positions in sector against the 35th Guards Rifle Division. The division lost six NCOs/enlisted killed in action; 21 NCOs/enlisted were wounded in action. To the northeast was the 76th Infantry Division; to the southwest was the 71st Infantry Division.

Fourth *Panzer* Army – The army headquarters was located east of Abganerovo.

IV Corps

94th Infantry Division – The division defended a blocking position northeast of Tinguta Rail Station opposite the 422nd Rifle Division. To the southeast were elements of the 29th Infantry Division (Motorized); to the southwest was the 371st Infantry Division. ***Generalleutnant*** Georg Pfeiffer served as the division commander. The division was authorized 17,734 men, including 8,000 infantrymen and 779 combat engineers; also authorized were 36 medium anti-tank guns, 20 light howitzers (7.5cm), 36 medium howitzers (10.5cm), 18 heavy howitzers (15cm) and 4,842 horses.

297th Infantry Division – The division defended a blocking position near 74 Kilometer Rail Station. To the northeast was the 371st Infantry Division; to the southwest was the 20th Romanian Infantry Division.

371st Infantry Division – The division defended a blocking position at Tinguta Rail Station and conducted a limited attack northwest. The division lost 11 NCOs/enlisted killed in action; three officers and 62 NCOs/enlisted were wounded in action. To the northeast was the 94th Infantry Division; to the southwest was the 297th Infantry Division. ***Generalmajor*** Richard Stempel served as division commander. The division was authorized 17,734 men, including 8,000 infantrymen and 779 combat engineers; also authorized were 36 medium anti-tank guns, 20 light howitzers (7.5cm), 36 medium howitzers (10.5cm), 18 heavy howitzers (15cm) and 4,842 horses.

XXXXVIII *Panzer* Corps

14th Panzer Division – The division attacked in zone northward, trailing the 29th Infantry Division (Motorized), seizing Hill 162.0 from elements of the 64th Army. The division lost 45 NCOs/enlisted killed in action; one officer and 120 NCOs/enlisted were wounded in action; 11 men were reported missing in action. ***Generalmajor*** Ferdinand Heim served as division commander. The division was authorized 15,600 men, including 5,500 infantrymen and 779 combat engineers; also authorized were 75 medium anti-tank guns, 18 light guns (7.5cm), 36 medium howitzers (10.5cm), 16 heavy howitzers (15cm), 165 armored fighting vehicles (including 22 Mark II tanks, 87 Mark III tanks and 26 Mark IV tanks) and 2,800 motor transport vehicles.

24th Panzer Division – The division attacked in zone north against elements of the 64th Army, seizing Hill 124, Farm Nr.1, Blinikov, Hill 130, Sety and Hill 174.0. The division lost eight NCOs/enlisted killed in action; four officers and 70 NCOs/enlisted were wounded in action; one man died of his wounds in hospital later in the day; two men were reported missing in action. To the east was the 29th Infantry Division (Motorized.)

29th Infantry Division (Motorized) – The bulk of the division attacked in zone northward to the east of the 24th ***Panzer*** Division, against the 138th Rifle Division, seizing Iurkino. Elements of the division defended in sector south of the 94th Infantry Division near Lake Zaza against the 302nd Rifle Division. The division lost two officers and 17 NCOs/enlisted killed in action; 71 NCOs/enlisted were wounded in action. ***Generalmajor*** Max Fremerey served as division commander. The division was authorized 16,400 men, including 7,100 infantrymen and 779 combat engineers; also authorized were 63 medium anti-tank guns, 20 light guns (7.5cm), 36 medium howitzers (10.5cm), 12 heavy howitzers (15cm), 77 ***panzers*** (20 Mark II tanks, 42 Mark III tanks and 15 Mark IV tanks) and 2,800 motor transport vehicles.

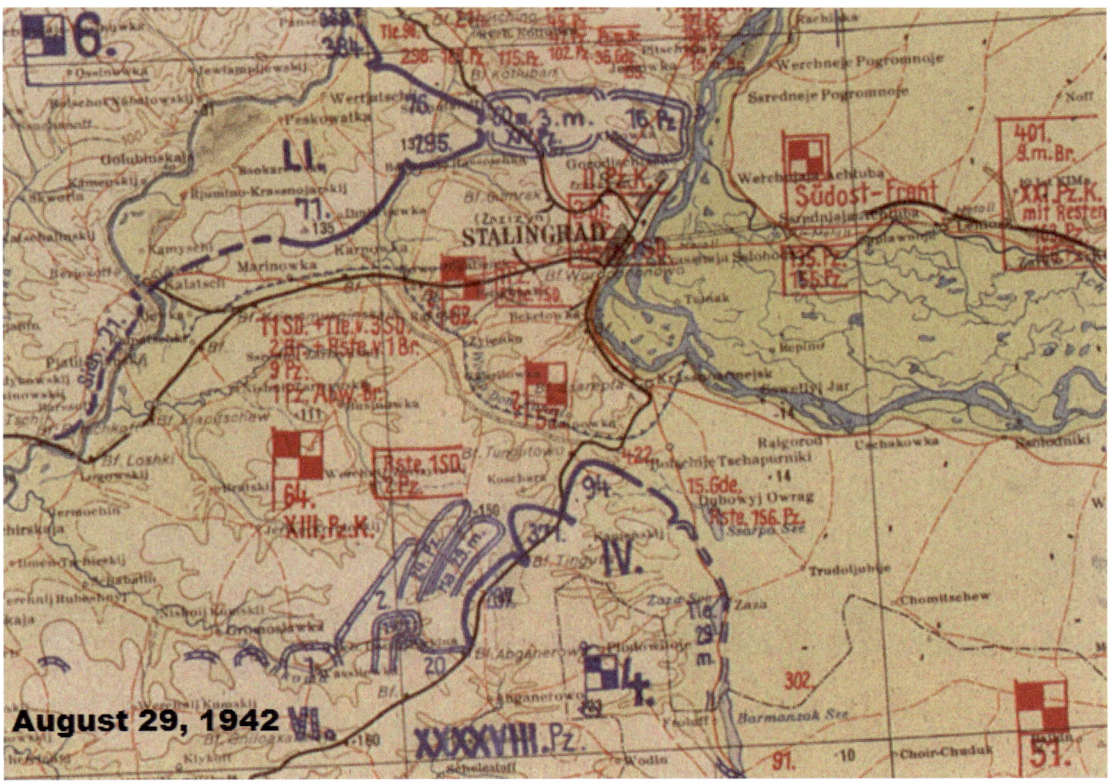

Sources, August 29, 1942: *Oberkommando des Heeres, Lage Ost: Stand: 29.8.42, Eastern Front Situation Map, National Archives Identifier: 559733, Record Group 242 – National Archives Collection of Foreign Records Seized, 1675-1958, National Archives, College Park, Maryland; Ia, Armeeoberkommando 6, "Morgen Meldung" and assorted reports, Kriegstagebuch 13, 30 August 1942, as found in Microfilm Series, T-312, Records of German Field Commands, Armies, Roll 1682, National Archives and Records Service, College Park, Maryland; Ia, XXXXVIII Panzerkorps, "Übersicht über die dem Korps Unterstellten Divisionen, 28. Juni 1942 – 11 October 1942," as found on T-314, Records of German Field Commands, Corps, Roll 1153, National Archives, College Park, Maryland; Korpsarzt, XXXXVIII Panzerkorps, "Meldung über Personelle Verluste," Stand 29.8.42, as found on T-314, Records of German Field Commands, Corps, Roll 1158, National Archives, College Park, Maryland; 22nd Panzer Division, Kriegstagebuch 2, 29 August 1942, as found in Microfilm Series T-315, Roll 784, National Archives and Records Service, College Park, Maryland; 371st Infantry Division, Kriegstagebuch, 29 August 1942, as found in Microfilm Series T-315, Roll 2164, National Archives and Records Service, College Park, Maryland; 384th Infantry Division, Kriegstagebuch, 29 August 1942, as found in Microfilm Series T-315, Roll 2188, National Archives and Records Service, College Park, Maryland; Antony Beevor, Stalingrad: The Fateful Siege: 1942-1943, London: Penguin Books, 1998, 116; James F. Dunnigan, War in the East: The Russo-German Conflict, 1941-45, Strategy & Tactics Staff Study Nr.1, New York: Simulations Publications Incorporated, 1977, 141-146; David M. Glantz, & Jonathan M. House, To the Gates of Stalingrad: Soviet-German Combat Operations, April-August 1942, (The Stalingrad Trilogy, Volume 1), Lawrence, Kansas: University Press of Kansas, 2009, 362-363, 370-374, 384-393; Joachim Lemelsen, 29. Division, Bad Nauheim, FRG: Podzun Verlag, 1960, 196; Jason Mark, Death of the Leaping Horseman: 24. Panzer-Division in Stalingrad, Sydney, Australia: Leaping Horsemen Books, 2003, Sydney, Australia: Leaping Horsemen Books, 2003, 81-91; Janusz Piekalkiewicz, Stalingrad: Anatomie einer Schlacht, München, BRD: Wilhelm Heyne Verlag, 1977, 122-123; Anton Schimak, Karl Lamprecht & Friedrich Dettmer, Die 44. Infanterie Division: Tagebuch der Hoch- und Deutschmeister, Wien: Verlag Austria Press, 169, 233 and Map: Marschweg der 44. Infanterie Division im Russland.*

"The Good Days of Summer." German troopers south of Stalingrad in the summer of 1942, riding a camel.

***Generaloberst* Hermann Hoth, Commander of the Fourth *Panzer* Army.**

"The Bad Days of Summer." Wounded German troopers near Stalingrad in the late summer of 1942, await evacuation.

August 30, 1942
Weather: sunny, bright, light clouds, 73° F, 41° F at night, good road conditions
Sunrise: 5:15 a.m.; **Sunset:** 6:50 p.m.
Moon: Waxing Gibbous; 79% illumination

Sixth Army – The army headquarters was located at Ossinowskij.

VIII Corps – The corps suffered the following officer casualties: one killed in action; two wounded in action.

305th Infantry Division – The division defended in sector near the Don River. The division reported four NCOs/enlisted wounded in action. To the west was the 44th Infantry Division; to the south was the 389th Infantry Division.

384th Infantry Division – The division defended in sector north of Vertiachii. The division lost one officer and four NCOs/enlisted wounded in action. To the north was the 389th Infantry Division; to the southeast was the 76th Infantry Division.

389th Infantry Division – The division defended its positions east of the Don River outside Pan'shino. The division suffered five NCOs/enlisted killed in action; one officer and 17 NCOs/enlisted were wounded in action. To the north was the 305th Infantry Division; to the southeast was the 384th Infantry Division.

XI Corps

22nd Panzer Division – The division, interspersed with the 79th Infantry Division, defended in sector south of Serafimovich. The division reported one man killed in action. Part of the division occupied an assembly area in the XI Corps sector.

44th Infantry Division – The division defended in sector Kurchajessowskij-Kamyshinskiy-Hill 171.0-Hill 180.9-Sirotinskaya-Khmelevskoy, against the 40th Guards Rifle Division. The division suffered three NCOs/enlisted killed in action; 12 NCOs/enlisted were wounded in action. The division headquarters was located at Verkhne-Golubaja. To the east was the 305th Infantry Division; to the west was the 100th ***Jäger*** Division.

100th Jäger Division – The division defended in sector near Blizhniaia-Perekopka. The division lost two NCOs/enlisted killed in action; 12 NCOs/enlisted were wounded in action. To the east was the 44th Infantry Division; to the west was the 376th Infantry Division. The division headquarters was located in Perekopskoi.

376th Infantry Division – The division defended in sector southwest of Perekopka. The division reported that it had no casualties. To the west was an assortment of battle groups; to the east was the 100th ***Jäger*** Division. The division headquarters was located in Ventsy.

XIV *Panzer* Corps – The 51st ***Werfer*** Regiment was assigned to support the corps. The corps suffered the following officer casualties: two killed in action; seven wounded in action.

3rd Infantry Division (Motorized) – The division conducted hedgehog defenses in the corridor centered on Kuz'michi to the north and Konnaia Station to the south. The division lost one officer and 24 NCOs/enlisted killed in action; one officer and 23 NCOs/enlisted were wounded in action. To the east was the 16th ***Panzer*** Division; to the west was the 60th Infantry Division (Motorized.)

16th Panzer Division – The division continued to hold terrain just north of Stalingrad; enemy artillery barrages blocked contact with the 3rd Infantry Division (Motorized.)

60th Infantry Division (Motorized) – The division conducted hedgehog defenses in the corridor. To the east was the 3rd Infantry

Division (Motorized); to the west were the 76th Infantry Division and the 295th Infantry Division.

XVII Corps – The corps suffered the following officer casualties: two wounded in action.

79th Infantry Division – The division defended in sector from Bol'shoy-Verkhne-Kalmykovskii-Verkhne-Fomichinskii-Baskowskij. The division headquarters was located at Karagichev. The division reported (late) 17 NCOs/enlisted killed in action; one officer and 108 NCOs/enlisted were wounded in action; seven NCOs/enlisted were reported missing in action. To the west was the XXXV Corps of the Italian Eighth Army; to the southeast was the 113th Infantry Division.

113th Infantry Division – The division defended in sector along the Don River west of Kletskiy. The division lost four NCOs/enlisted killed in action; ten NCOs/enlisted were wounded in action; one man was missing in action. To the northwest was the 79th Infantry Division; to the east was an assortment of battle groups.

LI Corps – The corps suffered the following officer casualties: one killed in action; eight wounded in action.

71st Infantry Division – The division continued to attack east in zone and reached the Rossoschka River north and south of Malaia Rossoschka. The division lost four NCOs/enlisted killed in action; one officer and 14 NCOs/enlisted were wounded in action; one NCO/enlisted was missing in action. To the northeast was the 295th Infantry Division; to the south was an open flank.

76th Infantry Division – The division defended in sector. The division suffered six NCOs/enlisted killed in action; 36 NCOs/enlisted were wounded in action. To the northwest was the 384th Infantry Division; to the south was the 295th Infantry Division; to the east was the 60th Infantry Division (Motorized.)

295th Infantry Division – The division defended in sector. The division reported three NCOs/enlisted killed in action; 31 NCOs/enlisted were wounded in action. To the north was the 76th Infantry Division; to the southwest was the 71st Infantry Division.

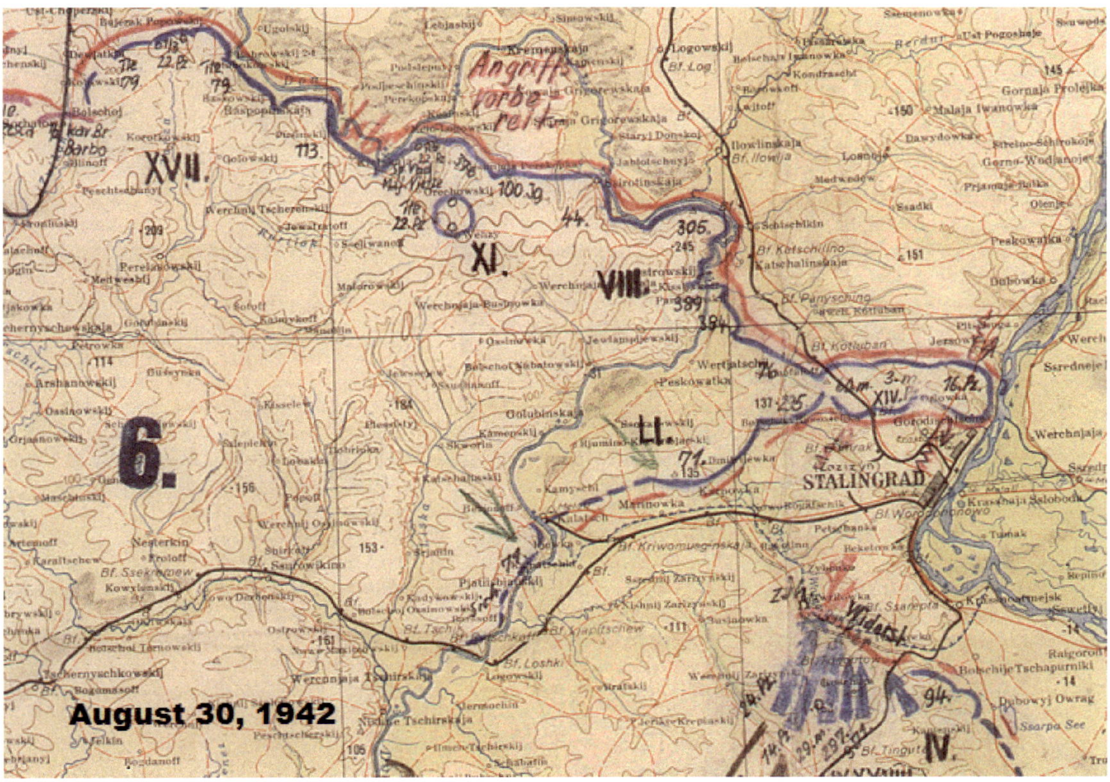

August 30, 1942

Fourth *Panzer* Army – The army headquarters was located east of Abganerovo.

IV Corps – The corps headquarters was located north of Abganerovo.

94th Infantry Division – The division attacked northwest in zone from a blocking position northeast of Tinguta Rail Station. To the southeast were elements of the 29th Infantry Division (Motorized); to the west was the 371st Infantry Division.

297th Infantry Division – The division attacked north in zone. To the east was the 371st Infantry Division; to the west was the 29th Infantry Division (Motorized.)

371st Infantry Division – The division attacked north in zone. The division then defended a bridgehead over the Chervlenoye River northwest of Ivanovka. The division suffered one officer and 15 NCOs/enlisted killed in action; 11 officers and 117 NCOs/enlisted were wounded in action; two men were reported missing in action. To the east was the 94th Infantry Division; to the west was the 297th Infantry Division.

XXXXVIII *Panzer* Corps – The corps headquarters was located in Gavrilovka.

14th Panzer Division – The division attacked in zone north and northeast. The division lost four officers and 30 NCOs/enlisted killed in action; four officers and 30 NCOs/enlisted were wounded in action; four officers and 83 NCOs/enlisted were reported missing in action. To the west was the 24th ***Panzer*** Division; to the east was the 29th Infantry Division (Motorized.) ***Generalleutnant*** Ferdinand Heim received the Knight's Cross.

24th Panzer Division – The division attacked in zone north and northeast over the Karpovka River, seizing Hill 150.0 and Nariman. The division lost one officer and 28 NCOs/enlisted killed in action; three officers and 53 NCOs/enlisted were wounded in action. To the east was the 14th ***Panzer*** Division; to the west was an open flank.

29th Infantry Division (Motorized) – The division attacked in zone north and northeast against the 208th Rifle Division near Verkhne-Zaryzinskij and then defended a bridgehead over the Chervlenoye River north of Nariman. Elements of the division defended in sector south of the 94th Infantry Division. The division lost 18 NCOs/enlisted killed in action; eight officers and 100 NCOs/enlisted were wounded in action. To the east was the 297th Infantry Division; to the west was the 14th ***Panzer*** Division.

Sources, August 30, 1942: ***Oberkommando des Heeres, Lage Ost: Stand: 30.8.42, Eastern Front Situation Map, National Archives Identifier: 559733, Record Group 242 – National Archives Collection of Foreign Records Seized, 1675-1958, National Archives, College Park, Maryland; Ia, Armeeoberkommando 6, "Morgen Meldung" and other reports, Kriegstagebuch 13, 31 August 1942, as found in Microfilm Series, T-312, Records of German Field Commands, Armies, Roll 1682, National Archives and Records Service, College Park, Maryland; Ia, Armeeoberkommando 6, "Morgen Meldung" and assorted reports, Kriegstagebuch 13, 30 August 1942, as found in Microfilm Series, T-312, Records of German Field Commands, Armies, Roll 1685, National Archives and Records Service, College Park, Maryland; Ia, XXXXVIII Panzerkorps, "Übersicht über die dem Korps Unterstellten Divisionen, 28. Juni 1942 – 11 October 1942," as found on T-314, Records of German Field Commands, Corps, Roll 1153, National Archives, College Park, Maryland; Korpsarzt, XXXXVIII Panzerkorps, "Meldung über Personelle Verluste," Stand 30.8.42, as found on T-314, Records of German Field Commands, Corps, Roll 1158, National Archives, College Park, Maryland; 22nd Panzer Division, Kriegstagebuch 2, 30 August 1942, as found in Microfilm Series T-315, Roll 784, National Archives and Records Service, College Park, Maryland; 79th Infantry Division, Kriegstagebuch, 30 August 1942, as found in Microfilm Series T-315, Roll 1108, National Archives and Records Service, College Park, Maryland; 371st Infantry Division, Kriegstagebuch, 30 August 1942, as found in Microfilm Series T-315, Roll 2164, National Archives and Records Service, College Park, Maryland; 384th Infantry Division, Kriegstagebuch, 30 August 1942, as found in Microfilm Series T-315, Roll 2188, National Archives and Records Service, College Park, Maryland; David M. Glantz, & Jonathan M. House, To the Gates of Stalingrad: Soviet-German Combat Operations, April-August 1942, (The Stalingrad Trilogy, Volume 1), Lawrence, Kansas: University Press of Kansas, 2009, 363-364, 373-375, 384-393; Joachim Lemelsen, 29. Division, Bad Nauheim, FRG: Podzun Verlag, 1960, 197; Jason Mark, Death of the Leaping Horseman: 24. Panzer-Division in Stalingrad, Sydney, Australia: Leaping Horsemen Books, 2003, Sydney, Australia: Leaping Horsemen Books, 2003, 92-96; Janusz Piekalkiewicz, Stalingrad: Anatomie einer Schlacht, München, BRD: Wilhelm Heyne Verlag, 1977, 124; Anton Schimak, Karl Lamprecht & Friedrich Dettmer, Die 44. Infanterie Division: Tagebuch der Hoch- und Deutschmeister, Wien: Verlag Austria Press, 169, 233 and Map: Marschweg der 44. Infanterie Division im Russland.***

Zum Andenken

an unseren unvergeßlichen Sohn und Bruder

Engelbert Gradinger

Unteroffizier in einem Infanterie-Regiment
Inhaber des E. K. 2. Klasse, des Infanterie-Sturm-abzeichens und des Verwundetenabzeichens

Hofbauersohn von Pimberg, Pf. Aspach

welcher am 30. August 1942 im 26. Lebensjahre an der Ostfront in treuer soldatischer Pflichterfüllung den Heldentod fand.

Geliebter Sohn, Bruder,
Du liegst begraben
In fremder Erde Schoß,
Als Held bist Du gefallen,
Das Leid um Dich ist groß.
Lebe wohl, geliebter Sohn, Bruder,
Der Abschied war so schwer,
Deine Lieben mußtest Du so früh
verlassen,
Seh'n Dich auf dieser Welt nicht mehr.
Beendet ist Dein junges Leben,
Reichst uns nicht mehr zum Gruß die Hand,
Dein Herz hat ausgeschlagen
Im Kampf fürs Vaterland.

Zeilinger, Aspach. 3519—42

***Unteroffizier* Engelbert Gradinger**, the son of a farmer, was born in Pimberg near Aspach in the district of Braunau am Inn, in Austria on July 24, 1917. Assigned to an infantry regiment in the 297th Infantry Division, and the winner of the Iron Cross 2nd Class, Infantry Assault Badge and Wound Badge in Black, he was killed in action on August 30, 1942 two miles west of Koschary. His name is listed in the remembrance book at the German Military Cemetery at Rossoschka.

August 31, 1942
Weather: clear, warming, good road conditions
Sunrise: 5:16 a.m.; **Sunset:** 6:48 p.m.
Moon: Waxing Gibbous; 70% illumination

Sixth Army – The army headquarters was located at Ossinowskij.

VIII Corps

305th Infantry Division – The division expanded its sector and defended along the Don River bend south of Ilowlinskaja opposite the 39th Guards Rifle Division. The division lost three NCOs/enlisted wounded in action. To the west was the 44th Infantry Division; to the south was the 384th Infantry Division.

384th Infantry Division – The division defended in sector northeast of Vertiachii opposite the 214th Rifle Division. The division suffered 11 NCOs/enlisted killed in action; 63 NCOs/enlisted were wounded in action; 18 men were reported missing in action. From August 15 through August 31, the division lost 16 officers, 101 NCOs and 408 enlisted men killed in action; 54 officers, 317 NCOs and 1,705 enlisted men were wounded in action; one officer, 13 NCOs and 141 enlisted men were missing in action. To the north was the 305th Infantry Division; to the southeast was the 76th Infantry Division.

389th Infantry Division – The division withdrew from its defensive sector east of the Don River outside Pan'shino to an assembly area southwest, near Akimovskii, for rest and refit operations. The division lost 15 NCOs/enlisted wounded in action.

XI Corps – The corps suffered the following officer casualties: one killed in action; two wounded in action.

22nd Panzer Division – The division defended in sector with the 79th Infantry Division. Part of the division continued to occupy an assembly area in the XI Corps sector. The division reported two NCOs/enlisted killed in action and eight NCOs/enlisted wounded in action. During recent fighting, the division lost an aggregate of six officers and 139 NCOs/enlisted killed in action; 57 officers and 1,430 NCOs/enlisted were wounded in action; three officers and 17 NCOs/enlisted were reported missing in action.

44th Infantry Division – The division defended in the sector Kurchajessowskij-Kamyshinskiy-Hill 171.0-Hill 180.9-Sirotinskaya-Khmelevskoy, against the 40th Guards Rifle Division and the 4th Guards Rifle Division. The division lost six NCOs/enlisted killed in action; two officers and 21 NCOs/enlisted were wounded in action. The division headquarters was located in Verkhne-Golubaja. To the east was the 305th Infantry Division; to the west was the 100th ***Jäger*** Division.

100th Jäger Division – The division defended in sector near Blizhniaia-Perekopka, repelling an enemy attack from the north by the 23rd Rifle Division and 38th Guards Rifle Division. The division reported one officer and eight NCOs/enlisted killed in action; one officer and 30 NCOs/enlisted were wounded in action. To the east was the 44th Infantry Division; to the west was the 376th Infantry Division.

376th Infantry Division – The division defended in sector southwest of Perekopka against the 63rd Rifle Division. The division suffered one NCO/enlisted killed in action; four NCOs/enlisted were wounded in action. To the west was an assortment of battle groups; to the east was the 100th ***Jäger*** Division.

XIV *Panzer* Corps – The corps suffered the following officer casualties: two wounded in action.

3rd Infantry Division (Motorized) – The division conducted hedgehog defenses in the corridor centered on Kuz'michi to the north – against the 4th Tank Corps – and Konnaia Station to the south. The division reported 14 men killed in action; 54 NCOs/enlisted were wounded in action. To the east was the 16th ***Panzer*** Division; to the west was the 60th Infantry Division (Motorized.)

16th Panzer Division – The division continued to hold terrain just north of Stalingrad against the 16th Tank Corps. The division reported nine men killed in action; 64 NCOs/enlisted were wounded in action. To the west was the 3rd Infantry Division (Motorized.) The division repelled an enemy attack from the south.

60th Infantry Division (Motorized) – The division conducted hedgehog defenses in the corridor against the 28th Tank Corps. To the east was the 3rd Infantry Division (Motorized); to the west were the 76th Infantry Division and the 295th Infantry Division.

XVII Corps – The corps suffered the following officer casualties: two wounded in action.

79th Infantry Division – The division defended in sector from Bol'shoy-Verkhne-Kalmykovskii-Verkhne-Fomichinskii-Baskowskij, opposite the 304th Rifle Division. The division headquarters was located at Karagichev. To the west was the XXXV Corps of the Italian Eighth Army; to the southeast was the 113th Infantry Division. The division lost 60 casualties. From August 1, 1942 through August 31, 1942, the division suffered 13 officers and 338 NCOs/enlisted killed in action; 40 officers and 1,453 NCOs/enlisted were wounded in action; three officers and 213 NCOs/enlisted were missing in action.

113th Infantry Division – The division defended in sector along the Don River west of Kletskiy, opposite the 278th Rifle Division and the 76th Rifle Division. The division reported two NCOs/enlisted killed in action and four NCOs/enlisted wounded in action. To the northwest was the 79th Infantry Division; to the east was an assortment of battle groups.

LI Corps – The 245th ***Sturmgeschütz*** Detachment was assigned to the corps. The corps suffered the following officer casualties: two killed in action; three wounded in action.

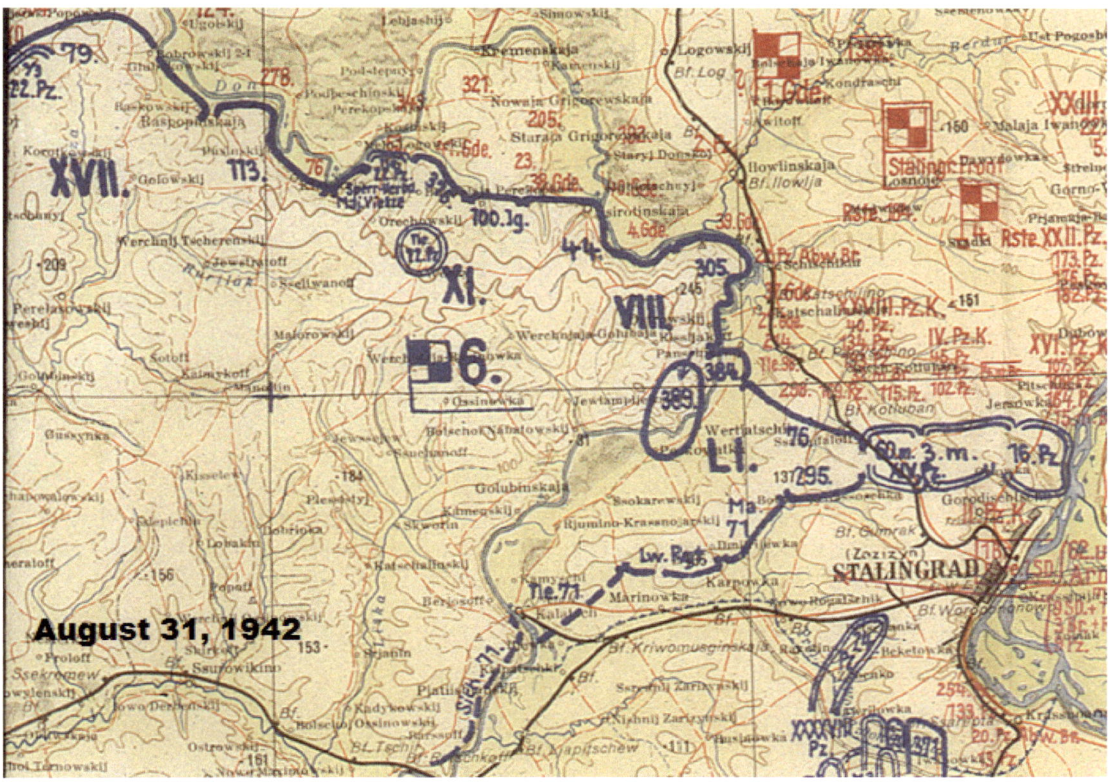

71st Infantry Division – The division continued to attack east in zone, reaching the Rossoschka River north and south of Malaia Rossoschka. The division reported two NCOs/enlisted wounded in action. To the north was the 295th Infantry Division; to the south was an open flank. The infantry regiment detached to the 295th Infantry Division returned to the division. A ***Luftwaffe*** ground regiment reinforced the division.

76th Infantry Division – The division defended in sector at the Kotluban' Balka against the 298th Rifle Division. The division suffered seven NCOs/enlisted killed in action; 34 NCOs/enlisted were wounded in action; two men were missing in action. To the northwest was the 384th Infantry Division; to the south was the 295th Infantry Division; to the east was the 60th Infantry Division (Motorized.) The division reported that from August 1 through August 31, 1942, 26 officers and 456 NCOs/enlisted were killed in action; 79 officers and 1,815 NCOs/enlisted were wounded in action; 64 NCOs/enlisted were missing in action.

295th Infantry Division – The division attacked in zone near Rossoschka, west of Gumrak, in the inner fortified zone of Stalingrad. To the north was the 76th Infantry Division; to the south was the 71st Infantry Division; to the east was the 60th Infantry Division (Motorized.)

Fourth *Panzer* Army – The aim of the army was to attack Stalingrad from the south and sever all lines of communication to it west of the Volga River. The army headquarters was located east of Abganerovo.

IV Corps – The aim of the corps was to protect the right flank of the XXXXVIII ***Panzer*** Corps. The corps headquarters was located north of Abganerovo.

94th Infantry Division – The division prepared to attack. To the west was the 371st Infantry Division; to the south were elements of the 29th Infantry Division (Motorized.)

297th Infantry Division – The division defended a bridgehead over the Chervlenoye River near Andreevka and then attacked north. To the east was the 371st Infantry Division; to the west was the 14th ***Panzer*** Division.

371st Infantry Division – The division defended a bridgehead over the Chervlenoye River near Andreevka and then attacked north. The division suffered two officers and 13 NCOs/enlisted killed in action; seven officers and 100 NCOs/enlisted were wounded in action; one man was reported missing in action. To the east was the 94th Infantry Division; to the west was the 297th Infantry Division.

XXXXVIII *Panzer* Corps – The aim of the corps, as the main effort for the Fourth ***Panzer*** Army, was to penetrate to the southern suburbs of Stalingrad. The corps headquarters was located in Gavrilovka.

14th Panzer Division – The division attacked in zone to the east of the 24th ***Panzer*** Division to cross the Chervlenaya Balka, and seize Hill 128.2 and Yagodnyi. The division lost 16 NCOs/enlisted killed in action; one officer and 45 NCOs/enlisted were wounded in action. To the east was the 297th Infantry Division.

24th Panzer Division – The division attacked in zone northward through Hill 112.5, Gavrilovka, Varvarovka, Zybenko, Hill 111.5, Hill 128.5 to cut the Bassargino-Stalingrad railway line. The division suffered one officer and ten NCOs/enlisted killed in action; four officers and 96 NCOs/enlisted were wounded in action. To the southeast was the 14th ***Panzer*** Division; to the west was an open flank; to the south was the 20th Romanian Infantry Division of the Romanian VI Corps.

29th Infantry Division (Motorized) – The division followed the 24th ***Panzer*** Division and then advanced to protect the east flank of the 24th ***Panzer*** Division. The division lost one officer and 15 NCOs/enlisted killed in action; three officers and 52 NCOs/enlisted were wounded in action.

20th Romanian Infantry Division – The division attacked in zone behind the 24th ***Panzer*** Division, reaching south of the Volga-Don Canal.

Sources, August 31, 1942: *Oberkommando des Heeres, Lage Ost: Stand: 31.8.42, Eastern Front Situation Map, National Archives Identifier: 559733, Record Group 242 – National Archives Collection of Foreign Records Seized, 1675-1958, National Archives, College Park, Maryland; Ia, Armeeoberkommando 6, "Morgen Meldung" and assorted reports, Kriegstagebuch 13, 1 September 1942, as found in Microfilm Series, T-312, Records of German Field Commands, Armies, Roll 1685, National Archives and Records Service, College Park, Maryland; Ia, XXXXVIII Panzerkorps, "Übersicht über die dem Korps Unterstellten Divisionen, 28. Juni 1942 – 11 October 1942," as found on T-314, Records of German Field Commands, Corps, Roll 1153, National Archives, College Park, Maryland; Korpsarzt, XXXXVIII Panzerkorps, "Meldung über Personelle Verluste," Stand 31.8.42, as found on T-314, Records of German Field Commands, Corps, Roll 1158, National Archives, College Park, Maryland; 22nd Panzer Division, Kriegstagebuch 2, 31 August 1942, as found in Microfilm Series T-315, Roll 784, National Archives and Records Service, College Park, Maryland; 76th Infantry Division, Kriegstagebuch, 31 August 1942, as found in Microfilm Series T-315, Roll 1090, National Archives and Records Service, College Park, Maryland; 79th Infantry Division, Kriegstagebuch, 31 August 1942, as found in Microfilm Series T-315, Roll 1108, National Archives and Records Service, College Park, Maryland; 371st Infantry Division, Kriegstagebuch, 31 August 1942, as found in Microfilm Series T-315, Roll 2164, National Archives and Records Service, College Park, Maryland; 384th Infantry Division, Kriegstagebuch, 31 August 1942, as found in Microfilm Series T-315, Roll 2188, National Archives and Records Service, College Park, Maryland; David M. Glantz, & Jonathan M. House, To the Gates of Stalingrad: Soviet-German Combat Operations, April-August 1942, (The Stalingrad Trilogy, Volume 1), Lawrence, Kansas: University Press of Kansas, 2009, 363-364, 373-376, 384-393; Joachim Lemelsen, 29. Division, Bad Nauheim, FRG: Podzun Verlag, 1960, 197; Jason Mark, Death of the Leaping Horseman: 24. Panzer-Division in Stalingrad, Sydney, Australia: Leaping Horsemen Books, 2003, Sydney, Australia: Leaping Horsemen Books, 2003, 96-104; Anton Schimak, Karl Lamprecht & Friedrich Dettmer, Die 44. Infanterie Division: Tagebuch der Hoch- und Deutschmeister, Wien: Verlag Austria Press, 169, 233 and Map: Marschweg der 44. Infanterie Division im Russland.*

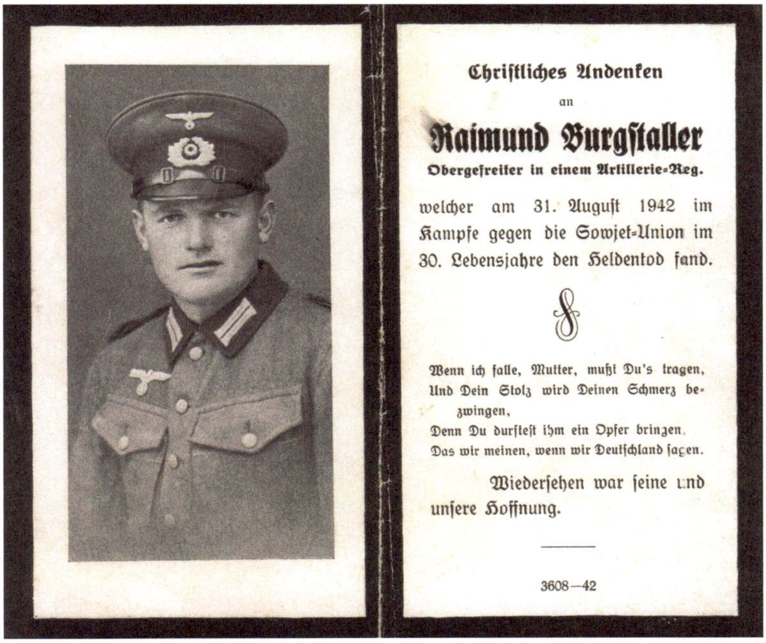

Obergefreiter **Raimund Burgstaller** was born in Reichersberg near Ried in Upper Austria on August 28, 1912. He was killed in action on August 31, 1942 southwest Tscherwjenaja, while assigned to an artillery regiment.

September, 1942

September 1, 1942
Weather: falling temperatures, increasing cloudiness, light precipitation, cool wind, good road conditions
Sunrise: 5:18 a.m.; **Sunset:** 6:46 p.m.
Moon: Waxing Gibbous; 61% illumination

Sixth Army – The army headquarters was located at Ossinowskij.

VIII Corps

305th Infantry Division – The division defended in sector along the Don River bend south of Ilowlinskaja. The division lost two men killed in action and two men wounded in action. To the west was the 44th Infantry Division; to the south was the 384th Infantry Division.

384th Infantry Division – The division defended its positions east of the Don River outside Pan'shino. The division reported two NCOs/enlisted wounded in action. To the north was the 305th Infantry Division; to the southeast was the 76th Infantry Division.

389th Infantry Division – The division occupied an assembly area south of the 389th Infantry Division and conducted rest and refit operations. The division lost two men wounded in action.

XI Corps – The corps suffered the following officer casualties: one wounded in action.

22nd Panzer Division – Elements of the division attacked northwest along the western flank of the 79th Infantry Division, driving the enemy back several miles. Another part of the division assisted the 376th Infantry Division defend in sector, while a third element of the division occupied an assembly area near Ventsy. The division reported seven men killed in action and 18 men wounded in action.

44th Infantry Division – The division defended in sector Kurchajessowskij-Kamyshinskiy-Hill 171.0-Hill 180.9-Sirotinskaya-Khmelevskoy, against the 40th Guards Rifle Division. The division lost two men killed in action and seven men wounded in action. The division headquarters was located at Verkhne-Golubaja. To the east was the 305th Infantry Division; to the west was the 100th ***Jäger*** Division.

100th Jäger Division – The division defended in sector near Blizhniaia-Perekopka. The division lost three men killed in action; one officer and seven NCOs/enlisted men were wounded in action. To the east was the 44th Infantry Division; to the west was the 376th Infantry Division.

376th Infantry Division – The division defended in sector near Blizhniaia-Perekopka. The division reported five men killed in action; one officer and 32 NCOs/enlisted were wounded in action. To the west was an assortment of battle groups; to the east was the 100th ***Jäger*** Division.

XIV *Panzer* Corps – Heavy enemy attacks struck throughout the corps sector but were repulsed. The corps suffered the following officer casualties: one wounded in action.

3rd Infantry Division (Motorized) – The division conducted hedgehog defenses in the corridor centered on Kuz'michi to the north and Konnaia Station to the south. The division lost eight NCOs/enlisted killed in action; one officer and 48 NCOs/enlisted were wounded in action; two men were reported missing in action. To the east was the 16th ***Panzer*** Division; to the west was the 60th Infantry Division (Motorized.)

16th Panzer Division – The division continued to hold terrain just north of Stalingrad; to the west was the 3rd Infantry Division (Motorized.)

60th Infantry Division (Motorized) – The division conducted hedgehog defenses in the corridor. To the east was the 3rd Infantry Division (Motorized); to the west was the 76th Infantry Division.

XVII Corps – The corps suffered the following officer casualties: one killed in action; one wounded in action.

79th Infantry Division – The division defended in sector from Bol'shoy-Verkhne-Kalmykovskii-Verkhne-Fomichinskii-Baskowskij. The division suffered one officer and 52 NCOs/enlisted killed in action; two officers and 221 NCOs/enlisted were wounded in action; 30 NCOs/enlisted were missing in action. The division headquarters was located at Karagichev. To the west was the XXXV Corps of the Italian Eighth Army; to the southeast was the 113th Infantry Division.

113th Infantry Division – The division defended in sector along the Don River west of Kletskiy. The division lost two NCOs/enlisted wounded in action. To the northwest was the 79th Infantry Division; to the east was an assortment of battle groups.

LI Corps – The 245th ***Sturmgeschütz*** Detachment was assigned to the corps. The corps suffered the following officer casualties: two wounded in action.

71st Infantry Division – The division moved northwest to a new attack position. The division reported one officer and one NCO wounded in action. To the northeast was the 76th Infantry Division; to the south was an open flank; to the northeast was the 295th Infantry Division. A ***Luftwaffe*** regiment of ground troops was attached to the division for combat.

76th Infantry Division – The division defended just north of Stalingrad at the Kotluban' Balka. The division reported six enlisted men wounded in action. To the northwest was the 384th Infantry Division; to the southeast was the 295th Infantry Division; to the east was the 60th Infantry Division (Motorized.)

295th Infantry Division – The division attacked near Rossoschka west of Gumrak in the inner fortified zone of Stalingrad. To the north was the 76th Infantry Division; to the south was the 71st Infantry Division; to the east was the 60th Infantry Division (Motorized.)

Fourth *Panzer* Army – The army headquarters was located at Plodowitoje.

IV Corps – The corps headquarters was located north of Abganerovo.

94th Infantry Division – The division moved north in preparation for offensive operations; it captured Dubovi-Ovrag. To the west was the 371st Infantry Division.

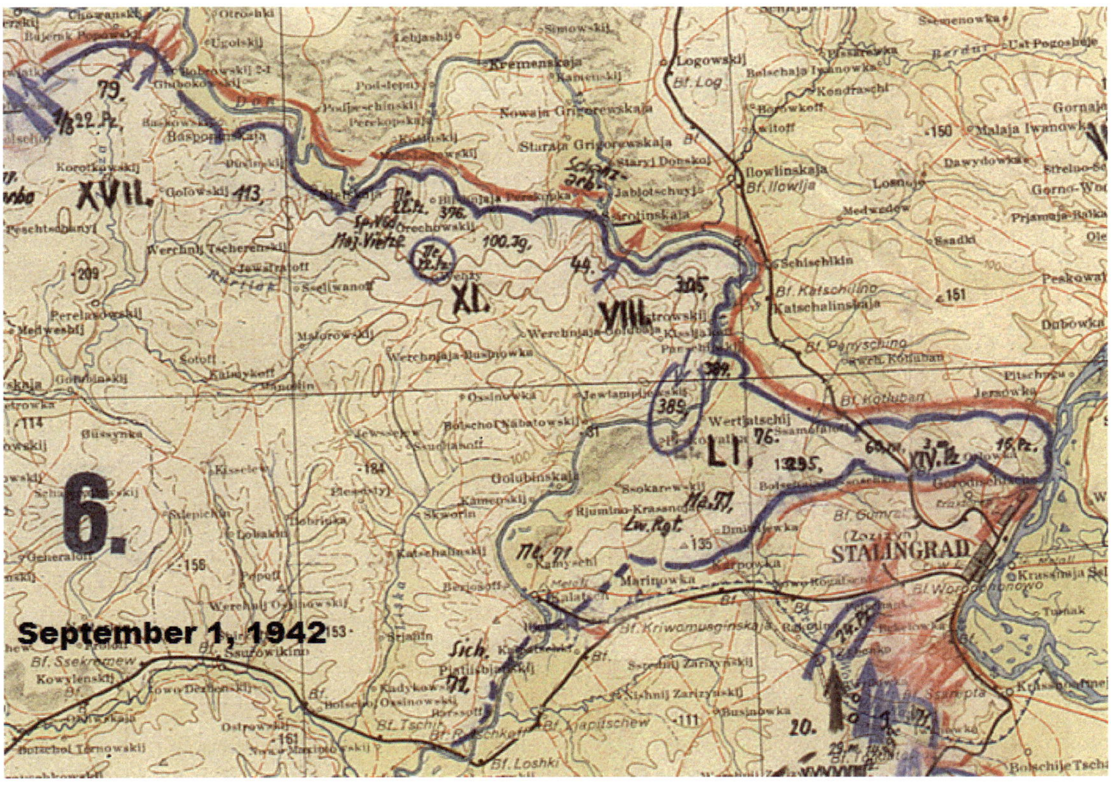

297th Infantry Division – The division defended a bridgehead over the Chervlenoye River near Andreevka. To the east was the 371st Infantry Division; to the west was the 14th ***Panzer*** Division.

371st Infantry Division – The division defended a bridgehead over the Chervlenoye River near Andreevka. The division lost 23 NCOs/enlisted killed in action; 140 NCOs/enlisted were wounded in action; five men were reported missing in action. To the east was the 94th Infantry Division; to the west was the 297th Infantry Division.

XXXXVIII *Panzer* Corps – Corps support units suffered four NCOs/enlisted killed in action; one officer and 13 NCOs/enlisted were wounded in action. The corps headquarters was located in Gavrilovka.

14th Panzer Division – The division consolidated its gains near Iagoniki. The division lost 23 NCOs/enlisted killed in action; one officer and 75 NCOs/enlisted were wounded in action. To the east was the 297th Infantry Division.

24th Panzer Division – The division consolidated its gains from the previous day – after briefly reaching Peschanka and then withdrawing – occupying Hill 128.5, 116.1, and repelling an enemy attack from the northeast. The division suffered 14 NCOs/enlisted killed in action; three officers and 92 NCOs/enlisted were wounded in action; two men were reported missing in action. To the southeast was the 29th Infantry Division (Motorized); to the west was an open flank. Operational tank strength in the division stood at 56.

29th Infantry Division (Motorized) – The division consolidated gains south of the 24th ***Panzer*** Division, including occupying Hill 111.5 near Gavrilovka against the 36th Guards Rifle Division.

20th Romanian Infantry Division – The division advanced north behind the 24th ***Panzer*** Division.

Innermost Russian anti-tank defensive ditch on the western edge of Stalingrad. The photo was taken by a member of the 524th Infantry Regiment of the 297th Infantry Division.

Sources, September 1, 1942: ***Oberkommando des Heeres, Lage Ost: Stand: 1.9.42, Eastern Front Situation Map, National Archives Identifier: 559733, Record Group 242 – National Archives Collection of Foreign Records Seized, 1675-1958, National Archives, College Park, Maryland; Ia, Armeeoberkommando 6, "Morgen Meldung" and assorted reports, Kriegstagebuch 13, 2 September 1942, as found in Microfilm Series, T-312, Records of German Field Commands, Armies, Roll 1685, National Archives and Records Service, College Park, Maryland; Ia, XXXXVIII Panzerkorps, "Übersicht über die dem Korps Unterstellten Divisionen, 28. Juni 1942 – 11 October 1942," as found on T-314, Records of German Field Commands, Corps, Roll 1153, National Archives, College Park, Maryland; Korpsarzt, XXXXVIII Panzerkorps, "Meldung über Personelle Verluste," Stand 1.9.42, as found on T-314, Records of German Field Commands, Corps, Roll 1158, National Archives, College Park, Maryland; 371st Infantry Division, Kriegstagebuch, 1 September 1942, as found in Microfilm Series T-315, Roll 2164, National Archives and Records Service, College Park, Maryland; David M. Glantz, & Jonathan M. House, To the Gates of Stalingrad: Soviet-German Combat Operations, April-August 1942, (The Stalingrad Trilogy, Volume 1), Lawrence, Kansas: University Press of Kansas, 2009, 375-381; Joachim Lemelsen, 29. Division, Bad Nauheim, FRG: Podzun Verlag, 1960, 197; Jason Mark, Death of the Leaping Horseman: 24. Panzer-Division in Stalingrad, Sydney, Australia: Leaping Horsemen Books, 2003, 104-109; Kurt Mehner, Die Geheimen Tagesberichte der Deutschen Wehrmachtführung im Zweiten Weltkrieg 1939-1945, Band 5: 1. Juni 1942 – 30. November 1942, Osnabrück, Germany: Biblio Verlag, 1991, 169; Anton Schimak, Karl Lamprecht & Friedrich Dettmer, Die 44. Infanterie Division: Tagebuch der Hoch- und Deutschmeister, Wien: Verlag Austria Press, 169, 233 and Map: Marschweg der 44. Infanterie Division im Russland.***

September 2, 1942
Weather: sunny, bright, cool, 64° F, light rain at night
Sunrise: 5:19 a.m.; **Sunset:** 6:44 p.m.
Moon: Last Quarter; 50% illumination

Sixth Army – The army headquarters was located at Ossinowskij.

VIII Corps – The corps repulsed attacks by elements of the 4th Tank Army. The corps received attachment of the 244th ***Sturmgeschütz*** Detachment.

76th Infantry Division – The division defended in sector just north of Stalingrad at the Kotluban' Balka. The division repelled attacks from the 298th Rifle Division from the north. The division suffered four NCOs/enlisted killed in action; 24 NCOs/enlisted were wounded in action. To the northwest was the 384th Infantry Division; to the southeast was the 295th Infantry Division; to the east was the 60th Infantry Division (Motorized.)

305th Infantry Division – The division defended in sector at the Don River bend south of Ilowlinskaja, opposite the 22nd Anti-Tank Brigade. One infantry regiment occupied an assembly area. The division began to exchange positions with the 384th Infantry Division. The division had two men wounded in action. To the west was the 44th Infantry Division; to the south was the 384th Infantry Division.

384th Infantry Division – The division defended in sector northeast of Vertiachii and repelled attacks by the 27th Guards Rifle Division and the 214th Rifle Division. The division began to exchange defensive positions with the 305th Infantry Division. The division lost six NCOs/enlisted killed in action and ten NCOs/enlisted wounded in action. To the north was the 305th Infantry Division; to the southeast was the 76th Infantry Division.

389th Infantry Division – The division occupied an assembly area near Vertyachiy and conducted rest and refit operations. The division then began to move east for future operations with the LI Corps. The division reported no casualties.

XI Corps – The corps suffered the following officer casualties: one killed in action; one wounded in action.

22nd Panzer Division – The division moved northeast to engage an enemy penetration on the right flank of the 79th Infantry Division. Elements of the division occupied two assembly areas behind the front line. The division reported three NCOs/enlisted killed in action and five NCOs/enlisted wounded in action.

44th Infantry Division – The division defended in sector Kurchajessowskij-Kamyshinskiy-Hill 171.0-Hill 180.9-Sirotinskaya-Khmelevskoy, against the 40th Guards Rifle Division and 4th Guards Rifle Division. The division lost one officer and six NCOs/enlisted killed in action; two officers and 38 NCOs/enlisted were wounded in action. The division headquarters was located in Verkhne-Golubaja. To the northwest was the 100th ***Jäger*** Division; to the east was the 305th Infantry Division.

100th Jäger Division – The division defended in sector near Blizhniaia-Perekopka, opposite the 23rd Rifle Division. The division suffered five NCOs/enlisted killed in action; one officer and 16 NCOs/enlisted were wounded in action. To the east was the 44th Infantry Division; to the west was the 376th Infantry Division.

376th Infantry Division – The division defended in sector near Blizhniaia-Perekopka against the 41st Guards Rifle Division. The division lost seven NCOs/enlisted wounded in action and one NCO/enlisted missing in action. To the west was an assortment of battle groups; to the east was the 100th ***Jäger*** Division.

XIV *Panzer* Corps – The corps suffered the following officer casualties: two killed in action; one wounded in action.

3rd Infantry Division (Motorized) – The division conducted hedgehog defenses in the corridor centered on Kuz'michi to the north and Konnaia Station to the south. The division lost two officers and seven NCOs/enlisted killed in action; one officer and 57 NCOs/enlisted were wounded in action; one man was reported missing in action. To the east was the 16th ***Panzer*** Division; to the west was the 60th Infantry Division (Motorized.)

16th Panzer Division – The division continued to hold terrain just north of Stalingrad against the 16th Tank Corps. To the west was the 3rd Infantry Division (Motorized.)

60th Infantry Division (Motorized) – The division conducted hedgehog defenses in the corridor, repelling an enemy attack from the north by the 4th Tank Corps. The division also attacked south. To the east was the 3rd Infantry Division (Motorized); to the west was the 76th Infantry Division.

XVII Corps – The corps suffered the following officer casualties: three wounded in action.

79th Infantry Division – The division defended in sector from Bol'shoy-Verkhne-Kalmykovskii-Verkhne-Fomichinskii-Baskowskij. The division headquarters was located at Karagichev. The 124th Rifle Division and the 96th Rifle Division attacked in the eastern half of the sector and gained several miles of terrain. The division lost 11 NCOs/enlisted killed in action; three officers and 52 NCOs/enlisted were wounded in action; nine NCOs/enlisted were missing in action. To the west was the XXXV Corps of the Italian Eighth Army; to the southeast was the 113th Infantry Division. The division reported the following anti-tank guns as operational: five 7.5cm, one Russian 7.62cm, three 5cm and four French 4.7cm.

113th Infantry Division – The division defended in sector along the Don River west of Kletskiy, against the 76th Rifle Division and the 278th Rifle Division. The division reported seven NCOs/enlisted killed in action; 15 NCOs/enlisted were wounded in action. To the northwest was the 79th Infantry Division; to the east was an assortment of battle groups. The division reported the following anti-tank guns as operational: four 7.5cm and fifteen 5cm.

LI Corps – The 245th ***Sturmgeschütz*** Detachment was assigned to the corps. The 851st Heavy Artillery Detachment was assigned to support the corps. The corps suffered the following officer casualties: five wounded in action.

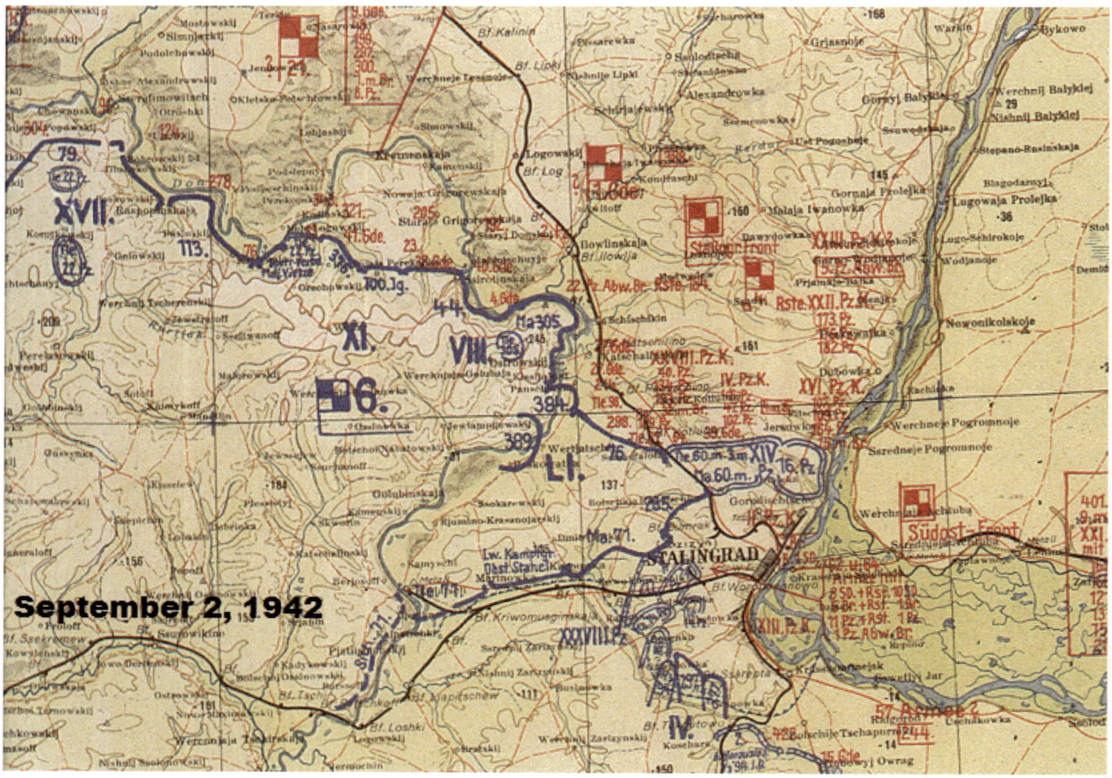

71st Infantry Division – The division made contact with the Fourth ***Panzer*** Army's 20th Romanian Infantry Division at the Voroponovo Rail Station and the 24th ***Panzer*** Division north of the rail line. ***Luftwaffe*** Battle Group Stahel, attached to the division, defended in sector between Marinovka and Karpovka. The division lost two NCOs/enlisted killed in action. To the northeast was the 295th Infantry Division.

295th Infantry Division – The division attacked to the southeast near Rossoschka and Gumrak in the inner fortified zone of Stalingrad. The division lost two NCOs/enlisted killed in action and five NCOs/enlisted were wounded in action. To the north was the 76th Infantry Division; to the south was the 71st Infantry Division.

Fourth *Panzer* Army – The army headquarters was located at Plodowitoje.

IV Corps – The corps headquarters was located north of Abganerovo.

94th Infantry Division – The division moved west and then north in preparation for offensive operations. To the east was the 297th Infantry Division; to the north was the 29th Infantry Division (Motorized.)

297th Infantry Division – The division defended a bridgehead over the Chervlenoye River near Andreevka. To the east was the 371st Infantry Division; to the west was the 94th Infantry Division.

371st Infantry Division – The division defended a bridgehead over the Chervlenoye River near Andreevka. The division lost five NCOs/enlisted killed in action; 44 NCOs/enlisted were wounded in action. To the west was the 297th Infantry Division; to the east was an open flank.

XXXXVIII *Panzer* Corps – The corps headquarters was located in Gavrilovka.

14th Panzer Division – The division attacked to the northeast along the eastern flank of the 24th ***Panzer*** Division toward Peschanka. The division lost 14 NCOs/enlisted killed in action; five officers and 46 NCOs/enlisted were wounded in action. To the west was the 24th ***Panzer*** Division; to the east was the 29th Infantry Division (Motorized.)

24th Panzer Division – The division attacked northeast and captured Hill 151.7 and Farm Nr.2; it also made contact with the 71st Infantry Division to the northwest. The division suffered one officer and 55 NCOs/enlisted killed in action; four officers and 153 NCOs/enlisted were wounded in action. To the east was the 14th ***Panzer*** Division; to the west was the 20th Romanian Infantry Division.

29th Infantry Division (Motorized) – The division attacked along the eastern flank of the 14th ***Panzer*** Division toward the northeast through Elkhi. The division lost 15 NCOs/enlisted killed in action; 56 NCOs/enlisted were wounded in action. To the west was the 14th ***Panzer*** Division.

20th Romanian Infantry Division – The division linked-up with the Sixth Army's 71st Infantry Division at the Voroponovo Rail Station. To the east was the 24th ***Panzer*** Division. The division was under the command of Major General Nicolae Tataranu.

Sources, September 2, 1942: ***Oberkommando des Heeres, Lage Ost: Stand: 2.9.42, Eastern Front Situation Map, National Archives Identifier: 559733, Record Group 242 – National Archives Collection of Foreign Records Seized, 1675-1958, National Archives, College Park, Maryland; Ia, Armeeoberkommando 6, "Morgen Meldung" and assorted reports, Kriegstagebuch 13, 3 September 1942, as found in Microfilm Series, T-312, Records of German Field Commands, Armies, Roll 1685, National Archives and Records Service, College Park, Maryland; Ia, XXXXVIII Panzerkorps, "Übersicht über die dem Korps Unterstellten Divisionen, 28. Juni 1942 – 11 October 1942," as found on T-314, Records of German Field Commands, Corps, Roll 1153, National Archives, College Park, Maryland; Korpsarzt, XXXXVIII Panzerkorps, "Meldung über Personelle Verluste," Stand 2.9.42, as found on T-314, Records of German Field Commands, Corps, Roll 1158, National Archives, College Park, Maryland; 76th Infantry Division, Kriegstagebuch, 2 September 1942, as found in Microfilm Series T-315, Roll 1090, National Archives and Records Service, College Park, Maryland; 371st Infantry Division, Kriegstagebuch, 2 September 1942, as found in Microfilm Series T-315, Roll 2164, National Archives and Records Service, College Park, Maryland; David M. Glantz, & Jonathan M. House, To the Gates of Stalingrad: Soviet-German Combat Operations, April-August 1942, (The Stalingrad Trilogy, Volume 1), Lawrence, Kansas: University Press of Kansas, 2009, 379; David M. Glantz & Jonathan M. House, Armageddon in Stalingrad: September-November 1942, (The Stalingrad Trilogy, Volume 2), Lawrence, Kansas: University Press of Kansas, 2009, 29-33; Joachim Lemelsen, 29. Division, Bad Nauheim, FRG: Podzun Verlag, 1960, 197; Jason Mark, Death of the Leaping Horseman: 24. Panzer-Division in Stalingrad, Sydney, Australia: Leaping Horsemen Books, 2003, 109-114; Janusz Piekalkiewicz, Stalingrad: Anatomie einer Schlacht, München, BRD: Wilhelm Heyne Verlag, 1977, 137; Anton Schimak, Karl Lamprecht & Friedrich Dettmer, Die 44. Infanterie Division: Tagebuch der Hoch- und Deutschmeister, Wien: Verlag Austria Press, 169, 233 and Map: Marschweg der 44. Infanterie Division im Russland; Georg Tessin, Verbände und Truppen der deutschen Wehrmacht und Waffen-SS im Zweiten Weltkrieg 1939-1945, Dritter Band: Die Landstreitkräfte 6-14, Osnabrück, FRG, 1974, 3.***

Zur frommen Erinnerung im Gebete

an unseren unvergeßlichen Sohn

Rudolf Süß

Obergefreiter in einer Radfahrerschwadron

Inhaber des E. K. 2. Kl. und des Sturm-abzeichens in Silber

Hausbesitzerssohn von Weeg, Pf. Raab

welcher am 2. September 1942 an der Ostfront im 24. Lebensjahre für Führer, Volk und Vaterland sein Leben gab.

Mit frohem Mute zog ich aus,
Leb' wohl, mein geliebtes Vaterhaus.
Lebt wohl, ihr Lieben, weinet nicht,
Gehorsam ist Soldatenpflicht.
Hast du gekämpft mit starker Hand,
Die Schlacht war heiß in Feindesland,
Da färbte sich mein Waffenrock;
Auch mein Stahlhelm blutig rot:
Mein Los war der Soldatentod.
Dein Grab im fernen Lande
Ist uns wohl eine schwere Pein,
Doch nimm dies Wort zum Unterpfande,
Dein Grab soll nicht verlassen sein.
Allabends, wenn die Glocken läuten,
Zieht liebend unser Geist dorthin
Und streut dir betend Andachtsblumen
Aufs Heldengrab mit frommem Sinn.

„Barmherziger Jesus, gib ihm die ewige Ruhe!" — (Ablaß von sieben Jahren und sieben Quadragenen.)

Auzinger, Er... 3517—42

Obergefreiter **Rudolf Süss** was born at Weeg near Raab, Austria on April 5, 1919. A winner of the Iron Cross 2nd Class and an Infantry Assault Badge in Silver, he was assigned to a bicycle battalion – probably in the 376th Infantry Division – before his death in combat at Perekopka on September 2, 1942. His name is listed in the remembrance book at the German Military Cemetery at Rossoschka.

In Gottes hl. Frieden

ruht fern von seinen Lieben

mein lieber Sohn, unser unvergeßlicher Bruder und Gatte

Josef Socher

Obergefreiter in einem Pion.Panz.Rgt.

geboren am 18. Okt. 1912 in Westendorf
gefallen am 2. September 1942
bei Jebanka, südwestl. Stalingrad.

Im fernen Osten, ins stille Grab
Da senkten sie unsern Helden hinab,
Man hörte keiner Glocke Klang,
Auch tönte kein ernster Grabgesang.
Wir in der Heimat hofften noch fort:
Der Sohn u. Bruder er kämpfet noch dort.
Doch ehe ein Abend brach herein,
Wir wußten, er kehrt nimmer heim.
Wir schauen hoffend zum Himmel hinauf
O, Lenker der Schlachten, nimm du ihn auf
Und mußt ohn' Abschied er von uns gehn
Dort oben, da gibt's ein Wiedersehn.

Obergefreiter **Josef Socher** was born in Westendorf, Germany on October 18, 1912. He was married and was assigned to the combat engineer battalion of the 24th ***Panzer*** Division. He was killed in action on September 2, 1942 north of Zybenko; his name is listed in the remembrance book at the German Military Cemetery at Rossoschka.

September 3, 1942
Weather: sunny, clear, light northeast wind, 77° F, good road conditions
Sunrise: 5:20 a.m.; **Sunset:** 6:42 p.m.
Moon: Waning Crescent; 42% illumination

Sixth Army – Bombers and dive-bombers from the ***Luftwaffe***'s VIII Air Corps pounded Stalingrad in a 24-hour, round-the-clock raid on the city. Pitomnik Airfield fell to German forces. The army headquarters was located at Ossinowskij.

VIII Corps – The corps suffered the following officer casualties: two wounded in action.

76th Infantry Division – The division defended in sector southwest of Samofalovka and north of Borodkin against the 298th Rifle Division, the 173rd Rifle Division and the 221st Rifle Division. The division reported two NCOs/enlisted killed in action; 37 NCOs/enlisted were wounded in action. To the west was the 384th Infantry Division; to the east was the 60th Infantry Division (Motorized.)

305th Infantry Division – The division defended in sector at the Don River bend south of Ilowlinskaja, opposite the 22nd Anti-Tank Brigade. Part of the division occupied an assembly area west of the front. The division continued to exchange positions with the 384th Infantry Division. The division suffered three NCOs/enlisted wounded in action. To the west was the 44th Infantry Division; to the south was the 384th Infantry Division.

384th Infantry Division – The division defended in sector northeast of Vertiachii near Nizhne-Gnilovskii against the 214th Rifle Division and the 27th Guards Rifle Division. The division continued to exchange positions with the 305th Infantry Division. The division lost five NCOs/enlisted wounded in action. To the north was the 305th Infantry Division; to the southeast was the 76th Infantry Division.

XI Corps – The corps suffered the following officer casualties: one wounded in action.

44th Infantry Division – The division defended in sector at Kurchajessowskij-Kamyshinskiy-Hill 171.0-Hill 180.9-Sirotinskaya-Khmelevskoy, against the 40th Guards Rifle Division. The division suffered four NCOs/enlisted killed in action; 23 NCOs/enlisted were wounded in action. The division headquarters was located at Verkhne-Golubaja. To the west was 100th ***Jäger*** Division; to the east was the 305th Infantry Division.

100th Jäger Division – The division defended in sector near Blizhniaia-Perekopka against the 23rd Rifle Division and the 343rd Rifle Division. The division lost two NCOs/enlisted killed in action; one officer and four NCOs/enlisted were wounded in action. To the east was the 44th Infantry Division; to the west was the 376th Infantry Division.

376th Infantry Division – The division defended in sector near Blizhniaia-Perekopka against the 41st Guards Rifle Division and the 321st Rifle Division. The division reported two NCOs/enlisted killed in action and five NCOs/enlisted killed in action. To the west was an assortment of battle groups; to the east was the 100th ***Jäger*** Division.

XIV *Panzer* Corps – The 51st ***Werfer*** Regiment was assigned to support the corps. The corps suffered the following officer casualties: four killed in action; nine wounded in action.

3rd Infantry Division (Motorized) – The division defended in sector, from the Tartar Hill-Hill 111.1-Hill 129.6-Hill 131.2. Heavy fighting occurred at Hill 139.7, Kuz'michi and the Konnaia Balka against the 116th Rifle Division, the 84th Rifle Division, the 39th Guards Rifle Division, the 315th Rifle Division, the 64th Rifle Division and the 120th Rifle Division. The division lost one officer and 74 NCOs/enlisted killed in action; four officers and 174 NCOs/enlisted were wounded in action; 14 men were reported missing in action. To the east was the 16th ***Panzer*** Division; to the west was the 60th Infantry Division (Motorized.)

16th Panzer Division – The division defended in sector, from Hill 139.7 to the Volga and from the Volga southwest to Hill 145.1, north of Orlovka against the 99th Rifle Division and the 213th Rifle Division. In the northern sector, to the west was the 3rd Infantry Division (Motorized.) In the southern sector, to the west was the 60th Infantry Division (Motorized.)

60th Infantry Division (Motorized) – The division defended in the corps' narrow sector to the Volga, from south of Kotluban' Station near Borodkin to Kuz'michi against the 24th Rifle Division and the 207th Rifle Division. Along the division's northern sector, to the west was the 76th Infantry Division; to the east was the 3rd Infantry Division (Motorized.) Along the division's southern sector to the east was the 16th ***Panzer*** Division.

XVII Corps – The Romanian V Corps was subordinated to the corps.

22nd Panzer Division – The division occupied assembly areas south of the 79th Infantry Division. The division reported five NCOs/enlisted wounded in action and one NCO/enlisted missing in action.

79th Infantry Division – The division defended in sector from Bol'shoy-Verkhne-Kalmykovskii-Verkhne-Fomichinskii-Baskowskij against the 304th Rifle Division, the 124th Rifle Division and the 96th Rifle Division. The division lost 18 NCOs/enlisted killed in action; 41 NCOs/enlisted were wounded in action; one man was missing in action. The division headquarters was located at Karagichev. To the west was the XXXV Corps of the Italian Eighth Army; to the southeast was the 113th Infantry Division.

113th Infantry Division – The division defended in sector along the Don River west of Kletskiy against the 278th Rifle Division and the 76th Rifle Division. The division reported seven men wounded in action. To the northwest was the 79th Infantry Division; to the east was an assortment of battle groups.

298th Infantry Division – The division moved separately from the Romanian V Corps northeast along the Italian Eighth Army and Sixth Army boundary.

1st Romanian Cavalry Division – The division moved northwest from Kamenschachtinskij.

6th Romanian Infantry Division – The division moved northeast behind the 13th Romanian Infantry Division.

13th Romanian Infantry Division – The division moved northeast behind the 1st Romanian Cavalry Division.

LI Corps – The corps headquarters was located at Nizhne-Alexejewskij. The corps suffered the following officer casualties: 12 wounded in action.

71st Infantry Division – The division attacked in zone eastward along the rail line Kalach-Stalingrad, capturing Hill 151.0, Hill 133.8 and the rail station at Gumrak, defeating the 112th Rifle Division and decimating the 87th Rifle Division and the 196th Rifle Division. The division reported 27 NCOs/enlisted killed in action; seven officers and 138 NCOs/enlisted were wounded in action; 20 NCOs/enlisted were missing in action. To the north was the 295th Infantry Division; to the south was the 24th ***Panzer*** Division. The division headquarters was located at Krassnyj Pachar.

295th Infantry Division – The division attacked in zone near Rossoschka west of Gumrak in the inner fortified zone of Stalingrad, through the Novaia Nadezhda Collective Farm, reaching Hill 143.3 and Hill 144.1 against the 399th Rifle Division. The division lost ten NCOs/enlisted killed in action; two officers and 50 NCOs/enlisted were wounded in action. To the northwest was the 76th Infantry Division; to the northeast was the 60th Infantry Division (Motorized); to the south was the 71st Infantry Division.

Battle Group Stahel – The battle group was commanded by ***Luftwaffe Oberst*** Rainer Stahel. It defended in sector between Marinovka and Karpovka. To the east and west were elements of the 71st Infantry Division.

Sixth Army Reserve

389th Infantry Division – The division moved to a new assembly area near Bol'shaya Rossoschka. One third of the division occupied an assembly area just west of the Don River. The division headquarters was located at Baburkin.

Fourth *Panzer* Army – The army headquarters was located at Plodowitoje.

IV Corps – The corps headquarters was located at Plantator.

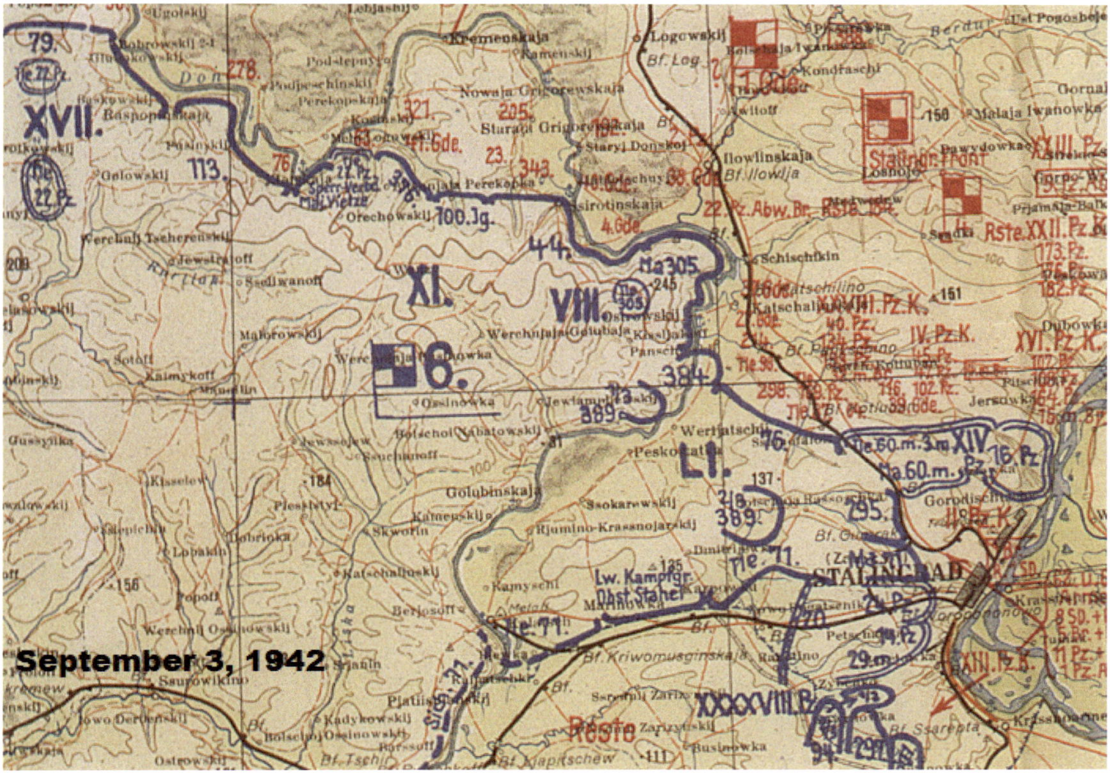

94th Infantry Division – The division defended in sector west of Beketovka against the 29th Rifle Division. To the north was the 29th Infantry Division (Motorized); to the southeast was the 297th Infantry Division.

297th Infantry Division – The division defended in sector south of Elkhi against the 38th Rifle Division and the 133rd Tank Brigade. To the northwest was the 94th Infantry Division; to the southeast was the 371st Infantry Division.

371st Infantry Division – The division defended in sector near Ivanovka and the Tundutovo Rail Station against the 36th Guards Rifle Division and the 422nd Rifle Division. The division lost seven NCOs/enlisted killed in action; 34 NCOs/enlisted were wounded in action; one man was reported missing in action. To the northwest was the 297th Infantry Division; to the south was the 2nd Romanian Infantry Division of the Romanian VI Corps.

XXXXVIII *Panzer* Corps

14th Panzer Division – The division attacked in zone northeast, overrunning the 33rd Guards Rifle Division and the 20th Destroyer Brigade. The division lost one officer and 17 NCOs/enlisted killed in action; one officer and 38 NCOs/enlisted were wounded in action; 12 NCOs/enlisted were reported missing in action. To the north was the 20th Romanian Infantry Division; to the south was the 29th Infantry Division (Motorized.)

24th Panzer Division – The division attacked in zone northeast, seizing Alexeyevka, Hill 153.2 and Krutenkiy, and overrunning the 33rd Guards Rifle Division and the 20th Destroyer Brigade. The division suffered two officers and 20 NCOs/enlisted killed in action; four officers and 112 NCOs/enlisted were wounded in action (one man died of his wounds the following day); four NCOs/ enlisted were reported missing in action. To the north was the 71st Infantry Division of the Sixth Army; to the south was the 20th Romanian Infantry Division.

29th Infantry Division (Motorized) – The division attacked in zone northeast, overrunning the 33rd Guards Rifle Division and the 20th Destroyer Brigade as it attacked toward the Voroponovo Rail Station. The division lost nine NCOs/enlisted killed in action; two officers and 16 NCOs/enlisted were wounded in action. To the north was the 14th ***Panzer*** Division; to the south was the 94th Infantry Division.

20th Romanian Infantry Division – Occupied a defensive position, oriented west, between the 24th ***Panzer*** Division to the north and the 14th ***Panzer*** Division to the south.

Sources, September 3, 1942: *Oberkommando des Heeres, Lage Ost: Stand: 3.9.42, Eastern Front Situation Map, National Archives Identifier: 559733, Record Group 242 – National Archives Collection of Foreign Records Seized, 1675-1958, National Archives, College Park, Maryland; Ia, Armeeoberkommando 6, "Morgen Meldung" and assorted reports, Kriegstagebuch 13, 4 September 1942, as found in Microfilm Series, T-312, Records of German Field Commands, Armies, Roll 1685, National Archives and Records Service, College Park, Maryland; Ia, XXXXVIII Panzerkorps, "Übersicht über die dem Korps Unterstellten Divisionen, 28. Juni 1942 – 11 October 1942," as found on T-314, Records of German Field Commands, Corps, Roll 1153, National Archives, College Park, Maryland; Korpsarzt, XXXXVIII Panzerkorps, "Meldung über Personelle Verluste," Stand 3.9.42, as found on T-314, Records of German Field Commands, Corps, Roll 1158, National Archives, College Park, Maryland; 371st Infantry Division, Kriegstagebuch, 3 September 1942, as found in Microfilm Series T-315, Roll 2164, National Archives and Records Service, College Park, Maryland; Die 71. Infanterie-Division, 1939-1945: Gefechts- und Erlebnisberichte aus Kämpfen der "Gluckhaften Division" von Verdun bis Stalingrad, vom Monte Cassino bis zum Plattensee, Eggolsheim, FRG: Edition Dörfler, 1973, 226; David M. Glantz & Jonathan M. House, Armageddon in Stalingrad: September-November 1942, (The Stalingrad Trilogy, Volume 2), Lawrence, Kansas: University Press of Kansas, 2009, 37-48, 58-69; Joachim Lemelsen, 29. Division, Bad Nauheim, FRG: Podzun Verlag, 1960, 197-198; Jason Mark, Death of the Leaping Horseman: 24. Panzer-Division in Stalingrad, Sydney, Australia: Leaping Horsemen Books, 2003, 115-119; Anton Schimak, Karl Lamprecht & Friedrich Dettmer, Die 44. Infanterie Division: Tagebuch der Hoch- und Deutschmeister, Wien: Verlag Austria Press, 169, 233 and Map: Marschweg der 44. Infanterie Division im Russland.*

Funkgefreiter **Paul Brandel** was born in Euerwang, Bavaria on October 21, 1921. Assigned as a radio operator in a ***flak*** regiment of the ***Luftwaffe***'s 9th ***Flak*** Division, he was killed in action on Hill 151 some six miles west of Stalingrad on September 3, 1942.

September 4, 1942
Weather: no clouds, dry, clear, sunny, 88° F, good road conditions
Sunrise: 5:22 a.m.; **Sunset:** 6:40 p.m.
Moon: Waning Crescent; 33% illumination

Sixth Army – ***General der Panzertruppe*** Friedrich Paulus submitted a plan to the Army High Command (OKH) for the Sixth Army to go into winter quarters once the enemy and been eliminated from the west bank of the Volga River. Bombers and dive-bombers from the ***Luftwaffe***'s VIII Air Corps pounded Stalingrad in large-scale attacks. The army headquarters was located at Ossinowskij.

VIII Corps – The aim of the corps was to exchange defensive sectors between the 305th Infantry Division and the 384th Infantry Division. The corps suffered the following officer casualties: one killed in action; one wounded in action.

76th Infantry Division – The division defended in sector southwest of Samofalovka and north of Borodkin against the 298th Rifle Division, the 173rd Rifle Division and the 221st Rifle Division. The division suffered five NCOs/enlisted killed in action; 23 NCOs/enlisted were wounded in action. To the northwest was the 384th Infantry Division; to the east was the 60th Infantry Division (Motorized.)

305th Infantry Division – The division defended in sector at the Don River bend southwest of Ilowlinskaja opposite the 22nd Anti-Tank Brigade and the 37th Guards Rifle Division. Part of the division occupied an assembly area southwest of the front line. The division continued to exchange positions with the 384th Infantry Division. The division reported two NCOs/enlisted wounded in action. To the west was the 44th Infantry Division; to the south was the 384th Infantry Division.

384th Infantry Division – The division defended in sector north of Vertiachii near Nizhne-Gnilovskii against the 214th Rifle Division and the 27th Guards Rifle Division. The division continued to exchange positions with the 305th Infantry Division. The division reported it had sustained no casualties. To the north was the 305th Infantry Division; to the southeast was the 76th Infantry Division.

XI Corps – The 521st ***Panzerjäger*** Detachment was attached to the corps.

44th Infantry Division – The division defended in sector at Kurchajessowskij-Kamyshinskiy-Hill 171.0-Hill 180.9-Sirotinskaya-Khmelevskoy, against the 40th Guards Rifle Division and the 343rd Rifle Division. The division lost 26 NCOs/enlisted killed in action; 47 NCOs/enlisted were wounded in action. The division headquarters was located at Verkhne-Golubaja. To the west was 100th ***Jäger*** Division; to the east was the 305th Infantry Division.

100th Jäger Division – The division defended in sector near Blizhniaia-Perekopka against the 23rd Rifle Division. Part of the division began moving southeast. The division suffered five NCOs/enlisted killed in action and 28 NCOs/enlisted wounded in action. To the east was the 44th Infantry Division; to the west was the 376th Infantry Division.

376th Infantry Division – The division defended in sector near Blizhniaia-Perekopka against the 63rd Rifle Division and the 321st Rifle Division. The division reported one NCO/enlisted wounded in action. To the west was an assortment of battle groups; to the east was the 100th ***Jäger*** Division.

XIV *Panzer* Corps – The corps suffered the following officer casualties: three killed in action; ten wounded in action; one missing in action.

3rd Infantry Division (Motorized) – The division defended in sector, from the Tartar Hill-Hill 111.1-Hill 129.6-Hill 131.2. Heavy fighting occurred at Hill 139.7, Kuz'michi and the Konnaia Balka against the 116th Rifle Division, the 84th Rifle Division, the 39th Guards Rifle Division, the 315th Rifle Division, the 64th Rifle Division and the 120th Rifle Division. The defensive line was pushed three miles south, but it did not break. The division lost one officer and 44 NCOs/enlisted killed in action; five officers and 111 NCOs/enlisted were wounded in action; one officer and nine men were reported missing in action. To the east was the 16th ***Panzer*** Division; to the west was the 60th Infantry Division (Motorized.)

16th Panzer Division – The division defended in sector, from Hill 139.7 to the Volga and from the Volga southwest to Hill 145.1, north of Orlovka against the 99th Rifle Division and the 213th Rifle Division. On the south of the corridor, the division's western neighbor was the 60th Infantry Division (Motorized); on the north of the corridor to the west was the 3rd Infantry Division (Motorized.)

60th Infantry Division (Motorized) – The division defended in sector from south of Kotluban' Station near Borodkin to Kuz'michi against the 24th Rifle Division and the 207th Rifle Division. To the east was the 16th ***Panzer*** Division; to the southwest was the 389th Infantry Division; to the west was the 76th Infantry Division.

XVII Corps – The Romanian V Corps was subordinated to the corps.

22nd Panzer Division – The division served as the XVII Corps reserve, occupying two assembly areas. The enemy launched a diversionary attack with the 304th Rifle Division and the 124th Rifle Division to tie down German forces and prevent them from moving east. The division reported two NCOs/enlisted killed in action; eight NCOs/enlisted were wounded in action.

79th Infantry Division – The division defended in sector from Bol'shoy-Verkhne-Kalmykovskii-Verkhne-Fomichinskii-Baskowskij. The division headquarters was located at Karagichev. The enemy launched a diversionary attack with the 304th Rifle Division and the 124th Rifle Division to tie down German forces and prevent them from moving east. The division reported seven NCOs/enlisted killed in action and 21 NCOs/enlisted wounded in action. To the west was the XXXV Corps of the Italian Eighth Army; to the east was the 113th Infantry Division.

113th Infantry Division – The division defended in sector along the Don River west of Kletskiy against the 278th Rifle Division and the 76th Rifle Division. The division reported sustaining four NCOs/enlisted killed in action and 21 NCOs/enlisted wounded in action. To the northwest was the 79th Infantry Division; to the east was an assortment of battle groups.

298th Infantry Division – The division moved separately from the Romanian V Corps northeast along the Italian Eighth Army and Sixth Army boundary.

1st Romanian Cavalry Division – The division, with 6,599 troops and 4,526 horses, moved northwest to Karnakoff.

6th Romanian Infantry Division – The division, with 15,986 troops and 7,374 horses, moved northeast behind the 13th Romanian Infantry Division.

13th Romanian Infantry Division – The division, with 15,700 troops and 7,307 horses, moved northeast behind the 1st Romanian Cavalry Division.

LI Corps – The aim of the corps was to continue to attack east toward Stalingrad. The corps headquarters was located at Nizhne-Alexejewskij. The corps suffered the following officer casualties: one killed in action; eight wounded in action.

71st Infantry Division – The division attacked in zone and seized a railway embankment, pushing the remnants of the 112th Rifle Division, the 196th Rifle Division and the 87th Rifle Division to the east. Part of the division that had been defending to the west began moving east. The division sustained seven officers and 182 NCOs/enlisted casualties. To the north was the 295th Infantry Division; to the south was the 24th ***Panzer*** Division, XXXXVIII ***Panzer*** Corps, of the Fourth ***Panzer*** Army; to the southwest was Battle Group Stahel. The division headquarters was located at Krassnyj Pachar.

295th Infantry Division – The division attacked in zone near Gumrak, clearing the remnants of the 112th Rifle Division from the airfield and the Gumrak Rail Station. The division lost 16 NCOs/enlisted killed in action; two officers and 91 NCOs/enlisted were wounded in action. To the north was the 60th Infantry Division (Motorized); to the south was the 71st Infantry Division.

389th Infantry Division – The division began arriving at its new attack zone near Kul'tstan, and assuming part of the 295th Infantry Division's zone against the 399th Rifle Division. One third of the division remained in an assembly area near the Don River. The division headquarters was located at Baburkin. The division reported five NCOs/enlisted wounded in action. To the east was the 60th Infantry Division (Motorized); to the south was the re-deployed 295th Infantry Division.

Battle Group Stahel – The battle group occupied an assembly area near Dmitriyevka.

Fourth *Panzer* Army – The army headquarters was located at Plodowitoje.

IV Corps – The corps headquarters was located at Plantator.

94th Infantry Division – The division defended positions west of Beketovka against the 29th Rifle Division. To the north was the 29th Infantry Division (Motorized); to the south was the 297th Infantry Division. The division began to move northwest behind the front.

297th Infantry Division – The division occupied positions south of Elkhi and the Volga-Don Canal against the 38th Rifle Division and the 133rd Tank Brigade. The division lost one officer killed in action; 32 NCOs/enlisted were wounded in action. To the north was the 94th Infantry Division; to the south was the 371st Infantry Division.

371st Infantry Division – The division defended in sector near Ivanovka and the Tundutovo Rail Station east of the Volga-Don Canal against the 36th Guards Rifle Division and the 422nd Rifle Division. The division suffered one officer and 25 NCOs/enlisted killed in action; four officers and 94 NCOs/enlisted were wounded in action. To the northwest was the 297th Infantry Division; to the south was the 2nd Romanian Infantry Division of the Romanian VI Corps.

XXXXVIII *Panzer* Corps

14th Panzer Division – The division attacked east in zone; the attack stalled just short of Peschanka. The division lost 27 NCOs/enlisted killed in action; three officers and 117 NCOs/enlisted were wounded in action. To the north was the 20th Romanian Infantry Division; to the south was the 29th Infantry Division (Motorized.)

24th Panzer Division – The division attacked northeast in zone, consolidating gains

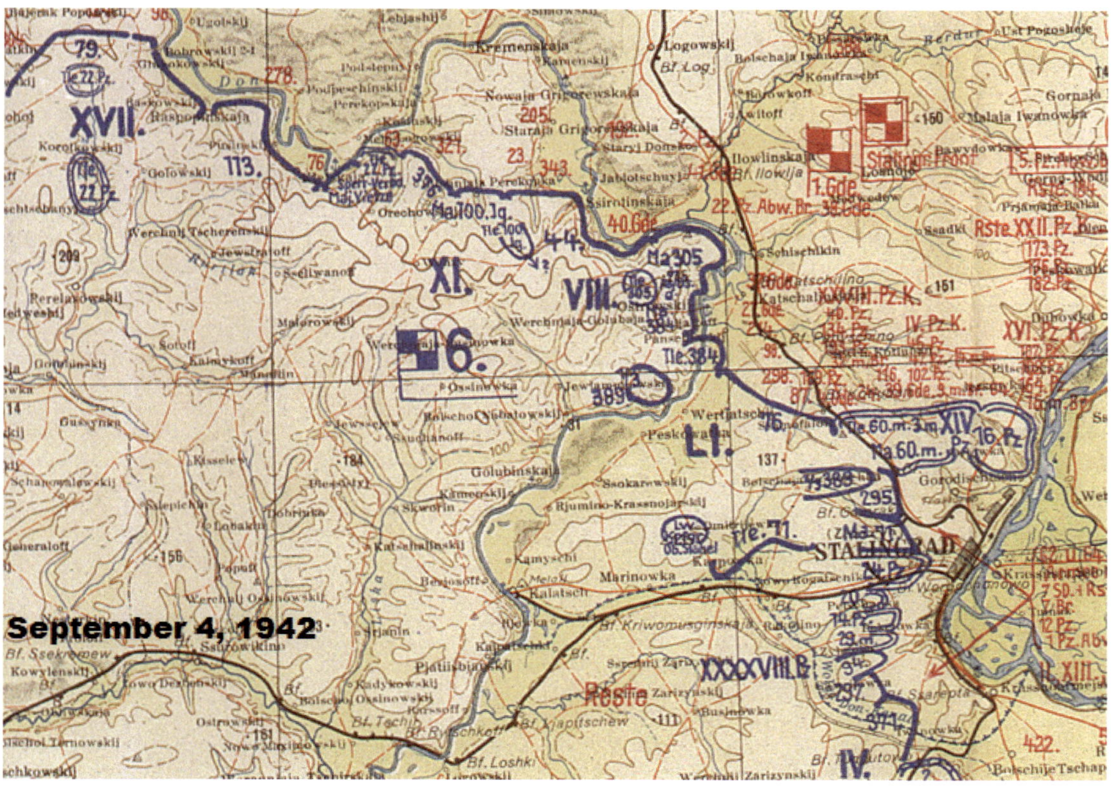

at Krutenkiy, Voroponovo, Hill 145.8 and Hill 147.5 against the 131st Rifle Division. Later in the day, advance elements reached the edge of Stalingrad. The division suffered two officers and 20 NCOs/enlisted killed in action; three officers and 127 NCOs/enlisted were wounded in action (three men later died of wounds); three men was reported missing in action. To the north was the 71st Infantry Division; to the south was the 20th Romanian Infantry Division.

29th Infantry Division (Motorized) – The division attacked northeast in zone, reaching Elkhi. The division lost 57 NCOs/enlisted killed in action; four officers and 144 NCOs/enlisted were wounded in action. To the north was the 14th ***Panzer*** Division; to the south was the 94th Infantry Division.

20th Romanian Infantry Division – The division attacked east in zone between the 24th ***Panzer*** Division to the north and the 14th ***Panzer*** Division to the south.

Für Führer, Volk
u. Heimat starb
den Heldentod
unser über alles
geliebter, her-
zensguter Sohn, Bruder, Schwa-
ger, Onkel und Neffe
FRIEDL SCHERTLER
Ober-Grenadier in einem Sturmbataillon
bei Stalingrad am 4. Sept. 1942 in
der Blüte der Jugend von 20
Jahren. Sein Heldengrab liegt
bei einer Milchfarm auf der Stra-
ße von Orlovka nach Jesovka.
In schwerem Leid:
Eltern und Geschwister.
Ach, der Heimat galt mein Sehnen
Meiner Augen letzter Blick;
Und nun fließen dort die Tränen,
Nimmermehr kehr' ich zurück.
Bin als Held im Feld gefallen,
Starb so jung auf steiler Höh';
Durfte früh zum Himmel wallen,
Wo ich euch einst wiederseh'.
Lebt drum wohl, ihr meine Lieben,
Eltern und Geschwister mein,
Immer denk' ich euer drüben,
Schließt auch mich ins Beten ein.
R/0375

Gefreiter Friedrich "Friedl" Schertler was born on June 17, 1922 at Mährisch Trübau in Bohemia. He was married. Assigned to the 16th ***Panzer*** Division, Schertler was killed in action northeast of Orlovka on September 4, 1942 and was initially buried at a milk farm on the road between Orlovka and Jersovka.

Sources, September 4, 1942: ***Oberkommando des Heeres, Lage Ost: Stand: 4.9.42, Eastern Front Situation Map, National Archives Identifier: 559733, Record Group 242 – National Archives Collection of Foreign Records Seized, 1675-1958, National Archives, College Park, Maryland; Ia, Armeeoberkommando 6, "Morgen Meldung" and assorted reports, Kriegstagebuch 13, 5 September 1942, as found in Microfilm Series, T-312, Records of German Field Commands, Armies, Roll 1685, National Archives and Records Service, College Park, Maryland; Ia, XXXXVIII Panzerkorps, "Übersicht über die dem Korps Unterstellten Divisionen, 28. Juni 1942 – 11 October 1942," as found on T-314, Records of German Field Commands, Corps, Roll 1153, National Archives, College Park, Maryland; Korpsarzt, XXXXVIII Panzerkorps, "Meldung über Personelle Verluste," Stand 4.9.42, as found on T-314, Records of German Field Commands, Corps, Roll 1158, National Archives, College Park, Maryland; 79th Infantry Division, Kriegstagebuch, 4 September 1942, as found in Microfilm Series T-315, Roll 1108, National Archives and Records Service, College Park, Maryland; 371st Infantry Division, Kriegstagebuch, 4 September 1942, as found in Microfilm Series T-315, Roll 2164, National Archives and Records Service, College Park, Maryland; Die 71. Infanterie-Division, 1939-1945: Gefechts- und Erlebnisberichte aus Kämpfen der "Gluckhaften Division" von Verdun bis Stalingrad, vom Monte Cassino bis zum Plattensee, Eggolsheim, FRG: Edition Dörfler, 1973, 227; David M. Glantz & Jonathan M. House, Armageddon in Stalingrad: September-November 1942, (The Stalingrad Trilogy, Volume 2), Lawrence, Kansas: University Press of Kansas, 2009, 45-71; Joachim Lemelsen, 29. Division, Bad Nauheim, FRG: Podzun Verlag, 1960, 198; Jason Mark, Death of the Leaping Horseman: 24. Panzer-Division in Stalingrad, Sydney, Australia: Leaping Horsemen Books, 2003, 119-124; Kurt Mehner, Die Geheimen Tagesberichte der Deutschen Wehrmachtführung im Zweiten Weltkrieg 1939-1945, Band 5: 1. Juni 1942 – 30. November 1942, Osnabrück, Germany: Biblio Verlag, 1991, 175; Anton Schimak, Karl Lamprecht & Friedrich Dettmer, Die 44. Infanterie Division: Tagebuch der Hoch- und Deutschmeister, Wien: Verlag Austria Press, 169, 233 and Map: Marschweg der 44. Infanterie Division im Russland.***

September 5, 1942
Weather: dry, light clouds, generally clear, local rain showers, 90° F, good road conditions
Sunrise: 5:23 a.m.; **Sunset:** 6:38 p.m.
Moon: Waning Crescent; 24% illumination

Sixth Army – The army headquarters was located at Golubinskaya.

VIII Corps – The 521st ***Panzerjäger*** Detachment, minus one company, was attached to the corps. The corps suffered the following officer casualties: four killed in action; four wounded in action.

76th Infantry Division – The division defended in sector southwest of Samofalovka and north of Borodkin. There was heavy fighting at Hill 93.1 and Hill 13.4, as the division repelled the 298th Rifle Division, the 173rd Rifle Division and the 221st Rifle Division. The division lost four NCOs/enlisted killed in action; 24 NCOs/enlisted were wounded in action. To the west was the 384th Infantry Division; to the east was the 60th Infantry Division (Motorized.)

305th Infantry Division – The division defended in sector at the Don River bend south of Ilowlinskaja opposite the 22nd Anti-Tank Brigade. The division continued to exchange positions with the 384th Infantry Division. The division reported two officers and ten NCOs/enlisted killed in action; two officers and 42 NCOs/enlisted wounded in action. To the west was the 44th Infantry Division; to the south was the 384th Infantry Division.

384th Infantry Division – The division defended in sector from the Don River, north of Nizhne-Gnilovskii to west of Kotluban'. Heavy fighting raged throughout the sector against the 27th Guards Rifle Division and the 214th Rifle Division. The division continued to exchange positions with the 305th Infantry Division. The division suffered five NCOs/enlisted killed in action and 33 NCOs/enlisted wounded in action. To the southeast was the 76th Infantry Division; to the north was the 305th Infantry Division.

XI Corps

44th Infantry Division – The division defended in sector oriented northward at Kurchajessowskij-Kamyshinskiy-Hill 171.0-Hill 180.9-Sirotinskaya-Khmelevskoy, against the 40th Guards Rifle Division. The division reported nine NCOs/enlisted killed in action and 27 NCOs/enlisted wounded in action. The division headquarters was located at Verkhne-Golubaja. To the west was 100th ***Jäger*** Division; to the east was the 305th Infantry Division.

100th Jäger Division – The division defended in sector near Blizhniaia-Perekopka. The division suffered three NCOs/enlisted killed in action and 13 NCOs/enlisted wounded in action. To the east was the 44th Infantry Division; to the west was the 376th Infantry Division.

376th Infantry Division – The division defended in sector southwest of Perekopka. The division reported one NCO/enlisted wounded in action. To the west was an assortment of battle groups; to the east was the 100th ***Jäger*** Division.

XIV *Panzer* Corps – The 1st Guards Army and 24th Army attacked along the corps front, in some places gaining two to three miles, but both were repulsed. The corps suffered the following officer casualties: two killed in action; 13 wounded in action.

3rd Infantry Division (Motorized) – The division defended in sector, from the Tartar Hill-Hill 111.1-Hill 129.6-Hill 131.2. Heavy fighting again occurred at Hill 139.7, Kuz'michi and the Konnaia Balka against the 116th Rifle Division, the 84th Rifle Division, the 39th Guards Rifle Division, the 315th Rifle Division, the 64th Rifle Division and the 120th Rifle Division. The division lost one officer and 67 NCOs/enlisted killed in action; two officers and 177 NCOs/enlisted were wounded in action; five men were reported missing in action. To the east was the 16th ***Panzer*** Division; to the west was the 60th Infantry Division (Motorized.)

16th Panzer Division – The division defended in sector, from Hill 139.7 to the Volga

and from the Volga southwest to Hill 145.1, north of Orlovka; it repelled attacks by the 299th Rifle Division and the 120th Rifle Division between Akatovka and the Sukhaia Mechetka Balka. On the north of the corridor, to the west was the 3rd Infantry Division (Motorized): on the south of the corridor, to the west was the 389th Infantry Division.

60th Infantry Division (Motorized) – The division defended in sector to the Volga, from south of Kotluban' Station near Borodkin to Kuz'michi against the 24th Rifle Division and the 207th Rifle Division. To the east was the 3rd Infantry Division (Motorized); to the west was the 76th Infantry Division.

XVII Corps – The Romanian V Corps was subordinated to the corps.

22nd Panzer Division – The division occupied assembly areas south of the 79th Infantry Division. The division lost one NCO/enlisted killed in action and four NCOs/enlisted wounded in action.

79th Infantry Division – The division defended in sector from Bol'shoy-Verkhne-Kalmykovskii-Verkhne-Fomichinskii-Baskowskij. The division lost three NCOs/enlisted killed in action and 11 NCOs/enlisted wounded in action. The division headquarters was located at Karagichev. To the west was the XXXV Corps of the Italian Eighth Army; to the southeast was the 113th Infantry Division.

113th Infantry Division – The division defended in sector along the Don River west of Kletskiy. The division reported no casualties. To the northwest was the 79th Infantry Division; to the east was an assortment of battle groups.

298th Infantry Division – The division moved separately from the Romanian V Corps northeast along the Italian Eighth Army and Sixth Army boundary.

1st Romanian Cavalry Division – The division moved northwest to Selivanovka.

6th Romanian Infantry Division – The division moved northeast behind the 13th Romanian Infantry Division.

13th Romanian Infantry Division – The division moved northeast behind the 1st Romanian Cavalry Division.

LI Corps – The 244th ***Sturmgeschütz*** Detachment and the 245th ***Sturmgeschütz*** Detachment were assigned to the corps. The 2nd ***Werfer*** Regiment was assigned to support the corps. The corps suffered the following officer casualties: seven killed in action; eight wounded in action.

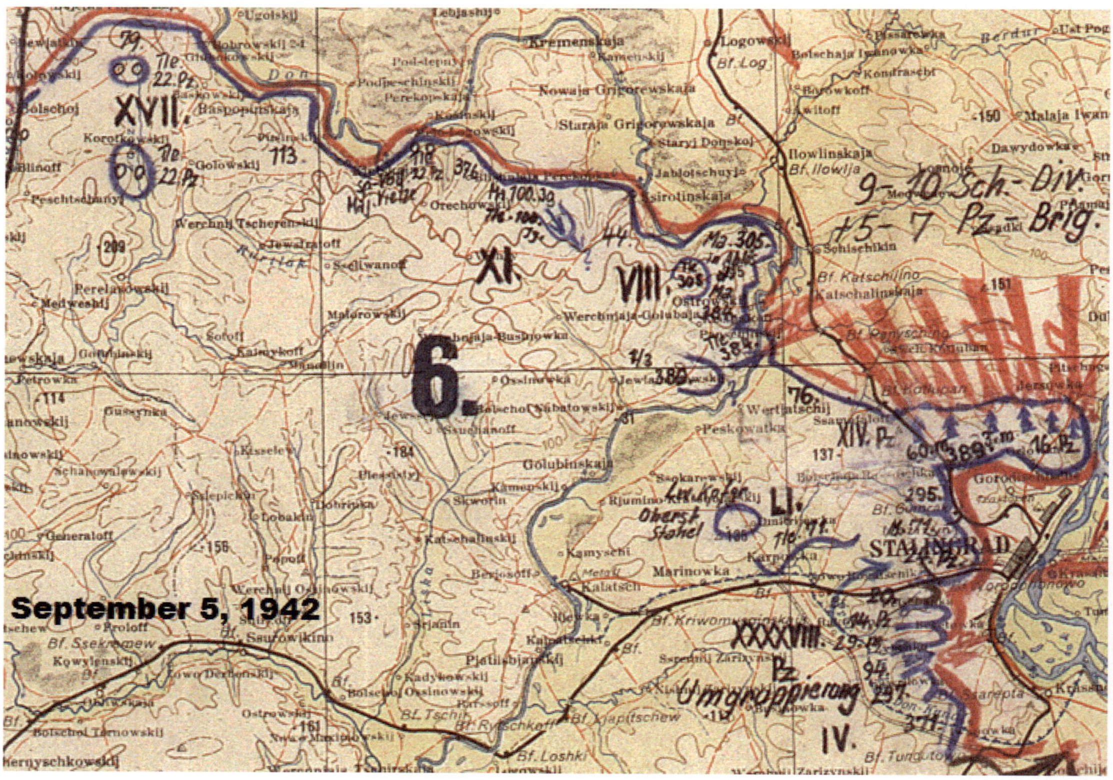

71st Infantry Division – The division attacked in zone and reached the inner line of defenses around Stalingrad against the 131st Rifle Division. The division lost four officers and 21 NCOs/enlisted killed in action; two officers and 86 NCOs/enlisted were wounded in action; six NCOs/enlisted were missing in action. To the north was the 295th Infantry Division; to the south was the 24th ***Panzer*** Division. The division headquarters was located at Krassnyj Pachar.

295th Infantry Division – The division attacked in zone near Gumrak and the Gumrak Rail Station opposite Stalingradskii against the 399th Rifle Division. The 87th Rifle Division counterattacked and retook a foothold of the Opytnaia Rail Station from the division. The division reported 20 NCOs/enlisted killed in action; 101 NCOs/enlisted were wounded in action; two men were missing in action. To the north was the 389th Infantry Division; to the south was the 71st Infantry Division.

389th Infantry Division – The division attacked east in zone from the Konnaia Rail Station toward Gorodishche against elements of the 23rd Tank Corps. The division suffered six NCOs/enlisted wounded in action. To the north was the 60th Infantry Division (Motorized); to the south was the 295th Infantry Division. The division headquarters was located just east of Nadezhda.

Battle Group Stahel – The battle group occupied as assembly area near Dmitriyevka.

Fourth *Panzer* Army – The army headquarters was located at Plodowitoje.

IV Corps – The corps headquarters was located at Plantator.

94th Infantry Division – The division defended in sector west of Beketovka against the 29th Rifle Division. To the north was the 29th Infantry Division (Motorized); to the south was the 297th Infantry Division. Elements of the division continued to move northwest behind the front.

297th Infantry Division – The division defended in sector south of Elkhi against the 38th Rifle Division and the 133rd Tank Brigade. To the north was the 94th Infantry Division; to the southeast was the 371st Infantry Division.

371st Infantry Division – The division defended in sector near Ivanovka and the Tundutovo Rail Station against the 36th Guards Rifle Division and the 422nd Rifle Division. The division lost six NCOs/enlisted killed in action; one officer and 23 NCOs/enlisted were wounded in action. To the north was the 297th Infantry Division; to the south was the 2nd Romanian Infantry Division of the Romanian VI Corps.

XXXXVIII *Panzer* Corps

14th Panzer Division – The division attempted to attack east in zone, but was quickly stopped by enemy action. The division lost one NCO/enlisted killed in action; two officers and 13 NCOs/enlisted were wounded in action. To the north was the 20th Romanian Infantry Division; to the south was the 29th Infantry Division (Motorized.)

24th Panzer Division – The division consolidated its gains of the previous day. The division suffered one officer and 19 NCOs/enlisted killed in action; three officers and 70 NCOs/enlisted were wounded in action. To the north was the 71st Infantry Division; to the south was the 20th Romanian Infantry Division. The division reported that only 34 tanks were operational.

29th Infantry Division (Motorized) – The division attempted to attack east in zone, but was quickly stopped by enemy action. The division lost 12 NCOs/enlisted killed in action; one officer and 32 NCOs/enlisted were wounded in action. To the north was the 14th ***Panzer*** Division; to the south was the 94th Infantry Division.

20th Romanian Infantry Division – The division occupied a defensive position between the 24th ***Panzer*** Division to the north and the 14th ***Panzer*** Division to the south.

Sixth Army Reserve

One company of the 521st ***Panzerjäger*** Detachment

Sources, September 5, 1942: ***Oberkommando des Heeres, Lage Ost: Stand: 5.9.42, Eastern Front Situation Map, National Archives Identifier: 559733, Record Group 242 – National Archives Collection of Foreign Records Seized, 1675-1958, National Archives, College Park, Maryland; Ia, Armeeoberkommando 6, "Morgen Meldung" and assorted reports, Kriegstagebuch 13, 6 September 1942, as found in Microfilm Series, T-312, Records of German Field Commands, Armies, Roll 1685, National Archives and Records Service, College Park, Maryland; Ia, XXXXVIII Panzerkorps, "Übersicht über die dem Korps Unterstellten Divisionen, 28. Juni 1942 – 11 October 1942," as found on T-314, Records of German Field Commands, Corps, Roll 1153, National Archives, College Park, Maryland;***

Korpsarzt, XXXXVIII Panzerkorps, "Meldung über Personelle Verluste," Stand 5.9.42, as found on T-314, Records of German Field Commands, Corps, Roll 1158, National Archives, College Park, Maryland; 371st Infantry Division, Kriegstagebuch, 5 September 1942, as found in Microfilm Series T-315, Roll 2164, National Archives and Records Service, College Park, Maryland; John Erickson, The Road to Stalingrad, New York: Harper & Row, 1975, 385; Die 71. Infanterie-Division, 1939-1945: Gefechts- und Erlebnisberichte aus Kämpfen der "Gluckhaften Division" von Verdun bis Stalingrad, vom Monte Cassino bis zum Plattensee, Eggolsheim, FRG: Edition Dörfler, 1973, 227; David M. Glantz & Jonathan M. House, Armageddon in Stalingrad: September-November 1942, (The Stalingrad Trilogy, Volume 2), Lawrence, Kansas: University Press of Kansas, 2009, 43-74; Jason Mark, Death of the Leaping Horseman: 24. Panzer-Division in Stalingrad, Sydney, Australia: Leaping Horsemen Books, 2003, 124-128; Kurt Mehner, Die Geheimen Tagesberichte der Deutschen Wehrmachtführung im Zweiten Weltkrieg 1939-1945, Band 5: 1. Juni 1942 – 30. November 1942, Osnabrück, Germany: Biblio Verlag, 1991, 179; Anton Schimak, Karl Lamprecht & Friedrich Dettmer, Die 44. Infanterie Division: Tagebuch der Hoch- und Deutschmeister, Wien: Verlag Austria Press, 169, 233 and Map: Marschweg der 44. Infanterie Division im Russland.

Wiederſehen war ſeine und unſere Hoffnung.

Chriſtliches Andenken

an unſeren lieben Bruder

Gefreiter in einem Infanterie-Regiment

Joſef Aſchenberger

Aſchenbergerſohn in Maad Nr. 13, Pfarre Taufkirchen a. d. Pram

welcher am 5. September 1942 im 38. Lebensjahre in treuer Pflichterfüllung an der Oſtfront den Heldentod gefunden hat.

Mich rief die Pflicht zum Kampf hinaus,
Mit Gott ſchied ich vom Elternhaus,
O, meine Lieben, immerfort
Dacht' ich an Euch vom fernen Ort.
Ich hoffte auf ein Wiederſeh'n,
Wenn Krieg und Sturm zu Ende geh'n.
Doch anders hat es Gott gefallen
Ich mußte im Oſten fallen;
Für's Vaterland bin ich geſtorben,
Hab' mir des Himmels Heil erworben,
Ich bin befreit vom Erdenleid,
Legt deshalb ab die Traurigkeit
Und weinet nicht. Das wahre Glück,
Das hat mir Gott, der Herr, geſchickt.

Ebner, Taufkirchen a. d. Pr. 3562—42

Gefreiter* Josef Aschenberger** was born on July 22, 1905 in Eggerding, near Taufkirchen, in Austria. An infantryman, likely assigned to the 16th ***Panzer Division, he was killed in action three miles south of Jersovka on September 5, 1942. His name is displayed on the war memorial at Taufkirchen an der Pram, Austria.

September 6, 1942
Weather: heavy morning fog, later clearing and sunny, light clouds, 93° F
Sunrise: 5:25 a.m.; **Sunset:** 6:36 p.m.
Moon: Waning Crescent; 17% illumination

Sixth Army – The army headquarters was located at Golubinskaya.

VIII Corps – The 521st ***Panzerjäger*** Detachment was assigned to the corps. The corps suffered the following officer casualties: five killed in action; seven wounded in action.

76th Infantry Division – The division defended in sector southwest of Samofalovka and north of Borodkin against the 298th Rifle Division, the 173rd Rifle Division and the 221st Rifle Division, repelling attacks by all three. The division lost 18 NCOs/enlisted killed in action; 120 NCOs/enlisted were wounded in action. To the northwest was the 305th Infantry Division; to the east was 60th Infantry Division (Motorized.)

305th Infantry Division – The division defended in sector from the Don River, north of Nizhne-Gnilovskii, to west of Kotluban'. Heavy fighting raged throughout the sector with the 279th Rifle Division. The division reported 12 NCOs/enlisted killed in action; one officer and 20 NCOs/enlisted were wounded in action; three NCOs/enlisted were missing in action. To the southeast was the 76th Infantry Division; to the north was the 384th Infantry Division.

XI Corps

44th Infantry Division – The division defended in sector Kurchajessowskij-Kamyshinskiy-Hill 171.0-Hill 180.9-Sirotinskaya-Khmelevskoy against the 40th Guards Rifle Division and the 343rd Rifle Division. The division reported two NCOs/enlisted killed in action and six NCOs/enlisted wounded in action. The division headquarters was located in Verkhne-Golubaja. To the northwest was 100th ***Jäger*** Division; to the east was the 384th Infantry Division.

100th Jäger Division – The division defended in sector near Blizhniaia-Perekopka against the 23rd Rifle Division. The division suffered three NCOs/enlisted wounded in action and one NCO/enlisted missing in action. To the east was the 44th Infantry Division; to the west was the 376th Infantry Division. Elements of the division continued to move southeast.

376th Infantry Division – The division defended in sector near Blizhniaia-Perekopka against the 321st Rifle Division. The division reported four NCOs/enlisted killed in action; ten NCOs/enlisted were wounded in action. To the west was an assortment of battle groups; to the east was the 100th ***Jäger*** Division.

384th Infantry Division – The division defended in sector west of the Don River near Trekhostrovskaia to Podgorskii against the 4th Guards Rifle Division and the 22nd Anti-Tank Brigade. The division suffered four NCOs/enlisted killed in action and six NCOs/enlisted were wounded in action. To the west was the 44th Infantry Division; to the south was the 305th Infantry Division.

XIV *Panzer* Corps – The corps suffered the following officer casualties: one killed in action; five wounded in action.

3rd Infantry Division (Motorized) – The division defended in sector, from the Tartar Hill-Hill 111.1-Hill 129.6-Hill 131.2 against the 116th Rifle Division, the 84th Rifle Division, the 39th Guards Rifle Division, the 315th Rifle Division, the 64th Rifle Division and the 120th Rifle Division. The division attacked south on a converging axis with the 389th Infantry Division, gaining several miles and collapsing the defenses of the 399th Rifle Division and the 189th Tank Brigade. The division lost one officer and 31 NCOs/enlisted killed in action; two officers and 78 NCOs/enlisted were wounded in action. To the east was the 16th ***Panzer*** Division; to the west was the 60th Infantry Division (Motorized.)

16th Panzer Division – The division defended in sector along the north of the corridor, from Hill 139.7 to the Volga and from the Volga southwest to Hill 145.1, north of Orlovka; heavy fighting continued with the 299th Rifle Division and the 120th Rifle Division between Akatovka and the Sukhaia Mechetka Balka. On the south, to the west was part of the 60th Infantry Division (Motorized.)

60th Infantry Division (Motorized) – The division defended in sector from south of Kotluban' Station near Borodkin to Kuz'michi against the 24th Rifle Division and the 207th Rifle Division. To the east was the 3rd Infantry Division (Motorized); to the west was the 76th Infantry Division. Along the south of the corridor, the division defended in sector with the 16th ***Panzer*** Division to the east and the 389th Infantry Division to the southwest.

XVII Corps – The Romanian V Corps was subordinated to the corps. The corps reported an accidental detonation of T-mines that killed four NCOs and 21 enlisted men. The corps suffered the following officer casualties: three killed in action; one wounded in action.

22nd Panzer Division – The division served as the XVII Corps reserve, occupying two assembly areas south of the 79th Infantry Division. The division lost three NCO/enlisted wounded in action.

79th Infantry Division – The division defended in sector from Bol'shoy-Verkhne-Kalmykovskii-Verkhne-Fomichinskii-Baskowskij opposite the 96th Rifle Division, the 304th Rifle Division and the 124th Rifle Division. The division headquarters was located at Karagichev. The division lost two officers and 13 NCOs/enlisted killed in action; one officer and 36 NCOs/enlisted were wounded in action. To the west was the XXXV Corps of the Italian Eighth Army; to the southeast was the 113th Infantry Division.

113th Infantry Division – The division defended in sector along the Don River west of Kletskiy against the 278th Rifle Division and the 76th Rifle Division. The division reported six NCOs/enlisted killed in action and ten NCOs/enlisted were wounded in action. To the northwest was the 79th Infantry Division; to the east was an assortment of battle groups.

298th Infantry Division – The division moved separately from the Romanian V Corps northeast along the Italian Eighth Army and the Sixth Army boundary.

1st Romanian Cavalry Division – The division moved northwest to Tschernyschewshja.

6th Romanian Infantry Division – The division moved northeast behind the 13th Romanian Infantry Division.

13th Romanian Infantry Division – The division moved northeast behind the 1st Romanian Cavalry Division.

LI Corps – The 244th ***Sturmgeschütz*** Detachment and the 245th ***Sturmgeschütz*** Detachment were assigned to the corps. The corps suffered the following officer casualties: two killed in action; 11 wounded in action.

71st Infantry Division – The division attacked in zone and reached the inner line of defenses around Stalingrad. The division lost 14 NCOs/enlisted killed in action; three officers and 67 NCOs/enlisted were wounded in action. To the north was the 295th Infantry Division; to the south was the 24th ***Panzer*** Division. The division headquarters was located at Krassnyj Pachar.

295th Infantry Division – The division attacked in zone near Gumrak and the Gumrak Rail Station opposite Stalingradskii. The division reported one officer and one NCO/enlisted killed in action; five officers and 69 NCOs/enlisted were wounded in action; one man was missing in action. To the north was the 389th Infantry Division; to the south was the 71st Infantry Division.

389th Infantry Division – The division attacked east in zone from the Konnaia Rail Station toward Gorodishche, gaining three miles and collapsing the defenses of the 399th Rifle Division and the 189th Tank Brigade. The division suffered one officer and 35 NCOs/enlisted killed in action; one officer and 120 NCOs/enlisted were wounded in action. To the east was the 60th Infantry Division (Motorized); to the south was the 295th Infantry Division. The division headquarters was located just east of Nadezhda.

Battle Group Stahel – The battle group occupied an assembly area near Dmitriyevka.

Fourth *Panzer* Army – The army headquarters was located at Plodowitoje.

IV Corps – The corps headquarters was located at Plantator.

94th Infantry Division – The division defended in sector west of Beketovka. To the north was the 20th Romanian Infantry Division; to the south was the 297th Infantry Division. Elements of the division continued to move northwest behind the front.

297th Infantry Division – The division defended in sector south of Elkhi against the 38th Rifle Division and the 133rd Tank Brigade. To the north was the 94th Infantry Division; to the south was the 371st Infantry Division.

371st Infantry Division – The division defended in sector near Ivanovka and the Tundutovo Rail Station against the 36th Guards Rifle Division and the 422nd Rifle Division. The division lost five NCOs/enlisted killed in action; 16 NCOs/enlisted were wounded in action; three men were reported missing in action. To the north was the 297th Infantry Division; to the south was the 2nd Romanian Infantry Division of the Romanian VI Corps.

XXXXVIII *Panzer* Corps

14th Panzer Division – The division occupied an assembly area west of Stalingrad and prepared to conduct future offensive operations. The division lost four NCOs/enlisted killed in action; one officer and 48 NCOs/enlisted were wounded in action. To the southeast was the 20th Romanian Infantry Division; to the east was the 24th ***Panzer*** Division.

24th Panzer Division – The division prepared to conduct future offensive operations. The division suffered one officer and ten NCOs/enlisted killed in action; 67 NCOs/enlisted were wounded in action. To the north was the 71st Infantry Division of the Sixth Army; to the south was the 20th Romanian Infantry Division.

29th Infantry Division (Motorized) – The division prepared to conduct future offensive operations. The division lost one officer and three NCOs/enlisted killed in action; eight NCOs/enlisted were wounded in action. To the north was the 71st Infantry Division; to the south was the 20th Romanian Infantry Division.

20th Romanian Infantry Division – The division occupied a defensive position between the 24th ***Panzer*** Division and 14th ***Panzer*** Division to the north and the 94th Infantry Division to the south.

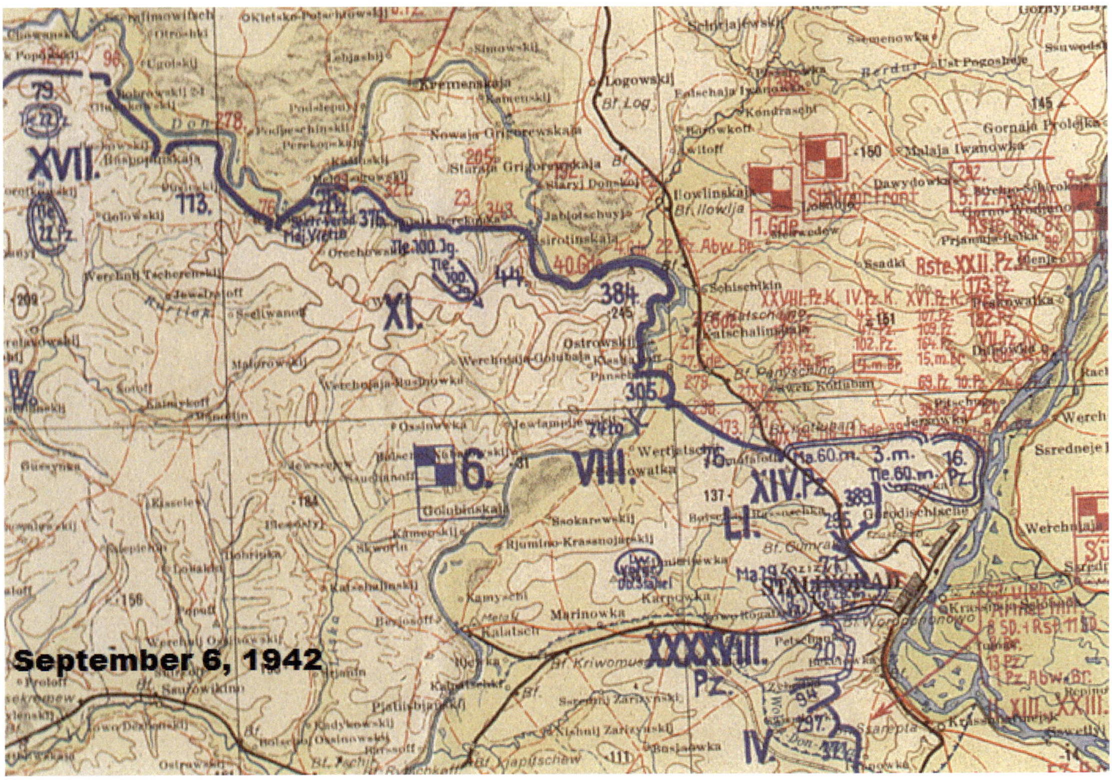

Sources, September 6, 1942: ***Oberkommando des Heeres, Lage Ost: Stand: 6.9.42, Eastern Front Situation Map, National Archives Identifier: 559733, Record Group 242 – National Archives Collection of Foreign Records Seized, 1675-1958, National Archives, College Park, Maryland; Ia, Armeeoberkommando 6, "Morgen Meldung" and assorted reports, Kriegstagebuch 13, 7 September 1942, as found in Microfilm Series, T-312, Records of German Field Commands, Armies, Roll 1685, National Archives and Records Service, College Park, Maryland; Ia, XXXXVIII Panzerkorps, "Übersicht über die dem Korps Unterstellten Divisionen, 28. Juni 1942 – 11 October 1942," as found on T-314, Records of German Field Commands, Corps, Roll 1153, National Archives, College Park, Maryland; Korpsarzt, XXXXVIII Panzerkorps, "Meldung über Personelle Verluste," Stand 6.9.42, as found on T-314, Records of German Field Commands, Corps, Roll 1158, National Archives, College Park, Maryland; 79th Infantry Division, Kriegstagebuch, 6 September 1942, as found in Microfilm Series T-315, Roll 1108, National Archives and Records Service, College Park, Maryland; 371st Infantry Division, Kriegstagebuch, 6 September 1942, as found in Microfilm Series T-315, Roll 2164, National Archives and Records Service, College Park, Maryland; David M. Glantz & Jonathan M. House, Armageddon in Stalingrad: September-November 1942, (The Stalingrad Trilogy, Volume 2), Lawrence, Kansas: University Press of Kansas, 2009, 72-78; Jochen Löser, Bittere Pflicht: Kampf und Untergang der 76. Berlin-Brandenburgischen Infanterie-Division, Osnabrück, FRG: Biblio Verlag, 1986, 208; Jason Mark, Death of the Leaping Horseman: 24. Panzer-Division in Stalingrad, Sydney, Australia: Leaping Horsemen Books, 2003, 128-130; Anton Schimak, Karl Lamprecht & Friedrich Dettmer, Die 44. Infanterie Division: Tagebuch der Hoch- und Deutschmeister, Wien: Verlag Austria Press, 169, 233 and Map: Marschweg der 44. Infanterie Division im Russland.***

Zur frommen Gebetserinnerung
an den Herrn
Karl Brunnhölzl
Gefreiter in einem Inf.-Regt.
Landwirtssohn von Kirchl
welcher am 6. September 1942 bei den schweren Kämpfen nordwestlich von Stalingrad im Alter von 20 Jahren den Heldentod fürs Vaterland starb.

Betet für ihn ein Vater unser
O Herr, gib ihm die ewige Ruhe!

Du hast gekämpft fürs Vaterland,
Wie war der Abschied schwer.
Nun ruhest du im fremden Land,
Wir sehen uns nicht mehr.
Treugeliebter, ruh in Frieden
Die fremde Erde sei dir leicht.
Wir tragen gern, was Gott beschieden,
Auch unser Weg nach oben zeigt.

Gefreiter **Karl Brunnhölzl** was born on July 13, 1922 at Kirchl, near Hohenau, in Bavaria. He was killed in action northwest of Alexandrovka on September 6, 1942, while assigned to an infantry regiment, probably in the 295th Infantry Division.

Photo taken by "Rudi," at sunrise dated September 6, 1942, stating that they were 25 kilometers from the Volga River. Rudi was the commander of the 13th Company in the 669th Infantry Regiment of the 371st Infantry Division.

September 7, 1942
Weather: morning ground fog, sunny, bright, later increasing cloudiness, 88° F
Sunrise: 5:26 a.m.; **Sunset:** 6:33 p.m.
Moon: Waning Crescent; 10% illumination

Sixth Army – The army headquarters was located at Golubinskaya.

VIII Corps – The corps suffered the following officer casualties: 12 wounded in action.

76th Infantry Division – The division defended in sector southwest of Samofalovka and north of Borodkin, against the 298th Rifle Division, the 173rd Rifle Division and the 221st Rifle Division. To the northwest was the 305th Infantry Division; to the east was the 60th Infantry Division (Motorized.) The division lost 40 NCOs/enlisted killed in action; 199 NCOs/enlisted were wounded in action. The division reported that of its nine infantry battalions, one was medium-strong, six were average and two were weak in combat power.

305th Infantry Division – The division defended in sector from the Don River, north of Nizhne-Gnilovskii, to west of Kotluban' against the 279th Rifle Division. Heavy fighting raged throughout the sector. To the east was the 76th Infantry Division; to the north was the 384th Infantry Division. The division reported seven NCOs/enlisted killed in action; two officers and 28 NCOs/enlisted were wounded in action. The division reported that of its nine infantry battalions, two were strong, one was medium-strong and six were average in combat power.

XI Corps – The corps suffered the following officer casualties: three wounded in action.

44th Infantry Division – The division defended in sector Kurchajessowskij-Kamyshinskiy-Hill 171.0-Hill 180.9-Sirotinskaya-Khmelevskoy against the 40th Guards Rifle Division and the 343rd Rifle Division. The division headquarters was located in Verkhne-Golubaja. To the west was the 100th ***Jäger*** Division; to the east was the 384th Infantry Division. The division reported three NCOs/enlisted killed in action; four officers and 27 NCOs/enlisted were wounded in action; two NCOs/enlisted were missing in action. The division reported that of its nine infantry battalions, five were average, two were weak and two were exhausted in combat power.

100th Jäger Division – The division defended in sector near Blizhniaia-Perekopka against the 23rd Rifle Division. To the east was the 44th Infantry Division; to the northwest was the 376th Infantry Division. Elements of the division continued to move southeast. The division suffered one NCO/enlisted killed in action; six NCOs/enlisted were wounded in action. The division reported that of its four ***Jäger*** battalions, all four were average in combat power, while the Croatian infantry battalion was strong in combat power.

376th Infantry Division – The division defended in sector southwest of Perekopka against the 321st Rifle Division. To the west was an assortment of battle groups; to the east was the 100th ***Jäger*** Division. The division reported one NCO/enlisted killed in action; four NCOs/enlisted were wounded in action. The division reported that of its eight infantry battalions, three were average and five were weak in combat power.

384th Infantry Division – The division defended in sector west of the Don River near Trekhostrovskaia to Podgorskii against the 22nd Anti-Tank Brigade and the 4th Guards Rifle Division. To the west was the 44th Infantry Division; to the south was the 305th Infantry Division. The division suffered three NCOs/enlisted killed in action; 16 NCOs/enlisted were wounded in action. The division reported that of its six infantry battalions, five were average and one was exhausted in combat power.

XIV *Panzer* Corps – The corps headquarters was located west of Nadezhda. The corps suffered the following officer casualties: four killed in action; eight wounded in action.

3rd Infantry Division (Motorized) – The division defended in sector, from the Tartar Hill-Hill 111.1-Hill 129.6-Hill 131.2 against the 116th Rifle Division, the 84th Rifle Division, the 39th Guards Rifle Division, the 315th Rifle Division, the 64th Rifle Division and the 120th Rifle Division. To the east was the 16th ***Panzer*** Division; to the west was the 60th Infantry Division (Motorized.) Heavy fighting occurred throughout the sector. The division reported 13 NCOs/enlisted killed in action; six officers and 83 NCOs/enlisted were wounded in action; one man was reported missing in action. The division reported that of its five motorized infantry battalions, three were medium-strong, one was average and one was weak in combat power.

16th Panzer Division – The division defended in sector from Hill 139.7 to the Volga and from the Volga southwest to Hill 145.1, north of Orlovka against the 99th Rifle Division and the 213th Rifle Division. Heavy fighting continued throughout the sector. On the south of the corridor to the west were elements of the 60th Infantry Division (Motorized); on the north of the corridor, to the west was the 3rd Infantry Division (Motorized.) The division reported that of its five ***panzer*** grenadier battalions, all five were medium-strong in combat power.

60th Infantry Division (Motorized) – The division defended sector from south of Kotluban' Station near Borodkin to Kuz'michi against the 24th Rifle Division and the 207th Rifle Division. Heavy fighting occurred throughout the sector. To the east was the 16th ***Panzer*** Division; to the southwest was the 389th Infantry Division. The division suffered one officer and 14 NCOs/enlisted killed in action; one officer and 44 NCOs/enlisted were wounded in action. The division reported that of its seven motorized infantry battalions, three were medium-strong and four were average in combat power.

XVII Corps – The Romanian V Corps was subordinated to the corps. The corps suffered the following officer casualties: one killed in action.

22nd Panzer Division – The division occupied assembly areas south of the 79th Infantry Division. The division lost three NCOs/enlisted killed in action and ten NCOs/enlisted wounded in action. The division reported that of its three ***panzer*** grenadier battalions, one was medium-strong, one was average and one was weak in combat power.

79th Infantry Division – The division defended in sector from Bol'shoy-Verkhne-Kalmykovskii-Verkhne-Fomichinskii-Baskow-skij, opposite the 96th Rifle Division. The division headquarters was located at Karagichev. To the west was the XXXV Corps of the Italian Eighth Army; to the southeast was the 113th Infantry Division. The division lost two NCOs/enlisted killed in action; 16 NCOs/enlisted were wounded in action; four NCOs/enlisted were posted missing in action. The division reported that of its nine infantry battalions, six were average and three were weak in combat power.

113th Infantry Division – The division defended in sector along the Don River west of Kletskiy, opposite the 278th Rifle Division. To the northwest was the 79th Infantry Division; to the east was an assortment of battle groups. The division reported 14 NCOs/enlisted wounded in action. The division reported that of its seven infantry battalions, six were strong and one was medium-strong in combat power.

298th Infantry Division – The division moved separately from the Romanian V Corps northeast along the Italian Eighth Army and the Sixth Army boundary.

1st Romanian Cavalry Division – The division moved northeast to south of the 79th Infantry Division.

6th Romanian Infantry Division – The division moved northeast behind the 13th Romanian Infantry Division.

13th Romanian Infantry Division – The division moved northeast behind the 1st Romanian Cavalry Division.

LI Corps – The 53rd ***Werfer*** Regiment and the 101st Heavy Artillery Detachment were assigned to support the corps. The corps suffered the following officer casualties: six killed in action; 16 wounded in action.

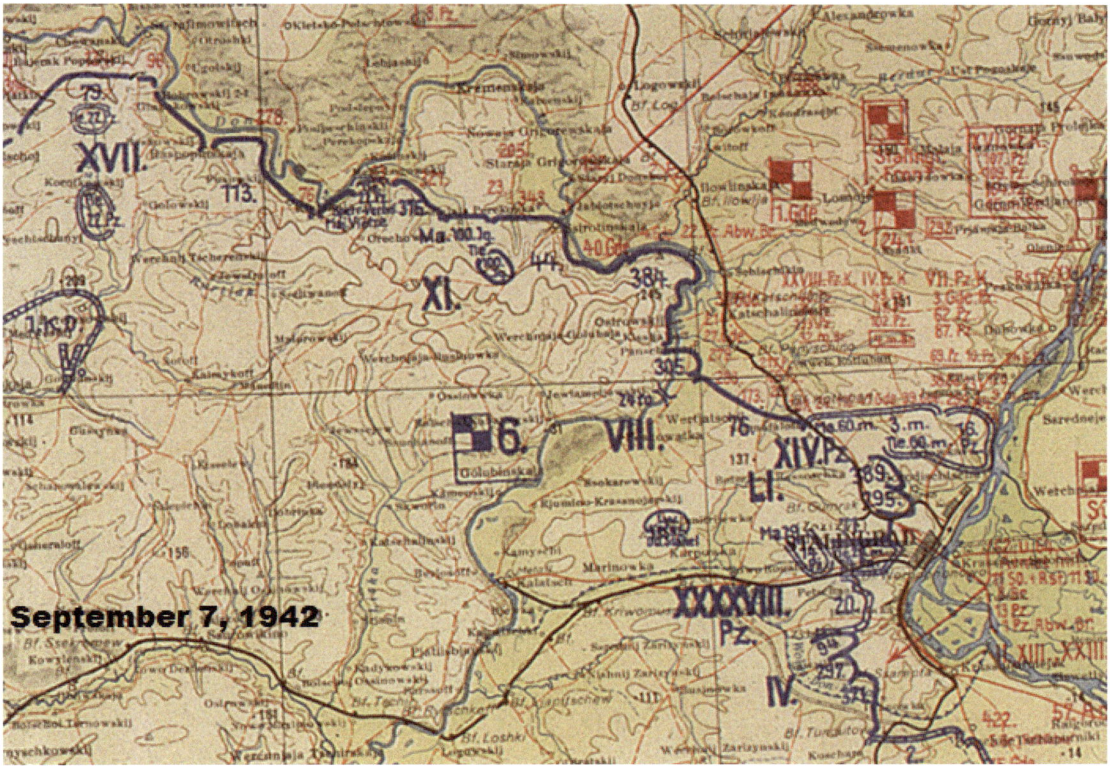

71st Infantry Division – The division attacked in zone and seized Experimental Station Nr.6. To the north was the 295th Infantry Division; to the south was the 24th *Panzer* Division. The division headquarters was located west of Gontschara. The division lost two officers and 11 NCOs/enlisted killed in action; three officers and 49 NCOs/enlisted were wounded in action; 24 NCOs/enlisted were missing in action. The division reported that of its nine infantry battalions, five were average and four were weak in combat power.

295th Infantry Division – The division attacked east in zone and seized a portion of the Tartar Ditch, as well as part of Gorodishche and the Razgulyayevka Rail Station, five miles northeast of the Mamayev Hill. The division headquarters was located at Gumrak. To the north was the 389th Infantry Division; to the south was the 71st Infantry Division. The division reported one officer and 12 NCOs/enlisted killed in action; three officers and 61 NCOs/enlisted were wounded in action. The division reported that of its seven infantry battalions, two were average and five were weak in combat power.

389th Infantry Division – The division attacked east in zone toward the bluffs overlooking Stalingrad. Enemy artillery and aircraft hit the division hard. To the northeast was the 60th Infantry Division (Motorized); to the south was the 295th Infantry Division. The division headquarters was located just east of Nadezhda. The division suffered one officer and 24 NCOs/enlisted killed in action; three officers and 14 NCOs were wounded in action. The division reported that of its six infantry battalions, five were medium-strong and one was average in combat power, while the combat engineer battalion was average in combat power.

Battle Group Stahel – The battle group occupied an assembly area near Dmitriyevka.

Fourth *Panzer* Army – The army headquarters was located at Plodowitoje.

IV Corps – The corps headquarters was located at Plantator.

94th Infantry Division – The division defended in sector west of Beketovka. To the north was the 20th Romanian Infantry Division; to the south was the 297th Infantry Division. Elements of the division continued to move northwest behind the front.

297th Infantry Division – The division defended in sector south of Elkhi against the 38th Rifle Division and the 133rd Tank Brigade. To the north was the 94th Infantry Division; to the south was the 371st Infantry Division.

371st Infantry Division – The division defended in sector near Ivanovka and the Tundutovo Rail Station against the 36th Guards Rifle Division and the 422nd Rifle Division. To the north was the 297th Infantry Division; to the south was the 2nd Romanian Infantry Division of the Romanian VI Corps. The division lost two NCOs/enlisted killed in action; one officer and 18 NCOs/enlisted were wounded in action.

XXXXVIII *Panzer* Corps – ***General der Panzertruppe*** Werner Kempf was lightly wounded in a night air attack.

14th Panzer Division – The division prepared to conduct future offensive operations. To the north was the 29th Infantry Division (Motorized); to the south was the 20th Romanian Infantry Division.

24th Panzer Division – The division prepared to conduct future offensive operations. To the north was the 71st Infantry Division of the Sixth Army; to the south was the 20th Romanian Infantry Division. The division suffered 14 NCOs/enlisted killed in action; 52 NCOs/enlisted were wounded in action.

29th Infantry Division (Motorized) – The division prepared to conduct future offensive operations. To the east was the 24th ***Panzer*** Division; to the south was the 20th Romanian Infantry Division. The division lost two NCOs/enlisted killed in action; one officer and five NCOs/enlisted were wounded in action.

20th Romanian Infantry Division – The division occupied a defensive position to the east of the 29th Infantry Division (Motorized.)

Sources, September 7, 1942: ***Oberkommando des Heeres, Lage Ost: Stand: 7.9.42, Eastern Front Situation Map, National Archives Identifier: 559733, Record Group 242 – National Archives Collection of Foreign Records Seized, 1675-1958, National Archives, College Park, Maryland; Ia, Armeeoberkommando 6, "Morgen Meldung" and assorted reports, Kriegstagebuch 13, 8 September 1942, as found in Microfilm Series, T-312, Records of German Field Commands, Armies, Roll 1685, National Archives and Records Service, College Park, Maryland; Ia, XXXXVIII Panzerkorps, "Übersicht über die dem Korps Unterstellten Divisionen, 28. Juni 1942 – 11 October 1942," as found on T-314, Records of German Field Commands, Corps, Roll 1153, National Archives, College Park, Maryland; Korpsarzt, XXXXVIII Panzerkorps, "Meldung über Personelle Verluste," Stand 7.9.42, as found on T-314, Records of German Field Commands, Corps, Roll 1158, National Archives, College Park, Maryland; 79th Infantry Division, Kriegstagebuch, 7 September 1942, as found in Microfilm Series T-315, Roll 1108, National Archives and Records Service, College Park, Maryland; 371st Infantry Division, Kriegstagebuch, 7 September 1942, as found in Microfilm Series T-315, Roll 2164, National Archives and Records Service, College Park, Maryland; Die 71. Infanterie-Division, 1939-1945: Gefechts- und Erlebnisberichte aus Kämpfen der "Gluckhaften Division" von Verdun bis Stalingrad, vom Monte Cassino bis zum Plattensee, Eggolsheim, FRG: Edition Dörfler, 1973, 228; David M. Glantz & Jonathan M. House, Armageddon in Stalingrad: September-November 1942, (The Stalingrad Trilogy, Volume 2), Lawrence, Kansas: University Press of Kansas, 2009, 43-76; Jason Mark, Death of the Leaping Horseman: 24. Panzer-Division in Stalingrad, Sydney, Australia: Leaping Horsemen Books, 2003, Sydney, Australia, Leaping Horsemen Books, 130-134; Anton Schimak, Karl Lamprecht & Friedrich Dettmer, Die 44. Infanterie Division: Tagebuch der Hoch- und Deutschmeister, Wien: Verlag Austria Press, 169, 233 and Map: Marschweg der 44. Infanterie Division im Russland.***

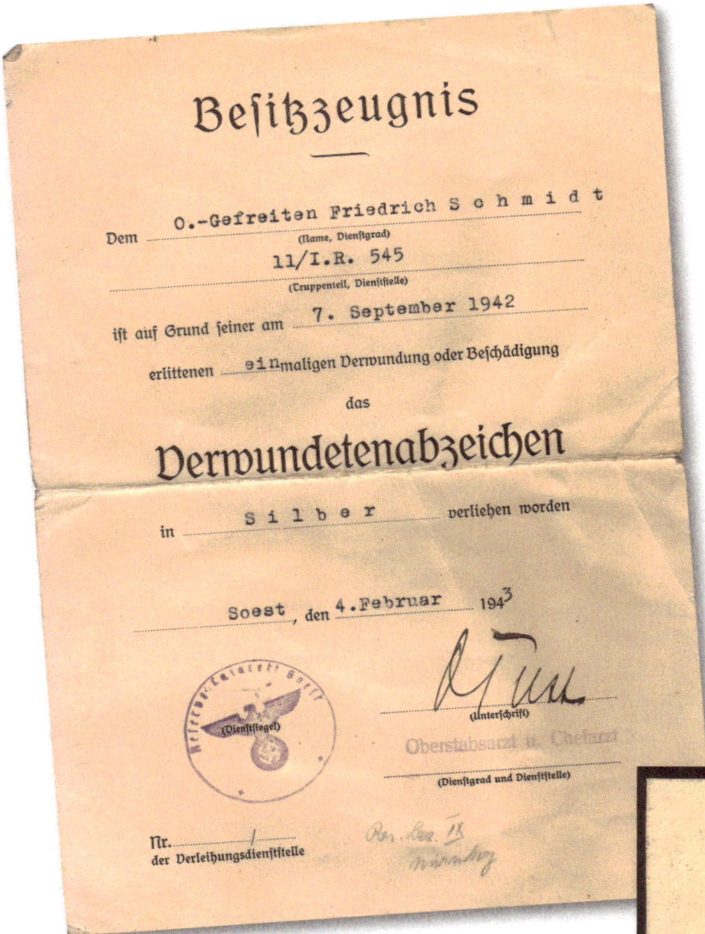
Besitzzeugnis

Dem O.-Gefreiten Friedrich Schmidt
(Name, Dienstgrad)
11/I.R. 545
(Truppenteil, Dienststelle)
ist auf Grund seiner am 7. September 1942
erlittenen einmaligen Verwundung oder Beschädigung
das

Verwundetenabzeichen

in Silber verliehen worden

Soest, den 4. Februar 1943

(Dienstsiegel)
(Unterschrift)
Oberstabsarzt u. Chefarzt
(Dienstgrad und Dienststelle)

Nr. 1
der Verleihungsdienststelle

Obergefreiter **Friedrich Schmidt**, of the 11th Company in the 545th Infantry Regiment of the 389th Infantry Division, was wounded on September 7, 1942 near Gorodishche. He was subsequently evacuated from Stalingrad and sent to the reserve hospital at Soest, Germany. He was awarded the Wound Badge in Silver in February 1943 in this document, which indicates that he probably lost a limb or an eye due to the wound.

In Gottes heiligem Frieden
ruht fern von seinen Lieben
unser innigstgeliebter, unvergeßlicher Sohn und Bruder
Obergefreiter Georg Petrich
in einer Panzerjäger-Abteilung
Inhaber des E.K. II
des Infanterie-Sturm- und Verwundeten-Abzeichens
geboren am 23. März 1912
gefallen am 7. September 1942 bei Stalingrad

Die Pflicht rief mich zum Krieg hinaus,
Mit Gott ging ich vom Elternhaus.
Ich dachte euer fort und fort,
Wenn ich auch an fremdem Ort,
Und freute mich auf's Wiedersehn,
Wenn Sturm und Krieg zu Ende geh'n.
Doch anders hat's der Herr gewollt
Und hat von hier mich abgeholt,
Weiß nichts von Krieg und Erdenleid
Und bin von jeder Sorg' befreit,
Drum tröstet, Liebste, euch daran:
„Was Gott tut, das ist wohlgetan!"

Obergefreiter **Georg Petrich** was born in Staig-Krugzell near Altusried, Austria on March 23, 1912. He was assigned to an anti-tank detachment and had won the Iron Cross 2nd Class, the Infantry Assault Badge and the Wound Badge in Black. He died of his wounds on September 7, 1942 at the 1/225 Medical Company near Stalingrad. He is buried at the German Military Cemetery at Rossoschka in Block 19, Row 22, in Grave 861.

September 8, 1942
Weather: dry, increasing cloudiness, 90° F
Sunrise: 5:27 a.m.; **Sunset:** 6:31 p.m.
Moon: Waning Crescent; 5% illumination

Sixth Army – The army headquarters was located at Golubinskaya.

VIII Corps – The corps suffered the following officer casualties: three wounded in action.

76th Infantry Division – The division defended in sector southwest of Samofalovka and north of Borodkin, against the 298th Rifle Division, the 173rd Rifle Division and the 221st Rifle Division. To the east was the 60th Infantry Division (Motorized); to the northwest was the 305th Infantry Division. Heavy fighting raged throughout the sector. The division lost eight NCOs/enlisted killed in action; 67 NCOs/enlisted were wounded in action.

305th Infantry Division – The division defended in sector from the Don River, north of Nizhne-Gnilovskii, to west of Kotluban' against the 279th Rifle Division. Heavy fighting raged throughout the sector. To the southeast was the 76th Infantry Division; to the north was the 384th Infantry Division. The division reported four NCOs/enlisted killed in action; one officer and 29 NCOs/enlisted were wounded in action.

XI Corps

44th Infantry Division – The division defended in sector Kurchajessowskij-Kamyshinskiy-Hill 171.0-Hill 180.9-Sirotinskaya-Khmelevskoy against the 40th Guards Rifle Division and the 343rd Rifle Division. The division headquarters was located at Verkhne-Golubaja. To the west was 100th ***Jäger*** Division; to the east was the 384th Infantry Division. The division reported one NCO/enlisted killed in action and one NCO/enlisted wounded in action.

100th Jäger Division – The division defended in sector near Blizhniaia-Perekopka, against the 23rd Rifle Division, but 50% of the division had moved southeastward to an assembly area. To the east was the 44th Infantry Division; to the west was the 376th Infantry Division. The division suffered four NCOs/enlisted wounded in action.

376th Infantry Division – The division defended in sector southwest of Perekopka against the 321st Rifle Division. To the west was an assortment of battle groups; to the east was the 100th ***Jäger*** Division. The division reported four NCOs/enlisted wounded in action.

384th Infantry Division – The division defended in sector west of the Don River near Trekhostrovskaia to Podgorskii against the 4th Guards Rifle Division. To the west was the 44th Infantry Division; to the south was the 305th Infantry Division. The division reported one NCO/enlisted killed in action and one NCO/enlisted wounded in action.

XIV *Panzer* Corps – The corps headquarters was located west of Nadezhda. The corps suffered the following officer casualties: three killed in action; 16 wounded in action.

3rd Infantry Division (Motorized) – The division defended in sector, from the Tartar Hill-Hill 111.1-Hill 129.6-Hill 131.2 against the 116th Rifle Division, the 84th Rifle Division, the 39th Guards Rifle Division, the 315th Rifle Division, the 64th Rifle Division and the 120th Rifle Division. To the east was the 16th ***Panzer*** Division; to the west was the 60th Infantry Division (Motorized.) Heavy fighting raged throughout the sector. The division lost four officers and 11 NCOs/enlisted killed in action; one officer and 84 NCOs/enlisted were wounded in action.

16th Panzer Division – The division defended in sector from Hill 139.7 to the Volga and from the Volga southwest to Hill 145.1, north of Orlovka against the 99th Rifle Division and the 213th Rifle Division. On the south of the corridor, to the west was the 60th Infantry Division (Motorized); on the north of the corridor to the west was the 3rd Infantry Division (Motorized.)

60th Infantry Division (Motorized) – The division defended in sector from south of Kotluban' Station near Borodkin to Kuz'michi against the 39th Guards Rifle Division, the 316th Rifle Division, the 24th Rifle Division and the 207th Rifle Division. On the south of the corridor to the east was the 16th ***Panzer*** Division; to the southwest was the 389th Infantry Division. On the north of the corridor to the east was the 3rd Infantry Division (Motorized); to the west was the 76th Infantry Division. Heavy fighting raged throughout the sector.

XVII Corps – The Romanian V Corps was subordinated to the corps. The corps suffered the following officer casualties: one wounded in action.

22nd Panzer Division – The division occupied assembly areas south of the 79th Infantry Division. The division lost one NCO killed in action and six NCOs/enlisted wounded in action.

79th Infantry Division – The division defended in sector from Bol'shoy-Verkhne-Kalmykovskii-Verkhne-Fomichinskii-Baskowskij against the 96th Rifle Division and the 304th Rifle Division. The division headquarters was located at Karagichev. To the west was the XXXV Corps of the Italian Eighth Army; to the south was the 113th Infantry Division. The division lost four NCOs/enlisted killed in action; three NCOs/enlisted were wounded in action; one NCO/enlisted was reported missing in action.

113th Infantry Division – The division defended in sector along the Don River west of Kletskiy against the 76th Rifle Division and the 278th Rifle Division. To the north was the 79th Infantry Division; to the east was an assortment of battle groups. The division lost one NCO/enlisted killed in action; five NCOs/enlisted were wounded in action.

298th Infantry Division – The division moved separately from the Romanian V Corps northeast along the Italian Eighth Army and Sixth Army boundary.

1st Romanian Cavalry Division – The division moved northeast to south of the 113th Infantry Division.

6th Romanian Infantry Division – The division moved northeast behind the 13th Romanian Infantry Division.

13th Romanian Infantry Division – The division moved northeast behind the 1st Romanian Cavalry Division.

LI Corps – The corps suffered the following officer casualties: one killed in action; six wounded in action.

71st Infantry Division – The division attacked in zone and approached the main Stalingrad hospital, scattering the 87th Rifle Division. The division repelled an enemy armored counter-attack aimed at the boundary between the 71st Infantry Division and its neighbor to the north, the 295th Infantry Division. The division headquarters was located west of Gontschara. To the south was the 24th ***Panzer*** Division. The division lost about ten officers and 100 NCO/enlisted casualties.

295th Infantry Division – The division attacked east in zone and pushed the 23rd Tank Corps' tank brigades into Alexandrovka, while seizing Hill 154.8 and the Tartar Wall. The division headquarters was located at Gumrak. To the north was the 389th Infantry Division; to the south was the 71st Infantry Division.

389th Infantry Division – The division moved into assault positions for an attack northeastward toward Orlovka; the division seized portions of the Tartar Wall. The division lost one officer and three NCOs/enlisted killed in action; 20 NCOs/enlisted were wounded in action. The division headquarters was located just east of Nadezhda. To the east was the 60th Infantry Division (Motorized); to the south was the 295th Infantry Division.

Battle Group Stahel – The battle group moved to an assembly area near Bol'shaya Rossoschka.

Fourth *Panzer* Army – The army headquarters was located at Plodowitoje.

IV Corps – The corps headquarters was located at Plantator.

94th Infantry Division – The division defended in sector west of Beketovka. To the north was the 20th Romanian Infantry Division; to the south was the 297th Infantry Division. Elements of the division continued to move northwest behind the front.

297th Infantry Division – The division defended in sector south of Elkhi against the 38th Rifle Division and the 133rd Tank Brigade. To the north was the 94th Infantry Division; to the south was the 371st Infantry Division.

371st Infantry Division – The division defended in sector near Ivanovka and the Tundutovo Rail Station against the 36th Guards Rifle Division and the 422nd Rifle Division. To the north was the 297th Infantry Division; to the south was the 2nd Romanian Infantry Division of the Romanian VI

Corps. The division lost three NCOs/enlisted killed in action; seven NCOs/enlisted were wounded in action.

XXXXVIII *Panzer* Corps

14th Panzer Division – The division attacked east in zone, penetrating the 131st Rifle Division, and seized Hill 144.9 and the Radio Station. To the south was the 29th Infantry Division (Motorized); to the north was the 24th ***Panzer*** Division. The division lost 42 NCOs/enlisted killed in action; ten officers and 160 NCOs/enlisted were wounded in action; one NCO/enlisted was reported missing in action.

24th Panzer Division – The division attacked east in zone through the Sadovaia Rail Station and seized the Leather Factory – crushing the 244th Rifle Division in the process. To the north was the 71st Infantry Division; to the south was the 14th ***Panzer*** Division. The division suffered one officer and 36 NCOs/enlisted killed in action; eight officers and 163 NCOs/enlisted were wounded in action; four men later died of their wounds. The division commander, ***Generalmajor*** Bruno ***Ritter*** von Hauenschild was seriously wounded by mortar fire.

29th Infantry Division (Motorized) – The division attacked east in zone and seized Verkhne-El'shanka. To the north was the 14th ***Panzer*** Division; to the south was the 20th Romanian Infantry Division. The division lost one officer and 54 NCOs/enlisted killed in action; nine officers and 197 NCOs/enlisted were wounded in action; nine NCOs/enlisted were reported missing in action.

20th Romanian Infantry Division – The division defended in sector. To the north was the 29th Infantry Division (Motorized); to the south was the 94th Infantry Division.

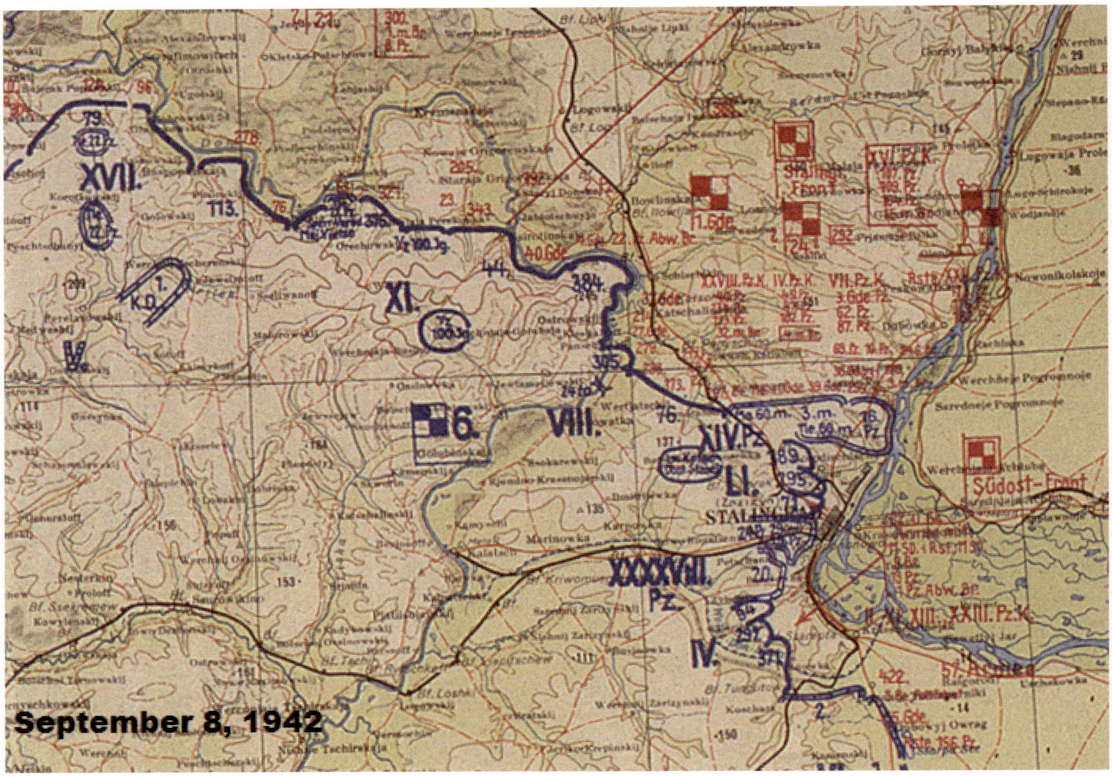

Sources, September 8, 1942: ***Oberkommando des Heeres, Lage Ost: Stand: 8.9.42, Eastern Front Situation Map, National Archives Identifier: 559733, Record Group 242 – National Archives Collection of Foreign Records Seized, 1675-1958, National Archives, College Park, Maryland; Ia, Armeeoberkommando 6, "Morgen Meldung" and assorted reports, Kriegstagebuch 13, 9 September 1942, as found in Microfilm Series, T-312, Records of German Field Commands, Armies, Roll 1685, National Archives and Records Service, College Park, Maryland; Ia, XXXXVIII Panzerkorps, "Übersicht über die dem Korps Unterstellten Divisionen, 28. Juni 1942 – 11 October 1942," as found on T-314, Records of German Field Commands, Corps, Roll 1153, National Archives, College Park, Maryland; Korpsarzt, XXXXVIII Panzerkorps, "Meldung über Personelle Verluste," Stand***

8.9.42, as found on T-314, Records of German Field Commands, Corps, Roll 1158, National Archives, College Park, Maryland; 79th Infantry Division, Kriegstagebuch, 8 September 1942, as found in Microfilm Series T-315, Roll 1108, National Archives and Records Service, College Park, Maryland; 371st Infantry Division, Kriegstagebuch, 8 September 1942, as found in Microfilm Series T-315, Roll 2164, National Archives and Records Service, College Park, Maryland; Die 71. Infanterie-Division, 1939-1945: Gefechts- und Erlebnisberichte aus Kämpfen der "Gluckhaften Division" von Verdun bis Stalingrad, vom Monte Cassino bis zum Plattensee, Eggolsheim, FRG: Edition Dörfler, 1973, 228; David M. Glantz & Jonathan M. House, Armageddon in Stalingrad: September-November 1942, (The Stalingrad Trilogy, Volume 2), Lawrence, Kansas: University Press of Kansas, 2009, 76-80; Joachim Lemelsen, 29. Division, Bad Nauheim, FRG: Podzun Verlag, 1960, 198; Jason Mark, Death of the Leaping Horseman: 24. Panzer-Division in Stalingrad, Sydney, Australia: Leaping Horsemen Books, 2003, 135-143; Anton Schimak, Karl Lamprecht & Friedrich Dettmer, Die 44. Infanterie Division: Tagebuch der Hoch- und Deutschmeister, Wien: Verlag Austria Press, 169, 233 and Map: Marschweg der 44. Infanterie Division im Russland.

Letter from *Gefreiter* Heinrich Meyer dated September 8, 1942 to his family. Meyer was assigned to the 1st Battery, 1st Battalion, of the 171st Artillery Regiment in the 71st Infantry Division. In his letter, he writes:

> "Two days ago, we finally reached our new destination and two letters from you were waiting for me, from August 22nd and 24th. Many thanks to all. I am glad to hear that you are all well; from Grandma I got a parcel with 60 cigarettes; give her my thanks. I hope you have good weather like we have; we are almost in Stalingrad now and building our gun positions. It won't be long now until the main attack will go in. Our Luftwaffe is busy every day over the city. Our artillery observer, my comrade Georg Fühl has a detailed view and knows everything that is going on at the front. We truly believe that by October the battle is over, not many enemy attacks here, only artillery fire from across the river. We live like moles now, digging bunkers and gun positions. The food is good; today we had bean soup with sheep meat; Sergeant Schüpper even had a bottle of good Häger Schnapps. There is no mess hall here, but our mood is good. We look forward to things to come, and awaiting the end of the war this year. You have to believe too."

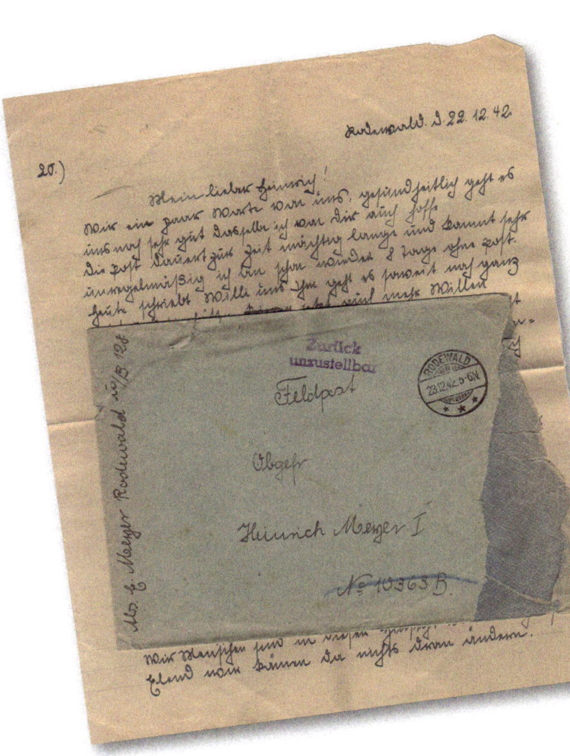

Undeliverable letter to the same *Obergefreiter* Heinrich Meyer. Meyer was assigned to the 1st Battery, 1st Battalion, of the 171st Artillery Regiment in the 71st Infantry Division. Meyer was from Rodewald near Hannover and was married. The letter was written on December 22, 1942, but could not be flown into the encirclement. Several hundred thousand letters meant for soldiers at Stalingrad met this same fate, marked with the dreaded "Zurück unrustellbar."

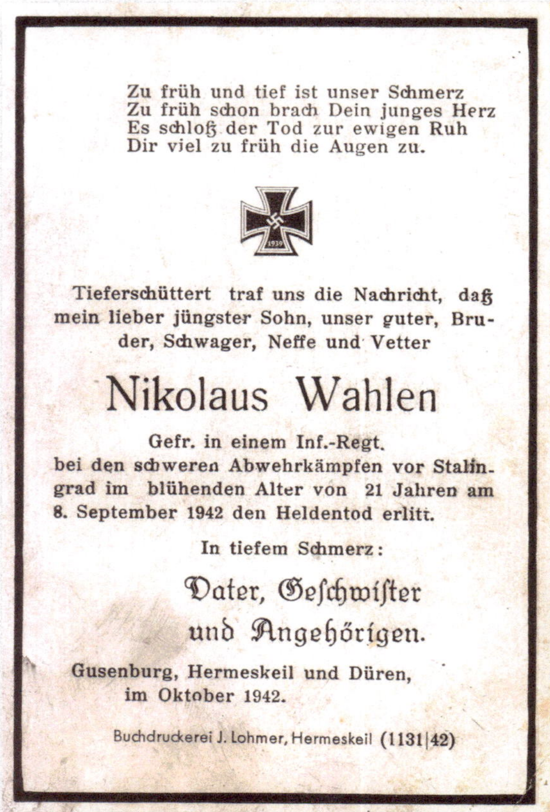

Zu früh und tief ist unser Schmerz
Zu früh schon brach Dein junges Herz
Es schloß der Tod zur ewigen Ruh
Dir viel zu früh die Augen zu.

Tieferschüttert traf uns die Nachricht, daß mein lieber jüngster Sohn, unser guter, Bruder, Schwager, Neffe und Vetter

Nikolaus Wahlen

Gefr. in einem Inf.-Regt.
bei den schweren Abwehrkämpfen vor Stalingrad im blühenden Alter von 21 Jahren am 8. September 1942 den Heldentod erlitt.

In tiefem Schmerz:

Vater, Geschwister
und Angehörigen.

Gusenburg, Hermeskeil und Düren,
im Oktober 1942.

Buchdruckerei J. Lohmer, Hermeskeil (1131|42)

Oberschütze **Niklolaus Wahlen** was born on April 24, 1921 in Gusenburg, near Trier in the Rhineland Palatinate. The youngest son in the family, he was married. Wahlen was killed in action at Hill 144.9, southwest of Stalingrad, on September 8, 1942, while serving in the 14th ***Panzer*** Division. He is listed in the remembrance book at the German Military Cemetery at Rossoschka.

Oberschütze **Niklolaus Wahlen**.

September 9, 1942
Weather: clear and warm, 90° F
Sunrise: 5:29 a.m.; **Sunset:** 6:29 p.m.
Moon: Waning Crescent; 1% illumination

Sixth Army – The army headquarters was located at Golubinskaya. Bombers and dive-bombers from the ***Luftwaffe***'s VIII Air Corps pounded Stalingrad in large-scale attacks.

VIII Corps – The corps suffered the following officer casualties: one killed in action; seven wounded in action.

76th Infantry Division – The division defended in sector southwest of Samofalovka and north of Borodkin against several enemy attacks by the 298th Rifle Division, the 173rd Rifle Division and the 221st Rifle Division. To the northwest was the 305th Infantry Division; to the east was the 60th Infantry Division (Motorized.) The division lost 16 NCOs/enlisted killed in action; 84 NCOs/enlisted were wounded in action.

305th Infantry Division – The division defended in sector from the Don River, north of Nizhne-Gnilovskii, to west of Kotluban' against the 27th Guards Rifle Division and the 279th Rifle Division. To the southeast was the 76th Infantry Division; to the north was the 384th Infantry Division. The division lost four NCOs/enlisted killed in action; 12 NCOs/enlisted were wounded in action.

XI Corps – The corps suffered the following officer casualties: one killed in action; two wounded in action.

44th Infantry Division – The division defended in sector Kurchajessowskij-Kamyshinskiy-Hill 171.0-Hill 180.9-Sirotinskaya-Khmelevskoy against the 343rd Rifle Division and the 40th Guards Rifle Division. The division headquarters was located at Verkhne-Golubaja. To the west was 100th ***Jäger*** Division; to the east was the 384th Infantry Division. The division lost four NCOs/enlisted killed in action; one officer and 14 NCOs/enlisted were wounded in action.

100th Jäger Division – The division defended in sector near Blizhniaia-Perekopka against the 23rd Rifle Division. To the east was the 44th Infantry Division; to the northwest was the 376th Infantry Division. One-half of the division occupied an assembly area south of the sector. The division lost three NCOs/enlisted wounded in action.

376th Infantry Division – The division defended in sector near Blizhniaia-Perekopka against the 321st Rifle Division. To the west was an assortment of battle groups; to the east was the 100th ***Jäger*** Division. The division lost one officer and four NCOs/enlisted killed in action; one officer and three NCOs/enlisted were wounded in action.

384th Infantry Division – The division defended in sector west of the Don River near Trekhostrovskaia to Podgorskii against the 4th Guards Rifle Division and the 22nd Anti-Tank Brigade. To the west was the 44th Infantry Division; to the south was the 305th Infantry Division. The 244th ***Sturmgeschütz*** Detachment was attached to the division. The division lost four NCOs/enlisted wounded in action.

XIV *Panzer* Corps – The corps headquarters was located west of Nadezhda. The corps suffered the following officer casualties: two killed in action; ten wounded in action.

3rd Infantry Division (Motorized) – The division defended in sector, from the Tartar Hill-Hill 111.1-Hill 129.6-Hill 131.2 against the 116th Rifle Division, the 84th Rifle Division, the 39th Guards Rifle Division, the 315th Rifle Division, the 64th Rifle Division and the 120th Rifle Division. To the east was the 16th ***Panzer*** Division; to the west was the 60th Infantry Division (Motorized.) Heavy fighting occurred throughout the sector. The division lost one officer and 33 NCOs/enlisted killed in action; 89 NCOs/enlisted were wounded in action; one man was reported missing in action.

16th Panzer Division – The division defended in sector from Hill 139.7 to the Volga and from the Volga southwest to Hill 145.1, north of Orlovka against the 99th Rifle Division and the 213th Rifle Division. Heavy fighting occurred throughout the sector. On the south of the corridor, to the west was the 60th Infantry Division (Motorized.) Along the north of the corridor to the west was the 3rd Infantry Division (Motorized.) The division lost two officers and 99 NCOs/enlisted as casualties.

60th Infantry Division (Motorized) – The division defended in sector from south of Kotluban' Station near Borodkin to Kuz'michi against the 39th Guards Rifle Division, the 316th Rifle Division, the 24th Rifle Division and the 207th Rifle Division. Heavy fighting occurred throughout the sector. Along the south of the corridor, to the east was the 16th ***Panzer*** Division; to the west was the 389th Infantry Division. Along the north of the corridor, to the east was the 3rd Infantry Division (Motorized); to the west was the 76th Infantry Division. The division lost five officers and 235 NCOs/enlisted as casualties.

XVII Corps – The Romanian V Corps was subordinated to the corps.

22nd Panzer Division – The division occupied assembly areas south of the 79th Infantry Division.

79th Infantry Division – The division defended in sector from Bol'shoy-Verkhne-Kalmykovskii-Verkhne-Fomichinskii-Baskowskij against the 96th Rifle Division. The division headquarters was located at Karagichev. To the west was the XXXV Corps of the Italian Eighth Army; to the south was the 113th Infantry Division. The division lost three NCOs/enlisted killed in action; 13 NCOs/enlisted were wounded in action.

113th Infantry Division – The division defended in sector along the Don River west of Kletskiy against the 278th Rifle Division and the 76th Rifle Division. To the northwest was the 79th Infantry Division; to the east was an assortment of battle groups. The division lost two NCOs/enlisted killed in action; ten NCOs/enlisted were wounded in action.

298th Infantry Division – The division moved separately from the Romanian V Corps northeast along the Italian Eighth Army and the Sixth Army boundary.

1st Romanian Cavalry Division – The division moved northeast to the southwest of the 376th Infantry Division.

6th Romanian Infantry Division – The division moved northeast behind the 13th Romanian Infantry Division.

13th Romanian Infantry Division – The division moved northeast behind the 1st Romanian Cavalry Division.

LI Corps – The corps suffered the following officer casualties: seven killed in action; 14 wounded in action.

71st Infantry Division – The division attacked in zone, incurring heavy losses. To the south was the 24th ***Panzer*** Division; to the north was the 295th Infantry Division. The division headquarters was located west of Gontschara. The division lost four officers and 12 NCOs/enlisted killed in action; five officers and 76 NCOs/enlisted were wounded in action; one man was reported missing in action.

295th Infantry Division – The division attacked east in zone and captured the western section of Alexandrovka. To the north was the 389th Infantry Division; to the south was the 71st Infantry Division. The division headquarters was located at Gumrak. The division lost eight NCOs/enlisted killed in action; two officers and 79 NCOs/enlisted were wounded in action.

389th Infantry Division – The division attacked east in zone and captured Gorodishche. To the northeast was the 60th Infantry Division (Motorized); to the south was the 295th Infantry Division. The division headquarters was located just east of Nadezhda. The division lost 15 NCOs/enlisted killed in action; two officers and 29 NCOs/enlisted were wounded in action.

Battle Group Stahel – The battle group occupied an assembly area near Bol'shaya Rossoschka.

Fourth *Panzer* Army – The army headquarters was located at Plodowitoje.

IV Corps – The corps headquarters was located at Plantator.

297th Infantry Division – The division defended in sector south of Elkhi against the 38th Rifle Division and the 133rd Tank Brigade. To the north was the 94th Infantry Division; to the south was the 371st Infantry Division.

371st Infantry Division – The division defended in sector near Ivanovka and the Tundutovo Rail Station against the 36th Guards Rifle Division and the 422nd Rifle Division. To the north was the 297th Infantry Division; to the south was the 2nd Romanian Infantry Division of the Romanian VI Corps. The division suffered one officer and four NCOs/enlisted killed in action; eight NCOs/enlisted were wounded in action.

XXXXVIII *Panzer* Corps

14th Panzer Division – The division attacked east in zone and seized Peschanka. To the south was the 29th Infantry Division (Motorized.) The division lost 33 NCOs/enlisted killed in action; seven officers and 107 NCOs/enlisted were wounded in action; one NCO/enlisted was reported missing in action.

24th Panzer Division – The division consolidated its gains from the day before. To the north was the 71st Infantry Division. The division suffered one officer and seven NCOs/enlisted killed in action; four officers and 67 NCOs/enlisted were wounded in action; one man later died of his wounds; one man was reported missing in action.

29th Infantry Division (Motorized) – The division attacked east in zone on the right flank of the 14th ***Panzer*** Division, approaching the Volga River. To the north was the 14th ***Panzer*** Division; to the south was the 20th Romanian Infantry Division. The division lost 26 NCOs/enlisted killed in action; one officer and 121 NCOs/enlisted were wounded in action; one officer and four NCOs/enlisted were reported missing in action.

94th Infantry Division – The division was subordinated to the XXXXVIIII ***Panzer*** Corps for anticipated operations inside Stalingrad. The division lost four NCOs/enlisted killed in action; 12 NCOs/enlisted were wounded in action; one NCO/enlisted was reported missing in action.

20th Romanian Infantry Division – The division occupied a defensive position. To the north was the 14th ***Panzer*** Division; to the south was the 94th Infantry Division.

Sources, September 9, 1942: *Oberkommando des Heeres, Lage Ost: Stand: 9.9.42, Eastern Front Situation Map, National Archives Identifier: 559733, Record Group 242 – National Archives Collection of Foreign Records Seized, 1675-1958, National Archives, College Park, Maryland; Ia, Armeeoberkommando 6, "Morgen Meldung" and assorted reports, Kriegstagebuch 13, 10 September 1942, as found in Microfilm Series, T-312, Records of German Field Commands, Armies, Roll 1685, National Archives and Records Service, College Park, Maryland; Ia, XXXXVIII Panzerkorps, "Übersicht über die dem Korps Unterstellten Divisionen, 28. Juni 1942 – 11 October 1942," as found on T-314, Records of German Field Commands, Corps, Roll 1153, National Archives, College Park, Maryland; Korpsarzt, XXXXVIII Panzerkorps, "Meldung über Personelle Verluste," Stand 9.9.42, as found on T-314, Records of German Field Commands, Corps, Roll 1158, National Archives, College Park, Maryland; 79th Infantry Division, Kriegstagebuch, 9 September 1942, as found in Microfilm Series T-315, Roll 1108, National Archives and Records Service, College Park, Maryland; 371st Infantry Division, Kriegstagebuch, 9 September 1942, as found in Microfilm Series T-315, Roll 2164, National Archives and Records Service, College Park, Maryland; David M. Glantz & Jonathan M. House, Armageddon in Stalingrad: September-November 1942, (The Stalingrad Trilogy, Volume 2), Lawrence, Kansas: University Press of Kansas, 2009, 80-89; Joachim Lemelsen, 29. Division, Bad Nauheim, FRG: Podzun Verlag, 1960, 198; Jochen Löser, Bittere Pflicht: Kampf und Untergang der 76. Berlin-Brandenburgischen Infanterie-Division, Osnabrück, FRG: Biblio Verlag, 1986, 208; Jason Mark, Death of the Leaping Horseman: 24. Panzer-Division in Stalingrad, Sydney, Australia: Leaping Horsemen Books, 2003, 143-146; Anton Schimak, Karl Lamprecht & Friedrich Dettmer, Die 44. Infanterie Division: Tagebuch der Hoch- und Deutschmeister, Wien: Verlag Austria Press, 169, 233 and Map: Marschweg der 44. Infanterie Division im Russland; Franz Thomas, & Günter Wegmann, Die Ritterkreuzträger der Deutschen Wehrmacht, 1939-1945, Teil 1: Sturmartillerie, Osnabrück, FRG: Biblio Verlag, 1985, 218.*

Obergefreiter **Josef Nagler** was born in Arberg near Gunzenhausen, Bavaria on March 7, 1911. He was killed in action on September 9, 1942 near Stalingrad.

Feldwebel **Jakob Waldhier** was born in Hemau near Ratisbon in Bavaria on November 14, 1915. He fought in the 1939 Polish Campaign, the 1940 French Campaign and the Russian Campaign, winning the Iron Cross 2nd Class and the Infantry Assault Badge in Silver. Assigned to an infantry regiment, he was killed in action eight miles north of Stalingrad on September 9, 1942; he was buried in a military cemetery five miles north of the city. Jakob Waldhier's older brother, Josef, was killed in action on the Russian Front on January 7, 1942.

September 10, 1942
Weather: sunny, warm, 91° F, good road conditions
Sunrise: 5:30 a.m.; **Sunset:** 6:27 p.m.
Moon: New Moon; 0% illumination

Sixth Army – The army headquarters was located at Golubinskaya.

VIII Corps – The corps suffered the following officer casualties: four wounded in action.

76th Infantry Division – The division defended in sector southwest of Samofalovka and north of Borodkin against several enemy attacks by the 308th Rifle Division, 298th Rifle Division, the 173rd Rifle Division and the 221st Rifle Division. To the northwest was the 305th Infantry Division; to the east was the 60th Infantry Division (Motorized.) The division lost nine NCOs/enlisted killed in action; 38 NCOs/enlisted were wounded in action.

305th Infantry Division – The division defended in sector from just west of the Don River eastward, north of Nizhne-Gnilovskii to the west of Kotluban' against the 279th Rifle Division. To the southeast was the 76th Infantry Division; to the north was the 384th Infantry Division. The division lost four NCOs/enlisted killed in action; one officer and nine NCOs/enlisted were wounded in action.

XI Corps – The corps suffered the following officer casualties: three wounded in action.

44th Infantry Division – The division defended in sector Kurchajessowskij-Kamyshinskiy-Hill 171.0-Hill 180.9-Sirotinskaya-Khmelevskoy against the 343rd Rifle Division and the 40th Guards Rifle Division. The division headquarters was located at Verkhne-Golubaja. To the west was 100th ***Jäger*** Division; to the east was the 384th Infantry Division. ***Generalmajor*** Heinrich-Anton von Deboi was awarded the Knight's Cross.

100th Jäger Division – The division defended in sector near Blizhniaia-Perekopka against the 23rd Rifle Division. To the east was the 44th Infantry Division; to the west was the 376th Infantry Division.

376th Infantry Division – The division defended in sector near Blizhniaia-Perekopka against the 321st Rifle Division. To the west was an assortment of battle groups; to the east was the 100th ***Jäger*** Division.

384th Infantry Division – The division defended in sector west of the Don River near Trekhostrovskaia to Podgorskii against the 22nd Anti-Tank Brigade and the 4th Guards Rifle Division. To the west was the 44th Infantry Division; to the south was the 305th Infantry Division. The 244th ***Sturmgeschütz*** Detachment was attached to the division.

XIV *Panzer* Corps – The corps attacked and eliminated two small penetrations of the front. The corps headquarters was located west of Nadezhda. The corps suffered the following officer casualties: 11 wounded in action.

3rd Infantry Division (Motorized) – The division defended in sector, from the Tartar Hill-Hill 111.1-Hill 129.6-Hill 131.2 against the 116th Rifle Division, the 84th Rifle Division, the 39th Guards Rifle Division, the 315th Rifle Division, the 64th Rifle Division and the 120th Rifle Division. To the east was the 16th ***Panzer*** Division; to the west was the 60th Infantry Division (Motorized.) For the period August 25, 1942 to September 9, 1942, the division lost 21 officers and 509 NCOs/enlisted killed in action; 32 officers and 1,499 NCOs/enlisted were wounded in action; one officer and 137 men were reported missing in action.

16th Panzer Division – The division defended in sector from Hill 139.7 to the Volga and from the Volga southwest to Hill 145.1, north of Orlovka against the 299th Rifle Division, the 84th Rifle Division and the 64th Rifle Division. On the south of the corridor, to the west was the 60th Infantry Division (Motorized), but this unit had only two battalions facing south. Along the north of the corridor, to the west was the 3rd Infantry Division (Motorized.) The division reported that from August 24, 1942 to September 10, 1942 the division suffered 74 officer and 2,035 NCI/enlisted casualties.

60th Infantry Division (Motorized) – The division defended in sector from south of Kotluban' Station near Borodkin to Kuz'michi against the 308th Rifle Division, the 39th Guards Rifle Division, the 316th Rifle Division, the 24th Rifle Division and the 207th Rifle Division. Extremely heavy fighting occurred at Hill 139.7, where the division repulsed several enemy divisions; all but two battalions now defended to the north. To the west was the 76th Infantry Division; to the east was the 3rd Infantry Division (Motorized.) The division reported that from August 24, 1942 to September 9, 1942, there were 51 officer and 1,692 NCO/enlisted casualties.

Battle Group Stahel – The battle group served as the corps reserve; it was located at an assembly area near Bol'shaya Rossoschka.

XVII Corps – The Romanian V Corps was subordinated to the corps. The corps suffered the following officer casualties: one killed in action; three wounded in action.

22nd Panzer Division – The division was located in assembly areas south of the 79th Infantry Division.

79th Infantry Division – The division defended in sector Bol'shoy-Verkhne-Kalmykovskii-Verkhne-Fomichinskii-Baskowskij against the 124th Rifle Division and the 304th Rifle Division. The division headquarters was located at Karagichev. To the west was the XXXV Corps of the Italian Eighth Army; to the southeast was the 113th Infantry Division. The division lost one officer and 15 NCOs/enlisted killed in action; 17 NCOs/enlisted were wounded in action.

113th Infantry Division – The division defended in sector along the Don River west of Kletskiy against the 278th Rifle Division and the 76th Rifle Division. To the northwest was the 79th Infantry Division; to the east was an assortment of battle groups. The division lost one officer and 15 NCOs/enlisted killed in action; 17 NCOs/enlisted were wounded in action.

298th Infantry Division – The division moved separately from the Romanian V Corps northeast along the Italian Eighth Army and the Sixth Army boundary.

1st Romanian Cavalry Division – The division occupied an assembly area southwest of the 376th Infantry Division.

6th Romanian Infantry Division – The division moved northeast behind the 13th Romanian Infantry Division.

13th Romanian Infantry Division – The division moved northeast behind the 1st Romanian Cavalry Division.

LI Corps – The 53rd ***Werfer*** Regiment was assigned to support the corps. The corps suffered the following officer casualties: five killed in action; 16 wounded in action.

71st Infantry Division – The division attacked in zone, creeping closer to the city's edge against the 399th Rifle Division. To the south was the 24th ***Panzer*** Division; to the north was the 295th Infantry Division. The division headquarters was located west of Gontschara. The division lost four NCOs/enlisted killed in action; 30 NCOs/enlisted were wounded in action; two men were reported missing in action.

295th Infantry Division – The division attacked east in zone and pushed to south of the Razgulyayevka Rail Station against the 112th Rifle Division. To the north was the 389th Infantry Division; to the south was the 71st Infantry Division. The division headquarters was located at Gumrak. The division lost 18 NCOs/enlisted killed in action; three officers and 89 NCOs/enlisted were wounded in action.

389th Infantry Division – The division attacked in zone to the east, reaching southwest of Orlovka. The division headquarters was located just east of Nadezhda. To the south was the 295th Infantry Division; to the northeast was the 16th ***Panzer*** Division. The division lost two officers and 12 NCOs/enlisted killed in action; one officer and 60 NCOs/enlisted were wounded in action.

Fourth *Panzer* Army – The army headquarters was located at Plodowitoje.

IV Corps – The corps headquarters was located at Plantator.

297th Infantry Division – The division defended in sector south of Elkhi against the 38th Rifle Division and the 133rd Tank Brigade. To the north was the 20th Romanian Infantry Division; to the south was the 371st Infantry Division.

371st Infantry Division – The division defended in sector near Ivanovka and the Tundutovo Rail Station against the 36th Guards Rifle Division and the 422nd Rifle Division. To the north was the 297th

Infantry Division; to the south was the 2nd Romanian Infantry Division of the Romanian VI Corps. The division suffered 15 NCOs/enlisted wounded in action.

XXXXVIII *Panzer* Corps

14th Panzer Division – The division attacked east in zone near Voroponovo against the 35th Guards Rifle Division. To the south was the 29th Infantry Division (Motorized); to the north was the 24th ***Panzer*** Division. The division lost two officers and 30 NCOs/enlisted killed in action; nine officers and 108 NCOs/enlisted were wounded in action.

24th Panzer Division – The division consolidated its gains from the day before against the 244th Rifle Division. To the north was the 71st Infantry Division. The division suffered three officers and 26 NCOs/enlisted killed in action; one officer and 18 NCOs/enlisted were wounded in action; one NCO/enlisted was reported missing in action.

29th Infantry Division (Motorized) – The division attacked east in zone and reached the Volga River at Kuporosnoye against the 131st Rifle Division. To the south was the 94th Infantry Division; to the north was the 14th ***Panzer*** Division. The division lost one officer and 26 NCOs/enlisted killed in action; four officers and 82 NCOs/enlisted were wounded in action; three NCOs/enlisted were reported missing in action.

94th Infantry Division – The division prepared to relieve the 24th ***Panzer*** Division in some of its positions. The division lost three NCOs/enlisted killed in action; 17 NCOs/enlisted were wounded in action.

20th Romanian Infantry Division – The division occupied a defensive position to the north of the 297th Infantry Division.

Sources, September 10, 1942: *Oberkommando des Heeres, Lage Ost: Stand: 10.9.42, Eastern Front Situation Map, National Archives Identifier: 559733, Record Group 242 – National Archives Collection of Foreign Records Seized, 1675-1958, National Archives, College Park, Maryland; Ia, Armeeoberkommando 6, "Morgen Meldung" and assorted reports, Kriegstagebuch 13, 11 September 1942, as found in Microfilm Series, T-312, Records of German Field Commands, Armies, Roll 1685, National Archives and Records Service, College Park, Maryland; Ia, XXXXVIII Panzerkorps, "Übersicht über die dem*

Korps Unterstellten Divisionen, 28. Juni 1942 – 11 October 1942," as found on T-314, Records of German Field Commands, Corps, Roll 1153, National Archives, College Park, Maryland; Korpsarzt, XXXXVIII Panzerkorps, "Meldung über Personelle Verluste," Stand 10.9.42, as found on T-314, Records of German Field Commands, Corps, Roll 1158, National Archives, College Park, Maryland; 79th Infantry Division, Kriegstagebuch, 10 September 1942, as found in Microfilm Series T-315, Roll 1108, National Archives and Records Service, College Park, Maryland; 371st Infantry Division, Kriegstagebuch, 10 September 1942, as found in Microfilm Series T-315, Roll 2164, National Archives and Records Service, College Park, Maryland; Division der Wehrmacht: 71. Infanterie-Division, 389. Infanterie-Division, 295. Infanterie-Division, 79. Infanterie-Division, 260. Infanterie-Division, 305. Infanterie-Division, 73. Infanterie-Division, 18. Infanterie-Division, 100. Jäger-Division, 94. Infanterie-Division, Germany: Books LLC, 2010, 187; David M. Glantz & Jonathan M. House, Armageddon in Stalingrad: September-November 1942, (The Stalingrad Trilogy, Volume 2), Lawrence, Kansas: University Press of Kansas, 2009, 52, 84-90; Joachim Lemelsen, 29. Division, Bad Nauheim, FRG: Podzun Verlag, 1960, 198; Jochen Löser, Bittere Pflicht: Kampf und Untergang der 76. Berlin-Brandenburgischen Infanterie-Division, Osnabrück, FRG: Biblio Verlag, 1986, 208; Jason Mark, Death of the Leaping Horseman: 24. Panzer-Division in Stalingrad, Sydney, Australia: Leaping Horsemen Books, 2003, 146-148; Kurt Mehner, Die Geheimen Tagesberichte der Deutschen Wehrmachtführung im Zweiten Weltkrieg 1939-1945, Band 5: 1. Juni 1942 – 30. November 1942, Osnabrück, Germany: Biblio Verlag, 1991, 186; Anton Schimak, Karl Lamprecht & Friedrich Dettmer, Die 44. Infanterie Division: Tagebuch der Hoch- und Deutschmeister, Wien: Verlag Austria Press, 169, 233 and Map: Marschweg der 44. Infanterie Division im Russland; Franz Thomas, & Günter Wegmann, Die Ritterkreuzträger der Deutschen Wehrmacht, 1939-1945, Teil 1: Sturmartillerie, Osnabrück, FRG: Biblio Verlag, 1985, 218.

Fern von der Heimat starb bei den Kämpfen in Sowjet-Rußland unser lieber guter Sohn und Bruder

Anton Knoll

Gefreiter u. MG.-Schütze in einem Inf.-Rgt.
Inhaber des EK. II und des Inf.-Sturmabzeichens.
Teilnehmer an den Feldzügen in Polen und Sowjet-Rußland.

Geboren am 17. Oktober 1912 in Rufen.
Gefallen am 10. September 1942 bei Stalingrad.

Du warst so gut, du starbst zu früh,
Wer dich gekannt, vergißt dich nie.

Barmherziger Jesus gib ihm die ewige Ruhe!
Vater unser. Ave Maria.

Mindelheimer Neueste Nachrichten

Gefreiter **Anton Knoll** was born in Oberkammlach near Memmingen in Bavaria on October 17, 1912. A veteran of the Polish Campaign and a machine-gunner in an infantry regiment, he had received the Iron Cross 2nd Class and the Infantry Assault Badge. Knoll was killed in action two miles west of Stalingrad on September 10, 1942. He is listed in the remembrance book at the German Military Cemetery at Rossoschka.

Obergefreiter **Helwig Felix Walter Paul Selig** was born in Kassel in Hesse on April 10, 1920. Assigned to the 15th Infantry Regiment (Motorized) of the 29th Infantry Division (Motorized), he was killed in action just south of Stalingrad on September 10, 1942. He is buried at the German Military Cemetery at Rossoschka in Block 5, Row 22, in Grave 858. His name is here shown on the family grave marker in Kassel, Germany.

September 11, 1942
Weather: warm, dry, increasing cloudiness, light overcast, 91° F, good road conditions
Sunrise: 5:32 a.m.; **Sunset:** 6:25 p.m.
Moon: Waxing Crescent; 1% illumination

Sixth Army – The army headquarters was located at Golubinskaya. The army reported 202 medium and 162 heavy anti-tank guns operational.

VIII Corps – The 521st ***Panzerjäger*** Detachment was assigned to the corps. The detachment reported eight medium and five heavy anti-tank guns operational.

76th Infantry Division – The division defended in sector southwest of Samofalovka and north of Borodkin against several enemy attacks from the 308th Rifle Division, the 298th Rifle Division, the 173rd Rifle Division and the 221st Rifle Division. To the northwest was the 305th Infantry Division; to the east was the 60th Infantry Division (Motorized.) The division reported 14 medium and 14 heavy anti-tank guns operational. The division lost five NCOs/enlisted killed in action; 32 NCOs/enlisted were wounded in action.

305th Infantry Division – The division defended in sector from the Don River, north of Nizhne-Gnilovskii, to west of Kotluban' against the 279th Rifle Division and the 27th Guards Rifle Division. To the southeast was the 76th Infantry Division; to the north was the 384th Infantry Division. The division reported 17 medium and 13 heavy anti-tank guns operational. The division lost four NCOs/enlisted killed in action; five NCOs/enlisted were wounded in action.

XI Corps – The 177th ***Sturmgeschütz*** Detachment, with seven Mark III-Long and four Mark III-Short assault guns operational, was assigned to the corps.

44th Infantry Division – The division defended in sector Kurchajessowskij-Kamyshinskiy-Hill 171.0-Hill 180.9-Sirotinskaya-Khmelevskoy against the 343rd Rifle Division and the 40th Guards Rifle Division. The division headquarters was located at Verkhne-Golubaja. To the west was 100th ***Jäger*** Division; to the east was the 384th Infantry Division. The division reported 11 medium and 20 heavy anti-tank guns operational. The division lost five NCOs/enlisted killed in action; six NCOs/enlisted were wounded in action.

100th Jäger Division – The division defended in sector near Blizhniaia-Perekopka against the 23rd Rifle Division. To the east was the 44th Infantry Division; to the west was the 376th Infantry Division. One-half of the division occupied an assembly area south of the sector at Verkhne-Golubaja. The division reported 14 medium and ten heavy anti-tank guns operational. The division lost one NCO/enlisted killed in action; six NCOs/enlisted wounded in action.

376th Infantry Division – The division defended in sector near Blizhniaia-Perekopka against the 321st Rifle Division. To the west, part of the 1st Romanian Cavalry Division began occupying a defensive sector; to the east was the 100th ***Jäger*** Division. The division reported five medium and 19 heavy anti-tank guns operational. The division lost one NCO/enlisted wounded in action.

384th Infantry Division – The division defended in sector west of the Don River near Trekhostrovskaia to Podgorskii against the 4th Guards Rifle Division and the 37th Guards Rifle Division. To the west was the 44th Infantry Division; to the south was the 305th Infantry Division. The division reported 12 medium and four heavy anti-tank guns operational. The division lost one NCO/enlisted killed in action; four NCOs/enlisted were wounded in action.

XIV *Panzer* Corps – The corps headquarters was located west of Nadezhda. The corps suffered the following officer casualties: two killed in action; six wounded in action.

3rd Infantry Division (Motorized) – The division defended in sector, from the Tartar Hill-Hill

111.1-Hill 129.6-Hill 131.2 against the 116th Rifle Division, the 84th Rifle Division, the 39th Guards Rifle Division, the 315th Rifle Division, the 64th Rifle Division and the 120th Rifle Division. To the east was the 16th ***Panzer*** Division; to the west was the 60th Infantry Division (Motorized.) The division reported seven medium and six heavy anti-tank guns operational. The division reported the following operational ***panzer*** strength: seven Mark II, 18 Mark III-Long and one Mark IV-Short tanks.

16th Panzer Division – The division defended in sector from Hill 139.7 to the Volga and from the Volga southwest to Hill 145.1, north of Orlovka against the 299th Rifle Division, the 64th Rifle Division and the 84th Rifle Division. On the south of the corridor, to the west were two battalions of the 60th Infantry Division (Motorized); on the north of the corridor, to the west was the 3rd Infantry Division (Motorized.) The division reported 21 medium and five heavy anti-tank guns operational. The division reported the following operational ***panzer*** strength: six Mark III-Short, 47 Mark III-Long and five Mark IV-Short tanks.

60th Infantry Division (Motorized) – The division defended in sector from south of Kotluban' Station near Borodkin to Kuz'michi against the 308th Rifle Division, the 39th Guards Rifle Division, the 316th Rifle Division, the 24th Rifle Division and the 207th Rifle Division. Along the southern corridor, to the east was the 16th ***Panzer*** Division; to the southwest was the 389th Infantry Division. Along the northern corridor, to the west was the 76th Infantry Division; to the east was the 3rd Infantry Division (Motorized.) The division reported 17 medium and five heavy anti-tank guns operational. The division reported the following operational ***panzer*** strength: five Mark II, 15 Mark III-Long and two Mark IV-Short tanks.

XVII Corps – The Romanian V Corps was subordinated to the corps.

22nd Panzer Division – The division occupied assembly areas south of the 79th Infantry Division. The division reported five medium and five heavy anti-tank guns operational. The division reported the following operational ***panzer*** strength: three Mark II, two Mark III-Long, one Mark IV-Short and 14 Mark 38(t) tanks.

79th Infantry Division – The division defended in sector Bol'shoy-Verkhne-Kalmykovskii-Verkhne-Fomichinskii-Baskowskij against the 124th Rifle Division and the 96th Rifle Division. The division headquarters was located at Karagichev. To the west was the XXXV Corps of the Italian Eighth Army; to the southeast was the 113th Infantry Division. The division lost four NCOs/enlisted killed in action; 12 NCOs/enlisted were wounded in action. The division reported ten medium and seven heavy anti-tank guns operational.

113th Infantry Division – The division defended in sector along the Don River west of Kletskiy against the 278th Rifle Division and the 76th Rifle Division. To the northwest was the 79th Infantry Division; to the east was an assortment of battle groups. The division reported 13 medium and ten heavy anti-tank guns operational. The division lost four NCOs/enlisted killed in action; 13 NCOs/enlisted were wounded in action.

298th Infantry Division – The division moved separately from the Romanian V Corps northeast along the Italian Eighth Army and Sixth Army boundary. The division reported 11 medium and 11 heavy anti-tank guns operational.

1st Romanian Cavalry Division – The division began to relieve elements of the 22nd ***Panzer*** Division from its defensive sector west of the 376th Infantry Division.

6th Romanian Infantry Division – The division moved northeast behind the 13th Romanian Infantry Division.

13th Romanian Infantry Division – The division moved northeast behind the 1st Romanian Cavalry Division.

LI Corps – The corps headquarters was located at Gumrak. The 244th ***Sturmgeschütz*** Detachment, with seven Mark III-Long and four Mark III-Short assault guns operational, and the 245th ***Sturmgeschütz*** Detachment, with six Mark III-Long and nine Mark III-Short assault guns operational, were assigned to the corps. The corps suffered the following officer casualties: two killed in action; six wounded in action.

71st Infantry Division – The division attacked in zone against fierce resistance by the 399th Rifle Division and the 95th Rifle Division. To the north was the 295th Infantry Division; to the south was the 24th ***Panzer*** Division. The division reported 13 medium and four heavy anti-tank guns operational. The division lost two officers and eight NCOs/enlisted killed in action; one officer and 22 NCOs/enlisted were wounded in action.

295th Infantry Division – The division attacked east in zone against the 112th Rifle Division. To the south was the 71st Infantry Division; to the north was the 389th Infantry Division. The division reported eight medium and ten heavy anti-tank guns operational. The division lost two NCOs/enlisted killed in action; 59 NCOs/enlisted were wounded in action; nine men were reported missing in action.

389th Infantry Division – The division attacked in zone southwest of Orlovka, reinforced by a tank detachment from the 16th ***Panzer*** Division. To the south was the 295th Infantry Division; to the northeast was Battle Group Stahel. The division headquarters was located just east of Nadezhda. The division reported 16 medium and nine heavy anti-tank guns operational. The division lost one officer and ten NCOs/enlisted killed in action; 80 NCOs/enlisted were wounded in action.

Battle Group Stahel – The battle group assumed the left zone of attack of the 389th Infantry Division to tie down enemy forces near Orlovka and allow the division to concentrate against the city of Stalingrad.

Fourth *Panzer* Army – The army headquarters was located at Plodowitoje.

IV Corps – The corps headquarters was located at Plantator.

297th Infantry Division – The division defended in sector south of Elkhi against the 38th Rifle Division and the 133rd Tank Brigade. To the north was the 20th Romanian Infantry Division; to the south was the 371st Infantry Division.

371st Infantry Division – The division defended in sector near Ivanovka and the Tundutovo Rail Station against the 36th Guards Rifle Division and the 422nd Rifle Division. To the north was the 297th Infantry Division; to the south was the 2nd Romanian Infantry Division of the Romanian VI Corps. The division lost four NCOs/enlisted killed in action; one officer and 16 NCOs/enlisted were wounded in action.

XXXXVIII *Panzer* Corps – The 53rd ***Werfer*** Regiment was assigned to support the corps.

14th Panzer Division – The division attacked east in zone against the 35th Guards Rifle Division. To the north was the 29th Infantry Division (Motorized); to the south was the 20th Romanian Infantry Division. The division lost 29 NCOs/enlisted killed in action; five officers and 109 NCOs/enlisted were wounded in action. The 2nd Battalion of the 72nd Artillery Regiment, the 1st Battalion of the 12th ***Flak*** Regiment and the 1st

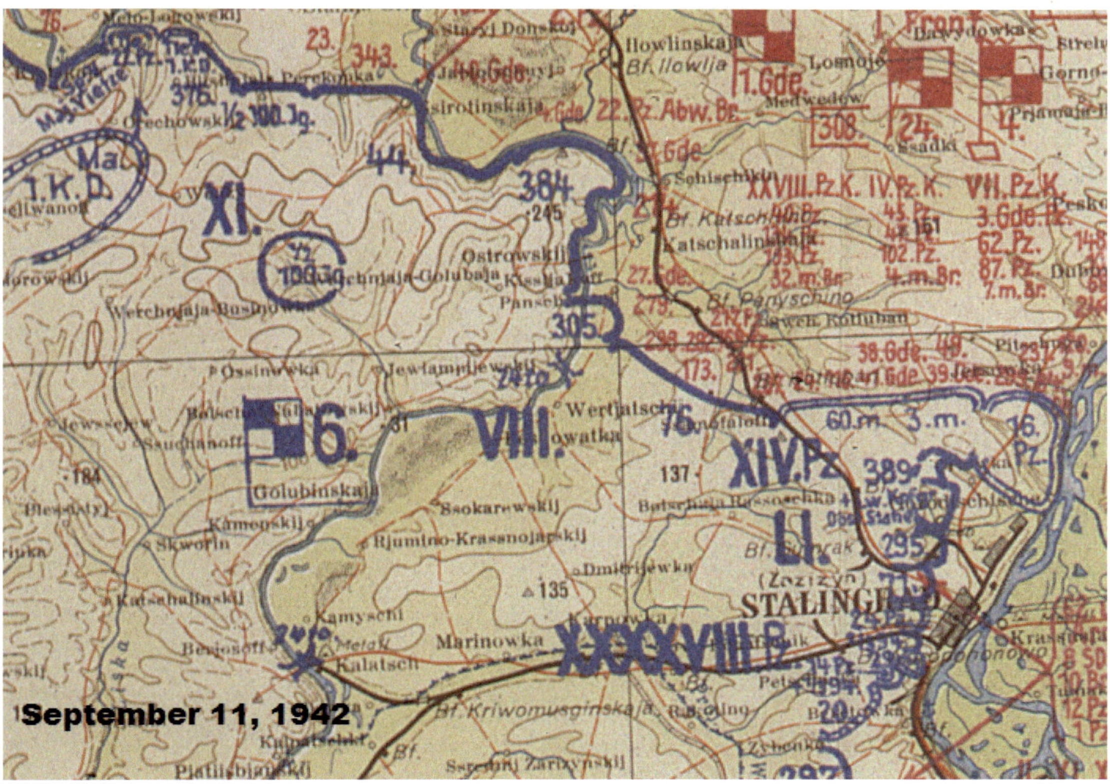

Battalion of the 25th ***Flak*** Regiment were attached to the division.

24th Panzer Division – The division consolidated its gains against the 244th Rifle Division and shortened its front. To the north was the 71st Infantry Division; to the south was the 94th Infantry Division. The division suffered eight NCOs/enlisted killed in action; one officer and 45 NCOs/enlisted were wounded in action. The division reported a combat strength of 8,714 men; it fielded only 14 operational tanks. The 635th Pioneer Battalion (Motorized), the 602nd ***Flak*** Detachment (Motorized) and the 670th ***Panzerjäger*** Detachment were attached to the division.

29th Infantry Division (Motorized) – The division attacked in zone, reaching a railway embankment against the 131st Rifle Division. Fierce fighting occurred in Kuperossnoje. To the north was the 94th Infantry Division; to the south was the 14th ***Panzer*** Division. The division lost one officer and nine NCOs/enlisted killed in action; 26 NCOs/enlisted were wounded in action.

94th Infantry Division – The division defended in sector between the 24th ***Panzer*** Division and the 29th Infantry Division (Motorized) against the 131st Rifle Division. The division lost seven NCOs/enlisted killed in action; 43 NCOs/enlisted were wounded in action. The 430th Heavy Artillery Detachment and the 1st Battalion of the 5th ***Flak*** Regiment were attached to the division.

20th Romanian Infantry Division – The division defended in sector west of Beketovka. To the south was the 297th Infantry Division; to the north was the 14th ***Panzer*** Division.

Another assault infantry squad in a balka outside of Stalingrad. Photo appears to have been taken in September 1942.

Sources, September 11, 1942: *Oberkommando des Heeres, Lage Ost: Stand: 11.9.42, Eastern Front Situation Map, National Archives Identifier: 559733, Record Group 242 – National Archives Collection of Foreign Records Seized, 1675-1958, National Archives, College Park, Maryland; Ia, Armeeoberkommando 6, "Morgen Meldung" and assorted reports, Kriegstagebuch 13, 12 September 1942, as found in Microfilm Series, T-312, Records of German Field Commands, Armies, Roll 1685, National Archives and Records Service, College Park, Maryland; Ia, XXXXVIII Panzerkorps, "Übersicht über die dem Korps Unterstellten Divisionen, 28. Juni 1942 – 11 October 1942," as found on T-314, Records of German Field Commands, Corps, Roll 1153, National Archives, College Park, Maryland; Korpsarzt, XXXXVIII Panzerkorps, "Meldung über Personelle Verluste," Stand 11.9.42, as found on T-314, Records of German Field Commands, Corps, Roll 1158, National Archives, College Park, Maryland; 79th Infantry Division, Kriegstagebuch, 11 September 1942, as found in Microfilm Series T-315, Roll 1108, National Archives and Records Service, College Park, Maryland; 371st Infantry Division, Kriegstagebuch, 11 September 1942, as found in Microfilm Series T-315, Roll 2164, National Archives and Records Service, College Park, Maryland; David M. Glantz & Jonathan M. House, Armageddon in Stalingrad: September-November 1942, (The Stalingrad Trilogy, Volume 2), Lawrence, Kansas: University Press of Kansas, 2009, 89-99; Joachim Lemelsen, 29. Division, Bad Nauheim, FRG: Podzun Verlag, 1960, 198; Jochen Löser, Bittere Pflicht: Kampf und Untergang der 76. Berlin-Brandenburgischen Infanterie-Division, Osnabrück, FRG: Biblio Verlag, 1986, 208; Jason Mark, Death of the Leaping Horseman: 24. Panzer-Division in Stalingrad, Sydney, Australia: Leaping Horsemen Books, 2003, 148-152; Kurt Mehner, Die Geheimen Tagesberichte der Deutschen Wehrmachtführung im Zweiten Weltkrieg 1939-1945, Band 5: 1. Juni 1942 – 30. November 1942, Osnabrück, Germany: Biblio Verlag, 1991, 188; Anton Schimak, Karl Lamprecht & Friedrich Dettmer, Die 44. Infanterie Division: Tagebuch der Hoch- und Deutschmeister, Wien: Verlag Austria Press, 169, 233 and Map: Marschweg der 44. Infanterie Division im Russland.*

September 12, 1942
Weather: clear and sunny, 90° F
Sunrise: 5:33 a.m.; **Sunset:** 6:23 p.m.
Moon: Waxing Crescent; 4% illumination

Sixth Army – The army headquarters was located at Golubinskaya.

VIII Corps – The corps suffered the following officer casualties: six wounded in action.

76th Infantry Division – The division defended in sector southwest of Samofalovka and north of Borodkin against several enemy attacks from the 308th Rifle Division, the 298th Rifle Division, the 173rd Rifle Division and the 221st Rifle Division. To the northwest was the 305th Infantry Division; to the east was the 60th Infantry Division (Motorized.) The division lost 16 NCOs/enlisted killed in action; 41 NCOs/enlisted were wounded in action.

305th Infantry Division – The division defended in sector from the Don River, north of Nizhne-Gnilovskii, to west of Kotluban' against the 279th Rifle Division. To the east was the 76th Infantry Division; to the north was the 384th Infantry Division. The division lost one officer and six NCOs/enlisted wounded in action.

XI Corps – The corps suffered the following officer casualties: one wounded in action.

44th Infantry Division – The division defended in sector Kurchajessowskij-Kamyshinskiy-Hill 171.0-Hill 180.9-Sirotinskaya-Khmelevskoy against the 343rd Rifle Division and the 40th Guards Rifle Division. The division headquarters was located at Verkhne-Golubaja. To the west was 100th ***Jäger*** Division; to the east was the 384th Infantry Division. The division lost six NCOs/enlisted killed in action; one officer and 22 NCOs/enlisted were wounded in action.

100th Jäger Division – The division defended in sector near Blizhniaia-Perekopka against the 23rd Rifle Division. To the east was the 44th Infantry Division; to the west was the 376th Infantry Division. One-half of the division occupied an assembly area south of the sector at Verkhne-Golubaja. The division lost seven NCOs/enlisted wounded in action.

376th Infantry Division – The division defended in sector near Blizhniaia-Perekopka against the 321st Rifle Division. To the west was the 1st Romanian Cavalry Division; to the east was the 100th ***Jäger*** Division.

384th Infantry Division – The division defended in sector west of the Don River near Trekhostrovskaia to Podgorskii against the 4th Guards Rifle Division and the 214th Rifle Division. To the west was the 44th Infantry Division; to the south was the 305th Infantry Division. The division lost three NCOs/enlisted wounded in action.

XIV *Panzer* Corps – The corps headquarters was located west of Nadezhda. The corps suffered the following officer casualties: three killed in action; three wounded in action.

3rd Infantry Division (Motorized) – The division defended in sector, from the Tartar Hill-Hill 111.1-Hill 129.6-Hill 131.2 against the 116th Rifle Division, the 84th Rifle Division, the 39th Guards Rifle Division, the 315th Rifle Division, the 64th Rifle Division and the 120th Rifle Division. To the east was the 16th ***Panzer*** Division; to the west was the 60th Infantry Division (Motorized.)

16th Panzer Division – The division defended in sector from Hill 139.7 to the Volga and from the Volga southwest to Hill 145.1, north of Orlovka against the 299th Rifle Division, the 84th Rifle Division and the 64th Rifle Division. On the south of the corridor, to the west was the 60th Infantry Division (Motorized), but this unit had only two battalions facing south. Along the northern corridor, to the west was the 3rd Infantry Division (Motorized.)

60th Infantry Division (Motorized) – The division defended in sector from south of Kotluban'

Station near Borodkin to Kuz'michi, against the 308th Rifle Division, the 39th Guards Rifle Division, the 316th Rifle Division, the 24th Rifle Division and the 207th Rifle Division. Along the southern corridor, to the east was the 16th ***Panzer*** Division; to the west was the 389th Infantry Division. Along the northern corridor, to the east was the 3rd Infantry Division (Motorized); to the west was the 76th Infantry Division.

XVII Corps – The Romanian V Corps was subordinated to the corps. The corps suffered the following officer casualties: three wounded in action.

22nd Panzer Division – The division began withdrawing from positions to become the Army Group B Reserve.

79th Infantry Division – The division defended in sector from Bol'shoy-Verkhne-Kalmykovskii-Verkhne-Fomichinskii-Baskowskij against the 124th Rifle Division and the 96th Rifle Division. The division headquarters was located at Karagichev. To the west was the XXXV Corps of the Italian Eighth Army; to the southeast was the 113th Infantry Division. The division lost 15 NCOs/enlisted killed in action; two officers and 52 NCOs/enlisted were wounded in action; one NCO/enlisted was reported missing in action.

113th Infantry Division – The division defended in sector along the Don River west of Kletskiy against the 278th Rifle Division and the 76th Rifle Division. To the northwest was the 79th Infantry Division; to the east were the 1st Romanian Cavalry Division and an assortment of battle groups. The division lost one NCO/enlisted killed in action; one officer and 15 NCOs/enlisted were wounded in action.

298th Infantry Division – The division moved separately from the Romanian V Corps northeast along the Italian Eighth Army and Sixth Army boundary.

1st Romanian Cavalry Division – The division defended in sector against the 63rd Rifle Division. To the west was the 376th Infantry Division; to the west were assorted battle groups.

6th Romanian Infantry Division – The division moved northeast behind the 13th Romanian Infantry Division.

13th Romanian Infantry Division – The division moved northeast; lead elements were located south of the 113th Infantry Division.

LI Corps – The corps headquarters was located at Gumrak. The corps suffered the following officer casualties: one killed in action; two wounded in action.

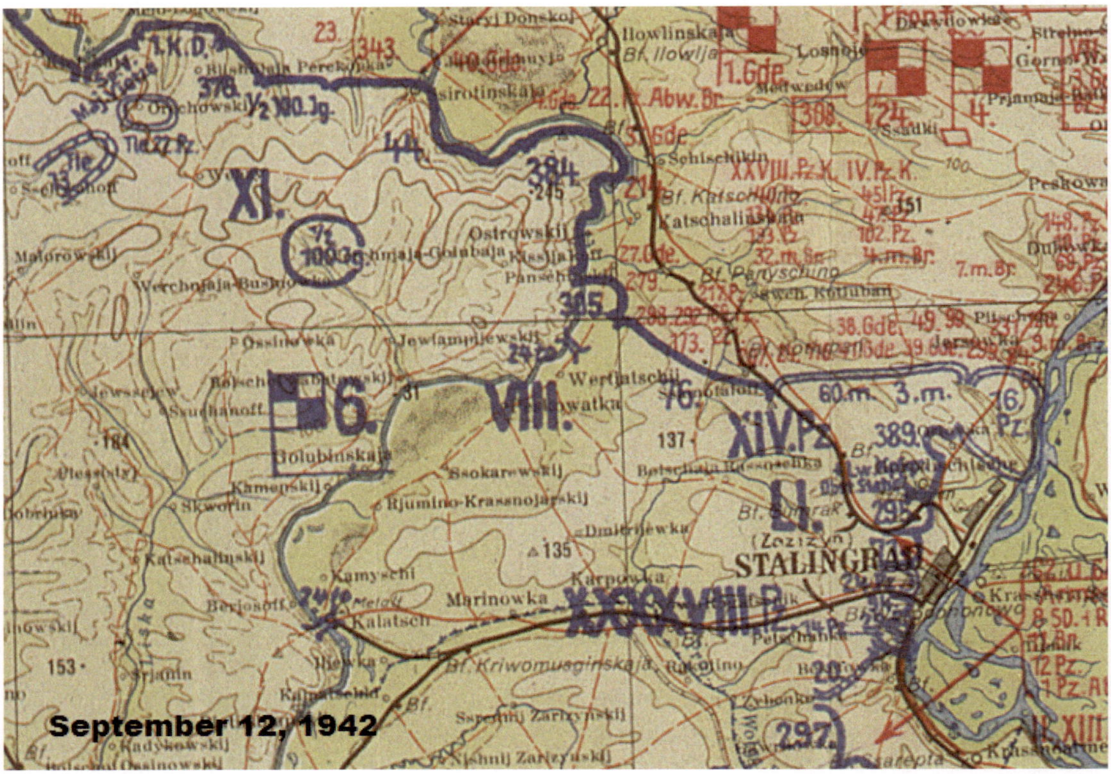

71st Infantry Division – The division attacked in zone west of the Krasny Oktyabr Workers' Settlement against the 112th Rifle Division. To the north was the 295th Infantry Division; to the south was the 24th ***Panzer*** Division. The division lost three NCOs/enlisted killed in action; 20 NCOs/enlisted were wounded in action.

295th Infantry Division – The division attacked east in zone at the Motor Tractor Station (one mile northeast of Razgulyayevka Station) against the 112th Rifle Division. To the south was the 71st Infantry Division; to the north was the 389th Infantry Division. The division lost one NCO/enlisted killed in action; 13 NCOs/enlisted were wounded in action.

389th Infantry Division – The division attacked in zone east of Gorodishche to southwest of Orlovka. To the south was the 295th Infantry Division. To the north was Battle Group Stahel. The division headquarters was located just east of Nadezhda.

Battle Group Stahel – The battle group defended in sector northwest of Orlovka to contain enemy forces.

Fourth *Panzer* Army – The army headquarters was located at Plodowitoje.

IV Corps – The corps headquarters was located at Plantator.

297th Infantry Division – The division defended in sector south of Elkhi against the 38th Rifle Division and the 133rd Tank Brigade. To the north was the 20th Romanian Infantry Division; to the south was the 371st Infantry Division.

371st Infantry Division – The division defended in sector near Ivanovka and the Tundutovo Rail Station against the 36th Guards Rifle Division and the 422nd Rifle Division. To the north was the 297th Infantry Division; to the south was the 2nd Romanian Infantry Division of the Romanian VI Corps. The division lost one NCO/enlisted killed in action; 13 NCOs/enlisted were wounded in action; one man was reported missing in action.

XXXXVIII *Panzer* Corps

14th Panzer Division – The division attacked east in zone into Kuporosnoye against the 35th Guards Rifle Division. To the north was the 29th Infantry Division (Motorized.) To the south was the 20th Romanian Infantry Division. The division then pulled west. The division lost ten NCOs/enlisted killed in action; 41 NCOs/enlisted were wounded in action; four NCOs/enlisted were reported missing in action.

24th Panzer Division – The division attacked in zone towards Stalingrad and reached the outer southwestern suburbs against the 131st Rifle Division. The division suffered one officer and 13 NCOs/enlisted killed in action; three officers and 135 NCOs/enlisted were wounded in action. To the north was the 71st Infantry Division of the Sixth Army; to the south was the 94th Infantry Division.

29th Infantry Division (Motorized) – The division attacked east in zone at Minina-Kuporosnoye against the 131st Rifle Division. To the north was the 94th Infantry Division; to the south was the 14th ***Panzer*** Division. The division lost three officers and 30 NCOs/enlisted killed in action; three officers and 133 NCOs/enlisted were wounded in action; nine NCOs/enlisted were reported missing in action.

94th Infantry Division – The division attacked east in zone to west of Sadovaia Station-Minina against the 131st Rifle Division. To the north was the 24th ***Panzer*** Division; to the south was the 29th Infantry Division (Motorized.) The division lost 20 NCOs/enlisted killed in action; 75 NCOs/enlisted were wounded in action; one NCO/enlisted was reported missing in action.

20th Romanian Infantry Division – The division defended in sector west of Gornaia-Poliana against the 157th Rifle Division. To the north was the 14th ***Panzer*** Division; to the south was the 297th Infantry Division.

Sources, September 12, 1942: ***Oberkommando des Heeres, Lage Ost: Stand: 12.9.42, Eastern Front Situation Map, National Archives Identifier: 559733, Record Group 242 – National Archives Collection of Foreign Records Seized, 1675-1958, National Archives, College Park, Maryland; Ia, Armeeoberkommando 6, "Morgen Meldung" and assorted reports, Kriegstagebuch 13, 13 September 1942, as found in Microfilm Series, T-312, Records of German Field Commands, Armies, Roll 1685, National Archives and Records Service, College Park, Maryland; Ia, XXXXVIII Panzerkorps, "Übersicht über die dem Korps Unterstellten Divisionen, 28. Juni 1942 – 11 October 1942," as found on T-314, Records of German Field Commands, Corps, Roll 1153, National Archives, College Park, Maryland; Korpsarzt, XXXXVIII Panzerkorps, "Meldung über Personelle Verluste," Stand 12.9.42, as found on T-314, Records of German Field Commands, Corps, Roll 1158, National Archives, College Park, Maryland; 79th Infantry Division, Kriegstagebuch, 12 September 1942, as found in Microfilm Series T-315, Roll 1108, National Archives and Records Service, College Park, Maryland; 371st Infantry Division, Kriegstagebuch, 12 September 1942, as found in Microfilm Series T-315, Roll 2164, National Archives and Records Service, College Park, Maryland; David M. Glantz & Jonathan M. House, Armageddon in Stalingrad: September-November 1942, (The Stalingrad Trilogy, Volume 2), Lawrence, Kansas:***

University Press of Kansas, 2009, 92-94, 101-104; Joachim Lemelsen, 29. Division, Bad Nauheim, FRG: Podzun Verlag, 1960, 199; Jochen Löser, Bittere Pflicht: Kampf und Untergang der 76. Berlin-Brandenburgischen Infanterie-Division, Osnabrück, FRG: Biblio Verlag, 1986, 208; Jason Mark, Death of the Leaping Horseman: 24. Panzer-Division in Stalingrad, Sydney, Australia: Leaping Horsemen Books, 2003, 152-156; Anton Schimak, Karl Lamprecht & Friedrich Dettmer, Die 44. Infanterie Division: Tagebuch der Hoch- und Deutschmeister, Wien: Verlag Austria Press, 169, 233 and Map: Marschweg der 44. Infanterie Division im Russland.

Letter from "Rudi" to his girlfriend Maria in Mainz dated September 12, 1942. Rudi was a lieutenant and the commander of the 13th Company in the 669th Infantry Regiment of the 371st Infantry Division. In his letter, he writes:

> "Tomorrow it will be 2 weeks since I have had mail from you. What is the matter? Are you pressed for time, or? Please remember, we are here fighting an enormous battle, far from home, and every little card or letter is doubly welcome. Please, let me hear from you. I do not complain; I am well, but other comrades are starting to get worried. I am confident that we will win this struggle but then: 'don't praise the day before the evening.' Much could happen, but believe me; it will be all over before winter arrives. The weather is still good, except at night it gets cooler. Please send me some writing paper and a pencil; these things have become luxuries here now. Many kisses and greetings."

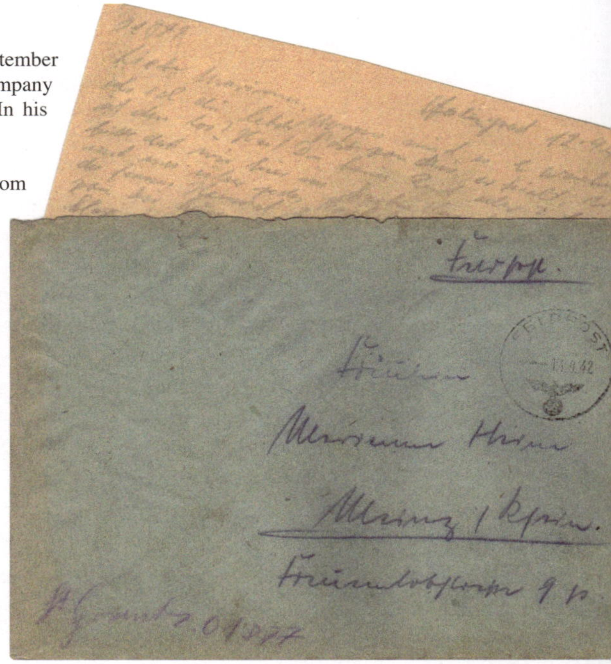

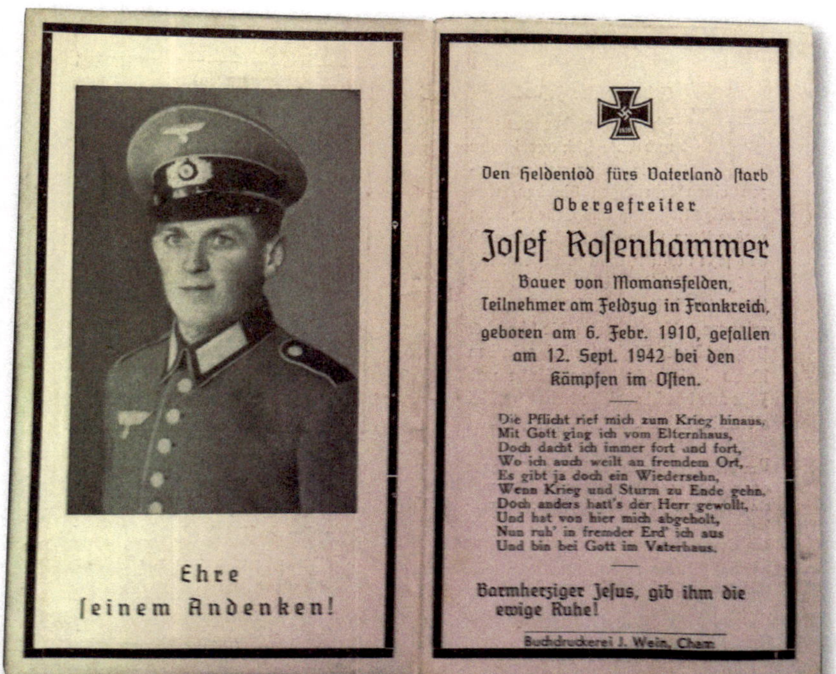

Ehre
seinem Andenken!

Den Heldentod fürs Vaterland starb
Obergefreiter
Josef Rosenhammer
Bauer von Momansfelden,
Teilnehmer am Feldzug in Frankreich,
geboren am 6. Febr. 1910, gefallen
am 12. Sept. 1942 bei den
Kämpfen im Osten.

Die Pflicht rief mich zum Krieg hinaus,
Mit Gott ging ich vom Elternhaus,
Doch dacht ich immer fort und fort,
Wo ich auch weilt an fremdem Ort,
Es gibt ja doch ein Wiedersehn,
Wenn Krieg und Sturm zu Ende gehn.
Doch anders hatt's der Herr gewollt,
Und hat von hier mich abgeholt,
Nun ruh' in fremder Erd' ich aus
Und bin bei Gott im Vaterhaus.

Barmherziger Jesus, gib ihm die
ewige Ruhe!

Buchdruckerei J. Wein, Cham

Obergefreiter* Josef Rosenhammer** was born in Momannsfelden near Roding, Bavaria on February 2, 1910. A participant in the French and Russian Campaigns, and assigned to the 16th ***Panzer Division, he was killed in action near Jersovka. He was buried near Orlovka, but his remains were never found after the war.

September 13, 1942
Weather: clear and warm, 93° F
Sunrise: 5:34 a.m.; **Sunset:** 6:21 p.m.
Moon: Waxing Crescent; 9% illumination

Sixth Army – Bombers and dive-bombers from the ***Luftwaffe***'s VIII Air Corps pounded Stalingrad in large-scale attacks. The army headquarters was located at Golubinskaya. In Moscow, Soviet leaders began to contemplate a counter-offensive to entrap the Sixth Army at Stalingrad.

VIII Corps – The corps suffered the following officer casualties: four wounded in action.

76th Infantry Division – The division defended in sector southwest of Samofalovka and north of Borodkin against several enemy attacks by the 308th Rifle Division, the 173rd Rifle Division and the 298th Rifle Division. To the northwest was the 305th Infantry Division; to the east was the 60th Infantry Division (Motorized.) The division lost nine NCOs/enlisted killed in action; 40 NCOs/enlisted were wounded in action.

305th Infantry Division – The division defended in sector from the Don River, north of Nizhne-Gnilovskii, to west of Kotluban' against the 27th Guards Rifle Division and the 279th Rifle Division. To the southeast was the 76th Infantry Division; to the north was the 384th Infantry Division. The division suffered three officers and five NCOs/enlisted wounded in action.

XI Corps – The 177th ***Sturmgeschütz*** Detachment, with ten Mark III-Long and four Mark III-Short assault guns operational, was assigned to the corps. The corps suffered the following officer casualties: one killed in action; one wounded in action.

44th Infantry Division – The division defended in sector Kurchajessowskij-Kamyshinskiy-Hill 171.0-Hill 180.9-Sirotinskaya-Khmelevskoy against the 343rd Rifle Division, repelling a night attack at 2:00 a.m. The division headquarters was located at Verkhne-Golubaja. To the west was 100th ***Jäger*** Division; to the east was the 384th Infantry Division. The division lost four NCOs/enlisted killed in action; one officer and 21 NCOs/enlisted were wounded in action.

100th Jäger Division – The division defended in sector near Blizhniaia-Perekopka against the 23rd Rifle Division. To the east was the 44th Infantry Division; to the west was the 376th Infantry Division. One-half of the division occupied an assembly area south of the sector at Verkhne-Golubaja. The division lost two NCOs/enlisted killed in action; nine NCOs/enlisted were wounded in action.

376th Infantry Division – The division defended in sector near Blizhniaia-Perekopka against the 321st Rifle Division. To the west was the 1st Romanian Cavalry Division; to the east was the 100th ***Jäger*** Division.

384th Infantry Division – The division defended in sector west of the Don River near Trekhostrovskaia to Podgorskii against the 4th Guards Rifle Division and the 37th Guards Rifle Division. To the west was the 44th Infantry Division; to the south was the 305th Infantry Division. The division lost two NCOs/enlisted wounded in action.

XIV *Panzer* Corps – The corps headquarters was located west of Nadezhda. The corps suffered the following officer casualties: two killed in action; two wounded in action.

3rd Infantry Division (Motorized) – The division defended in sector, from the Tartar Hill-Hill 111.1-Hill 129.6-Hill 131.2. The division repelled several enemy attacks by the 38th Guards Rifle Division, the 39th Guards Rifle Division and the 41st Guards Rifle Division. To the east was the 16th ***Panzer*** Division; to the west was the 60th Infantry Division (Motorized.)

16th Panzer Division – The division defended in sector from Hill 139.7 to the Volga and from the Volga southwest to Hill 145.1, north of Orlovka against the 299th Rifle Division, the 84th Rifle Division and the 64th Rifle Division. On the south of the corridor, to the west were two battalions of the 60th Infantry Division (Motorized); along the north of the corridor to the west was the 3rd Infantry Division (Motorized.)

60th Infantry Division (Motorized) – The division defended in sector, from south of Kotluban' Station near Borodkin to Kuz'michi against the 308th Rifle Division, the 24th Rifle Division and the 116th Rifle Division. To the east was the 16th ***Panzer*** Division; to the west was the 76th Infantry Division.

XVII Corps – The Romanian V Corps was subordinated to the corps. The corps suffered the following officer casualties: one accidental death.

79th Infantry Division – The division defended in sector from Bol'shoy-Verkhne-Kalmykovskii-Verkhne-Fomichinskii-Baskowskij against the 124th Rifle Division and the 96th Rifle Division. The division headquarters was located at Karagichev. To the west was the XXXV Corps of the Italian Eighth Army; to the southeast was the 113th Infantry Division. The division suffered two NCOs/enlisted killed in action; five NCOs/enlisted were wounded in action.

113th Infantry Division – The division defended in sector along the Don River west of Kletskiy against the 278th Rifle Division and the 76th Rifle Division. To the northwest was the 79th Infantry Division; to the east were assorted battle groups and the 1st Romanian Cavalry Division. The division lost one NCO/enlisted killed in action; five NCOs/enlisted were wounded in action.

298th Infantry Division – The division moved separately from the Romanian V Corps northeast along the Italian Eighth Army and the Sixth Army boundary.

1st Romanian Cavalry Division – The division defended in sector near Mołologowskij against the 63rd Rifle Division. To the west was the 113th Infantry Division; to the east was the 376th Infantry Division.

6th Romanian Infantry Division – The division moved northeast behind the 13th Romanian Infantry Division.

13th Romanian Infantry Division – The division moved northeast; lead elements were located southeast of the 113th Infantry Division.

LI Corps – Corps elements captured Gorodishche, Alexandrovka and Aviagorodok. The 244th ***Sturmgeschütz*** Detachment, with three Mark III-Long and three Mark III-Short assault guns operational, and the 245th ***Sturmgeschütz*** Detachment, with eight Mark III-Long and nine Mark III-Short assault guns operational, were assigned to the corps. The corps suffered the following officer casualties: six killed in action; 27 wounded in action. Corps artillery was located just west of Razgulyayevka.

71st Infantry Division – The division attacked in zone and reached the Brick Works, capturing Aviagorodok and reaching the approaches to Hill 112.5 against the 133rd Tank Brigade. To the north was the 295th Infantry Division; to the south was the 24th ***Panzer*** Division. The division lost two officers and 31 NCOs/enlisted killed in action; five officers and 169 NCOs/enlisted were wounded in action; four NCOs/enlisted were reported missing in action.

295th Infantry Division – The division attacked in zone south of Gorodishche, capturing Hill 126.3 and Hill 153.7 against the 38th Naval Infantry Brigade. The division suffered three officers and 47 NCOs/enlisted killed in action; ten officers and 224 NCOs/enlisted were wounded in action; two NCOs/enlisted were reported missing in action. To the south was the 71st Infantry Division; to the north was the 389th Infantry Division.

389th Infantry Division – The division attacked in zone, reaching east of Gorodishche and pushing a regiment into Razgulyayevka. To the south was the 295th Infantry Division; to the northeast was Battle Group Stahel. The division headquarters was located just east of Nadezhda. The division lost one officer and 27 NCOs/enlisted killed in action; five officers and 159 NCOs/enlisted were wounded in action.

Battle Group Stahel – The battle group defended northwest of Orlovka to contain enemy forces.

Fourth *Panzer* Army – The army headquarters was located at Plodowitoje.

IV Corps – The corps headquarters was located at Plantator.

297th Infantry Division – The division defended in sector south of Elkhi against the 38th Rifle Division and the 133rd Tank Brigade. To the north was the 20th Romanian Infantry Division; to the south was the 371st Infantry Division.

371st Infantry Division – The division defended in sector near Ivanovka and the Tundutovo Rail Station against the 36th Guards Rifle Division. To the north was the 297th Infantry Division; to the south was the 2nd Romanian Infantry Division of the Romanian VI Corps. The division lost one NCO/enlisted killed in action; five NCOs/enlisted were wounded in action; three men were reported missing in action.

XXXXVIII *Panzer* Corps

14th Panzer Division – The division attacked in zone in the vicinity of Verkhne-El'shanka against a hill southeast of Peschanka held by the 35th Guards Rifle Division. The division repelled strong enemy infantry attacks in the morning and late afternoon, as it attempted to maintain contact with the 29th Infantry Division (Motorized) to the north. To the south was the 20th Romanian Infantry Division. The division lost two officers and 26 NCOs/enlisted killed in action; two officers and 56 NCOs/enlisted were wounded in action.

24th Panzer Division – The division consolidated its positions and repelled an attack by the 244th Rifle Division. The division lost 26 NCOs/enlisted killed in action; one officer and 83 NCOs/enlisted were wounded in action. To the north was the 71st Infantry Division; to the south was the 94th Infantry Division.

29th Infantry Division (Motorized) – The division attacked in zone, capturing the southwest section of Minina from the 35th Guards Rifle Division and the 131st Rifle Division. The division lost two officers and 28 NCOs/enlisted killed in action; 85 NCOs/enlisted were wounded in action. To the north was the 94th Infantry Division; to the south was the 14th ***Panzer*** Division.

94th Infantry Division – The division attacked in zone, reaching the western outskirts of Minina against the 131st Rifle Division, the 271st NKVD Regiment and the 10th Replacement Rifle Brigade. The division lost 66 NCOs/enlisted killed in action; eight officers and 175 NCOs/enlisted were wounded in action; three NCOs/enlisted were reported missing in action. To the north was the 24th ***Panzer*** Division; to the south was the 29th Infantry Division (Motorized.)

20th Romanian Infantry Division – The division defended in sector west of Gornaia-Poliana against the 157th Rifle Division. To the north was the 14th ***Panzer*** Division; to the south was the 297th Infantry Division.

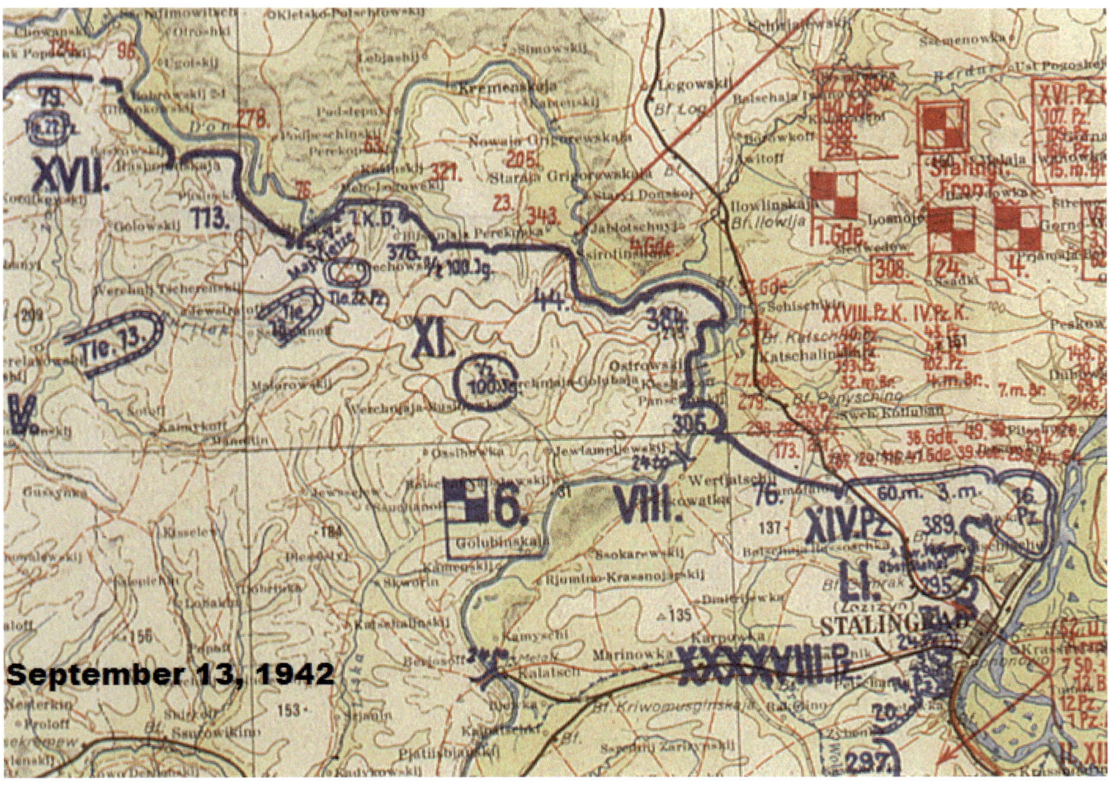

Sources, September 13, 1942: *Oberkommando des Heeres, Lage Ost: Stand: 13.9.42, Eastern Front Situation Map, National Archives Identifier: 559733, Record Group 242 – National Archives Collection of Foreign Records Seized, 1675-1958, National Archives, College Park, Maryland; Ia, Armeeoberkommando 6, "Morgen Meldung" and assorted reports, Kriegstagebuch 13, 14 September 1942, as found in Microfilm Series, T-312, Records of German Field Commands, Armies, Roll 1685, National Archives and Records Service, College Park, Maryland; Ia, XXXXVIII Panzerkorps, "Übersicht über die dem Korps Unterstellten Divisionen, 28. Juni 1942 – 11 October 1942," as found on T-314, Records of German Field Commands, Corps, Roll 1153, National Archives, College Park, Maryland; Korpsarzt, XXXXVIII Panzerkorps, "Meldung über Personelle Verluste," Stand 13.9.42, as found on T-314, Records of German Field Commands, Corps, Roll 1158, National Archives, College Park, Maryland; 79th Infantry Division, Kriegstagebuch, 13 September 1942, as found in Microfilm Series T-315, Roll 1108, National Archives and Records Service, College Park, Maryland; 371st Infantry Division, Kriegstagebuch, 13 September 1942, as found in Microfilm Series T-315, Roll 2164, National Archives and Records Service, College Park, Maryland; Florian Freiherr von und zu Aufsess, Die Anlagenbände zu den Kriegstagebüchern der 6. Armee vom 14.09.1942 bis 24.11.1942, Band 1, Schwabach, Germany: Selbstverlag, 2006, 6, 27; John Erickson, The Road to Stalingrad, New York: Harper & Row, 1975, 390-391; Die 71. Infanterie-Division, 1939-1945: Gefechts- und Erlebnisberichte aus Kämpfen der "Gluckhaften Division" von Verdun bis Stalingrad, vom Monte Cassino bis zum Plattensee, Eggolsheim, FRG: Edition Dörfler, 1973, 238; David M. Glantz & Jonathan M. House, Armageddon in Stalingrad: September-November 1942, (The Stalingrad Trilogy, Volume 2), Lawrence, Kansas: University Press of Kansas, 2009, 101-117; Joachim Lemelsen, 29. Division, Bad Nauheim, FRG: Podzun Verlag, 1960, 202; Jochen Löser, Bittere Pflicht: Kampf und Untergang der 76. Berlin-Brandenburgischen Infanterie-Division, Osnabrück, FRG: Biblio Verlag, 1986, 208; Jason Mark, Death of the Leaping Horseman: 24. Panzer-Division in Stalingrad, Sydney, Australia: Leaping Horsemen Books, 2003, 156-159; Janusz Piekalkiewicz, Stalingrad: Anatomie einer Schlacht, München, BRD: Wilhelm Heyne Verlag, 1977, 192; Anton Schimak, Karl Lamprecht & Friedrich Dettmer, Die 44. Infanterie Division: Tagebuch der Hoch- und Deutschmeister, Wien: Verlag Austria Press, 169, 233 and Map: Marschweg der 44. Infanterie Division im Russland.*

Gefreiter **Josef Walter** was born in Röfingen near Günzburg, Bavaria on April 10, 1922. Assigned to an infantry regiment, he was killed in action near Stalingrad on September 13, 1942. He is listed in the remembrance book at the German Military Cemetery at Rossoschka.

Gefreiter **Max Engl** was born near Regensburg, Bavaria on February 20, 1906. Assigned to an infantry regiment, he was killed in action on September 13, 1942 at Alexandrovka, probably with the 295th Infantry Division. He is listed in the remembrance book at the German Military Cemetery at Rossoschka.

September 14, 1942
Weather: cloudy, afternoon light rain showers, 95° F
Sunrise: 5:36 a.m.; **Sunset:** 6:19 p.m.
Moon: Waxing Crescent; 17% illumination

Sixth Army – The army headquarters was located at Golubinskaya. ***General der Panzertruppe*** Paulus visited the LI Corps and the 389th Infantry Division. The OKH informed the army that Hitler had decided that the 22nd ***Panzer*** Division and the 113th Infantry Division would not be available for use in Stalingrad, due to the enemy situation opposite the Italian Eighth Army.

VIII Corps – The corps suffered the following officer casualties: two killed in action; one wounded in action.

76th Infantry Division – The division defended in sector southwest of Samofalovka and north of Borodkin against several enemy attacks by the 308th Rifle Division, the 298th Rifle Division, 292nd Rifle Division and the 173rd Rifle Division. To the northwest was the 305th Infantry Division; to the east was the 60th Infantry Division (Motorized.) The division reported that of its nine infantry battalions, five were medium-strong and four average in combat power, while the combat engineer battalion was average in combat power. The division lost six NCOs/enlisted killed in action; 22 NCOs/enlisted were wounded in action.

305th Infantry Division – The division defended in sector from the Don River, north of Nizhne-Gnilovskii, to west of Kotluban' against the 27th Guards Rifle Division and the 279th Rifle Division. To the southeast was the 76th Infantry Division; to the north was the 384th Infantry Division. The division reported that of its nine infantry battalions, three were strong, two were medium-strong and four were average in combat power, while the combat engineer battalion was average in combat power. The division lost two officers and eight NCOs/enlisted killed in action; nine NCOs/enlisted were wounded in action.

XI Corps

44th Infantry Division – The division defended in sector Kurchajessowskij-Kamyshinskiy-Hill 171.0-Hill 180.9-Sirotinskaya-Khmelevskoy against the 343rd Rifle Division. The division headquarters was located at Verkhne-Golubaja. To the west was 100th ***Jäger*** Division; to the east was the 384th Infantry Division. The division reported that of its nine infantry battalions, seven were average and two were weak in combat power, while the combat engineer battalion was average in combat power. The division lost one NCO/enlisted killed in action; 24 NCOs/enlisted were wounded in action.

100th Jäger Division – Part of the division defended in sector near Blizhniaia-Perekopka against the 23rd Rifle Division. To the east was the 44th Infantry Division; to the west was the 376th Infantry Division. Much of the division now occupied an assembly area near Verkhne-Golubaja. The division reported that of its four infantry battalions, all four were strong in combat power, while the combat engineer battalion was also strong in combat power. The division lost one NCO/enlisted wounded in action; one NCO/enlisted was wounded in action.

376th Infantry Division – The division defended in sector near Blizhniaia-Perekopka. To the west was the 1st Romanian Cavalry Division; to the east was the 100th ***Jäger*** Division. The division reported that of its seven infantry battalions, six were average and one was weak in combat power, while the combat engineer battalion was average in combat power. The division lost one NCO/enlisted wounded in action.

384th Infantry Division – The division defended in sector west of the Don River near Trekhostrovskaia to Podgorskii against the 4th Guards Rifle Division and the 214th Rifle Division. To the west was the 44th Infantry Division; to the south was the 305th Infantry Division. The division reported that of its six infantry battalions, three were strong, one was medium-strong and two were average in combat power, while the combat engineer battalion posted a rating of strong in combat power. The division lost two NCOs/enlisted wounded in action.

XIV *Panzer* Corps – ***General der Infanterie*** Anton von Wietersheim was relieved of command of the corps for suggesting a withdrawal from Stalingrad. The corps headquarters was located west of Nadezhda. The corps suffered the following officer casualties: three wounded in action.

3rd Infantry Division (Motorized) – The division defended in sector, from the Tartar Hill-Hill 111.1-Hill 129.6-Hill 131.2 against the 39th Guards Rifle Division and the 41st Guards Rifle Division. To the east was the 16th ***Panzer*** Division; to the west was the 60th Infantry Division (Motorized.) The division reported that of its five motorized infantry battalions, two were medium-strong, two were average and one was weak in combat power; the division combat engineer battalion was weak in combat power. The division lost seven NCOs/enlisted killed in action; 16 NCOs/enlisted were wounded in action.

16th Panzer Division – The division defended in sector from Hill 139.7 to the Volga and from the Volga southwest to Hill 145.1, north of Orlovka against the 299th Rifle Division, the 64th Rifle Division and the 84th Rifle Division. Along the north of the corridor, to the west was the 3rd Infantry Division (Motorized); on the south of the corridor, to the west was the 60th Infantry Division (Motorized.) The division reported that of its five ***panzer*** grenadier battalions, three were medium-strong and two average in combat power, while the combat engineer battalion was average in combat power.

60th Infantry Division (Motorized) – The division defended in sector from south of Kotluban' Station near Borodkin to Kuz'michi against the 308th Rifle Division, the 24th Rifle Division and the 116th Rifle Division. Along the north of the corridor, to the east was the 3rd Infantry Division (Motorized); to the west was the 76th Infantry Division. The division reported that of its seven motorized infantry battalions, one was medium-strong and six were average in combat power; the division combat engineer battalion was reported average in combat power.

XVII Corps – The Romanian V Corps was subordinated to the corps.

79th Infantry Division – The division defended in sector from Bol'shoy-Verkhne-Kalmykovskii-Verkhne-Fomichinskii-Baskowskij against the 124th Rifle Division and the 96th Rifle Division. The division headquarters was located at Karagichev. To the west was the XXXV Corps of the Italian Eighth Army; to the southeast was the 113th Infantry Division. The division suffered two NCOs/enlisted wounded in action. The division reported that of its nine infantry battalions, six were average and three were weak in combat power, while the combat engineer battalion was average in combat power.

113th Infantry Division – The division defended in sector along the Don River west of Kletskiy against the 278th Rifle Division and the 76th Rifle Division, and began to turn over responsibility for its sector to the 13th Romanian Infantry Division. To the northwest was the 79th Infantry Division; to the southeast were an assortment of battle groups and the 1st Romanian Cavalry Division. The division lost two NCOs/enlisted killed in action and two NCOs/enlisted wounded in action. The division reported that of its eight infantry battalions, five were strong and three were medium-strong in combat power, while the combat engineer battalion was average in combat power.

298th Infantry Division – The division occupied an assembly area along the Sixth Army's western boundary, behind the front line. The division reported that of its six infantry battalions, all six were strong in combat power; the combat engineer battalion was also strong in combat power.

1st Romanian Cavalry Division – The division defended in sector near Molologowskij against the 63rd Rifle Division. To the west were several battle groups; to the east was the 376th Infantry Division. The division reported that of its four cavalry detachments (battalions), all four were strong in combat power. The division was under the command of Brigadier General Constantin Brătescu.

6th Romanian Infantry Division – The division moved northeast behind the 13th Romanian Infantry Division.

13th Romanian Infantry Division – The division began to assume the defensive sector of the 113th Infantry Division along the Don River. The division reported that of its seven infantry battalions, all seven were strong in combat power.

LI Corps – The 245th ***Sturmgeschütz*** Detachment was assigned to the corps. The corps suffered the following officer casualties: two killed in action; 22 wounded in action. The corps headquarters was located three miles southwest of Gorodishche.

71st Infantry Division – The division initially repelled an enemy counterattack from the 399th Rifle Division; it then attacked in zone, seizing Hill 112.5, and reached Stalingrad's Central Railway Station at noon (the station changed hands at least five times that day), with one regiment reaching the Volga River and encountering the 13th Guards Rifle Division. The division also seized the waterworks. The 245th ***Sturmgeschütz*** Detachment was attached to the division. To the north was the 295th Infantry Division; to the south was the 24th ***Panzer*** Division. The division lost 38 NCOs/enlisted killed in action; six officers and 120 NCOs/enlisted were wounded in action; one man was reported missing in action. The division reported that all eight infantry battalions were weak in combat power, while the combat engineer battalion was average in combat power. The division headquarters was located three miles southwest of Gorodishche.

295th Infantry Division – The division initially repelled an enemy counterattack from the 10th NKVD Division; it then attacked northeast in zone and reached the Volga River. To the south was the 71st Infantry Division; to the north was the 389th Infantry Division. The division suffered one officer and 17 NCOs/enlisted killed in action; seven officers and 157 NCOs/enlisted were wounded in action; one man was reported missing in action. The division reported that of its seven infantry battalions, two were medium-strong, three were average and two were weak in combat power; the division rated its combat engineer battalion as average.

389th Infantry Division – The division attacked northeast in zone and seized Hill 98.9. The division lost one officer and 44 NCOs/enlisted killed in action; six officers and 140 NCOs/enlisted were wounded in action. The division reported that of its six infantry battalions, one was medium-strong, three were average and two were weak in combat power; the division rated its combat engineer battalion as average. To the south was the 295th Division; to the northeast was Battle Group Stahel. The division headquarters was located one mile west of Schischjankin.

Battle Group Stahel – The battle group defended northwest of Orlovka to contain enemy forces.

Fourth *Panzer* Army – The army headquarters was located at Plodowitoje.

IV Corps – The corps headquarters was located at Plantator.

297th Infantry Division – The division defended in sector south of Elkhi against the 38th Rifle Division and the 133rd Tank Brigade. To the north was the 20th Romanian Division; to the south was the 371st Infantry Division.

371st Infantry Division – The division defended in sector near the Volga-Don Canal against the 36th Guards Rifle Division. The division lost two NCOs/enlisted killed in action; eight NCOs/enlisted were wounded in action. To the north was the 297th Infantry Division; to the south was the 2nd Romanian Infantry Division of the Romanian VI Corps.

XXXXVIII *Panzer* Corps

14th Panzer Division – The division attacked in zone near Verkhne-El'shanka against the 35th Guards Rifle Division. To the northwest was the 29th Infantry Division (Motorized); to the south was the 20th Romanian Infantry Division. The division lost four NCOs/enlisted killed in action; 30 NCOs/enlisted were wounded in action.

24th Panzer Division – The division attacked east in zone to the north of the El'shanka River against the 244th Rifle Division. To the north was the 71st Infantry Division; to the south was the 94th Infantry Division. The division lost five NCOs/enlisted killed in action; 29 NCOs/enlisted were wounded in action.

29th Infantry Division (Motorized) – The division attacked northeast in zone to seize northern Kuporosnoye and attempted to clear the 35th Guards Rifle Division from eastern Kuporosnoye. To the northwest was the 94th Infantry Division; to the south was the 14th ***Panzer*** Division. The division lost three officers and 35 NCOs/enlisted killed in action; three officers and 107 NCOs/enlisted were wounded in action; 30 NCOs/enlisted were reported missing in action.

94th Infantry Division – The division attacked to the northeast to seize Minina and El'shanka against elements of the 244th Rifle Division, the 271st NKVD Regiment and the 131st Rifle Division. To the north was the 24th ***Panzer*** Division; to the southeast was the 29th Infantry Division (Motorized.) The division lost two officers and 18 NCOs/enlisted killed in action; one officer and 69 NCOs/enlisted were wounded in action.

20th Romanian Infantry Division – The division defended in sector west of Beketovka against the 157th Rifle Division. To the northeast was the 14th ***Panzer*** Division; to the south was the 297th Infantry Division.

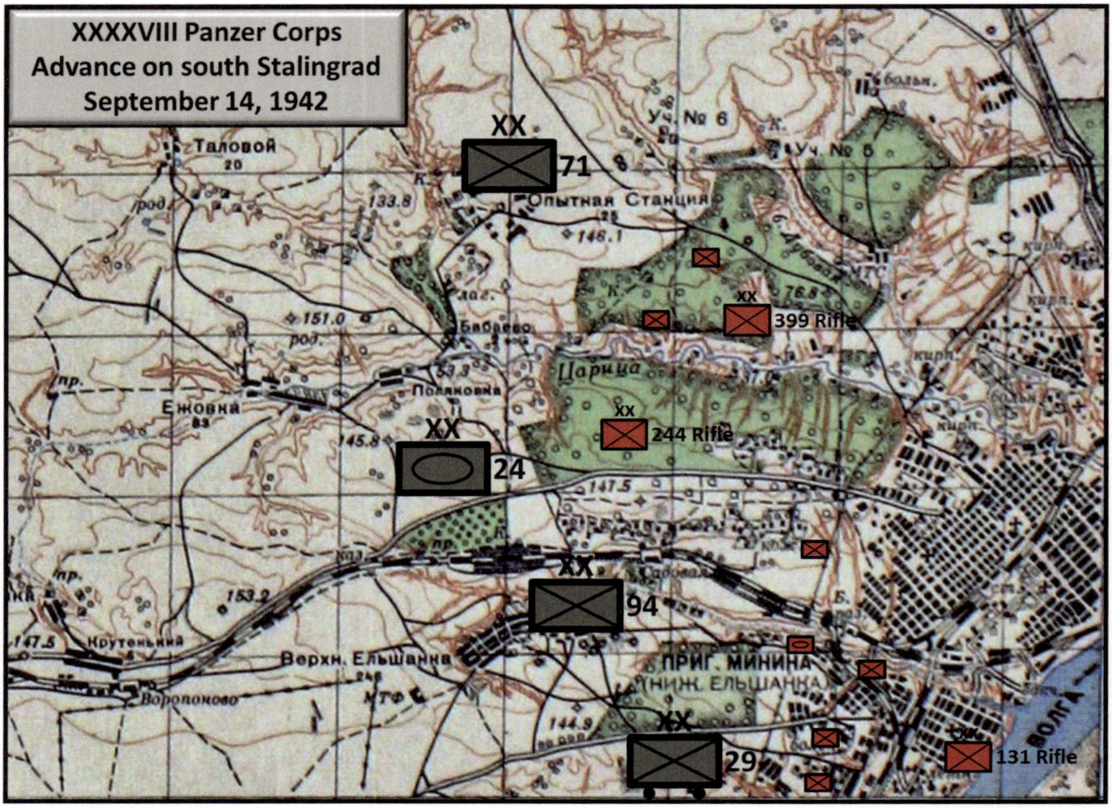
XXXXVIII Panzer Corps
Advance on south Stalingrad
September 14, 1942
XX
71
Опытная Станция
Таловой
Ежовка
Бабаево
Поляковка
Царица
399 Rifle
244 Rifle
XX
24
XX
94
Верхн. Ельшанка
Крутенький
Воропоново
ПРИГ. МИНИНА
(НИЖ. ЕЛЬШАНКА)
XX
29
131 Rifle
ВОЛГА

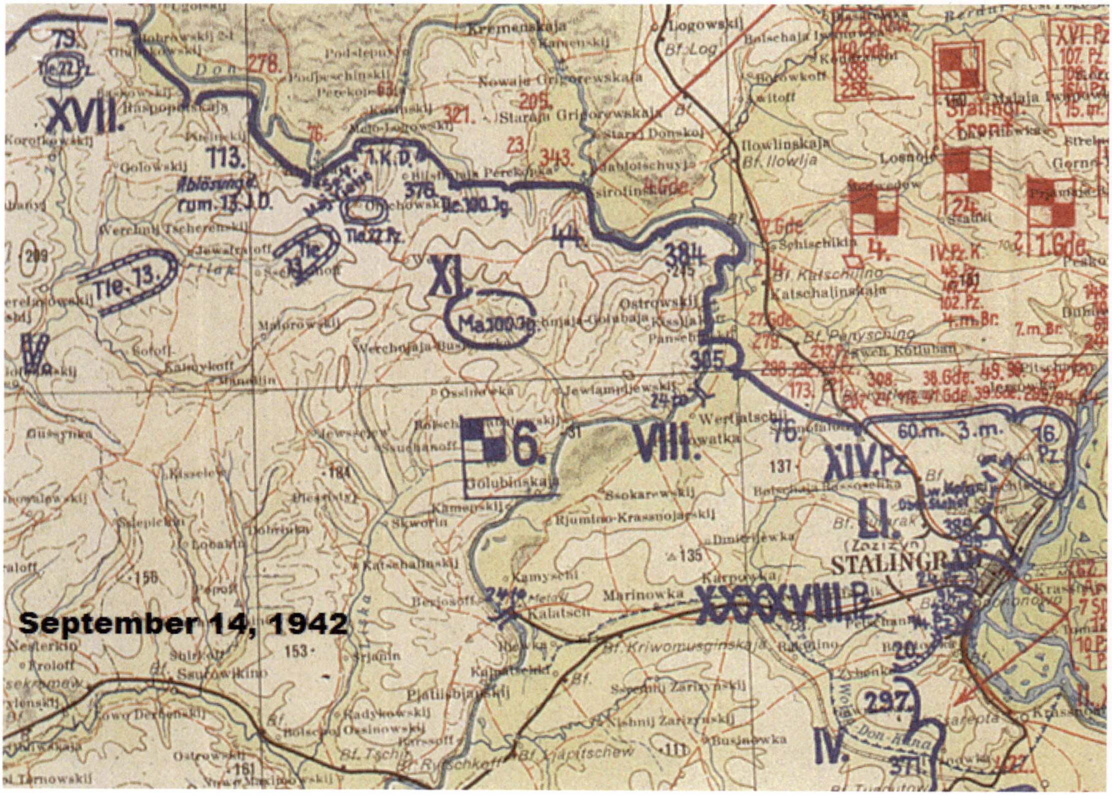
September 14, 1942
XVII.
XI.
VIII.
XIV.Pz
LI.
STALINGRAD
XXXXVIII.B
IV.

Sources, September 14, 1942: *Oberkommando des Heeres, Lage Ost: Stand: 14.9.42, Eastern Front Situation Map, National Archives Identifier: 559733, Record Group 242 – National Archives Collection of Foreign Records Seized, 1675-1958, National Archives, College Park, Maryland; Ia, Armeeoberkommando 6, "Morgen Meldung" and assorted reports, Kriegstagebuch 13, 15 September 1942, as found in Microfilm Series, T-312, Records of German Field Commands, Armies, Roll 1685, National Archives and Records Service, College Park, Maryland; Ia, XXXXVIII Panzerkorps, "Übersicht über die dem Korps Unterstellten Divisionen, 28. Juni 1942 – 11 October 1942," as found on T-314, Records of German Field Commands, Corps, Roll 1153, National Archives, College Park, Maryland; Korpsarzt, XXXXVIII Panzerkorps, "Meldung über Personelle Verluste," Stand 14.9.42, as found on T-314, Records of German Field Commands, Corps, Roll 1158, National Archives, College Park, Maryland; 371st Infantry Division, Kriegstagebuch, 14 September 1942, as found in Microfilm Series T-315, Roll 2164, National Archives and Records Service, College Park, Maryland; Florian Freiherr von und zu Aufsess, Die Anlagenbände zu den Kriegstagebüchern der 6. Armee vom 14.09.1942 bis 24.11.1942, Band 1, Schwabach, Germany: Selbstverlag, 2006, 6-15, 18-19 and 27; Antony Beevor, Stalingrad: The Fateful Siege: 1942-1943, London: Penguin Books, 1998, 131; John Erickson, The Road to Stalingrad, New York: Harper & Row, 1975, 404; Die 71. Infanterie-Division, 1939-1945: Gefechts- und Erlebnisberichte aus Kämpfen der "Gluckhaften Division" von Verdun bis Stalingrad, vom Monte Cassino bis zum Plattensee, Eggolsheim, FRG: Edition Dörfler, 1973, 238; David M. Glantz & Jonathan M. House, Armageddon in Stalingrad: September-November 1942, (The Stalingrad Trilogy, Volume 2), Lawrence, Kansas: University Press of Kansas, 2009, 117-123; Helmuth Greiner, "Greiner Diary Notes, 12 August 1942 – 12 March 1943," MS #C-065a, Heidelberg, Germany: Historical Division, Headquarters, United States Army Europe, 1949, 63; Joachim Lemelsen, 29. Division, Bad Nauheim, FRG: Podzun Verlag, 1960, 202; Jochen Löser, Bittere Pflicht: Kampf und Untergang der 76. Berlin-Brandenburgischen Infanterie-Division, Osnabrück, FRG: Biblio Verlag, 1986, 208; Jason Mark, Death of the Leaping Horseman: 24. Panzer-Division in Stalingrad, Sydney, Australia: Leaping Horsemen Books, 2003, 159-162; Anton Schimak, Karl Lamprecht & Friedrich Dettmer, Die 44. Infanterie Division: Tagebuch der Hoch- und Deutschmeister, Wien: Verlag Austria Press, 169, 233 and Map: Marschweg der 44. Infanterie Division im Russland; Janusz Piekalkiewicz, Stalingrad: Anatomie einer Schlacht, München, BRD: Wilhelm Heyne Verlag, 1977, 191; Franz Thomas, & Günter Wegmann, Die Ritterkreuzträger der Deutschen Wehrmacht, 1939-1945, Teil 1: Sturmartillerie, Osnabrück, FRG: Biblio Verlag, 1985, 180.*

Zur Erinnerung
an den Heldentod
unseres guten Sohnes

ROBERT BEUTEL

Gefreiter in einem Panzer-Reg.
Inhaber des EK 2., des Inf.-Sturm-
abzeichen und Verwundetenabz.

geboren am 8. 5. 1920

gefallen am 14. 9. 1942
bei Stalingrad

Richter

Gefreiter **Robert Beutel** was born in Niederwildgrub near Troppau in Austria on May 8, 1920. The area later became part of the Sudetenland, before returning to Germany in 1938. Beutel was a winner of the Iron Cross 2nd Class, the Infantry Assault Badge and the Wound Badge in Black. Last assigned to a ***panzer*** regiment (probably in either the 24th ***Panzer*** Division or the 14th ***Panzer*** Division); he was killed in action at Stalingrad on September 14, 1942. He is listed in the remembrance book at the German Military Cemetery at Rossoschka.

1939

In der Blüte der schönsten Jahre
Brach der Tod Dein junges Herz.
Ruhe sanft in fremder Erde
Uns bleibt nur der Trennungsschmerz.
Denn Du warst uns Alles
Doch das Schicksal wollt' es nicht
Die Heimat und Deine Lieben wiederzusehn.

Gefreiter **Robert Beutel**

September 15, 1942
Weather: windy, cool, 52° F, local rain showers
Sunrise: 5:37 a.m.; **Sunset:** 6:17 p.m.
Moon: Waxing Crescent; 26% illumination

Sixth Army – ***General der Panzertruppe*** Paulus ordered ***General der Artillerie*** von Seydlitz (LI Corps) to join forces with the XXXXVIII ***Panzer*** Corps to clean out central and southern Stalingrad. The army headquarters was located at Golubinskaya. Bombers and dive-bombers from the ***Luftwaffe***'s VIII Air Corps pounded Stalingrad in large-scale attacks.

VIII Corps – The corps suffered the following officer casualties: one wounded in action.

76th Infantry Division – The division defended in sector southwest of Samofalovka and north of Borodkin against several enemy attacks by the 308th Rifle Division, the 298th Rifle Division and the 173rd Rifle Division. To the northwest was the 305th Infantry Division; to the east was the 60th Infantry Division (Motorized.) The division lost three NCOs/enlisted killed in action; 18 NCOs/enlisted were wounded in action.

305th Infantry Division – The division defended in sector from the Don River, north of Nizhne-Gnilovskii, to west of Kotluban' against the 279th Rifle Division. To the southeast was the 76th Infantry Division; to the north was the 384th Infantry Division. The division lost two NCOs/enlisted wounded in action.

XI Corps – The 177th ***Sturmgeschütz*** Detachment, with ten Mark III-Long and four Mark III-Short assault guns operational, was assigned to the corps.

44th Infantry Division – The division defended in sector Kurchajessowskij-Kamyshinskiy-Hill 171.0-Hill 180.9-Sirotinskaya-Khmelevskoy, against the 40th Guards Rifle Division. The division headquarters was located at Verkhne-Golubaja. To the west was 100th ***Jäger*** Division; to the east was the 384th Infantry Division. The division lost four NCOs/enlisted wounded in action.

100th Jäger Division – The division defended in sector near Blizhniaia-Perekopka. To the east was the 44th Infantry Division; to the west was the 376th Infantry Division. The division lost six NCOs/enlisted wounded in action.

376th Infantry Division – The division defended in sector southwest of Perekopka. To the west was the 113th Infantry Division; to the east was the 100th ***Jäger*** Division. The division lost one NCO/enlisted wounded in action.

384th Infantry Division – The division defended in sector west of the Don River near Trekhostrovskaia to Podgorskii against the 214th Rifle Division. To the west was the 44th Infantry Division; to the south was the 305th Infantry Division. The division lost two NCOs/enlisted wounded in action.

XIV *Panzer* Corps – The corps headquarters was located west of Nadezhda.

3rd Infantry Division (Motorized) – The division defended in sector, from the Tartar Hill-Hill 111.1-Hill 129.6-Hill 131.2 against the 41st Guards Rifle Division and the 39th Guards Rifle Division. To the east was the 16th ***Panzer*** Division; to the west was the 60th Infantry Division (Motorized.)

16th Panzer Division – The division defended in sector from Hill 139.7 to the Volga and from the Volga southwest to Hill 145.1, north of Orlovka against the 299th Rifle Division, the 84th Rifle Division and the 64th Rifle Division. Along the northern corridor, to the west was the 3rd Infantry Division (Motorized.) On the southern corridor, to the west was Battle Group Stahel.

60th Infantry Division (Motorized) – The division defended in sector, from south of Kotluban' Station near Borodkin to Kuz'michi against the 308th Rifle Division, the 24th Rifle Division, the 38th Guards Rifle Division and the 116th Rifle Division. To the east was the 3rd Infantry Division (Motorized); to the west was the 76th Infantry Division.

XVII Corps – The corps suffered the following officer casualties: one wounded in action.

79th Infantry Division – The division defended in sector from Bol'shoy-Verkhne-Kalmykovskii-Verkhne-Fomichinskii-Baskowskij against the 124th Rifle Division and the 96th Rifle Division. The division headquarters was located at Karagichev. To the west was the XXXV Corps of the Italian Eighth Army; to the southeast was the 13th Romanian Infantry Division. The division lost eight NCOs/enlisted killed in action; 12 NCOs/enlisted were wounded in action.

113th Infantry Division – The division moved from its defensive sector toward the southeast. Part of the division defended in sector between the 13th Romanian Infantry Division and several battle groups. The division lost three NCOs/enlisted killed in action; five NCOs/enlisted were wounded in action; one man was reported missing in action.

298th Infantry Division – The division occupied an assembly area along the Sixth Army's western boundary, behind the front line.

1st Romanian Cavalry Division – The division defended in sector near Molologowskij against the 63rd Rifle Division. To the west were assorted battle groups; to the southeast was the 376th Infantry Division. In the previous 48 hours, the division lost three NCOs/enlisted killed in action; four officers and 123 NCOs/enlisted were wounded in action; one officer and two men were reported missing in action.

6th Romanian Infantry Division – The division moved northeast behind the 13th Romanian Infantry Division.

13th Romanian Infantry Division – The division defended in sector along the Don River west of Kletskiy against the 278th Rifle Division and the 76th Rifle Division. To the northwest was the 79th Infantry Division; to the east was part of the 113th Infantry Division.

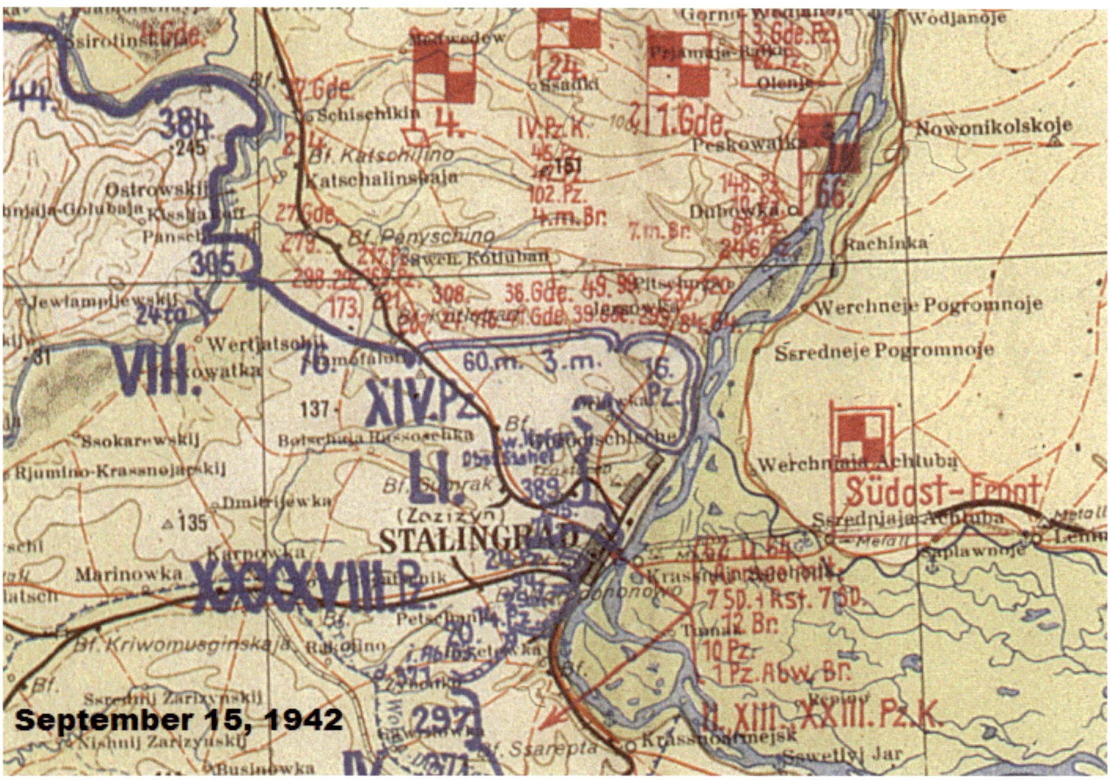

September 15, 1942

LI Corps – The corps headquarters was located three miles southwest of Gorodishche. The corps suffered the following officer casualties: five killed in action; seven wounded in action.

71st Infantry Division – The division attacked in zone at Railway Station Nr.1 and advanced eastward along the northern bank of the Tsaritsa River against the 13th Guards Rifle Division. The 245th ***Sturmgeschütz*** Detachment was attached to the division. To the north was the 295th Infantry Division; to the south was the 24th ***Panzer*** Division. The division lost one officer and 11 NCOs/enlisted killed in action; one officer and 64 NCOs/enlisted were wounded in action.

295th Infantry Division – The division attacked eastward in zone to the heights overlooking the Krasny Oktyabr Workers' Settlement and toward the Mamayev Kurgan [Hill 102] against the 112th Rifle Division and the 13th Guards Rifle Division. To the north was the 389th Infantry Division; to the south was the 71st Infantry Division. The division headquarters was located at Gumrak. The division lost 17 NCOs/enlisted killed in action; five officers and 68 NCOs/enlisted were wounded in action.

389th Infantry Division – The division consolidated its gains. To the north was Battle Group Stahel; to the south was the 295th Infantry Division.

Battle Group Stahel – The battle group defended northwest of Orlovka to contain enemy forces. To the northeast was the 16th ***Panzer*** Division; to the south was the 389th Infantry Division.

Fourth *Panzer* Army – The army headquarters was located at Plodowitoje.

IV Corps – The corps headquarters was located at Plantator.

297th Infantry Division – The division defended in sector south of Elkhi against the 38th Rifle Division and the 133rd Tank Brigade. To the north was the 371st Infantry Division; to the south was the 20th Romanian Division.

371st Infantry Division – The division exchanged defensive sectors with the 20th Romanian Division. To the north now was the 14th ***Panzer*** Division; to the south now was the 297th Infantry Division. The division lost one officer and four NCOs/enlisted wounded in action.

XXXXVIII *Panzer* Corps – The corps suffered the following officer casualties: one killed in action.

14th Panzer Division – The division defended in sector south of Kuporosnoye and north of Beketovka against the 35th Guards Rifle Division. To the north was the 29th Infantry Division (Motorized); to the south was the 371st Infantry Division. The division lost 42 NCOs/enlisted killed in action; four officers and 101 NCOs/enlisted were wounded in action; one NCO/enlisted was reported missing in action.

24th Panzer Division – The division attacked east in zone into Stalingrad, seizing the Stalingrad Rail Station Nr.2 (Southern Railway Station) and advancing in a narrow corridor northeast to a railway bridge over the Tsaritsa River. To the north was the 71st Infantry Division; to the south was the 94th Infantry Division. The division lost 23 NCOs/enlisted killed in action; four officers and 61 NCOs/enlisted were wounded in action; one officer and two NCOs/enlisted were reported missing in action.

29th Infantry Division (Motorized) – The division attacked north in zone into Stalingrad, seizing the Lumber Factory Nr.2 and the Elektroles 25 October Power Plant against the 35th Guards Rifle Division and the 10th Tank Destroyer Brigade. To the north was the 94th Infantry Division; to the south was the 14th ***Panzer*** Division. The division lost 37 NCOs/enlisted killed in action; 100 NCOs/enlisted were wounded in action; two NCOs/enlisted were reported missing in action.

94th Infantry Division – The division attacked in north in zone into Stalingrad, clearing the 131st Rifle Division from Minina and El'shanka and seizing a railroad bridge over the El'shanka River. To the north was the 24th ***Panzer*** Division; to the south was the 29th Infantry Division (Motorized.) The division lost 36 NCOs/enlisted killed in action; five officers and 32 NCOs/enlisted were wounded in action.

20th Romanian Infantry Division – The division exchanged defensive sectors with the 371st Infantry Division. To the north now was the 297th Infantry Division; to the south was the 2nd Romanian Infantry Division of the Romanian VI Corps.

German officer at field accommodations outside Stalingrad. His small tent is in the background. He sits at a rough-hewn wooden table, decorated with a tablecloth and ample foodstuffs.

Sources, September 15, 1942: *Oberkommando des Heeres, Lage Ost: Stand: 15.9.42, Eastern Front Situation Map, National Archives Identifier: 559733, Record Group 242 – National Archives Collection of Foreign Records Seized, 1675-1958, National Archives, College Park, Maryland; Ia, Armeeoberkommando 6, "Morgen Meldung" and assorted reports, Kriegstagebuch 13, 16 September 1942, as found in Microfilm Series, T-312, Records of German Field Commands, Armies, Roll 1685, National Archives and Records Service, College Park, Maryland; Ia, XXXXVIII Panzerkorps, "Übersicht über die dem Korps Unterstellten Divisionen, 28. Juni 1942 – 11 October 1942," as found on T-314, Records of German Field Commands, Corps, Roll 1153, National Archives, College Park, Maryland; Korpsarzt, XXXXVIII Panzerkorps, "Meldung über Personelle Verluste," Stand 15.9.42, as found on T-314, Records of German Field Commands, Corps, Roll 1158, National Archives, College Park, Maryland; 79th Infantry Division, Kriegstagebuch, 15 September 1942, as found in Microfilm Series T-315, Roll 1108, National Archives and Records Service, College Park, Maryland; 371st Infantry Division, Kriegstagebuch, 15 September 1942, as found in Microfilm Series T-315, Roll 2164, National Archives and Records Service, College Park, Maryland; Florian Freiherr von und zu Aufsess, Die Anlagenbände zu den Kriegstagebüchern der 6. Armee vom 14.09.1942 bis 24.11.1942, Band 1, Schwabach, Germany: Selbstverlag, 2006, 15-17 and 27; John Erickson, The Road to Stalingrad, New York: Harper & Row, 1975, 404; Die 71. Infanterie-Division, 1939-1945: Gefechts- und Erlebnisberichte aus Kämpfen der "Gluckhaften Division" von Verdun bis Stalingrad, vom Monte Cassino bis zum Plattensee, Eggolsheim, FRG: Edition Dörfler, 1973, 245; Division der Wehrmacht: 71. Infanterie-Division, 389. Infanterie-Division, 295. Infanterie-Division, 79. Infanterie-Division, 260. Infanterie-Division, 305. Infanterie-Division, 73. Infanterie-Division, 18. Infanterie-Division, 100. Jäger-Division, 94. Infanterie-Division, Germany: Books LLC, 2010, 565; David M. Glantz & Jonathan M. House, Armageddon in Stalingrad: September-November 1942, (The Stalingrad Trilogy, Volume 2), Lawrence, Kansas: University Press of Kansas, 2009, 124-138; Jochen Löser, Bittere Pflicht: Kampf und Untergang der 76. Berlin-Brandenburgischen Infanterie-Division, Osnabrück, FRG: Biblio Verlag, 1986, 208; Jason Mark, Death of the Leaping Horseman: 24. Panzer-Division in Stalingrad, Sydney, Australia: Leaping Horsemen Books, 2003, 162-174; Kurt Mehner, Die Geheimen Tagesberichte der Deutschen Wehrmachtführung im Zweiten Weltkrieg 1939-1945, Band 5: 1. Juni 1942 – 30. November 1942, Osnabrück, Germany: Biblio Verlag, 1991, 195; Anton Schimak, Karl Lamprecht & Friedrich Dettmer, Die 44. Infanterie Division: Tagebuch der Hoch- und Deutschmeister, Wien: Verlag Austria Press, 169, 233 and Map: Marschweg der 44. Infanterie Division im Russland; Franz Thomas, & Günter Wegmann, Die Ritterkreuzträger der Deutschen Wehrmacht, 1939-1945, Teil 1: Sturmartillerie, Osnabrück, FRG: Biblio Verlag, 1985, 180.*

September 16, 1942
Weather: very cloudy, light rain showers, windy, falling temperatures, 54° F
Sunrise: 5:39 a.m.; **Sunset:** 6:15 p.m.
Moon: Waxing Crescent; 36% illumination

Sixth Army – The army headquarters was located at Golubinskaya. Enemy forces (13th Guards Rifle Division) re-captured Mamayev Kurgan. Hitler ordered that all forces committed to the battle for Stalingrad would be placed under the unified command of the Sixth Army.

VIII Corps – The corps suffered the following officer casualties: one killed in action; four wounded in action.

76th Infantry Division – The division defended in sector southwest of Samofalovka and north of Borodkin against the 308th Rifle Division, the 298th Rifle Division and the 173rd Rifle Division. To the west was the 305th Infantry Division; to the east was the 60th Infantry Division (Motorized.) Russian attacks were greatly reduced. The division lost six NCOs/enlisted killed in action; 19 NCOs/enlisted were wounded in action.

305th Infantry Division – The division defended in sector from the Don River, north of Nizhne-Gnilovskii, to west of Kotluban' against the 27th Guards Rifle Division and the 278th Rifle Division. To the southeast was the 76th Infantry Division; to the north was the 384th Infantry Division. The division lost two NCOs/enlisted wounded in action.

XI Corps – The 177th ***Sturmgeschütz*** Detachment, with ten Mark III-Long and four Mark III-Short assault guns operational, was assigned to the corps.

44th Infantry Division – The division defended in sector Kurchajessowskij-Kamyshinskiy-Hill 171.0-Hill 180.9-Sirotinskaya-Khmelevskoy against the 343rd Rifle Division. The division headquarters was located at Verkhne-Golubaja. To the west was 100th ***Jäger*** Division; to the east was the 384th Infantry Division. The division lost one NCO/enlisted killed in action.

100th Jäger Division – Part of the division defended in sector near Blizhniaia-Perekopka against the 23rd Rifle Division. To the east was the 44th Infantry Division; to the west was the 376th Infantry Division. The bulk of the division remained in an assembly area south of the sector. The division lost eight NCOs/enlisted wounded in action.

376th Infantry Division – The division defended in sector near Blizhniaia-Perekopka against the 321st Rifle Division. To the west was the 1st Romanian Cavalry Division; to the east was part of the 100th ***Jäger*** Division.

384th Infantry Division – The division defended in sector west of the Don River near Trekhostrovskaia to Podgorskii against the 4th Guards Rifle Division and the 214th Rifle Division. To the west was the 44th Infantry Division; to the south was the 305th Infantry Division. The division lost two NCOs/enlisted wounded in action.

XIV *Panzer* Corps – ***Generalleutnant*** Hans Valentin Hube assumed command of the corps. The corps headquarters was located west of Nadezhda.

3rd Infantry Division (Motorized) – The division defended in sector, from the Tartar Hill-Hill 111.1-Hill 129.6-Hill 131.2 against the 41st Guards Rifle Division and the 39th Guards Rifle Division. To the east was the 16th ***Panzer*** Division; to the west was the 60th Infantry Division (Motorized.)

16th Panzer Division – The division defended in sector, from Hill 139.7 to the Volga and from the Volga southwest to Hill 145.1, north of Orlovka against the 299th Rifle Division, the 64th Rifle Division and the 84th Rifle Division. To the west was the 3rd Infantry Division (Motorized); to the southwest was Battle Group Stahel. ***Generalleutnant*** Hans Valentin Hube relinquished command of the division.

60th Infantry Division (Motorized) – The division defended in sector, from south of Kotluban' Station near Borodkin to Kuz'michi against the 308th Rifle Division, the 24th Rifle Division and the 116th Rifle Division. To the east was the 3rd Infantry Division (Motorized); to the west was the 76th Infantry Division.

XVII Corps – The corps suffered the following officer casualties: one wounded in action.

79th Infantry Division – The division defended in sector from Bol'shoy-Verkhne-Kalmykovskii-Verkhne-Fomichinskii-Baskowskij against the 124th Rifle Division and the 96th Rifle Division. The division headquarters was located at Karagichev. To the west was the XXXV Corps of the Italian Eighth Army; to the southeast was the 13th Romanian Infantry Division. The division suffered four NCOs/enlisted killed in action; one officer and 14 NCOs/enlisted were wounded in action.

113th Infantry Division – The division stopped moving south. Part of the division remained in sector with the 13th Romanian Infantry Division. Part of the division defended in sector between the 13th Romanian Infantry Division and several battle groups. The division lost ten NCOs/enlisted killed in action.

298th Infantry Division – The division occupied an assembly area along the Sixth Army's western boundary, behind the front line.

1st Romanian Cavalry Division – The division defended in sector near Mololologowskij, southeast of the Don River, against the 63rd Rifle Division. To the southwest was part of the 113th Infantry Division; to the southeast was the 376th Infantry Division.

6th Romanian Infantry Division – The division moved northeast behind the 13th Romanian Infantry Division.

13th Romanian Infantry Division – Part of the division defended in sector along the Don River west of Kletskiy against the 278th Rifle Division and the 76th Rifle Division. To the northwest was the 79th Infantry Division; to the southeast was part of the 113th Infantry Division.

XXXXVIII *Panzer* Corps – The corps was subordinated to the Sixth Army from the Fourth ***Panzer*** Army. The corps suffered the following officer casualties: two killed in action; two wounded in action.

14th Panzer Division – The division defended in sector south of Kuporosnoye and north of Beketovka against the 35th Guards Rifle Division. To the north was the 29th Infantry Division (Motorized); to the south was the 371st Infantry Division. The division lost one officer and 22 NCOs/enlisted killed in action; one officer and 50 NCOs/enlisted were wounded in action; three NCOs/enlisted were reported missing in action.

24th Panzer Division – The division attacked in north and west in zone inside Stalingrad, seizing a crossing of the Tsaritsa Balka in the north and Barracks Hill in the west, and reaching the area of Railroad Station Nr.2 against the 244th Rifle Division. To the north was the 71st Infantry Division; to the south was the 94th Infantry Division. The division lost one officer and 18 NCOs/enlisted killed in action; two officers and 48 NCOs/enlisted were wounded in action; one man died later of his wounds; one man was reported missing in action. Operational tank strength in the division was 19.

29th Infantry Division (Motorized) – The division attacked north in zone in southern Stalingrad against the 35th Guards Rifle Division and the 10th Tank Destroyer Brigade. To the north was the 94th Infantry Division; to the south was the 14th ***Panzer*** Division. The division lost one officer and 23 NCOs/enlisted killed in action; 49 NCOs/enlisted were wounded in action; two NCOs/enlisted were reported missing in action.

94th Infantry Division – The division attacked north in zone inside Stalingrad in the vicinity of the Railway Station Nr.2 toward the Grain Elevator – held by the 35th Guards Rifle Division – seizing part of the Food Combine from the 271st NKVD Regiment. To the northwest was the 24th ***Panzer*** Division; to the southeast was the 29th Infantry Division (Motorized.) The division lost one officer and 21 NCOs/enlisted killed in action; one officer and 88 NCOs/enlisted were wounded in action.

LI Corps – The corps headquarters was located three miles southwest of Gorodishche. The corps suffered the following officer casualties: one killed in action; ten wounded in action.

71st Infantry Division – The division attacked east in zone, gaining parts of the Dol'gii Balka and Krutoi Balka against the 13th Guards Rifle Division. The division lost one officer and ten NCOs/enlisted killed in action; 50 NCOs/enlisted were wounded in action; ten NCOs/enlisted were reported missing in action. To the north was the 295th Infantry Division; to the south was the 24th *Panzer* Division.

295th Infantry Division – The division attacked in zone toward Mamayev Kurgan (gaining the summit before losing it) and from Hill 126.3 to the western edge of the Krasny Oktyabr Workers' Settlement against the 112th Rifle Division, the 13th Guards Rifle Division, the 6th Guards Tank Brigade and the 189th Tank Brigade. The division suffered one officer and 38 NCOs/enlisted killed in action; seven officers and 123 NCOs/enlisted were wounded in action; nine NCOs/enlisted were reported missing in action. To the north was the 389th Infantry Division; to the south was the 71st Infantry Division. The division headquarters was located at Gumrak.

389th Infantry Division – The division attempted to attack northeast in zone but the attack stalled. The division suffered five NCOs/enlisted killed in action; four NCOs/enlisted were wounded in action. To the north was Battle Group Stahel; to the south was the 295th Infantry Division.

Battle Group Stahel – The battle group defended northwest of Orlovka to contain enemy forces.

Fourth *Panzer* Army – The army headquarters was located at Plodowitoje.

IV Corps – The corps headquarters was located at Plantator.

297th Infantry Division – The division defended in sector south of Elkhi against the 29th Rifle Division. To the north was the 371st Infantry Division; to the south was the 20th Romanian Division.

371st Infantry Division – The division defended in sector near Peschanka against the 157th Rifle Division. To the north was the 14th *Panzer* Division; to the south was the 297th Infantry Division. The division lost one officer and four NCOs/enlisted wounded in action.

20th Romanian Infantry Division – The division defended in sector near the Volga-Don Canal against the 36th Guards Rifle Division. To the north was the 297th Infantry Division; to the south was the 2nd Romanian Infantry Division of the Romanian VI Corps.

Sources, September 16, 1942: *Oberkommando des Heeres, Lage Ost: Stand: 16.9.42, Eastern Front Situation Map, National Archives Identifier: 559733, Record Group 242 – National Archives Collection of Foreign Records Seized, 1675-1958, National Archives, College Park, Maryland; Ia, Armeeoberkommando 6, "Morgen Meldung" and assorted reports, Kriegstagebuch 13, 17 September 1942, as found in Microfilm Series, T-312, Records of German Field Commands, Armies, Roll 1686, National Archives and Records Service, College Park, Maryland; Ia, XXXXVIII Panzerkorps, "Übersicht über die dem Korps Unterstellten Divisionen, 28. Juni 1942 – 11 October 1942," as found on T-314, Records of German Field Commands, Corps, Roll 1153, National Archives, College Park, Maryland; Korpsarzt, XXXXVIII Panzerkorps, "Meldung über Personelle Verluste," Stand 16.9.42, as found on T-314, Records of German Field Commands, Corps, Roll 1158, National Archives, College Park, Maryland; 371st Infantry Division, Kriegstagebuch, 16 September 1942, as found in Microfilm Series T-315, Roll 2164, National Archives and Records Service, College Park, Maryland; Florian Freiherr von und zu Aufsess, Die Anlagenbände zu den Kriegstagebüchern der 6. Armee vom 14.09.1942 bis 24.11.1942, Band 1, Schwabach, Germany: Selbstverlag, 2006, 20-25 and 27-28, 32; Dermot Bradley, Die Generale des Heeres, 1921-1945, Band 6: Hochbaum – Klutmann, Bissendorf, Germany: Biblio Verlag, 2002, 162-163; Paul Carell, Stalingrad: The Defeat of the German Sixth Army, Atglen, Pennsylvania: Schiffer Publishing, 1993, 141; Die 71. Infanterie-Division, 1939-1945: Gefechts- und Erlebnisberichte aus Kämpfen der "Gluckhaften Division" von Verdun bis Stalingrad, vom Monte Cassino bis zum Plattensee, Eggolsheim, FRG: Edition Dörfler, 1973, 245; Division der Wehrmacht: 71. Infanterie-Division, 389. Infanterie-Division, 295. Infanterie-Division, 79. Infanterie-Division, 260. Infanterie-Division, 305. Infanterie-Division, 73. Infanterie-Division, 18. Infanterie-Division, 100. Jäger-Division, 94. Infanterie-Division, Germany: Books LLC, 2010, 564; David M. Glantz & Jonathan M. House, Armageddon in Stalingrad: September-November 1942, (The Stalingrad Trilogy, Volume 2), Lawrence, Kansas: University Press of Kansas, 2009, 124-138; Helmuth Greiner, "Greiner Diary Notes, 12 August 1942 – 12 March 1943," MS #C-065a, Heidelberg, Germany: Historical Division, Headquarters, United States Army Europe, 1949, 65; Joachim Lemelsen, 29. Division, Bad Nauheim, FRG: Podzun Verlag, 1960, 202; Jochen Löser, Bittere Pflicht: Kampf und Untergang der 76. Berlin-Brandenburgischen Infanterie-Division, Osnabrück, FRG: Biblio Verlag, 1986, 208; Jason Mark, Death of the Leaping Horseman: 24. Panzer-Division in Stalingrad, Sydney, Australia: Leaping Horsemen Books, 2003, 174-182; Kurt Mehner, Die Geheimen Tagesberichte der Deutschen Wehrmachtführung im Zweiten Weltkrieg 1939-1945, Band 5: 1. Juni 1942 – 30. November 1942, Osnabrück, Germany: Biblio Verlag, 1991, 197; Anton Schimak, Karl Lamprecht & Friedrich Dettmer, Die 44. Infanterie Division: Tagebuch der Hoch- und Deutschmeister, Wien: Verlag Austria Press, 169, 233 and Map: Marschweg der 44. Infanterie Division im Russland.*

Commanding General of the 295th Infantry Division, Rolf Wuthmann (facing camera behind thermos jug.)
He is in conversation with ***General der Panzertruppe*** Friedrich Paulus (back to camera) in Stalingrad.

***Generalleutnant* Hans Valentin Hube assumed command of the XIV *Panzer* Corps.**

Leutnant* Helwig Luz**, the son of ***Generalleutnant Helwig Luz, was born in Straubing, Bavaria on June 25, 1921. Assigned to the 10th Company of the 24th ***Panzer*** Regiment in the 24th ***Panzer*** Division, he was killed in action near Barracks Hill in Stalingrad on September 16, 1942. ***Leutnant*** Luz is buried at the German Military Cemetery at Rossoschka in Block 2, Row 6, in Grave 222. His name is here shown on the family grave marker in Germany; the general lost two sons during the war.

September 17, 1942
Weather: sunny, bright, almost cloudless, warming after noon, 73° F significant cooling in the evening, good road conditions
Sunrise: 5:40 a.m.; **Sunset:** 6:12 p.m.
Moon: First Quarter; 50% illumination

Sixth Army – Forces from the LI Corps and the XXXXVIII ***Panzer*** Corps made contact on the Tsaritsa River. The army headquarters was located at Golubinskaya. ***General der Panzertruppe*** Paulus visited the LI Corps, the 94th Infantry Division and the 389th Infantry Division.

VIII Corps

76th Infantry Division – The division defended in sector southwest of Samofalovka and north of Borodkin against the 308th Rifle Division, the 298th Rifle Division and the 173rd Rifle Division. To the northwest was the 305th Infantry Division; to the east was the 60th Infantry Division (Motorized.) The division lost three NCOs/enlisted killed in action; 14 NCOs/enlisted were wounded in action. One infantry company had only eight men left; its commander was a junior enlisted man.

305th Infantry Division – The division defended in sector from the Don River, north of Nizhne-Gnilovskii, to west of Kotluban' against the 27th Guards Rifle Division and the 279th Rifle Division. To the east was the 76th Infantry Division; to the north was the 384th Infantry Division. The division suffered one NCO/enlisted killed in action; three NCOs/enlisted were wounded in action.

XI Corps

44th Infantry Division – The division defended in sector Kurchajessowskij-Kamyshinskiy-Hill 171.0-Hill 180.9-Sirotinskaya-Khmelevskoy against the 343rd Rifle Division. The division headquarters was located at Verkhne-Golubaja. To the west was the 100th ***Jäger*** Division; to the east was the 384th Infantry Division. The division lost one NCO/enlisted killed in action; three NCOs/enlisted were wounded in action.

100th Jäger Division – The division defended in sector near Blizhniaia-Perekopka against the 23rd Rifle Division. To the east was the 44th Infantry Division; to the west was the 376th Infantry Division. The division lost one NCO/enlisted killed in action; six NCOs/enlisted were wounded in action.

376th Infantry Division – The division defended in sector near Blizhniaia-Perekopka. To the west was the 1st Romanian Cavalry Division; to the east was the 100th ***Jäger*** Division.

384th Infantry Division – The division defended in sector west of the Don River near Trekhostrovskaia to Podgorskii against the 4th Guards Rifle Division and the 214th Rifle Division. To the west was the 44th Infantry Division; to the south was the 305th Infantry Division. The division lost one NCO/enlisted wounded in action.

XIV *Panzer* Corps – The corps headquarters was located east of Ssadtschi-Kowa. The corps suffered the following officer casualties: one wounded in action.

3rd Infantry Division (Motorized) – The division defended in sector from the Tartar Hill-Hill 111.1-Hill 129.6-Hill 131.2 against the 39th Guards Rifle Division and the 49th Rifle Division. To the east was the 16th ***Panzer*** Division; to the west was the 60th Infantry Division (Motorized.)

16th Panzer Division – The division defended in sector from Hill 139.7 to the Volga and from the Volga southwest to Hill 145.1, north of Orlovka against the 299th Rifle Division, the 64th Rifle Division and the 84th Rifle Division. To the west was the 3rd Infantry Division (Motorized); to the southwest was Battle Group Stahel.

60th Infantry Division (Motorized) – The division defended in sector from south of

Kotluban' Station near Borodkin to Kuz'michi against the 308th Rifle Division, the 116th Rifle Division, the 29th Rifle Division and the 41st Guards Rifle Division. To the east was the 3rd Infantry Division (Motorized); to the west was the 76th Infantry Division.

XVII Corps – The corps suffered the following officer casualties: one killed in action; two wounded in action.

79th Infantry Division – The division defended in sector from Bol'shoy-Verkhne-Kalmykovskii-Verkhne-Fomichinskii-Baskowskij against the 121st Rifle Division and the 96th Rifle Division. The division headquarters was located at Karagichev. To the west was the XXXV Corps of the Italian Eighth Army; to the southeast was the 13th Romanian Infantry Division. The division lost two NCOs/enlisted killed in action; 13 NCOs/enlisted were wounded in action.

113th Infantry Division – Part of the division defended in sector with the 13th Romanian Division against the 278th Rifle Division and the 304th Rifle Division. Part of the division moved back towards the sector from the southeast. The division lost one officer and 21 NCOs/enlisted killed in action; two officers and 73 NCOs/enlisted were wounded in action.

298th Infantry Division – The division occupied an assembly area along the Sixth Army's western boundary, behind the front line.

1st Romanian Cavalry Division – The division defended in sector near Mololowgowskij south of the Don River against the 76th Rifle Division. To the west were several battle groups and the 13th Romanian Infantry Division; to the east was the 376th Infantry Division.

6th Romanian Infantry Division – The division moved northeast behind the 13th Romanian Infantry Division.

13th Romanian Infantry Division – The division defended in sector along the Don River west of Kletskiy against the 278th Rifle Division and the 304th Rifle Division. To the northwest was the 79th Infantry Division; to the southeast were several battle groups and the 1st Romanian Cavalry Division.

XXXXVIII *Panzer* Corps

14th Panzer Division – The division defended in sector south of Kuporosnoye and north of Beketovka against the 35th Guards Rifle Division. To the north was the 29th Infantry Division (Motorized); to the south was the 371st Infantry Division. The division lost one officer and four NCOs/enlisted killed in action; 25 NCOs/enlisted were wounded in action.

24th Panzer Division – The division attacked north in zone to clear the city of enemy forces west of the railway line, up to the Tsaritsa Balka against the 244th Rifle Division. Elements linked up with the 71st Infantry Division just south of the city center. The division lost 13 NCOs/enlisted killed in action; three officers and 46 NCOs/enlisted were wounded in action. To the north was the 71st Infantry Division; to the south was 94th Infantry Division.

29th Infantry Division (Motorized) – The division attacked in zone to seize the northern half of Lumber Factory Nr.2 and the northwestern section of El'shanka from the 35th Guards Rifle Division and the 10th Tank Destroyer Brigade. The division lost eight NCOs/enlisted killed in action; 50 NCOs/enlisted were wounded in action; 26 NCOs/enlisted were reported missing in action. To the north was the 94th Infantry Division; to the south was the 14th ***Panzer*** Division.

94th Infantry Division – The division attacked north in zone, re-taking Railroad Station Nr.2, solidifying its hold on the Food Combine and assaulting the Grain Elevator, now held by the Marine Infantry Brigade and the 35th Guards Rifle Division. The division lost three officers and 33 NCOs/enlisted killed in action; three officers and 76 NCOs/enlisted were wounded in action; six NCOs/enlisted were reported missing in action. To the north was the 24th ***Panzer*** Division; to the south was the 29th Infantry Division (Motorized.) The division headquarters was located north of Pestschanka.

LI Corps – The 244th ***Sturmgeschütz*** Detachment was assigned to the corps. The corps suffered the following officer casualties: three killed in action; five wounded in action. The corps headquarters was located at Gumrak.

71st Infantry Division – The division attacked in zone, linking up with the 24th ***Panzer*** Division just south of the city center and re-capturing Railroad Station Nr.1 (the station switched hands four times during the day) against the 13th Guards Rifle Division. The division lost

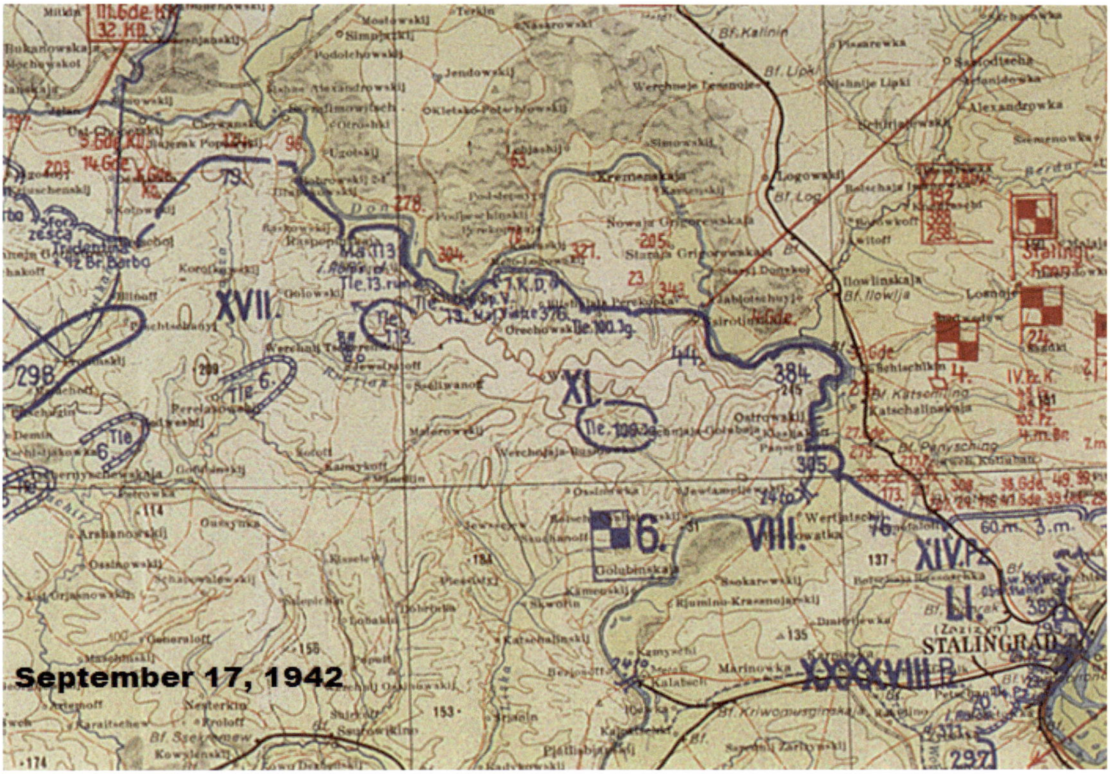

25 NCOs/enlisted killed in action; 57 NCOs/enlisted were wounded in action. To the north was the 295th Infantry Division; to the south was the 24th *Panzer* Division.

295th Infantry Division – The division attacked in zone, seizing the western edge of the Vishnevaia Balka and the northern slopes of Mamayev Kurgan. The division suffered one officer and 26 NCOs/enlisted killed in action; three officers and 99 NCOs/enlisted were wounded in action; one man was reported missing in action. To the north was the 389th Infantry Division; to the south was the 71st Infantry Division.

389th Infantry Division – The division attacked east in zone. Eight NCOs/enlisted were killed in action; five NCOs/enlisted were wounded in action. To the north was Battle Group Stahel; to the south was the 295th Infantry Division. The division headquarters was located one mile east of Schischjankin.

Battle Group Stahel – The battle group defended northwest of Orlovka to contain enemy forces. To the south was the 389th Infantry Division; to the northwest was the 16th *Panzer* Division.

Fourth *Panzer* Army – The army headquarters was located at Plodowitoje.

IV Corps – The corps headquarters was located at Plantator.

297th Infantry Division – The division defended in sector south of Elkhi against the 29th Rifle Division. To the north was the 371st Infantry Division; to the south was the 20th Romanian Infantry Division.

371st Infantry Division – The division defended in sector against the 157th Rifle Division. The division lost six NCOs/enlisted killed in action; two officers and eight NCOs/enlisted were wounded in action; two men were reported missing in action. To the north was the 14th *Panzer* Division; to the south was the 297th Infantry Division.

20th Romanian Infantry Division – The division defended in sector against the 36th Guards Rifle Division. To the north was the 297th Infantry Division; to the south was the 2nd Romanian Infantry Division of the Romanian VI Corps.

Ruined buildings in Stalingrad. In many south Stalingrad buildings, built predominantly of wood, only the chimneys remained after fire consumed the structures.

Sources, September 17, 1942: *Oberkommando des Heeres, Lage Ost: Stand: 17.9.42, Eastern Front Situation Map, National Archives Identifier: 559733, Record Group 242 – National Archives Collection of Foreign Records Seized, 1675-1958, National Archives, College Park, Maryland; Ia, Armeeoberkommando 6, "Morgen Meldung" and assorted reports, Kriegstagebuch 13, 18 September 1942, as found in Microfilm Series, T-312, Records of German Field Commands, Armies, Roll 1686, National Archives and Records Service, College Park, Maryland; Ia, XXXXVIII Panzerkorps, "Übersicht über die dem Korps Unterstellten Divisionen, 28. Juni 1942 – 11 October 1942," as found on T-314, Records of German Field Commands, Corps, Roll 1153, National Archives, College Park, Maryland; Korpsarzt, XXXXVIII Panzerkorps, "Meldung über Personelle Verluste," Stand 17.9.42, as found on T-314, Records of German Field Commands, Corps, Roll 1158, National Archives, College Park, Maryland; 79th Infantry Division, Kriegstagebuch, 17 September 1942, as found in Microfilm Series T-315, Roll 1108, National Archives and Records Service, College Park, Maryland; 371st Infantry Division, Kriegstagebuch, 17 September 1942, as found in Microfilm Series T-315, Roll 2164, National Archives and Records Service, College Park, Maryland; Florian Freiherr von und zu Aufsess, Die Anlagenbände zu den Kriegstagebüchern der 6. Armee vom 14.09.1942 bis 24.11.1942, Band 1, Schwabach, Germany: Selbstverlag, 2006, 28, 32; Alan Clark, Barbarossa: The Russian-German Conflict, 1941-45, New York: William Morrow and Company, 1965, 229; Die 71. Infanterie-Division, 1939-1945: Gefechts- und Erlebnisberichte aus Kämpfen der "Gluckhaften Division" von Verdun bis Stalingrad, vom Monte Cassino bis zum Plattensee, Eggolsheim, FRG: Edition Dörfler, 1973, 245; Division der Wehrmacht: 71. Infanterie-Division, 389. Infanterie-Division, 295. Infanterie-Division, 79. Infanterie-Division, 260. Infanterie-Division, 305. Infanterie-Division, 73. Infanterie-Division, 18. Infanterie-Division, 100. Jäger-Division, 94. Infanterie-Division, Germany: Books LLC, 2010, 565; David M. Glantz & Jonathan M. House, Armageddon in Stalingrad: September-November 1942, (The Stalingrad Trilogy, Volume 2), Lawrence, Kansas: University Press of Kansas, 2009, 145-161; Joachim Lemelsen, 29. Division, Bad Nauheim, FRG: Podzun Verlag, 1960, 203; Jochen Löser, Bittere Pflicht: Kampf und Untergang der 76. Berlin-Brandenburgischen Infanterie-Division, Osnabrück, FRG: Biblio Verlag, 1986, 209; Jason Mark, Death of the Leaping Horseman: 24. Panzer-Division in Stalingrad, Sydney, Australia: Leaping Horsemen Books, 2003, 182-188; Anton Schimak, Karl Lamprecht & Friedrich Dettmer, Die 44. Infanterie Division: Tagebuch der Hoch- und Deutschmeister, Wien: Verlag Austria Press, 169, 233 and Map: Marschweg der 44. Infanterie Division im Russland.*

September 18, 1942
Weather: changing cloudiness, warm, 73° F, frost at night
Sunrise: 5:42 a.m.; **Sunset:** 6:10 p.m.
Moon: Waxing Gibbous; 59% illumination

Sixth Army – The army headquarters was located at Golubinskaya.

VIII Corps – The aim of the corps was to defend the northern shoulder of the Sixth Army east of the Don River against the 4th Tank Army and the 24th Army. The 652nd Pioneer Battalion, the 177th ***Sturmgeschütz*** Detachment and the 521st ***Panzerjäger*** Detachment were assigned to the corps. The corps suffered the following officer casualties: four killed in action; 11 wounded in action; one accidental death.

76th Infantry Division – The division defended in sector southwest of Samofalovka and north of Borodkin against the 308th Rifle Division, the 173rd Rifle Division, the 298th Rifle Division and the 258nd Rifle Division. To the northwest was the 305th Infantry Division; to the east was the 60th Infantry Division (Motorized.) The 292nd Rifle Division and 12th Tank Brigade penetrated the division's defenses and advanced to the Borodkin State Farm, but the division later retook it. Heavy attacks by Stukas and bombers pummeled the attackers. The division lost 80 killed in action and 371 wounded in action.

305th Infantry Division – The division defended in sector from the Don River, north of Nizhne-Gnilovskii, to west of Kotluban' against the 27th Guards Rifle Division. To the southeast was the 76th Infantry Division; to the north was the 384th Infantry Division. The division lost one killed in action and four wounded in action.

XI Corps – The corps suffered the following officer casualties: one killed in action.

44th Infantry Division – The division defended in sector Kurchajessowskij-Kamyshinskiy-Hill 171.0-Hill 180.9-Sirotinskaya-Khmelevskoy against the 343rd Rifle Division. The division headquarters was located at Verkhne-Golubaja. To the west was 100th ***Jäger*** Division; to the east was the 384th Infantry Division. The division lost two NCOs/enlisted killed in action; nine NCOs/enlisted were wounded in action.

100th Jäger Division – The division prepared to be relieved of its defensive sector by the 376th Infantry Division; the bulk of the division was in an assembly area south of the sector.

376th Infantry Division – The division prepared to assume the sector of the 100th ***Jäger*** Division and continued to conduct defensive operations near Blizhniaia-Perekopka opposite the 321st Rifle Division and the 23rd Rifle Division. To the west was the 1st Romanian Cavalry Division; to the east was the 44th Infantry Division.

384th Infantry Division – The division defended in sector west of the Don River near Trekhostrovskaia to Podgorskii opposite the 4th Guards Division and the 37th Guards Rifle Division. To the west was the 44th Infantry Division; to the south was the 305th Infantry Division. The division lost two NCOs/enlisted killed in action; 14 NCOs/enlisted were wounded in action; one man was reported missing in action.

XIV *Panzer* Corps – The corps headquarters was located east of Ssadtschi-Kowa. The corps suffered the following officer casualties: one wounded in action.

3rd Infantry Division (Motorized) – The division defended in sector from the Tartar Hill-Hill 111.1-Hill 129.6-Hill 131.2 against the 84th Rifle Division, the 38th Guards Rifle Division, and the 116th Rifle Division. To the east was the 16th ***Panzer*** Division; to the west was the 60th Infantry Division (Motorized.) The division lost seven NCOs/enlisted killed in action; 21 NCOs/enlisted were wounded in action.

16th Panzer Division – The division defended in sector, from Hill 139.7 to the Volga and from the Volga southwest to Hill 145.1, north of Orlovka against the 299th Rifle Division, the 120th Rifle Division, the 231st Rifle Division and the 64th Rifle Division. The division repelled attacks against Hill 101.3 and Hill 135.4. To the west was the 3rd Infantry Division (Motorized); to the southwest was Battle Group Stahel.

60th Infantry Division (Motorized) – The division defended in sector from south of Kotluban' Station near Borodkin to Kuz'michi against the 116th Rifle Division, the 41st Guards Rifle Division, the 49th Rifle Division, the 24th Rifle Division, the 39th Guards Rifle Division, the 233rd Rifle Division, the 316th Rifle Division, the 292nd Rifle Division and the 308th Rifle Division. The 316th Rifle Division succeeded in seizing the 564 km Station and Hill 145.5, but the division later retook both. To the east was the 3rd Infantry Division (Motorized); to the west was the 76th Infantry Division.

XVII Corps – The aim of the corps was to defend in sector until the complete arrival of the Romanian V Corps. The corps suffered the following officer casualties: one killed in action.

79th Infantry Division – The division defended in sector from Bol'shoy-Verkhne-Kalmykovskii-Verkhne-Fomichinskii-Baskowskij against the 96th Rifle Division and the 124th Rifle Division. The division headquarters was located at Karagichev. To the west was the XXXV Corps of the Italian Eighth Army; to the southeast was the 13th Romanian Infantry Division. The division lost one officer and ten NCOs/enlisted killed in action; 39 NCOs/enlisted were wounded in action.

113th Infantry Division – The division defended in sector with the 13th Romanian Infantry Division against the 278th Rifle Division and the 304th Rifle Division. Part of the division occupied an assembly area south of the sector. The division lost 27 NCOs/enlisted killed in action; 104 NCOs/enlisted were wounded in action, when the division repelled an enemy attack near Raspopinskaja.

298th Infantry Division – The division occupied an assembly area along the Sixth Army's western boundary, behind the front line.

1st Romanian Cavalry Division – The division defended in sector near Mololologowskij south of the Don River against the 76th Rifle Division. To the west were assorted battle groups and the 13th Romanian Infantry

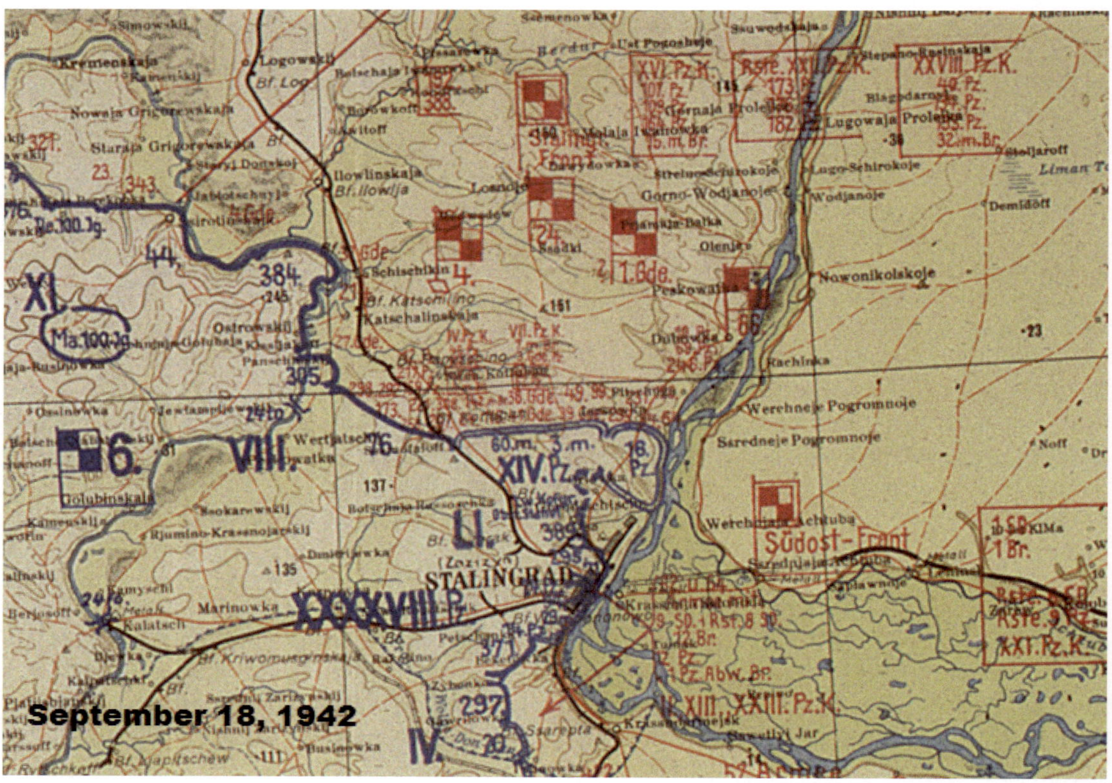

September 18, 1942

Division; to the southeast was the 376th Infantry Division.

6th Romanian Infantry Division – The division moved northeast behind the 79th Infantry Division.

13th Romanian Infantry Division – The division defended in sector along the Don River west of Kletskiy with the 113th Infantry Division against the 278th Rifle Division and the 304th Rifle Division. To the northwest was the 79th Infantry Division; to the east were assorted battle groups and the 1st Romanian Cavalry Division.

XXXXVIII *Panzer* Corps – The aim of the corps was to clear the southern suburbs and the southern part of the city of enemy forces. The corps suffered the following officer casualties: one wounded in action.

14th Panzer Division – The division defended in sector south of Kuporosnoye and north of Beketovka against the 35th Guards Rifle Division. To the north was the 29th Infantry Division (Motorized); to the south was the 371st Infantry Division.

24th Panzer Division – The division consolidated its position and provided fire support against the Grain Elevator – held by the Marine Infantry Brigade; the division also cleared a balka south of the Tsaritsa River against the 244th Rifle Division. The division lost four NCOs/enlisted killed in action; 20 NCOs/enlisted were wounded in action. During the period June 1, 1942 and September 9, 1942, the division suffered 36 officers and 719 NCOs/enlisted killed in action; 215 officers and 3,771 NCOs/enlisted were wounded in action; 47 NCOs/enlisted were reported missing in action. To the north was the 71st Infantry Division; to the southeast was the 94th Infantry Division.

29th Infantry Division (Motorized) – The division attacked in zone to clear all enemy forces south of the city center against the 35th Guards Rifle Division and the 10th Tank Destroyer Brigade. The division lost three NCOs/enlisted killed in action; two officers and 21 NCOs/enlisted were wounded in action. To the north was 94th Infantry Division; to the south was the 14th ***Panzer*** Division.

94th Infantry Division – The division attacked in zone against the Grain Elevator and captured a bridge over the Tsaritsa River against the 35th Guards Rifle Division. To the north was the 24th ***Panzer*** Division; to the south was the 29th Infantry Division (Motorized.) The division lost 22 NCOs/enlisted killed in action; one officer and 65 NCOs/enlisted were wounded in action; one NCO/enlisted was reported missing in action.

LI Corps – The aim of the corps was to clear the center portion of Stalingrad of all enemy forces. The corps headquarters was located at Gumrak. The 245th ***Sturmgeschütz*** Detachment was assigned to the corps. The corps suffered the following officer casualties: two wounded in action.

71st Infantry Division – The division attacked in its zone, culminating in the city center at Railroad Station Nr.1 and 9th of January Square against the 13th Guards Rifle Division. The division lost five NCOs/enlisted killed in action; three officers and 40 NCOs/enlisted were wounded in action. To the north was the 295th Infantry Division; to the south was the 24th ***Panzer*** Division.

295th Infantry Division – The division suffered 19 NCOs/enlisted killed in action; one officer and 68 NCOs/enlisted were wounded in action; one man was reported missing in action. To the north was the 389th Infantry Division; to the south was the 71st Infantry Division.

389th Infantry Division – The division conducted a counter-attack against enemy forces at Hill 126.6. The division lost one officer and two NCOs/enlisted killed in action; eight NCOs/enlisted were wounded in action. To the north was Battle Group Stahel; to the south was the 295th Infantry Division.

Battle Group Stahel – The battle group defended northwest of Orlovka to contain enemy forces. To the south was the 389th Infantry Division; to the northeast was the 16th ***Panzer*** Division.

Fourth *Panzer* Army – The army headquarters was located at Plodowitoje.

IV Corps – The corps headquarters was located at Plantator.

297th Infantry Division – The division defended in sector south of Elkhi against the 29th Rifle Division. To the north was the 371st Infantry Division; to the south was the 20th Romanian Division.

371st Infantry Division – The division defended in sector north of Peschanka to Elkhi against the 157th Rifle Division, the 136th Rifle Division and the 138th Rifle Division. The division headquarters was located west of Staro-Dubovka. The division lost two NCOs/enlisted killed in action; 13 NCOs/enlisted were wounded in action; one man was reported missing in action. To the north was the 14th ***Panzer*** Division; to the south was the 297th Infantry Division.

20th Romanian Infantry Division – The division defended in sector against the 36th Guards Rifle Division. To the north was the 297th Infantry Division; to the south was the 2nd Romanian Infantry Division of the Romanian VI Corps.

Zum frommen Andenken
an unseren unvergeßlichen Sohn u. Bruder
Johann Maier
Obergefreiter in einem Infanterie-Rgt,
gewesener Sekretärssohn, Pfarre Palting,
welcher im Kampfe um Stalingrad am 18. September 1942 schwer verwundet wurde und am 30. September 1942 im 31. Lebensjahre den Heldentod gestorben ist.

Siegeshoffend zog ich am 1. März 1940
vom Elternhaus
Februar 1941 kam ich wieder nach Haus.
Nach drei Wochen rückte ich wieder ein,
Mit der Hoffnung ich komme wieder
mal heim.
Drückte der Mutter die Hand,
Nicht ahnend, daß es das letztemal sein
kann.
21. Juni zog ich ins Feld, wo mich in
blutiger Schlacht, jetzt eine Kugel traf.
Man brachte mich in ein Feldlazarett,
Dort starb ich fürs Volk als christlicher
Held.
Meine lieben Angehörigen weinet nicht,
Sondern betet für mich, ich gehe
zu meinem Vater,
Der vor 12 Jahren gestorben ist.

Obergefreiter **Johann Maier** was born on October 31, 1911 at Perwang near Braunau am Inn, in Upper Austria. The son of a secretary, he was assigned to an infantry regiment in the 297th Infantry Division. Maier was seriously wounded on September 18, 1942. He died of his wounds at the 2nd Medical Company of the 297th Infantry Division near Gavrilovka on September 30, 1942. He was buried near that location, but today the location of his remains is unknown.

Sources, September 18, 1942: ***Oberkommando des Heeres, Lage Ost: Stand: 18.9.42, Eastern Front Situation Map, National Archives Identifier: 559733, Record Group 242 – National Archives Collection of Foreign Records Seized, 1675-1958, National Archives, College Park, Maryland; Ia, Armeeoberkommando 6, "Morgen Meldung" and assorted reports, Kriegstagebuch 13, 19 September 1942, as found in Microfilm Series, T-312, Records of German Field Commands, Armies, Roll 1686, National Archives and Records Service, College Park, Maryland; Ia, XXXXVIII Panzerkorps, "Übersicht über die dem Korps Unterstellten Divisionen, 28. Juni 1942 – 11 October 1942," as found on T-314, Records of German Field Commands, Corps, Roll 1153, National Archives, College Park, Maryland; Ia, XXXXVIII Panzerkorps, "Zahlenmässige Verlustmeldung der Unterstellten Divisionen und Heerestruppen in der Zeit vom 1. April 1942 bis 31. Oktober 1942," as found in T-314, Records of German Field Commands, Corps, Roll 1153, National Archives, College Park, Maryland; Korpsarzt, XXXXVIII Panzerkorps, "Meldung über Personelle Verluste," Stand 18.9.42, as found on T-314, Records of German Field Commands, Corps, Roll 1158, National Archives, College Park, Maryland; 79th Infantry Division, Kriegstagebuch, 18 September 1942, as found in Microfilm Series T-315, Roll 1108, National Archives and Records Service, College Park, Maryland; 371st Infantry Division, Kriegstagebuch, 18 September 1942, as found in Microfilm Series T-315, Roll 2164, National Archives and Records Service, College Park, Maryland; Florian Freiherr von und zu Aufsess, Die Anlagenbände zu den Kriegstagebüchern der 6. Armee vom 14.09.1942 bis 24.11.1942, Band 1, Schwabach, Germany: Selbstverlag, 2006, 29-31; Alan Clark, Barbarossa: The Russian-German Conflict, 1941-45, New York: William Morrow and Company, 1965, 229; Die 71. Infanterie-Division, 1939-1945: Gefechts- und Erlebnisberichte aus Kämpfen der "Gluckhaften Division" von Verdun bis Stalingrad, vom Monte Cassino bis zum Plattensee, Eggolsheim, FRG: Edition Dörfler, 1973, 246; Division der Wehrmacht: 71. Infanterie-Division, 389. Infanterie-Division, 295. Infanterie-Division, 79. Infanterie-Division, 260. Infanterie-Division, 305. Infanterie-Division, 73. Infanterie-Division, 18. Infanterie-Division, 100. Jäger-Division, 94. Infanterie-Division, Germany: Books LLC, 2010, 321, 565; David M. Glantz & Jonathan M. House, Armageddon in Stalingrad: September-November 1942, (The Stalingrad Trilogy, Volume 2), Lawrence, Kansas: University Press of Kansas, 2009, 161-176; Joachim Lemelsen, 29. Division, Bad Nauheim, FRG: Podzun Verlag, 1960, 203; Jochen Löser, Bittere Pflicht: Kampf und Untergang der 76. Berlin-Brandenburgischen Infanterie-Division, Osnabrück, FRG: Biblio Verlag, 1986, 209; Jason Mark, Death of the Leaping Horseman: 24. Panzer-Division in Stalingrad, Sydney, Australia: Leaping Horsemen Books, 2003, 188-191; Kurt Mehner, Die Geheimen Tagesberichte der Deutschen Wehrmachtführung im Zweiten Weltkrieg 1939-1945, Band 5: 1. Juni 1942 – 30. November 1942, Osnabrück, Germany: Biblio Verlag, 1991, 201; Hans Neidhardt, Mit Tanne und Eichenlaub: Kriegschronik der 100. Jäger Division vormals 100. leichte Infanterie Division, Graz, Austria: Leopold Stocker Verlag, 1981, 206; Anton Schimak, Karl Lamprecht & Friedrich Dettmer, Die 44. Infanterie Division: Tagebuch der Hoch- und Deutschmeister, Wien: Verlag Austria Press, 169, 233 and Map: Marschweg der 44. Infanterie Division im Russland.***

September 19, 1942
Weather: changing cloudiness, warm, 72° F, dry, windy, rain at dusk
Sunrise: 5:43 a.m.; **Sunset:** 6:08 p.m.
Moon: Waxing Gibbous; 70% illumination

Sixth Army – The army headquarters was located at Golubinskaya.

VIII Corps – The 177th ***Sturmgeschütz*** Detachment was assigned to the corps. The corps suffered the following officer casualties: two killed in action; ten wounded in action.

76th Infantry Division – The division defended in sector southwest of Samofalovka and north of Borodkin, against the 308th Rifle Division, the 173rd Rifle Division, the 298th Rifle Division and the 258nd Rifle Division. To the northwest was the 305th Infantry Division; to the east was the 60th Infantry Division (Motorized.) Enemy attacks were supported by heavy artillery fire and rockets. The division lost 42 NCOs/enlisted killed in action; eight officers and 178 NCOs/enlisted were wounded in action; one officer and ten men were listed as missing in action.

305th Infantry Division – The division defended in sector from the Don River, north of Nizhne-Gnilovskii, to west of Kotluban' against the 27th Guards Rifle Division. To the east was the 76th Infantry Division; to the north was the 384th Infantry Division. The division lost 11 NCOs/enlisted killed in action; 21 NCOs/enlisted were wounded in action.

XI Corps – The corps suffered the following officer casualties: three wounded in action; one missing in action.

44th Infantry Division – The division defended in sector Kurchajessowskij-Kamyshinskiy-Hill 171.0-Hill 180.9-Sirotinskaya-Khmelevskoy against the 343rd Rifle Division. The division headquarters was located at Verkhne-Golubaja. To the west was 376th Infantry Division; to the east was the 384th Infantry Division. The division lost two NCOs/enlisted wounded in action.

100th Jäger Division – The division began moving east toward Stalingrad. The bulk of the division reached the Don River near Bol'shaya Nabatowskij.

376th Infantry Division – The division defended in sector near Blizhniaia-Perekopka, against the 321st Rifle Division. To the west was the 1st Romanian Cavalry Division; to the east was the 44th Infantry Division. The division lost two NCOs/enlisted killed in action; one officer and 18 NCOs/enlisted were wounded in action.

384th Infantry Division – The division defended in sector west of the Don River near Trekhostrovskaia to Podgorskii against the 4th Guards Rifle Division, the 214th Rifle Division and the 27th Guards Rifle Division. To the west was the 44th Infantry Division; to the south was the 305th Infantry Division. The division lost one officer and 30 NCOs/enlisted killed in action; 60 NCOs/enlisted were wounded in action; one man was reported missing in action.

XIV *Panzer* Corps – The corps headquarters was located east of Ssadtschi-Kowa. The corps suffered the following officer casualties: one wounded in action.

3rd Infantry Division (Motorized) – The division defended in sector, from the Tartar Hill-Hill 111.1-Hill 129.6-Hill 131.2 against the 84th Rifle Division, the 38th Guards Rifle Division, and the 116th Rifle Division. To the east was the 16th ***Panzer*** Division; to the west was the 60th Infantry Division (Motorized.)

16th Panzer Division – The division defended in sector, from Hill 139.7 to the Volga and from the Volga southwest to Hill 145.1, north of Orlovka against the 299th Rifle Division,

120th Rifle Division, the 231st Rifle Division and the 64th Rifle Division. To the west was the 3rd Infanterie Division (Motorized); to the southwest was Battle Group Stahel.

60th Infantry Division (Motorized) – The division defended in sector, from south of Kotluban' Station near Borodkin to Kuz'michi, against the 116th Rifle Division, the 41st Guards Rifle Division, the 49th Rifle Division, the 24th Rifle Division, the 39th Guards Rifle Division, the 233rd Rifle Division, the 316th Rifle Division, the 292nd Rifle Division and the 308th Rifle Division. To the east was the 3rd Infantry Division (Motorized); to the west was the 76th Infantry Division.

XVII Corps – The corps suffered the following officer casualties: one wounded in action.

79th Infantry Division – The division defended in sector from Bol'shoy-Verkhne-Kalmykovskii-Verkhne-Fomichinskii-Baskowskij against the 124th Rifle Division. The division headquarters was located at Karagichev. To the west was the XXXV Corps of the Italian Eighth Army; to the east was the 13th Romanian Infantry Division. The division lost seven NCOs/enlisted killed in action; one NCO/enlisted were wounded in action.

113th Infantry Division – Two-thirds of the division moved south. One-third of the division remained in defensive positions with the 13th Romanian Infantry Division against the 278th Rifle Division and the 304th Rifle Division. The division lost five NCOs/enlisted killed in action; 62 NCOs/enlisted were wounded in action; 12 men were reported missing in action.

298th Infantry Division – The division occupied three assembly areas along the Sixth Army's western boundary and south of the 79th Infantry Division.

1st Romanian Cavalry Division – The division defended in sector near Mololologowskij south of the Don River against the 76th Rifle Division. To the west were assorted battle groups and the 13th Romanian Infantry Division; to the east was the 376th Infantry Division.

6th Romanian Infantry Division – The division moved northeast to positions behind the 79th Infantry Division.

13th Romanian Infantry Division – The division defended in sector along the Don River west of Kletskiy against the 278th Rifle Division and the 304th Rifle Division. To the northwest was the 79th Infantry Division; to the east were assorted battle groups and the 1st Romanian Cavalry Division.

XXXXVIII *Panzer* Corps

14th Panzer Division – The division defended in sector south of Kuporosnoye and north of Beketovka against the 35th Guards Rifle Division. To the north was the 29th Infantry Division (Motorized); to the south was the 371st Infantry Division.

29th Infantry Division (Motorized) – The division attacked in zone, clearing enemy forces across the El'shanka River and defeating the 35th Guards Rifle Division and the 131st Rifle Division. The division assumed responsibility for the southern zone of the 94th Infantry Division. To the north was the 94th Infantry Division; to the south was the 14th ***Panzer*** Division. The division lost three NCOs/enlisted killed in action; eight NCOs/enlisted were wounded in action.

94th Infantry Division – The division attacked in zone in the center of the city down the Tsaritsa Gulley toward the Volga River, reaching the river with small elements against the 131st Rifle Division. The division relinquished the southern portion of its attack zone to the 29th Infantry Division (Motorized.) To the northwest was the 24th ***Panzer*** Division; to the south was the 29th Infantry Division (Motorized.) The division lost 19 NCOs/enlisted killed in action; three officers and 86 NCOs/enlisted were wounded in action; three NCOs/enlisted were reported missing in action.

LI Corps – The corps headquarters was located at Gumrak. The corps suffered the following officer casualties: one wounded in action.

24th Panzer Division – The division was transferred from the XXXXVIII ***Panzer*** Corps to the LI Corps, and prepared to withdraw from its positions inside Stalingrad and assemble in the Voroponovo area to rest. The division lost five NCOs/enlisted killed in action; one officer and 25 NCOs/enlisted were wounded in action; one officer was missing in action.

71st Infantry Division – The division defended in sector, repelling the 13th Guards Rifle Division and then attacked to clear the western portion of the city of enemy forces north of the Tsaritsa River. To the north was the 295th Infantry

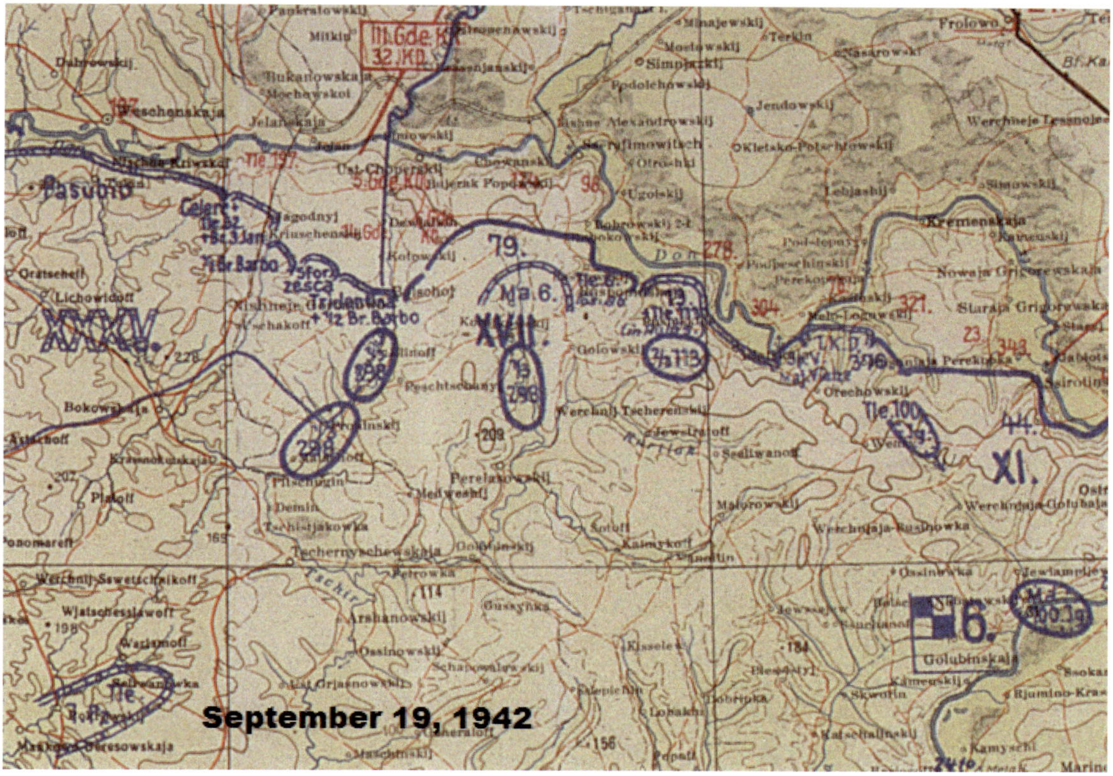

Division; to the south was the 94th Infantry Division. The division lost one officer and 12 NCOs/enlisted killed in action; three officers and 60 NCOs/enlisted were wounded in action.

295th Infantry Division – The division defended in the north of sector, losing Hill 126 against the 95th Rifle Division. To the south, it continued its fight for Mamayev Kurgan [Hill 102.] To the north was the 389th Infantry Division; to the south was the 94th Infantry Division. The division lost one officer and 16 NCOs/enlisted killed in action; one officer and 78 NCOs/enlisted were wounded in action.

389th Infantry Division – The division attacked east in zone. To the south was the 295th Infantry Division; to the north was Battle Group Stahel. The division lost five NCOs/enlisted killed in action; ten NCOs/enlisted were wounded in action.

Battle Group Stahel – The battle group defended northwest of Orlovka to contain enemy forces. To the south was the 389th Infantry Division; to the northeast was the 16th ***Panzer*** Division.

Fourth *Panzer* Army – The army headquarters was located at Plodowitoje.

IV Corps – The corps headquarters was located at Plantator.

297th Infantry Division – The division defended in sector south of Elkhi against the 29th Rifle Division. To the north was the 371st Infantry Division; to the south was the 20th Romanian Infantry Division.

371st Infantry Division – The division defended in sector north of Peschanka to Elkhi against the 157th Rifle Division, the 136th Rifle Division and the 138th Rifle Division. The division headquarters was located west of Staro-Dubovka. To the northeast was the 14th ***Panzer*** Division; to the southwest was the 297th Infantry Division. The division lost five NCOs/enlisted killed in action; one officer and 30 NCOs/enlisted were wounded in action.

20th Romanian Infantry Division – The division defended in sector north of the Volga-Don Canal against the 36th Guards Rifle Division. To the north was the 297th Infantry Division; to the south was the 2nd Romanian Infantry Division of the Romanian VI Corps.

Sources, September 19, 1942: *Oberkommando des Heeres, Lage Ost: Stand: 19.9.42, Eastern Front Situation Map, National Archives Identifier: 559733, Record Group 242 – National Archives Collection of Foreign Records Seized, 1675-1958, National Archives, College Park, Maryland; Ia, Armeeoberkommando 6, "Morgen Meldung" and assorted reports, Kriegstagebuch 13, 20 September 1942, as found in Microfilm Series, T-312, Records of German Field Commands, Armies, Roll 1686, National Archives and Records Service, College Park, Maryland; Ia, XXXXVIII Panzerkorps, "Übersicht über die dem Korps Unterstellten Divisionen, 28. Juni 1942 – 11 October 1942," as found on T-314, Records of German Field Commands, Corps, Roll 1153, National Archives, College Park, Maryland; Korpsarzt, XXXXVIII Panzerkorps, "Meldung über Personelle Verluste," Stand 19.9.42, as found on T-314, Records of German Field Commands, Corps, Roll 1158, National Archives, College Park, Maryland; 79th Infantry Division, Kriegstagebuch, 19 September 1942, as found in Microfilm Series T-315, Roll 1108, National Archives and Records Service, College Park, Maryland; 371st Infantry Division, Kriegstagebuch, 19 September 1942, as found in Microfilm Series T-315, Roll 2164, National Archives and Records Service, College Park, Maryland; Florian Freiherr von und zu Aufsess, Die Anlagenbände zu den Kriegstagebüchern der 6. Armee vom 14.09.1942 bis 24.11.1942, Band 1, Schwabach, Germany: Selbstverlag, 2006, 33-36; Die 71. Infanterie-Division, 1939-1945: Gefechts- und Erlebnisberichte aus Kämpfen der "Gluckhaften Division" von Verdun bis Stalingrad, vom Monte Cassino bis zum Plattensee, Eggolsheim, FRG: Edition Dörfler, 1973, 246; David M. Glantz & Jonathan M. House, Armageddon in Stalingrad: September-November 1942, (The Stalingrad Trilogy, Volume 2), Lawrence, Kansas: University Press of Kansas, 2009, 108, 109, 187-191; Joachim Lemelsen, 29. Division, Bad Nauheim, FRG: Podzun Verlag, 1960, 203; Jochen Löser, Bittere Pflicht: Kampf und Untergang der 76. Berlin-Brandenburgischen Infanterie-Division, Osnabrück, FRG: Biblio Verlag, 1986, 209; Jason Mark, Death of the Leaping Horseman: 24. Panzer-Division in Stalingrad, Sydney, Australia: Leaping Horsemen Books, 2003, 191-192; Anton Schimak, Karl Lamprecht & Friedrich Dettmer, Die 44. Infanterie Division: Tagebuch der Hoch- und Deutschmeister, Wien: Verlag Austria Press, 169, 233 and Map: Marschweg der 44. Infanterie Division im Russland; Dr. F.M. von Senger und Etterlin, Jr., Die 24. Panzer-Division vormals 1. Kavallerie-Division 1939-1945, Neckargemünd, FRG: Kurt Vowinckel Verlag, 1962, 121.*

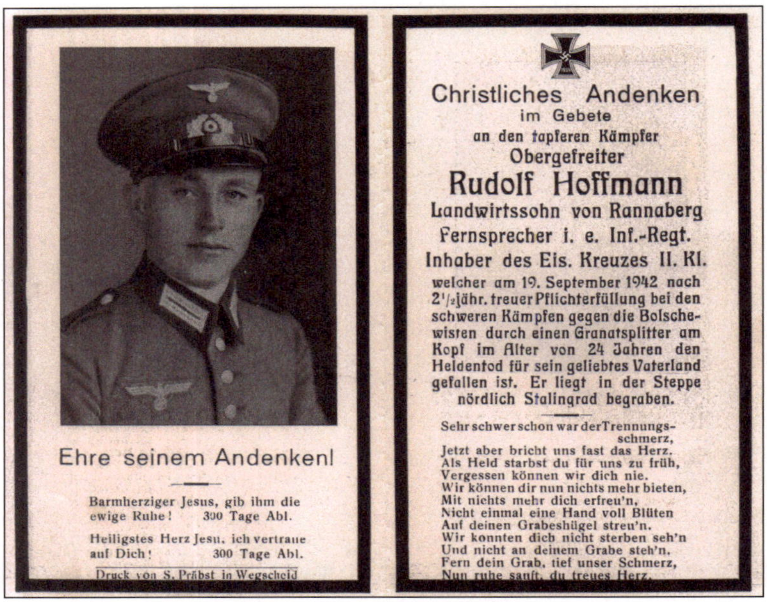
Ehre seinem Andenken!

Barmherziger Jesus, gib ihm die ewige Ruhe! 300 Tage Abl.

Heiligstes Herz Jesu, ich vertraue auf Dich! 300 Tage Abl.

Druck von S. Präbst in Wegscheid

Christliches Andenken
im Gebete
an den tapferen Kämpfer
Obergefreiter
Rudolf Hoffmann
Landwirtssohn von Rannaberg
Fernsprecher i. e. Inf.-Regt.
Inhaber des Eis. Kreuzes II. Kl.

welcher am 19. September 1942 nach 2½ jähr. treuer Pflichterfüllung bei den schweren Kämpfen gegen die Bolschewisten durch einen Granatsplitter am Kopf im Alter von 24 Jahren den Heldentod für sein geliebtes Vaterland gefallen ist. Er liegt in der Steppe nördlich Stalingrad begraben.

Sehr schwer schon war der Trennungsschmerz,
Jetzt aber bricht uns fast das Herz.
Als Held starbst du für uns zu früh,
Vergessen können wir dich nie.
Wir können dir nun nichts mehr bieten,
Mit nichts mehr dich erfreu'n,
Nicht einmal eine Hand voll Blüten
Auf deinen Grabeshügel streu'n.
Wir konnten dich nicht sterben seh'n
Und nicht an deinem Grabe steh'n.
Fern dein Grab, tief unser Schmerz,
Nun ruhe sanft, du treues Herz.

Obergefreiter **Rudolf Hoffmann** was born at Rannaberg near Sonnen in Bavaria on June 3, 1918. The winner of the Iron Cross 2nd Class, he was a telephone operator in an infantry regiment. On September 19, 1942 he was hit in the head by shrapnel and was killed near Kuz'michi, possibly while assigned to the 3rd Infantry Division (Motorized.) He is buried at the German Military Cemetery at Rossoschka in Block 9, Row 21, in Grave 807.

September 20, 1942
Weather: clear, windy, significant cooling in the evening, good road conditions
Sunrise: 5:44 a.m.; **Sunset:** 6:06 p.m.
Moon: Waxing Gibbous; 80% illumination

Sixth Army – Friedrich Paulus reported to Army Group B: "The infantry strength of the army has been so weakened by our own and the Russian attacks of recent days that a supplement is needed to activate it." Bombers and dive-bombers from the ***Luftwaffe***'s VIII Air Corps pounded Stalingrad in large-scale attacks, especially at the railway station. The army headquarters was located at Golubinskaya.

VIII Corps – The corps suffered the following officer casualties: two killed in action; one wounded in action.

76th Infantry Division – The division defended in sector southwest of Samofalovka and north of Borodkin against attacks by the 308th Rifle Division, the 173rd Rifle Division, the 298th Rifle Division, 260th Rifle Division and the 258nd Rifle Division, which were supported by heavy artillery and rocket fire. To the northwest was the 305th Infantry Division; to the east was the 60th Infantry Division (Motorized.) The division lost 13 NCOs/enlisted killed in action; four officers and 101 NCOs/enlisted were wounded in action.

305th Infantry Division – The division defended in sector from the Don River, north of Nizhne-Gnilovskii, to west of Kotluban', against the 260th Rifle Division. To the southeast was the 76th Infantry Division; to the north was the 384th Infantry Division. The division lost eight NCOs/enlisted wounded in action.

XI Corps – The corps suffered the following officer casualties: five wounded in action.

44th Infantry Division – The division defended in sector Kurchajessowskij-Kamyshinskiy-Hill 171.0-Hill 180.9-Sirotinskaya-Khmelevskoy against the 343rd Rifle Division. The division headquarters was located at Verkhne-Golubaja. To the west was 376th Infantry Division; to the east was the 384th Infantry Division.

100th Jäger Division – The division moved east toward Stalingrad. Lead elements reached west of Zapadnovka.

376th Infantry Division – The division defended in sector near Blizhniaia-Perekopka against the 321st Rifle Division. To the west was the 1st Romanian Cavalry Division; to the east was the 44th Infantry Division. The division lost four NCOs/enlisted wounded in action.

384th Infantry Division – The division defended in sector west of the Don River near Trekhostrovskaia to Podgorskii against the 4th Guards Rifle Division. To the west was the 44th Infantry Division; to the south was the 305th Infantry Division.

XIV *Panzer* Corps – The corps headquarters was located east of Ssadtschi-Kowa. The corps suffered the following officer casualties: two killed in action; five wounded in action.

3rd Infantry Division (Motorized) – The division defended in sector, from the Tartar Hill-Hill 111.1-Hill 129.6-Hill 131.2 against the 84th Rifle Division, the 38th Guards Rifle Division, and the 116th Rifle Division. To the east was the 16th ***Panzer*** Division; to the west was the 60th Infantry Division (Motorized.)

16th Panzer Division – The division defended in sector, from Hill 139.7 to the Volga and from the Volga southwest to Hill 145.1, north of Orlovka against the 299th Rifle Division, the 120th Rifle Division, the 231st Rifle Division and the 64th Rifle Division. To the west was the 3rd Infantry Division (Motorized); to the southwest was Battle Group Stahel.

60th Infantry Division (Motorized) – The division defended in sector, from south of Kotluban' Station near Borodkin to Kuz'michi against the 116th Rifle Division, the 41st Guards Rifle Division, the 49th Rifle Division, the 24th Rifle Division, the 39th Guards

Rifle Division, the 233rd Rifle Division, the 316th Rifle Division, the 292nd Rifle Division and the 308th Rifle Division. To the east was the 3rd Infantry Division (Motorized); to the west was the 76th Infantry Division.

XVII Corps

79th Infantry Division – The division defended in sector from Bol'shoy-Verkhne-Kalmykovskii-Verkhne-Fomichinskii-Baskowskij against the 124th Rifle Division and the 96th Rifle Division. The division headquarters was located at Karagichev. To the west was the XXXV Corps of the Italian Eighth Army; to the south was the 13th Romanian Infantry Division. The division lost three NCOs/enlisted killed in action; two NCOs/enlisted were wounded in action.

113th Infantry Division – The division occupied an assembly area south of the front. Part of the division defended in sector south of the Don River with the 13th Romanian Infantry Division against the 278th Rifle Division and the 304th Rifle Division

298th Infantry Division – The division occupied three assembly areas along the Sixth Army's western boundary and south of the 79th Infantry Division.

1st Romanian Cavalry Division – The division defended in sector near Mololologowskij south of the Don River against the 76th Rifle Division. To the west was the 13th Romanian Infantry Division; to the east was the 376th Infantry Division.

1st Romanian Armored Division – The division moved from the south toward the western part of the corps sector.

6th Romanian Infantry Division – The division moved northeast behind the 79th Infantry Division.

13th Romanian Infantry Division – The division defended in sector along the Don River west of Kletskiy against the 278th Rifle Division and the 304th Rifle Division. To the northwest was the 79th Infantry Division; to the east was the 1st Romanian Cavalry Division.

XXXXVIII *Panzer* Corps

14th Panzer Division – The division defended in sector south of Kuporosnoye and north of Beketovka against the 35th Guards Rifle Division. To the northeast was the 29th Infantry Division (Motorized); to the southwest was the 371st Infantry Division. The division lost six NCOs/enlisted killed in action; one officer and 21 NCOs/enlisted were wounded in action; two NCOs/enlisted were reported missing in action.

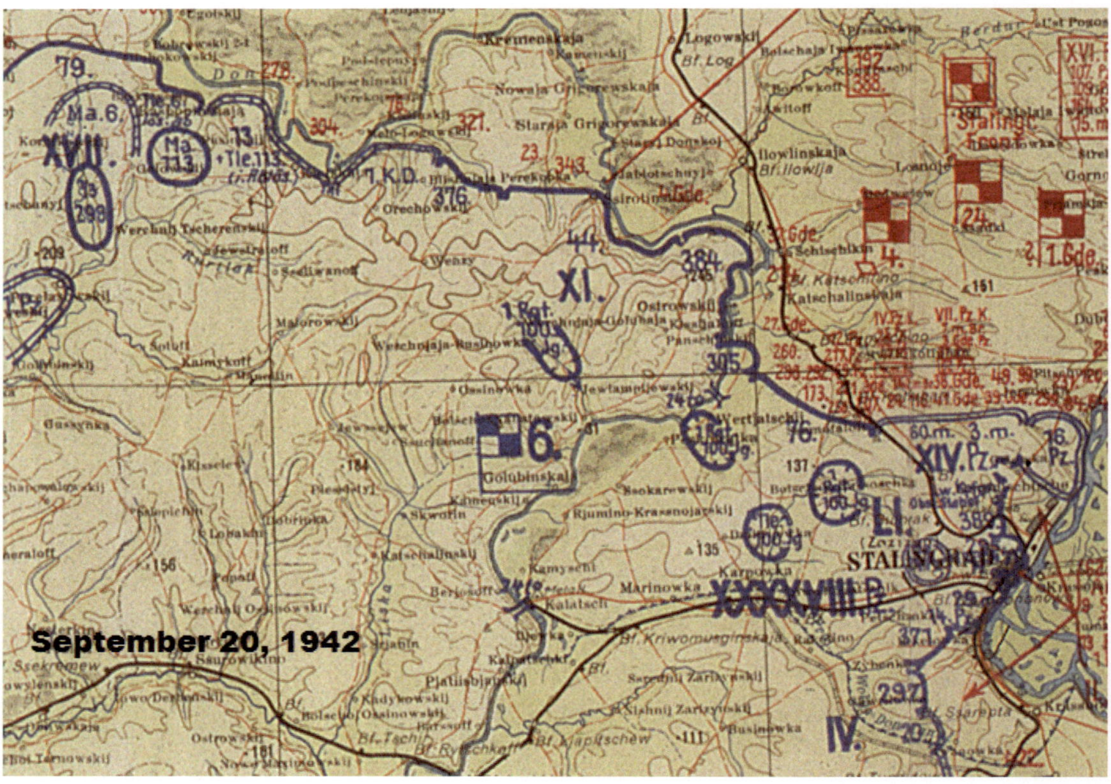

29th Infantry Division (Motorized) – The division continued to attack in southern Stalingrad near the Tsaritsa River and the Grain Elevator, held by the Marine Infantry Brigade. The division lost four NCOs/enlisted killed in action; 25 NCOs/enlisted were wounded in action. To the north was the 94th Infantry Division; to the south was the 14th ***Panzer*** Division.

94th Infantry Division – The division attacked in sector, attempting to seize the Grain Elevator from the Marine Infantry Brigade. To the north was the 71st Infantry Division; to the south was the 29th Infantry Division (Motorized.) The division lost one officer and 31 NCOs/enlisted killed in action; two officers and 163 NCOs/enlisted were wounded in action; one NCO/enlisted was reported missing in action.

LI Corps – The corps headquarters was located at Gumrak. The corps suffered the following officer casualties: ten wounded in action.

24th Panzer Division – The division began a relief in place of the 295th Infantry Division at Mamayev Kurgan (Hill 102.) The division lost four NCOs/enlisted killed in action; 25 NCOs/enlisted were wounded in action.

71st Infantry Division – The division attacked in its zone in the center of the city against the 13th Guards Rifle Division. To the northwest was the 295th Infantry Division; to the south was the 94th Infantry Division. The division lost ten NCOs/enlisted killed in action; 60 NCOs/enlisted were wounded in action.

295th Infantry Division – The division attacked to attempt to seize the crest of Mamayev Kurgan against the 95th Rifle Division and the 112th Rifle Division. The division later began to be relieved in place from some of its positions west of Mamayev Kurgan (Hill 102) by the 24th ***Panzer*** Division. To the north was the 389th Infantry Division; to the south was the 71st Infantry Division. The division suffered 22 NCOs/enlisted killed in action; two officers and 77 NCOs/enlisted were wounded in action.

389th Infantry Division – The division attacked north in zone. To the north was Battle Group Stahel; to the south was the 295th Infantry Division. The division lost two NCOs/enlisted killed in action; 60 NCOs/enlisted were wounded in action.

Battle Group Stahel – The battle group defended northwest of Orlovka to contain enemy forces. To the northwest was the 16th ***Panzer*** Division; to the south was the 389th Infantry Division.

Fourth *Panzer* Army – The army headquarters was located at Plodowitoje.

IV Corps – The corps headquarters was located at Plantator.

297th Infantry Division – The division defended in sector east of Elkhi against the 29th Rifle Division. To the north was the 371st Infantry Division; to the south was the 20th Romanian Infantry Division.

371st Infantry Division – The division defended in sector north of Peschanka to Elkhi against the 138th Rifle Division. The division headquarters was located west of Staro-Dubovka. To the north was the 14th ***Panzer*** Division; to the south was the 297th Infantry Division. The division lost one officer and four NCOs/enlisted killed in action; 36 NCOs/enlisted were wounded in action; two men were reported missing in action.

20th Romanian Infantry Division – The division defended in sector north of the Volga-Don Canal against the 36th Guards Rifle Division. To the north was the 297th Infantry Division; to the south was the 2nd Romanian Infantry Division of the Romanian VI Corps.

Sources, September 20, 1942: *Oberkommando des Heeres, Lage Ost: Stand: 20.9.42, Eastern Front Situation Map, National Archives Identifier: 559733, Record Group 242 – National Archives Collection of Foreign Records Seized, 1675-1958, National Archives, College Park, Maryland; Ia, Armeeoberkommando 6, "Morgen Meldung" and assorted reports, Kriegstagebuch 13, 21 September 1942, as found in Microfilm Series, T-312, Records of German Field Commands, Armies, Roll 1686, National Archives and Records Service, College Park, Maryland; Ia, XXXXVIII Panzerkorps, "Übersicht über die dem Korps Unterstellten Divisionen, 28. Juni 1942 – 11 October 1942," as found on T-314, Records of German Field Commands, Corps, Roll 1153, National Archives, College Park, Maryland; Korpsarzt, XXXXVIII Panzerkorps, "Meldung über Personelle Verluste," Stand 20.9.42, as found on T-314, Records of German Field Commands, Corps, Roll 1158, National Archives, College Park, Maryland; 79th Infantry Division, Kriegstagebuch, 20 September 1942, as found in Microfilm Series T-315, Roll 1108, National Archives and Records Service, College Park, Maryland; 371st Infantry Division, Kriegstagebuch, 20 September 1942, as found in Microfilm Series T-315, Roll 2164, National Archives and Records Service, College Park, Maryland; Florian Freiherr von und zu Aufsess, Die Anlagenbände zu den Kriegstagebüchern der 6. Armee vom 14.09.1942 bis 24.11.1942, Band 1, Schwabach, Germany: Selbstverlag, 2006, 36-40; Alan Clark, Barbarossa: The Russian-German Conflict, 1941-45, New York: William Morrow and Company, 1965, 229; John Erickson, The Road to Stalingrad, New York: Harper & Row, 1975, 407; Die 71. Infanterie-Division, 1939-1945: Gefechts- und Erlebnisberichte aus*

Kämpfen der "Gluckhaften Division" von Verdun bis Stalingrad, vom Monte Cassino bis zum Plattensee, Eggolsheim, FRG: Edition Dörfler, 1973, 250; John Erickson, The Road to Stalingrad, New York: Harper & Row, 1975, 407; David M. Glantz & Jonathan M. House, Armageddon in Stalingrad: September-November 1942, (The Stalingrad Trilogy, Volume 2), Lawrence, Kansas: University Press of Kansas, 2009, 192-197; Joachim Lemelsen, 29. Division, Bad Nauheim, FRG: Podzun Verlag, 1960, 203; Jochen Löser, Bittere Pflicht: Kampf und Untergang der 76. Berlin-Brandenburgischen Infanterie-Division, Osnabrück, FRG: Biblio Verlag, 1986, 209; Jason Mark, Death of the Leaping Horseman: 24. Panzer-Division in Stalingrad, Sydney, Australia: Leaping Horsemen Books, 2003, 193-194; Kurt Mehner, Die Geheimen Tagesberichte der Deutschen Wehrmachtführung im Zweiten Weltkrieg 1939-1945, Band 5: 1. Juni 1942 – 30. November 1942, Osnabrück, Germany: Biblio Verlag, 1991, 205; Anton Schimak, Karl Lamprecht & Friedrich Dettmer, Die 44. Infanterie Division: Tagebuch der Hoch- und Deutschmeister, Wien: Verlag Austria Press, 169, 233 and Map: Marschweg der 44. Infanterie Division im Russland.

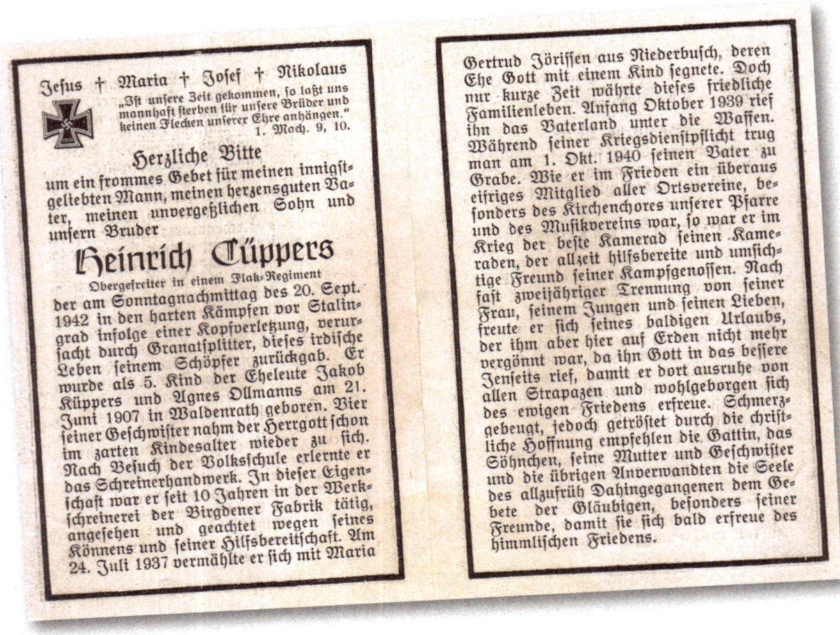
Jesus † Maria † Josef † Nikolaus

„Ist unsere Zeit gekommen, so laßt uns mannhaft sterben für unsere Brüder und keinen Flecken unserer Ehre anhängen."
1. Mach. 9, 10.

Herzliche Bitte

um ein frommes Gebet für meinen innigst-geliebten Mann, meinen herzensguten Vater, meinen unvergeßlichen Sohn und unsern Bruder

Heinrich Cüppers

Obergefreiter in einem Flak-Regiment

der am Sonntagnachmittag des 20. Sept. 1942 in den harten Kämpfen vor Stalingrad infolge einer Kopfverletzung, verursacht durch Granatsplitter, dieses irdische Leben seinem Schöpfer zurückgab. Er wurde als 5. Kind der Eheleute Jakob Küppers und Agnes Ollmanns am 21. Juni 1907 in Waldenrath geboren. Vier seiner Geschwister nahm der Herrgott schon im zarten Kindesalter wieder zu sich. Nach Besuch der Volksschule erlernte er das Schreinerhandwerk. In dieser Eigenschaft war er seit 10 Jahren in der Werkschreinerei der Birgdener Fabrik tätig, angesehen und geachtet wegen seines Könnens und seiner Hilfsbereitschaft. Am 24. Juli 1937 vermählte er sich mit Maria Gertrud Jörissen aus Niederbusch, deren Ehe Gott mit einem Kind segnete. Doch nur kurze Zeit währte dieses friedliche Familienleben. Anfang Oktober 1939 rief ihn das Vaterland unter die Waffen. Während seiner Kriegsdienstpflicht trug man am 1. Okt. 1940 seinen Vater zu Grabe. Wie er im Frieden ein überaus eifriges Mitglied aller Ortsvereine, besonders des Kirchenchores unserer Pfarre und des Musikvereins war, so war er im Krieg der beste Kamerad seinen Kameraden, der allzeit hilfsbereite und umsichtige Freund seiner Kampfgenossen. Nach fast zweijähriger Trennung von seiner Frau, seinem Jungen und seinen Lieben, freute er sich seines baldigen Urlaubs, der ihm aber hier auf Erden nicht mehr vergönnt war, da ihn Gott in das bessere Jenseits rief, damit er dort ausruhe von allen Strapazen und wohlgeborgen sich des ewigen Friedens erfreue. Schmerzgebeugt, jedoch getröstet durch die christliche Hoffnung empfehlen die Gattin, das Söhnchen, seine Mutter und Geschwister und die übrigen Anverwandten die Seele des allzufrüh Dahingegangenen dem Gebete der Gläubigen, besonders seiner Freunde, damit sie sich bald erfreue des himmlischen Friedens.

Luftwaffe Obergefreiter **Heinrich Cüppers (Küppers)** was born in Waldenrath near Geilenkirchen in North Rhine-Westphalia on June 21, 1907. Assigned to a ***flak*** regiment in the 9th ***Flak*** Division, he was hit in the head by shrapnel and killed on September 20, 1942, one mile south of Point 456, near Stalingrad. He is listed in the remembrance book at the German Military Cemetery at Rossoschka.

Der bitt're Tod, er hat dich uns entrissen,
Fern von der Heimat in des Feindes Land,
Für's Vaterland hast du ihn kosten müssen,
Beweint von allen, die dich geliebt, gekannt.
Nie mehr können wir in deine Augen blicken,
Du kannst uns nicht mehr reichen deine Hand.
Wer hätt' geahnt, daß du schon scheiden mußtest
Aus unserm friedlichen Familienband.
Doch wird auch einstens jener Tag erscheinen,
Der uns im Himmel wird vereinen,
Dort wo des Friedens Palmen wehn,
Winkt uns ein frohes Wiedersehn.

Gütige Mutter Maria,
bitte für die armen Seelen!
Betrübte Mutter Maria,
tröste sie!

Lasset uns beten.

Gott, himmlischer Vater, wir bitten Dich durch die Wunden und den blutigen Tod Deines eingeborenen Sohnes, Du mögest ihm, der in treuer Erfüllung seiner Pflicht die Todeswunde empfangen hat, ein gnädiger Richter und Belohner sein.

Karl Becker. Geilenkirchen.

In Rußlands Erde, schwer und müde,
Sank hin dein Haupt zur ew'gen Ruh.
Fürs Vaterland gabst du dein Leben,
Schlaf wohl, du tapferer Krieger, du.
Du warst so jung, du starbst so früh,
Wer dich gekannt, vergißt dich nie.

Luftwaffe Obergefreiter **Heinrich Cüppers (Küppers)**

September 21, 1942
Weather: dry, very windy, 68° F, changing cloudiness, night rain, good road conditions
Sunrise: 5:46 a.m.; **Sunset:** 6:04 p.m.
Moon: Waxing Gibbous; 88% illumination

Sixth Army – The aim of the army was to rush the 79th Infantry Division, the 113th Infantry Division and the 100th ***Jäger*** Division to Stalingrad for the latest offensive. The army headquarters was located at Golubinskaya.

VIII Corps – The 177th ***Sturmgeschütz*** Detachment and the 521st ***Panzerjäger*** Detachment were assigned to the corps. The corps suffered the following officer casualties: three killed in action; six wounded in action.

76th Infantry Division – The division defended in sector southwest of Samofalovka and north of Borodkin, against the 308th Rifle Division, the 173rd Rifle Division, the 298th Rifle Division, the 260th Rifle Division and the 258nd Rifle Division. To the northwest was the 305th Infantry Division; to the east was the 60th Infantry Division (Motorized.) Enemy attacks were supported by heavy artillery fire and rockets. The division lost 24 NCOs/enlisted killed in action; 130 NCOs/enlisted were wounded in action; eight men were reported missing in action.

305th Infantry Division – The division defended in sector from the Don River, north of Nizhne-Gnilovskii, to west of Kotluban' against the 27th Guards Rifle Division and the 260th Rifle Division. To the east was the 76th Infantry Division; to the north was the 384th Infantry Division. The division lost one officer and two NCOs/enlisted killed in action; one officer and nine NCOs/enlisted were wounded in action.

XI Corps

44th Infantry Division – The division defended in sector Kurchajessowskij-Kamyshinskiy-Hill 171.0-Hill 180.9-Sirotinskaya-Khmelevskoy against the 343rd Rifle Division. The division headquarters was located at Verkhne-Golubaja. To the west was 376th Infantry Division; to the east was the 384th Infantry Division. Two NCOs/enlisted were wounded in action.

100th Jäger Division – The division moved east toward Stalingrad. Lead elements reached Bol'shaya Rossoschka; trail elements reached the Don River. The division lost one NCO/enlisted wounded in action.

376th Infantry Division – The division defended in sector near Blizhniaia-Perekopka against the 321st Rifle Division. To the west was the 1st Romanian Cavalry Division; to the east was the 44th Infantry Division. Three NCOs/enlisted were wounded in action.

384th Infantry Division – The division defended in sector west of the Don River near Trekhostrovskaia to Podgorskii against the 37th Guards Rifle Division and the 214th Rifle Division, repulsing an attack against Hill 130. To the west was the 44th Infantry Division; to the south was the 305th Infantry Division. The division lost six NCOs/enlisted killed in action; 47 NCOs/enlisted were wounded in action.

XIV *Panzer* Corps – The aim of the corps was to defend the northern shoulder of the Sixth Army east of the Don River against attacks by the 4th Tank Army and the 24th Army. The corps headquarters was located east of Ssadtschi-Kowa. The corps suffered the following officer casualties: 11 killed in action; four wounded in action.

3rd Infantry Division (Motorized) – The division defended in sector, from the Tartar Hill-Hill 111.1-Hill 129.6-Hill 131.2 against the 84th Rifle Division, the 38th Guards Rifle Division and the 116th Rifle Division. To the east was the 16th ***Panzer*** Division; to the west was the 60th Infantry Division (Motorized.)

16th Panzer Division – The division defended in sector, from Hill 139.7 to the Volga and from the Volga southwest to Hill 145.1, north of Orlovka, against the 299th Rifle Division, the 120th Rifle Division, the 231st Rifle Division and the 64th Rifle Division. To the west was the 3rd Infantry Division (Motorized); to the southwest was Battle Group Stahel.

60th Infantry Division (Motorized) – The division defended in sector, from south of Kotluban' Station near Borodkin to Kuz'michi against the 116th Rifle Division, the 41st Guards Rifle Division, the 49th Rifle Division, the 24th Rifle Division, the 39th Guards Rifle Division, the 233rd Rifle Division, the 316th Rifle Division, the 292nd Rifle Division and the 308th Rifle Division. To the east was the 3rd Infantry Division (Motorized); to the west was the 76th Infantry Division.

Battle Group Stahel – The battle group defended northwest of Orlovka to contain enemy forces. To the northwest was the 16th ***Panzer*** Division; to the southwest was the 389th Infantry Division.

XVII Corps

79th Infantry Division – The division defended in sector from Bol'shoy-Verkhne-Kalmykovskii-Verkhne-Fomichinskii-Baskowskij against the 124th Rifle Division and the 96th Rifle Division. The 6th Romanian Infantry Division assumed the eastern portion of the sector. The division headquarters was located at Karagichev. To the west was the XXXV Italian Corps; to the east was the 6th Romanian Infantry Division. The division suffered one NCO/enlisted wounded in action; one NCO/enlisted was reported missing in action.

113th Infantry Division – The division moved to the southeast toward the Don River. Lead elements reached Verkhne-Businovka.

298th Infantry Division – The division occupied three assembly areas along the Sixth Army's western boundary and south of the 79th Infantry Division.

1st Romanian Cavalry Division – The division defended in sector near Molologowskij south of the Don River against the 76th Rifle

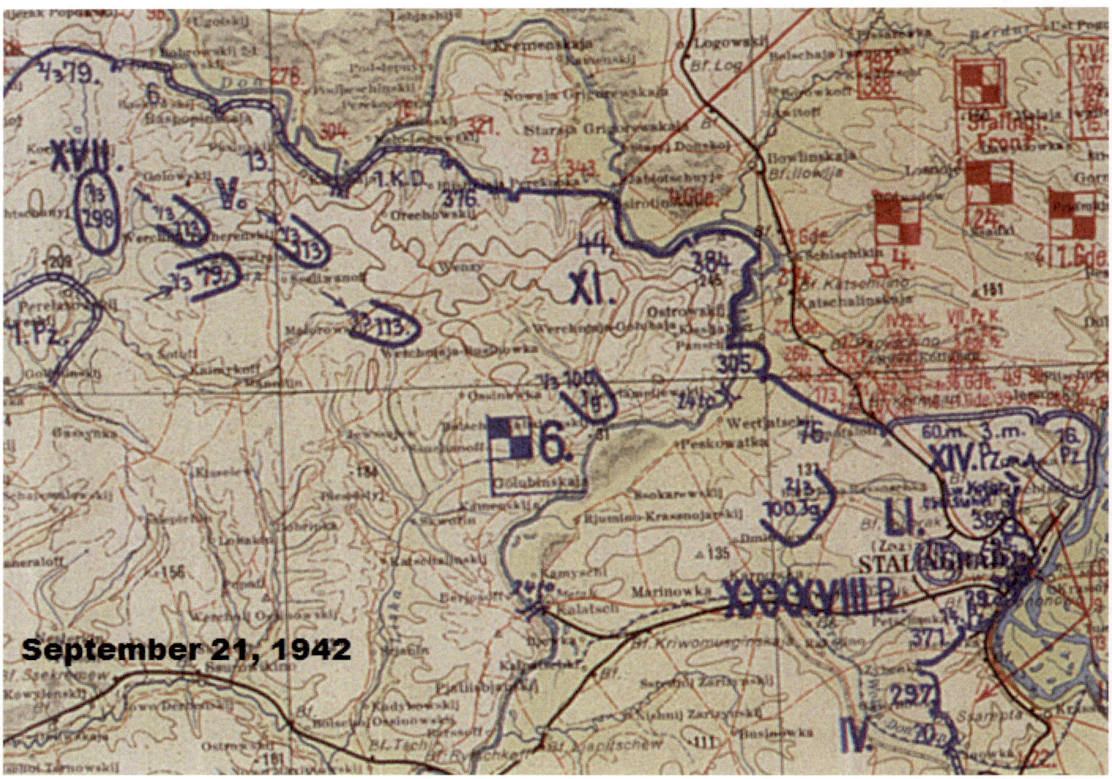

Division. To the west was the 13th Romanian Infantry Division; to the east was the 376th Infantry Division.

1st Romanian Armored Division – The division moved from the south toward the western part of the corps sector.

6th Romanian Infantry Division – The division defended in sector south of the Don River against the 96th Rifle Division. To the west was the 79th Infantry Division; to the southeast was the 13th Romanian Infantry Division.

13th Romanian Infantry Division – The division defended in sector along the Don River west of Kletskiy against the 278th Rifle Division and the 304th Rifle Division. To the northwest was the 6th Romanian Infantry Division; to the east was the 1st Romanian Cavalry Division.

XXXXVIII *Panzer* Corps – The corps suffered the following officer casualties: two killed in action; two wounded in action.

14th Panzer Division – The division defended in sector south of Kuporosnoye and north of Beketovka, smashing enemy probes against its sector. To the north was the 29th Infantry Division (Motorized); to the south was the 371st Infantry Division. The division lost one officer and 14 NCOs/enlisted killed in action; two officers and 56 NCOs/enlisted were wounded in action; three NCOs/enlisted were reported missing in action.

29th Infantry Division (Motorized) – The division attacked in zone to sweep remaining enemy units from the southern portion of the city. Bitter fighting occurred at the Grain Elevator against the Marine Infantry Brigade, with the division seizing the southwest portion of the area. To the north was the 94th Infantry Division; to the south was the 14th ***Panzer*** Division. The division lost one officer and 33 NCOs/enlisted killed in action; one officer and 72 NCOs/enlisted were wounded in action.

94th Infantry Division – The division attacked in zone, planting the German flag on the Grain Elevator at 10:00 p.m. and controlling all crossing sites over the Tsaritsa River. To the north was the 71st Infantry Division; to the south was the 29th Infantry Division (Motorized.) The division lost one officer and 12 NCOs/enlisted killed in action; one officer and 88 NCOs/enlisted were wounded in action.

LI Corps – The corps headquarters was located at Gumrak. The corps suffered the following officer casualties: one killed in action; one wounded in action.

24th Panzer Division – The division completed a relief in place of the 295th Infantry Division at Mamayev Kurgan (Hill 102.) To the northwest was the 389th Infantry Division; to the southeast was the 295th Infantry Division. The division suffered seven NCOs/enlisted killed in action; 24 NCOs/enlisted were wounded in action.

71st Infantry Division – The division attacked in zone in the center of the city, with heavy fighting at Kommunisticheskaia Street, Respublikanskaia Street, Krasnopiterskaia Street, Stalinskaia Street and Naberezhnaia Street against the 13th Guards Rifle Division. To the south was the 94th Infantry Division; to the north was the 295th Infantry Division. The division lost 12 NCOs/enlisted killed in action; 45 NCOs/enlisted were wounded in action.

295th Infantry Division – The division completed having its western elements relieved in place by the 24th ***Panzer*** Division at Mamayev Kurgan (Hill 102) against the 95th Rifle Division and the 112th Rifle Division. To the east, it initially gave ground to the 137th Tank Brigade at the Bannyi Balka, but later forced the enemy to withdraw. The division suffered 27 NCOs/enlisted killed in action; five officers and 101 NCOs/enlisted were wounded in action; one man was reported missing in action. To the west was the 24th ***Panzer*** Division; to the south was the 71st Infantry Division.

389th Infantry Division – The division consolidated its earlier gains in fierce fighting. The division lost 32 NCOs/enlisted killed in action; 25 NCOs/enlisted were wounded in action. To the south was the 24th ***Panzer*** Division; to the northeast was Battle Group Stahel.

Battle Group Stahel – The battle group defended northwest of Orlovka to contain enemy forces. To the northwest was the 16th ***Panzer*** Division; to the south was the 389th Infantry Division.

Fourth *Panzer* Army – The army headquarters was located at Plodowitoje.

IV Corps – The corps headquarters was located at Plantator.

297th Infantry Division – The division defended in sector east of Elkhi. To the north was the 371st Infantry Division; to the south was the 20th Romanian Infantry Division.

371st Infantry Division – The division defended in sector north of Peschanka to Elkhi, repelling heavy enemy attacks to its left flank; the division headquarters was located west of Staro-Dubovka. To the northeast was the 14th ***Panzer*** Division; to the south was the 297th Infantry Division. The division lost five NCOs/enlisted killed in action; 25 NCOs/enlisted were wounded in action.

20th Romanian Infantry Division – The division defended in sector north of the Volga-Don River. To the north was the 297th Infantry Division; to the south was the 2nd Romanian Infantry Division of the Romanian VI Corps.

Sources, September 21, 1942: *Oberkommando des Heeres, Lage Ost: Stand: 21.9.42, Eastern Front Situation Map, National Archives Identifier: 559733, Record Group 242 – National Archives Collection of Foreign Records Seized, 1675-1958, National Archives, College Park, Maryland; Ia, Armeeoberkommando 6, "Morgen Meldung" and assorted reports, Kriegstagebuch 13, 22 September 1942, as found in Microfilm Series, T-312, Records of German Field Commands, Armies, Roll 1686, National Archives and Records Service, College Park, Maryland; Ia, XXXXVIII Panzerkorps, "Übersicht über die dem Korps Unterstellten Divisionen, 28. Juni 1942 – 11 October 1942," as found on T-314, Records of German Field Commands, Corps, Roll 1153, National Archives, College Park, Maryland; Korpsarzt, XXXXVIII Panzerkorps, "Meldung über Personelle Verluste," Stand 21.9.42, as found on T-314, Records of German Field Commands, Corps, Roll 1158, National Archives, College Park, Maryland; 79th Infantry Division, Kriegstagebuch, 21 September 1942, as found in Microfilm Series T-315, Roll 1108, National Archives and Records Service, College Park, Maryland; 371st Infantry Division, Kriegstagebuch, 21 September 1942, as found in Microfilm Series T-315, Roll 2164, National Archives and Records Service, College Park, Maryland; Florian Freiherr von und zu Aufsess, Die Anlagenbände zu den Kriegstagebüchern der 6. Armee vom 14.09.1942 bis 24.11.1942, Band 1, Schwabach, Germany: Selbstverlag, 2006, 43-44; Alan Clark, Barbarossa: The Russian-German Conflict, 1941-45, New York: William Morrow and Company, 1965, 229; Die 71. Infanterie-Division, 1939-1945: Gefechts- und Erlebnisberichte aus Kämpfen der "Gluckhaften Division" von Verdun bis Stalingrad, vom Monte Cassino bis zum Plattensee, Eggolsheim, FRG: Edition Dörfler, 1973, 250; David M. Glantz & Jonathan M. House, Armageddon in Stalingrad: September-November 1942, (The Stalingrad Trilogy, Volume 2), Lawrence, Kansas: University Press of Kansas, 2009, 193-199; Joachim Lemelsen, 29. Division, Bad Nauheim, FRG: Podzun Verlag, 1960, 203; Jochen Löser, Bittere Pflicht: Kampf und Untergang der 76. Berlin-Brandenburgischen Infanterie-Division, Osnabrück, FRG: Biblio Verlag, 1986, 209; Jason Mark, Death of the Leaping Horseman: 24. Panzer-Division in Stalingrad, Sydney, Australia: Leaping Horsemen Books, 2003, 195-202; Kurt Mehner, Die Geheimen Tagesberichte der Deutschen Wehrmachtführung im Zweiten Weltkrieg 1939-1945, Band 5: 1. Juni 1942 – 30. November 1942, Osnabrück, Germany: Biblio Verlag, 1991, 206; Anton Schimak, Karl Lamprecht & Friedrich Dettmer, Die 44. Infanterie Division: Tagebuch der Hoch- und Deutschmeister, Wien: Verlag Austria Press, 169, 233 and Map: Marschweg der 44. Infanterie Division im Russland.*

Photo taken by "Rudi" sometime in September 1942 of the graves of his comrades at a small Military Cemetery near Gorodishche. Rudi was the commander of the 13th Company in the 669th Infantry Regiment of the 371st Infantry Division.

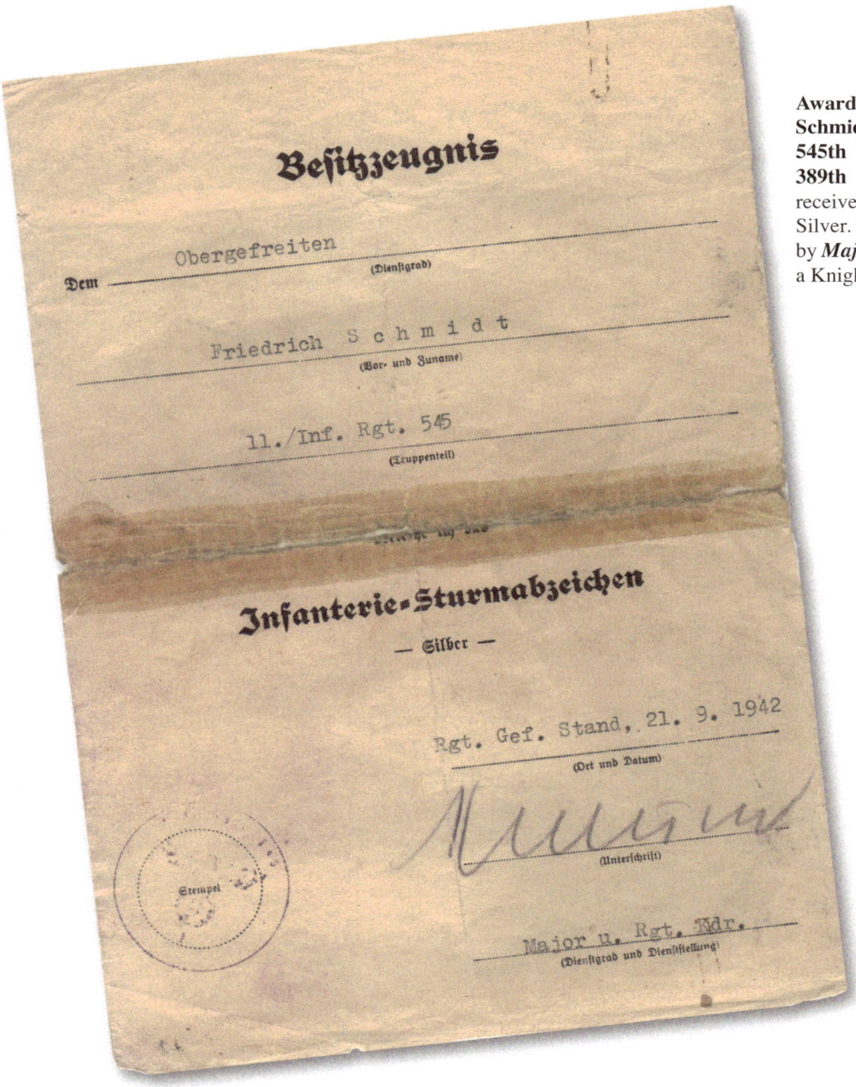

Besitzzeugnis

Dem Obergefreiten
(Dienstgrad)

Friedrich Schmidt
(Vor- und Zuname)

11./Inf. Rgt. 545
(Truppenteil)

Infanterie-Sturmabzeichen
— Silber —

Rgt. Gef. Stand, 21. 9. 1942
(Ort und Datum)

(Unterschrift)

Stempel

Major u. Rgt. Kdr.
(Dienstgrad und Dienststellung)

Award document to Friedrich Schmidt, 11th Company of the 545th Infantry Regiment in the 389th Infantry Division. Schmidt received the Infantry Assault Badge in Silver. The award document is signed by ***Major*** Hans von Schmidt, who was a Knights Cross winner.

September 22, 1942
Weather: clear, sunny, cool, no clouds, strong north wind, 55° F
Sunrise: 5:47 a.m.; **Sunset:** 6:02 p.m.
Moon: Waxing Gibbous; 85% illumination

Sixth Army – Bombers and dive-bombers from the ***Luftwaffe***'s VIII Air Corps pounded Stalingrad in large-scale attacks, especially at Mamayev Kurgan. The army headquarters was located at Golubinskaya.

VIII Corps – The corps suffered the following officer casualties: two killed in action; seven wounded in action.

76th Infantry Division – The division defended in sector southwest of Samofalovka and north of Borodkin, against the 308th Rifle Division, the 173rd Rifle Division, the 298th Rifle Division, the 260th Rifle Division and the 258nd Rifle Division. To the northwest was the 305th Infantry Division; to the east was the 60th Infantry Division (Motorized.) Enemy attacks were supported by heavy artillery fire and rockets. The division lost 30 NCOs/enlisted killed in action; 80 NCOs/enlisted were wounded in action.

305th Infantry Division – The division defended in sector from the Don River, north of Nizhne-Gnilovskii, to west of Kotluban' against the 260th Rifle Division. To the east was the 76th Infantry Division; to the north was the 384th Infantry Division. The division lost one NCO/enlisted killed in action; eight NCOs/enlisted were wounded in action.

XI Corps – The corps suffered the following officer casualties: two wounded in action; two missing in action.

44th Infantry Division – The division defended in sector Kurchajessowskij-Kamyshinskiy-Hill 171.0-Hill 180.9-Sirotinskaya-Khmelevskoy against the 343rd Rifle Division, the 40th Guards Rifle Division and 4th Guards Rifle Division. The division headquarters was located at Verkhne-Golubaja. To the west was 376th Infantry Division; to the east was the 384th Infantry Division. The division lost one NCO/enlisted killed in action; one NCO/enlisted was wounded in action.

100th Jäger Division – The division moved east toward Stalingrad reaching Bol'shaya Rossoschka.

376th Infantry Division – The division defended in sector near Blizhniaia-Perekopka against the 321st Rifle Division. To the west was the 1st Romanian Cavalry Division; to the east was the 44th Infantry Division. The division lost one NCO/enlisted wounded in action.

384th Infantry Division – The division defended in sector west of the Don River near Trekhostrovskaia to Podgorskii against the 37th Guards Rifle Division, the 214th Rifle Division and the 27th Guards Rifle Division. To the west was the 44th Infantry Division; to the south was the 305th Infantry Division. The division lost two officers and 15 NCOs/enlisted killed in action; four officers and 77 NCOs/enlisted were wounded in action; two officers and 61 men were reported missing in action.

XIV *Panzer* Corps – The corps headquarters was located east of Ssadtschi-Kowa. The corps suffered the following officer casualties: three wounded in action.

3rd Infantry Division (Motorized) – The division defended in sector, from the Tartar Hill-Hill 111.1-Hill 129.6-Hill 131.2 against the 84th Rifle Division, the 38th Guards Rifle Division, and the 116th Rifle Division. To the east was the 16th ***Panzer*** Division; to the west was the 60th Infantry Division (Motorized.)

16th Panzer Division – The division defended in sector, from Hill 139.7 to the Volga and from the Volga southwest to Hill 145.1, north of Orlovka against the 299th Rifle Division, the

120th Rifle Division, the 231st Rifle Division and the 64th Rifle Division. To the west was the 3rd Infantry Division (Motorized); to the southwest was Battle Group Stahel.

60th Infantry Division (Motorized) – The division defended in sector, from south of Kotluban' Station near Borodkin to Kuz'michi against the 116th Rifle Division, the 41st Guards Rifle Division, the 49th Rifle Division, the 24th Rifle Division, the 39th Guards Rifle Division, the 233rd Rifle Division, the 316th Rifle Division, the 292nd Rifle Division and the 308th Rifle Division. To the east was the 3rd Infantry Division (Motorized); to the west was the 76th Infantry Division.

Battle Group Stahel – The battle group defended northwest of Orlovka to contain enemy forces. To the northwest was the 16th ***Panzer*** Division; to the south was the 389th Infantry Division.

XVII Corps

79th Infantry Division – The bulk of the division defended in sector from Bol'shoy-Verkhne-Kalmykovskii-Verkhne-Fomichinskii-Baskowskij against the 124th Rifle Division, repelling a night attack at 1:30 a.m. against Hill 188. The division headquarters was located at Karagichev. To the west was the Italian XXXV Corps; to the east was the 6th Romanian Infantry Division. Part of the division moved southeast toward Stalingrad. The division lost one NCO/ enlisted wounded in action.

113th Infantry Division – The division moved to the southeast toward the Don River. Lead elements reached Verkhne-Businovka.

298th Infantry Division – The division occupied three assembly areas along the Sixth Army's western boundary and south of the 79th Infantry Division.

1st Romanian Cavalry Division – The division defended in sector near Molologowskij south of the Don River against the 76th Rifle Division. To the west was the 13th Romanian Infantry Division; to the east was the 376th Infantry Division.

1st Romanian Armored Division – The division occupied an assembly area in the western part of the corps sector.

6th Romanian Infantry Division – The division defended in sector south of the Don River against the 96th Rifle Division. To the west was part of the 79th Infantry Division; to the southeast was the 13th Romanian Infantry Division.

13th Romanian Infantry Division – The division defended in sector along the Don River west of Kletskiy against the 278th Rifle Division and the 304th Rifle Division. To the northwest was the 6th Romanian Infantry Division; to the east was the 1st Romanian Cavalry Division.

XXXXVIII *Panzer* Corps – The corps suffered the following officer casualties: three wounded in action.

14th Panzer Division – The division attacked in zone; it later repelled an attack against its right flank. The division lost 19 NCOs/enlisted killed in action; one officer and 57 NCOs/enlisted were wounded in action; one officer and four NCOs/enlisted were reported missing in action. To the northwest was the 29th Infantry Division (Motorized); to the south was the 371st Infantry Division.

29th Infantry Division (Motorized) – The division attacked in zone near the Grain Elevator. The division reported no casualties. To the northwest was the 94th Infantry Division; to the southeast was the 14th ***Panzer*** Division.

94th Infantry Division – The division seized the Grain Elevator at 4:00 a.m. and continued to attack east in zone near the Tsaritsa River. During the period August 25, 1942 to September 22, 1942, the division lost seven officers and 339 NCOs/enlisted killed in action; 42 officers and 1,232 NCOs/enlisted were wounded in action; one officer and 26 NCOs/enlisted were reported missing in action. To the north was the 71st Infantry Division; to the southeast was the 29th Infantry Division (Motorized.)

LI Corps – Heavy enemy attacks were reported at Hill 102. The corps headquarters was located at Gumrak. The corps suffered the following officer casualties: four killed in action; 13 wounded in action.

24th Panzer Division – The division repulsed several enemy attacks along the western edge of Hill 102 (Mamayev Kurgan.) The division suffered one officer and 11 NCOs/enlisted killed in action; two officers and 11 NCOs/enlisted were wounded in action. To the north was the 389th Infantry Division; to the southeast was the 295th Infantry Division.

71st Infantry Division – The division attacked in its zone against the 13th Guards Rifle Division. The division gained ground south of the Dol'gii Balka, seized a housing block east of the Communist Party area and reached the Volga River at several points, using underground sewers to do so – but had to withdraw that night. To the north was the 295th Infantry Division; to the south was the 94th Infantry Division. The division lost ten NCOs/enlisted killed in action; three officers and 40 NCOs/enlisted were wounded in action.

295th Infantry Division – The division conducted an attack from southeast of Hill 102 to the north attempting to seize the hill from the 95th Rifle Division and the 112th Rifle Division. The 284th Rifle Division began infiltrating positions of the division. The division lost 46 NCOs/enlisted killed in action; seven officers and 164 NCOs/enlisted were wounded in action; four NCOs/enlisted were posted missing in action. To the northwest was the 24th ***Panzer*** Division; to the south was the 71st Infantry Division.

389th Infantry Division – The division attacked east in zone. To the south was the 24th ***Panzer*** Division; to the northeast was Battle Group Stahel. The division lost five NCOs/enlisted wounded in action.

Battle Group Stahel – The battle group defended northwest of Orlovka to contain enemy forces. To the northwest was the 16th ***Panzer*** Division; to the south was the 389th Infantry Division.

Fourth *Panzer* Army – The army headquarters was located at Plodowitoje.

IV Corps – The corps headquarters was located at Plantator.

297th Infantry Division – The division defended in sector east of Elkhi. To the north was the 371st Infantry Division; to the south was the 20th Romanian Infantry Division.

371st Infantry Division – The division defended in sector north of Peschanka to Elkhi; the division headquarters was located west of Staro-Dubovka. To the north was the 14th ***Panzer*** Division; to the south was the 297th Infantry Division. The division lost three NCOs/enlisted killed in action; one officer and 14 NCOs/enlisted were wounded in action.

20th Romanian Infantry Division – The division defended in sector north of the Volga-Don Canal. To the north was the 297th Infantry Division; to the south was the 2nd Romanian Infantry Division of the Romanian VI Corps.

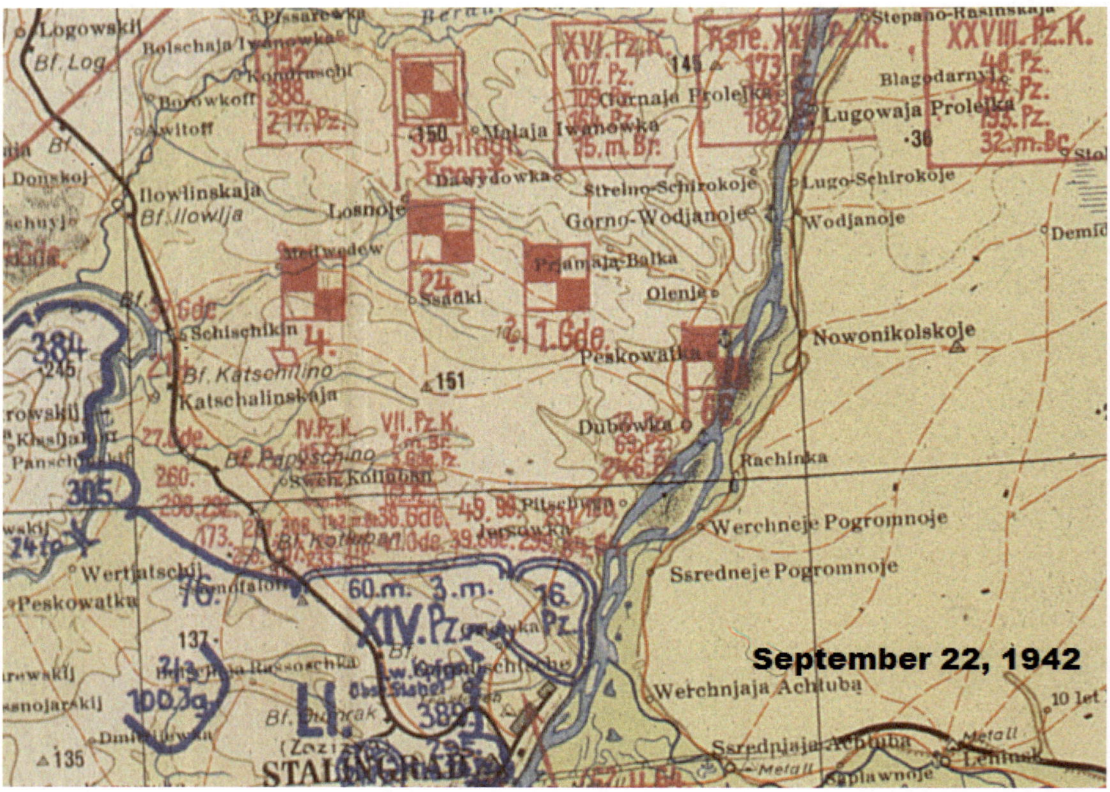

September 22, 1942

Sources, September 22, 1942: *Oberkommando des Heeres, Lage Ost: Stand: 22.9.42, Eastern Front Situation Map, National Archives Identifier: 559733, Record Group 242 – National Archives Collection of Foreign Records Seized, 1675-1958, National Archives, College Park, Maryland; Ia, Armeeoberkommando 6, "Morgen Meldung" and assorted reports, Kriegstagebuch 13, 23 September 1942, as found in Microfilm Series, T-312, Records of German Field Commands, Armies, Roll 1686, National Archives and Records Service, College Park, Maryland; Ia, XXXXVIII Panzerkorps, "Übersicht über die dem Korps Unterstellten Divisionen, 28. Juni 1942 – 11 October 1942," as found on T-314, Records of German Field Commands, Corps, Roll 1153, National Archives, College Park, Maryland; Ia, XXXXVIII Panzerkorps, "Zahlenmässige Verlustmeldung der Unterstellten Divisionen und Heerestruppen in der Zeit vom 1. April 1942 bis 31. Oktober 1942," as found in T-314, Records of German Field Commands, Corps, Roll 1153, National Archives, College Park, Maryland; Korpsarzt, XXXXVIII Panzerkorps, "Meldung über Personelle Verluste," Stand 22.9.42, as found on T-314, Records of German Field Commands, Corps, Roll 1158, National Archives, College Park, Maryland; 79th Infantry Division, Kriegstagebuch, 22 September 1942, as found in Microfilm Series T-315, Roll 1108, National Archives and Records Service, College Park, Maryland; 371st Infantry Division, Kriegstagebuch, 22 September 1942, as found in Microfilm Series T-315, Roll 2164, National Archives and Records Service, College Park, Maryland; Florian Freiherr von und zu Aufsess, Die Anlagenbände zu den Kriegstagebüchern der 6. Armee vom 14.09.1942 bis 24.11.1942, Band 1, Schwabach, Germany: Selbstverlag, 2006, 43-45; Paul Carell, Stalingrad: The Defeat of the German Sixth Army, Atglen, Pennsylvania: Schiffer Publishing, 1993, 145; Alan Clark, Barbarossa: The Russian-German Conflict, 1941-45, New York: William Morrow and Company, 1965, 229; Die 71. Infanterie-Division, 1939-1945: Gefechts- und Erlebnisberichte aus Kämpfen der "Gluckhaften Division" von Verdun bis Stalingrad, vom Monte Cassino bis zum Plattensee, Eggolsheim, FRG: Edition Dörfler, 1973, 250; David M. Glantz & Jonathan M. House, Armageddon in Stalingrad: September-November 1942, (The Stalingrad Trilogy, Volume 2), Lawrence, Kansas: University Press of Kansas, 2009, 199-203; Joachim Lemelsen, 29. Division, Bad Nauheim, FRG: Podzun Verlag, 1960, 203; Jochen Löser, Bittere Pflicht: Kampf und Untergang der 76. Berlin-Brandenburgischen Infanterie-Division, Osnabrück, FRG: Biblio Verlag, 1986, 209; Jason Mark, Death of the Leaping Horseman: 24. Panzer-Division in Stalingrad, Sydney, Australia: Leaping Horsemen Books, 2003, 202-203; Kurt Mehner, Die Geheimen Tagesberichte der Deutschen Wehrmachtführung im Zweiten Weltkrieg 1939-1945, Band 5: 1. Juni 1942 – 30. November 1942, Osnabrück, Germany: Biblio Verlag, 1991, 208; Janusz Piekalkiewicz, Stalingrad: Anatomie einer Schlacht, München, BRD: Wilhelm Heyne Verlag, 1977, 234; Anton Schimak, Karl Lamprecht & Friedrich Dettmer, Die 44. Infanterie Division: Tagebuch der Hoch- und Deutschmeister, Wien: Verlag Austria Press, 169, 233 and Map: Marschweg der 44. Infanterie Division im Russland.*

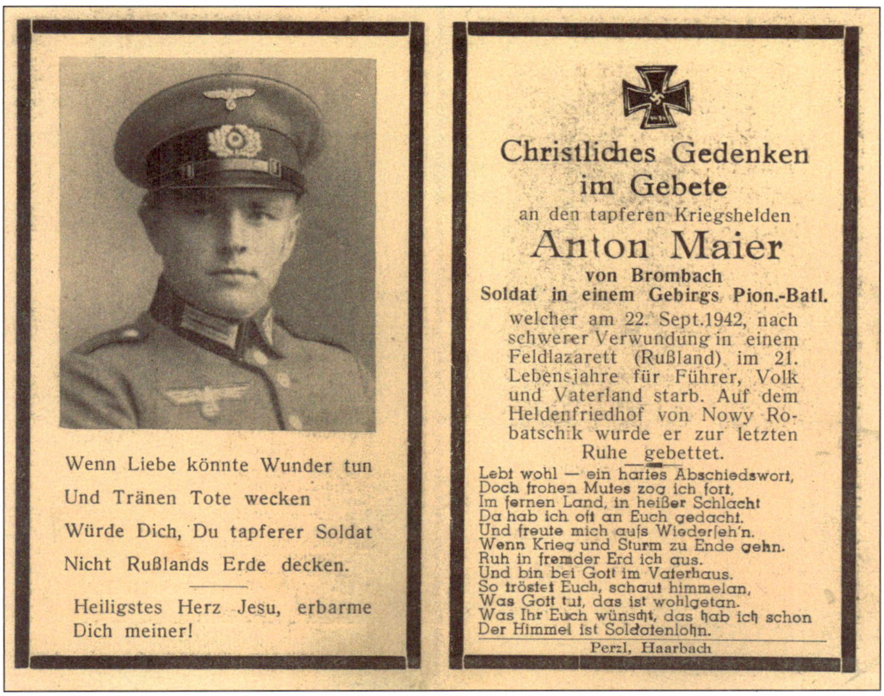

Wenn Liebe könnte Wunder tun
Und Tränen Tote wecken
Würde Dich, Du tapferer Soldat
Nicht Rußlands Erde decken.

Heiligstes Herz Jesu, erbarme Dich meiner!

Christliches Gedenken
im Gebete
an den tapferen Kriegshelden
Anton Maier
von Brombach
Soldat in einem Gebirgs Pion.-Batl.
welcher am 22. Sept.1942, nach schwerer Verwundung in einem Feldlazarett (Rußland) im 21. Lebensjahre für Führer, Volk und Vaterland starb. Auf dem Heldenfriedhof von Nowy Robatschik wurde er zur letzten Ruhe gebettet.

Lebt wohl — ein hartes Abschiedswort,
Doch frohen Mutes zog ich fort,
Im fernen Land, in heißer Schlacht
Da hab ich oft an Euch gedacht.
Und freute mich aufs Wiederseh'n.
Wenn Krieg und Sturm zu Ende gehn.
Ruh in fremder Erd ich aus.
Und bin bei Gott im Vaterhaus.
So tröstet Euch, schaut himmelan,
Was Gott tut, das ist wohlgetan.
Was Ihr Euch wünscht, das hab ich schon
Der Himmel ist Soldatenlohn.

Perzl, Haarbach

Pionier* Anton Maier** was born in Brombach near Pfarrkirchen in Bavaria on January 17, 1922. Assigned to the 100th Combat Engineer Battalion of the 100th ***Jäger Division, he was seriously wounded on September 22, 1942 and taken to the 2nd Medical Company of the 696th Casualty Collection Point at Novvy Rogachik, where he died the same day. He is buried at the German Military Cemetery at Rossoschka in Block 26, Row 10 in Grave 377.

September 23, 1942
Weather: sunny, clear, 56° F, slight warming after noon
Sunrise: 5:49 a.m.; **Sunset:** 6:00 p.m.
Moon: Waxing Gibbous; 99% illumination

Sixth Army – Enemy air attacks at night and artillery fire by day limited Sixth Army operations in Stalingrad. The army headquarters was located at Golubinskaya.

VIII Corps – The 53rd ***Werfer*** Regiment and the 855th Heavy Artillery Detachment were assigned to support the corps; the 652nd Pioneer Battalion and the 177th ***Sturmgeschütz*** Detachment were assigned to the corps. The corps suffered the following officer casualties: three killed in action; 17 wounded in action; one missing in action.

76th Infantry Division – The division defended in sector southwest of Samofalovka and north of Borodkin, against the 308th Rifle Division, the 298th Rifle Division and the 173rd Rifle Division. To the northwest was the 305th Infantry Division; to the east was the 60th Infantry Division (Motorized.) Enemy forces achieved a small penetration, before withdrawing under a counter-attack. The division shortened its defensive sector, with the 305th Infantry Division assuming the northwest half.

305th Infantry Division – The division defended in sector from the Don River, north of Nizhne-Gnilovskii, to west of Kotluban' against the 27th Guards Rifle Division and the 260th Rifle Division. The division also assumed the northwest half of the defensive sector of the 76th Infantry Division. To the southeast was the 76th Infantry Division; to the north was the 384th Infantry Division. The division lost two officers and seven NCOs/enlisted killed in action; 16 NCOs/enlisted were wounded in action; two men were reported missing in action.

XI Corps – The corps suffered the following officer casualties: one killed in action; three wounded in action.

44th Infantry Division – The division defended in sector Kurchajessowskij-Kamyshinskiy-Hill 171.0-Hill 180.9-Sirotinskaya-Khmelevskoy against the 343rd Rifle Division and the 40th Guards Rifle Division. The division headquarters was located at Verkhne-Golubaja. To the west was 376th Infantry Division; to the east was the 384th Infantry Division.

100th Jäger Division – Advance units of the division began arriving at Stalingrad. The bulk of the division reached Bol'shaya Rossoschka.

376th Infantry Division – The division defended in sector near Blizhniaia-Perekopka, against the 321st Rifle Division. To the west was the 1st Romanian Cavalry Division; to the east was the 44th Infantry Division. The division lost two NCOs/enlisted wounded in action.

384th Infantry Division – The division defended in sector west of the Don River near Trekhostrovskaia to Podgorskii, against the 37th Guards Rifle Division and the 214th Rifle Division. To the west was the 44th Infantry Division; to the south was the 305th Infantry Division. The division suffered one officer and eight NCOs/enlisted killed in action; one officer and 18 NCOs/enlisted were wounded in action.

XIV *Panzer* Corps – The corps headquarters was located east of Ssadtschi-Kowa. The corps suffered the following officer casualties: five killed in action; nine wounded in action.

3rd Infantry Division (Motorized) – The division defended in sector, from the Tartar Hill-Hill 111.1-Hill 129.6-Hill 131.2, against the 299th Rifle Division, the 38th Guards Rifle Division, the 116th Rifle Division and the 343rd Rifle Division. To the east was the 16th ***Panzer*** Division; to the west was the 60th Infantry Division (Motorized.)

16th Panzer Division – The division defended in sector, from Hill 139.7 to the Volga and from the Volga southwest to Hill 145.1, north of Orlovka against the 120th Rifle Division, the 84th Rifle Division and the 64th Rifle Division. To the southwest was Battle Group Stahel; to the west was the 3rd Infantry Division (Motorized.)

60th Infantry Division (Motorized) – The division defended in sector, from south of Kotluban' Station near Borodkin to Kuz'michi, against the 308th Rifle Division, the 41st Guards Rifle Division, the 49th Rifle Division, the 231st Rifle Division, the 233rd Rifle Division, the 39th Guards Rifle Division, the 316th Rifle Division and the 207th Rifle Division. To the east was the 3rd Infantry Division (Motorized); to the west was the 76th Infantry Division. Heavy fighting occurred at Hill 111.1.

Battle Group Stahel – The battle group defended northwest of Orlovka to contain enemy forces. To the south was the 389th Infantry Division; to the north was the 16th ***Panzer*** Division.

XVII Corps – The corps suffered the following officer casualties: two wounded in action.

79th Infantry Division – The division defended in sector from Bol'shoy-Verkhne-Kalmykovskii-Verkhne-Fomichinskii-Baskowskij, against the 124th Rifle Division. The division headquarters was located at Karagichev. To the west was the Italian XXXV Corps; to the east was the 6th Romanian Infantry Division. The division lost two officers and six NCOs/enlisted wounded in action.

113th Infantry Division – The division moved to the southeast toward the Don River, reaching Jewlampijewskij.

298th Infantry Division – The division occupied three assembly areas along the Sixth Army's western boundary and south of the 79th Infantry Division.

1st Romanian Cavalry Division – The division defended in sector near Mololegowskij south of the Don River against the 76th Rifle Division. To the west was the 13th Romanian Infantry Division; to the east was the 376th Infantry Division.

1st Romanian Armored Division – The division moved from the south toward the western part of the corps sector.

6th Romanian Infantry Division – The division defended in sector south of the Don River near Baskowskij against the 96th Rifle Division. To the west was the 79th Infantry Division; to the southeast was the 13th Romanian Infantry Division.

13th Romanian Infantry Division – The division defended in sector along the Don River west of Kletskiy to Raspopinskaja against the 278th Rifle Division and the 304th Rifle Division. To the northwest was the 6th Romanian Infantry Division; to the east was the 1st Romanian Cavalry Division.

XXXXVIII *Panzer* Corps – Corps support troops lost three NCOs/enlisted killed in action and 13 NCOs/enlisted wounded in action.

14th Panzer Division – The division defended in sector along the Volga River. To the north was the 29th Infantry Division (Motorized); to the south was the 371st Infantry Division. The division lost three NCOs/enlisted killed in action; five NCOs/enlisted were wounded in action.

29th Infantry Division (Motorized) – The division defended in sector along the Volga River. To the north was the 94th Infantry Division; to the south was the 14th ***Panzer*** Division. The division lost one officer and five NCOs/enlisted wounded in action.

LI Corps – The corps headquarters was located at Gumrak. The corps suffered the following officer casualties: one killed in action; ten wounded in action.

24th Panzer Division – The division repulsed several enemy attacks against Hill 102 (Mamayev Kurgan) against the 95th Rifle Division. The division suffered 13 NCOs/enlisted killed in action; one officer and 40 NCOs/enlisted were wounded in action; five NCOs/enlisted were reported missing in action. To the northwest was the 389th Infantry Division; to the southeast was the 295th Infantry Division.

71st Infantry Division – The division attacked in its zone, advancing against the 13th Guards Rifle Division from the Krutoi Balka to the base of Kievskaia Street. To the north was the 295th Infantry Division; to the south was the 94th Infantry Division. The division suffered 14 NCOs/enlisted killed in action; 35 NCOs/enlisted were wounded in action.

94th Infantry Division – The division transferred to the LI Corps. To the north was the 71st Infantry Division; to the south was the 29th

Infantry Division (Motorized.) The division lost one NCO/enlisted killed in action; one officer and 12 NCOs/enlisted were wounded in action.

295th Infantry Division – The division attacked in zone east of the main train station against the 95th Rifle Division and the 284th Rifle Division. To the south was the 71st Infantry Division; to the west was the 24th ***Panzer*** Division. The division lost one NCO/enlisted killed in action; one officer and 35 NCOs/enlisted were wounded in action; one man was reported missing in action.

389th Infantry Division – The division consolidated its gains. To the north was Battle Group Stahel; to the south was the 24th ***Panzer*** Division. The division suffered five NCOs/enlisted wounded in action.

Fourth *Panzer* Army – The army headquarters was located at Plodowitoje.

IV Corps – The corps headquarters was located at Plantator.

297th Infantry Division – The division defended in sector east of Elkhi. To the north was the 371st Infantry Division; to the south was the 14th ***Panzer*** Division.

371st Infantry Division – The division defended in sector north of Peschanka to Elkhi; the division headquarters was located west of Staro-Dubovka. To the northeast was the 14th ***Panzer*** Division; to the south was the 297th Infantry Division. The division lost six NCOs/enlisted killed in action; 26 NCOs/enlisted were wounded in action; two men were reported missing in action.

20th Romanian Infantry Division – The division defended in sector north of the Volga-Don Canal. To the north was the 297th Infantry Division; to the south was the 2nd Romanian Infantry Division of the Romanian VI Corps.

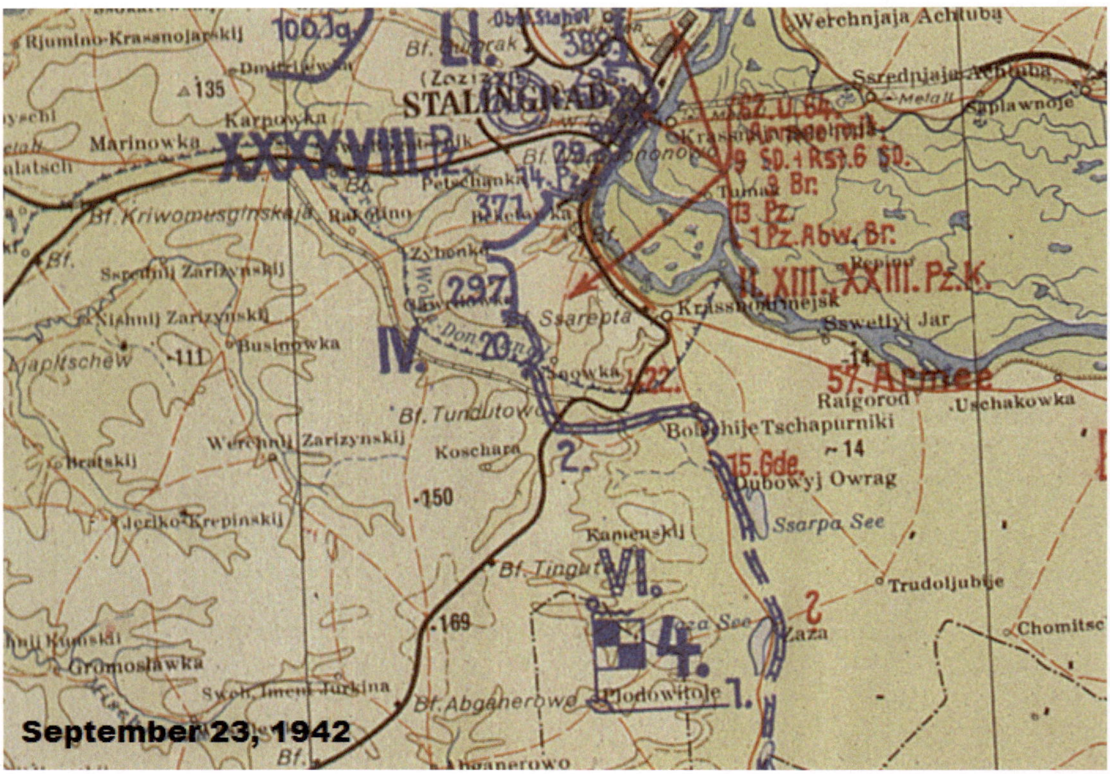

September 23, 1942

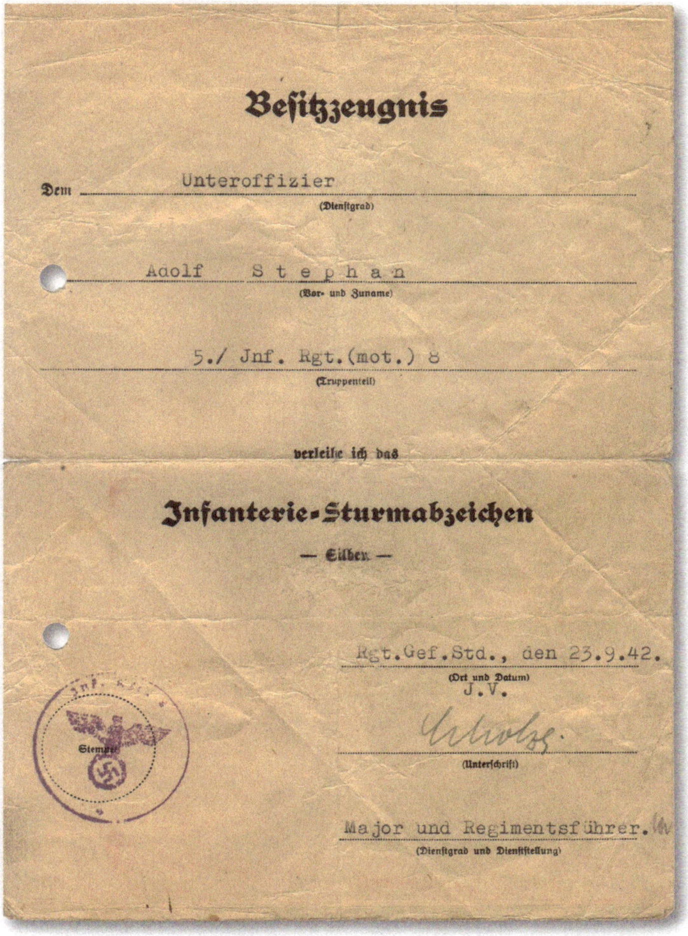
Besitzzeugnis

Dem Unteroffizier
(Dienstgrad)

Adolf Stephan
(Vor- und Zuname)

5./ Jnf. Rgt.(mot.) 8
(Truppenteil)

verleihe ich das

Infanterie-Sturmabzeichen

— Silber —

Rgt.Gef.Std., den 23.9.42.
(Ort und Datum)

J.V.

Scholze
(Unterschrift)

Major und Regimentsführer.
(Dienstgrad und Dienststellung)

Unteroffizier **Adolf Stephan** in the 5th Company of the 8th Motorized Infantry Regiment in the 3rd Infantry Division (Motorized) was awarded the Infantry Assault Badge on September 23, 1942. Stephan, who was born on September 15, 1921, was posted missing in action in Stalingrad on January 1, 1943. The document is signed by ***Major*** Scholze, who normally commanded the regiment's 2nd battalion.

Sources, September 23, 1942: *Oberkommando des Heeres, Lage Ost: Stand: 23.9.42, Eastern Front Situation Map, National Archives Identifier: 559733, Record Group 242 – National Archives Collection of Foreign Records Seized, 1675-1958, National Archives, College Park, Maryland; Ia, Armeeoberkommando 6, "Morgen Meldung" and assorted reports, Kriegstagebuch 13, 24 September 1942, as found in Microfilm Series, T-312, Records of German Field Commands, Armies, Roll 1686, National Archives and Records Service, College Park, Maryland; Ia, XXXXVIII Panzerkorps, "Übersicht über die dem Korps Unterstellten Divisionen, 28. Juni 1942 – 11 October 1942," as found on T-314, Records of German Field Commands, Corps, Roll 1153, National Archives, College Park, Maryland; Korpsarzt, XXXXVIII Panzerkorps, "Meldung über Personelle Verluste," Stand 23.9.42, as found on T-314, Records of German Field Commands, Corps, Roll 1158, National Archives, College Park, Maryland; 79th Infantry Division, Kriegstagebuch, 23 September 1942, as found in Microfilm Series T-315, Roll 1108, National Archives and Records Service, College Park, Maryland; 371st Infantry Division, Kriegstagebuch, 23 September 1942, as found in Microfilm Series T-315, Roll 2164, National Archives and Records Service, College Park, Maryland; Florian Freiherr von und zu Aufsess, Die Anlagenbände zu den Kriegstagebüchern der 6. Armee vom 14.09.1942 bis 24.11.1942, Band 1, Schwabach, Germany: Selbstverlag, 2006, 48; Die 71. Infanterie-Division, 1939-1945: Gefechts- und Erlebnisberichte aus Kämpfen der "Gluckhaften Division" von Verdun bis Stalingrad, vom Monte Cassino bis zum Plattensee, Eggolsheim, FRG: Edition Dörfler, 1973, 250; David M. Glantz & Jonathan M. House, Armageddon in Stalingrad: September-November 1942, (The Stalingrad Trilogy, Volume 2), Lawrence, Kansas: University Press of Kansas, 2009, 203-207; Joachim Lemelsen, 29. Division, Bad Nauheim, FRG: Podzun Verlag, 1960, 203; Jochen Löser, Bittere Pflicht: Kampf und Untergang der 76. Berlin-Brandenburgischen Infanterie-Division, Osnabrück, FRG: Biblio Verlag, 1986, 209; Jason Mark, Death of the Leaping Horseman: 24. Panzer-Division in Stalingrad, Sydney, Australia: Leaping Horsemen Books, 2003, 204-205; Kurt Mehner, Die Geheimen Tagesberichte der Deutschen Wehrmachtführung im Zweiten Weltkrieg 1939-1945, Band 5: 1. Juni 1942 – 30. November 1942, Osnabrück, Germany: Biblio Verlag, 1991, 210; Hans Neidhardt, Mit Tanne und Eichenlaub: Kriegschronik der 100. Jäger Division vormals 100. leichte Infanterie Division, Graz, Austria: Leopold Stocker Verlag, 1981, 208; Anton Schimak, Karl Lamprecht & Friedrich Dettmer, Die 44. Infanterie Division: Tagebuch der Hoch- und Deutschmeister, Wien: Verlag Austria Press, 169, 233 and Map: Marschweg der 44. Infanterie Division im Russland.*

September 24, 1942
Weather: sunny, clear, 70° F, light warming after noon
Sunrise: 5:50 a.m.; **Sunset:** 5:58 p.m.
Moon: Full Moon; 100% illumination

Sixth Army – Bombers and dive-bombers from the ***Luftwaffe***'s VIII Air Corps pounded the Volga River shore in Stalingrad in large-scale attacks. The army headquarters was located at Golubinskaya. Adolf Hitler relieved ***Generaloberst*** Franz Halder as Chief of the General Staff.

VIII Corps – The 754th Pioneer Battalion and the 177th ***Sturmgeschütz*** Detachment were assigned to the corps. The 53rd ***Werfer*** Regiment was assigned to support the corps. The corps suffered the following officer casualties: one killed in action; five wounded in action.

76th Infantry Division – The division defended in sector southwest of Samofalovka and north of Borodkin against the 308th Rifle Division, the 173rd Rifle Division and the 16th Tank Corps, losing Hill 130.4 in heavy fighting. To the northwest was the 305th Infantry Division; to the east was the 60th Infantry Division (Motorized.) The division lost 22 NCOs/enlisted killed in action; 110 NCOs/enlisted were wounded in action.

305th Infantry Division – The division defended in sector from the Don River, north of Nizhne-Gnilovskii, to west of Kotluban', against the 260th Rifle Division, the 27th Guards Rifle Division and the 298th Rifle Division. To the east was the 76th Infantry Division; to the north was the 384th Infantry Division. The division lost six NCOs/enlisted killed in action; 17 NCOs/enlisted were wounded in action; five men were reported missing in action.

XI Corps

44th Infantry Division – The division defended in sector Kurchajessowskij-Kamyshinskiy-Hill 171.0-Hill 180.9-Sirotinskaya-Khmelevskoy, against the 23rd Rifle Division, the 343rd Rifle Division and the 40th Guards Rifle Division, repelling an attack at 2:15 a.m. The division headquarters was located at Verkhne-Golubaja. To the west was the 376th Infantry Division; to the east was the 384th Infantry Division. The division lost two NCOs/enlisted killed in action; ten NCOs/enlisted were wounded in action; one man was reported missing in action.

376th Infantry Division – The division defended in sector near Blizhniaia-Perekopka against the 321st Infantry Division. To the west was the 1st Romanian Cavalry Division; to the east was the 44th Infantry Division.

384th Infantry Division – The division defended in sector west of the Don River near Trekhostrovskaia to Podgorskii against the 37th Guards Rifle Division and the 214th Rifle Division. To the west was the 44th Infantry Division; to the south was the 305th Infantry Division. The division suffered one officer and eight NCOs/enlisted killed in action; one officer and 18 NCOs/enlisted were wounded in action.

XIV *Panzer* Corps – The corps headquarters was located east of Ssadtschi-Kowa. The corps suffered the following officer casualties: four wounded in action.

3rd Infantry Division (Motorized) – The division defended in sector, from the Tartar Hill-Hill 111.1-Hill 129.6-Hill 131.2, against the 299th Rifle Division, the 38th Guards Rifle Division, the 116th Rifle Division and the 343rd Rifle Division. To the east was the 16th ***Panzer*** Division; to the west was the 60th Infantry Division (Motorized.)

16th Panzer Division – The division defended in sector, from Hill 139.7 to the Volga and from the Volga southwest to Hill 145.1, north of Orlovka against the 120th Rifle Division, the 84th Rifle Division and the 64th Rifle Division. To the southwest was Battle Group Stahel; to the west was the 3rd Infantry Division (Motorized.)

60th Infantry Division (Motorized) – The division defended in sector, from south of Kotluban' Station near Borodkin to Kuz'michi, repelling the 308th Rifle Division, the 41st Guards Rifle Division, the 49th Rifle Division, the 231st Rifle Division, the 233rd Rifle Division, the 39th Guards Rifle Division, the 316th Rifle Division and the 207th Rifle Division. The 221st Rifle Division seized 564 km Station from the 9th Machine Gun Battalion, attached to the division. To the west was the 76th Infantry Division; to the east was the 3rd Infantry Division (Motorized.)

Battle Group Stahel – The battle group defended northwest of Orlovka to contain enemy forces. To the south was the 389th Infantry Division; to the northeast was the 16th ***Panzer*** Division.

XVII Corps

79th Infantry Division – The division defended in sector from Bol'shoy-Verkhne-Kalmykovskii-Verkhne-Fomichinskii-Baskowskij, against the 124th Rifle Division. The division headquarters was located at Karagichev. To the west was the XXXV Italian Corps; to the southeast was the 6th Romanian Infantry Division. The division lost two NCOs/enlisted killed in action.

113th Infantry Division – The division moved to the southeast; lead elements reached the Don River.

298th Infantry Division – The division occupied three assembly areas along the Sixth Army's western boundary and south of the 79th Infantry Division.

1st Romanian Cavalry Division – The division defended in sector near Molologowskij south of the Don River against the 76th Rifle Division and 63rd Rifle Division. To the west was the 13th Romanian Infantry Division; to the east was the 376th Infantry Division.

1st Romanian Armored Division – The division moved from the south toward the western part of the corps sector.

6th Romanian Infantry Division – The division defended in sector south of the Don River against the 96th Rifle Division. To the west was the 79th Infantry Division; to the southeast was the 13th Romanian Infantry Division.

13th Romanian Infantry Division – The division defended in sector along the Don River west of Kletskiy against the 278th Rifle Division and the 304th Rifle Division. To the northwest was the 6th Romanian Infantry Division; to the east was the 1st Romanian Cavalry Division.

XXXXVIII *Panzer* Corps – Corps troops lost one NCO/enlisted wounded in action. The corps suffered the following officer casualties: one wounded in action.

14th Panzer Division – The division defended in sector south of Kuporosnoye and north of Beketovka. To the north was the 29th Infantry Division (Motorized); to the south was the 371st Infantry Division. The division lost five NCOs/enlisted killed in action; 16 NCOs/enlisted were wounded in action.

29th Infantry Division (Motorized) – The division defended in sector along the Volga River. To the north was the 94th Infantry Division; to the south was the 14th ***Panzer*** Division. The division lost three NCOs/enlisted killed in action; one officer and 14 NCOs/enlisted were wounded in action.

LI Corps – The corps headquarters was located at Gumrak. The 244th ***Sturmgeschütz*** Detachment was assigned to the corps. The corps suffered the following officer casualties: six killed in action; 14 wounded in action.

24th Panzer Division – The division defended in sector against several enemy attacks against Hill 102 (Mamayev Kurgan), by the 95th Rifle Division and the 137th Tank Brigade, but the enemy achieved a 400-yard penetration; it was later sealed. To the northwest was the 389th Infantry Division; to the east was the 295th Infantry Division. The division suffered 19 NCOs/enlisted killed in action; one officer and 56 NCOs/enlisted were wounded in action; two men were posted missing in action.

71st Infantry Division – The division attacked in its zone, pushing toward the Volga River on both sides of the Tsaritsa River, against the 10th NKVD Division, the 244th Rifle Division, the 13th Guards Rifle Division and the 115th Fortified Division. To the south was the 94th Infantry Division; to the north was the 295th Infantry Division. The division lost one officer and 18 NCOs/enlisted killed in action; one officer and 52 NCOs/enlisted were wounded in action.

94th Infantry Division – The division attacked in zone, pushing toward the Volga River. To the north was the 71st Infantry Division; to the south was the 29th Infantry Division (Motorized.) The division suffered one officer and 19 NCOs/enlisted killed in action; 54 NCOs/enlisted were wounded in action.

100th Jäger Division – The division arrived at Stalingrad and prepared to relieve elements of the 24th ***Panzer*** Division in sector. The division suffered one officer and two NCOs/enlisted killed in action; two officers and six NCOs/enlisted were wounded in action.

295th Infantry Division – The division defended in sector against the attacks by the 95th Rifle Division and the 137th Tank Brigade that penetrated to Kolodeznaia Street and the Dol'gii Balka. To the west was the 24th ***Panzer*** Division; to the south was the 71st Infantry Division. The division lost one officer and 14 enlisted killed in action; three officers and 54 NCOs/enlisted were wounded in action; two men were reported missing in action.

389th Infantry Division – The division prepared for offensive operations. To the north was Battle Group Stahel; to the south was the 295th Infantry Division. The division lost three NCOs/enlisted killed in action; 12 NCOs/enlisted were wounded in action.

Fourth *Panzer* Army – The army headquarters was located at Plodowitoje.

IV Corps – The corps headquarters was located at Plantator.

297th Infantry Division – The division The division defended in sector east of Elkhi against the 154th Marine Infantry Brigade and the 36th Guards Rifle Division. To the north was the 371st Infantry Division; to the south was the 20th Romanian Infantry Division.

371st Infantry Division – The division defended in sector north of Peschanka to Elkhi against elements of the 422nd Rifle Division. The division headquarters was located west of Staro-Dubovka. To the north was the 14th ***Panzer*** Division; to the south was the 297th Infantry Division. The division lost three NCOs/enlisted killed in action; 19 NCOs/enlisted were wounded in action.

20th Romanian Infantry Division – The division defended in sector north of the Volga-Don Canal against the 38th Rifle Division. To the north was the 297th Infantry Division; to the south was the 2nd Romanian Infantry Division of the Romanian VI Corps.

Sources, September 24, 1942: *Oberkommando des Heeres, Lage Ost: Stand: 24.9.42, Eastern Front Situation Map, National Archives Identifier: 559733, Record Group 242 – National Archives Collection of Foreign Records Seized, 1675-1958, National Archives, College Park, Maryland; Ia, Armeeoberkommando 6, "Morgen Meldung" and assorted reports, Kriegstagebuch 13, 25 September 1942, as found in Microfilm Series, T-312, Records of German Field Commands, Armies, Roll 1686, National Archives and Records Service, College Park, Maryland; Ia, XXXXVIII Panzerkorps, "Übersicht über die dem Korps Unterstellten Divisionen, 28. Juni 1942 – 11 October 1942," as found on T-314, Records of German Field Commands, Corps, Roll 1153, National Archives, College Park, Maryland; Korpsarzt, XXXXVIII Panzerkorps, "Meldung über Personelle Verluste," Stand 24.9.42, as found on T-314, Records of German Field Commands, Corps, Roll 1158, National Archives, College Park, Maryland; 79th Infantry Division, Kriegstagebuch, 24 September 1942, as found in Microfilm Series T-315, Roll 1108, National Archives and Records Service, College Park, Maryland; 371st Infantry Division, Kriegstagebuch, 24 September 1942, as found in Microfilm Series T-315, Roll 2164, National Archives and Records Service, College Park, Maryland; Florian Freiherr von und zu Aufsess, Die Anlagenbände zu den Kriegstagebüchern der 6. Armee vom 14.09.1942 bis 24.11.1942, Band 1, Schwabach, Germany: Selbstverlag, 2006, 49-52; Die 71. Infanterie-Division, 1939-1945: Gefechts- und Erlebnisberichte aus Kämpfen der "Gluckhaften Division" von Verdun bis Stalingrad, vom Monte Cassino bis zum Plattensee, Eggolsheim, FRG: Edition Dörfler, 1973, 250; David M. Glantz & Jonathan M. House, Armageddon in Stalingrad: September-November 1942, (The Stalingrad Trilogy, Volume 2), Lawrence, Kansas: University Press of Kansas, 2009, 180, 202-214; Adalbert Holl, An Infantryman in Stalingrad, translated by Jason D. Mark and Neill Page, Sydney, Australia: Leaping Horseman Books, 2005, 25, 34; Joachim Lemelsen, 29. Division, Bad Nauheim, FRG: Podzun Verlag, 1960, 203; Jochen Löser, Bittere Pflicht: Kampf und Untergang der 76. Berlin-Brandenburgischen Infanterie-Division, Osnabrück, FRG: Biblio Verlag, 1986, 209 and 241; Jason Mark, Death of the Leaping Horseman: 24. Panzer-Division in Stalingrad, Sydney, Australia: Leaping Horsemen Books, 2003, 205-208; Kurt Mehner, Die Geheimen Tagesberichte der Deutschen Wehrmachtführung im Zweiten Weltkrieg 1939-1945, Band 5: 1. Juni 1942 – 30. November 1942, Osnabrück, Germany: Biblio Verlag, 1991, 212; Hans Neidhardt, Mit Tanne und Eichenlaub: Kriegschronik der 100. Jäger Division vormals 100. leichte Infanterie Division, Graz, Austria: Leopold Stocker Verlag, 1981, 208; Anton Schimak, Karl Lamprecht & Friedrich Dettmer, Die 44. Infanterie Division: Tagebuch der Hoch- und Deutschmeister, Wien: Verlag Austria Press, 169, 233 and Map: Marschweg der 44. Infanterie Division im Russland.*

Pionier **Josef Schmid** was born on June 21, 1922 at Bärnham near Wasserburg am Inn, Bavaria. The son of a cooper, Schmid was assigned to a mountain infantry regiment in the 100th *Jäger* Division. He was killed in action on September 24, 1942 at Stalingrad. He is listed in the remembrance book at the German Military Cemetery at Rossoschka.

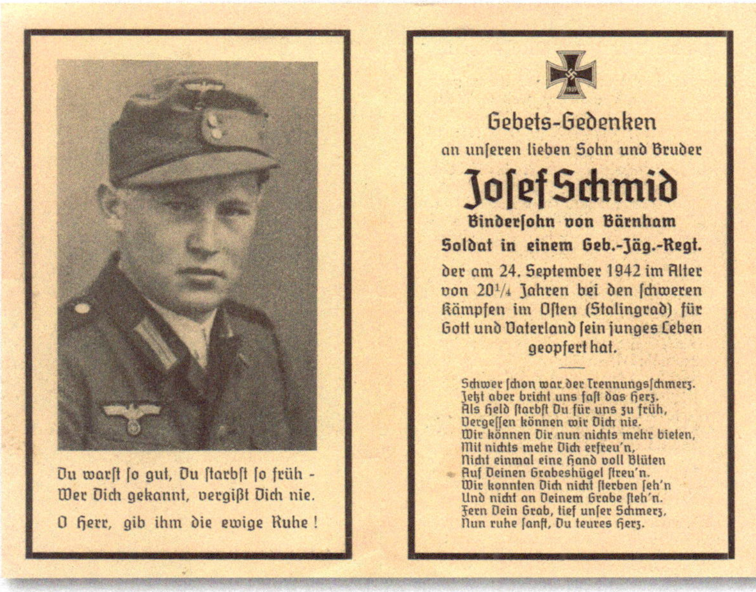

Franz Halder, Chief of the General Staff until Hitler relieved him on September 24, 1942. Halder would never have another position in the ***Wehrmacht***.

Franz Halder. When he was relieved, Halder told Hitler: "Out there, brave men and young officers are falling in thousands simply because their commanders are not allowed to make the only reasonable decision and have their hands tied behind their backs."

September 25, 1942
Weather: sunny, warm, 70° F, clear, good road conditions
Sunrise: 5:51 a.m.; **Sunset:** 5:55 p.m.
Moon: Waning Gibbous; 99% illumination

Sixth Army – The army headquarters was located at Golubinskaya.

VIII Corps – The 521st ***Panzerjäger*** Detachment was assigned to the corps. The 53rd ***Werfer*** Regiment was assigned to support the corps. The corps suffered the following officer casualties: two killed in action; four wounded in action.

76th Infantry Division – The division defended in sector southwest of Samofalovka and north of Borodkin, against the 173rd Rifle Division and the 282nd Rifle Division. To the west was the 305th Infantry Division; to the east was the 60th Infantry Division (Motorized.) A counter-attack recovered all lost positions from the day before. The division lost 23 NCOs/enlisted killed in action; two officers and 16 NCOs/enlisted were wounded in action. Between September 7 and September 25, at least 12 enemy rifle divisions and nine tank brigades conducted attacks against the division.

305th Infantry Division – The division defended in sector from the Don River, north of Nizhne-Gnilovskii, to west of Kotluban' against the 260th Rifle Division and the 298th Rifle Division. To the southeast was the 76th Infantry Division; to the north was the 384th Infantry Division. The division suffered nine NCOs/enlisted killed in action; 23 NCOs/enlisted were wounded in action.

XI Corps

44th Infantry Division – The division defended in sector Kurchajessowskij-Kamyshinskiy-Hill 171.0-Hill 180.9-Sirotinskaya-Khmelevskoy, against the 23rd Rifle Division, the 343rd Rifle Division and the 40th Guards Rifle Division. The division headquarters was located at Verkhne-Golubaja. To the west was 376th Infantry Division; to the east was the 384th Infantry Division. The division lost four NCOs/enlisted killed in action; 15 NCOs/enlisted were wounded in action.

376th Infantry Division – The division defended in sector near Blizhniaia-Perekopka against the 321st Rifle Division. To the west was the 1st Romanian Cavalry Division; to the east was the 44th Infantry Division. The division lost two NCOs/enlisted wounded in action.

384th Infantry Division – The division defended in sector west of the Don River near Trekhostrovskaia to Podgorskii against the 4th Guards Rifle Division, the 37th Guards Rifle Division and the 214th Rifle Division. To the west was the 44th Infantry Division; to the south was the 305th Infantry Division. The division suffered one officer and eight NCOs/enlisted killed in action; one officer and 18 NCOs/enlisted were wounded in action.

XIV *Panzer* Corps – The corps headquarters was located east of Ssadtschi-Kowa. The 51st ***Werfer*** Regiment was assigned to support the corps. The corps suffered the following officer casualties: two killed in action; eight wounded in action.

3rd Infantry Division (Motorized) – The division defended in sector, from the Tartar Hill-Hill 111.1-Hill 129.6-Hill 131.2, against the 299th Rifle Division, the 38th Guards Rifle Division, the 116th Rifle Division and the 343rd Rifle Division. To the east was the 16th ***Panzer*** Division; to the west was the 60th Infantry Division (Motorized.) The division lost five NCOs/enlisted killed in action; one officer and 12 NCOs/enlisted were wounded in action.

16th Panzer Division – The division defended in sector, from Hill 139.7 to the Volga and from the Volga southwest to Hill 145.1, north of Orlovka, against the 120th Rifle Division, the

84th Rifle Division and the 64th Rifle Division. The enemy attacked from south of Erzovka. To the southwest was Battle Group Stahel; to the west was the 3rd Infantry Division (Motorized.) ***Generalmajor*** Günther Angern assumed command of the division.

60th Infantry Division (Motorized) – The division defended in sector, from south of Kotluban' Station near Borodkin to Kuz'michi, against the 41st Guards Rifle Division, the 49th Rifle Division, the 231st Rifle Division, the 233rd Rifle Division, the 39th Guards Rifle Division, the 316th Rifle Division and the 207th Rifle Division. To the west was the 76th Infantry Division; to the east was the 3rd Infantry Division (Motorized.)

Battle Group Stahel – The battle group defended northwest of Orlovka to contain enemy forces. To the northeast was the 16th ***Panzer*** Division; to the south was the 389th Infantry Division.

XVII Corps – The corps suffered the following officer casualties: two wounded in action.

79th Infantry Division – The division defended in sector from Bol'shoy-Verkhne-Kalmykovskii-Verkhne-Fomichinskii-Baskowskij, against the 124th Rifle Division. The division headquarters was located at Karagichev. To the west was the Romanian V Corps; to the southeast was the 6th Romanian Infantry Division.

113th Infantry Division – The division occupied an assembly area just west of the Don River.

298th Infantry Division – The division occupied three assembly areas along the Sixth Army's western boundary and south of the 79th Infantry Division.

1st Romanian Cavalry Division – The division defended in sector near Mololologowskij south of the Don River against the 76th Rifle Division and 63rd Rifle Division. To the west was the 13th Romanian Infantry Division; to the east was the 376th Infantry Division. The division suffered one NCO/enlisted killed in action; eight NCOs/enlisted were wounded in action; one NCO/enlisted was reported missing in action.

1st Romanian Armored Division – The division occupied an assembly in the western part of the corps sector.

6th Romanian Infantry Division – The division defended in sector south of the Don River near Raspopinskaja against the 69th Rifle Division. To the west was the 79th Infantry Division; to the southeast was the 13th Romanian Infantry

Division. The division lost 21 NCOs/enlisted killed in action; two officers and 82 NCOs/enlisted were wounded in action.

13th Romanian Infantry Division – The division defended in sector along the Don River west of Kletskiy against the 278th Rifle Division and the 69th Rifle Division. To the northwest was the 6th Romanian Infantry Division; to the east was the 1st Romanian Cavalry Division. The division suffered 21 NCOs/enlisted killed in action; six officers and 302 NCOs/enlisted were wounded in action; five men were reported missing in action.

XXXXVIII *Panzer* Corps – The corps suffered the following officer casualties: one wounded in action.

14th Panzer Division – The division defended in sector south of Kuporosnoye and north of Beketovka. To the north was the 29th Infantry Division (Motorized); to the south was the 371st Infantry Division. The division lost three NCOs/enlisted killed in action; nine NCOs/enlisted were wounded in action.

29th Infantry Division (Motorized) – The division defended in sector along the Volga River. To the north was the 94th Infantry Division; to the south was the 14th ***Panzer*** Division. The division lost two NCOs/enlisted killed in action; 16 NCOs/enlisted were wounded in action. ***Generalmajor*** Max Fremerey was relieved of command of the division. He was replaced by ***Generalmajor*** Hans-Georg Leyser.

LI Corps – The corps headquarters was located at Gumrak. The corps suffered the following officer casualties: one killed in action; 14 wounded in action.

24th Panzer Division – The division counterattacked the enemy penetration of the 95th Rifle Division and eliminated it. The division was relieved from its positions on Hill 102 by the 100th ***Jäger*** Division. To the west of the division was the 389th Infantry Division; to the east was the 100th ***Jäger*** Division. The division suffered 15 NCOs/enlisted killed in action; four officers and 41 NCOs/enlisted were wounded in action.

71st Infantry Division – The division attacked in zone, seizing the Communist party and government buildings near 9th of January Square against the 13th Guards Rifle Division. To the north was the 295th Infantry Division; to the south was the 94th Infantry Division. The division suffered ten NCOs/enlisted killed in action; one officer and 42 NCOs/enlisted were wounded in action.

94th Infantry Division – The division attacked in zone, seizing the Tsaritsa Gulley all the way to its mouth against the 13th Guards Rifle Division. To the north was the 71st Infantry Division; to the south was the 29th Infantry Division (Motorized.) The division lost nine NCOs/enlisted killed in action; two officers and three NCOs/enlisted were wounded in action.

100th Jäger Division – The division finished moving to Stalingrad and conducted a relief in place of the 24th ***Panzer*** Division on Hill 102 against the 95th Rifle Division. To the west was the 24th ***Panzer*** Division; to the east was the 295th Infantry Division. The division suffered one officer killed in action; ten NCOs/enlisted were wounded in action.

295th Infantry Division – The division defended in sector against the 95th Rifle Division. To the west was the 100th ***Jäger*** Division; to the south was the 71st Infantry Division. The division lost 17 NCOs/enlisted killed in action; one officer and 72 NCOs/enlisted were wounded in action.

389th Infantry Division – The division defended in sector. To the north was Battle Group Stahel; to the southeast was the 24th ***Panzer*** Division. The division suffered one NCO/enlisted killed in action; 16 NCOs/enlisted were wounded in action.

Fourth *Panzer* Army – The army headquarters was located at Plodowitoje.

IV Corps – The corps headquarters was located at Plantator.

297th Infantry Division – The division The division defended in sector east of Elkhi against the 157th Rifle Division. To the north was the 371st Infantry Division; to the south was the 20th Romanian Infantry Division.

371st Infantry Division – The division defended in sector north of Peschanka to Elkhi against part of the 422nd Rifle Division. The division headquarters was located west of Staro-Dubovka. To the north was the 14th ***Panzer*** Division; to the south was the 297th Infantry Division. The division lost one officer and four NCOs/enlisted killed in action; three officers and 16 NCOs/enlisted were wounded in action.

20th Romanian Infantry Division – The division defended in sector north of the Volga-Don Canal against the 38th Rifle Division. To the north was the 297th Infantry Division; to the south was the 2nd Romanian Infantry Division of the Romanian VI Corps.

Sources, September 25, 1942: ***Oberkommando des Heeres, Lage Ost: Stand: 25.9.42, Eastern Front Situation Map, National Archives Identifier: 559733, Record Group 242 – National Archives Collection of Foreign Records Seized, 1675-1958, National Archives, College Park, Maryland; Ia, Armeeoberkommando 6, "Morgen Meldung" and assorted reports, Kriegstagebuch 13, 26 September 1942, as found in Microfilm Series, T-312, Records of German Field Commands, Armies, Roll 1686, National Archives and Records Service, College Park, Maryland; Ia, XXXXVIII Panzerkorps, "Übersicht über die dem Korps Unterstellten Divisionen, 28. Juni 1942 – 11 October 1942," as found on T-314, Records of German Field Commands, Corps, Roll 1153, National Archives, College Park, Maryland; Korpsarzt, XXXXVIII Panzerkorps, "Meldung über Personelle Verluste," Stand 25.9.42, as found on T-314, Records of German Field Commands, Corps, Roll 1158, National Archives, College Park, Maryland; 371st Infantry Division, Kriegstagebuch, 25 September 1942, as found in Microfilm Series T-315, Roll 2164, National Archives and Records Service, College Park, Maryland; Florian Freiherr von und zu Aufsess, Die Anlagenbände zu den Kriegstagebüchern der 6. Armee vom 14.09.1942 bis 24.11.1942, Band 1, Schwabach, Germany: Selbstverlag, 2006, 56-58; Dermot Bradley, Karl-Friedrich Hildebrand & Markus Rövekamp, Die Generale des Heeres, 1921-1945, Band 1: Abberger – Bitthorn, Osnabrück, Germany: Biblio Verlag, 1993, 75-76; Die 71. Infanterie-Division, 1939-1945: Gefechts- und Erlebnisberichte aus Kämpfen der "Gluckhaften Division" von Verdun bis Stalingrad, vom Monte Cassino bis zum Plattensee, Eggolsheim, FRG: Edition Dörfler, 1973, 250; David M. Glantz & Jonathan M. House, Armageddon in Stalingrad: September-November 1942, (The Stalingrad Trilogy, Volume 2), Lawrence, Kansas: University Press of Kansas, 2009, 196, 202-214; Joachim Lemelsen, 29. Division, Bad Nauheim, FRG: Podzun Verlag, 1960, 203-204; Jochen Löser, Bittere Pflicht: Kampf und Untergang der 76. Berlin-Brandenburgischen Infanterie-Division, Osnabrück, FRG: Biblio Verlag, 1986, 209 and 210; Jason Mark, Death of the Leaping Horseman: 24. Panzer-Division in Stalingrad, Sydney, Australia: Leaping Horsemen Books, 2003, 209-210; Kurt Mehner, Die Geheimen Tagesberichte der Deutschen Wehrmachtführung im Zweiten Weltkrieg 1939-1945, Band 5: 1. Juni 1942 – 30. November 1942, Osnabrück, Germany: Biblio Verlag, 1991, 213; Hans Neidhardt, Mit Tanne und Eichenlaub: Kriegschronik der 100. Jäger Division vormals 100. leichte Infanterie Division, Graz, Austria: Leopold Stocker Verlag, 1981, 208; Anton Schimak, Karl Lamprecht & Friedrich Dettmer, Die 44. Infanterie Division: Tagebuch der Hoch- und Deutschmeister, Wien: Verlag Austria Press, 169, 233 and Map: Marschweg der 44. Infanterie Division im Russland.***

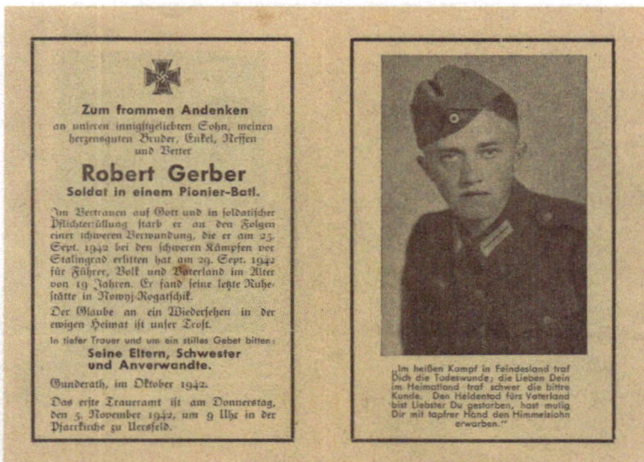

Zum frommen Andenken
an unseren innigstgeliebten Sohn, meinen herzensguten Bruder, Enkel, Neffen und Vetter

Robert Gerber
Soldat in einem Pionier-Batl.

Im Vertrauen auf Gott und in soldatischer Pflichterfüllung starb er an den Folgen einer schweren Verwundung, die er am 25. Sept. 1942 bei den schweren Kämpfen vor Stalingrad erlitten hat am 29. Sept. 1942 für Führer, Volk und Vaterland im Alter von 19 Jahren. Er fand seine letzte Ruhestätte in Nowyj-Rogatschik.

Der Glaube an ein Wiedersehen in der ewigen Heimat ist unser Trost.

In tiefer Trauer und um ein stilles Gebet bitten:
Seine Eltern, Schwester und Anverwandte.

Gunderath, im Oktober 1942.

Das erste Traueramt ist am Donnerstag, den 5. November 1942, um 9 Uhr in der Pfarrkirche zu Uersfeld.

„Im heißen Kampf in Feindesland traf Dich die Todeswunde; die Lieben Dein im Heimatland traf schwer die bittre Kunde. Den Heldentod fürs Vaterland bist Liebster Du gestorben, hast mutig Dir mit tapfrer Hand den Himmelslohn erworben."

Pionier **Robert Gerber** was born at Gunderath near Kelberg in the Rhineland-Palatinate on June 13, 1923. Likely assigned to the combat engineer battalion of the 14th ***Panzer*** Division, he was seriously wounded at Novyy Rogachik on September 25, 1942. He died of his wounds four days later. He is buried at the German Military Cemetery in Block 26, Row 1, in Grave 9.

Gebets-Andenken
an Herrn

Bernhard Lenz
Obergefreiter in einer Pionier-Abtlg.
Bauerssohn von Kreuzberg

gefallen am 25. September 1942 bei der Abwehrkämpfen bei Stalingrad im 25. Lebensjahr fürs Vaterland.
Ehre seinem Andenken!

Buchdruckerei Fuchs, Freyung

Obergefreiter **Bernhard Lenz**, a farmer's son, was born in Kreuzberg near Freyung on August 17, 1917. Assigned to an engineer battalion, he was killed in action at Bol'shaya Rossoschka on September 25, 1942.

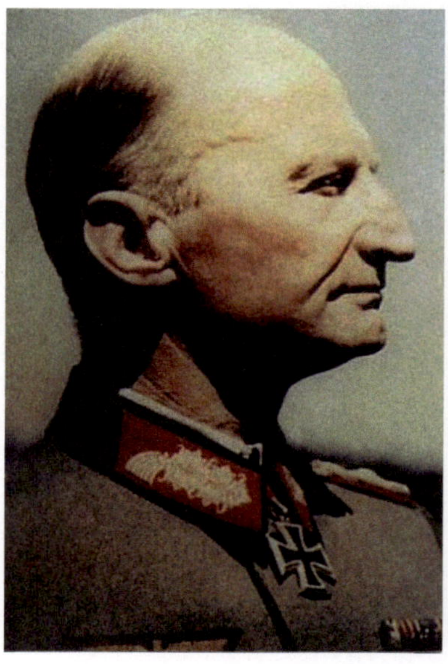

Generalmajor **Max Fremerey.** He was relieved of command of the 29th Infantry Division (Motorized) on September 25, 1942 and placed in the ***Führer*** Reserve officer pool.

September 26, 1942
Weather: clear, sunny, changing temperatures, 75° F
Sunrise: 5:53 a.m.; **Sunset:** 5:53 p.m.
Moon: Waning Gibbous; 96% illumination

Sixth Army – The army headquarters was located at Golubinskaya.

VIII Corps – The corps suffered the following officer casualties: one killed in action; five wounded in action.

76th Infantry Division – The division defended in sector southwest of Samofalovka and north of Borodkin against the 173rd Rifle Division. To the northwest was the 305th Infantry Division; to the east was the 60th Infantry Division (Motorized.) The enemy attacked, supported by heavy artillery and mortar fire, but made no progress. Between September 2 and September 26, division medics treated 5,400 patients. The division lost 20 NCOs/enlisted killed in action; 60 NCOs/enlisted were wounded in action.

305th Infantry Division – The division defended in sector from the Don River, north of Nizhne-Gnilovskii, to west of Kotluban', against the 298th Rifle Division and the 260th Rifle Division. To the southeast was the 76th Infantry Division; to the north was the 384th Infantry Division. The division suffered five NCOs/enlisted killed in action; two officers and nine NCOs/enlisted were wounded in action.

XI Corps – The corps suffered the following officer casualties: two wounded in action.

44th Infantry Division – The division defended in sector Kurchajessowskij-Kamyshinskiy-Hill 171.0-Hill 180.9-Sirotinskaya-Khmelevskoy, against the 40th Guards Rifle Division and the 343rd Rifle Division. The division headquarters was located at Verkhne-Golubaja. To the west was 376th Infantry Division; to the east was the 384th Infantry Division. The division lost one NCO/enlisted killed in action; one officer and 11 NCOs/enlisted were wounded in action.

376th Infantry Division – The division defended in sector against the 321st Rifle Division near Blizhniaia-Perekopka. To the west was the 1st Romanian Cavalry Division; to the east was the 44th Infantry Division. To consolidate combat power, **the division disbanded the 1st Battalion of the 672nd Infantry Regiment and the 1st Battalion of the 673rd Infantry Regiment** and transferred these soldiers to other units. The division lost 17 NCOs/enlisted killed in action; 41 NCOs/enlisted were wounded in action; seven men were reported missing in action.

384th Infantry Division – The division defended in sector west of the Don River near Trekhostrovskaia to Podgorskii against the 4th Guards Rifle Division, the 27th Guards Rifle Division and the 214th Rifle Division. To the west was the 44th Infantry Division; to the south was the 305th Infantry Division. To consolidate combat power, **the division disbanded the 3rd Battalion of the 534th Infantry Regiment, the 3rd Battalion of the 535th Infantry Regiment and the 1st Battalion of the 536th Infantry Regiment** and transferred these soldiers to other units. The division lost one NCO/enlisted killed in action; 19 NCOs/enlisted were wounded in action; seven men were reported missing in action.

XIV *Panzer* Corps – The corps headquarters was located east of Ssadtschi-Kowa. The corps suffered the following officer casualties: four killed in action; eight wounded in action; one missing in action.

3rd Infantry Division (Motorized) – The division defended in sector, from the Tartar Hill-Hill 111.1-Hill 129.6-Hill 131.2 against the 299th Rifle Division, the 38th Guards Rifle Division, the 116th Rifle Division and the 343rd Rifle Division. To the east was the 16th ***Panzer*** Division; to the west was the 60th Infantry Division (Motorized.) To consolidate combat power, **the division disbanded the 2nd Battalion of the 8th Infantry Regiment and the 3rd Battalion of the 29th Infantry Regiment** and transferred these soldiers to bring other units up to strength.

16th Panzer Division – The division defended in sector, from Hill 139.7 to the Volga and from the Volga southwest to Hill 145.1, north of Orlovka, against the 120th Rifle Division, the 84th Rifle Division and the 64th Rifle Division. To the southwest was Battle Group Stahel; to the west was the 3rd Infantry Division (Motorized.)

60th Infantry Division (Motorized) – The division defended in sector, from south of Kotluban' Station near Borodkin to Kuz'michi, against the 41st Guards Rifle Division, the 49th Rifle Division, the 231st Rifle Division, the 233rd Rifle Division, the 39th Guards Rifle Division, the 316th Rifle Division and the 207th Rifle Division. To the west was the 76th Infantry Division; to the east was the 3rd Infantry Division (Motorized.)

Battle Group Stahel – The battle group defended northwest of Orlovka to contain enemy forces. To the northwest was the 16th ***Panzer*** Division; to the southwest was the 389th Infantry Division.

XVII Corps

79th Infantry Division – The division defended in sector from Bol'shoy-Verkhne-Kalmykovskii-Verkhne-Fomichinskii-Baskowskij against the 124th Rifle Division. The division headquarters was located at Karagichev. To the west was the Italian XXXV Corps; to the south was the 6th Romanian Infantry Division. The division lost five NCOs/enlisted wounded in action.

113th Infantry Division – The division occupied an assembly area just west of the Don River. To consolidate combat power, **the division disbanded the 2nd Battalion of the 260th Infantry Regiment** and transferred these soldiers to other units.

298th Infantry Division – The division occupied three assembly areas along the Sixth Army's western boundary and south of the 79th Infantry Division. To consolidate combat power, **the division disbanded the 1st Battalion of the 525th Infantry Regiment, the 2nd Battalion of the 526th Infantry Regiment and the 3rd Battalion of the 527th Infantry Regiment** and transferred these soldiers to other units.

1st Romanian Cavalry Division – The division defended in sector near Mololologowskij south of the Don River against the 76th Rifle Division and 63rd Rifle Division. To the west was the 13th Romanian Infantry Division; to the east was the 376th Infantry Division. The division suffered one NCO/enlisted killed in action; two NCOs/enlisted were wounded in action.

1st Romanian Armored Division – The division occupied an assembly in the western part of the corps sector.

6th Romanian Infantry Division – The division defended in sector south of the Don River against the 96th Rifle Division. To the west was the 79th Infantry Division; to the southeast was the 13th Romanian Infantry Division. The division lost five NCOs/enlisted killed in action; 32 NCOs/enlisted were wounded in action.

13th Romanian Infantry Division – The division defended in sector along the Don River west of Kletskiy against the 278th Rifle Division and the 63rd Rifle Division. To the northwest was the 6th Romanian Infantry Division; to the east was the 1st Romanian Cavalry Division. The division suffered two officers and 23 NCOs/enlisted killed in action; three officers and 68 NCOs/enlisted were wounded in action; seven men were reported missing in action.

XXXXVIII *Panzer* Corps – Corps troops lost one NCO/enlisted killed in action and two NCOs/enlisted wounded in action. The corps suffered the following officer casualties: two wounded in action.

14th Panzer Division – The division conducted consolidation operations in sector. To the north was the 29th Infantry Division (Motorized); to the south was the 371st Infantry Division. The division lost three NCOs/enlisted killed in action; 16 NCOs/enlisted were wounded in action; two NCOs/enlisted were reported missing in action.

29th Infantry Division (Motorized) – The division conducted consolidation operations in sector and assisted the 94th Infantry Division seize the quay near the Tsaritsa River and the Volga River. To the north was the 94th Infantry Division; to the south was the 14th ***Panzer*** Division. The division lost one NCO/enlisted killed in action; four NCOs/enlisted were wounded in action.

LI Corps – The corps headquarters was located at Gumrak. The corps suffered the following officer casualties: three killed in action; eight wounded in action.

24th Panzer Division – The division prepared for its attack the following day to seize

Ovrashnaya, Hill 107.5 and the Krasny Oktyabr Steel Factory Workers' Settlement against the 95th Rifle Division and the 193rd Rifle Division. To the west was the 389th Infantry Division; to the east was the 100th ***Jäger*** Division. The division suffered two NCOs/enlisted killed in action; one officer and 18 NCOs/enlisted were wounded in action.

71st Infantry Division – The division attacked in its zone, seizing the Gorki Theater and the Stalingrad Communist Party Headquarters, and reaching the Volga River shoreline, fighting against the 13th Guards Rifle Division. To the north was the 295th Infantry Division; to the south was the 94th Infantry Division. The division also defended against attacks at Respublikanskaia Street, Kievskaia Street, Tobol'skaia Street and Tambovskaia Street.

94th Infantry Division – The division attacked in zone, cleaning out the south bank of the Tsaritsa River to its mouth, defeating the 92nd Rifle Brigade. The division received orders to be prepared to move north. The division lost one officer and ten NCOs/enlisted killed in action; 35 NCOs/enlisted were wounded in action. To the north was the 71st Infantry Division; to the south was the 29th Infantry Division (Motorized.)

100th Jäger Division – The division relieved the 295th Infantry Division from its positions against the 95th Rifle Division. To the west was the 24th ***Panzer*** Division; to the east was the 295th Infantry Division. The division suffered four NCOs/enlisted killed in action; two officers and 29 NCOs/enlisted were wounded in action. To consolidate combat power, **the division disbanded the 3rd Battalion of the 54th *Jäger* Regiment and the 3rd Battalion of the 227th *Jäger* Regiment** and transferred these soldiers to other units.

295th Infantry Division – The division relinquished some of its positions to the 100th ***Jäger*** Division to prepare to attack Mamayev Kurgan [Hill 102] against the 95th Rifle Division. To the west was the 100th ***Jäger*** Division; to the south was the 71st Infantry Division. The division suffered seven NCOs/enlisted killed in action; one officer and 43 NCOs/enlisted were wounded in action. To consolidate combat power, **the division disbanded the 1st Battalion of the 516th Infantry Regiment and the 3rd Battalion of the 516th Infantry Regiment** and transferred these soldiers to other units.

389th Infantry Division – The division prepared for offensive operations. To the northeast

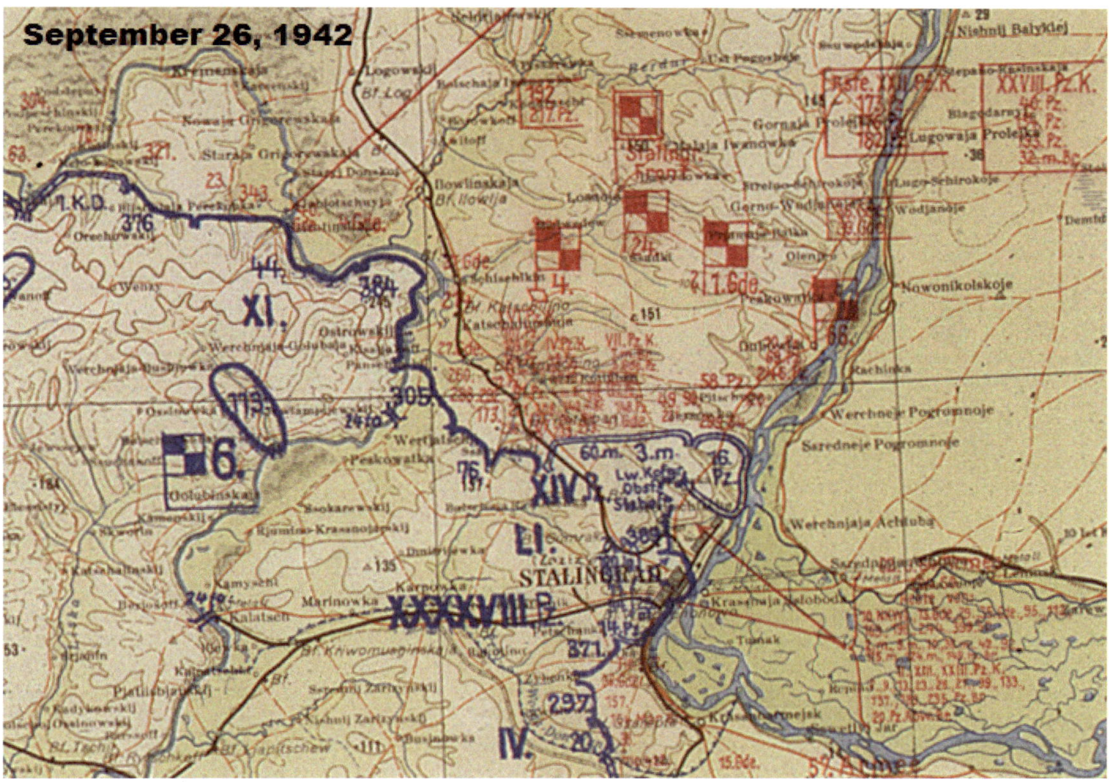

was Battle Group Stahel; to the southeast was the 24th ***Panzer*** Division. The division lost three NCOs/enlisted killed in action; seven NCOs/enlisted were wounded in action. To consolidate combat power, **the division disbanded the 2nd Battalion of the 544th Infantry Regiment, the 2nd Battalion of the 545th Infantry Regiment and the 2nd Battalion of the 546th Infantry Regiment** and transferred these soldiers to other units.

Fourth *Panzer* Army – The army headquarters was located at Plodowitoje.

IV Corps – The corps headquarters was located at Plantator.

297th Infantry Division – The division The division defended in sector east of Elkhi against the 157th Rifle Division and the 38th Guards Rifle Division. To the north was the 371st Infantry Division; to the south was the 20th Romanian Infantry Division.

371st Infantry Division – The division defended in sector north of Peschanka to Elkhi against elements of the 422nd Rifle Division. The division headquarters was located west of Staro-Dubovka. To the north was the 14th ***Panzer*** Division; to the south was the 297th Infantry Division. The division lost one officer and 11 NCOs/enlisted killed in action; 64 NCOs/enlisted were wounded in action.

20th Romanian Infantry Division – The division defended in sector north of the Volga-Don Canal against the 157th Rifle Division. To the north was the 297th Infantry Division; to the south was the 2nd Romanian Infantry Division of the Romanian VI Corps.

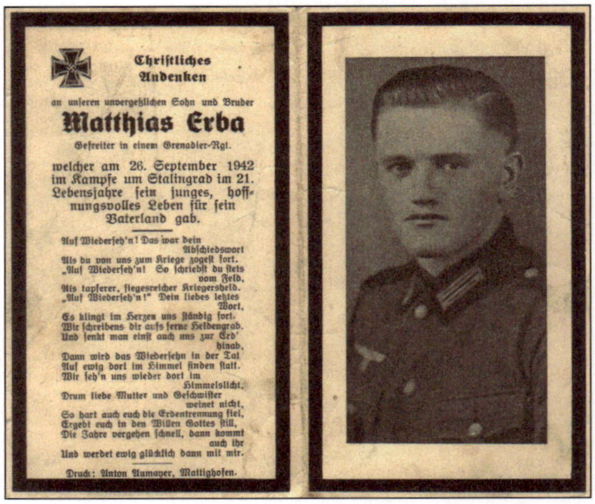
Christliches Andenken

an unseren unvergeßlichen Sohn und Bruder

Matthias Erba

Gefreiter in einem Grenadier-Rgt.

welcher am 26. September 1942 im Kampfe um Stalingrad im 21. Lebensjahre sein junges, hoffnungsvolles Leben für sein Vaterland gab.

Auf Wiederseh'n! Das war dein Abschiedswort
Als du von uns zum Kriege zogest fort.
„Auf Wiederseh'n! So schriebst du stets vom Feld,
Als tapferer, siegesreicher Kriegersheld.
„Auf Wiederseh'n!" Dein liebes letztes Wort,
Es klingt im Herzen uns ständig fort.
Wir schreibens dir aufs ferne Heldengrab.
Und senkt man einst auch uns zur Erd' hinab,
Dann wird das Wiedersehn in der Tat
Auf ewig dort im Himmel finden statt.
Wir seh'n uns wieder dort im Himmelslicht.
Drum liebe Mutter und Geschwister weinet nicht,
So hart auch euch die Erdentrennung fiel,
Ergebt euch in den Willen Gottes still,
Die Jahre vergehen schnell, dann kommt auch ihr
Und werdet ewig glücklich dann mit mir.

Druck: Anton Aumayer, Mattighofen.

Gefreiter **Matthias Erba** was born in Poschnig near Mattighofen on August 26, 1921. He was killed in action at Malaia Rossoschka on September 26, 1942.

Sources, September 26, 1942: ***Oberkommando des Heeres, Lage Ost: Stand: 26.9.42, Eastern Front Situation Map, National Archives Identifier: 559733, Record Group 242 – National Archives Collection of Foreign Records Seized, 1675-1958, National Archives, College Park, Maryland; Ia, Armeeoberkommando 6, "Morgen Meldung" and assorted reports, Kriegstagebuch 13, 27 September 1942, as found in Microfilm Series, T-312, Records of German Field Commands, Armies, Roll 1686, National Archives and Records Service, College Park, Maryland; Ia, XXXXVIII Panzerkorps, "Übersicht über die dem Korps Unterstellten Divisionen, 28. Juni 1942 – 11 October 1942," as found on T-314, Records of German Field Commands, Corps, Roll 1153, National Archives, College Park, Maryland; Korpsarzt, XXXXVIII Panzerkorps, "Meldung über Personelle Verluste," Stand 26.9.42, as found on T-314, Records of German Field Commands, Corps, Roll 1158, National Archives, College Park, Maryland; 371st Infantry Division, Kriegstagebuch, 26 September 1942, as found in Microfilm Series T-315, Roll 2164, National Archives and Records Service, College Park, Maryland; Division der Wehrmacht: 71. Infanterie-Division, 389. Infanterie-Division, 295. Infanterie-Division, 79. Infanterie-Division, 260. Infanterie-Division, 305. Infanterie-Division, 73. Infanterie-Division, 18. Infanterie-Division, 100. Jäger-Division, 94. Infanterie-Division, Germany: Books LLC, 2010, 13; Florian Freiherr von und zu Aufsess, Die Anlagenbände zu den Kriegstagebüchern der 6. Armee vom 14.09.1942 bis 24.11.1942, Band 1, Schwabach, Germany: Selbstverlag, 2006, 59-66, 73, 79-80; John Erickson, The Road to Stalingrad, New York: Harper & Row, 1975, 409; David M. Glantz & Jonathan M. House, Armageddon in Stalingrad: September-November 1942, (The Stalingrad Trilogy, Volume 2), Lawrence, Kansas: University Press of Kansas, 2009, 202-214; Adalbert Holl, An Infantryman in Stalingrad, translated by Jason D. Mark and Neill Page, Sydney, Australia: Leaping Horseman Books, 2005, 65-67; Jochen Löser, Bittere Pflicht: Kampf und Untergang der 76. Berlin-Brandenburgischen Infanterie-Division, Osnabrück, FRG: Biblio Verlag, 1986, 209 and 211; Jason Mark, Death of the Leaping Horseman: 24. Panzer-Division in Stalingrad, Sydney, Australia: Leaping Horsemen Books, 2003, 214-215; Janusz Piekalkiewicz, Stalingrad: Anatomie einer Schlacht, München, BRD: Wilhelm Heyne Verlag, 1977, 235; Anton Schimak, Karl Lamprecht & Friedrich Dettmer, Die 44. Infanterie Division: Tagebuch der Hoch- und Deutschmeister, Wien: Verlag Austria Press, 169, 233 and Map: Marschweg der 44. Infanterie Division im Russland.***

September 27, 1942
Weather: sunny, clear, warm, cool morning, after noon warming, 79° F, good road conditions
Sunrise: 5:54 a.m.; **Sunset:** 5:51 p.m.
Moon: Waning Gibbous; 91% illumination

Sixth Army – Bombers and dive-bombers from the ***Luftwaffe***'s VIII Air Corps pounded Stalingrad in large-scale attacks, disrupting planned Soviet counter-attacks. Army headquarters was located at Golubinskaya.

VIII Corps – The 177th ***Sturmgeschütz*** Detachment and the 754th Pioneer Battalion were assigned to the corps; the 849th Heavy Artillery Detachment was assigned to support the corps. The corps suffered the following officer casualties: four wounded in action.

76th Infantry Division – The division defended in sector southwest of Samofalovka and north of Borodkin, against the 260th Rifle Division and the 173rd Rifle Division. To the northwest was the 305th Infantry Division; to the east was the 60th Infantry Division (Motorized.) The enemy, supported by heavy artillery and mortar fire, attacked unsuccessfully. The division lost 25 NCOs/enlisted killed in action; 120 NCOs/enlisted were wounded in action.

305th Infantry Division – The division defended in sector from the Don River, north of Nizhne-Gnilovskii, to west of Kotluban' against the 298th Rifle Division. To the east was the 76th Infantry Division; to the north was the 384th Infantry Division. The division lost six NCOs/enlisted killed in action; 17 NCOs/enlisted were wounded in action.

XI Corps – The 614th ***Flak*** Battalion (Motorized) was assigned to the corps. The corps suffered the following officer casualties: nine wounded in action.

44th Infantry Division – The division defended in sector Kurchajessowskij-Kamyshinskiy-Hill 171.0-Hill 180.9-Sirotinskaya-Khmelevskoy against the 343rd Rifle Division and the 40th Guards Rifle Division. The division headquarters was located at Verkhne-Golubaja. To the west was 376th Infantry Division; to the east was the 384th Infantry Division. The division lost five NCOs/enlisted killed in action; 23 NCOs/enlisted were wounded in action.

376th Infantry Division – The division defended in sector near Blizhniaia-Perekopka against the 23rd Rifle Division. To the east was the 44th Infantry Division; to the west was the 1st Romanian Cavalry Division. The division lost two NCOs/enlisted killed in action; one NCO/enlisted was wounded in action.

384th Infantry Division – The division defended in sector west of the Don River near Trekhostrovskaia to Podgorskii, against the 4th Guards Rifle Division and the 37th Guards Rifle Division. To the west was the 44th Infantry Division; to the south was the 305th Infantry Division. During the night, enemy bombers struck hard at Hill 130.1 and Hill 110.2. The division lost 11 NCOs/enlisted killed in action; eight officers and 29 NCOs/enlisted were wounded in action.

XIV *Panzer* Corps – The corps headquarters was located east of Ssadtschi-Kowa. The corps suffered the following officer casualties: two killed in action; four wounded in action.

3rd Infantry Division (Motorized) – The division defended in sector, from the Tartar Hill-Hill 111.1-Hill 129.6-Hill 131.2 against the 299th Rifle Division, the 38th Guards Rifle Division, the 116th Rifle Division and the 343rd Rifle Division. To the east was the 16th ***Panzer*** Division; to the west was the 60th Infantry Division (Motorized.) The division lost one NCO/enlisted killed in action; three NCOs/enlisted were wounded in action.

16th Panzer Division – The division defended in sector, from Hill 139.7 to the Volga

and from the Volga southwest to Hill 145.1, north of Orlovka, against the 120th Rifle Division, the 84th Rifle Division and the 64th Rifle Division. A local division attack near the Volga captured many enemy prisoners. To the west was the 3rd Infantry Division (Motorized); to the southwest was Battle Group Stahel.

60th Infantry Division (Motorized) – The division defended in sector, from south of Kotluban' Station near Borodkin to Kuz'michi, against the 41st Guards Rifle Division, the 49th Rifle Division, the 231st Rifle Division, the 233rd Rifle Division, the 39th Guards Rifle Division, the 316th Rifle Division and the 207th Rifle Division. To the west was the 76th Infantry Division; to the east was the 3rd Infantry Division (Motorized.)

Battle Group Stahel – The battle group defended northwest of Orlovka to contain enemy forces. To the northeast was the 16th ***Panzer*** Division; to the southwest was the 389th Infantry Division.

XVII Corps

79th Infantry Division – The division defended in sector from Bol'shoy-Verkhne-Kalmykovskii-Verkhne-Fomichinskii-Baskowskij, against the 124th Rifle Division. The division headquarters was located at Karagichev. To the west was the Italian XXXV Corps; to the east was the 6th Romanian Infantry Division. The division lost three NCOs wounded in action.

113th Infantry Division – The division moved toward Stalingrad. Lead elements reached Bol'shaya Rossoschka, while trail elements were at the Don River.

298th Infantry Division – The division occupied three assembly areas along the Sixth Army's western boundary and south of the 79th Infantry Division.

1st Romanian Cavalry Division – The division defended in sector near Mologowskij south of the Don River against the 76th Rifle Division and 63rd Rifle Division. To the west was the 13th Romanian Infantry Division; to the east was the 376th Infantry Division.

1st Romanian Armored Division – The division occupied an assembly in the western part of the corps sector.

6th Romanian Infantry Division – The division defended in sector south of the Don River against the 96th Rifle Division. To the west was the 79th Infantry Division; to the southeast was the 13th Romanian Infantry Division. The division lost nine NCOs/enlisted killed in action; five officers and 97 NCOs/enlisted were wounded in action.

13th Romanian Infantry Division – The division defended in sector along the Don River west of Kletskiy against the 278th Rifle Division and the 63rd Rifle Division. To the northwest was the 6th Romanian Infantry Division; to the east was the 1st Romanian Cavalry Division. The division lost 35 NCOs/enlisted killed in action; four officers and 100 NCOs/enlisted were wounded in action.

XXXXVIII *Panzer* Corps – Corps troops lost one NCO/enlisted wounded in action. The corps suffered the following officer casualties: one wounded in action.

14th Panzer Division – The division conducted consolidation operations in sector. To the north was the 29th Infantry Division (Motorized); to the south was the 371st Infantry Division. The division lost five NCOs/enlisted killed in action; 27 NCOs/enlisted were wounded in action.

29th Infantry Division (Motorized) – The division conducted consolidation operations in sector. To the north was the 94th Infantry Division; to the south was the 14th ***Panzer*** Division. The division lost three NCOs/enlisted killed in action; seven NCOs/enlisted were wounded in action.

LI Corps – The corps headquarters was located at Gumrak. The corps suffered the following officer casualties: seven killed in action; 33 wounded in action.

24th Panzer Division – The division initially repulsed an enemy attack on its positions and then attacked north in zone, seizing Ovrashnaya, Hill 107.5 and the northwest section of the Krasny Oktyabr Steel Factory Workers' Settlement, driving back the 112th Rifle Division and parts of the 95th Rifle Division. The division suffered one officer and 27 NCOs/enlisted killed in action; eight officers and 120 NCOs/enlisted were wounded in action. To the west was the 389th Infantry Division; to the southeast was the 100th ***Jäger*** Division. ***Generalmajor*** Bruno ***Ritter*** von Hauenschild, former division commander, was awarded the Oak Leaves to the Knight's Cross.

71st Infantry Division – The division attacked in zone to clear enemy forces from north of the Tsaritsa River; heavy fighting occurred at the House of Specialists and Pavlov's House

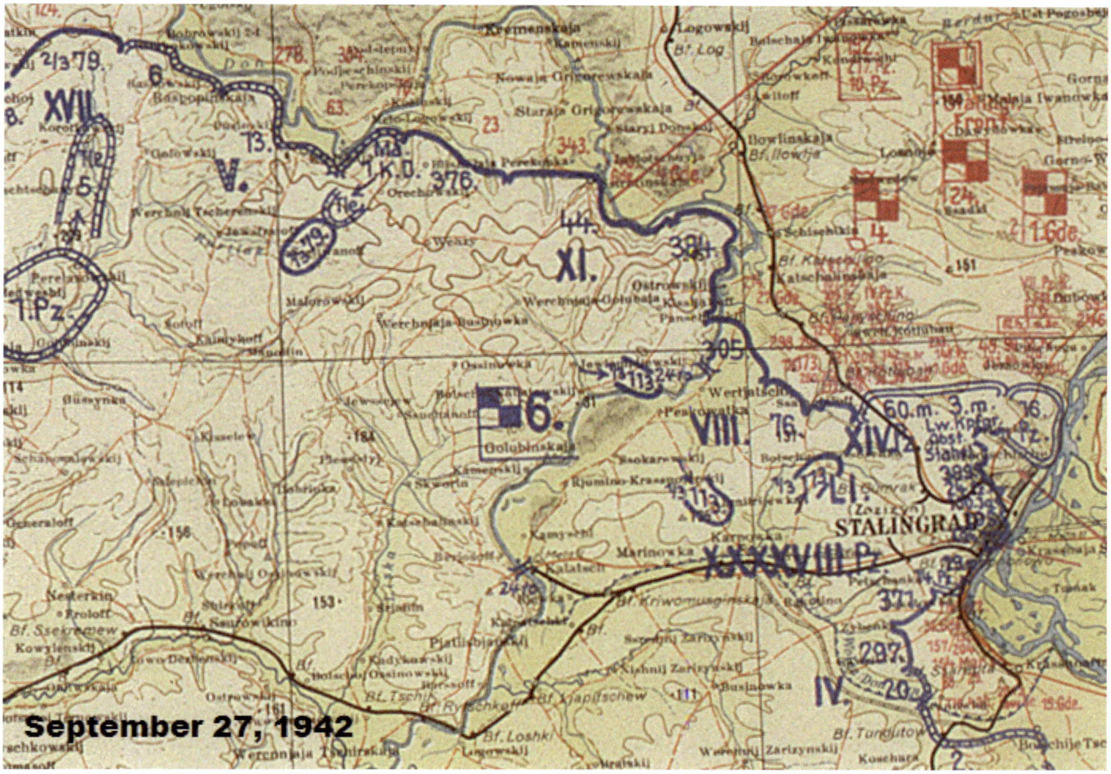

September 27, 1942

against the 13th Guards Rifle Division. To the northwest was the 295th Infantry Division; to the south was the 94th Infantry Division. The division headquarters was located in the Dubowaja Balka. By the end of the day, the division assumed the entire sector along the western bank of the Volga River from the Dol'gii Balka southward to the northern outskirts of Kuporosnoye.

94th Infantry Division – The division attacked in zone, clearing enemy forces of the 13th Guards Rifle Division from south of the Tsaritsa River. Late in the day the division transferred two regiments northward toward the Krasny Oktyabr Workers' Settlement. The division lost four NCOs/enlisted killed in action; two officers and 20 NCOs/enlisted were wounded in action. To the north was the 71st Infantry Division; to the south was the 29th Infantry Division (Motorized.)

100th Jäger Division – The division attacked north in zone from Hill 107.5, protecting the right flank of the 24th ***Panzer*** Division, seizing the crest of Hill 102 against the 95th Rifle Division and the 284th Rifle Division. The division suffered four officers and 144 NCOs/enlisted killed in action; 13 officers and 334 NCOs/enlisted were wounded in action. To the west was the 24th ***Panzer*** Division; to the southeast was the 295th Infantry Division.

295th Infantry Division – The division attempted to seize more of Hill 102 against the 95th Rifle Division and the 284th Rifle Division. To the northwest was the 100th ***Jäger*** Division; to the southeast was the 71st Infantry Division. The division suffered ten NCOs/enlisted killed in action; 48 NCOs/enlisted were wounded in action.

389th Infantry Division – The division attacked north in zone along the west flank of the 24th ***Panzer*** Division, seizing the railroad line southeast of Gorodishche, as well as Hill 109.4 and Hill 97.7 against the 112th Rifle Division and the 308th Rifle Division. To the east was the 24th ***Panzer*** Division; to the northeast was Battle Group Stahel.

Fourth *Panzer* Army – The army headquarters was located at Plodowitoje.

IV Corps – The corps headquarters was located at Plantator.

297th Infantry Division – The division defended in sector east of Elkhi against the 157th

Rifle Division and the 154th Marine Infantry Brigade. To the north was the 371st Infantry Division; to the south was the 20th Romanian Infantry Division.

371st Infantry Division – The division defended in sector north of Peschanka to Elkhi, against the 157th Rifle Division and elements of the 422nd Rifle Division. The division headquarters was located west of Staro-Dubovka. To the north was the 14th ***Panzer*** Division; to the southwest was the 297th Infantry Division. The division lost one officer and three NCOs/enlisted killed in action; two officers and 66 NCOs/enlisted were wounded in action.

20th Romanian Infantry Division – The division defended in sector north of the Volga-Don Canal against elements of the 422nd Rifle Division. To the north was the 297th Infantry Division; to the south was the 2nd Romanian Infantry Division of the Romanian VI Corps.

Sources, September 27, 1942: ***Oberkommando des Heeres, Lage Ost: Stand: 27.9.42, Eastern Front Situation Map, National Archives Identifier: 559733, Record Group 242 – National Archives Collection of Foreign Records Seized, 1675-1958, National Archives, College Park, Maryland; Ia, Armeeoberkommando 6, "Morgen Meldung" and assorted reports, Kriegstagebuch 13, 28 September 1942, as found in Microfilm Series, T-312, Records of German Field Commands, Armies, Roll 1686, National Archives and Records Service, College Park, Maryland; Ia, XXXXVIII Panzerkorps, "Übersicht über die dem Korps Unterstellten Divisionen, 28. Juni 1942 – 11 October 1942," as found on T-314, Records of German Field Commands, Corps, Roll 1153, National Archives, College Park, Maryland; Korpsarzt, XXXXVIII Panzerkorps, "Meldung über Personelle Verluste," Stand 27.9.42, as found on T-314, Records of German Field Commands, Corps, Roll 1158, National Archives, College Park, Maryland; 79th Infantry Division, Kriegstagebuch, 27 September 1942, as found in Microfilm Series T-315, Roll 1108, National Archives and Records Service, College Park, Maryland; 371st Infantry Division, Kriegstagebuch, 27 September 1942, as found in Microfilm Series T-315, Roll 2164, National Archives and Records Service, College Park, Maryland; Florian Freiherr von und zu Aufsess, Die Anlagenbände zu den Kriegstagebüchern der 6. Armee vom 14.09.1942 bis 24.11.1942, Band 1, Schwabach, Germany: Selbstverlag, 2006, 66-72; Paul Carell, Stalingrad: The Defeat of the German Sixth Army, Atglen, Pennsylvania: Schiffer Publishing, 1993, 145; Division der Wehrmacht: 71. Infanterie-Division, 389. Infanterie-Division, 295. Infanterie-Division, 79. Infanterie-Division, 260. Infanterie-Division, 305. Infanterie-Division, 73. Infanterie-Division, 18. Infanterie-Division, 100. Jäger-Division, 94. Infanterie-Division, Germany: Books LLC, 2010, 321; Die 71. Infanterie-Division, 1939-1945: Gefechts- und Erlebnisberichte aus Kämpfen der "Gluckhaften Division" von Verdun bis Stalingrad, vom Monte Cassino bis zum Plattensee, Eggolsheim, FRG: Edition Dörfler, 1973, 250-252; David M. Glantz & Jonathan M. House, Armageddon in Stalingrad: September-November 1942, (The Stalingrad Trilogy, Volume 2), Lawrence, Kansas: University Press of Kansas, 2009, 234, 246-258; Adalbert Holl, An Infantryman in Stalingrad, translated by Jason D. Mark and Neill Page, Sydney, Australia: Leaping Horseman Books, 2005, 73; Jochen Löser, Bittere Pflicht: Kampf und Untergang der 76. Berlin-Brandenburgischen Infanterie-Division, Osnabrück, FRG: Biblio Verlag, 1986, 209; Jason Mark, Death of the Leaping Horseman: 24. Panzer-Division in Stalingrad, Sydney, Australia: Leaping Horsemen Books, 2003, 215-228; Kurt Mehner, Die Geheimen Tagesberichte der Deutschen Wehrmachtführung im Zweiten Weltkrieg 1939-1945, Band 5: 1. Juni 1942 – 30. November 1942, Osnabrück, Germany: Biblio Verlag, 1991, 215; Hans Neidhardt, Mit Tanne und Eichenlaub: Kriegschronik der 100. Jäger Division vormals 100. leichte Infanterie Division, Graz, Austria: Leopold Stocker Verlag, 1981, 209; Janusz Piekalkiewicz, Stalingrad: Anatomie einer Schlacht, München, BRD: Wilhelm Heyne Verlag, 1977, 251; Anton Schimak, Karl Lamprecht & Friedrich Dettmer, Die 44. Infanterie Division: Tagebuch der Hoch- und Deutschmeister, Wien: Verlag Austria Press, 169, 233 and Map: Marschweg der 44. Infanterie Division im Russland; Stephen Walsh, Stalingrad: The Infernal Cauldron, 1942-1943, New York: Thomas Dunne Books/St. Martin's Press, 2000, 77.***

Schütze* Ferdinand Doblhammer** was born on November 11, 1922 in Aigerding, near St. Florian, Austria. Assigned to the 100th ***Jäger Division, he was killed in action at Stalingrad on September 27, 1942. At the time of his death, he had received the Iron Cross 2nd Class and the Infantry Assault Badge. He is listed in the remembrance book at the German Military Cemetery at Rossoschka.

Zur frommen Erinnerung
an unſeren lieben Sohn und Bruder
Soldat in einem Gebirgsjäger-Regiment
Ferdinand Doblhammer
Mörtlbauernſohn von Aigerding,
Pfarre St. Florian
Inhaber des Eiſernen Kreuzes II. Klaſſe
und des Infanterie-Sturmabzeichens
welcher am 27. September 1942
im 20. Lebensjahre im Kampfe
gegen Sowjetrußland den Helden-
tod für Volk und Heimat ſtarb.

Behüt Euch Gott, war's letzte Wort,
Als ich ging von meinen Lieben fort'
Auf Wiederſeh'n hab' ich geſagt,
Doch anders hat's der Herr bedacht.
Und weil mich traf das kalte Erz,
O, nicht zu tief ſei Euer Schmerz,
Der liebe Gott, der alle Menſchen liebt,
Er hat dies alles ſo gefügt.
Und fern lieg' ich als Held begraben,
Wohl in den ſchönſten Lebensjahren.
Ich bitte all' die Lieben mein,
Ich komme zu Euch nimmer heim,
Als mein Auge war gebrochen,
Sah ich ſchon den Himmel offen.

Buchdruckerei Dees, Schärding.

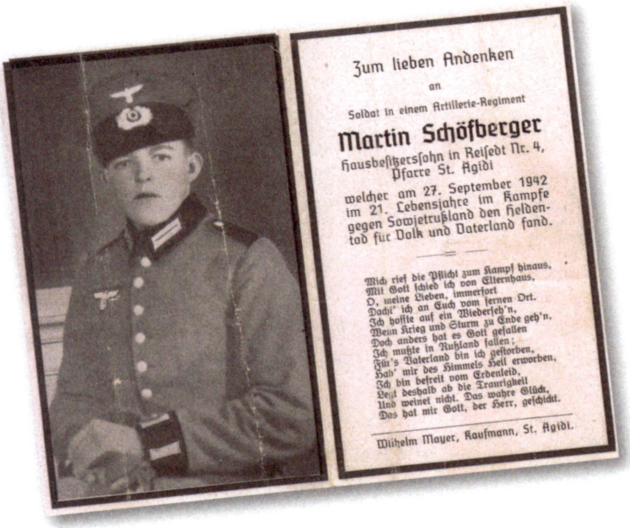

Zum lieben Andenken
an
Soldat in einem Artillerie-Regiment
Martin Schöfberger
Hausbeſitzersſohn in Reiſedt Nr. 4,
Pfarre St. Ägidi
welcher am 27. September 1942
im 21. Lebensjahre im Kampfe
gegen Sowjetrußland den Helden-
tod für Volk und Vaterland fand.

Mich rief die Pflicht zum Kampf hinaus,
Mit Gott ſchied ich von Elternhaus,
O, meine Lieben, immerfort
Dacht' ich an Euch vom fernen Ort.
Ich hoffte auf ein Wiederſeh'n,
Wenn Krieg und Sturm zu Ende geh'n.
Doch anders hat es Gott gefallen
Ich mußte in Rußland fallen;
Für's Vaterland bin ich geſtorben,
Hab' mir des Himmels Heil erworben,
Ich bin befreit vom Erdenleid,
Legt deshalb ab die Traurigkeit
Und weinet nicht. Das wahre Glück,
Das hat mir Gott, der Herr, geſchickt.

Wilhelm Mayer, Kaufmann, St. Ägidi.

***Kanonier* Martin Schöfberger** was born in St. Ägidi in Upper Austria on June 16, 1922. An artilleryman, he was killed in action at Hill 252, west of Chlebnyj, on September 27, 1942.

Unteroffizier* Friedrich Schmiedl** was born in Taufkirchen, Austria on August 17, 1919. The previous winner of the Iron Cross 2nd Class and the Infantry Assault Badge, Schmiedel was assigned to the 100th ***Jäger Division. He was killed in action at Stalingrad on September 27, 1942. He is listed in the remembrance book at the German Military Cemetery at Rossoschka. It is also displayed on the war memorial at Taufkirchen an der Pram, Austria.

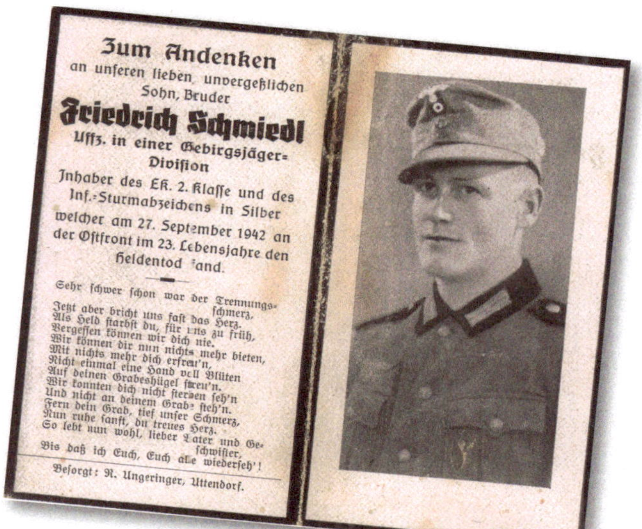

Zum Andenken
an unſeren lieben unvergeßlichen
Sohn, Bruder
Friedrich Schmiedl
Uffz. in einer Gebirgsjäger=
Diviſion
Inhaber des EK. 2. Klaſſe und des
Inf.=Sturmabzeichens in Silber
welcher am 27. September 1942 an
der Oſtfront im 23. Lebensjahre den
Heldentod fand.

Sehr ſchwer ſchon war der Trennungs-
ſchmerz,
Jetzt aber bricht uns faſt das Herz.
Als Held ſtarbſt du, für uns zu früh,
Vergeſſen können wir dich nie.
Wir können dir nun nichts mehr bieten,
Mit nichts mehr dich erfreu'n,
Nicht einmal eine Hand voll Blüten
Auf deinen Grabeshügel ſtreu'n.
Wir konnten dich nicht ſterben ſeh'n
Und nicht an deinem Grabe ſteh'n.
Fern dein Grab, tief unſer Schmerz,
Nun ruhe ſanft, du treues Herz.
So lebt nun wohl, lieber Vater und Ge-
ſchwiſter,
Bis daß ich Euch, Euch alle wiederſeh'!

Beſorgt: R. Ungeringer, Uttendorf.

September 28, 1942
Weather: sunny, bright, changing temperatures, 81° F
Sunrise: 5:56 a.m.; **Sunset:** 5:49 p.m.
Moon: Waning Gibbous; 84% illumination

Sixth Army – Bombers and dive-bombers from the ***Luftwaffe***'s VIII Air Corps pounded Stalingrad in large-scale attacks, concentrating on Volga shipping and the Volga west bank. The army headquarters was located at Golubinskaya.

VIII Corps – The aim of the corps was to prepare to exchange defensive sectors of the divisions. The 754th Pioneer Battalion was assigned to the corps. The corps suffered the following officer casualties: two killed in action; eight wounded in action.

76th Infantry Division – The division defended in sector southwest of Samofalovka and north of Borodkin, against the 260th Rifle Division and the 173rd Rifle Division. To the northwest was the 305th Infantry Division; to the east was the 60th Infantry Division (Motorized.) Enemy attacks were supported by heavy mortar and artillery fire, but were repelled. The division reported that of its nine infantry battalions, two were average and seven were weak in combat power; the division rated its combat engineer battalion as average. The division lost eight NCOs/enlisted killed in action; four officers and 30 NCOs/enlisted were wounded in action.

305th Infantry Division – The division defended in sector from the Don River, north of Nizhne-Gnilovskii, to west of Kotluban', against the 298th Rifle Division. To the east was the 76th Infantry Division; to the north was the 384th Infantry Division. The division reported that of its nine infantry battalions, three were strong, three were medium-strong and three were average in combat power; the division rated its combat engineer battalion as strong. The division lost two NCOs/enlisted killed in action; one officer and 11 NCOs/enlisted were wounded in action.

XI Corps – The corps suffered the following officer casualties: four wounded in action.

44th Infantry Division – The division defended in sector Kurchajessowskij-Kamyshinskiy-Hill 171.0-Hill 180.9-Sirotinskaya-Khmelevskoy, against the 343rd Rifle Division. The division headquarters was located at Verkhne-Golubaja. To the west was the 376th Infantry Division; to the east was the 384th Infantry Division. The division reported that of its nine infantry battalions, five were strong, three were medium-strong and one was weak in combat power; the division rated its combat engineer battalion as strong. The division lost two NCOs/enlisted killed in action; ten NCOs/enlisted were wounded in action.

376th Infantry Division – The division defended in sector near Blizhniaia-Perekopka, against the 23rd Rifle Division. To the west was the 1st Romanian Cavalry Division; to the east was the 44th Infantry Division. The division reported that of its seven infantry battalions, four were average and three were weak in combat power; the division rated its combat engineer battalion as weak. The division lost six NCOs/enlisted killed in action; 21 NCOs/enlisted were wounded in action; 15 men were reported missing in action.

384th Infantry Division – The division defended in sector west of the Don River near Trekhostrovskaia to Podgorskii, against attacks by the 27th Guards Rifle Division, but gave up terrain near the river short of Hill 245. To the west was the 44th Infantry Division; to the south was the 305th Infantry Division. The division reported that of its six infantry battalions, three were average and three were weak in combat power; the division rated its combat engineer battalion as weak. The division lost five NCOs/enlisted killed in action; one officer and 15 NCOs/enlisted were wounded in action.

XIV *Panzer* Corps – The corps headquarters was located east of Ssadtschi-Kowa. The corps suffered the following officer casualties: three killed in action; seven wounded in action.

3rd Infantry Division (Motorized) – The division defended in sector, from the Tartar Hill-Hill 111.1-Hill 129.6-Hill 131.2, against the 299th Rifle Division, the 38th Guards Rifle Division, the 116th Rifle Division and the 343rd Rifle Division. To the east was the 16th ***Panzer*** Division; to the west was the 60th Infantry Division (Motorized.) The division reported that of its five motorized infantry battalions, four were average and one was weak in combat power; the division rated its combat engineer battalion as average.

16th Panzer Division – The division defended in sector, from Hill 139.7 to the Volga and from the Volga southwest to Hill 145.1, north of Orlovka, against the 120th Rifle Division, the 84th Rifle Division and the 64th Rifle Division. Along its southern front, the division defended to contain enemy forces at Orlovka. To the west was the 3rd Infantry Division (Motorized); to the southwest was Battle Group Stahel. The division reported that of its five ***panzer*** grenadier battalions, three were medium-strong and two were average in combat power; the division rated its combat engineer battalion as average.

60th Infantry Division (Motorized) – The division defended in sector, from south of Kotluban' Station near Borodkin to Kuz'michi against the 41st Guards Rifle Division, the 49th Rifle Division, the 231st Rifle Division, the 233rd Rifle Division, the 39th Guards Rifle Division, the 316th Rifle Division and the 207th Rifle Division. Along its southern front, the division defended to contain enemy forces at Orlovka. To the west was the 76th Infantry Division; to the east was the 3rd Infantry Division (Motorized.) The division reported that of its seven motorized infantry battalions, four were average, two were weak and one was exhausted in combat power; the division rated its combat engineer battalion as exhausted.

94th Infantry Division – The division withdrew from its attack zone in central Stalingrad – south of the 71st Infantry Division and north of the 29th Infantry Division (Motorized) – and moved north. The division transferred the 276th Infantry Regiment to the 24th ***Panzer*** Division. The division lost ten NCOs/enlisted killed in action; ten NCOs/enlisted were wounded in action. The division reported that of its seven infantry battalions, all seven were weak in combat power; the division rated its combat engineer battalion as average.

Battle Group Stahel – The battle group defended northwest of Orlovka to contain enemy forces. To the southwest was the 389th Infantry Division; to the northeast was the 16th ***Panzer*** Division.

XVII Corps

79th Infantry Division – The division defended in sector from Bol'shoy-Verkhne-Kalmykovskii-Verkhne-Fomichinskii-Baskowskij, against the 124th Rifle Division. The division headquarters was located at Karagichev. To the west was the XXXV Italian Corps; to the east was the 6th Romanian Infantry Division. The division reported that of its six infantry battalions, four were average and two were weak in combat power; the division rated its combat engineer battalion as average.

113th Infantry Division – The division swung north and moved toward the rear of the 76th Infantry Division. The division reported that of its eight infantry battalions, six were strong, one was medium-strong and one was exhausted in combat power; the division rated its combat engineer battalion as medium-strong.

298th Infantry Division – The division occupied three assembly areas along the Sixth Army's western boundary and south of the 79th Infantry Division.

1st Romanian Cavalry Division – The division defended in sector near Molologowskij against the 76th Rifle Division and the 63rd Rifle Division. To the west was the 13th Romanian Infantry Division; to the east was the 376th Infantry Division.

1st Romanian Armored Division – The division occupied an assembly in the western part of the corps sector.

5th Romanian Infantry Division – The division moved to the north of the 1st Romanian Armored Division.

6th Romanian Infantry Division – The division defended in sector south of the Don River against the 96th Rifle Division. To the west was the 79th Infantry Division; to the southeast was the 13th Romanian Infantry Division.

13th Romanian Infantry Division – The division defended in sector along the Don River west of Kletskiy against the 278th Rifle Division and the 63rd Rifle Division. To the northwest was the 6th Romanian Infantry Division; to the east was the 1st Romanian Cavalry Division.

XXXXVIII *Panzer* Corps

14th Panzer Division – The division conducted consolidation operations in sector. To the north was the 29th Infantry Division (Motorized); to the south was the 371st Infantry Division. The division lost one officer and nine NCOs/enlisted killed in action; 62 NCOs/enlisted were wounded in action; three NCOs/enlisted were reported missing in action.

29th Infantry Division (Motorized) – The division conducted consolidation operations in sector. To the north was the 71st Infantry Division; to the south was the 14th ***Panzer*** Division. The division lost five NCOs/enlisted wounded in action; one NCO/enlisted was reported missing in action. The division reported that of its six motorized infantry battalions, three were medium-strong and three were average in combat power; the division rated its combat engineer battalion as strong and its motorcycle battalion as strong.

71st Infantry Division – The division, now subordinated to the XXXXVIII ***Panzer*** Corps, defended in its sector against the 13th Guards Rifle Division, with the 29th Infantry Division (Motorized) to the south and the 295th Infantry Division to the north. The division reported that of its eight infantry battalions, one was weak and seven were exhausted in combat power; the division rated its combat engineer battalion as average.

LI Corps – The corps seized about half of the Barrikady Gun Factory Workers' Settlement. The corps headquarters was located at Gumrak. The 101st Heavy Artillery Detachment and the 616th Heavy Artillery Detachment were assigned to support the corps. The corps suffered the following officer casualties: five killed in action; 30 wounded in action.

24th Panzer Division – The division initially repulsed an enemy attack on its positions and then continued to attack north in zone, seizing Silikat Factory Nr.3 against the 112th Rifle Division. The division received the attachment of the 276th Infantry Regiment from the 94th Infantry Division. The division suffered two officers and 22 NCOs/enlisted killed in action; two officers and 89 NCOs/enlisted were wounded in action. The division reported that of its four ***panzer*** grenadier battalions, two were average and two were weak in combat power; the division rated its combat engineer battalion as average. To the northwest was the 389th Infantry Division; to the south was the 100th ***Jäger*** Division.

100th Jäger Division – The division attacked north in zone, seizing the water tower on Hill 102 against the 95th Rifle Division and the 284th Rifle Division, gaining positions in the Krasny Oktyabr Steel Factory Workers' Settlement and seizing two-thirds of the Meat Combine (west of the "Tennis Racquet."). To the north was the 24th ***Panzer*** Division; to the south was the 295th Infantry Division. The division suffered three officers and 67 NCOs/enlisted killed in action; five officers and 271 NCOs/enlisted were wounded in action. The division reported that all four ***jäger*** battalions were strong in combat power; the one Croatian infantry battalion was strong in combat power; the division rated its combat engineer battalion as medium-strong.

295th Infantry Division – The division attacked in zone on and near Hill 102 against the 95th Rifle Division and the 284th Rifle Division. To the north was the 100th ***Jäger*** Division; to the south was the 71st Infantry Division. The division lost 16 NCOs/enlisted killed in action; two officers and 42 NCOs/enlisted were wounded in action. The division reported that of its seven infantry battalions, four were weak and three were exhausted in combat power; the division rated its combat engineer battalion as average.

389th Infantry Division – The division attacked northeast in zone, protecting the flank of the 24th ***Panzer*** Division and seizing the edge of the Barrikady Gun Factory Workers' Settlement against the 308th Rifle Division. To the east was the 24th ***Panzer*** Division; to the northeast was Battle Group Stahel. The division suffered three NCOs/enlisted killed in action; ten NCOs/enlisted were wounded in action. The division reported that of its six infantry battalions, all six were weak in combat power; the division rated its combat engineer battalion as weak.

Fourth *Panzer* Army – The army headquarters was located at Plodowitoje.

IV Corps – The corps headquarters was located at Plantator.

297th Infantry Division – The division defended in sector against the 157th Rifle Division and the 154th Marine Infantry Brigade. To the north was the 371st Infantry Division; to the south was the 20th Romanian Infantry Division.

371st Infantry Division – The division defended in sector north of Peschanka to Elkhi against elements of the 422nd Rifle Division. The division headquarters was located west of Staro-Dubovka. To the north was the 14th ***Panzer*** Division; to the south was the 297th Infantry Division. The division suffered eight NCOs/enlisted killed in action; one officer and 27 NCOs/enlisted were wounded in action.

20th Romanian Infantry Division – The division defended in sector north of the Volga-Don Canal against the 154th Marine Infantry Brigade and the 38th Rifle Division. To the north was the 297th Infantry Division; to the south was the 2nd Romanian Infantry Division of the Romanian VI Corps.

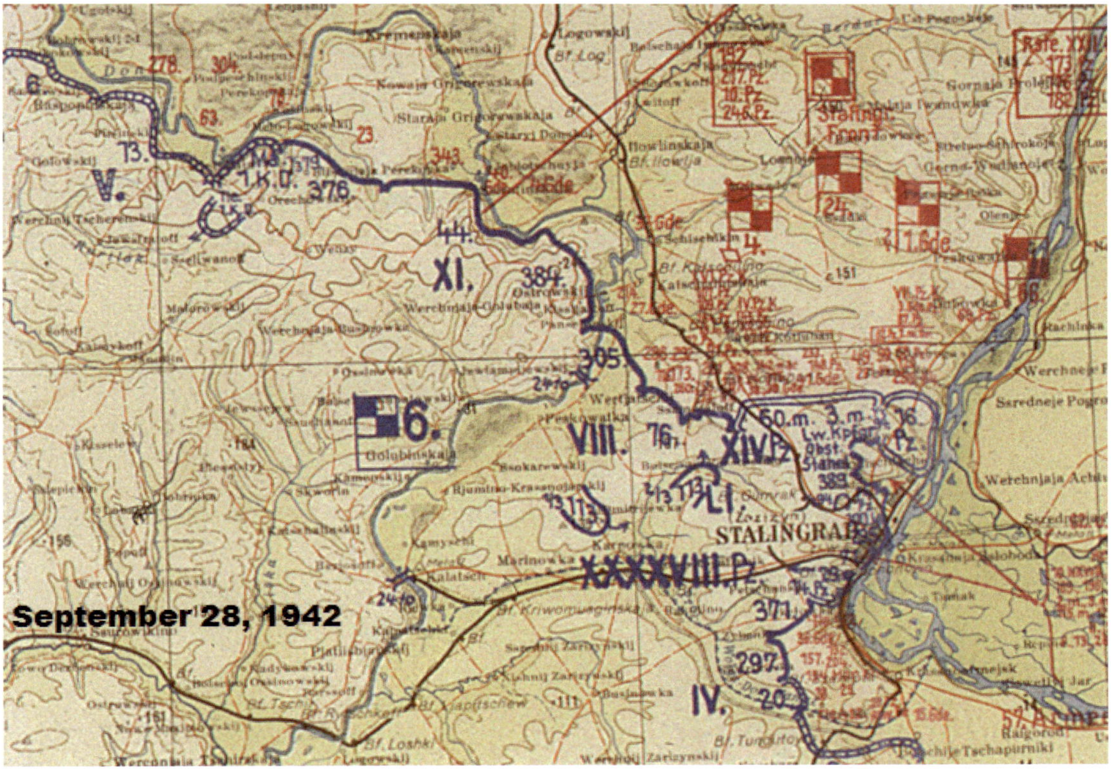

Sources, September 28, 1942: *Oberkommando des Heeres, Lage Ost: Stand: 28.9.42, Eastern Front Situation Map, National Archives Identifier: 559733, Record Group 242 – National Archives Collection of Foreign Records Seized, 1675-1958, National Archives, College Park, Maryland; Ia, Armeeoberkommando 6, "Morgen Meldung" and assorted reports, Kriegstagebuch 13, 29 September 1942, as found in Microfilm Series, T-312, Records of German Field Commands, Armies, Roll 1686, National Archives and Records Service, College Park, Maryland; Ia, XXXXVIII Panzerkorps, "Übersicht über die dem Korps Unterstellten Divisionen, 28. Juni 1942 – 11 October 1942," as found on T-314, Records of German Field Commands, Corps, Roll 1153, National Archives, College Park, Maryland; Korpsarzt, XXXXVIII Panzerkorps, "Meldung über Personelle Verluste," Stand 28.9.42, as found on T-314, Records of German Field Commands, Corps, Roll 1158, National Archives, College Park, Maryland; 371st Infantry Division, Kriegstagebuch, 28 September 1942, as found in Microfilm Series T-315, Roll 2164, National Archives and Records Service, College Park, Maryland; Florian Freiherr von und zu Aufsess, Die Anlagenbände zu den Kriegstagebüchern der 6. Armee vom 14.09.1942 bis 24.11.1942, Band 1, Schwabach, Germany: Selbstverlag, 2006, 74-86; Antony Beevor, Stalingrad: The Fateful Siege: 1942 – 1943, London: Penguin Books, 1998, 162; Die 71. Infanterie-Division, 1939-1945: Gefechts- und Erlebnisberichte aus Kämpfen der "Gluckhaften Division" von Verdun bis Stalingrad, vom Monte Cassino bis zum Plattensee, Eggolsheim, FRG: Edition Dörfler, 1973, 252; Division der Wehrmacht: 71. Infanterie-Division, 389. Infanterie-Division, 295. Infanterie-Division, 79. Infanterie-Division, 260. Infanterie-Division, 305. Infanterie-Division, 73. Infanterie-Division, 18. Infanterie-Division, 100. Jäger-Division, 94. Infanterie-Division, Germany: Books LLC, 2010, 565; John Erickson, The Road to Stalingrad, New York: Harper & Row, 1975, 412; David M. Glantz & Jonathan M. House, Armageddon in Stalingrad: September-November 1942, (The Stalingrad Trilogy, Volume 2), Lawrence, Kansas: University Press of Kansas, 2009, 234, 258-272; Adalbert Holl, An Infantryman in Stalingrad, translated by Jason D. Mark and Neill Page, Sydney, Australia: Leaping Horseman Books, 2005, 73; Jochen Löser, Bittere Pflicht: Kampf und Untergang der 76. Berlin-Brandenburgischen Infanterie-Division, Osnabrück, FRG: Biblio Verlag, 1986, 209; Jason Mark, Death of the Leaping Horseman: 24. Panzer-Division in Stalingrad, Sydney, Australia: Leaping Horsemen Books, 2003, 228-234; Hans Neidhardt, Mit Tanne und Eichenlaub: Kriegschronik der 100. Jäger Division vormals 100. leichte Infanterie Division, Graz, Austria: Leopold Stocker Verlag, 1981, 211; Anton Schimak, Karl Lamprecht & Friedrich Dettmer, Die 44. Infanterie Division: Tagebuch der Hoch- und Deutschmeister, Wien: Verlag Austria Press, 169, 233 and Map: Marschweg der 44. Infanterie Division im Russland.*

Jäger **Josef Steinbacher** was born on December 21, 1923 at Schildorn, near Eberschwang, in Austria. He was killed in the fighting for Hill 102 at Stalingrad on September 28, 1942, while a member of the 8th Company in the 227th Infantry Regiment of the 100th *Jäger* Division. Josef Steinbacher, whose remains were never found for proper burial, is listed in the remembrance book at the German Military Cemetery at Rossoschka.

Zum Andenken
an Gebirgsjäger
Josef Steinbacher
Hausbesitzerssohn in Kronawitten

welcher am 28. September 1942 in Stalingrad im 19. Lebensjahre im Kampfe gegen den Bolschewismus den Heldentod für Führer, Volk und Vaterland starb.

Eltern, Geschwister und Freunde mein!
So gern schrieb ich aus der Ferne heim;
Doch heut ist's zum letztenmal,
Daß ich Euch grüße tausendmal
Und sage Dank für jede Gab',
Die ich von Euch empfangen hab'.
Richte an Euch die letzte Bitt':
Vergeßt ja im Gebet mich nicht.
Nur keine Träne, keine Klag',
Der liebe Gott, der mir das Leben gab,
Rief mich so früh ins Heldengrab.
Und ich werde in des Himmels Auen,
Im Lorbeerkranz Euch wiederschauen.

4187—42

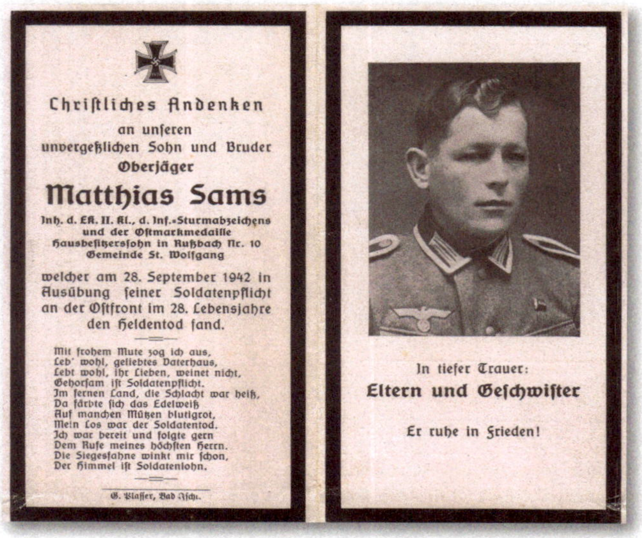

Christliches Andenken
an unseren
unvergeßlichen Sohn und Bruder
Oberjäger
Matthias Sams
Inh. d. EK. II. Kl., d. Inf.-Sturmabzeichens
und der Ostmarkmedaille
Hausbesitzerssohn in Rußbach Nr. 10
Gemeinde St. Wolfgang

welcher am 28. September 1942 in Ausübung seiner Soldatenpflicht an der Ostfront im 28. Lebensjahre den Heldentod fand.

Mit frohem Mute zog ich aus,
Leb' wohl, geliebtes Vaterhaus,
Lebt wohl, ihr Lieben, weinet nicht,
Gehorsam ist Soldatenpflicht.
Im fernen Land, die Schlacht war heiß,
Da färbte sich das Edelweiß
Auf manchen Mützen blutigrot,
Mein Los war der Soldatentod.
Ich war bereit und folgte gern
Dem Rufe meines höchsten Herrn.
Die Siegesfahne winkt mir schon,
Der Himmel ist Soldatenlohn.

G. Plasser, Bad Ischl.

In tiefer Trauer:
Eltern und Geschwister

Er ruhe in Frieden!

Oberjäger **Matthias Sams** was born in Sankt Wolfgang near Salzburg in Upper Austria on February 4, 1915. He previous won the Iron Cross 2nd Class, the Infantry Assault Badge and the Eastern Front Medal. He was killed in action west of Stalingrad on September 28, 1942 while a member of the 100th *Jäger* Division. His name is listed in the remembrance book at the German Military Cemetery at Rossoschka.

Jäger **Johann Hager** was born in Hochburg near Braunau in Upper Austria on May 28, 1923. Assigned to an infantry regiment in the 100th *Jäger* Division, he was killed in the fighting for Hill 102 at Stalingrad on September 28, 1942.

Zur frommen Erinnerung
an unseren unvergeßlichen Sohn
und Bruder
Johann Hager
Gebirgsjäger
in einem Infanterie-Regiment

welcher am 28. September 1942 bei Stalingrad im 20. Lebensjahre den Heldentod fand.

Weinet nicht in stillen Stunden,
Lieb' Eltern, Geschwister und Verwandte mein,
Hab' ja mein Glück gefunden,
Darf ewig im Himmel sein.
Beim täglichen Abendsegen,
Schickt mir einen Gruß hinab
Und Euren heiligen Segen
Zum fernen Soldatengrab.

Barmherziger Jesus, gib ihm die ewige Ruhe!

Innviertler Verlagsgesellschaft Braunau.

September 29, 1942
Weather: warm, dry, sunny, late afternoon northeast winds, morning and evening cold, 73° F, good road conditions
Sunrise: 5:57 a.m.; **Sunset:** 5:47 p.m.
Moon: Waning Gibbous; 77% illumination

Sixth Army – Bombers and dive-bombers from the ***Luftwaffe***'s VIII Air Corps pounded the factory district, setting the Dzerzhinsky Tractor Factory ablaze, and hitting the Orlovka salient. The army headquarters was located at Golubinskaya. ***General der Panzertruppe*** Paulus visited the VIII Corps, the LI Corps, the 24th ***Panzer*** Division, the 100th ***Jäger*** Division, the 113th Infantry Division and the 76th Infantry Division.

VIII Corps – The 177th ***Sturmgeschütz*** Detachment was assigned to the corps. The corps suffered the following officer casualties: two wounded in action. The corps headquarters was located at Peskowatka.

76th Infantry Division – The division was relieved in sector by the 113th Infantry Division and withdrew to an assembly area near the Don River to rest and refit. The division lost ten NCOs/enlisted killed in action; 45 NCOs/enlisted were wounded in action. Within one regiment, one infantry company had only seven men, another had six and a third company had only two men fit for combat.

113th Infantry Division – The division conducted a relief in place of the 76th Infantry Division in sector. The division defended in sector southwest of Samofalovka and north of Borodkin against the 173rd Rifle Division. To the west was the 305th Infantry Division; to the east was the 60th Infantry Division (Motorized.)

305th Infantry Division – The division defended in sector from the Don River, north of Nizhne-Gnilovskii, to west of Kotluban', against the 298th Rifle Division and the 173rd Rifle Division. To the southeast was the 113th Infantry Division; to the north was the 384th Infantry Division. The division suffered seven NCOs/enlisted wounded in action.

XI Corps

44th Infantry Division – The division defended in sector Kurchajessowskij-Kamyshinskiy-Hill 171.0-Hill 180.9-Sirotinskaya-Khmelevskoy against the 343rd Rifle Division and the 40th Guards Rifle Division. The division headquarters was located at Verkhne-Golubaja. To the west was 376th Infantry Division; to the east was the 384th Infantry Division. The division lost one NCO/enlisted killed in action; five NCOs/enlisted were wounded in action.

376th Infantry Division – The division defended in sector near Blizhniaia-Perekopka, against the 23rd Rifle Division. The division received the attachment of one infantry regiment from the 79th Infantry Division. To the east was the 44th Infantry Division; to the west was the 1st Romanian Cavalry Division. The division lost one NCO/enlisted killed in action; one NCO/enlisted was wounded in action.

384th Infantry Division – The division defended in sector west of the Don River near Trekhostrovskaia to Podgorskii against the 37th Guards Rifle Division, the 214th Rifle Division and the 27th Guards Rifle Division. To the west was the 44th Infantry Division; to the south was the 305th Infantry Division. The division lost five NCOs/enlisted killed in action; three NCOs/enlisted were wounded in action.

XIV *Panzer* Corps – The corps headquarters was located east of Ssadtschi-Kowa. The corps suffered the following officer casualties: 12 wounded in action.

3rd Infantry Division (Motorized) – The division defended in sector, from the Tartar Hill-Hill 111.1-Hill 129.6-Hill 131.2, against the 299th Rifle Division, the 38th Guards Rifle Division, the 116th Rifle Division and the 343rd Rifle Division. To the east was the 16th ***Panzer*** Division; to the west was the 60th Infantry Division (Motorized.)

16th Panzer Division – The division defended in sector, from Hill 139.7 to the Volga and from the Volga southwest to Hill 145.1, north of Orlovka against the 120th Rifle Division, the 84th Rifle Division and the 64th Rifle Division. Along its southern front, the division, with the attached 651st Pioneer Battalion, attacked to destroy the Orlovka pocket, held by the 112th Rifle Division. To the west was the 3rd Infantry Division (Motorized); to the southwest was Battle Group Stahel.

60th Infantry Division (Motorized) – The division defended in sector, from south of Kotluban' Station near Borodkin to Kuz'michi, against the 41st Guards Rifle Division, the 49th Rifle Division, the 231st Rifle Division, the 233rd Rifle Division, the 39th Guards Rifle Division, the 316th Rifle Division and the 207th Rifle Division. Along its southern front, the division attacked to destroy the Orlovka pocket. To the west was the 113th Infantry Division; to the east was the 3rd Infantry Division (Motorized.)

94th Infantry Division – The division moved north toward Gorodishche and attacked the enemy salient at Orlovka, held by the 112th Rifle Division. To the south was the 389th Infantry Division; to the north was Battle Group Stahel.

Battle Group Stahel – The battle group defended northwest of Orlovka to contain enemy forces of the 112th Rifle Division. To the south was the 94th Infantry Division; to the northeast was the 16th ***Panzer*** Division.

XVII Corps

79th Infantry Division – The division defended in sector from Bol'shoy-Verkhne-Kalmykovskii-Verkhne-Fomichinskii-Baskowskij against the 124th Rifle Division. The division headquarters was located at Karagichev. The division detached one infantry Regiment to the 376th Infantry Division. To the west was the 298th Infantry Division; to the southeast was the 6th Romanian Infantry Division.

298th Infantry Division – Division elements defended in sector. To the west was the Italian XXXV Corps; to the east was the 79th Infantry Division. The bulk of the division occupied assembly areas along the Sixth Army's western boundary.

1st Romanian Cavalry Division – The division defended in sector near Mololologowskij south of the Don River against the 76th Rifle

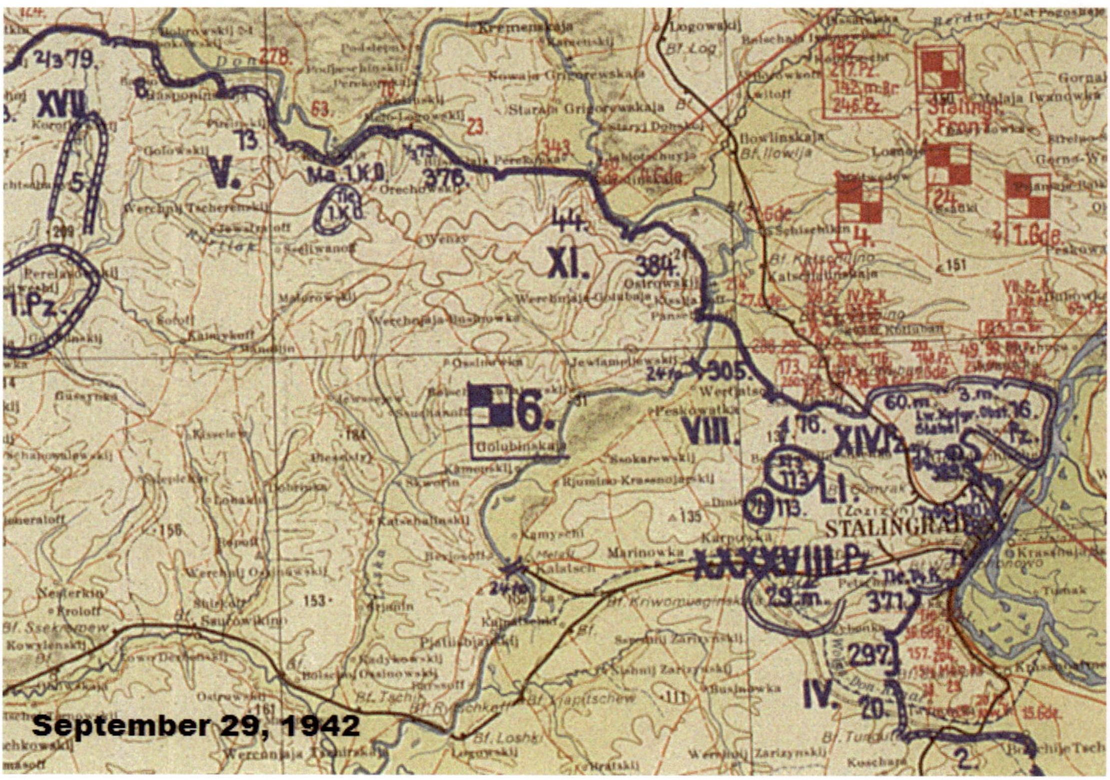

September 29, 1942

Division and 63rd Rifle Division. To the west was the 13th Romanian Infantry Division; to the east was the 376th Infantry Division. The division lost two NCOs/enlisted wounded in action. Part of the division occupied an assembly area south of the sector.

1st Romanian Armored Division – The division occupied an assembly in the western part of the corps sector.

5th Romanian Infantry Division – The division moved to the north of the 1st Romanian Armored Division.

6th Romanian Infantry Division – The division defended in sector south of the Don River against the 96th Rifle Division. To the west was the 79th Infantry Division; to the southeast was the 13th Romanian Infantry Division. The division lost 15 NCOs/enlisted killed in action; 56 NCOs/enlisted wounded in action; 21 NCOs/enlisted were reported missing in action.

13th Romanian Infantry Division – The division defended in sector along the Don River west of Kletskiy against the 278th Rifle Division and the 63rd Rifle Division. To the northwest was the 6th Romanian Infantry Division; to the east was the 1st Romanian Cavalry Division. The division suffered one officer and seven NCOs/enlisted killed in action; one officer and 18 NCOs/enlisted were wounded in action; 14 NCOs/enlisted were reported missing in action.

XXXXVIII *Panzer* Corps

14th Panzer Division – The division was relieved in sector by the 371st Infantry Division; most of the division then moved south toward an assembly area near the Tundutovo Rail Station to rest and refit. The division lost one NCO/enlisted killed in action; five NCOs/enlisted were wounded in action.

29th Infantry Division (Motorized) – The division moved west and occupied an assembly area west of Zybenko and Varvarovka, along the Volga-Don Canal, to prepare for future operations. The division lost two NCOs/enlisted killed in action.

71st Infantry Division – The division defended in its sector, attempting to clear the remnants of the 13th Guards Rifle Division from the city center along the Volga. To the south were some elements of the 14th ***Panzer*** Division and the 371st Infantry Division; to the north was the 295th Infantry Division.

LI Corps – The 2nd ***Werfer*** Regiment, the 616th Heavy Artillery Detachment, the 733rd Heavy Artillery Detachment and the 2nd Battalion of the 64th Artillery Regiment were assigned to support the corps. The corps suffered the following officer casualties: six killed in action; 18 wounded in action. The corps headquarters was located at Gumrak.

24th Panzer Division – The division initially repulsed an enemy attack on its positions by the 193rd Rifle Division and then attacked northeast in zone, seizing the northeast half of the Barrikady Gun Factory Workers' Settlement held by the Siberian 308th Rifle Division. The division suffered two officers and 25 NCOs/enlisted killed in action; two officers and 53 NCOs/enlisted were wounded in action; eight men were reported missing in action. To the northwest was the 389th Infantry Division; to the south was the 100th ***Jäger*** Division.

100th Jäger Division – The division attacked northeast in zone and gained more positions in the Krasny Oktyabr Steel Factory Workers' Settlement toward the Krasny Oktyabr Steel Factory; it later captured Hill 107.5 as well as some bunkers in the Bannyi Balka against the 95th Rifle Division. The division reported 70 killed in action, 276 wounded in action and ten missing in action. To the north was the 24th ***Panzer*** Division; to the south was the 295th Infantry Division.

295th Infantry Division – The division attacked northeast in zone against the 95th Rifle Division and the 284th Rifle Division. It lost nine NCOs/enlisted killed in action; 48 NCOs/enlisted were wounded in action. To the north was the 100th ***Jäger*** Division; to the south was the 71st Infantry Division.

389th Infantry Division – The division attacked along the Vishnevaia Balka toward the northwestern edge of the Barrikady Gun Factory Workers' Settlement, and then crossed the Mechetka River against the 112th Rifle Division and Kazennaia Balka toward Orlovka. The division reported 30-35 casualties overall. To the southeast was the 24th ***Panzer*** Division; to the north was the 94th Infantry Division.

Fourth *Panzer* Army – The army headquarters was located at Plodowitoje.

IV Corps – The corps headquarters was located at Plantator.

297th Infantry Division – The division defended in sector east of Elkhi and Iagodniki against the 157th Rifle Division, the 204th Rifle Division and the 154th Marine Infantry Brigade. To the north was the 371st Infantry Division; to the south was the 20th Romanian Infantry Division.

371st Infantry Division – The division relieved the 14th ***Panzer*** Division of its sector and continued to defend in its own sector against elements of the 422nd Rifle Division. The division lost two NCOs/enlisted killed in action; one officer and four NCOs/enlisted were wounded in action.

20th Romanian Infantry Division – The division defended in sector, west of the Tundutovo Rail Station and east of Andreevka against the 15th Guards Rifle Division. To the north was the 297th Infantry Division; to the south was the 2nd Romanian Infantry Division.

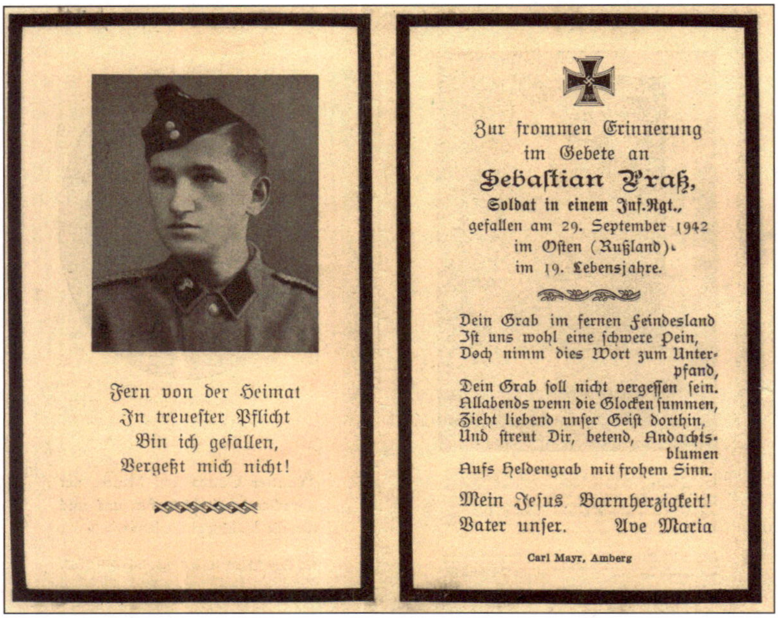

Schütze **Sebastian Prass** was born in the small village of Ammersvichl, Bavaria on August 17, 1923. Assigned to an infantry regiment in the 44th Infantry Division, he was killed in action at Kamyshinskiy (36 miles north of Kalach) on September 29, 1942. He is buried in the unknown section at the German Military Cemetery at Rossoschka.

Sources, September 29, 1942: *Oberkommando des Heeres, Lage Ost: Stand: 29.9.42, Eastern Front Situation Map, National Archives Identifier: 559733, Record Group 242 – National Archives Collection of Foreign Records Seized, 1675-1958, National Archives, College Park, Maryland; Ia, Armeeoberkommando 6, "Morgen Meldung" and assorted reports, Kriegstagebuch 13, 30 September 1942, as found in Microfilm Series, T-312, Records of German Field Commands, Armies, Roll 1686, National Archives and Records Service, College Park, Maryland; Ia, XXXXVIII Panzerkorps, "Übersicht über die dem Korps Unterstellten Divisionen, 28. Juni 1942 – 11 October 1942," as found on T-314, Records of German Field Commands, Corps, Roll 1153, National Archives, College Park, Maryland; Korpsarzt, XXXXVIII Panzerkorps, "Meldung über Personelle Verluste," Stand 29.9.42, as found on T-314, Records of German Field Commands, Corps, Roll 1158, National Archives, College Park, Maryland; 371st Infantry Division, Kriegstagebuch, 29 September 1942, as found in Microfilm Series T-315, Roll 2164, National Archives and Records Service, College Park, Maryland; Florian Freiherr von und zu Aufsess, Die Anlagenbände zu den Kriegstagebüchern der 6. Armee vom 14.09.1942 bis 24.11.1942, Band 1, Schwabach, Germany: Selbstverlag, 2006, 87-95; Antony Beevor, Stalingrad: The Fateful Siege: 1942-1943, London: Penguin Books, 1998, 162, 188; Division der Wehrmacht: 71. Infanterie-Division, 389. Infanterie-Division, 295. Infanterie-Division, 79. Infanterie-Division, 260. Infanterie-Division, 305. Infanterie-Division, 73. Infanterie-Division, 18. Infanterie-Division, 100. Jäger-Division, 94. Infanterie-Division, Germany: Books LLC, 2010, 14; John Erickson, The Road to Stalingrad, New York: Harper & Row, 1975, 414; David M. Glantz & Jonathan M. House, Armageddon in Stalingrad: September-November 1942, (The Stalingrad Trilogy, Volume 2), Lawrence, Kansas: University Press of Kansas, 2009, 182, 275-280, 293-294; Rolf Grams, Die 14. Panzer-Division, 1940-1945, Friedberg, FRG: Podzun Pallas Verlag, 1986, 53; Joachim Lemelsen, 29. Division, Bad Nauheim, FRG: Podzun Verlag, 1960, 205; Jochen Löser, Bittere Pflicht: Kampf und Untergang der 76. Berlin-Brandenburgischen Infanterie-Division, Osnabrück, FRG: Biblio Verlag, 1986, 209; Jason Mark, Death of the Leaping Horseman: 24. Panzer-Division in Stalingrad, Sydney, Australia: Leaping Horsemen Books, 2003, 234-236; Kurt Mehner, Die Geheimen Tagesberichte der Deutschen Wehrmachtführung im Zweiten Weltkrieg 1939-1945, Band 5: 1. Juni 1942 – 30. November 1942, Osnabrück, Germany: Biblio Verlag, 1991, 217; Anton Schimak, Karl Lamprecht & Friedrich Dettmer, Die 44. Infanterie Division: Tagebuch der Hoch- und Deutschmeister, Wien: Verlag Austria Press, 169, 233 and Map: Marschweg der 44. Infanterie Division im Russland.*

September 30, 1942
Weather: cool, 70° F, sunny, bright, clear, windy, good road conditions
Sunrise: 5:59 a.m.; **Sunset:** 5:45 p.m.
Moon: Waning Gibbous; 68% illumination

Sixth Army – Bombers and dive-bombers from the ***Luftwaffe***'s VIII Air Corps pounded the factory district. The army headquarters was located at Golubinskaya.

VIII Corps – The corps suffered the following officer casualties: two killed in action; two wounded in action.

76th Infantry Division – The division moved toward an assembly area north of Kalach at Bol'shenabatovskiy for rest and refit.

113th Infantry Division – The division defended in sector southwest of Samofalovka and north of Borodkin against the 173rd Rifle Division and the 260th Rifle Division. To the northwest was the 305th Infantry Division; to the east was the 60th Infantry Division (Motorized.) The division lost one officer and six NCOs/enlisted killed in action; one officer and nine NCOs/enlisted were wounded in action.

305th Infantry Division – The division defended in sector from the Don River, north of Nizhne-Gnilovskii, to west of Kotluban' against the 298th Rifle Division and the 292nd Rifle Division. To the southeast was the 113th Infantry Division; to the northwest was the 384th Infantry Division. The division lost three NCOs/enlisted killed in action; one officer and ten NCOs/enlisted were wounded in action; one man was reported missing in action.

XI Corps

44th Infantry Division – The division defended in sector Kurchajessowskij-Kamyshinskiy-Hill 171.0-Hill 180.9-Sirotinskaya-Khmelevskoy against the 40th Guards Rifle Division, the 4th Guards Rifle Division and the 343rd Rifle Division. The division headquarters was located at Verkhne-Golubaja. To the west was 376th Infantry Division; to the east was the 384th Infantry Division. The division lost two NCOs/enlisted killed in action; 12 NCOs/enlisted were wounded in action.

376th Infantry Division – The division, reinforced with one infantry regiment from the 79th Infantry Division, defended in sector near Blizhniaia-Perekopka against the 23rd Rifle Division. To the east was the 44th Infantry Division; to the west was the 1st Romanian Cavalry Division. The division lost five NCOs/enlisted killed in action; 15 NCOs/enlisted were wounded in action.

384th Infantry Division – The division defended in sector west of the Don River near Trekhostrovskaia to Podgorskii against the 37th Guards Rifle Division, the 214th Rifle Division and the 27th Guards Rifle Division. To the west was the 44th Infantry Division; to the south was the 305th Infantry Division. The division lost one NCO/enlisted killed in action; one NCO/enlisted was wounded in action.

XIV *Panzer* Corps – Elements of the Don Front attacked the corps in the north. The corps broke into Orlovka from the north. The corps headquarters was located east of Ssadtschi-Kowa. The corps suffered the following officer casualties: two killed in action; ten wounded in action.

3rd Infantry Division (Motorized) – The division defended in sector, from the Tartar Hill-Hill 111.1-Hill 129.6-Hill 131.2 against the 299th Rifle Division, the 38th Guards Rifle Division, the 116th Rifle Division and the 343rd Rifle Division. To the east was the 16th ***Panzer*** Division; to the west was the 60th Infantry Division (Motorized.)

16th Panzer Division – The division defended in sector, from Hill 139.7 to the Volga and from the Volga southwest to Hill 145.1, north of Orlovka against the 120th Rifle Division, the 84th

Rifle Division and the 64th Rifle Division. In the division's southern sector, the division attacked to reduce the enemy salient at Orlovka. In the north, the division repelled several armored and infantry attacks. To the west was the 3rd Infantry Division (Motorized.)

60th Infantry Division (Motorized) – The division defended in sector, from south of Kotluban' Station near Borodkin to Kuz'michi, repelling several armor and infantry attacks from the 41st Guards Rifle Division, the 49th Rifle Division, the 231st Rifle Division, the 233rd Rifle Division, the 316th Rifle Division and the 207th Rifle Division. To the west was the 113th Infantry Division; to the east was the 3rd Infantry Division (Motorized.) In the division's southern sector, the division attacked to reduce the enemy salient at Orlovka.

94th Infantry Division – The division detached the 276th Infantry Regiment to the 24th ***Panzer*** Division. The division attacked in zone to reduce the enemy salient at Orlovka. To the north was Battle Group Stahel; to the south was the 389th Infantry Division. At least two officers were killed in action.

Battle Group Stahel – The battle group attacked northwest toward Orlovka to contain enemy forces. To the south was the 94th Infantry Division; to the northeast was the 16th ***Panzer*** Division.

XVII Corps

79th Infantry Division – The division defended in sector from Bol'shoy-Verkhne-Kalmykovskii-Verkhne-Fomichinskii-Baskowskij against the 124th Rifle Division. The division headquarters was located at Karagichev. The division was replaced in part of its sector by the 5th Romanian Infantry Division. To the west were elements of the 298th Infantry Division; to the east was the 6th Romanian Infantry Division.

298th Infantry Division – Division elements defended in sector against the 14th Guards Rifle Division. To the west was the Italian XXXV Corps; to the east was the 79th Infantry Division. The bulk of the division occupied assembly areas along the Sixth Army's western boundary.

1st Romanian Cavalry Division – The division defended in sector near Mololologowskij south of the Don River against the 76th Rifle Division and the 63rd Rifle Division. To the west was the 13th Romanian Infantry Division; to the east was the 376th Infantry Division.

1st Romanian Armored Division – The division occupied an assembly in the western part of the corps sector.

5th Romanian Infantry Division – The division moved to the north of the 1st Romanian Armored Division. One-third of the division assumed part of the 79th Infantry Division's defensive sector against the 124th Rifle Division.

6th Romanian Infantry Division – The division defended in sector south of the Don River against the 96th Rifle Division. To the west was the 79th Infantry Division; to the southeast was the 13th Romanian Infantry Division. The division lost three NCOs/enlisted killed in action; nine NCOs/enlisted were wounded in action.

13th Romanian Infantry Division – The division defended in sector along the Don River west of Kletskiy against the 278th Rifle Division and the 63rd Rifle Division. To the northwest was the 6th Romanian Infantry Division; to the east was the 1st Romanian Cavalry Division. The division lost 11 NCOs/enlisted killed in action; 19 NCOs/enlisted were wounded in action.

XXXXVIII *Panzer* Corps

29th Infantry Division (Motorized) – The division occupied an assembly area west of Zybenko and Varvarovka, along the Volga-Don Canal, to prepare for future operations. During the period July 11, 1942 to September 30, 1942, the division lost 45 officers and 975 NCOs/enlisted killed in action; 169 officers and 4,509 NCOs/enlisted were wounded in action; one officer and 199 NCOs/enlisted were reported missing in action.

71st Infantry Division – The division attacked positions of the 13th Guards Rifle Division along the Volga, but made little progress. To the north was the 295th Infantry Division; to the south was the 371st Infantry Division.

LI Corps – The corps headquarters was located at Gumrak. The corps suffered the following officer casualties: one killed in action; six wounded in action.

24th Panzer Division – The division received the attachment of the 276th Infantry Regiment. The division attacked, making slow progress into the western section of the Krasny Oktyabr Workers' Settlement against the 112th Rifle Division. To the northwest was the 389th Infantry Division; to the south was the 100th ***Jäger***

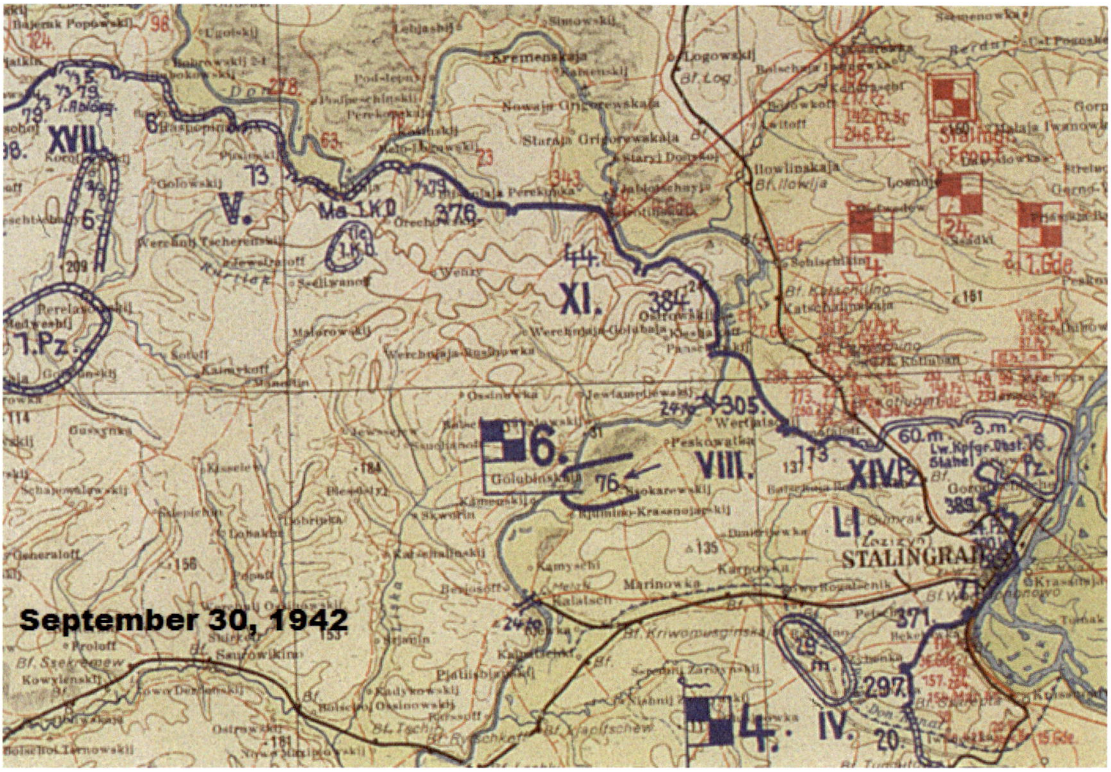

Division. The division suffered 11 NCOs/enlisted killed in action; one officer and 40 NCOs/enlisted were wounded in action.

100th Jäger Division – The division attacked northeast and gained more positions in the Krasny Oktyabr Steel Factory Workers' Settlement, gaining the railroad line against the 295th Rifle Division and the 39th Guards Rifle Division. To the north was the 24th ***Panzer*** Division; to the south was the 295th Infantry Division. The division suffered 15 NCOs/enlisted killed in action; two officers and 68 NCOs/enlisted were wounded in action; seven men were reported missing in action.

295th Infantry Division – The division continued to attack, attempting to seize the northern and eastern slopes of Mamayev Kurgan (Hill 102), the southern portion of the Meat Combine, the "Tennis Racquet" and the Dol'gii and Krutoi Balkas against the 95th Rifle Division, the 13th Guards Rifle Division and the 284th Rifle Division. An enemy counterattack recaptured part of the Meat Combine. To the north was the 100th ***Jäger*** Division; to the south was the 71st Infantry Division. The division lost 11 NCO/enlisted killed in action; 45 NCOs/enlisted were wounded in action.

389th Infantry Division – The division attacked north and northeast along the northern bank of the Mechetka River against the 112th Rifle Division. To the north was the 94th Infantry Division; to the south was the 24th ***Panzer*** Division. The division suffered one NCO/enlisted killed in action; ten NCOs/enlisted were wounded in action.

Fourth *Panzer* Army – The army headquarters was located east of Verkhne-Zaryzinskij.

IV Corps – The corps headquarters was located at Plantator.

297th Infantry Division – The division defended in sector east of Elkhi and Iagodniki against the 157th Rifle Division and the 154th Marine Infantry Brigade. To the north was the 371st Infantry Division; to the south was the 20th Romanian Infantry Division.

371st Infantry Division – The division defended in sector east of Peschanka against the 36th Guards Rifle Division and part of the 422nd

Rifle Division. To the north was the 71st Infantry Division; to the south was the 297th Infantry Division. The division lost one officer and ten NCOs/enlisted killed in action; two officers and 33 NCOs/enlisted were wounded in action.

20th Romanian Infantry Division – The division defended in sector, west of the Tundutovo Rail Station and east of Andreevka against part of the 422nd Rifle Division. To the north was the 297th Infantry Division; to the south was the 2nd Romanian Infantry Division of the Romanian VI Corps.

Fourth *Panzer* Army Reserve

14th Panzer Division – The division moved southeast from its assembly area to positions northwest of Lake Barmantsak and at Sadovia, in the Romanian VI Corps area of operations. The division lost six NCOs/enlisted wounded in action.

Zur frommen Erinnerung
im Gebete an unseren innigstgeliebten unvergeßlichen Sohn, Bruder, Schwager und Onkel
Josef Geyer
Jäger in einer M. G.-Abteilung
welcher am 30. September 1942 bei den schweren Kämpfen in Stalingrad im 20. Lebensjahre den Heldentod gefunden hat.

Ach, es ist ja kaum zu fassen,
Daß Du nicht mehr kehrst zurück,
So jung mußtest Du Dein Leben lassen
Und zerstört ist unser Glück.
Ein jeder, der Dich hat gekannt
Und auch Dein treues Herz,
Der drückt uns nur noch stumm die Hand
In tiefem, tiefem Schmerz.
Du gutes Herz, ruh still in Frieden,
Ewig beweint von Deinen Lieben.

In tiefer Trauer:
Deine Eltern und Schwestern.

Jäger **Josef Geyer** was born in Schirmsdorf on August 30, 1923. He was assigned to the 9th Machine Gun Battalion, which was attached to the 60th Infantry Division (Motorized.) Geyer was killed in action on September 30, 1942 at Malaia Rossoschka. He is listed in the remembrance book at the German Military Cemetery at Rossoschka.

Sources, September 30, 1942: ***Oberkommando des Heeres, Lage Ost: Stand: 30.9.42, Eastern Front Situation Map, National Archives Identifier: 559733, Record Group 242 – National Archives Collection of Foreign Records Seized, 1675-1958, National Archives, College Park, Maryland; Ia, Armeeoberkommando 6, "Morgen Meldung" and assorted reports, Kriegstagebuch 13, 1 October 1942, as found in Microfilm Series, T-312, Records of German Field Commands, Armies, Roll 1686, National Archives and Records Service, College Park, Maryland; Ia, XXXXVIII Panzerkorps, "Übersicht über die dem Korps Unterstellten Divisionen, 28. Juni 1942 – 11 October 1942," as found on T-314, Records of German Field Commands, Corps, Roll 1153, National Archives, College Park, Maryland; Ia, XXXXVIII Panzerkorps, "Zahlenmässige Verlustmeldung der Unterstellten Divisionen und Heerestruppen in der Zeit vom 1. April 1942 bis 31. Oktober 1942," as found in T-314, Records of German Field Commands, Corps, Roll 1153, National Archives, College Park, Maryland; Korpsarzt, XXXXVIII Panzerkorps, "Meldung über Personelle Verluste," Stand 30.9.42, as found on T-314, Records of German Field Commands, Corps, Roll 1158, National Archives, College Park, Maryland; 371st Infantry Division, Kriegstagebuch, 30 September 1942, as found in Microfilm Series T-315, Roll 2164, National Archives and Records Service, College Park, Maryland; Florian Freiherr von und zu Aufsess, Die Anlagenbände zu den Kriegstagebüchern der 6. Armee vom 14.09.1942 bis 24.11.1942, Band 1, Schwabach, Germany: Selbstverlag, 2006, 92-98, 104; Antony Beevor, Stalingrad: The Fateful Siege: 1942-1943, London: Penguin Books, 1998, 163, 188; David M. Glantz & Jonathan M. House, Armageddon in Stalingrad: September-November 1942, (The Stalingrad Trilogy, Volume 2), Lawrence, Kansas: University Press of Kansas, 2009, 280-286, 289-298, 305-307; Rolf Grams, Die 14. Panzer-Division, 1940-1945, Friedberg, FRG: Podzun Pallas Verlag, 1986, 53; Adalbert Holl, An Infantryman in Stalingrad, translated by Jason D. Mark and Neill Page, Sydney, Australia: Leaping Horseman Books, 2005, 87; Jochen Löser, Bittere Pflicht: Kampf und Untergang der 76. Berlin-Brandenburgischen Infanterie-Division, Osnabrück, FRG: Biblio Verlag, 1986, 215; Jason Mark, Death of the Leaping Horseman: 24. Panzer-Division in Stalingrad, Sydney, Australia: Leaping Horsemen Books, 2003, 236-241; Anton Schimak, Karl Lamprecht & Friedrich Dettmer, Die 44. Infanterie Division: Tagebuch der Hoch- und Deutschmeister, Wien: Verlag Austria Press, 169, 233 and Map: Marschweg der 44. Infanterie Division im Russland.***

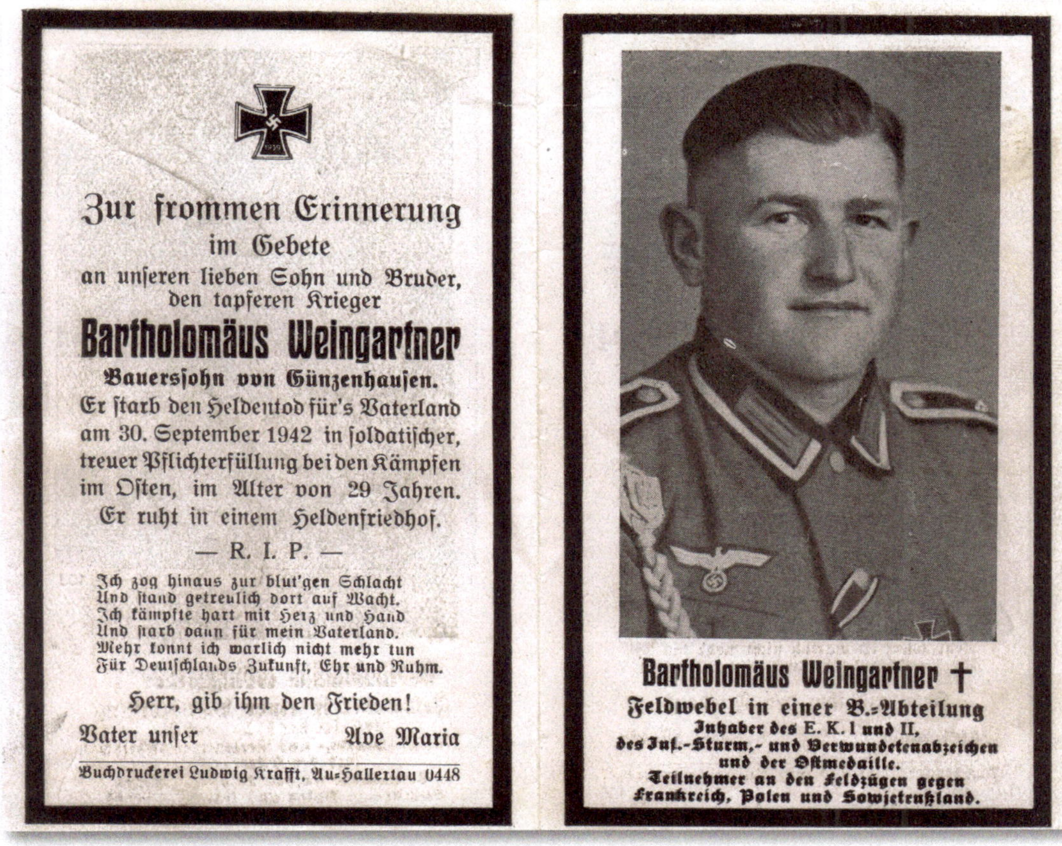

Zur frommen Erinnerung
im Gebete
an unseren lieben Sohn und Bruder,
den tapferen Krieger
Bartholomäus Weingartner
Bauerssohn von Günzenhausen.
Er starb den Heldentod für's Vaterland
am 30. September 1942 in soldatischer,
treuer Pflichterfüllung bei den Kämpfen
im Osten, im Alter von 29 Jahren.
Er ruht in einem Heldenfriedhof.

— R. I. P. —

Ich zog hinaus zur blut'gen Schlacht
Und stand getreulich dort auf Wacht.
Ich kämpfte hart mit Herz und Hand
Und starb dann für mein Vaterland.
Mehr konnt ich warlich nicht mehr tun
Für Deutschlands Zukunft, Ehr und Ruhm.

Herr, gib ihm den Frieden!

Vater unser Ave Maria

Buchdruckerei Ludwig Krafft, Au-Hallertau 0448

Bartholomäus Weingartner †
Feldwebel in einer B.-Abteilung
Inhaber des E. K. I und II,
des Inf.-Sturm,- und Verwundetenabzeichen
und der Ostmedaille.
Teilnehmer an den Feldzügen gegen
Frankreich, Polen und Sowjetrußland.

Wachtmeister **Bartholomäus Weingartner**, a farmer's son, was born in Günzenhausen, Bavaria on October 21, 1913. A veteran soldier, he fought in the Polish Campaign in 1939 and the 1940 French Campaign, receiving the Iron Cross 2nd and 1st Class, the Infantry Assault Badge, the Wound Badge in Black and the Eastern Front Medal. Bartholomäus Weingartner was killed in action on September 30, 1942 at Gorodishche, while in the 389th Infantry Division. He is listed in the remembrance book at the German Military Cemetery at Rossoschka.

OCTOBER, 1942

October 1, 1942
Weather: clear, sunny, 75° F, good road conditions
Sunrise: 6:00 a.m.; Sunset: 5:43 p.m.
Moon: Waning Gibbous; 59% illumination

Sixth Army – The army headquarters was located at Golubinskaya.

VIII Corps – The corps headquarters was located at Peskovatka. The corps suffered the following officer casualties: two wounded in action.

113th Infantry Division – The division defended in sector southwest of Samofalovka and north of Borodkin against the 260th Rifle Division, the 24th Rifle Division, the 292nd Rifle Division, the 173rd Rifle Division and the 258th Rifle Division. To the northwest was the 305th Infantry Division; to the east was the 60th Infantry Division (Motorized.) The division lost one officer and 16 NCOs/enlisted killed in action; 68 NCOs/enlisted were wounded in action.

305th Infantry Division – The division defended in sector from the Don River, north of Nizhne-Gnilovskii, to west of Kotluban' against the 298th Rifle Division. To the southeast was the 113th Infantry Division; to the northwest was the 384th Infantry Division. The division lost two NCOs/enlisted killed in action; 12 NCOs/enlisted were wounded in action.

XI Corps

44th Infantry Division – The division defended in sector Kurchajessowskij-Kamyshinskiy-Hill 171.0-Hill 180.9-Sirotinskaya-Khmelevskoy against the 23rd Rifle Division, the 4th Guards Rifle Division and the 40th Guards Rifle Division. The division headquarters was located at Verkhne-Golubaja. To the west was the 376th Infantry Division; to the east was the 384th Infantry Division. The division lost two NCOs/enlisted killed in action; three NCOs/enlisted were wounded in action.

376th Infantry Division – The division, with an infantry regiment attached from the 79th Infantry Division, defended in sector near Blizhniaia-Perekopka against the 23rd Rifle Division. To the east was the 44th Infantry Division; to the west was the 1st Romanian Cavalry Division. The division lost four NCOs/enlisted wounded in action.

384th Infantry Division – The division defended in sector west of the Don River near Trekhostrovskaia to Podgorskii against the 27th Guards Rifle Division and the 214th Rifle Division. To the northwest was the 44th Infantry Division; to the southeast was the 305th Infantry Division.

XIV *Panzer* Corps – The corps headquarters was located east of Ssadtschi-Kowa. The 651st Pioneer Battalion was assigned to the corps. The corps suffered the following officer casualties: one killed in action; seven wounded in action; three missing in action.

3rd Infantry Division (Motorized) – The division defended in sector, from the Tartar Hill-Hill 111.1-Hill 129.6-Hill 131.2 against the 299th Rifle Division, the 38th Guards Rifle Division, the 116th Rifle Division and the 343rd Rifle Division. To the east was the 16th ***Panzer*** Division; to the west was the 60th Infantry Division (Motorized.)

16th Panzer Division – The division defended in sector, from Hill 139.7 to the Volga and from the Volga southwest to Hill 145.1, north of Orlovka against the 120th Rifle Division, the 84th Rifle Division and the 64th Rifle Division. In the division's southern sector, the division attacked against the Orlovka salient and captured most of the village. To the west was the 3rd Infantry Division (Motorized); to the southwest was Battle Group Stahel.

60th Infantry Division (Motorized) – The division defended in sector, from south of Kotluban' Station near Borodkin to Kuz'michi against the 41st Guards Rifle Division, the 49th Rifle Division, the 231st Rifle Division, the 233rd Rifle Division, the 316th Rifle Division and the 207th Rifle Division.

To the west was the 113th Infantry Division; to the east was the 3rd Infantry Division (Motorized.) In the division's southern sector, the division attacked to reduce the enemy salient at Orlovka.

94th Infantry Division – The division attacked in zone against the Orlovka salient and captured the cemetery. Heavy fighting occurred at Hill 104.6. To the north was Battle Group Stahel; to the south was the 389th Infantry Division.

Battle Group Stahel – The battle group defended northwest of Orlovka to contain enemy forces. To the northeast was the 16th ***Panzer*** Division; to the south was the 94th Infantry Division.

XVII Corps

79th Infantry Division – The division defended in sector from Bol'shoy-Verkhne-Kalmykovskii-Verkhne-Fomichinskii-Baskowskij against the 124th Rifle Division. The division headquarters was located at Karagichev. To the west was the 298th Infantry Division; to the east was the 5th Romanian Infantry Division. The division lost one NCO/enlisted killed in action; one NCO/enlisted was reported missing in action.

298th Infantry Division – Division elements defended in sector, against the 14th Guards Rifle Division. To the west was the Italian XXXV Corps; to the east was the 79th Infantry Division. The bulk of the division occupied assembly areas along the Sixth Army's western boundary.

1st Romanian Cavalry Division – The division defended in sector near Molologowskij south of the Don River against the 76th Rifle Division and 63rd Rifle Division; enemy forces broke through the sector. To the west was the 13th Romanian Infantry Division; to the east was the 376th Infantry Division. The division lost 2 NCOs/enlisted killed in action; seven NCOs/enlisted were wounded in action.

1st Romanian Armored Division – The division occupied an assembly in the western part of the corps sector.

5th Romanian Infantry Division – Elements of the division defended in sector south of the Don River. To the west was the 79th Infantry Division; to the east was the 6th Romanian Infantry Division. The rest of the division occupied assembly areas south of the front.

6th Romanian Infantry Division – The division defended in sector south of the Don River against the 96th Rifle Division. To the west was the 79th Infantry Division; to the southeast was the 13th Romanian Infantry Division. The division suffered four NCOs/enlisted killed in action; 14 NCOs/enlisted were wounded in action.

13th Romanian Infantry Division – The division defended in sector along the Don River west of Kletskiy against the 278th Rifle Division and the 63rd Rifle Division. To the northwest was the 6th Romanian Infantry Division; to the east was the 1st Romanian Cavalry Division. The division defended in sector. The division lost three NCOs/enlisted killed in action; three NCOs/enlisted were wounded in action.

XXXXVIII *Panzer* Corps

29th Infantry Division (Motorized) – The division occupied an assembly area west of Zybenko and Varvarovka, along the Volga-Don Canal, to prepare for future operations. The division lost four NCOs/enlisted wounded in action.

71st Infantry Division – The division defended in sector to retain previous gains against the 13th Guards Rifle Division. To the north was the 295th Infantry Division; to the south was the 371st Infantry Division.

LI Corps – The corps headquarters was located at Gumrak. The 71st Pioneer Battalion and the 635th Pioneer Battalion (Motorized) were assigned to the corps. The corps suffered the following officer casualties: two killed in action; nine wounded in action; two missing in action.

24th Panzer Division – The division defended, repulsing an enemy attack and then driving a wedge between the 112th Rifle Division and the 193rd Rifle Division south of Silikat Factory Nr.3. To the west was the 389th Infantry Division; to the south was the 100th ***Jäger*** Division. The division lost eight NCOs/enlisted killed in action; one officer and 24 NCOs/enlisted were wounded in action. Combat strength of the division fell to 6,943: the 24th ***Panzer*** Regiment reported a combat strength of 1,089; the 21st ***Panzer*** Grenadier Regiment reported a combat strength of 896 and the 26th ***Panzer*** Grenadier Regiment reported a combat strength of 923.

100th Jäger Division – The division consolidated its gains against the 95th Rifle Division and the 284th Rifle Division. To the north was the 24th ***Panzer*** Division; to the south was the 295th Infantry Division. The division suffered 16 NCOs/enlisted killed in action; 50 NCOs/enlisted were wounded in action.

295th Infantry Division – Elements of the division moved through the Krutoi Balka to reach the

Volga River, surprising the 34th Guards Rifle Regiment of the 13th Guards Rifle Division and the 284th Rifle Division. To the north was the 100th ***Jäger*** Division; to the south was the 71st Infantry Division. The division lost four NCOs/enlisted killed in action; one officer and 21 NCOs/enlisted were wounded in action.

389th Infantry Division – The division deployed southward to the valley of the Mechetka River against elements of the 112th Rifle Division. To the north was the 94th Infantry Division; to the south was the 24th ***Panzer*** Division. The division reported ten overall casualties.

Sixth Army Reserve

76th Infantry Division – The division conducted rest and refit operations at an assembly area north of Kalach at Bol'shenabatovskiy.

Fourth *Panzer* Army – The army headquarters was located east of Verkhne-Zaryzinskij.

IV Corps – The corps headquarters was located at Plantator.

297th Infantry Division – The division defended in sector east of Elkhi and Iagodniki against the 157th Rifle Division, the 138th Rifle Division, the 204th Rifle Division, the 29th Rifle Division and the 106th Rifle Division. To the north was the 371st Infantry Division; to the south was the 20th Romanian Infantry Division.

371st Infantry Division – The division defended in sector east of Peschanka to Kuporosnoye against the 422nd Rifle Division and the 36th Guards Rifle Division. To the north was the 71st Infantry Division; to the south was the 297th Infantry Division. The division lost six NCOs/enlisted killed in action; one officer and 24 NCOs/enlisted were wounded in action.

20th Romanian Infantry Division – The division defended in sector, west of the Tundutovo Rail Station and east of Andreevka against the 154th Marine Infantry Brigade. To the north was the 297th Infantry Division; to the south was the 2nd Romanian Infantry Division of the Romanian VI Corps.

Fourth *Panzer* Army Reserve

14th Panzer Division – The division defended in sectors northwest of Lake Barmantsak and at Sadovia and counter-attacked advancing enemy forces in the Romanian VI Corps sector. The division lost six NCOs/enlisted killed in action; 24 NCOs/enlisted were wounded in action.

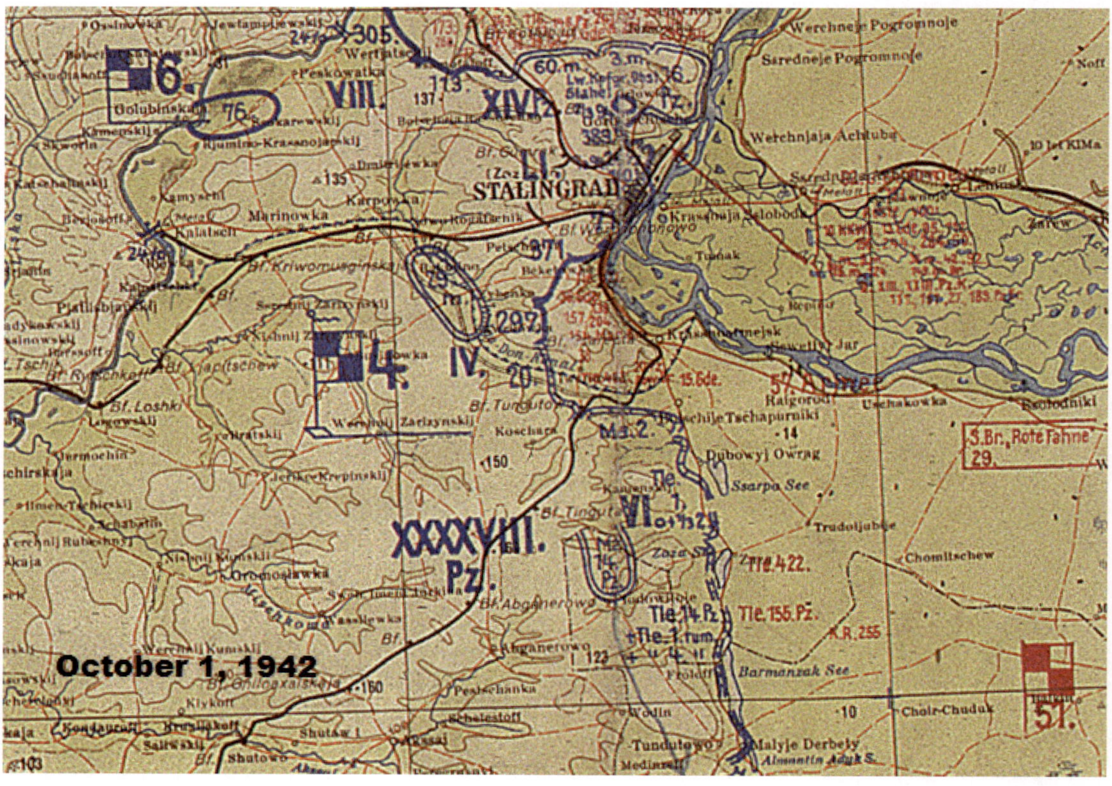

Christliches Andenken an Obergefreiten
Karl Hinterberger
Inhaber des E. K. II. Klasse, des Infanterie-Sturm-Abzeichens sowie der Ostmedaille, wohnhaft Raiben Nr. 2, Pfarre Hartkirchen
welcher am 1. Oktober 1942, an der Ostfront, im 24. Lebensjahre den Heldentod fand.

Die Pflicht rief mich zum Krieg hinaus
Mit Gott ging ich vom Vaterhaus,
Ich dachte ewig fort und fort,
Wenn ich auch weilt an fremdem Ort,
Und freute mich aufs Wiedersehn,
Wenn Krieg und Sturm zu Ende gehn.
Doch anders hat's der Herr gewollt
Und hat von hier mich abgeholt.
Nun ruh' in fremder Erd' mich aus
Und bin in Gottes Vaterhaus,
Ruh aus von Krieg und Erdenleid
Und bin von jeder Sorg' befreit,
Drum tröstet, ihr Lieben, euch daran,
Was Gott tut, das ist wohlgetan".

Besteller: J. Schindlbauer, Hartkirchen 36
Druck: „Welsermühl", Wels

Obergefreiter **Karl Hinterberger** was born on June 5, 1919 at Hartkirchen, Upper Austria. The recipient of the Iron Cross 2nd Class, Infantry Assault Badge, and Eastern Front Medal, he was killed in action on October 1, 1942 at Stalingrad. His name is listed in the remembrance book at the German Military Cemetery at Rossoschka. It is also listed on the war memorial in the village of Hartkirchen, Austria.

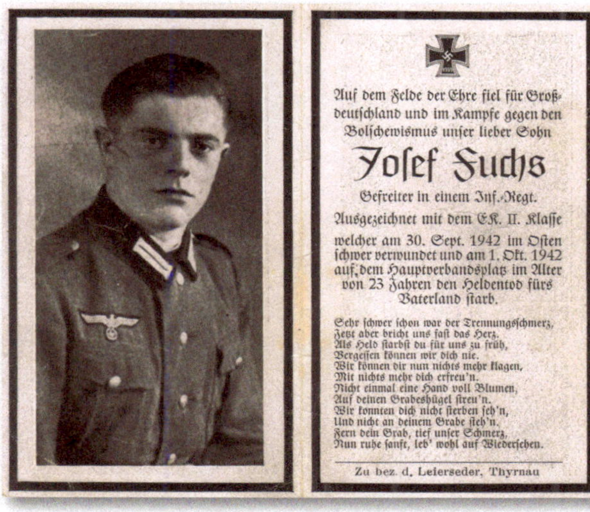
Auf dem Felde der Ehre fiel für Großdeutschland und im Kampfe gegen den Bolschewismus unser lieber Sohn
Josef Fuchs
Gefreiter in einem Inf.-Regt.
Ausgezeichnet mit dem EK. II. Klasse
welcher am 30. Sept. 1942 im Osten schwer verwundet und am 1. Okt. 1942 auf dem Hauptverbandsplatz im Alter von 23 Jahren den Heldentod fürs Vaterland starb.

Sehr schwer schon war der Trennungsschmerz,
Jetzt aber bricht uns fast das Herz.
Als Held starbst du für uns zu früh,
Vergessen können wir dich nie.
Wir können dir nun nichts mehr klagen,
Mit nichts mehr dich erfreu'n.
Nicht einmal eine Hand voll Blumen,
Auf deinen Grabeshügel streu'n.
Wir konnten dich nicht sterben seh'n,
Und nicht an deinem Grabe steh'n.
Fern dein Grab, tief unser Schmerz,
Nun ruhe sanft, leb' wohl auf Wiedersehen.

Zu bez. d. Leiserseder, Thyrnau

Gefreiter **Joseph Fuchs** was born in Gosting near Thyrnau in Bavaria on February 1, 1920. Assigned to an infantry regiment, most likely in the 305th Infantry Division, he was previously awarded the Iron Cross 2nd Class. He was severely wounded on September 30, 1942 and evacuated to a field hospital at Vertyachiy on the Don River; he died there the following day on October 1, 1942. He is buried in the German Military Cemetery at Rossoschka in Block 11, Row 11 in Grave 432.

Sources, October 1, 1942: *Oberkommando des Heeres, Lage Ost: Stand: 1.10.42, Eastern Front Situation Map, National Archives Identifier: 559733, Record Group 242 – National Archives Collection of Foreign Records Seized, 1675-1958, National Archives, College Park, Maryland; Ia, Armeeoberkommando 6, "Morgen Meldung" and assorted reports, Kriegstagebuch 13, 2 October 1942, as found in Microfilm Series, T-312, Records of German Field Commands, Armies, Roll 1686, National Archives and Records Service, College Park, Maryland; Ia, XXXXVIII Panzerkorps, "Übersicht über die dem Korps Unterstellten Divisionen, 28. Juni 1942 – 11 October 1942," as found on T-314, Records of German Field Commands, Corps, Roll 1153, National Archives, College Park, Maryland; Korpsarzt, XXXXVIII Panzerkorps, "Meldung über Personelle Verluste," Stand 1.10.42, as found on T-314, Records of German Field Commands, Corps, Roll 1158, National Archives, College Park, Maryland; 79th Infantry Division, Kriegstagebuch, 1 October 1942, as found in Microfilm Series T-315, Roll 1108, National Archives and Records Service, College Park, Maryland; 371st Infantry Division, Kriegstagebuch, 1 October 1942, as found in Microfilm Series T-315, Roll 2164, National Archives and Records Service, College Park, Maryland; Florian Freiherr von und zu Aufsess, Die Anlagenbände zu den Kriegstagebüchern der 6. Armee vom 14.09.1942 bis 24.11.1942, Band 1, Schwabach, Germany: Selbstverlag, 2006, 100-111; Antony Beevor, Stalingrad: The Fateful Siege: 1942-1943, London: Penguin Books, 1998, 163; John Erickson, The Road to Stalingrad, New York: Harper & Row, 1975, 416; David M. Glantz & Jonathan M. House, Armageddon in Stalingrad: September-November 1942, (The Stalingrad Trilogy, Volume 2), Lawrence, Kansas: University Press of Kansas, 2009, 347, 287-296, 356-357; Jochen Löser, Bittere Pflicht: Kampf und Untergang der 76. Berlin-Brandenburgischen Infanterie-Division, Osnabrück, FRG: Biblio Verlag, 1986, 215; Jason Mark, Death of the Leaping Horseman: 24. Panzer-Division in Stalingrad, Sydney, Australia: Leaping Horsemen Books, 2003, 241; Kurt Mehner, Die Geheimen Tagesberichte der Deutschen Wehrmachtführung im Zweiten Weltkrieg 1939-1945, Band 5: 1. Juni 1942 – 30. November 1942, Osnabrück, Germany: Biblio Verlag, 1991, 220; Anton Schimak, Karl Lamprecht & Friedrich Dettmer, Die 44. Infanterie Division: Tagebuch der Hoch- und Deutschmeister, Wien: Verlag Austria Press, 169, 233 and Map: Marschweg der 44. Infanterie Division im Russland.*

October 2, 1942
Weather: clear, 73° F
Sunrise: 6:02 a.m.; **Sunset:** 5:41 p.m.
Moon: Last Quarter; 50% illumination

Sixth Army – Bombers and dive-bombers from the ***Luftwaffe***'s VIII Air Corps pounded Stalingrad in large-scale attacks, destroying numerous large oil-storage tanks. The army headquarters was located at Golubinskaya. The Sixth Army chief of staff informed Army Group B that "In spite of the most intensive efforts by all forces, the low combat strengths of the infantry will prolong the taking of Stalingrad indefinitely if reinforcements cannot be supplied."

VIII Corps – The corps headquarters was located at Peskovatka.

113th Infantry Division – The division defended in sector southwest of Samofalovka and north of Borodkin against the 260th Rifle Division, the 24th Rifle Division, the 292nd Rifle Division, the 173rd Rifle Division and the 258th Rifle Division. To the northwest was the 305th Infantry Division; to the east was the 60th Infantry Division (Motorized.) The division lost 20 NCOs/enlisted killed in action; 50 NCOs/ enlisted were wounded in action.

305th Infantry Division – The division defended in sector from the Don River, north of Nizhne-Gnilovskii, to west of Kotluban' against the 27th Guards Rifle Division and the 298th Rifle Division. To the southeast was the 113th Infantry Division; to the northwest was the 384th Infantry Division. The division lost one NCO/enlisted killed in action; three NCOs/ enlisted were wounded in action.

XI Corps

44th Infantry Division – The division defended in sector Kurchajessowskij-Kamyshinskiy-Hill 171.0-Hill 180.9-Sirotinskaya-Khmelevskoy against the 40th Guards Rifle Division and the 4th Guards Rifle Division. The division headquarters was located at Verkhne-Golubaja. To the west was 376th Infantry Division; to the east was the 384th Infantry Division. The division lost three NCOs/enlisted wounded in action.

376th Infantry Division – The division defended in sector, with an attached infantry regiment from the 79th Infantry Division, near Blizhniaia-Perekopka against the 23rd Rifle Division. To the east was the 44th Infantry Division; to the west were elements of the 1st Romanian Cavalry Division. The division lost one NCO/enlisted wounded in action.

384th Infantry Division – The division defended in sector west of the Don River near Trekhostrovskaia to Podgorskii against the 4th Guards Rifle Division, the 214th Rifle Division and the 27th Guards Rifle Division. To the northwest was the 44th Infantry Division; to the southeast was the 305th Infantry Division. The division lost one NCO/enlisted wounded in action.

XIV *Panzer* Corps – The corps headquarters was located east of Ssadtschi-Kowa. The 651st Pioneer Battalion was assigned to the corps. The corps suffered the following officer casualties: four killed in action; 12 wounded in action; and one missing in action.

3rd Infantry Division (Motorized) – The division defended in sector, from the Tartar Hill-Hill 111.1-Hill 129.6-Hill 131.2 against the 299th Rifle Division, the 38th Guards Rifle Division, the 116th Rifle Division and the 343rd Rifle Division. To the east was the 16th ***Panzer*** Division; to the west was the 60th Infantry Division (Motorized.) The division reported the following operational ***panzer*** status: five Mark II, 14 Mark III-Long, two Mark IV-Short and four Mark IV-Long tanks.

16th Panzer Division – The division defended in sector, from Hill 139.7 to the Volga and from the Volga southwest to Hill 145.1, north of Orlovka against the 120th Rifle Division, the 84th Rifle Division and the 64th Rifle Division. In the southern sector, elements of the division crushed final enemy resistance in the Orlovka salient. To the west was the 60th Infantry Division (Motorized); to the southwest was Battle Group Stahel. The division reported the following operational ***panzer*** status: 32 Mark III-Long, two Mark IV-Short and 11 Mark IV-Long tanks.

60th Infantry Division (Motorized) – The division defended in sector to the north, from south of Kotluban' Station near Borodkin to Kuz'michi against the 41st Guards Rifle Division, the 49th Rifle Division, the 231st Rifle Division, the 233rd Rifle Division, the 316th Rifle Division and the 207th Rifle Division. To the west was the 113th Infantry Division; to the east was the 3rd Infantry Division (Motorized.) In the southern sector, elements of the division crushed final enemy resistance in the Orlovka salient. The division reported the following operational ***panzer*** status: five Mark II, two Mark III-Short, nine Mark III-Long, four Mark IV-Short and two Mark IV-Long tanks.

94th Infantry Division – The division attacked seizing Hill 97.9, south of Orlovka, marking the final destruction of enemy resistance in the salient. To the north was Battle Group Stahel; to the south was the 389th Infantry Division.

Battle Group Stahel – The battle group attacked in zone to help crush final enemy resistance in the Orlovka salient. To the northeast was the 16th ***Panzer*** Division; to the south was the 94th Infantry Division.

XVII Corps

79th Infantry Division – One-third of the division defended in sector south of the Don River with the 376th Infantry Division. The division reported one regiment on the march at Platonov and one regiment on the march at Ivanuschinskij. The division lost two NCOs/enlisted wounded in action.

XXXXVIII *Panzer* Corps

29th Infantry Division (Motorized) – The division occupied an assembly area west

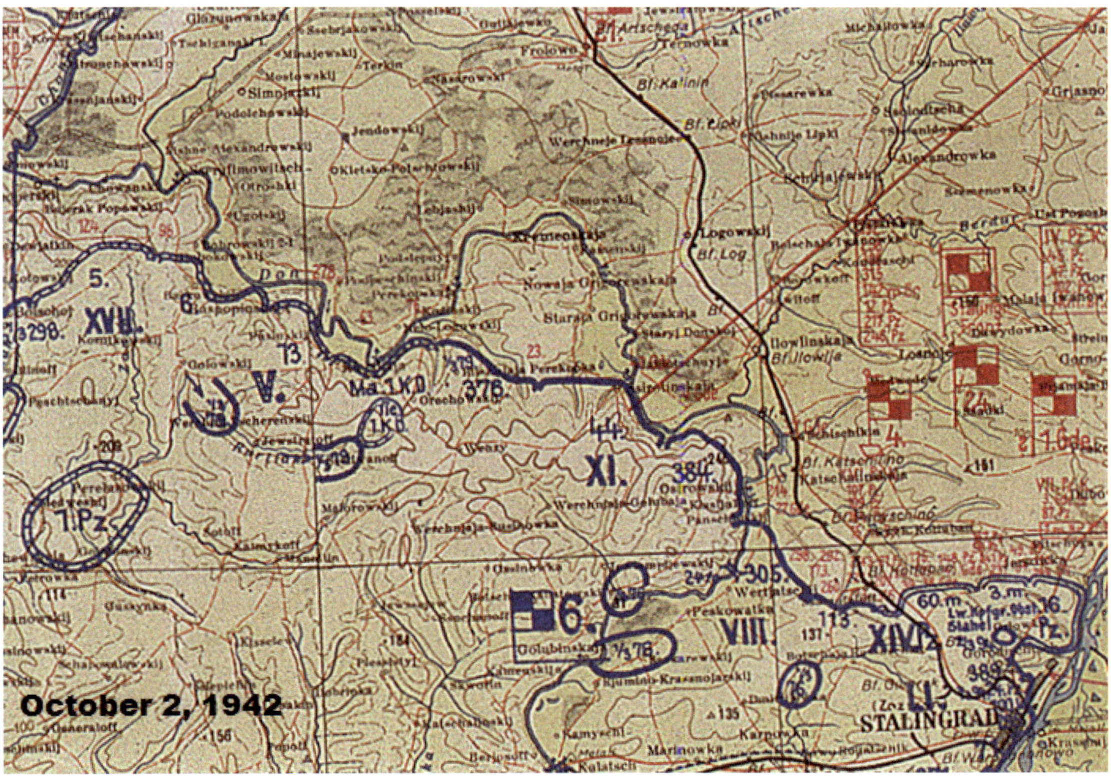

of Zybenko and Varvarovka, along the Volga-Don Canal, to prepare for future operations. The division lost six NCOs/enlisted wounded in action.

LI Corps – Units attacked the oil storage tanks. The corps headquarters was located at Gumrak. The corps reported that the attached 244th ***Sturmgeschütz*** Detachment had 17 operational assault guns and the 245th ***Sturmgeschütz*** Detachment had seven operational assault guns. The corps suffered the following officer casualties: nine wounded in action.

24th Panzer Division – The division defended in sector, repulsing enemy reconnaissance probes of the 308th Rifle Division, and prepared for further offensive operations against the 112th Rifle Division. The division lost 20 NCOs/enlisted killed in action; six officers and 132 NCOs/enlisted were wounded in action; four men were reported missing in action. The division reported the following operational ***panzer*** status: eight Mark II, four Mark III-Short, 11 Mark III-Long, two Mark IV-Short and three Mark IV-Long tanks. To the north was the 389th Infantry Division; to the south was the 100th ***Jäger*** Division.

71st Infantry Division – The division defended in sector to retain previous gains against the 13th Guards Rifle Division. To the north was the 295th Infantry Division; to the south was the 371st Infantry Division.

100th Jäger Division – The division repelled reconnaissance probes on Makeevskaia Street and Vinnitskaia Street by the 92nd Rifle Brigade, and took over part of the 24th ***Panzer*** Division's sector. To the north was the 24th ***Panzer*** Division; to the south was the 295th Infantry Division. The division suffered seven NCOs/enlisted killed in action; 31 NCOs/enlisted were wounded in action.

295th Infantry Division – The division continued small unit actions against the 95th Rifle Division and the 284th Rifle Division. To the north was the 100th ***Jäger*** Division; to the south was the 71st Infantry Division. The division lost five NCOs/enlisted killed in action; 25 NCOs/enlisted were wounded in action; five men were reported missing in action.

389th Infantry Division – The division attacked against the Orlovka salient, seeing heavy fighting at Hill 109.4 against elements of the 112th Rifle Division. The division lost 16 NCOs/enlisted killed in action; 55 NCOs/enlisted were wounded in action. To the north was the 94th Infantry Division; to the south was the 24th ***Panzer*** Division.

Romanian V Corps – The corps transferred to the Romanian Third Army.

Sixth Army Reserve

76th Infantry Division – The division conducted rest and refit operations at an assembly area north of Kalach at Bol'shenabatovskiy. The division reported one regiment at Baburkin, one at Malyj and one at Golubinskaya.

Fourth *Panzer* Army – The army headquarters was located east of Verkhne-Zaryzinskij.

IV Corps – The corps headquarters was located at Plantator.

297th Infantry Division – The division defended in sector east of Elkhi and Iagodniki against the 157th Rifle Division, the 138th Rifle Division, the 204th Rifle Division, the 29th Rifle Division and the 106th Rifle Division, repelling multiple attacks by the 157th Rifle Division. To the north was the 371st Infantry Division; to the south was the 20th Romanian Infantry Division.

371st Infantry Division – The division defended in sector east of Peschanka, repelling attacks by the 36th Guards Rifle Division and the 422nd Rifle Division from Peschanka to Zelenaia Poliana. To the north was the 71st Infantry Division; to the south was the 297th Infantry Division. The division lost 36 NCOs/enlisted killed in action; two officers and 111 NCOs/enlisted were wounded in action.

20th Romanian Infantry Division – The division defended in sector, west of the Tundutovo Rail Station and east of Andreevka against the 154th Marine Infantry Brigade. To the north was the 297th Infantry Division; to the south was the 2nd Romanian Division of the Romanian VI Corps.

Fourth *Panzer* Army Reserve

14th Panzer Division – The division attacked in zone northwest of Lake Barmantsak and at Sadovia, in the area of Plodowitoje, but failed to drive the 155th Tank Brigade and the 91st Rifle Division eastward.

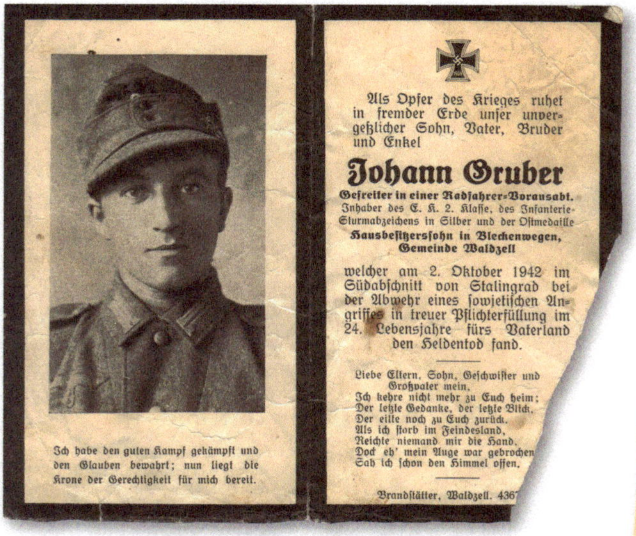

Ich habe den guten Kampf gekämpft und den Glauben bewahrt; nun liegt die Krone der Gerechtigkeit für mich bereit.

Als Opfer des Krieges ruhet in fremder Erde unser unvergeßlicher Sohn, Vater, Bruder und Enkel

Johann Gruber

Gefreiter in einer Radfahrer-Vorausabt.
Inhaber des E. K. 2. Klasse, des Infanterie-Sturmabzeichens in Silber und der Ostmedaille
Hausbesitzerssohn in Bleckenwegen, Gemeinde Waldzell

welcher am 2. Oktober 1942 im Südabschnitt von Stalingrad bei der Abwehr eines sowjetischen Angriffes in treuer Pflichterfüllung im 24. Lebensjahre fürs Vaterland den Heldentod fand.

Liebe Eltern, Sohn, Geschwister und
Großvater mein,
Ich kehre nicht mehr zu Euch heim;
Der letzte Gedanke, der letzte Blick,
Der eilte noch zu Euch zurück.
Als ich starb im Feindesland,
Reichte niemand mir die Hand.
Doch eh' mein Auge war gebrochen
Sah ich schon den Himmel offen.

Brandstätter, Waldzell. 436

Gefreiter **Johann Gruber** was born in Bleckenwegen, near Waldzell in Austria on May 29, 1919. Assigned to a bicycle battalion, he won the Iron Cross 2nd Class, Infantry Assault Badge and Eastern Front Medal. He was killed in action in southern Stalingrad on October 2, 1942. His name is listed in the remembrance book at the German Military Cemetery at Rossoschka.

Sanitäts-Obergefreiter **Alois Koller** was born on May 9, 1919 in Esternberg, near Passau, in Bavaria; he previously worked on a farm. A medic who had previously won the Iron Cross 2nd Class, he had fought in France, Belgium, Holland and Russia. Koller was killed in action on October 2, 1942 near Elkhi, assigned to the 297th Infantry Division.

Zum Andenken an den Sanitäts-Obergefreiten

Alois Koller

Landarbeiter in Hub, bei Esternberg
Träger des Eisernen Kreuzes II. Klasse
Teilnehmer an den Feldzügen in Frankreich, Belgien, Holland und Rußland

welcher am 2. Oktober 1942, in der Nähe von Stalingrad im Alter von 23 Jahren den Heldentod gestorben ist.

Innstadt-Druckerei Passau

Sources, October 2, 1942: *Oberkommando des Heeres, Lage Ost: Stand: 2.10.42, Eastern Front Situation Map, National Archives Identifier: 559733, Record Group 242 – National Archives Collection of Foreign Records Seized, 1675-1958, National Archives, College Park, Maryland; Ia, Armeeoberkommando 6, "Morgen Meldung" and assorted reports, Kriegstagebuch 13, 3 October 1942, as found in Microfilm Series, T-312, Records of German Field Commands, Armies, Roll 1686, National Archives and Records Service, College Park, Maryland; Ia, XXXXVIII Panzerkorps, "Übersicht über die dem Korps Unterstellten Divisionen, 28. Juni 1942 – 11 October 1942," as found on T-314, Records of German Field Commands, Corps, Roll 1153, National Archives, College Park, Maryland; Korpsarzt, XXXXVIII Panzerkorps, "Meldung über Personelle Verluste," Stand 2.10.42, as found on T-314, Records of German Field Commands, Corps, Roll 1158, National Archives, College Park, Maryland; 371st Infantry Division, Kriegstagebuch, 2 October 1942, as found in Microfilm Series T-315, Roll 2164, National Archives and Records Service, College Park, Maryland; Florian Freiherr von und zu Aufsess, Die Anlagenbände zu den Kriegstagebüchern der 6. Armee vom 14.09.1942 bis 24.11.1942, Band 1, Schwabach, Germany: Selbstverlag, 2006, 104-111; David M. Glantz & Jonathan M. House, Armageddon in Stalingrad: September-November 1942, (The Stalingrad Trilogy, Volume 2), Lawrence, Kansas: University Press of Kansas, 2009, 313-317, 356-357; Jason Mark, Death of the Leaping Horseman: 24. Panzer-Division in Stalingrad, Sydney, Australia: Leaping Horsemen Books, 2003, 241-245; Kurt Mehner, Die Geheimen Tagesberichte der Deutschen Wehrmachtführung im Zweiten Weltkrieg 1939-1945, Band 5: 1. Juni 1942 – 30. November 1942, Osnabrück, Germany: Biblio Verlag, 1991, 222; Hans Neidhardt, Mit Tanne und Eichenlaub: Kriegschronik der 100. Jäger Division vormals 100. leichte Infanterie Division, Graz, Austria: Leopold Stocker Verlag, 1981, 212; Anton Schimak, Karl Lamprecht & Friedrich Dettmer, Die 44. Infanterie Division: Tagebuch der Hoch- und Deutschmeister, Wien: Verlag Austria Press, 169, 233 and Map: Marschweg der 44. Infanterie Division im Russland.*

October 3, 1942
Weather: sunny, bright, warmer after noon, 73° F, changing cloudiness
Sunrise: 6:03 a.m.; **Sunset:** 5:39 p.m.
Moon: Waning Crescent; 40% illumination

Sixth Army – ***General der Panzertruppe*** Paulus told ***Generalfeldmarschall*** von Weichs: "At present, even the breaking out of individual blocks of houses can only be accomplished after lengthy regroupings to bring together the few combat-worthy assault elements that can still be found." The army headquarters was located at Golubinskaya.

VIII Corps – The corps headquarters was located at Peskovatka.

113th Infantry Division – The division defended in sector southwest of Samofalovka and north of Borodkin, against the 260th Rifle Division, the 24th Rifle Division, the 292nd Rifle Division, the 173rd Rifle Division and the 258th Rifle Division. To the northwest was the 305th Infantry Division; to the east was the 60th Infantry Division (Motorized.) The division lost nine NCOs/enlisted killed in action; 13 NCOs/enlisted were wounded in action.

305th Infantry Division – The division defended in sector from the Don River, north of Nizhne-Gnilovskii, to west of Kotluban' against the 298th Rifle Division. To the east was the 113th Infantry Division; to the northwest was the 384th Infantry Division. The division lost six NCOs/enlisted wounded in action.

XI Corps

44th Infantry Division – The division defended in sector Kurchajessowskij-Kamyshinskiy-Hill 171.0-Hill 180.9-Sirotin-skaya-Khmelevskoy against the 40th Guards Rifle Division and the 4th Guards Rifle Division. The division headquarters was located at Verkhne-Golubaja. To the west was 376th Infantry Division; to the east was the 384th Infantry Division. The division lost three NCOs/enlisted wounded in action.

376th Infantry Division – The division, with an attached infantry regiment from the 79th Infantry Division, defended in sector near Blizhniaia-Perekopka against the 23rd Rifle Division. To the east was the 44th Infantry Division; to the west was the 1st Romanian Cavalry Division. The division lost four NCOs/enlisted wounded in action.

384th Infantry Division – The division defended in sector west of the Don River near Trekhostrovskaia to Podgorskii against the 37th Guards Rifle Division, the 214th Rifle Division and the 27th Guards Rifle Division. To the northwest was the 44th Infantry Division; to the southeast was the 305th Infantry Division.

XIV *Panzer* Corps – The corps headquarters was located east of Ssadtschi-Kowa. The 521st ***Panzerjäger*** Detachment was assigned to the corps. The 51st ***Werfer*** Regiment was assigned to support the corps. The corps suffered the following officer casualties: five killed in action; three wounded in action.

3rd Infantry Division (Motorized) – The division defended in sector, from the Tartar Hill-Hill 111.1-Hill 129.6-Hill 131.2 against the 343rd Rifle Division, the 116th Rifle Division and the 38th Guards Rifle Division. To the east was the 16th ***Panzer*** Division; to the west was the 60th Infantry Division (Motorized.)

16th Panzer Division – The division defended in sector, from Hill 139.7 to the Volga and from the Volga southwest to Hill 145.1, north of Orlovka against the 299th Rifle Division and the 64th Rifle Division. At Orlovka, elements of the division mopped up remnants of the 112th Rifle Division. To the west was the 3rd Infantry Division (Motorized.)

60th Infantry Division (Motorized) – The division defended in sector to the north, from south of Kotluban' Station near Borodkin to Kuz'michi against the 41st Guards Rifle Division, the 221st Rifle Division and the 116th Rifle Division. To the west was the 113th Infantry Division; to the east was the 3rd Infantry Division (Motorized.)

94th Infantry Division – The division prepared for offensive operations. To the north was Battle Group Stahel; to the south was the 389th Infantry Division.

Battle Group Stahel – The battle group prepared for future operations. To the northeast was the 16th ***Panzer*** Division; to the south was the 94th Infantry Division.

XVII Corps

79th Infantry Division – One-third of the division defended in sector south of the Don River with the 376th Infantry Division. To the east was the 44th Infantry Division; to the west was the Romanian V Corps of the Romanian Third Army. The division reported one regiment on the march at Platonov and one regiment on the march at Ivanuschinskij.

XXXXVIII *Panzer* Corps

29th Infantry Division (Motorized) – The division occupied an assembly area west of Zybenko and Varvarovka, along the Volga-Don Canal, to prepare for future operations.

LI Corps – The corps headquarters was located at Gumrak. The corps suffered the following officer casualties: three killed in action; 11 wounded in action.

24th Panzer Division – The division attacked, reaching the western edge of Skulpturny Park and the southeast edge of the Schnellhefter Block against elements of the 308th Rifle Division and the 37th Guards Rifle Division. The division lost two officers and 27 NCOs/enlisted killed in action; five officers and 96 NCOs/enlisted were wounded in action; five NCOs/enlisted were reported missing in action. To the north was the 389th Infantry Division; to the south was the 100th ***Jäger*** Division. The division reported six heavy and 35 medium anti-tank guns to be operational. The division reported the following ***panzer***s as operational: two Mark II, nine Mark III-Short, 17 Mark III-Long, five Mark IV-Short and five Mark IV-Long tanks.

71st Infantry Division – The division attacked in zone against the 13th Guards Rifle Division. To the north was the 295th Infantry Division; to the south was the 371st Infantry Division.

100th Jäger Division – The division attacked east from Silikat Factory Nr.3 to the Krutoi Balka, gaining terrain at Bibliotechnaia Street, Karusel'naia Street, Bibleiskaia Street, Martovskaia Street and Tsekhovaia Street against the 193rd Rifle Division and the 39th Guards Rifle Division. To the north was the 24th ***Panzer*** Division; to the south was the 295th Infantry Division. The division suffered two officers and 17 NCOs/enlisted killed in action; two officers and 44 NCOs/enlisted were wounded in action. The 245th ***Sturmgeschütz*** Detachment, with 13 operational assault guns, was in direct support of the division. The division reported six heavy and 11 medium anti-tank guns to be operational.

295th Infantry Division – The division attacked east on the eastern slopes of Mamayev Kurgan (Hill 102) and along the Dol'gii and Krutoi Balkas against the 284th Rifle Division and 95th Rifle Division. To the north was the 100th ***Jäger*** Division; to the south was the 71st Infantry Division. The division lost one NCO/enlisted killed in action; one officer and 11 NCOs/enlisted were wounded in action. The division reported ten heavy and five medium anti-tank guns to be operational.

389th Infantry Division – The division attacked northeast and seized a small balka branching east from the Mokraya Mechetka River against elements of the 112th Rifle Division. The division lost two officers and three NCOs/enlisted killed in action; three officers and 40 men were wounded in action. To the north was the 94th Infantry Division; to the south was the 24th ***Panzer*** Division. The 244th ***Sturmgeschütz*** Detachment, with seven operational assault guns, was in direct support of the division. The division reported eight heavy and 13 medium anti-tank guns to be operational.

Sixth Army Reserve

76th Infantry Division – The division conducted rest and refit operations

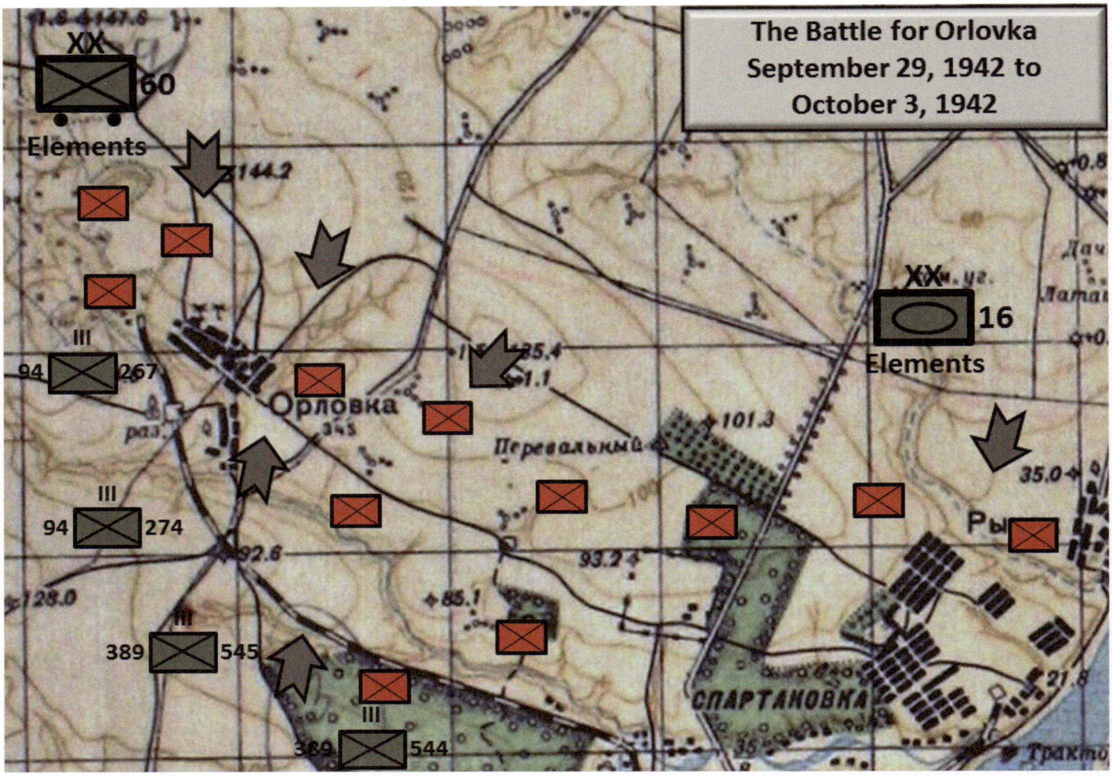
The Battle for Orlovka
September 29, 1942 to
October 3, 1942
XX
60
Elements
III
94
267
III
94
274
III
389
545
III
389
544
XX
16
Elements
Орловка
Перевальный
СПАРТАНОВКА

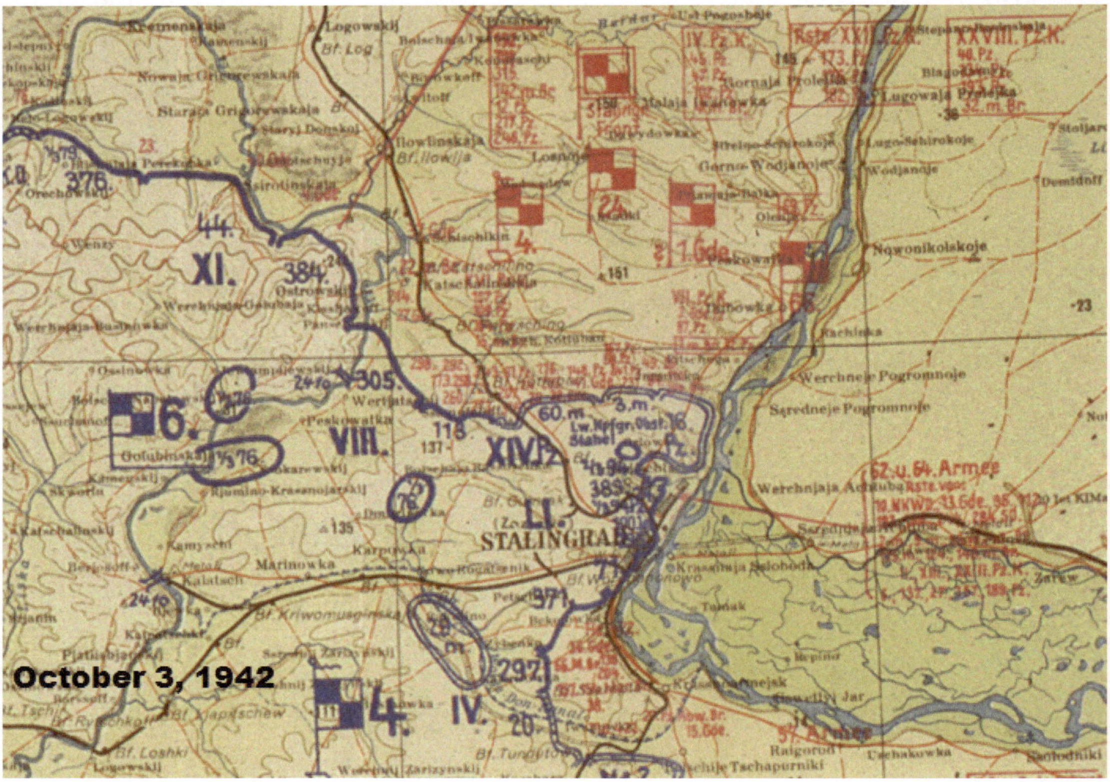
October 3, 1942
STALINGRAD
XI.
VIII.
XIV.Pz.
LI.
IV.
6.
4.
384.
305.
389.
371.
297.
62.u.64.Armee

at three assembly areas north of Kalach at Bol'shenabatovskiy. The division reported one regiment at Baburkin, one at Malyj and one at Golubinskaya.

Fourth *Panzer* Army – The army headquarters was located east of Verkhne-Zaryzinskij.

IV Corps

297th Infantry Division – The division defended in sector east of Elkhi and Iagodniki against the 157th Rifle Division and the 66th Marine Infantry Brigade. To the north was the 371st Infantry Division; to the south was the 20th Romanian Infantry Division.

371st Infantry Division – The division defended in sector against the 34th Guards Rifle Division, repelling several enemy attacks. The division lost six NCOs/enlisted killed in action; 22 NCOs/enlisted were wounded in action. To the north was the 71st Infantry Division; to the south was the 297th Infantry Division.

20th Romanian Infantry Division – The division defended in sector, west of the Tundutovo Rail Station and east of Andreevka against the 38th Rifle Division. To the north was the 297th Infantry Division; to the south was the 2nd Romanian Infantry Division of the Romanian VI Corps.

Fourth *Panzer* Army Reserve

14th Panzer Division – The division conducted combat operations in sector near Sadovia against the 155th Tank Brigade, the 422nd Rifle Division and the 91st Rifle Division. The division lost 13 NCOs/enlisted wounded in action.

Sources, October 3, 1942: *Oberkommando des Heeres, Lage Ost: Stand: 3.10.42, Eastern Front Situation Map, National Archives Identifier: 559733, Record Group 242 – National Archives Collection of Foreign Records Seized, 1675-1958, National Archives, College Park, Maryland; Ia, Armeeoberkommando 6, "Morgen Meldung" and assorted reports, Kriegstagebuch 13, 4 October 1942, as found in Microfilm Series, T-312, Records of German Field Commands, Armies, Roll 1686, National Archives and Records Service, College Park, Maryland; Ia, XXXXVIII Panzerkorps, "Übersicht über die dem Korps Unterstellten Divisionen, 28. Juni 1942 – 11 October 1942," as found on T-314, Records of German Field Commands, Corps, Roll 1153, National Archives, College Park, Maryland; Korpsarzt, XXXXVIII Panzerkorps, "Meldung über Personelle Verluste," Stand 3.10.42, as found on T-314, Records of German Field Commands, Corps, Roll 1158, National Archives, College Park, Maryland; 371st Infantry Division, Kriegstagebuch, 3 October 1942, as found in Microfilm Series T-315, Roll 2164, National Archives and Records Service, College Park, Maryland; Florian Freiherr von und zu Aufsess, Die Anlagenbände zu den Kriegstagebüchern der 6. Armee vom 14.09.1942 bis 24.11.1942, Band 1, Schwabach, Germany: Selbstverlag, 2006, 110-123; David M. Glantz & Jonathan M. House, Armageddon in Stalingrad: September-November 1942, (The Stalingrad Trilogy, Volume 2), Lawrence, Kansas: University Press of Kansas, 2009, 318-327; Jason Mark, Death of the Leaping Horseman: 24. Panzer-Division in Stalingrad, Sydney, Australia: Leaping Horsemen Books, 2003, 246-250; Anton Schimak, Karl Lamprecht & Friedrich Dettmer, Die 44. Infanterie Division: Tagebuch der Hoch- und Deutschmeister, Wien: Verlag Austria Press, 169, 233 and Map: Marschweg der 44. Infanterie Division im Russland; Stephen Walsh, Stalingrad: The Infernal Cauldron, 1942-1943, New York: Thomas Dunne Books/St. Martin's Press, 2000, 83.*

Gebets-Andenken
an
Georg Limmer
Jäger in einem Gebirgsjäger-Rgt.
Landwirtssohn von Unterdeggenbach.
Gefallen am 3. Oktober 1942 bei den
schweren Kämpfen um Stalingrad
im Alter von fast 33 Jahren.

O liebe Eltern und Geschwister mein,
Ich kehre nicht mehr zu Euch heim,
Der letzte Gedanke, der letzte Blick,
Sie eilten noch zu Euch zurück.
Als ich starb im Feindesland,
Reichte niemand mir die Hand,
Doch eh' mein Auge war gebrochen
Sah den Himmel ich schon offen.
Ihr Lieben mein,
Schließt in's Gebet mich ein,
Vergeßt Euern lieben Georg nicht,
Der im Feindesland begraben liegt.

Jäger **George Limmer** was born on January 5, 1910 in Unterdeggenbach near Schierling, Bavaria. The son of a farmer, he was killed in action on October 3, 1942 at Stalingrad while a member of the 100th ***Jäger*** Division. His name is listed in the remembrance book at the German Military Cemetery at Rossoschka.

Die fremde Erde sei Dir leicht
Wo Du als Kämpfer bist erbleicht.

Eine größere Liebe hat niemand
als wer sein Leben hingibt,
für seine Freunde!

Fern der Heimat im Kampfe gegen den Bolschewismus starb den Heldentod für Führer und Vaterland getreu seinem Fahneneid

Max Stumbeck
von **Herzogau**
Gefreiter in einem Jnf.-Rgt.,
gefallen am 3. Okt. 1942 im Alter
von 32 Jahren.

Beim heißen Kampf im Feindesland
Traf dich die Todesstunde
Die Lieben dein im Heimatland
Traf schwer die bittere Kunde:
Den Heldentod fürs Vaterland
Bist Liebster du gestorben,
Hast mutig dir mit tapferer Hand
Den Himmelslohn erworben.

Druckerei A. Lackerbauer, Regen Tel. 78

Gefreiter **Max Stumbeck** was born in Herzogau near Regen in Bavaria on January 4, 1910. Assigned to an infantry regiment in the 297th Infantry Division, he was seriously wounded on October 3, 1942 and died of his wounds at the 2nd Medical Company of the 297th Medical Detachment at Gavrilovka. His name is listed in the remembrance book at the German Military Cemetery at Rossoschka.

October 4, 1942
Weather: clear, sunny, 66° F
Sunrise: 6:04 a.m.; **Sunset:** 5:37 p.m.
Moon: Waning Crescent; 31% illumination

Sixth Army – Bombers and dive-bombers from the ***Luftwaffe***'s VIII Air Corps pounded enemy positions in front of the 24th ***Panzer*** Division and the 389th Infantry Division in preparation for their ground attacks. The army headquarters was located at Golubinskaya. The army chief of staff reported: "Without reinforcements, the army is not going to take Stalingrad very soon. The danger exists that were the Russians to make fairly strong counterattacks, our front might not hold, because there are no reserves behind it."

VIII Corps – The corps headquarters was located at Peskovatka. The corps suffered the following officer casualties: four wounded in action.

113th Infantry Division – The division defended in sector southwest of Samofalovka and north of Borodkin, against the 260th Rifle Division, the 24th Rifle Division, the 292nd Rifle Division, the 173rd Rifle Division and the 258th Rifle Division. To the west was the 305th Infantry Division; to the east was the 60th Infantry Division (Motorized.) The division reported that 20 heavy and 15 medium anti-tank guns were operational. The division lost 14 NCOs/enlisted killed in action; two officers and 51 NCOs/enlisted were wounded in action.

305th Infantry Division – The division defended in sector from the Don River, north of Nizhne-Gnilovskii, to west of Kotluban', against the 298th Rifle Division. To the southeast was the 113th Infantry Division; to the northwest was the 384th Infantry Division. The division reported that 15 heavy and 17 medium anti-tank guns were operational. The division lost two NCOs/enlisted wounded in action; one man was reported as missing in action.

XI Corps

44th Infantry Division – The division defended in sector Kurchajessowskij-Kamyshinskiy-Hill 171.0-Hill 180.9-Sirotinskaya-Khmelevskoy, against the 40th Guards Rifle Division and the 4th Guards Rifle Division. The division headquarters was located at Verkhne-Golubaja. To the west was 376th Infantry Division; to the east was the 384th Infantry Division. The division reported that 22 heavy and 11 medium anti-tank guns were operational. The division lost 14 NCOs/enlisted killed in action; 40 NCOs/enlisted were wounded in action.

376th Infantry Division – The division, reinforced by one infantry regiment from the 79th Infantry Division, defended in sector near Blizhniaia-Perekopka, against the 23rd Rifle Division. To the east was the 44th Infantry Division; to the west was the 1st Romanian Cavalry Division. The division reported that 18 heavy and nine medium anti-tank guns were operational. The division lost two NCOs/enlisted killed in action; 64 NCOs/enlisted were wounded in action.

384th Infantry Division – The division defended in sector west of the Don River near Trekhostrovskaia to Podgorskii, against the 4th Guards Rifle Division, the 27th Guards Rifle Division and the 214th Rifle Division. To the west was the 44th Infantry Division; to the southeast was the 305th Infantry Division. The division reported that eight heavy and 12 medium anti-tank guns were operational. The division lost three NCOs/enlisted killed in action; one NCO/enlisted was wounded in action.

XIV *Panzer* Corps – The corps headquarters was located east of Ssadtschi-Kowa. The corps suffered the following officer casualties: one wounded in action;

3rd Infantry Division (Motorized) – The division defended in sector, from the Tartar Hill-Hill 111.1-Hill 129.6-Hill 131.2 against the 343rd Rifle Division, the 116th Rifle Division and the 38th Guards Rifle Division. To the east was the 16th ***Panzer*** Division; to the west was the 60th Infantry Division (Motorized.)

16th Panzer Division – The division defended in sector, from Hill 139.7 to the Volga and from the Volga southwest to Hill 145.1, north of Orlovka against the 120th Rifle Division, the 84th Rifle Division, the 299th Rifle Division and the 64th Rifle Division. The division also attacked, defeating the 282nd NKVD Rifle Regiment at the State Farm, south of Hill 135.4. To the west was the 60th Infantry Division (Motorized.)

60th Infantry Division (Motorized) – The division defended in sector, from south of Kotluban' Station near Borodkin to Kuz'michi against the 41st Guards Rifle Division, the 221st Rifle Division and the 116th Rifle Division. To the west was the 113th Infantry Division; to the east was the 3rd Infantry Division (Motorized.)

94th Infantry Division – The division attempted to attack across the Mechetka River, but was repelled by the 112th Rifle Division and the 308th Rifle Division. To the north was Battle Group Stahel; to the south was the 389th Infantry Division.

Battle Group Stahel – The battle group prepared for future combat operations. To the northeast was the 16th ***Panzer*** Division; to the south was the 94th Infantry Division.

XVII Corps

79th Infantry Division – One-third of the division defended in sector south of the Don River with the 376th Infantry Division. To the east was the 44th Infantry Division; to the west was the Romanian V Corps of the Romanian Third Army. The rest of the division occupied an assembly area at Vlassoff.

XXXXVIII *Panzer* Corps

29th Infantry Division (Motorized) – The division occupied an assembly area west of Zybenko and Varvarovka, along the Volga-Don Canal, to prepare for future operations.

71st Infantry Division – The division made only small gains in its attack zone against the 13th Guards Rifle Division. To the north was

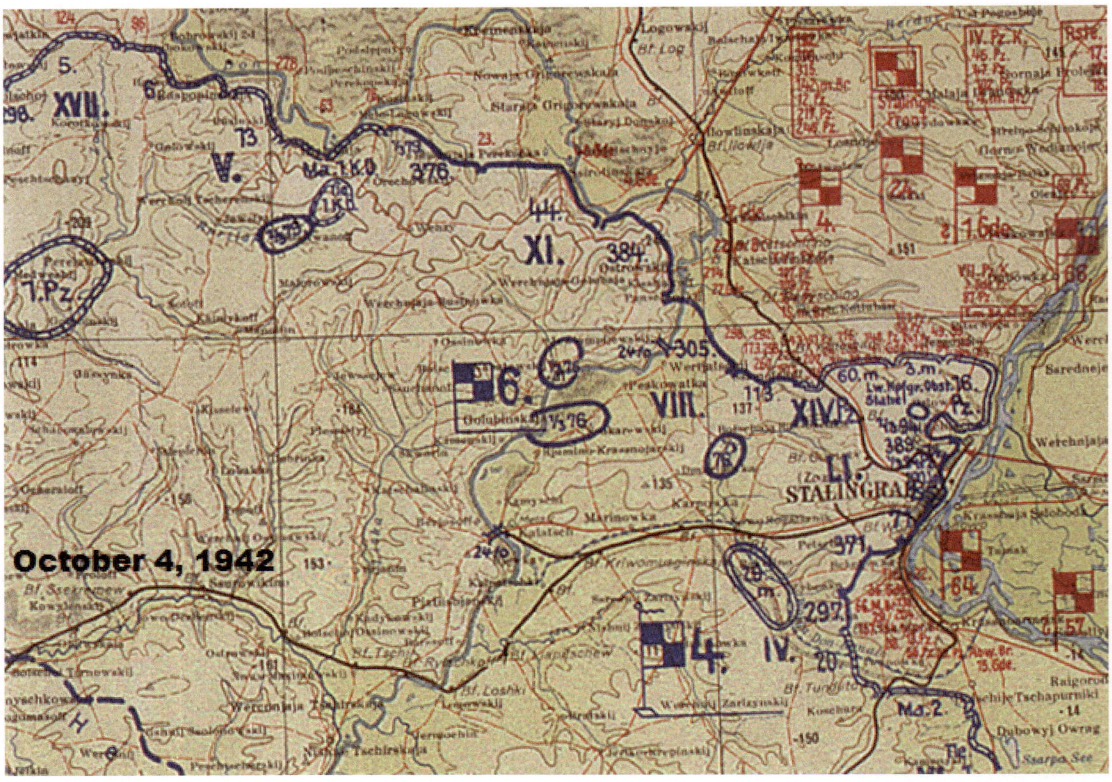

the 295th Infantry Division; to the south was the 371st Infantry Division.

LI Corps – The corps headquarters was located at Gumrak. The corps suffered the following officer casualties: four killed in action; seven wounded in action.

24th Panzer Division – The division attacked against the 112th Rifle Division and the 308th Rifle Division, attacking north and seizing the Schnellhefter Block and the neighboring Sports Ground (Stadium) as well as Mytischchi Street, Aviatornaia Street and Petrozavodskaia Street. The division lost 27 NCOs/enlisted killed in action; one officer and 66 NCOs/enlisted were wounded in action. The division reported that six heavy and 35 medium anti-tank guns were operational. Combat strength in the 21st ***Panzer*** Grenadier Regiment dropped to 265, while the combat strength of the 26th ***Panzer*** Regiment fell to 319. The combat strength of the division's 40th ***Panzer*** Combat Engineer Battalion stood at just 40 men. To the north was the 389th Infantry Division; to the south was the 100th ***Jäger*** Division.

100th Jäger Division – The division made only small gains in its attack zone, against the 193rd Rifle Division and the 39th Guards Rifle Division. To the north was the 24th ***Panzer*** Division; to the south was the 295th Infantry Division. The division reported that six heavy and 11 medium anti-tank guns were operational. The division suffered eight NCOs/enlisted killed in action; 36 NCOs/enlisted were wounded in action. The division also reported that in the attached 245th ***Sturmgeschütz*** Detachment, nine Mark III-Long and four Mark III-Short assault guns were operational, but did not have any ammunition.

295th Infantry Division – The division made only small gains in its attack zone against the 95th Rifle Division and the 284th Rifle Division. The division lost one NCO/enlisted killed in action; 13 NCOs/enlisted were wounded in action. The division reported that ten heavy and five medium anti-tank guns were operational. To the north was the 100th ***Jäger*** Division; to the south was the 71st Infantry Division.

389th Infantry Division – The division attacked northeast and seized what was called "the Burg," as well as Shchelkovskaia Street and the upper portion of the Dzerzhinsky Tractor Factory Workers' Settlement, crushing the 112th Rifle Division and engaging the 37th Guards Rifle Division. To the north was the 94th Infantry Division; to the south was the 24th ***Panzer*** Division. The division suffered two officers and ten NCOs/enlisted killed in action; 20 NCOs/enlisted were wounded in action. The division reported that eight heavy and 13 medium anti-tank guns were operational. The division also reported that in the attached 244th ***Sturmgeschütz*** Detachment, three Mark III-Long and four Mark III-Short assault guns were operational, but ammunition was low.

Sixth Army Reserve

76th Infantry Division – The division conducted rest and refit operations at three assembly areas north of Kalach at Bol'shenabatovskiy. The division reported one regiment at Baburkin, one at Malyj and one at Golubinskaya. The division reported that 11 heavy and four medium anti-tank guns were operational.

Fourth *Panzer* Army – The army headquarters was located east of Verkhne-Zaryzinskij.

IV Corps

297th Infantry Division – The division defended in sector east of Elkhi and Iagodniki, against the 66th Marine Infantry Brigade. To the north was the 371st Infantry Division; to the south was the 20th Romanian Infantry Division.

371st Infantry Division – The division defended in sector, repelling several enemy attacks against the 36th Guards Rifle Division. The division lost one NCO/enlisted killed in action; one officer and 15 NCOs/enlisted were wounded in action. To the north was the 71st Infantry Division; to the south was the 297th Infantry Division.

20th Romanian Infantry Division – The division defended in sector, west of the Tundutovo Rail Station and east of Andreevka, against the 38th Rifle Division. To the north was the 297th Infantry Division; to the south was the 2nd Romanian Infantry Division.

Fourth *Panzer* Army Reserve

14th Panzer Division – The division conducted combat operations in sector south of Sadovia against the 155th Tank Brigade, the 91st Rifle Division and the 254th Tank Brigade. The division lost one officer and two NCOs/enlisted killed in action; one officer and four NCOs/enlisted were wounded in action.

Christliches Andenken
an unseren unvergeßlichen Sohn und Bruder

Johann Schilcher

Gefreiter in einem Gebirgsjäger=Reg.

Inhaber des E. K. 2. Klasse und
des Infanterie=Sturmabzeichens

Schilchersohn in Gobrechtsham,
Pfarre Neuhofen

welcher am 2. Oktober 1942 an der Ostfront bei Stalingrad verwundet wurde und am 4. Oktober 1942 im 22. Lebensjahre den Heldentod gestorben ist.

Vater, Geschwister und Freunde mein!
So gern schrieb ich aus der Ferne heim,
Doch heut ist's zum letztenmal,
Daß ich Euch grüße tausendmal
Und sage Dank für jede Gab',
Die ich von Euch empfangen hab'.
Richte an Euch die letzte Bitt',
Vergeßt ja im Gebet mich nicht.
Nur keine Träne, keine Klag',
Der liebe Gott, der mir das Leben gab,
Rief mich so früh ins Heldengrab.
Auf meiner Brust sah man das Zeichen glänzen,
Das nur von Ruhm und Heldentaten spricht,
Und ich werde in des Himmels Auen
Im Lorbeerkranz Euch wiederschauen.

4380—42

Gefreiter **Johann Schilcher** was born on July 4, 1921 at Gobrechtsham, near Neuhofen, in Upper Austria. The winner of the Iron Cross 2nd Class, the Infantry Assault Badge and the Black Wound Badge, he was assigned to the 100th ***Jäger*** Division where he was seriously wounded at Stalingrad on October 2, 1942. He died of his wounds two days later on October 4, 1942.

Sources, October 4, 1942: ***Oberkommando des Heeres, Lage Ost: Stand: 4.10.42, Eastern Front Situation Map, National Archives Identifier: 559733, Record Group 242 – National Archives Collection of Foreign Records Seized, 1675-1958, National Archives, College Park, Maryland; Ia, Armeeoberkommando 6, "Morgen Meldung" and assorted reports, Kriegstagebuch 13, 5 October 1942, as found in Microfilm Series, T-312, Records of German Field Commands, Armies, Roll 1686, National Archives and Records Service, College Park, Maryland; Ia, XXXXVIII Panzerkorps, "Übersicht über die dem Korps Unterstellten Divisionen, 28. Juni 1942 – 11 October 1942," as found on T-314, Records of German Field Commands, Corps, Roll 1153, National Archives, College Park, Maryland; Korpsarzt, XXXXVIII Panzerkorps, "Meldung über Personelle Verluste," Stand 4.10.42, as found on T-314, Records of German Field Commands, Corps, Roll 1158, National Archives, College Park, Maryland; 371st Infantry Division, Kriegstagebuch, 4 October 1942, as found in Microfilm Series T-315, Roll 2164, National Archives and Records Service, College Park, Maryland; Florian Freiherr von und zu Aufsess, Die Anlagenbände zu den Kriegstagebüchern der 6. Armee vom 14.09.1942 bis 24.11.1942, Band 1, Schwabach, Germany: Selbstverlag, 2006, 116-124; David M. Glantz & Jonathan M. House, Armageddon in Stalingrad: September-November 1942, (The Stalingrad Trilogy, Volume 2), Lawrence, Kansas: University Press of Kansas, 2009, 327-333; Jason Mark, Death of the Leaping Horseman: 24. Panzer-Division in Stalingrad, Sydney, Australia: Leaping Horsemen Books, 2003, 250-259; Janusz Piekalkiewicz, Stalingrad: Anatomie einer Schlacht, München, BRD: Wilhelm Heyne Verlag, 1977, 299; Anton Schimak, Karl Lamprecht & Friedrich Dettmer, Die 44. Infanterie Division: Tagebuch der Hoch- und Deutschmeister, Wien: Verlag Austria Press, 169, 233 and Map: Marschweg der 44. Infanterie Division im Russland.***

October 5, 1942
Weather: generally sunny and bright, occasionally overcast, strong winds, 66° F, later cooling
Sunrise: 6:06 a.m.; **Sunset:** 5:34 p.m.
Moon: Waning Crescent; 22% illumination

Sixth Army – Bombers and dive-bombers from the ***Luftwaffe***'s VIII Air Corps pounded enemy positions in front of the 389th Infantry Division. The army headquarters was located at Golubinskaya.

VIII Corps – The corps headquarters was located at Peskovatka. The 36th Artillery Observation Detachment was assigned to the corps. The corps suffered the following officer casualties: two wounded in action; one accidental death. Eight NCOs/enlisted were killed in action; 47 NCOs/enlisted were wounded in action.

113th Infantry Division – The division defended in sector southwest of Samofalovka and north of Borodkin, against the 298th Rifle Division, the 258th Rifle Division, the 173rd Rifle Division, the 207th Rifle Division, the 292nd Rifle Division, the 221st Rifle Division and the 24th Rifle Division. To the west was the 305th Infantry Division; to the east was the 60th Infantry Division (Motorized.)

305th Infantry Division – The division defended in sector from the Don River, north of Nizhne-Gnilovskii, to west of Kotluban', against the 173rd Rifle Division and the 298th Rifle Division. To the east was the 113th Infantry Division; to the west was the 384th Infantry Division.

XI Corps

44th Infantry Division – The division defended in sector Kurchajessowskij-Kamyshinskiy-Hill 171.0-Hill 180.9-Sirotinskaya-Khmelevskoy, against the 40th Guards Rifle Division and the 4th Guards Rifle Division. The division headquarters was located at Verkhne-Golubaja. To the west was 376th Infantry Division; to the east was the 384th Infantry Division. The division lost two NCOs/enlisted killed in action; 15 NCOs/enlisted were wounded in action.

376th Infantry Division – The division, with an attached infantry regiment from the 79th Infantry Division, defended in sector near Blizhniaia-Perekopka, against the 23rd Rifle Division, losing ground at Hill 178, but repelling an attack at Hill 115.2. To the east was the 44th Infantry Division; to the west was the 1st Romanian Cavalry Division. The division lost 12 NCOs/enlisted killed in action; two NCOs/enlisted were wounded in action; 25 men were reported missing in action.

384th Infantry Division – The division defended in sector west of the Don River near Trekhostrovskaia to Podgorskii, against the 214th Rifle Division, the 37th Guards Rifle Division and the 27th Guards Rifle Division. To the west was the 44th Infantry Division; to the southeast was the 305th Infantry Division.

XIV *Panzer* Corps – The corps headquarters was located east of Ssadtschi-Kowa. The corps suffered the following officer casualties: three wounded in action; one missing in action. The 651st Pioneer Battalion and the 25th Artillery Observation Detachment were assigned to the corps.

3rd Infantry Division (Motorized) – The division defended in sector, from the Tartar Hill-Hill 111.1-Hill 129.6-Hill 131.2, against the 299th Rifle Division, the 38th Guards Rifle Division and the 343rd Rifle Division. To the east was the 16th ***Panzer*** Division; to the west was the 60th Infantry Division (Motorized.) The division reported that of its five motorized infantry battalions, three were average and two were weak in combat power; the division rated its combat engineer battalion as exhausted.

16th Panzer Division – The division defended in sector, from Hill 139.7 to the Volga and from the Volga southwest to Hill 145.1, north of Orlovka, against the 120th Rifle Division, the 84th Rifle Division, the 299th Rifle Division and the 64th Rifle Division. The division reported that of its five *panzer* grenadier battalions, three were medium-strong, one was average and one was weak in combat power; the division rated its combat engineer battalion as average.

60th Infantry Division (Motorized) – The division defended in sector, from south of Kotluban' Station near Borodkin to Kuz'michi against the 231st Rifle Division, the 49th Rifle Division, the 233rd Rifle Division and the 316th Rifle Division. To the west was the 113th Infantry Division; to the east was the 3rd Infantry Division (Motorized.) The division reported that of its seven motorized infantry battalions, four were average, two were weak and one was exhausted in combat power; the division rated its combat engineer battalion as exhausted.

94th Infantry Division – The division prepared for future combat operations opposite the 112th Rifle Division. To the south was the 389th Infantry Division; to the north was Battle Group Stahel. The division reported that of its seven infantry battalions, all seven were exhausted in combat power; the division rated its combat engineer battalion as average. The infantry strength of the division was only 535 soldiers.

Battle Group Stahel – The battle group prepared for future combat operations.

XVII Corps

79th Infantry Division – One-third of the division defended in sector south of the Don River. To the east was the 44th Infantry Division; to the west was the Romanian V Corps of the Romanian Third Army. The rest of the division occupied an assembly area at Vlassoff.

XXXXVIII *Panzer* Corps

29th Infantry Division (Motorized) – The division occupied an assembly area west of Zybenko and Varvarovka, along the Volga-Don Canal, to prepare for future operations.

71st Infantry Division – The division conducted limited offensive operations in zone against the 13th Guards Rifle Division. To the north was the 295th Infantry Division; to the south was the 371st Infantry Division.

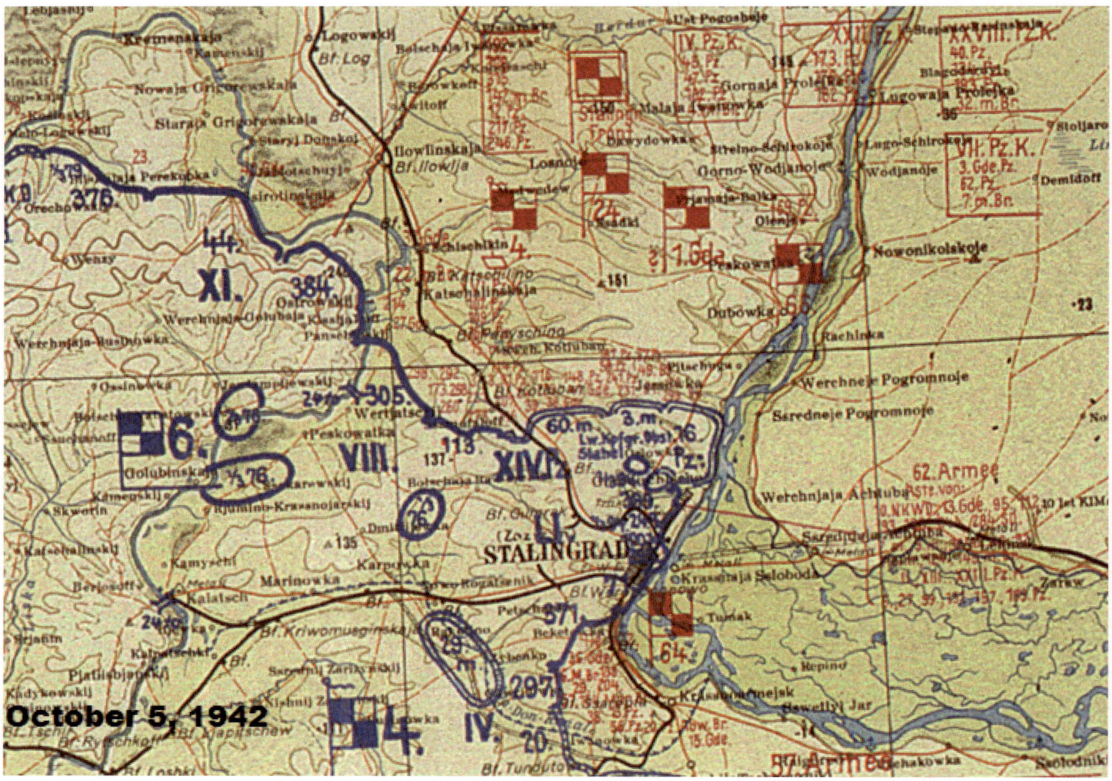

LI Corps – The corps headquarters was located at Gumrak. The 29th Artillery Observation Detachment, the 40th Artillery Observation Detachment and the 851st Heavy Artillery Detachment were assigned to support the corps. The corps suffered the following officer casualties: five killed in action; six wounded in action.

24th Panzer Division – The division switched to defensive operations at the northern part of the Barrikady Gun Factory Workers' Settlement, against the 308th Rifle Division, in preparation for future attacks; it also received heavy enemy artillery fire during the day. The division suffered one officer and 16 NCOs/enlisted killed in action; 47 NCOs/enlisted were wounded in action. To the north was the 389th Infantry Division; to the south was the 100th ***Jäger*** Division. The division reported that of its four ***panzer*** grenadier battalions, one was weak and three were exhausted in combat power; the division rated its combat engineer battalion as average. The division reported the following ***panzer***s as operational: two Mark II, five Mark III-Short, 16 Mark III-Long, three Mark IV-Short and four Mark IV-Long tanks.

100th Jäger Division – The division conducted limited offensive operations in zone. To the north was the 24th ***Panzer*** Division; to the south was the 295th Infantry Division. The division reported that of its five ***jäger*** battalions, four were average and one was weak in combat power; the division rated its combat engineer battalion as weak. The division reported five heavy and 11 medium anti-tank guns as operational. The division lost one officer and ten NCOs/enlisted killed in action; 29 NCOs/enlisted were wounded in action.

295th Infantry Division – The division conducted limited offensive operations in zone against the 95th Rifle Division. To the north was the 100th ***Jäger*** Division; to the south was the 71st Infantry Division. The division reported that of its seven infantry battalions, four were weak and three were exhausted in combat power; the division rated its combat engineer battalion as weak. The division lost one NCO/enlisted killed in action; seven NCOs/enlisted were wounded in action.

389th Infantry Division – The division conducted operations to straighten its front line in the vicinity of Hill 97.7, in and south of the Dzerzhinsky Tractor Factory Workers' Settlement against the 37th Guards Rifle Division and the 112th Rifle Division; it also received heavy enemy artillery fire during the day. To the north was the 94th Infantry Division; to the south was the 24th ***Panzer*** Division. The division reported that of its six infantry battalions, all six were weak in combat power; the division rated its combat engineer battalion as exhausted.

Sixth Army Reserve

76th Infantry Division – The division conducted rest and refit operations at three assembly areas north of Kalach at Bol'shenabatovskiy. The division reported one regiment at Baburkin, one at Malyj and one at Golubinskaya.

Fourth *Panzer* Army – The army headquarters was located east of Verkhne-Zaryzinskij.

IV Corps

297th Infantry Division – The division defended in sector east of Elkhi and Iagodniki, against the 29th Rifle Division and the 106th Rifle Division. To the north was the 371st Infantry Division; to the south was the 20th Romanian Infantry Division.

371st Infantry Division – The division defended in sector, from Kuporosnoye in the east to northwest of Gornaia Poliana, against the 35th Guards Rifle Division. To the north was the 71st Infantry Division; to the south was the 297th Infantry Division.

20th Romanian Infantry Division – The division defended in sector, west of the Tundutovo Rail Station and east of Andreevka, against the 57th Rifle Division. To the north was the 297th Infantry Division; to the south was the 2nd Romanian Infantry Division of the Romanian VI Corps.

Fourth *Panzer* Army Reserve

14th Panzer Division – The division attacked the 91st Rifle Division, the 254th Tank Brigade and the 302nd Rifle Division near Sadovia. The division lost one NCO/enlisted killed in action.

Andenken
an meinen lieben Sohn,
unseren guten Bruder
Josef Kratzer
Schütze in einem Infanterie-Regt.
geb. 2. Febr. 1922 in Reatshofen
gefallen 5. Okt. 1942 nordwestl. Stalingrad,
begraben auf d. Heldenfriedhof Mal Rossoschka

In Rußland liegt ein stiller Hügel
All unser Sehnen, Hoffen schließt
er ein,
Wenn uns die Liebe liehe Flügel
Nie, guter Sohn und Bruder,
Würdest Du dort einsam sein.

Bet' auch Du für mich,
Ich starb ja auch für Dich.

Schütze **Josef Kratzer** was born in Reatshofen near Dillingen an der Donau in Bavaria on February 2, 1922. Assigned to an infantry regiment in the 113th Infantry Division, he was killed in action three miles north of Malaia Rossoschka on October 5, 1942.

Sources, October 5, 1942: ***Oberkommando des Heeres, Lage Ost: Stand: 5.10.42, Eastern Front Situation Map, National Archives Identifier: 559733, Record Group 242 – National Archives Collection of Foreign Records Seized, 1675-1958, National Archives, College Park, Maryland; Ia, Armeeoberkommando 6, "Morgen Meldung" and assorted reports, Kriegstagebuch 14, 6 October 1942, as found in Microfilm Series, T-312, Records of German Field Commands, Armies, Roll 1453 and 1688, National Archives and Records Service, College Park, Maryland; Ia, XXXXVIII Panzerkorps, "Übersicht über die dem Korps Unterstellten Divisionen, 28. Juni 1942 – 11 October 1942," as found on T-314, Records of German Field Commands, Corps, Roll 1153, National Archives, College Park, Maryland; Korpsarzt, XXXXVIII Panzerkorps, "Meldung über Personelle Verluste," Stand 5.10.42, as found on T-314, Records of German Field Commands, Corps, Roll 1158, National Archives, College Park, Maryland; 371st Infantry Division, Kriegstagebuch, 5 October 1942, as found in Microfilm Series T-315, Roll 2164, National Archives and Records Service, College Park, Maryland; Florian Freiherr von und zu Aufsess, Die Anlagenbände zu den Kriegstagebüchern der 6. Armee vom 14.09.1942 bis 24.11.1942, Band 1, Schwabach, Germany: Selbstverlag, 2006, 124-134; David M. Glantz & Jonathan M. House, Armageddon in Stalingrad: September-November 1942, (The Stalingrad Trilogy, Volume 2), Lawrence, Kansas: University Press of Kansas, 2009, 334-336, 358, 369; Manfred Kehrig, Stalingrad: Analyse und Dokumentation einer Schlacht, Stuttgart, FRG: Deutsche Verlags-Anstalt, 1976, 37; Jason Mark, Death of the Leaping Horseman: 24. Panzer-Division in Stalingrad, Sydney, Australia: Leaping Horsemen Books, 2003, 261-263; Anton Schimak, Karl Lamprecht & Friedrich Dettmer, Die 44. Infanterie Division: Tagebuch der Hoch- und Deutschmeister, Wien: Verlag Austria Press, 169, 233 and Map: Marschweg der 44. Infanterie Division im Russland.***

October 6, 1942
Weather: sunny, bright, slight warming after noon, 66° F
Sunrise: 6:07 a.m.; **Sunset:** 5:32 p.m.
Moon: Waning Crescent; 15% illumination

Sixth Army – The Sixth Army reported: "The army's attack into Stalingrad had to be temporarily suspended because of the exceptionally low infantry combat strengths." Bombers and dive-bombers from the ***Luftwaffe***'s VIII Air Corps pounded enemy positions in the Dzerzhinsky Tractor Factory Workers' Settlement. The army headquarters was located at Golubinskaya.

VIII Corps – The corps headquarters was located at Peskovatka.

113th Infantry Division – The division defended in sector southwest of Samofalovka and north of Borodkin, against the 298th Rifle Division, the 258th Rifle Division, the 173rd Rifle Division, the 207th Rifle Division, the 292nd Rifle Division, the 221st Rifle Division and the 24th Rifle Division. To the west was the 305th Infantry Division; to the east was the 60th Infantry Division (Motorized.) The division lost nine NCOs/enlisted killed in action; 11 NCOs/enlisted were wounded in action.

305th Infantry Division – The division defended in sector from the Don River, north of Nizhne-Gnilovskii, to west of Kotluban', against the 298th Rifle Division and the 173rd Rifle Division. To the east was the 113th Infantry Division; to the northwest was the 384th Infantry Division. The division lost two NCOs/enlisted killed in action; five NCOs/enlisted were wounded in action.

XI Corps

44th Infantry Division – The division defended in sector Kurchajessowskij-Kamyshinskiy-Hill 171.0-Hill 180.9-Sirotinskaya-Khmelevskoy, against the 40th Guards Rifle Division and the 23rd Rifle Division. The division headquarters was located at Verkhne-Golubaja. To the west was 376th Infantry Division; to the east was the 384th Infantry Division. The division lost one NCO/enlisted killed in action; seven NCOs/enlisted were wounded in action.

376th Infantry Division – The division, reinforced with an infantry regiment from the 79th Infantry Division, defended in sector near Blizhniaia-Perekopka against the 23rd Rifle Division and the 331st Rifle Division. To the east was the 44th Infantry Division; to the west was the 1st Romanian Cavalry Division. The division lost four NCOs/enlisted killed in action; 35 NCOs/enlisted were wounded in action.

384th Infantry Division – The division defended in sector west of the Don River near Trekhostrovskaia to Podgorskii, against the 4th Guards Rifle Division, 37th Guards Rifle Division, 214th Rifle Division and the 27th Guards Rifle Division. To the northwest was the 44th Infantry Division; to the southeast was the 305th Infantry Division. The division lost one NCO/enlisted killed in action.

XIV *Panzer* Corps – The corps headquarters was located east of Ssadtschi-Kowa. The 177th ***Sturmgeschütz*** Detachment was assigned to the corps. The corps suffered the following officer casualties: three wounded in action.

3rd Infantry Division (Motorized) – The division defended in sector, from the Tartar Hill-Hill 111.1-Hill 129.6-Hill 131.2 against the 299th Rifle Division, the 38th Guards Rifle Division and the 343rd Rifle Division. To the east was the 16th ***Panzer*** Division; to the west was the 60th Infantry Division (Motorized.) The division lost six NCOs/enlisted killed in action; 30 NCOs/enlisted were wounded in action; five men were reported missing in action.

16th Panzer Division – The division defended in sector, from Hill 139.7 to the Volga and from the Volga southwest to Hill 145.1, north of Orlovka against the 120th Rifle Division, the 84th Rifle Division, the 299th Rifle Division and the 64th Rifle Division. To the west was the 3rd Infantry Division

(Motorized); to the southwest was the 94th Infantry Division. The division lost nine NCOs/enlisted killed in action; 32 NCOs/enlisted were wounded in action; one man was reported missing in action.

60th Infantry Division (Motorized) – The division defended in sector, from south of Kotluban' Station near Borodkin to Kuz'michi against the 231st Rifle Division, the 49th Rifle Division, the 233rd Rifle Division and the 316th Rifle Division. To the west was the 113th Infantry Division; to the east was the 3rd Infantry Division (Motorized.) The division lost five NCOs/enlisted killed in action; 15 NCOs/enlisted were wounded in action.

94th Infantry Division – The division prepared for future operations opposite the 112th Rifle Division. To the south was the 389th Infantry Division; to the northeast was the 16th *Panzer* Division. The division lost two NCOs/enlisted killed in action; four NCOs/enlisted were wounded in action.

Battle Group Stahel – The battle group occupied an assembly area and prepared for future operations.

XVII Corps

79th Infantry Division – One-third of the division defended in sector south of the Don River. To the east was the 376th Infantry Division; to the west was the Romanian V Corps of the Romanian Third Army. The rest of the division occupied an assembly area at Vlassoff.

XXXXVIII *Panzer* Corps

29th Infantry Division (Motorized) – The division occupied an assembly area west of Zybenko and Varvarovka, along the Volga-Don Canal, to prepare for future operations.

71st Infantry Division – The division defended in sector against the 13th Guards Rifle Division. To the north was the 295th Infantry Division; to the south was the 371st Infantry Division.

LI Corps – The corps headquarters was located at Gumrak. The corps suffered the following officer casualties: one killed in action; three wounded in action.

24th Panzer Division – The division defended at the northern part of the Barrikady Gun Factory Workers' Settlement in preparation for future attacks opposite the 308th Rifle Division; enemy artillery and rocket fire struck the front line the entire day. The division suffered nine NCOs/enlisted killed in action; one officer and 42 NCOs/enlisted were wounded in action. To the north was the 389th

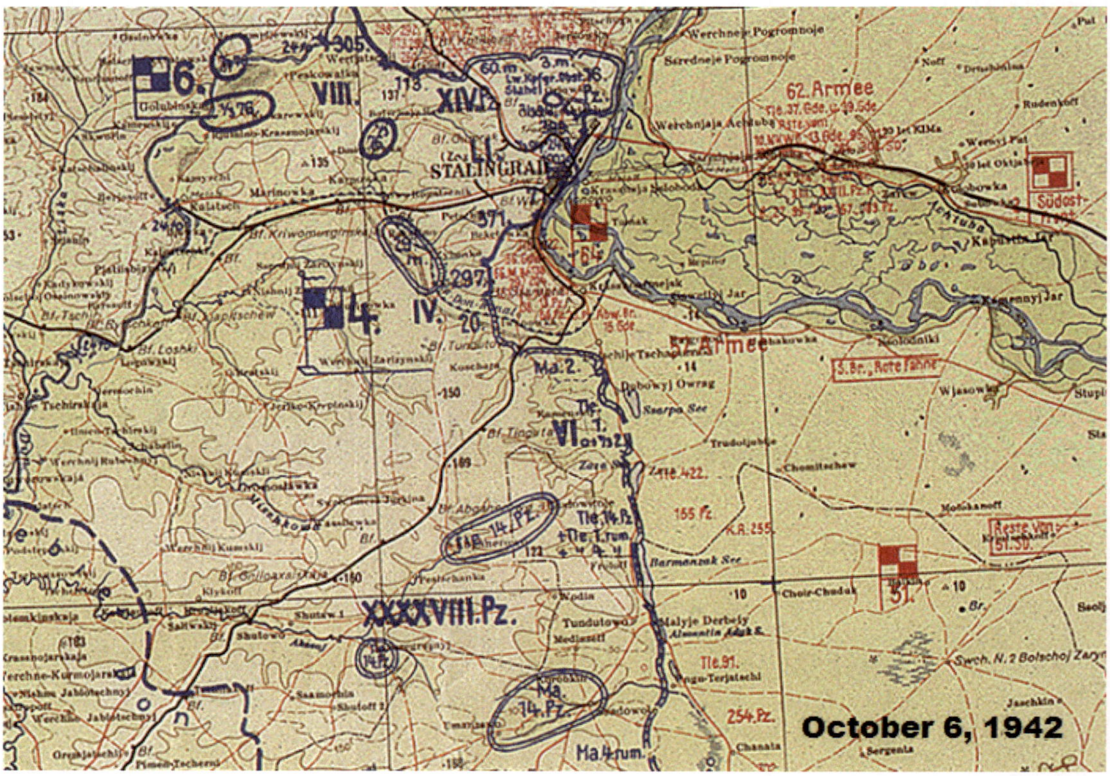

Infantry Division; to the south was the 100th ***Jäger*** Division.

100th Jäger Division – The division defended in sector. To the north was the 24th ***Panzer*** Division; to the south was the 295th Infantry Division. The division lost three NCOs/enlisted killed in action; two officers and 42 NCOs/enlisted were wounded in action.

295th Infantry Division – The division defended in sector against the 284th Rifle Division. To the north was the 100th ***Jäger*** Division; to the south was the 71st Infantry Division.

389th Infantry Division – The division defended in sector against the 37th Guards Rifle Division and the 112th Rifle Division in preparation for future attacks. To the north was the 94th Infantry Division; to the south was the 24th ***Panzer*** Division. The division lost three NCOs/enlisted killed in action; 16 NCOs/enlisted were wounded in action.

Sixth Army Reserve

76th Infantry Division – The division conducted rest and refit operations at three assembly areas north of Kalach at Bol'shenabatovskiy. The division reported one regiment at Baburkin, one at Malyj and one at Golubinskaya.

Fourth *Panzer* Army – The army headquarters was located east of Verkhne-Zaryzinskij.

IV Corps

297th Infantry Division – The division defended in sector east of Elkhi and Iagodniki. To the north was the 371st Infantry Division; to the south was the 20th Romanian Infantry Division.

371st Infantry Division – The division defended in sector from Kuporosnoye in the east to northwest of Gornaia Poliana. The division lost four NCOs/enlisted killed in action; 36 NCOs/enlisted were wounded in action. To the north was the 71st Infantry Division; to the south was the 297th Infantry Division.

20th Romanian Infantry Division – The division defended in sector, west of the Tundutovo Rail Station and east of Andreevka, against the 38th Rifle Division. To the north was the 297th Infantry Division; to the south was the 2nd Romanian Infantry Division of the Romanian VI Corps.

Fourth *Panzer* Army Reserve

14th Panzer Division – The division occupied assembly areas near Sadovia and Abganerovo.

Enlisted soldier on horseback from the 79th Infantry Division. Photo was taken outside of Stalingrad in the fall or early winter of 1942. The division was authorized 4,854 horses.

Sources, October 6, 1942: ***Oberkommando des Heeres, Lage Ost: Stand: 6.10.42, Eastern Front Situation Map, National Archives Identifier: 559733, Record Group 242 – National Archives Collection of Foreign Records Seized, 1675-1958, National Archives, College Park, Maryland; Ia, Armeeoberkommando 6, "Morgen Meldung" and assorted reports, Kriegstagebuch 14, 7 October 1942, as found in Microfilm Series, T-312, Records of German Field Commands, Armies, Roll 1453 and 1688 and 1688, National Archives and Records Service, College Park, Maryland; Korpsarzt, XXXXVIII Panzerkorps, "Meldung über Personelle Verluste," Stand 6.10.42, as found on T-314, Records of German Field Commands, Corps, Roll 1158, National Archives, College Park, Maryland; 371st Infantry Division, Kriegstagebuch, 6 October 1942, as found in Microfilm Series T-315, Roll 2164, National Archives and Records Service, College Park, Maryland; Florian Freiherr von und zu Aufsess, Die Anlagenbände zu den Kriegstagebüchern der 6. Armee vom 14.09.1942 bis 24.11.1942, Band 1, Schwabach, Germany: Selbstverlag, 2006, 132-136; David M. Glantz & Jonathan M. House, Armageddon in Stalingrad: September-November 1942, (The Stalingrad Trilogy, Volume 2), Lawrence, Kansas: University Press of Kansas, 2009, 337-339, 370; Jason Mark, Death of the Leaping Horseman: 24. Panzer-Division in Stalingrad, Sydney, Australia: Leaping Horsemen Books, 2003, 263-264; Anton Schimak, Karl Lamprecht & Friedrich Dettmer, Die 44. Infanterie Division: Tagebuch der Hoch- und Deutschmeister, Wien: Verlag Austria Press, 169, 233 and Map: Marschweg der 44. Infanterie Division im Russland.***

October 7, 1942

Weather: clear, hazy after noon, 66° F, powerful west winds, good road conditions
Sunrise: 6:09 a.m.; **Sunset:** 5:30 p.m.
Moon: Waning Crescent; 8% illumination

Sixth Army – The army headquarters was located at Golubinskaya. ***General der Panzertruppe*** Paulus visited the LI Corps, the XIV ***Panzer*** Corps and the 389th Infantry Division.

VIII Corps – The corps headquarters was located at Peskovatka.

113th Infantry Division – The division defended in sector southwest of Samofalovka and north of Borodkin, against the 298th Rifle Division, the 258th Rifle Division, the 173rd Rifle Division, the 207th Rifle Division, the 292nd Rifle Division, the 221st Rifle Division and the 24th Rifle Division. To the west was the 305th Infantry Division; to the east was the 60th Infantry Division (Motorized.) The division lost one NCO/enlisted killed in action; nine NCOs/enlisted were wounded in action.

305th Infantry Division – The division defended in sector from the Don River, north of Nizhne-Gnilovskii, to west of Kotluban', against the 27th Guards Rifle Division and the 298th Infantry Division. To the east was the 113th Infantry Division; to the northwest was the 384th Infantry Division. Elements from the 76th Infantry Division moved into sector to begin to assume the defensive sector. The division lost five NCOs/enlisted killed in action; six NCOs/enlisted were wounded in action.

XI Corps – The corps suffered the following officer casualties: one wounded in action.

44th Infantry Division – The division defended in sector Kurchajessowskij-Kamyshinskiy-Hill 171.0-Hill 180.9-Sirotinskaya-Khmelevskoy, against the 40th Guards Rifle Division and the 4th Guards Rifle Division. The division headquarters was located at Verkhne-Golubaja. To the west was 376th Infantry Division; to the east was the 384th Infantry Division. The division lost one NCO/enlisted killed in action; three NCOs/enlisted were wounded in action.

376th Infantry Division – The division defended in sector near Blizhniaia-Perekopka, against the 23rd Rifle Division. To the east was the 44th Infantry Division; to the west was the 1st Romanian Cavalry Division of the Romanian V Corps of the Romanian Third Army. The division lost two NCOs/enlisted wounded in action.

384th Infantry Division – The division defended in sector west of the Don River near Trekhostrovskaia to Podgorskii, against the 4th Guards Rifle Division, the 37th Guards Rifle Division and the 214th Rifle Division. To the west was the 44th Infantry Division; to the southeast was the 305th Infantry Division. The division lost one NCO/enlisted wounded in action.

XIV *Panzer* Corps – The corps headquarters was located east of Ssadtschi-Kowa. The 177th ***Sturmgeschütz*** Detachment was assigned to the corps. The corps suffered the following officer casualties: five wounded in action.

3rd Infantry Division (Motorized) – The division defended in sector, from the Tartar Hill-Hill 111.1-Hill 129.6-Hill 131.2 against the 299th Rifle Division, the 38th Guards Rifle Division and the 343rd Rifle Division. To the east was the 16th ***Panzer*** Division; to the west was the 60th Infantry Division (Motorized.) The division lost nine NCOs/enlisted killed in action; four officers and 22 NCOs/enlisted were wounded in action; two men were reported missing in action.

16th Panzer Division – The division defended in sector, from Hill 139.7 to the Volga and from the Volga southwest to Hill 145.1, north of Orlovka against the 120th Rifle Division, the 84th Rifle Division, the 299th Rifle Division and the 64th Rifle Division. The division lost 31 NCOs/enlisted wounded in action.

60th Infantry Division (Motorized) – The division defended in sector, from south of Kotluban'

Station near Borodkin to Kuz'michi against the 231st Rifle Division, the 49th Rifle Division, the 233rd Rifle Division and the 316th Rifle Division. To the west was the 113th Infantry Division; to the east was the 3rd Infantry Division (Motorized.) The division lost five NCOs/enlisted killed in action; 20 NCOs/enlisted were wounded in action.

94th Infantry Division – The division defended in sector, after the attack across the Mechetka River south of the railroad bridge against the 112th Rifle Division failed. To the south was the 389th Infantry Division; to the northeast was the 16th ***Panzer*** Division. The division lost one NCO/enlisted killed in action; four NCOs/enlisted were wounded in action.

Battle Group Stahel – The battle group occupied an assembly area and prepared for future operations.

XXXXVIII *Panzer* Corps

29th Infantry Division (Motorized) – The division occupied an assembly area west of Zybenko and Varvarovka, along the Volga-Don Canal, to prepare for future operations.

71st Infantry Division – The division defended in sector. To the north was the 295th Infantry Division; to the south was the 371st Infantry Division.

LI Corps – The 244th ***Sturmgeschütz*** Detachment was assigned to the corps. The corps suffered the following officer casualties: two killed in action; two wounded in action. The corps headquarters was located northwest of the Gumrak Rail Station.

24th Panzer Division – The division defended at the northern part of the Barrikady Gun Factory Workers' Settlement against the 308th Rifle Division in preparation for future attacks. Nighttime enemy air attacks struck the division, which also repelled enemy reconnaissance probes. The division suffered 19 NCOs/enlisted killed in action; one officer and 47 NCOs/enlisted were wounded in action. To the north was the 389th Infantry Division; to the south was the 100th ***Jäger*** Division.

100th Jäger Division – The division defended in sector and repelled an enemy counter-attack of regimental-size in sector. The division suffered 11 NCOs/enlisted killed in action; one officer and 51 NCOs/enlisted were wounded in action. To the north was the 24th ***Panzer*** Division; to the south was the 295th Infantry Division.

295th Infantry Division – The division defended in sector against the 284th Rifle Division. The division lost three NCOs/enlisted killed in action; 20 NCOs/enlisted were wounded in action. To the

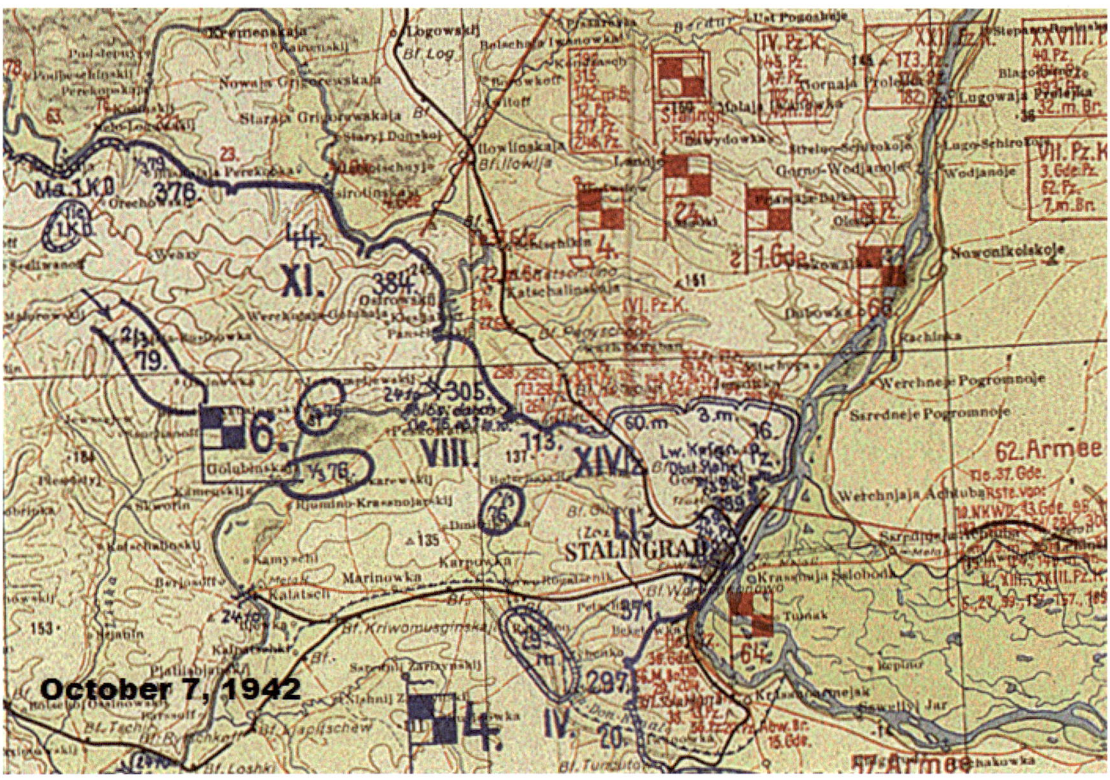

October 7, 1942

north was the 100th ***Jäger*** Division; to the south was the 71st Infantry Division.

389th Infantry Division – The division conducted limited offensive operations in sector against the 37th Guards Rifle Division and the 112th Rifle Division, in preparation for future attacks. With the attached 245th ***Sturmgeschütz*** Detachment, the division seized a block of worker's houses and approached the stadium. To the north was the 94th Infantry Division; to the south was the 24th ***Panzer*** Division. The division lost one officer and 19 NCOs/enlisted killed in action; 45 NCOs/enlisted were wounded in action.

Sixth Army Reserve

76th Infantry Division – The division conducted rest and refit operations at three assembly areas north of Kalach at Bol'shenabatovskiy. The division reported one regiment at Baburkin, one at Malyj and one at Golubinskaya. Advance elements of the division moved into the sector of the 305th Infantry Division to prepare to relieve it.

79th Infantry Division – One-third of the division defended in sector south of the Don River. To the east was the 376th Infantry Division; to the west was the Romanian V Corps of the Romanian Third Army. The rest of the division occupied an assembly area at Verkhne-Businovka.

Fourth *Panzer* Army – The army headquarters was located east of Verkhne-Zaryzinskij.

IV Corps

297th Infantry Division – The division defended in sector east of Elkhi and Iagodniki against the 196th Rifle Division and the 29th Rifle Division. To the north was the 371st Infantry Division; to the south was the 20th Romanian Infantry Division.

371st Infantry Division – The division defended in sector from Kuporosnoye in the east to northwest of Gornaia Poliana against the 36th Guards Rifle Division, the 157th Rifle Division and part of the 422nd Rifle Division. To the north was the 71st Infantry Division; to the south was the 297th Infantry Division. The division lost two NCOs/enlisted killed in action; nine NCOs/enlisted were wounded in action.

20th Romanian Infantry Division – The division defended in sector, west of the Tundutovo Rail Station and east of Andreevka, against the 38th Rifle Division. To the north was the 297th Infantry Division; to the south was the 2nd Romanian Infantry Division of the Romanian VI Corps.

Fourth *Panzer* Army Reserve

14th Panzer Division – The division occupied assembly areas near Sadovia and Abganerovo. The division lost three NCOs/enlisted killed in action; three NCOs/enlisted were wounded in action.

Schütze **Karl Schlicht** was born on November 4, 1911 in Köhlerlohe, near Bayreuth, in Bavaria and was assigned to the 546th Infantry Regiment of the 389th Infantry Division. He was severely wounded on October 7, 1942 in Stalingrad and evacuated to a casualty collection point operated by the 1st Medical Company of the 389th Infantry Division that was located at Gumrak. He died there the same day. His remains are buried in Block 10, Row 19 in Grave 739 at the German Military Cemetery at Rossoschka.

Sources, October 7, 1942: ***Oberkommando des Heeres, Lage Ost: Stand: 7.10.42, Eastern Front Situation Map, National Archives Identifier: 559733, Record Group 242 – National Archives Collection of Foreign Records Seized, 1675-1958, National Archives, College Park, Maryland; Ia, Armeeoberkommando 6, "Morgen Meldung" and assorted reports, Kriegstagebuch 14, 8 October 1942, as found in Microfilm Series, T-312, Records of German Field Commands, Armies, Roll 1453 and 1688 and 1688, National Archives and Records Service, College Park, Maryland; Ia, XXXXVIII Panzerkorps, "Übersicht über die dem Korps Unterstellten Divisionen, 28. Juni 1942 – 11 October 1942," as found on T-314, Records of German Field Commands, Corps, Roll 1153, National Archives, College Park, Maryland; Korpsarzt, XXXXVIII Panzerkorps, "Meldung über Personelle Verluste," Stand 7.10.42, as found on T-314, Records of German Field Commands, Corps, Roll 1158, National Archives, College Park, Maryland; 371st Infantry Division, Kriegstagebuch, 7 October 1942, as found in Microfilm Series T-315, Roll 2164, National Archives and Records Service, College Park, Maryland; Florian Freiherr von und zu Aufsess, Die Anlagenbände zu den Kriegstagebüchern der 6. Armee vom 14.09.1942 bis 24.11.1942, Band 1, Schwabach, Germany: Selbstverlag, 2006, 134-139, 141; David M. Glantz & Jonathan M. House, Armageddon in Stalingrad: September-November 1942, (The Stalingrad Trilogy, Volume 2), Lawrence, Kansas: University Press of Kansas, 2009, 338-340, 351; Jason Mark, Death of the Leaping Horseman: 24. Panzer-Division in Stalingrad, Sydney, Australia: Leaping Horsemen Books, 2003, 264; Hans Neidhardt, Mit Tanne und Eichenlaub: Kriegschronik der 100. Jäger Division vormals 100. leichte Infanterie Division, Graz, Austria: Leopold Stocker Verlag, 1981, 214; Anton Schimak, Karl Lamprecht & Friedrich Dettmer, Die 44. Infanterie Division: Tagebuch der Hoch- und Deutschmeister, Wien: Verlag Austria Press, 169, 233 and Map: Marschweg der 44. Infanterie Division im Russland.***

October 8, 1942
Weather: clear, sunny, hazy after noon, 59° F, good road conditions
Sunrise: 6:10 a.m.; **Sunset:** 5:28 p.m.
Moon: Waning Crescent; 3% illumination

Sixth Army – The army headquarters was located at Golubinskaya. Army Group B, commanded by ***Generaloberst*** Maximilian von Weichs, issued orders to the army to conduct another major offensive against northern Stalingrad to start no later than October 14.

VIII Corps – The aim of the corps was to begin to exchange the 76th Infantry Division for the 305th Infantry Division in sector. The corps headquarters was located at Peskovatka. The corps suffered the following officer casualties: three wounded in action.

113th Infantry Division – The division defended in sector southwest of Samofalovka and north of Borodkin, against the 298th Rifle Division, the 258th Rifle Division, the 173rd Rifle Division, the 207th Rifle Division, the 292nd Rifle Division, the 221st Rifle Division and the 24th Rifle Division. To the west was the 305th Infantry Division; to the east was the 60th Infantry Division (Motorized.) The division lost four NCOs/enlisted killed in action; 12 NCOs/enlisted were wounded in action.

305th Infantry Division – The division defended in sector from the Don River, north of Nizhne-Gnilovskii, to west of Kotluban', against the 298th Rifle Division and the 173rd Rifle Division. To the east was the 113th Infantry Division; to the northwest was the 384th Infantry Division. Elements of the 76th Infantry Division began to relieve parts of the division in sector. The division suffered one NCO/enlisted killed in action; one officer and 16 NCOs/enlisted were wounded in action.

XI Corps

44th Infantry Division – The division defended in sector Kurchajessowskij-Kamyshinskiy-Hill 171.0-Hill 180.9-Sirotinskaya-Khmelevskoy, against the 40th Guards Rifle Division. The division headquarters was located at Verkhne-Golubaja. To the west was 376th Infantry Division; to the east was the 384th Infantry Division. The division lost three NCOs/enlisted wounded in action.

376th Infantry Division – The division, with an attached infantry regiment from the 79th Infantry Division, defended in sector near Blizhniaia-Perekopka against the 23rd Rifle Division. The division repelled an enemy attack launched at 4:00 a.m. To the east was the 44th Infantry Division; to the west was the 1st Romanian Cavalry Division. The division lost six NCOs/enlisted killed in action; two officers and 36 NCOs/enlisted were wounded in action.

384th Infantry Division – The division defended in sector southwest of the Don River near Trekhostrovskaia to Podgorskii, against the 214th Rifle Division, the 37th Guards Rifle Division and the 4th Guards Rifle Division. To the west was the 44th Infantry Division; to the southeast was the 305th Infantry Division. The division lost one NCO/enlisted killed in action and one NCO/enlisted wounded in action.

XIV *Panzer* Corps – The corps headquarters was located east of Ssadtschi-Kowa. The corps suffered the following officer casualties: one killed in action; two wounded in action; and one missing in action.

3rd Infantry Division (Motorized) – The division defended in sector, from the Tartar Hill-Hill 111.1-Hill 129.6-Hill 131.2 against the 299th Rifle Division, the 38th Guards Rifle Division and the 343rd Rifle Division. To the east was the 16th ***Panzer*** Division; to the west was the 60th Infantry Division (Motorized.) The division lost one NCO/enlisted killed in action; one officer and 15 NCOs/enlisted were wounded in action.

16th Panzer Division – The division defended in sector, from Hill 139.7 to the Volga

and from the Volga southwest to Hill 145.1, north of Orlovka against the 120th Rifle Division, the 84th Rifle Division, the 299th Rifle Division and the 64th Rifle Division. To the west was the 3rd Infantry Division (Motorized); to the southwest was the 94th Infantry Division. The division suffered one officer killed in action; one officer and 19 NCOs/enlisted men were wounded in action.

60th Infantry Division (Motorized) – The division defended in sector, from south of Kotluban' Station near Borodkin to Kuz'michi against the 231st Rifle Division, the 49th Rifle Division, the 233rd Rifle Division and the 316th Rifle Division. To the west was the 113th Infantry Division; to the east was the 3rd Infantry Division (Motorized.) The division lost five NCOs/enlisted killed in action; 20 NCOs/enlisted were wounded in action.

94th Infantry Division – The division prepared for future offensive operations. To the south was the 389th Infantry Division; to the northwest was the 16th ***Panzer*** Division. The division lost two NCOs/enlisted wounded in action.

Battle Group Stahel – The battle group occupied an assembly area and prepared for future operations.

XXXXVIII *Panzer* Corps

29th Infantry Division (Motorized) – The division occupied an assembly area west of Zybenko and Varvarovka, along the Volga-Don Canal, to prepare for future operations. The division lost one NCO/enlisted killed in action and one NCO/enlisted wounded in action.

71st Infantry Division – The division defended in sector. To the north was the 295th Infantry Division; to the south was the 371st Infantry Division. ***Generalleutnant*** Alexander von Hartmann was awarded the Knight's Cross.

LI Corps – The corps headquarters was located at Gumrak. The 2nd ***Werfer*** Regiment was assigned to support the corps. The corps suffered the following officer casualties: two killed in action; five wounded in action.

24th Panzer Division – The division defended at the northern part of the Barrikady Gun Factory Workers' Settlement against the 37th Guards Rifle Division. The division suffered seven NCOs/enlisted killed in action; two officers and 23 NCOs/enlisted were wounded in action; one of the wounded died later that day. To the north was the

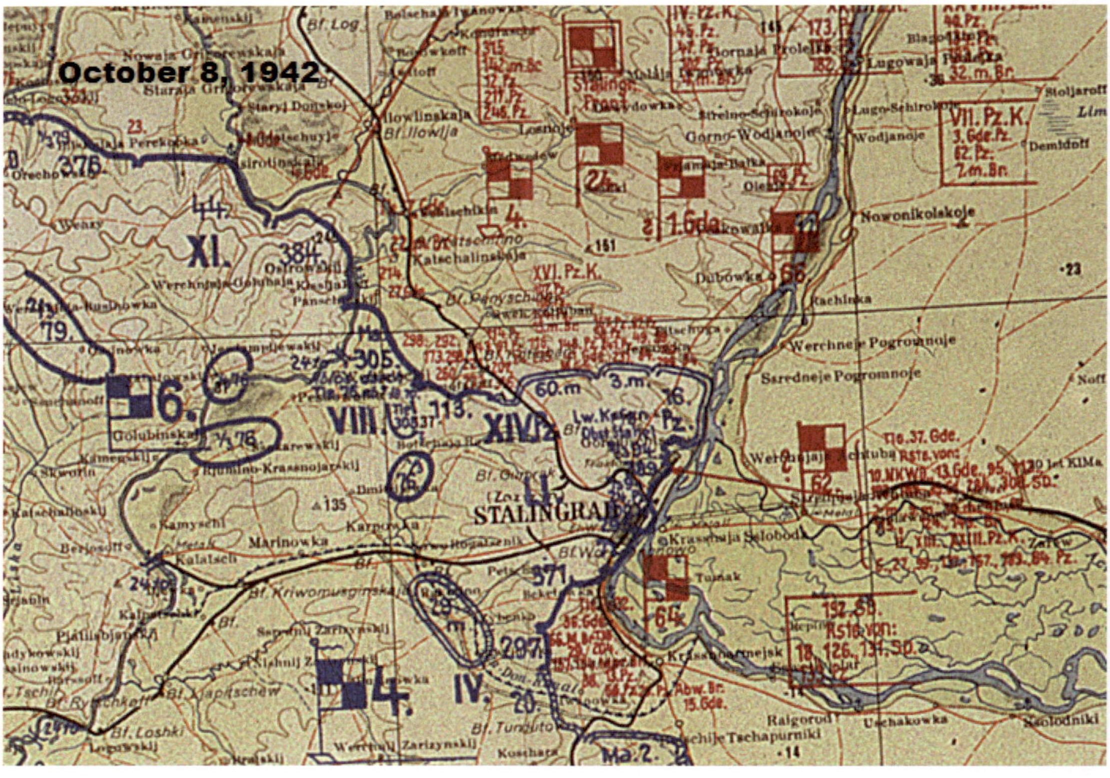

389th Infantry Division; to the south was the 100th *Jäger* Division.

100th Jäger Division – The division attacked in zone against the 95th Rifle Division. To the north was the 24th ***Panzer*** Division; to the south was the 295th Infantry Division. The division lost three NCOs/enlisted killed in action; 20 NCOs/enlisted were wounded in action.

295th Infantry Division – The division attacked in zone against the 95th Rifle Division. To the north was the 100th ***Jäger*** Division; to the south was the 71st Infantry Division. The division suffered two NCOs/enlisted killed in action; ten NCOs/enlisted were wounded in action.

389th Infantry Division – The division attempted to seize additional portions of the Dzerzhinsky Tractor Factory Workers' Settlement from the 37th Guards Rifle Division and the remnants of the 112th Rifle Division, but was repelled. To the north was the 94th Infantry Division; to the south was the 24th ***Panzer*** Division. The division lost six NCOs/enlisted killed in action; 23 NCOs/enlisted were wounded in action.

Sixth Army Reserve

76th Infantry Division – The division moved toward the sector of the 305th Infantry Division. Elements of the division relieved part of the 305th Infantry Division. The division consolidated its nine infantry battalions to six battalions because of previous losses. ***Generalleutnant*** Carl Rodenburg was awarded the Knight's Cross.

79th Infantry Division – One-third of the division defended in sector south of the Don River. To the east was the 376th Infantry Division; to the west was the Romanian V Corps of the Romanian Third Army. The rest of the division occupied an assembly area at Verkhne-Businovka.

Fourth *Panzer* Army – The army headquarters was located east of Verkhne-Zaryzinskij.

IV Corps

297th Infantry Division – The division defended in sector east of Elkhi and Iagodniki, against the 66th Marine Infantry Brigade and the 157th Rifle Division. To the north was the 371st Infantry Division; to the south was the 20th Romanian Infantry Division.

371st Infantry Division – The division defended against the 36th Guards Rifle Division and the 422nd Rifle Division in sector from Kuporosnoye, in the east, to northwest of Gornaia Poliana. To the north was the 71st Infantry Division; to the south was the 297th Infantry Division. The division lost four NCOs/enlisted killed in action; 31 NCOs/enlisted were wounded in action.

20th Romanian Infantry Division – The division defended in sector, west of the Tundutovo Rail Station and east of Andreevka, against the 38th Rifle Division. To the north was the 297th Infantry Division; to the south was the 2nd Romanian Infantry Division of the Romanian VI Corps.

Fourth *Panzer* Army Reserve

14th Panzer Division – The division occupied assembly areas near Sadovia, Abganerovo and Goncharovskoye.

Sources, October 8, 1942: ***Oberkommando des Heeres, Lage Ost: Stand: 8.10.42, Eastern Front Situation Map, National Archives Identifier: 559733, Record Group 242 – National Archives Collection of Foreign Records Seized, 1675-1958, National Archives, College Park, Maryland; Ia, Armeeoberkommando 6, "Morgen Meldung" and assorted reports, Kriegstagebuch 14, 9 October 1942, as found in Microfilm Series, T-312, Records of German Field Commands, Armies, Roll 1453 and 1688 and 1688, National Archives and Records Service, College Park, Maryland; Ia, XXXXVIII Panzerkorps, "Übersicht über die dem Korps Unterstellten Divisionen, 28. Juni 1942 – 11 October 1942," as found on T-314, Records of German Field Commands, Corps, Roll 1153, National Archives, College Park, Maryland; Korpsarzt, XXXXVIII Panzerkorps, "Meldung über Personelle Verluste," Stand 8.10.42, as found on T-314, Records of German Field Commands, Corps, Roll 1158, National Archives, College Park, Maryland; 371st Infantry Division, Kriegstagebuch, 8 October 1942, as found in Microfilm Series T-315, Roll 2164, National Archives and Records Service, College Park, Maryland; Florian Freiherr von und zu Aufsess, Die Anlagenbände zu den Kriegstagebüchern der 6. Armee vom 14.09.1942 bis 24.11.1942, Band 1, Schwabach, Germany: Selbstverlag, 2006, 136-147; Antony Beevor, Stalingrad: The Fateful Siege: 1942-1943, London: Penguin Books, 1998, 162, 191; David M. Glantz & Jonathan M. House, Armageddon in Stalingrad: September-November 1942, (The Stalingrad Trilogy, Volume 2), Lawrence, Kansas: University Press of Kansas, 2009, 351; Jason Mark, Death of the Leaping Horseman: 24. Panzer-Division in Stalingrad, Sydney, Australia: Leaping Horsemen Books, 2003, 264-265; Anton Schimak, Karl Lamprecht & Friedrich Dettmer, Die 44. Infanterie Division: Tagebuch der Hoch- und Deutschmeister, Wien: Verlag Austria Press, 169, 233 and Map: Marschweg der 44. Infanterie Division im Russland; Georg Tessin, Verbände und Truppen der deutschen Wehrmacht und Waffen-SS im Zweiten Weltkrieg 1939-1945, Dritter Band: Die Landstreitkräfte 6-14, Osnabrück, FRG, 1974, 3.***

Generalfeldmarschall **Maximilian von Weichs, Army Group B.**

Graves of troopers in the 297th Infantry Division outside of Stalingrad. Note that several birch crosses are topped with German helmets.

October 9, 1942
Weather: cooling, 59° F, partly cloudy, changing cloudiness, windy, overcast, good road conditions
Sunrise: 6:12 a.m.; **Sunset:** 5:26 p.m.
Moon: Waning Crescent; 1% illumination

Sixth Army – The army headquarters was located at Golubinskaya.

VIII Corps – The corps headquarters was located at Peskovatka. The corps suffered the following officer casualties: one wounded in action.

76th Infantry Division – The division conducted relief in place operations of the 305th Infantry Division and took over their defensive sector from the Don River, north of Nizhne-Gnilovskii, to west of Kotluban', against the 298th Rifle Division. To the east was the 113th Infantry Division; to the west was the 384th Infantry Division.

113th Infantry Division – The division defended in sector southwest of Samofalovka and north of Borodkin against the 298th Rifle Division, the 258th Rifle Division, the 173rd Rifle Division, the 207th Rifle Division, the 292nd Rifle Division, the 221st Rifle Division and the 24th Rifle Division. To the west was the 76th Infantry Division; to the east was the 60th Infantry Division (Motorized.) The division lost five NCOs/enlisted killed in action; 23 NCOs/enlisted were wounded in action.

305th Infantry Division – The division was relieved in place by the 76th Infantry Division and began moving toward Stalingrad, reaching Bol'shaya Rossoschka. The division suffered 14 NCOs/enlisted killed in action; one officer and 21 NCOs/enlisted were wounded in action.

XI Corps

44th Infantry Division – The division defended in sector Kurchajessowskij-Kamyshinskiy-Hill 171.0-Hill 180.9-Sirotinskaya-Khmelevskoy, against the 40th Guards Rifle Division. The division headquarters was located at Verkhne-Golubaja. To the west was 376th Infantry Division; to the east was the 384th Infantry Division. The division lost two NCOs/enlisted wounded in action.

376th Infantry Division – The division, with an attached infantry regiment from the 79th Infantry Division, defended in sector near Blizhniaia-Perekopka against the 321st Rifle Division and the 23rd Rifle Division. To the east was the 44th Infantry Division; to the west was the 1st Romanian Cavalry Division of the Romanian V Corps of the Romanian Third Army. The division lost two NCOs/enlisted killed in action; ten NCOs/enlisted were wounded in action.

384th Infantry Division – The division defended in sector west of the Don River near Trekhostrovskaia to Podgorskii, against the 4th Guards Rifle Division, the 214th Rifle Division and the 27th Guards Rifle Division. To the west was the 44th Infantry Division; to the southeast was the 76th Infantry Division. The division lost three NCOs/enlisted wounded in action.

XIV *Panzer* Corps – The corps headquarters was located east of Ssadtschi-Kowa. The corps suffered the following officer casualties: one killed in action; one accidental death; three wounded in action.

3rd Infantry Division (Motorized) – The division defended in sector, from the Tartar Hill-Hill 111.1-Hill 129.6-Hill 131.2, repelling attacks by the 299th Rifle Division, the 38th Guards Rifle Division and the 343rd Rifle Division. To the east was the 16th ***Panzer*** Division; to the west was the 60th Infantry Division (Motorized.) The division lost five NCOs/enlisted killed in action; one officer and 24 NCOs/enlisted were wounded in action.

16th Panzer Division – The division defended in sector, from Hill 139.7 to the Volga and from the Volga southwest to Hill 145.1, north of

Orlovka against the 120th Rifle Division, the 84th Rifle Division, the 299th Rifle Division and the 64th Rifle Division. To the west was the 3rd Infantry Division (Motorized); to the southwest was the 94th Infantry Division.

60th Infantry Division (Motorized) – The division defended in sector, from south of Kotluban' Station near Borodkin to Kuz'michi against the 231st Rifle Division, the 49th Rifle Division, the 233rd Rifle Division and the 316th Rifle Division. To the west was the 113th Infantry Division; to the east was the 3rd Infantry Division (Motorized.) The division lost 12 NCOs/enlisted killed in action; two officers and 28 NCOs/enlisted were wounded in action.

94th Infantry Division – The division defended in sector. To the south was the 389th Infantry Division; to the northeast was the 16th ***Panzer*** Division. The division lost five NCOs/enlisted wounded in action.

Battle Group Stahel – The battle group occupied an assembly area and prepared for future operations.

XXXXVIII *Panzer* Corps

29th Infantry Division (Motorized) – The division occupied an assembly area west of Zybenko and Varvarovka, along the Volga-Don Canal, to prepare for future operations.

71st Infantry Division – The division conducted limited attacks in zone, seizing little terrain. To the north was the 295th Infantry Division; to the south was the 371st Infantry Division.

LI Corps – The corps headquarters was located at Gumrak. The corps suffered the following officer casualties: two killed in action; two wounded in action.

24th Panzer Division – The division defended at the northern part of the Barrikady Gun Factory Workers' Settlement. The division suffered one officer and 11 NCOs/enlisted killed in action; 21 NCOs/enlisted were wounded in action; one of the wounded died later that day in hospital. To the north was the 389th Infantry Division; to the south was the 100th ***Jäger*** Division.

100th Jäger Division – The division conducted limited attacks in zone, seizing little terrain. To the north was the 24th ***Panzer*** Division; to the south was the 295th Infantry Division. The division suffered three NCOs/enlisted killed in action; 26 NCOs/enlisted were wounded in action.

295th Infantry Division – The division conducted limited attacks in zone, seizing little terrain

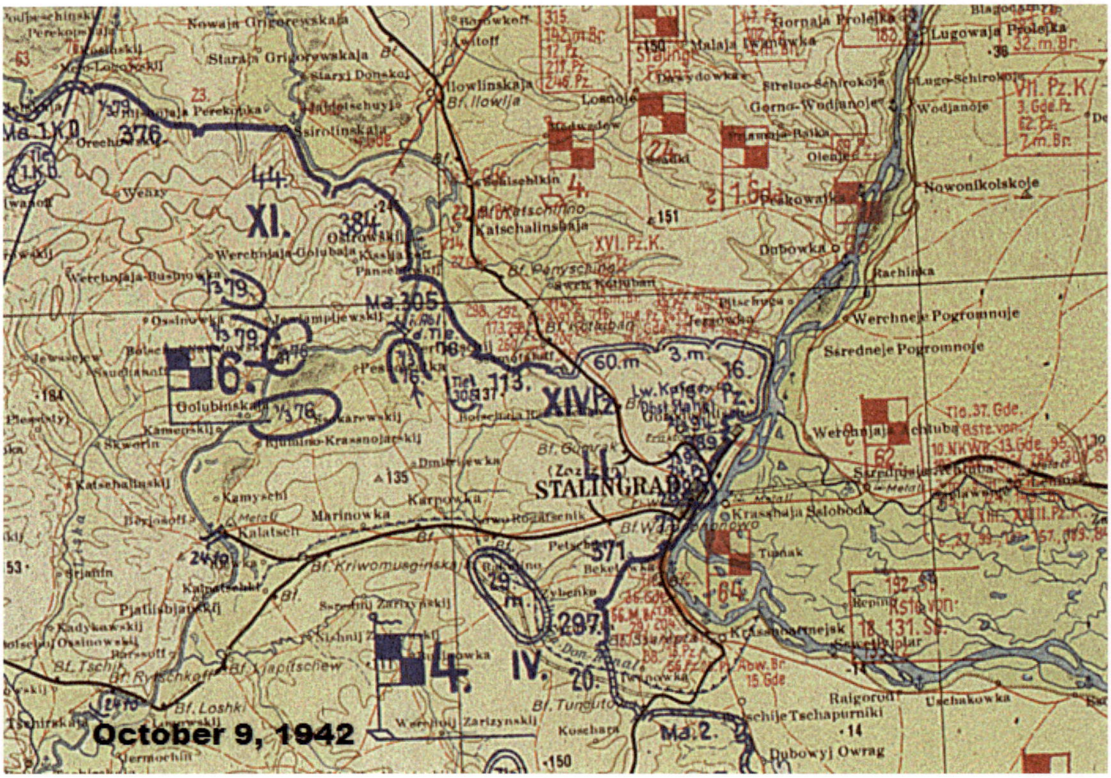

against the 284th Rifle Division. To the north was the 100th ***Jäger*** Division; to the south was the 71st Infantry Division. The division lost nine NCOs/enlisted men wounded in action.

389th Infantry Division – The division conducted limited attacks in zone, seizing little terrain. To the north was the 94th Infantry Division; to the south was the 24th ***Panzer*** Division. The division reported 30 overall casualties. ***Generalleutnant*** Erwin Jaenecke was awarded the Knight's Cross. The division headquarters was located two miles west of Gorodishche.

Sixth Army Reserve

79th Infantry Division – One-third of the division defended in sector south of the Don River with the 376th Infantry Division. To the east was the 44th Infantry Division; to the west was the Romanian V Corps of the Romanian Third Army. The rest of the division moved toward Stalingrad, reaching the Don River.

Fourth *Panzer* Army – The army headquarters was located east of Verkhne-Zaryzinskij.

IV Corps

297th Infantry Division – The division defended in sector east of Elkhi and Iagodniki, against the 66th Marine Infantry Brigade. To the north was the 371st Infantry Division; to the south was the 20th Romanian Infantry Division.

371st Infantry Division – The division defended in sector from Kuporosnoye in the east to northwest of Gornaia Poliana, against the 36th Guards Rifle Division. To the north was the 71st Infantry Division; to the south was the 297th Infantry Division. The division lost five NCOs/enlisted killed in action; one officer and 16 NCOs/enlisted were wounded in action.

20th Romanian Infantry Division – The division defended in sector, west of the Tundutovo Rail Station and east of Andreevka, against the 38th Rifle Division. To the north was the 297th Infantry Division; to the south was the 2nd Romanian Infantry Division of the Romanian VI Corps.

Fourth *Panzer* Army Reserve

14th Panzer Division – The division began moving northwest in the general direction of Karpovka.

Frommes Gebets-andenken
an unseren lieben Bruder
Jüngling
Karl Manglberger
Wastlseppsohn in Eichbichl
Pfarre Tarsdorf
Soldat in einem Pionier-Regiment
welcher am 9. Oktober 1942 bei Stalingrad im 21. Lebensjahre den Heldentod fand.

Fern vom lieben Elternhaus
Hauchtest du dein junges Leben aus,
Fürs Vaterland in Kriegesnot
Fand'st allzu früh den Heldentod.
Es deckt der grüne Rasen
Nun dich, du tapferer Held,
Du starbst den Tod der Ehre
Auf weitem blutigen Feld.

Barmherziger Jesu, gib ihm die ewige Ruhe!

Druck von Anton Pustet, Tittmoning

Pionier **Karl Manglberger** was born at Tarsdorf near Braunau am Inn in Austria on January 20, 1922. Assigned to the 100th Combat Engineer Battalion in the 100th ***Jäger*** Division, he died of his wounds at the divisional casualty collection point at Stalingrad on October 9, 1942. His name is listed in the remembrance book at the German Military Cemetery at Rossoschka.

Sources, October 9, 1942: ***Oberkommando des Heeres, Lage Ost: Stand: 9.10.42, Eastern Front Situation Map, National Archives Identifier: 559733, Record Group 242 – National Archives Collection of Foreign Records Seized, 1675-1958, National Archives, College Park, Maryland; Ia, Armeeoberkommando 6, "Morgen Meldung" and assorted reports, Kriegstagebuch 14, 10 October 1942, as found in Microfilm Series, T-312, Records of German Field Commands, Armies, Roll 1453 and 1688 and 1688, National Archives and Records Service, College Park, Maryland; Ia, XXXXVIII Panzerkorps, "Übersicht über die dem Korps Unterstellten Divisionen, 28. Juni 1942 – 11 October 1942," as found on T-314, Records of German Field Commands, Corps, Roll 1153, National Archives, College Park, Maryland; Korpsarzt, XXXXVIII Panzerkorps, "Meldung über Personelle Verluste," Stand 9.10.42, as found on T-314, Records of German Field Commands, Corps, Roll 1158, National Archives, College Park, Maryland; 371st Infantry Division, Kriegstagebuch, 9 October 1942, as found in Microfilm Series T-315, Roll 2164, National Archives and Records Service, College Park, Maryland; Florian Freiherr von und zu Aufsess, Die Anlagenbände zu den Kriegstagebüchern der 6. Armee vom 14.09.1942 bis 24.11.1942, Band 1, Schwabach, Germany: Selbstverlag, 2006, 147-148; David M. Glantz & Jonathan M. House, Armageddon in Stalingrad: September-November 1942, (The Stalingrad Trilogy, Volume 2), Lawrence, Kansas: University Press of Kansas, 2009, 349-350; Jochen Löser, Bittere Pflicht: Kampf und Untergang der 76. Berlin-Brandenburgischen Infanterie-Division, Osnabrück, FRG: Biblio Verlag, 1986, 215; Jason Mark, Death of the Leaping Horseman: 24. Panzer-Division in Stalingrad, Sydney, Australia: Leaping Horsemen Books, 2003, 265-266; Anton Schimak, Karl Lamprecht & Friedrich Dettmer, Die 44. Infanterie Division: Tagebuch der Hoch- und Deutschmeister, Wien: Verlag Austria Press, 169, 233 and Map: Marschweg der 44. Infanterie Division im Russland.***

October 10, 1942
Weather: cloudy to bright and sunny, windy, 63° F, changing cloudiness
Sunrise: 6:13 a.m.; **Sunset:** 5:24 p.m.
Moon: New Moon; 0% illumination

Sixth Army – The army headquarters was located at Golubinskaya.

VIII Corps – The corps headquarters was located at Peskovatka. The 177th ***Sturmgeschütz*** Detachment, with three Mark III-Long assault guns operational, was assigned to the corps.

76th Infantry Division – The division defended in sector, east of the Don River, north of Nizhne-Gnilovskii, to west of Kotluban' against the 298th Rifle Division and the 27th Guards Rifle Division. To the east was the 113th Infantry Division; to the northwest was the 384th Infantry Division. The division lost one NCO/enlisted killed in action; four NCOs/enlisted were wounded in action.

113th Infantry Division – The division defended in sector southwest of Samofalovka and north of Borodkin against the 298th Rifle Division, the 258th Rifle Division, the 173rd Rifle Division, the 207th Rifle Division, the 292nd Rifle Division, the 221st Rifle Division and the 24th Rifle Division. To the northwest was the 76th Infantry Division; to the east was the 60th Infantry Division (Motorized.) The division lost four NCOs/enlisted killed in action; 25 NCOs/enlisted were wounded in action.

305th Infantry Division – The division moved toward Stalingrad, reaching Bol'shaya Rossoschka.

XI Corps

44th Infantry Division – The division defended in sector Kurchajessowskij-Kamyshinskiy-Hill 171.0-Hill 180.9-Sirotinskaya-Khmelevskoy against the 40th Guards Rifle Division. The division headquarters was located at Verkhne-Golubaja. To the west was 376th Infantry Division; to the southeast was the 384th Infantry Division. The division lost two NCOs/enlisted wounded in action.

376th Infantry Division – The division, with an attached infantry regiment from the 79th Infantry Division, defended in sector near Blizhniaia-Perekopka against the 321st Rifle Division and the 23rd Rifle Division. To the east was the 44th Infantry Division; to the west was the 1st Romanian Cavalry Division of the Romanian V Corps in the Romanian Third Army. The division lost one NCO/enlisted killed in action; two NCOs/enlisted were wounded in action.

384th Infantry Division – The division defended in sector west of the Don River near Trekhostrovskaia to Podgorskii against the 4th Guards Rifle Division. To the west was the 44th Infantry Division; to the southeast was the 76th Infantry Division. The division lost one NCO/enlisted wounded in action.

XIV *Panzer* Corps – The corps headquarters was located east of Ssadtschi-Kowa. The 51st ***Werfer*** Regiment was assigned to support the corps. The corps suffered the following officer casualties: one killed in action; three wounded in action; and one missing in action.

3rd Infantry Division (Motorized) – The division defended in sector, from the Tartar Hill-Hill 111.1-Hill 129.6-Hill 131.2, repelling attacks by the 299th Rifle Division, the 38th Guards Rifle Division and the 343rd Rifle Division. To the east was the 16th ***Panzer*** Division; to the west was the 60th Infantry Division (Motorized.) The division lost one NCO/enlisted killed in action; one officer and ten NCOs/enlisted were wounded in action.

16th Panzer Division – The division defended in sector, from Hill 139.7 to the Volga and from the Volga southwest to Hill 145.1, north of Orlovka against the 120th Rifle Division, the 84th Rifle Division, the 299th Rifle Division and the 64th Rifle Division. The division lost six

NCOs/enlisted killed in action; one officer and 15 NCOs/enlisted were killed in action; one man was reported missing in action.

60th Infantry Division (Motorized) – The division defended in sector, from south of Kotluban' Station near Borodkin to Kuz'michi against the 231st Rifle Division, the 49th Rifle Division, the 233rd Rifle Division and the 316th Rifle Division. To the west was the 113th Infantry Division; to the east was the 3rd Infantry Division (Motorized.) The division suffered three NCOs/enlisted killed in action; two officers and 40 NCOs/enlisted were wounded in action; one man was reported missing in action.

94th Infantry Division – The division defended in sector. To the south was the 389th Infantry Division; to the northeast was the 16th ***Panzer*** Division. The division lost one NCO/enlisted killed in action.

Battle Group Stahel – The battle group defended in sector, south of Erzovka, from the Volga River to the west.

XXXXVIII *Panzer* Corps

14th Panzer Division – The division continued to march northwest, reaching Novyy Rogachik. The division lost one NCO/enlisted wounded in action. During the period August 1, 1942 to October 8, 1942, the division lost 27 officers and 550 NCOs/enlisted killed in action; 119 officers and 2,285 NCOs/enlisted were wounded in action; 12 NCOs/enlisted were reported missing in action.

29th Infantry Division (Motorized) – The division occupied an assembly area west of Zybenko and Varvarovka, along the Volga-Don Canal, to prepare for future operations. Part of the division assumed a defensive sector north of the Volga-Don Canal, against the 66th Marine Infantry Brigade. To the north was the 297th Infantry Division; to the south was the 20th Romanian Infantry Division.

71st Infantry Division – The division conducted limited attacks in zone, seizing little terrain. To the north was the 295th Infantry Division; to the south was the 371st Infantry Division.

LI Corps – The corps headquarters was located at Gumrak. The corps suffered the following officer casualties: two killed in action; four wounded in action.

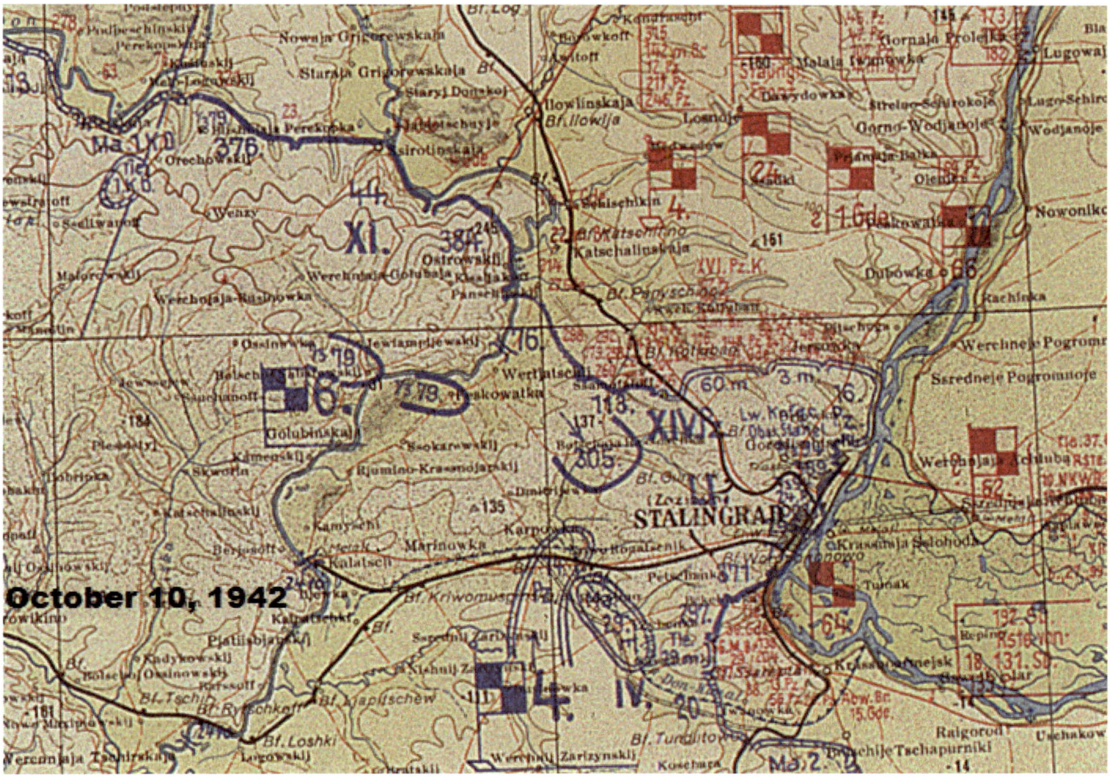

24th Panzer Division – The division defended in sector at the northern part of the Barrikady Gun Factory Workers' Settlement. The division suffered nine NCOs/enlisted killed in action; two officers and 24 NCOs/enlisted were wounded in action; two NCOs/enlisted were reported missing in action. To the north was the 389th Infantry Division; to the south was the 100th ***Jäger*** Division.

100th Jäger Division – The division defended in sector. To the north was the 24th ***Panzer*** Division; to the south was the 295th Infantry Division. The division lost one officer and five NCOs/enlisted killed in action; one officer and 17 NCOs/enlisted were wounded in action; one NCO was reported missing in action.

295th Infantry Division – The division defended in sector against the 284th Rifle Division. To the north was the 100th ***Jäger*** Division; to the south was the 71st Infantry Division. The division suffered four NCOs/enlisted killed in action; 14 NCOs/enlisted were wounded in action.

389th Infantry Division – The division defended in sector. To the north was the 94th Infantry Division; to the south was the 24th ***Panzer*** Division. The division lost three NCOs/enlisted killed in action; three officers and 20 NCOs/enlisted were wounded in action.

Sixth Army Reserve

79th Infantry Division – One-third of the division defended in sector south of the Don River with the 376th Infantry Division. To the east was the 44th Infantry Division; to the west was the Romanian V Corps of the Romanian Third Army. The division received orders to move from its location west of the Don River to Stalingrad for attachment to the LI Corps; lead elements reached Peskovatka.

Fourth *Panzer* Army – The army headquarters was located east of Verkhne-Zaryzinskij.

IV Corps

297th Infantry Division – The division defended in sector east of Elkhi and Iagodniki against the 38th Guards Rifle Division. To the northeast was the 371st Infantry Division; to the south was the 29th Infantry Division (Motorized.)

371st Infantry Division – The division defended in sector from Kuporosnoye in the east to northwest of Gornaia Poliana against part of the 422nd Rifle Division. The division lost four NCOs/enlisted killed in action; 15 NCOs/enlisted were wounded in action. During the period July 9, 1942 through October 10, 1942, the division lost 43 officers, 158 NCOs and 811 enlisted killed in action; 146 officers, 774 NCOs and 3,673 enlisted were wounded in action; two officers, ten NCOs and 114 enlisted were reported missing in action. To the north was the 71st Infantry Division; to the southwest was the 297th Infantry Division.

20th Romanian Infantry Division – The division defended in sector, west of the Tundutovo Rail Station and east of Andreevka against the 38th Rifle Division. To the north was the 29th Infantry Division (Motorized); to the south was the 2nd Romanian Infantry Division of the Romanian VI Corps.

Sources, October 10, 1942: *Oberkommando des Heeres, Lage Ost: Stand: 10.10.42, Eastern Front Situation Map, National Archives Identifier: 559733, Record Group 242 – National Archives Collection of Foreign Records Seized, 1675-1958, National Archives, College Park, Maryland; Ia, Armeeoberkommando 6, "Morgen Meldung" and assorted reports, Kriegstagebuch 14, 11 October 1942," as found in Microfilm Series, T-312, Records of German Field Commands, Armies, Roll 1453 and 1688 and 1688, National Archives and Records Service, College Park, Maryland; Ia, XXXXVIII Panzerkorps, "Übersicht über die dem Korps Unterstellten Divisionen, 28. Juni 1942 – 11 October 1942," as found on T-314, Records of German Field Commands, Corps, Roll 1153, National Archives, College Park, Maryland; Ia, XXXXVIII Panzerkorps, "Zahlenmässige Verlustmeldung der Unterstellten Divisionen und Heerestruppen in der Zeit vom 1. April 1942 bis 31. Oktober 1942," as found in T-314, Records of German Field Commands, Corps, Roll 1153, National Archives, College Park, Maryland; Korpsarzt, XXXXVIII Panzerkorps, "Meldung über Personelle Verluste," Stand 10.10.42, as found on T-314, Records of German Field Commands, Corps, Roll 1158, National Archives, College Park, Maryland; 371st Infantry Division, Kriegstagebuch, 10 October 1942, as found in Microfilm Series T-315, Roll 2164, National Archives and Records Service, College Park, Maryland; Florian Freiherr von und zu Aufsess, Die Anlagenbände zu den Kriegstagebüchern der 6. Armee vom 14.09.1942 bis 24.11.1942, Band 1, Schwabach, Germany: Selbstverlag, 2006, 150-155; David M. Glantz & Jonathan M. House, Armageddon in Stalingrad: September-November 1942, (The Stalingrad Trilogy, Volume 2), Lawrence, Kansas: University Press of Kansas, 2009, 349, 354; Jason Mark, Death of the Leaping Horseman: 24. Panzer-Division in Stalingrad, Sydney, Australia: Leaping Horsemen Books, 2003, 267-272; Hans Sänger, Die 79. Infanterie Division, Friedberg, FRG: Podzun-Pallas-Verlag, 1971, 70; Anton Schimak, Karl Lamprecht & Friedrich Dettmer, Die 44. Infanterie Division: Tagebuch der Hoch- und Deutschmeister, Wien: Verlag Austria Press, 169, 233 and Map: Marschweg der 44. Infanterie Division im Russland.*

Zur frommen Erinnerung
an unseren guten, unvergeßlichen Sohn und Bruder

Franz Entres

Schütze in einem Infanterieregiment,

welcher am 10. Oktober 1942 im 19. Lebensjahre nordwestlich Stalingrad den Heldentod fand.

Fern von der Heimat und den Lieben
Hat dich der Tod dahingerafft.
Du hast dem Vaterland geopfert
Dein Leben, deine Manneskraft.
Als Held ruhst du in fremder Erde,
Doch unvergessen, heiß beweint
Bleibst du den Herzen deiner Lieben,
Bis sie der Tod mit dir vereint.

Schütze **Franz Entres** was born in Aggsbach-Dorf along the Danube River in Austria on December 31, 1923. Assigned to an infantry regiment, he was killed in action on October 10, 1942 at Bol'shaya Rossoschka. His remains are buried in the section for the unknown at the German Military Cemetery at Rossoschka.

Wer im Herzen seiner Lieben lebt,
Der ist nicht tot, er ist nur fern.
Tot ist nur der, der vergessen wird.

Gebets-Andenken

an den Kriegshelden

Karl Haider

Wachtmeister und Offiziersanwärter in einer Abt. der Heeresartillerie

Inh. des E.K. 2. Kl, Teilnehmer an den Feldzügen Frankreich, Jugoslavien und Sowjetrußland, beschäftigt in der Deutschen Heraklith A.-G.

welcher am 10. Okt. 1942 im Alter von 32 Jahren bei Stalingrad den Heldentod erlitt.

R. I. P.

Du hast gekämpft fürs Vaterland,
Wie war der Abschied schwer;
Nun ruhest Du in fremdem Land,
Wir sehen uns nicht mehr.
Allabends, wenn die Glocken summen,
Zieht liebend unser Geist dorthin
Und streut Dir betend Andachtsblumen
Aufs Heldengrab mit frommem Sinn.

Druck: A. Lehner, Simbach-Inn

***Wachtmeister*, and officer candidate, Karl Haider** was born in Munich, Bavaria on July 20, 1910. He had previously been awarded the Iron Cross 2nd Class and had fought in the 1940 French Campaign and the 1941 Yugoslavian Campaign. Assigned to an army artillery detachment, he was killed in action south of Kot'luban on October 10, 1942. He is buried at the German Military Cemetery at Rossoschka in Block AT1, Row 20 in Grave 1182.

October 11, 1942
Weather: clear, dusty at noon, low cloud cover, windy, dry, early mist, good road conditions
Sunrise: 6:15 a.m.; **Sunset:** 5:22 p.m.
Moon: Waxing Crescent; 2% illumination

Sixth Army – The army headquarters was located at Golubinskaya.

VIII Corps – The corps suffered the following officer casualties: two wounded in action; one missing in action.

76th Infantry Division – The division defended in sector, east of the Don River, north of Nizhne-Gnilovskii, to west of Kotluban' against the 298th Rifle Division. To the southeast was the 113th Infantry Division; to the northwest was the 384th Infantry Division.

113th Infantry Division – The division defended in sector southwest of Samofalovka and north of Borodkin against the 298th Rifle Division, the 258th Rifle Division, the 173rd Rifle Division, the 207th Rifle Division, the 292nd Rifle Division, the 221st Rifle Division and the 24th Rifle Division, giving up no ground. To the northwest was the 76th Infantry Division; to the east was the 60th Infantry Division (Motorized.) The division lost 20 NCOs/enlisted killed in action; 35 NCOs/enlisted were wounded in action.

305th Infantry Division – The division moved toward Stalingrad, reaching Gorodishche.

XI Corps

44th Infantry Division – The division defended in sector Kurchajessowskij-Kamyshinskiy-Hill 171.0-Hill 180.9-Sirotinskaya-Khmelevskoy, against the 40th Guards Rifle Division. The division headquarters was located at Verkhne-Golubaja. To the west was 376th Infantry Division; to the east was the 384th Infantry Division. The division lost two NCOs/enlisted killed in action; seven NCOs/enlisted were wounded in action.

376th Infantry Division – The division, with an attached infantry regiment from the 79th Infantry Division, defended in sector near Blizhniaia-Perekopka against the 321st Rifle Division and the 23rd Rifle Division. To the east was the 44th Infantry Division; to the west was the 1st Romanian Cavalry Division of the Romanian V Corps in the Romanian Third Army. The division lost six NCOs/enlisted wounded in action.

384th Infantry Division – The division defended in sector west of the Don River near Trekhostrovskaia to Podgorskii, against the 214th Rifle Division and the 27th Guards Rifle Division. To the west was the 44th Infantry Division; to the southeast was the 76th Infantry Division. The division lost one NCO/enlisted wounded in action.

XIV *Panzer* Corps – The corps headquarters was located east of Ssadtschi-Kowa. The corps suffered the following officer casualties: one wounded in action.

3rd Infantry Division (Motorized) – The division defended in sector, from the Tartar Hill-Hill 111.1-Hill 129.6-Hill 131.2, repelling attacks by the 299th Rifle Division, the 38th Guards Rifle Division and the 343rd Rifle Division. To the east was the 16th ***Panzer*** Division; to the west was the 60th Infantry Division (Motorized.)

16th Panzer Division – The division defended in sector, from Hill 139.7 to the Volga and from the Volga southwest to Hill 145.1, north of Orlovka against the 120th Rifle Division, the 84th Rifle Division, the 299th Rifle Division and the 64th Rifle Division. To the west was the 3rd Infantry Division (Motorized); to the southwest was the 389th Infantry Division.

60th Infantry Division (Motorized) – The division defended in sector, from south of Kotluban' Station near Borodkin to Kuz'michi against the 231st Rifle Division, the 49th Rifle Division, the 233rd Rifle Division and the 316th Rifle Division. To the west was the 113th Infantry Division; to the east was the 3rd Infantry Division (Motorized.)

94th Infantry Division – The division defended in sector. To the south was the 389th Infantry Division; to the northeast was the 16th ***Panzer*** Division.

Battle Group Stahel – The battle group defended in sector, south of Erzovka, from the Volga River west.

XXXXVIII *Panzer* Corps

29th Infantry Division (Motorized) – The division occupied an assembly area west of Zybenko and Varvarovka, along the Volga-Don Canal, to prepare for future operations. The division also relinquished its defensive sector.

71st Infantry Division – The division conducted limited attacks in zone, seizing little terrain. To the north was the 295th Infantry Division; to the south was the 371st Infantry Division. The division lost one NCO/enlisted killed in action; five NCOs/enlisted were wounded in action.

LI Corps – The corps headquarters was located at Gumrak. The corps suffered the following officer casualties: three wounded in action.

14th Panzer Division – The division moved toward Stalingrad, reaching Pitomnik. The division was assigned to the LI Corps for operations in northern Stalingrad. The division lost one NCO/enlisted killed in action; six NCOs/enlisted were wounded in action.

24th Panzer Division – After attacking east of the stadium against the 37th Guards Rifle Division, the division defended in sector at the northern part of the Barrikady Gun Factory Workers' Settlement, repelling an attack by elements of the 84th Tank Brigade. To the north was the 389th Infantry Division; to the south was the 100th ***Jäger*** Division. The division suffered five NCOs/enlisted killed in action; six NCOs/enlisted were wounded in action.

100th Jäger Division – The division defended in sector. To the north was the 24th ***Panzer*** Division; to the south was the 295th Infantry Division. The division lost six NCOs/enlisted killed in action; 23 NCOs/enlisted were wounded in action; one man was reported missing in action.

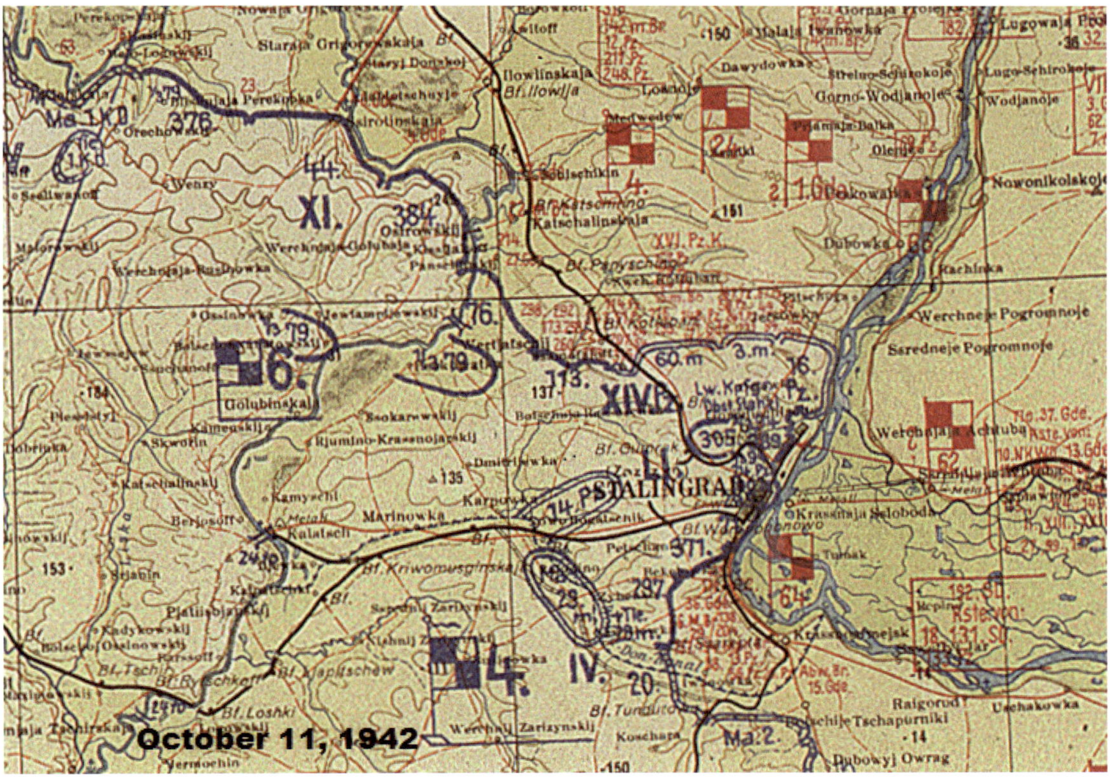

295th Infantry Division – The division defended in sector against the 284th Rifle Division. To the north was the 100th ***Jäger*** Division; to the south was the 71st Infantry Division. The division lost four NCOs/enlisted killed in action; two officers and 11 NCOs/enlisted were wounded in action.

389th Infantry Division – The division defended in sector. To the north was the 94th Infantry Division; to the south was the 24th ***Panzer*** Division. The division suffered 17 NCOs/enlisted killed in action; 45 NCOs/enlisted were wounded in action.

Sixth Army Reserve

79th Infantry Division – One-third of the division defended in sector south of the Don River with the 376th Infantry Division. To the east was the 44th Infantry Division; to the west was the Romanian V Corps of the Romanian Third Army. The rest of the division moved toward Stalingrad.

Fourth *Panzer* Army – The army headquarters was located east of Verkhne-Zaryzinskij.

IV Corps

297th Infantry Division – The division defended in sector east of Elkhi and Iagodniki against the 36th Guards Rifle Division. To the northwest was the 371st Infantry Division; to the south was the 20th Romanian Infantry Division.

371st Infantry Division – The division defended in sector from Kuporosnoye in the east to northwest of Gornaia Poliana against part of the 422nd Rifle Division. To the north was the 71st Infantry Division; to the southwest was the 297th Infantry Division.

20th Romanian Infantry Division – The division defended in sector, west of the Tundutovo Rail Station and east of Andreevka against the 38th Rifle Division. To the north was the 297th Infantry Division; to the southeast was the 2nd Romanian Infantry Division of the Romanian VI Corps.

Sources, October 11, 1942: ***Oberkommando des Heeres, Lage Ost: Stand: 11.10.42, Eastern Front Situation Map, National Archives Identifier: 559733, Record Group 242 – National Archives Collection of Foreign Records Seized, 1675-1958, National Archives, College Park, Maryland; Ia, Armeeoberkommando 6, "Morgen Meldung" and assorted reports, Kriegstagebuch 14, 12 October 1942, as found in Microfilm Series, T-312, Records of German Field Commands, Armies, Roll 1453 and 1688, National Archives and Records Service, College Park, Maryland; Ia, XXXXVIII Panzerkorps, "Übersicht über die dem Korps Unterstellten Divisionen, 28. Juni 1942 – 11 October 1942," as found on T-314, Records of German Field Commands, Corps, Roll 1153, National Archives, College Park, Maryland; Korpsarzt, XXXXVIII Panzerkorps, "Meldung über Personelle Verluste," Stand 11.10.42, as found on T-314, Records of German Field Commands, Corps, Roll 1158, National Archives, College Park, Maryland; Florian Freiherr von und zu Aufsess, Die Anlagenbände zu den Kriegstagebüchern der 6. Armee vom 14.09.1942 bis 24.11.1942, Band 1, Schwabach, Germany: Selbstverlag, 2006, 155-160; Antony Beevor, Stalingrad: The Fateful Siege: 1942-1943, London: Penguin Books, 1998, 162, 191; David M. Glantz & Jonathan M. House, Armageddon in Stalingrad: September-November 1942, (The Stalingrad Trilogy, Volume 2), Lawrence, Kansas: University Press of Kansas, 2009, 351; Jason Mark, Death of the Leaping Horseman: 24. Panzer-Division in Stalingrad, Sydney, Australia: Leaping Horsemen Books, 2003, 267-272; Hans Sänger, Die 79. Infanterie Division, Friedberg, FRG: Podzun-Pallas-Verlag, 1971, 70; Anton Schimak, Karl Lamprecht & Friedrich Dettmer, Die 44. Infanterie Division: Tagebuch der Hoch- und Deutschmeister, Wien: Verlag Austria Press, 169, 233 and Map: Marschweg der 44. Infanterie Division im Russland; Wolfgang Werthen, Geschichte der 16. Panzer-Division 1939-1945, Friedberg, FRG: Podzun-Pallas-Verlag, 1958, 114.***

Soldiers from the 44th Infantry Division escorting a coffin. Railyard is south of the Don River in the autumn of 1942. The casket is marked "Hentrup."

Letter from *Unteroffizier* Kurt Helbig, 9th Company, 54th *Jäger* Regiment, 100th *Jäger* Division, written on October 11, 1942. The letter from Stalingrad reads in part:

> "Health-wise I am OK and I thank God for it, because the fighting here is very vicious. Even right now, it is a hot situation outside...When I look outside of my bunker, I have a view of the city and the Volga River. But honestly, I rather would like to be far away from here and hope that the war will be over soon. The Russian is a very hard enemy...The nice summer has gone too, and the cold Russian winter knocks on the door. I do not look forward to it. I don't think there is a chance to get out of here."

Zum frommen Gedenken
im Gebet
an unseren lieben Sohn, Bruder, Schwager, Onkel und Neffen
Lukas Hammer
Obergefreiter in einem Inf.-Regt.
geboren am 13. April 1912
zu Völkersweiler
gefallen am 27. November 1943
in Rußland.

Ach Gott ich tausch Euch nimmermehr.
Mir ist ein lieblich Los gefallen,
Weit schöner als es drunten wär,
Das schönste Los von allen.
Herr, gib ihnen die ewige Ruhe!

Zum frommen Gedenken
im Gebet
an meinen innigstgeliebten Mann, den treusorgenden Vater seines Kindes, unseren lieben Sohn, Schwiegersohn, Bruder, Schwager und Neffen
Josef Hammer
Feldw. und Zugführer in einem Inf.-Regt.
geb. am 23. Aug. 1916 zu Völkersweiler
gefallen am 11. Okt. 1942 in Rußland.

O weint nicht mehr, Ihr Lieben mein.
Blickt nicht zum dunklen Grabe.
Nein blickt zum schönen Himmel ein,
Wo ich so gut es habe.
Vater unser . . Gegrüßest seist du Maria

***Feldwebel* Joseph Hammer** was born on August 23, 1916 in Völkersweiler near Landau in the Rhineland-Palatinate. Married with children, Hammer served as a platoon leader in an infantry regiment. He was killed in action at Stalingrad on October 11, 1942. His remains have never been located, but he is listed in the remembrance book at the German Military Cemetery at Rossoschka. His older brother Lukas (shown at left) was killed near Kirovograd in the Ukraine on November 27, 1943.

October 12, 1942
Weather: clear, warming, bright, sunny, dry
Sunrise: 6:16 a.m.; **Sunset:** 5:20 p.m.
Moon: Waxing Crescent; 7% illumination

Sixth Army – The army headquarters was located at Golubinskaya.

VIII Corps – The corps suffered the following officer casualties: one wounded in action.

76th Infantry Division – The division defended in sector, east of the Don River, north of Nizhne-Gnilovskii, to west of Kotluban', against the 298th Rifle Division and the 297th Rifle Division. To the southeast was the 113th Infantry Division; to the northwest was the 384th Infantry Division. The division reported that of its six infantry battalions, one was medium-strong and five were average in combat power; the division rated its combat engineer battalion as average. The division lost four NCOs/enlisted killed in action; five NCOs/enlisted were wounded in action; one man was reported missing in action.

113th Infantry Division – The division defended in sector southwest of Samofalovka and north of Borodkin, against the 173rd Rifle Division and the 260th Rifle Division. To the northwest was the 76th Infantry Division; to the east was the 60th Infantry Division (Motorized.) The division reported that of its seven infantry battalions, one was strong, three were medium-strong and three were average in combat power; the division rated its combat engineer battalion as medium-strong. The division lost four NCOs/enlisted killed in action; 11 NCOs/enlisted were wounded in action.

XI Corps – The corps suffered the following officer casualties: one wounded in action.

44th Infantry Division – The division defended in sector Kurchajessowskij-Kamyshinskiy-Hill 171.0-Hill 180.9-Sirotinskaya-Khmelevskoy, against the 40th Guards Rifle Division. The division headquarters was located at Verkhne-Golubaja. To the west was 376th Infantry Division; to the east was the 384th Infantry Division. The division reported that of its seven infantry battalions, five were medium-strong and two were average in combat power; the division rated its combat engineer battalion as average. The division lost one NCO/enlisted wounded in action.

376th Infantry Division – The division defended in sector, south of Perekopskaja, near Logowskii and Ossinskij, against the 321st Rifle Division and the 23rd Rifle Division. To the east was the 44th Infantry Division; to the west was the Romanian Third Army. The division reported that of its seven infantry battalions, three were average and four were weak in combat power; the division rated its combat engineer battalion as weak. The division lost one NCO/enlisted wounded in action.

384th Infantry Division – The division defended in sector west of the Don River near Trekhostrovskaia to Podgorskii, against the 214th Rifle Division. To the west was the 44th Infantry Division; to the east was the 76th Infantry Division. The division reported that of its six infantry battalions, three were average and three were weak in combat power; the division rated its combat engineer battalion as weak. The division lost one NCO/enlisted wounded in action.

XIV *Panzer* Corps – The corps headquarters was located east of Ssadtschi-Kowa. The corps suffered the following officer casualties: three killed in action; three wounded in action.

3rd Infantry Division (Motorized) – The division defended in sector, from the Tartar Hill-Hill 111.1-Hill 129.6-Hill 131.2 against the 231st Rifle Division. To the east was the 16th ***Panzer*** Division; to the west was the 60th Infantry Division (Motorized.) The division reported that of its five motorized infantry battalions, two were average, two were weak and one was exhausted in combat power; the division rated its combat engineer battalion as average. The division lost two NCOs/enlisted killed in action; six NCOs/enlisted were wounded in action.

16th Panzer Division – The division defended in sector, from Hill 139.7 to the Volga and from the Volga southwest to Hill 145.1, north of Orlovka. To the west was the 3rd Infantry Division (Motorized); to the southwest was the 94th Infantry Division. The division reported that of its five ***panzer*** grenadier battalions, two were medium-strong, two were average and one was weak in combat power; the division rated its combat engineer battalion as average. The division lost one officer killed in action; 18 NCOs/enlisted were wounded in action.

60th Infantry Division (Motorized) – The division defended in sector, from south of Kotluban' Station near Borodkin to Kuz'michi against the 41st Guards Rifle Division and the 231st Rifle Division. To the west was the 113th Infantry Division; to the east was the 3rd Infantry Division (Motorized.) The division reported that of its seven motorized infantry battalions, four were average, two were weak and one was exhausted in combat power; the division rated its combat engineer battalion as exhausted. The division lost one officer and four NCOs/enlisted killed in action;15 NCOs/enlisted were wounded in action.

94th Infantry Division – The division defended in sector. To the south was the 389th Infantry Division; to the northeast was the 16th ***Panzer*** Division. The division reported that of its seven infantry battalions, all seven were exhausted in combat power; the division rated its combat engineer battalion as weak. The division lost two NCOs/enlisted wounded in action.

Battle Group Stahel – The battle group defended in sector, south of Erzovka, from the Volga River west.

XXXXVIII *Panzer* Corps

29th Infantry Division (Motorized) – The division occupied an assembly area west of Zybenko and Varvarovka, along the Volga-Don Canal, to prepare for future operations. The division lost one NCO/enlisted killed in action; three NCOs/enlisted were wounded in action.

71st Infantry Division – The division defended in sector. To the north was the 295th

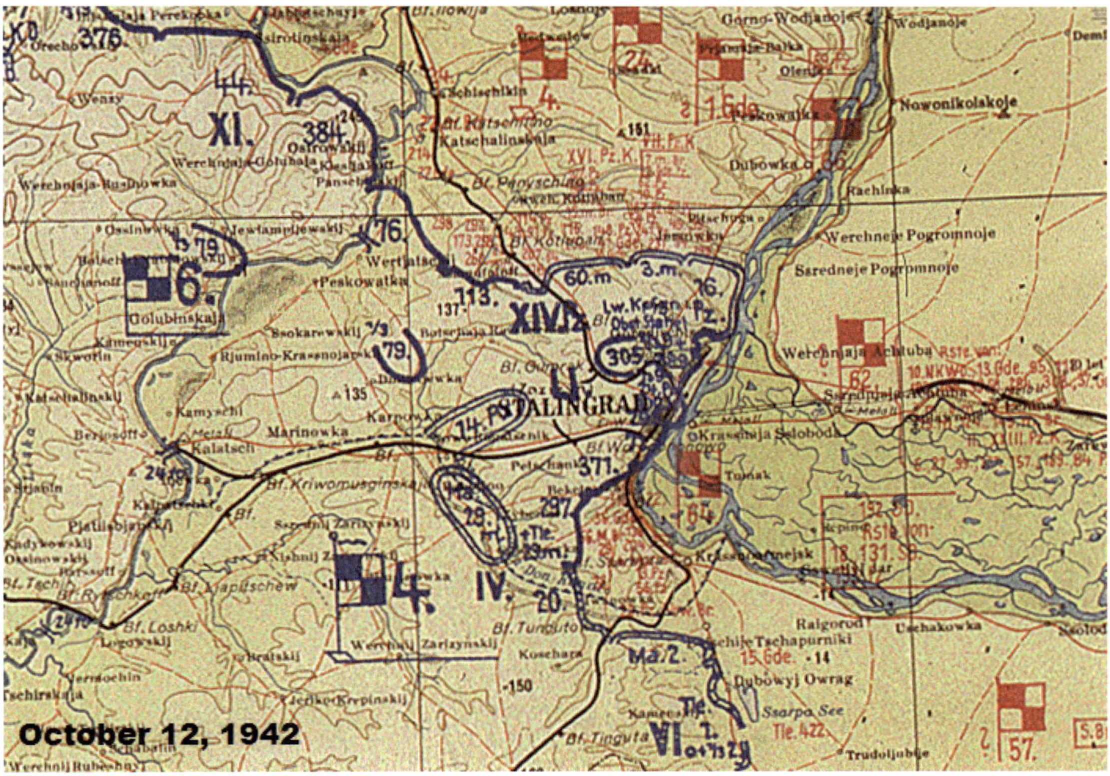

Infantry Division; to the south was the 371st Infantry Division. The division lost one officer and two NCOs/enlisted killed in action; 13 NCOs/enlisted were wounded in action. The division reported that of its seven infantry battalions, all seven were weak in combat power; the division rated its combat engineer battalion as weak.

LI Corps – The corps headquarters was located at Gumrak. The 53rd ***Werfer*** Regiment was assigned to support the corps. The corps suffered the following officer casualties: one killed in action; five wounded in action.

14th Panzer Division – The division moved north toward Stalingrad. The division suffered four NCOs/enlisted killed in action; one officer and 45 NCOs/enlisted were wounded in action.

24th Panzer Division – The division defended at the northern part of the Barrikady Gun Factory Workers' Settlement Barrikady, repelling attacks by the 308th Rifle Division and the 37th Guards Rifle Division. To the north was the 389th Infantry Division; to the south was the 100th ***Jäger*** Division. The division suffered 11 NCOs/enlisted killed in action; 27 NCOs/enlisted were wounded in action. The division reported that of its four ***panzer*** grenadier battalions, one was weak and three were exhausted in combat power; the division rated its combat engineer battalion as exhausted.

100th Jäger Division – The division defended in sector against the 39th Guards Rifle Division and the 193rd Rifle Division, repulsing strong enemy company-size reconnaissance probes of its positions. To the north was the 24th ***Panzer*** Division; to the south was the 295th Infantry Division. The division suffered two officers and three NCOs/enlisted killed in action; two officers and 21 NCOs/enlisted were wounded in action. The division reported that of its four ***jäger*** battalions, three were average and one was weak in combat power; the division rated its combat engineer battalion as weak.

295th Infantry Division – The division defended in sector against the 284th Rifle Division, repulsing strong enemy reconnaissance probes of its positions. To the north was the 100th ***Jäger*** Division; to the south was the 71st Infantry Division. The division lost ten NCOs/enlisted killed in action; one officer and 22 NCOs/enlisted wounded in action. The division reported that of its seven infantry battalions, four were weak and three were exhausted in combat power; the division rated its combat engineer battalion as weak.

389th Infantry Division – The division defended in sector, repulsing strong enemy reconnaissance patrols of its positions. To the north was the 94th Infantry Division; to the south was the 24th ***Panzer*** Division. The division lost four NCOs/enlisted killed in action; 19 NCOs/enlisted were wounded in action. The division reported that of its five infantry battalions, one was weak and four were exhausted in combat power; the division rated its combat engineer battalion as exhausted.

Sixth Army Reserve

79th Infantry Division – One-third of the division defended in sector south of the Don River. To the east was the 44th Infantry Division; to the west was the Romanian V Corps of the Romanian Third Army. The rest of the division moved toward Stalingrad, reaching Dmitriyevka. The division reported that of its eight infantry battalions, three were medium-strong, three were average and two were weak in combat power; the division rated its combat engineer battalion as medium-strong.

305th Infantry Division – The division moved toward Stalingrad. The division suffered one officer and four NCOs/enlisted killed in action; one officer and seven NCOs/enlisted were wounded in action. The division reported that of its nine infantry battalions, all nine were average in combat power; the division rated its combat engineer battalion as strong.

Fourth *Panzer* Army – The army headquarters was located east of Verkhne-Zaryzinskij.

IV Corps

297th Infantry Division – The division defended in sector east of Elkhi and Iagodniki against the 36th Guards Rifle Division. To the north was the 371st Infantry Division; to the south was the 20th Romanian Infantry Division.

371st Infantry Division – The division defended in sector from Kuporosnoye in the east to northwest of Gornaia Poliana, against the 66th Marine Infantry Brigade. To the north was the 71st Infantry Division; to the south was the 297th Infantry Division.

20th Romanian Infantry Division – The division defended in sector, west of the Tundutovo Rail Station and east of Andreevka against the 38th Rifle Division. To the north was the 297th Infantry Division; to the south was the 2nd Romanian Infantry Division of the Romanian VI Corps.

Obergefreiter **Albert Schneider** was born in Amberg, Bavaria on July 8, 1917. Assigned to an infantry regiment in the 113th Infantry Division, he was killed in action at Bol'shaya Rossoschka on October 12, 1942. His remains are buried in the section for the unknown at the German Military Cemetery at Rossoschka.

Sources, October 12, 1942: ***Oberkommando des Heeres, Lage Ost: Stand: 12.10.42, Eastern Front Situation Map, National Archives Identifier: 559733, Record Group 242 – National Archives Collection of Foreign Records Seized, 1675-1958, National Archives, College Park, Maryland; Ia, Armeeoberkommando 6, "Morgen Meldung" and assorted reports, Kriegstagebuch 14, 13 October 1942, as found in Microfilm Series, T-312, Records of German Field Commands, Armies, Roll 1453 and 1688, National Archives and Records Service, College Park, Maryland; Korpsarzt, XXXXVIII Panzerkorps, "Meldung über Personelle Verluste," Stand 12.10.42, as found on T-314, Records of German Field Commands, Corps, Roll 1158, National Archives, College Park, Maryland; Florian Freiherr von und zu Aufsess, Die Anlagenbände zu den Kriegstagebüchern der 6. Armee vom 14.09.1942 bis 24.11.1942, Band 1, Schwabach, Germany: Selbstverlag, 2006, 155-166; David M. Glantz & Jonathan M. House, Armageddon in Stalingrad: September-November 1942, (The Stalingrad Trilogy, Volume 2), Lawrence, Kansas: University Press of Kansas, 2009, 353, 358-359; Adalbert Holl, An Infantryman in Stalingrad, translated by Jason D. Mark and Neill Page, Sydney, Australia: Leaping Horseman Books, 2005, 108; Jason Mark, Death of the Leaping Horseman: 24. Panzer-Division in Stalingrad, Sydney, Australia: Leaping Horsemen Books, 2003, 267-272; Kurt Mehner, Die Geheimen Tagesberichte der Deutschen Wehrmachtführung im Zweiten Weltkrieg 1939-1945, Band 5: 1. Juni 1942 – 30. November 1942, Osnabrück, Germany: Biblio Verlag, 1991, 235; Anton Schimak, Karl Lamprecht & Friedrich Dettmer, Die 44. Infanterie Division: Tagebuch der Hoch- und Deutschmeister, Wien: Verlag Austria Press, 169, 233 and Map: Marschweg der 44. Infanterie Division im Russland.***

October 13, 1942
Weather: overcast, raining, poor conditions for aerial reconnaissance
Sunrise: 6:18 a.m.; **Sunset:** 5:18 p.m.
Moon: Waxing Crescent; 14% illumination

Sixth Army – The army headquarters was located at Golubinskaya.

VIII Corps – The corps suffered the following officer casualties: one wounded in action;

76th Infantry Division – The division defended in sector, east of the Don River, north of Nizhne-Gnilovskii, to west of Kotluban', against the 27th Guards Rifle Division and the 298th Rifle Division. To the southeast was the 113th Infantry Division; to the northwest was the 384th Infantry Division. The division lost eight NCOs/enlisted wounded in action.

113th Infantry Division – The division defended in sector southwest of Samofalovka and north of Borodkin against the 173rd Rifle Division, the 207th Rifle Division, the 221st Rifle Division and the 273rd Rifle Division. To the west was the 76th Infantry Division; to the east was the 60th Infantry Division (Motorized.) The division lost one NCO/enlisted killed in action; one NCO/enlisted was wounded in action.

XI Corps

44th Infantry Division – The division defended in sector Kurchajessowskij-Kamyshinskiy-Hill 171.0-Hill 180.9-Sirotinskaya-Khmelevskoy, against the 40th Guards Rifle Division and the 23rd Rifle Division. The division headquarters was located at Verkhne-Golubaja. To the west was 376th Infantry Division; to the east was the 384th Infantry Division. The division lost one NCO/enlisted wounded in action.

376th Infantry Division – The division defended in sector, south of Perekopskaja, near Logowskii and Ossinskij, against the 321st Rifle Division and the 23rd Rifle Division. To the east was the 44th Infantry Division; to the west was the Romanian Third Army. The division lost two NCOs/enlisted killed in action; two NCOs/enlisted were wounded in action.

384th Infantry Division – The division defended in sector west of the Don River near Trekhostrovskaia to Podgorskii, against the 214th Rifle Division. To the west was the 44th Infantry Division; to the southeast was the 76th Infantry Division. The division lost one NCO/enlisted killed in action; three NCOs/enlisted were wounded in action.

XIV *Panzer* Corps – The corps headquarters was located east of Ssadtschi-Kowa.

3rd Infantry Division (Motorized) – The division defended in sector, from the Tartar Hill-Hill 111.1-Hill 129.6-Hill 131.2 against the 343rd Rifle Division, the 116th Rifle Division, the 38th Guards Rifle Division and the 62nd Tank Brigade. To the east was the 16th ***Panzer*** Division; to the west was the 60th Infantry Division (Motorized.) The division lost one NCO/enlisted killed in action; four NCOs/enlisted were wounded in action.

16th Panzer Division – The division defended in sector, east of the 3rd Infantry Division (Motorized), from Hill 139.7 to the Volga and from the Volga southwest to Hill 145.1, north of Orlovka against the 299th Rifle Division, the 84th Rifle Division and the 99th Rifle Division. To the west was the 3rd Infantry Division (Motorized); to the southwest was the 94th Infantry Division.

60th Infantry Division (Motorized) – The division defended in sector, from south of Kotluban' Station near Borodkin to Kuz'michi against the 49th Rifle Division, the 41st Guards Rifle Division, the 233rd Rifle Division, the 318th Rifle Division and the 231st Rifle Division. To the west was the 113th Infantry Division; to the east was the 3rd Infantry Division (Motorized.) The division lost five NCOs/enlisted killed in action; 15 NCOs/enlisted were wounded in action.

94th Infantry Division – The division defended in sector. To the south was the 389th Infantry Division; to the northeast was the 16th ***Panzer*** Division.

Battle Group Stahel – The battle group occupied an assembly area west of Orlovka.

XXXXVIII *Panzer* Corps

29th Infantry Division (Motorized) – The division occupied an assembly area west of Zybenko and Varvarovka, along the Volga-Don Canal, to prepare for future operations. The division lost one NCO/enlisted killed in action; three NCOs/enlisted were wounded in action.

71st Infantry Division – The division defended in sector. To the north was the 295th Infantry Division; to the south was the 371st Infantry Division. The division reported three heavy anti-tank guns operational. The division lost one officer and two NCOs/enlisted killed in action; 13 NCOs/enlisted were wounded in action.

LI Corps – The corps headquarters was located at Gumrak. The 2nd ***Werfer*** Regiment was assigned to support the corps. The 244th ***Sturmgeschütz*** Detachment, with nine Mark III-Long and nine Mark III-Short assault guns operational, and the 245th ***Sturmgeschütz*** Detachment, with nine Mark III-Long and four Mark III-Short assault guns operational, were assigned to the corps. The corps suffered the following officer casualties: two killed in action; six wounded in action.

14th Panzer Division – The division moved into attack positions in northern Stalingrad; to the north was the 389th Infantry Division; to the south was the 305th Infantry Division.

24th Panzer Division – The division defended at the northern part of the Barrikady Gun Factory Workers' Settlement Barrikady and prepared for offensive operations. To the north was the 305th Infantry Division; to the south was the 100th ***Jäger*** Division. The division suffered one NCO/enlisted killed in action; 12 NCOs/enlisted were wounded in action. The division reported six heavy and 35 medium anti-tank guns operational.

100th Jäger Division – The division defended in sector against the 39th Guards Rifle Division and the 193rd Rifle Division, repulsing several enemy reconnaissance raids. To the north was the 24th ***Panzer*** Division; to the south was the 295th Infantry Division. From September 27 through October 13, the division's 369th Infantry Regiment lost 120 men killed in action, 352 men wounded in

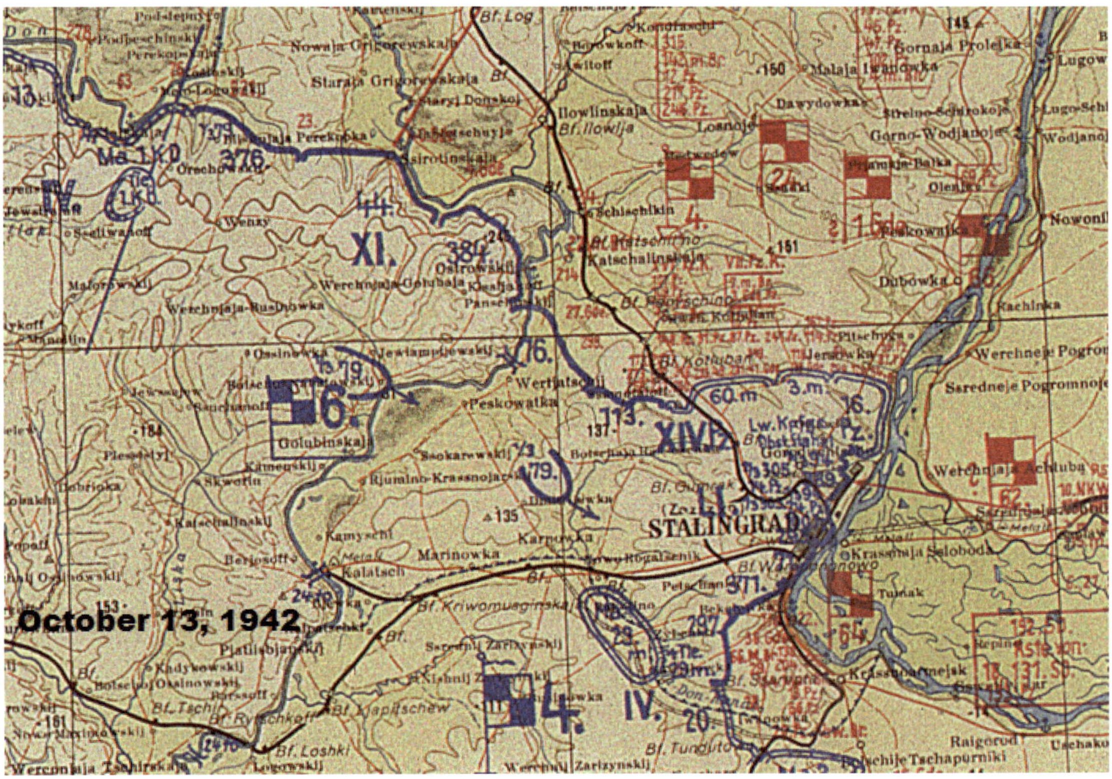

action and 50 men missing in action. The division reported six heavy and ten medium anti-tank guns operational. The division lost three NCOs/enlisted wounded in action.

295th Infantry Division – The division defended in sector against the 284th Rifle Division. To the north was the 100th ***Jäger*** Division; to the south was the 71st Infantry Division. The division reported 13 heavy and three medium anti-tank guns operational. The division lost nine NCOs/enlisted wounded in action.

305th Infantry Division – The division moved into attack positions in northern Stalingrad. To the north was the 14th ***Panzer*** Division; to the south was the 24th ***Panzer*** Division. The division reported 15 heavy and 17 medium anti-tank guns operational. The division lost one officer and four NCOs/enlisted killed in action; one officer and seven NCOs/enlisted were wounded in action.

389th Infantry Division – The division defended in sector, after two limited attacks against the 37th Guards Rifle Division were repelled. The division also repulsed several enemy reconnaissance raids. To the north was the 94th Infantry Division; to the south was the 14th ***Panzer*** Division. The division reported six heavy and 12 medium anti-tank guns operational.

Sixth Army Reserve

79th Infantry Division – One-third of the division defended in sector south of the Don River. To the east was the 376th Infantry Division; to the west was the Romanian V Corps of the Romanian Third Army. The rest of the division moved toward Stalingrad, reaching Pitomnik.

Fourth *Panzer* Army – The army headquarters was located east of Verkhne-Zaryzinskij.

IV Corps

297th Infantry Division – The division defended in sector east of Elkhi and Iagodniki, against the 66th Marine Infantry Brigade. To the north was the 371st Infantry Division; to the south was the 20th Romanian Infantry Division.

371st Infantry Division – The division defended in sector from Kuporosnoye in the east to northwest of Gornaia Poliana against part of the 422nd Rifle Division. To the north was the 71st Infantry Division; to the south was the 297th Infantry Division.

20th Romanian Infantry Division – The division defended in sector, west of the Tundutovo Rail Station and east of Andreevka against the 38th Rifle Division. To the north was the 297th Infantry Division; to the south was the 2nd Romanian Division of the Romanian VI Corps.

Gefreiter **Franz Hüttenberger** was born in Niederham near St. Marienkirchen in Austria. Twenty years old, he was the son of a homeowner and had won the Iron Cross 2nd Class. Hüttenberger died of his wounds at the 1/541 Field Hospital in Kalach on the Don on October 13, 1942. He is buried at Kalach.

Sources, October 13, 1942: *Oberkommando des Heeres, Lage Ost: Stand: 13.10.42, Eastern Front Situation Map, National Archives Identifier: 559733, Record Group 242 – National Archives Collection of Foreign Records Seized, 1675-1958, National Archives, College Park, Maryland; Ia, Armeeoberkommando 6, "Morgen Meldung" and assorted reports, Kriegstagebuch 14, 14 October 1942, as found in Microfilm Series, T-312, Records of German Field Commands, Armies, Roll 1453 and 1688, National Archives and Records Service, College Park, Maryland; Korpsarzt, XXXXVIII Panzerkorps, "Meldung über Personelle Verluste," Stand 13.10.42, as found on T-314, Records of German Field Commands, Corps, Roll 1158, National Archives, College Park, Maryland; Florian Freiherr von und zu Aufsess, Die Anlagenbände zu den Kriegstagebüchern der 6. Armee vom 14.09.1942 bis 24.11.1942, Band 1, Schwabach, Germany: Selbstverlag, 2006, 165-171; David M. Glantz & Jonathan M. House, Armageddon in Stalingrad: September-November 1942, (The Stalingrad Trilogy, Volume 2), Lawrence, Kansas: University Press of Kansas, 2009, 353, 372, 381; Jason Mark, Death of the Leaping Horseman: 24. Panzer-Division in Stalingrad, Sydney, Australia: Leaping Horsemen Books, 2003, 267-272; Kurt Mehner, Die Geheimen Tagesberichte der Deutschen Wehrmachtführung im Zweiten Weltkrieg 1939-1945, Band 5: 1. Juni 1942 – 30. November 1942, Osnabrück, Germany: Biblio Verlag, 1991, 237; Janusz Piekalkiewicz, Stalingrad: Anatomie einer Schlacht, München, BRD: Wilhelm Heyne Verlag, 1977, 272; Anton Schimak, Karl Lamprecht & Friedrich Dettmer, Die 44. Infanterie Division: Tagebuch der Hoch- und Deutschmeister, Wien: Verlag Austria Press, 169, 233 and Map: Marschweg der 44. Infanterie Division im Russland; Hans J. Wijers, Der Kampf um Stalingrad: Die Kämpfe im Industriegelände – 14. Oktober bis 19. November 1942, Selbstverlag, 155.*

Letter, dated October 13, 1942, from *Gefreiter* Helmuth Barth in the Heavy Company of the 29th Infantry Regiment in the 3rd Infantry Division (Motorized.) The letter is to his wife in the tiny village of Crottendorf in the Erzgebirge Mountains. He writes:

> "It was with great joy that I received your two letters today; one was from October 5. Thank you very much; I am well. We managed to push the Russians over the Volga and we do not have too much artillery fire from across the river. As long as we stay in this position here [north of Stalingrad,] we do not have much to do. Our bakery has not yet arrived. We get our supplies from the infantry, as the road to our own supply depot is too dangerous.
>
> Dear Ilse, yes I have heard that Minzel was killed in action. He had been back from furlough only two days when it happened. I was as shattered as you were. I would have loved to see him again before he went back. I was told that he died of loss of blood. But please do not tell anyone. I do not want to write much about these things.
>
> Yes, Ilse, as an observer, one is constantly in the front line. Let me know who else was killed. Karl Steier has a better job I suppose. He is always in the rear with the horses, far from the shooting war.
>
> I have remembered our wedding anniversary. How fast a year goes by. A year ago, everything was OK and now we are catching lice. I have caught 28 so far. The lice powder that you mailed me does not bother them, but thank you also for the two photos; I will keep them. Well, that is all for now, as the candle will go out soon. Greetings and kisses."

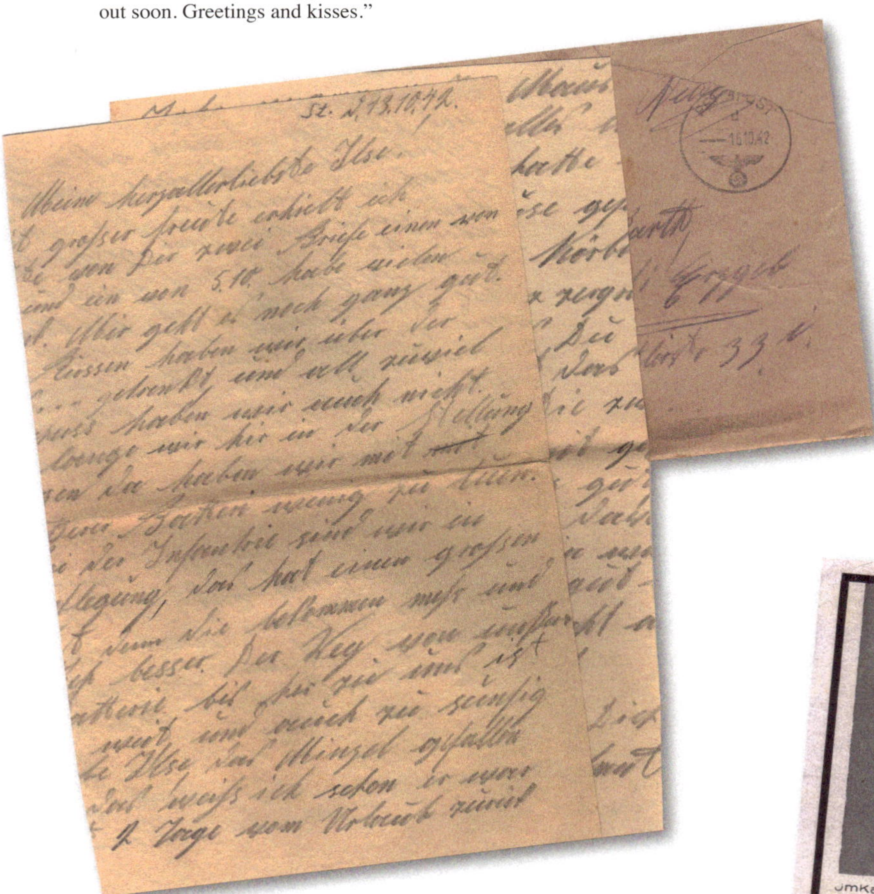

Im Kampf geg. den Bolschewismus starb den Heldentod fürs Vaterland

GEORG WEISS

Landwirtssohn, **Höllmannsried**

Gefreiter einer Granatwerfer-Abtlg gefallen am 13. Okt. 1942 im Blüten-Alter von 20 Jahren bei Stalingrad.

Heiß beweint von Deinen Lieben
Die gebeugt vor Schmerz und Gram
Du bist so schnell von uns geschieden
Und das hat nun der Krieg getan.
Ach es ist kaum zu fassen,
Daß Du nimmer kehrst zurück.
So jung mußtest Du dein Leben lassen
Zerstört ist unser ganzes Glück.
Nichts möge stören deine Grabesruh
Schlaf wohl guter Sohn u. Bruder du

Druckerei A. Lackerbauer, Regen Tel. 71

Gefreiter **Georg Weiss**, the son of a farmer from Höllmannsried near Regen, Bavaria, was born on December 5, 1922. Assigned to a mortar detachment, he was killed in action at the Barrikady Gun Factory on October 13, 1942. His remains have never been located, but he is listed in the remembrance book at the German Military Cemetery at Rossoschka.

October 14, 1942
Weather: clear and sunny morning, increasing cloudiness, cool
Sunrise: 6:19 a.m.; **Sunset:** 5:16 p.m.
Moon: Waxing Crescent; 23% illumination

Sixth Army – Bombers and dive-bombers from the ***Luftwaffe***'s VIII Air Corps pounded enemy positions in the northern half of Stalingrad. The army headquarters was located at Golubinskaya. The aim of the Sixth Army in the upcoming attack was initially to push the XIV ***Panzer*** Corps through Rynok and Spartakovka to the mouth of the Gorodishche River. The LI Corps would occupy the Dzerzhinsky Tractor Factory, the Brick Works and reach the bank of the Volga River. It would then turn south and seize the Barrikady Gun Factory, the Krasny Oktyabr Steel Factory and the Lazur Chemical Works.

VIII Corps – The 670th ***Panzerjäger*** Detachment was assigned to the corps. The corps suffered the following officer casualties: one wounded in action.

76th Infantry Division – The division defended in sector, east of the Don River, north of Nizhne-Gnilovskii, to west of Kotluban', against the 27th Guards Rifle Division and the 298th Rifle Division. To the southeast was the 113th Infantry Division; to the northwest was the 384th Infantry Division. The division suffered one NCO/enlisted killed in action; nine NCOs/enlisted were wounded in action.

113th Infantry Division – The division defended in sector southwest of Samofalovka and north of Borodkin against the 173rd Rifle Division, the 207th Rifle Division, the 221st Rifle Division and the 273rd Rifle Division. To the northwest was the 76th Infantry Division; to the east was the 60th Infantry Division (Motorized.) The division lost five NCOs/enlisted killed in action; 28 NCOs/ enlisted were wounded in action.

XI Corps

44th Infantry Division – The division defended in sector Kurchajessowskij-Kamyshinskiy-Hill 171.0-Hill 180.9-Sirotinskaya-Khmelevskoy against the 40th Guards Rifle Division and the 4th Guards Rifle Division. The division headquarters was located at Verkhne-Golubaja. To the west was 376th Infantry Division; to the southeast was the 384th Infantry Division. The division lost two NCOs/ enlisted wounded in action.

376th Infantry Division – The division defended in sector, south of Perekopskaja, near Logowskii and Ossinskij against the 23rd Rifle Division and the 321st Rifle Division. To the east was the 44th Infantry Division; to the west was the Romanian Third Army. The division lost one NCO/enlisted killed in action.

384th Infantry Division – The division defended in sector west of the Don River near Trekhostrovskaia to Podgorskii against the 214th Rifle Division. To the west was the 44th Infantry Division; to the southeast was the 76th Infantry Division.

XIV *Panzer* Corps – The aim of the corps was to attack through Rynok and Spartakovka to the mouth of the Gorodishche River. The corps suffered the following officer casualties: two wounded in action. The corps headquarters was located east of Ssadtschi-Kowa.

3rd Infantry Division (Motorized) – The division defended in sector, from the Tartar Hill-Hill 111.1-Hill 129.6-Hill 131.2 against the 343rd Rifle Division, the 116th Rifle Division, the 38th Guards Rifle Division and the 62nd Tank Brigade. To the east was the 16th ***Panzer*** Division; to the west was the 60th Infantry Division (Motorized.) The division lost two NCOs/enlisted wounded in action.

16th Panzer Division – The division defended in sector, from Hill 139.7 to the Volga and from the Volga southwest to Hill 145.1, north of Orlovka against the 299th Rifle Division, the 84th Rifle Division and the 99th Rifle Division. The division prepared to conduct offensive operations to destroy enemy forces at Hill 135.4, Spartakovka and Rynok north of the Mokraya Mechetka River against the 124th Rifle Brigade, the 149th Rifle Brigade, the 115th Rifle Brigade and the 2nd Motorized Rifle Brigade. The division was reinforced by the 651st Engineer Battalion. The division lost nine NCOs/enlisted wounded in action.

60th Infantry Division (Motorized) – The division defended in sector, from south of Kotluban' Station near Borodkin to Kuz'michi against the 49th Rifle Division, the 41st Guards Rifle Division, the 233rd Rifle Division, the 318th Rifle Division and the 231st Rifle Division. To the west was the 113th Infantry Division; to the east was the 3rd Infantry Division (Motorized.) The division lost three NCOs/enlisted killed in action; 20 NCOs/enlisted were wounded in action.

94th Infantry Division – The division defended in sector and prepared to attack against the 124th Rifle Brigade, the 149th Rifle Brigade, the 115th Rifle Brigade and the 2nd Motorized Rifle Brigade. To the south was the 389th Infantry Division; to the northeast was the 16th ***Panzer*** Division. The division lost seven NCOs/enlisted wounded in action.

Battle Group Stahel – The battle group occupied an assembly area west of Orlovka.

LI Corps – The initial aim of the corps was to seize the Dzerzhinsky Tractor Factory, the Brick Works and reach the bank of the Volga River. The corps headquarters was located at Gumrak. The corps suffered the following officer casualties: 11 killed in action; 37 wounded in action.

14th Panzer Division – The division attacked in zone, advancing through the southern portion of the Dzerzhinsky Tractor Factory, deflecting a counter-attack by the 84th Tank Brigade and crushing the 37th Guards Rifle Division. To the north was the 389th Infantry Division; to the south was the 305th Infantry Division. The division lost four officers and 27 NCOs/enlisted killed in action; nine officers and 96 NCOs/enlisted were wounded in action; two men were reported missing in action.

24th Panzer Division – The division attacked in zone at Skulpturny Park, the Brick Works and the southern part of the Dzerzhinsky Tractor Factory against the 112th Rifle Division

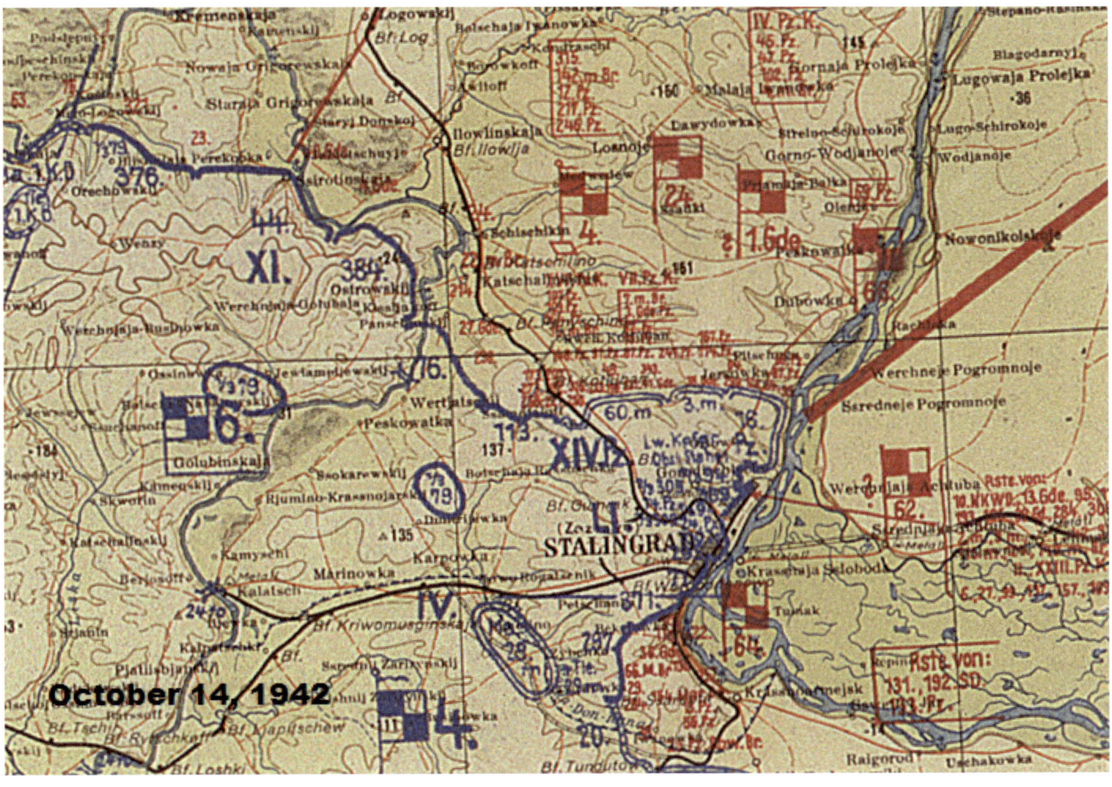

and part of the 37th Guards Rifle Division. To the north was the 305th Infantry Division; to the south was the 100th ***Jäger*** Division. The division suffered one officer and 31 NCOs/enlisted killed in action; two officers and 50 NCOs/enlisted were wounded in action; one man was reported missing in action. Eight tanks of the division were damaged in the attacks.

71st Infantry Division – The division defended in sector. To the north was the 295th Infantry Division; to the south was the 371st Infantry Division. The division lost three NCOs/enlisted killed in action; 12 NCOs/enlisted were wounded in action.

100th Jäger Division – The division conducted several reconnaissance-in-force operations against the 39th Guards Rifle Division and the 193rd Rifle Division to prevent enemy units from moving north. To the north was the 24th ***Panzer*** Division; to the south was the 295th Infantry Division. The division lost eight NCOs/enlisted killed in action; 29 NCOs/enlisted were wounded in action. The division received two "march-battalions" of replacements, each with 50 to 60 men.

295th Infantry Division – The division defended in sector against the 284th Rifle Division. To the north was the 100th ***Jäger*** Division; to the south was the 71st Infantry Division. The division suffered one officer and two NCOs/enlisted killed in action; one officer and 11 NCOs/enlisted were wounded in action.

305th Infantry Division – The division attacked in zone in the northwest portion of the Dzerzhinsky Tractor Factory and the housing area to the northeast against the 305th Rifle Division, the 95th Rifle Division and the 37th Guards Rifle Division. To the north was the 14th ***Panzer*** Division; to the south was the 24th ***Panzer*** Division. The division lost 84 NCOs/enlisted killed in action; seven officers and 276 NCOs/enlisted were wounded in action; 15 men were reported missing in action. The division was reinforced by the 244th ***Sturmgeschütz*** Detachment and the 245th ***Sturmgeschütz*** Detachment. Six assault guns of the 244th and seven assault guns of the 245th were damaged in the attacks.

389th Infantry Division – The division attacked in zone into the Dzerzhinsky Tractor Factory and the workers' settlement, overrunning the 112th Rifle Division and seizing terrain to the east. To the north was the 94th Infantry Division; to the south was the 14th ***Panzer*** Division.

Sixth Army Reserve

79th Infantry Division – One-third of the division defended in sector south of the Don River. To the east was the 44th Infantry Division; to the west was the Romanian V Corps of the Romanian Third Army. The rest of the division moved toward Stalingrad.

Fourth *Panzer* Army – The army headquarters was located east of Verkhne-Zaryzinskij.

IV Corps

297th Infantry Division – The division defended in sector east of Elkhi and Iagodniki, against the 66th Marine Infantry Brigade and the 29th Rifle Division. To the north was the 371st Infantry Division; to the south was the 20th Romanian Infantry Division.

371st Infantry Division – The division defended in sector from Kuporosnoye in the east to northwest of Gornaia Poliana against part of the 422nd Rifle Division. To the north was the 71st Infantry Division; to the south was the 297th Infantry Division.

20th Romanian Infantry Division – The division defended in sector, west of the Tundutovo Rail Station and east of Andreevka against the 38th Rifle Division. To the north was the 297th Infantry Division; to the south was the 2nd Romanian Infantry Division of the Romanian VI Corps.

Fourth *Panzer* Army Reserve

29th Infantry Division (Motorized) – The division occupied an assembly area west of Zybenko and Varvarovka, along the Volga-Don Canal, to prepare for future operations. The division lost two NCOs/enlisted wounded in action; two NCOs/enlisted were reported missing in action.

Gebets-Andenken
an
Josef Detterbeck
Funker in einer Nachrichten-Abtlg.
Finanzanwärter am Finanzamt
München-Süd
geboren am 12. Oktober 1922
gefallen am 14. Oktober 1942
in Stalingrad (Rußland)

Auf Feindesboden schwer und müd
sank hin Dein Haupt zur letzten Ruh,
fürs Vaterland gabst Du Dein Leben,
schlaf wohl, Du wackrer Streiter Du!
Warst noch so jung, starbst viel zu früh,
wer Dich gekannt, vergißt Dich nie.
Doch es lag in des Höchsten Plan
was Gott tut, das ist wohlgetan.

„Mein Jesus Barmherzigkeit!"

M. Wälischmiller, Dingolfing

Funker **Josef Detterbeck** was born in Straubing, Bavaria on October 12, 1922. Before entering the military, he worked in a finance office in south Munich. Detterbeck served as a radio operator in a signal unit, possibly as part of an artillery battalion. He was killed in action on October 14, 1942 at Stalingrad, just two days after his twentieth birthday. His remains are buried in the section for the unknown at the German Military Cemetery at Rossoschka.

Funker **Josef Detterbeck**

Sources, October 14, 1942: *Oberkommando des Heeres, Lage Ost: Stand: 14.10.42, Eastern Front Situation Map, National Archives Identifier: 559733, Record Group 242 – National Archives Collection of Foreign Records Seized, 1675-1958, National Archives, College Park, Maryland; Ia, Armeeoberkommando 6, "Morgen Meldung" and assorted reports, Kriegstagebuch 14, 15 October 1942, as found in Microfilm Series, T-312, Records of German Field Commands, Armies, Roll 1453 and 1688, National Archives and Records Service, College Park, Maryland; Korpsarzt, XXXXVIII Panzerkorps, "Meldung über Personelle Verluste," Stand 14.10.42, as found on T-314, Records of German Field Commands, Corps, Roll 1158, National Archives, College Park, Maryland; Florian Freiherr von und zu Aufsess, Die Anlagenbände zu den Kriegstagebüchern der 6. Armee vom 14.09.1942 bis 24.11.1942, Band 1, Schwabach, Germany: Selbstverlag, 2006, 168-175; Antony Beevor, Stalingrad: The Fateful Siege: 1942-1943, London: Penguin Books, 1998, 192-193; William Craig, Enemy at the Gates: The Battle for Stalingrad, New York: Readers' Digest Press, 1973, 135; David M. Glantz & Jonathan M. House, Armageddon in Stalingrad: September-November 1942, (The Stalingrad Trilogy, Volume 2), Lawrence, Kansas: University Press of Kansas, 2009, 355, 379-391; Adalbert Holl, An Infantryman in Stalingrad, translated by Jason D. Mark and Neill Page, Sydney, Australia: Leaping Horseman Books, 2005, 104; Jason Mark, Death of the Leaping Horseman: 24. Panzer-Division in Stalingrad, Sydney, Australia: Leaping Horsemen Books, 2003, 272-278; Jason Mark, Island of Fire: The Battle for the Barrikady Gun Factory in Stalingrad, November 1942 – February 1943, Sydney, Australia: Leaping Horsemen Books, 2006, 4; Kurt Mehner, Die Geheimen Tagesberichte der Deutschen Wehrmachtführung im Zweiten Weltkrieg 1939-1945, Band 5: 1. Juni 1942 – 30. November 1942, Osnabrück, Germany: Biblio Verlag, 1991, 239; Hans Neidhardt, Mit Tanne und Eichenlaub: Kriegschronik der 100. Jäger Division vormals 100. leichte Infanterie Division, Graz, Austria: Leopold Stocker Verlag, 1981, 215; Janusz Piekalkiewicz, Stalingrad: Anatomie einer Schlacht, München, BRD: Wilhelm Heyne Verlag, 1977, 300; Anton Schimak, Karl Lamprecht & Friedrich Dettmer, Die 44. Infanterie Division: Tagebuch der Hoch- und Deutschmeister, Wien: Verlag Austria Press, 169, 233 and Map: Marschweg der 44. Infanterie Division im Russland.*

October 15, 1942
Weather: fresh, dry, bright, sunny, changing cloudiness
Sunrise: 6:21 a.m.; **Sunset:** 5:14 p.m.
Moon: Waxing Crescent; 34% illumination

Sixth Army – Bombers and dive-bombers from the ***Luftwaffe***'s VIII Air Corps pounded enemy positions in the northern half of Stalingrad. The army headquarters was located at Golubinskaya.

VIII Corps

76th Infantry Division – The division defended in sector, east of the Don River, north of Nizhne-Gnilovskii, to west of Kotluban', against the 27th Guards Rifle Division and the 298th Rifle Division. To the southeast was the 113th Infantry Division; to the northwest was the 384th Infantry Division. The division suffered one NCO/enlisted killed in action; nine NCOs/enlisted were wounded in action. The division reported 19 heavy and four medium anti-tank guns operational.

113th Infantry Division – The division defended in sector southwest of Samofalovka and north of Borodkin, against the 258th Rifle Division, the 207th Rifle Division, the 221st Rifle Division, the 273rd Rifle Division and the 173rd Rifle Division. To the northwest was the 76th Infantry Division; to the east was the 60th Infantry Division (Motorized.) The division lost five NCOs/enlisted killed in action; 28 NCOs/enlisted were wounded in action. The division reported 19 heavy and 17 medium anti-tank guns operational.

XI Corps

44th Infantry Division – The division defended in sector Kurchajessowskij-Kamyshinskiy-Hill 171.0-Hill 180.9-Sirotinskaya-Khmelevskoy, against the 40th Guards Rifle Division and the 23rd Rifle Division. The division headquarters was located at Verkhne-Golubaja. To the west was 376th Infantry Division; to the southeast was the 384th Infantry Division.

376th Infantry Division – The division defended in sector, south of Perekopskaja, near Logowskii and Ossinskij, against the 321st Rifle Division and the 23rd Rifle Division. To the east was the 44th Infantry Division; to the west was the Romanian Third Army. The division lost one NCO/enlisted killed in action; three NCOs/enlisted were wounded in action.

384th Infantry Division – The division defended in sector west of the Don River near Trekhostrovskaia to Podgorskii, against the 214th Rifle Division and the 22nd Mechanized Brigade. To the west was the 44th Infantry Division; to the southeast was the 76th Infantry Division. The division lost two NCOs/enlisted wounded in action.

XIV *Panzer* Corps – The aim of the corps was to conduct offensive operations at Spartakovka and Rynok. The corps headquarters was located east of Ssadtschi-Kowa. The corps suffered the following officer casualties: four killed in action; eight wounded in action; and one missing in action.

3rd Infantry Division (Motorized) – The division defended in sector, from the Tartar Hill-Hill 111.1-Hill 129.6-Hill 131.2 against the 343rd Rifle Division, the 116th Rifle Division and the 114th Tank Brigade. To the east was the 16th ***Panzer*** Division; to the west was the 60th Infantry Division (Motorized.) The division lost one NCO/enlisted killed in action; three NCOs/enlisted were wounded in action.

16th Panzer Division – The division defended in sector, from Hill 139.7 to the Volga and from the Volga southwest to Hill 145.1, north of Orlovka against the 299th Rifle Division, the 64th Rifle Division, the 120th Rifle Division and the 99th Rifle Division. To the west was the 3rd Infantry Division (Motorized); to the southwest was the 94th Infantry Division. In its southern sector, the division – reinforced by the 651st Engineer Battalion – attacked at Spartakovka and Rynok against the 124th Rifle Brigade, the 149th Rifle Brigade, the 115th Rifle Brigade and the 2nd Motorized Rifle Brigade. The division reported the following ***panzer***s as operational: 36 Mark III-Long, three Mark IV-Short and 11 Mark IV-Long tanks. The division lost four officers and 41 NCOs/enlisted killed in action; five officers and 147 NCOs/enlisted were wounded in action; eight men were reported missing in action.

60th Infantry Division (Motorized) – The division defended in sector, from south of Kotluban' Station near Borodkin to Kuz'michi, against the 260th Rifle Division, the 49th Rifle Division and the 231st Rifle Division. To the west was the 113th Infantry Division; to the east was the 3rd Infantry Division (Motorized.) The division reported the following ***panzer***s as operational: four Mark II, one Mark III-Short, 13 Mark III-Long, three Mark IV-Short and 12 Mark IV-Long tanks. The division lost eight NCOs/enlisted wounded in action.

94th Infantry Division – The division attacked in zone, seizing terrain near the Orlovka River north of the Dzerzhinsky Tractor Factory Workers' Settlement against the 124th Rifle Brigade, the 149th Rifle Brigade, the 115th Rifle Brigade and the 2nd Motorized Rifle Brigade. To the south was the 389th Infantry Division; to the northeast was the 16th ***Panzer*** Division. The division lost three NCOs/enlisted wounded in action.

Battle Group Stahel – The battle group defended in sector, south of Erzovka, from the Volga River west.

LI Corps – The corps headquarters was located at Gumrak. The corps suffered the following officer casualties: one killed in action; 16 wounded in action; two missing in action.

14th Panzer Division – The division attacked in zone through the Dzerzhinsky Tractor Factory, against the 112th Rifle Division, the 37th Guards Rifle Division and the 95th Rifle Division, and reached the Volga River south of the fuel dump. To the north was the 389th Infantry Division; to the south was the 305th Infantry Division. The division reported the following

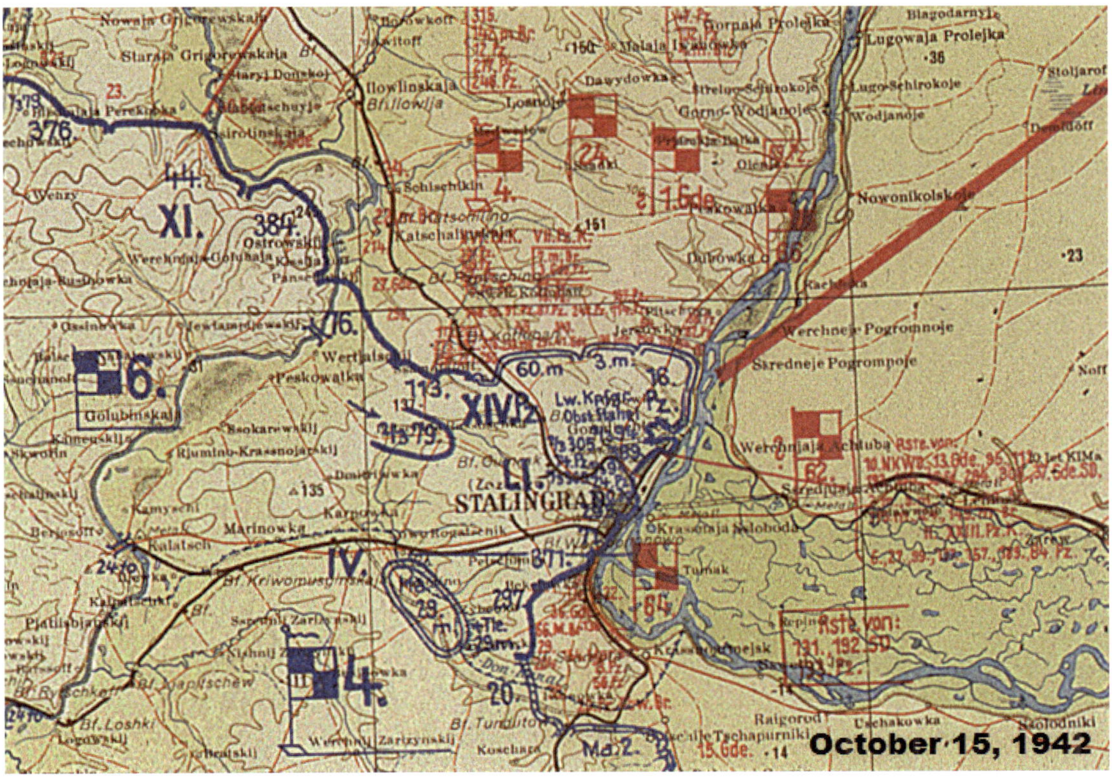

***panzer*s as operational: three Mark II, three Mark III-Short, nine Mark III-Long, two Mark IV-Short and four Mark IV-Long tanks. The division lost three NCOs/enlisted killed in action; two officers and 83 NCOs/enlisted were wounded in action.

24th Panzer Division – The division conducted consolidation operations at Skulpturny Park, the Brick Works and the southern part of the Dzerzhinsky Tractor Factory against elements of the 95th Rifle Division and the 37th Guards Rifle Division, and prepared to support an attack by the 14th ***Panzer*** Division and the 305th Infantry Division the following day. To the north was the 305th Infantry Division; to the south was the 100th ***Jäger*** Division. The division suffered one officer and seven NCOs/enlisted killed in action; 22 NCOs/enlisted were wounded in action; one of them died of wounds later in the day. The division reported the following ***panzer*s as operational: six Mark II, six Mark III-Short, ten Mark III-Long and four Mark IV-Short tanks.

71st Infantry Division – The division defended in sector. To the north was the 295th Infantry Division; to the south was the 371st Infantry Division. One man was reported missing in action.

100th Jäger Division – The division conducted several reconnaissance-in-force operations against the 39th Guards Rifle Division and the 193rd Rifle Division to prevent enemy units from moving north. To the north was the 24th ***Panzer*** Division; to the south was the 295th Infantry Division. The division lost seven NCOs/enlisted killed in action; 27 NCOs/enlisted were wounded in action.

295th Infantry Division – The division defended in sector against the 284th Rifle Division. To the north was the 100th ***Jäger*** Division; to the south was the 71st Infantry Division. The division lost two NCOs/enlisted killed in action; nine NCOs/enlisted were wounded in action.

305th Infantry Division – The division attacked in zone in the ruins of the Dzerzhinsky Tractor Factory and the Dzerzhinsky Tractor Factory Workers' Settlement against the 112th Rifle Division, capturing the landing south of the junction of the Volga and Mokraia Mechetka Rivers and penetrating southward to Pribaltiiskaia Street against elements of the 39th Guards Rifle Division. To the north was the 14th ***Panzer*** Division; to the south was the 24th ***Panzer*** Division. The division was reinforced by the 244th ***Sturmgeschütz*** Detachment and the 245th ***Sturmgeschütz*** Detachment. The division lost 53 NCOs/enlisted killed in action; seven officers and 122 NCOs/enlisted were wounded in action; one man was reported missing in action.

389th Infantry Division – The division attacked in zone into the Dzerzhinsky Tractor Factory and the Dzerzhinsky Tractor Factory Workers' Settlement against the 112th Rifle Division, while under heavy artillery fire from the Volga River's eastern bank. To the north was the 94th Infantry Division; to the south was the 14th ***Panzer*** Division.

Sixth Army Reserve

79th Infantry Division – One-third of the division defended in sector south of the Don River. To the east was the 44th Infantry Division; to the west was the Romanian V Corps of the Romanian Third Army. The rest of the division was in march-order from Bol'shaya Rossoschka to Zapadnovka. The division reported 16 heavy and ten medium anti-tank guns operational.

Fourth *Panzer* Army – The army headquarters was located east of Verkhne-Zaryzinskij.

IV Corps

297th Infantry Division – The division defended in sector east of Elkhi and Iagodniki, against the 36th Guards Rifle Division and the 29th Rifle Division. To the north was the 371st Infantry Division; to the south was the 20th Romanian Infantry Division.

371st Infantry Division – The division defended in sector from Kuporosnoye in the east to northwest of Gornaia Poliana against part of the 422nd Rifle Division. To the north was the 71st Infantry Division; to the south was the 297th Infantry Division.

20th Romanian Infantry Division – The division defended in sector, west of the Tundutovo Rail Station and east of Andreevka, against the 204th Rifle Division and the 38th Rifle Division. To the north was the 297th Infantry Division; to the south was the 2nd Romanian Infantry Division of the Romanian VI Corps.

Fourth *Panzer* Army Reserve

29th Infantry Division (Motorized) – The division occupied an assembly area west of Zybenko and Varvarovka, along the Volga-Don Canal, to prepare for future operations.

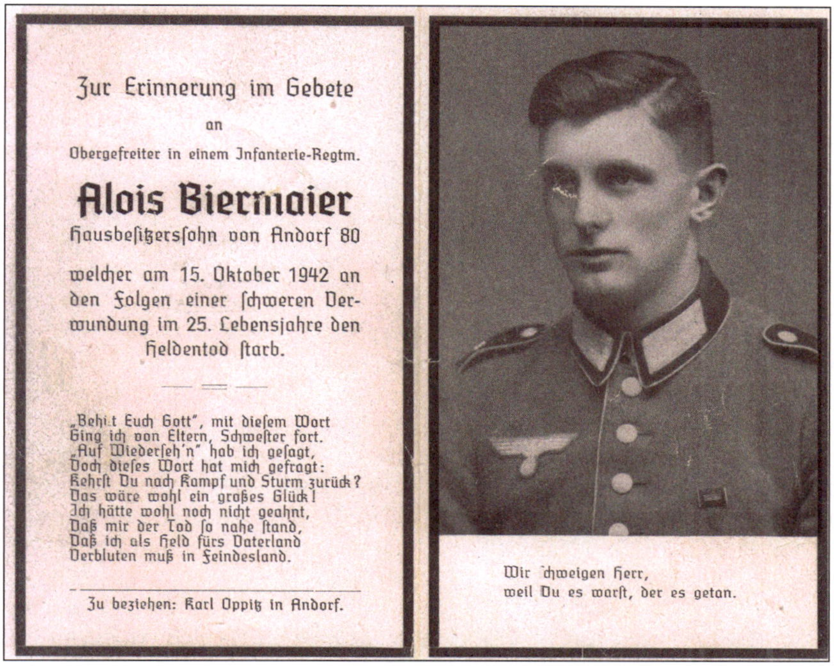
Zur Erinnerung im Gebete

an

Obergefreiter in einem Infanterie-Regtm.

Alois Biermaier

Hausbesitzerssohn von Andorf 80

welcher am 15. Oktober 1942 an den Folgen einer schweren Verwundung im 25. Lebensjahre den Heldentod starb.

„Behüt Euch Gott", mit diesem Wort
Ging ich von Eltern, Schwester fort.
„Auf Wiederseh'n" hab ich gesagt,
Doch dieses Wort hat mich gefragt:
Kehrst Du nach Kampf und Sturm zurück?
Das wäre wohl ein großes Glück!
Ich hätte wohl noch nicht geahnt,
Daß mir der Tod so nahe stand,
Daß ich als Held fürs Vaterland
Verbluten muß in Feindesland.

Zu beziehen: Karl Oppitz in Andorf.

Wir schweigen Herr,
weil Du es warst, der es getan.

Obergefreiter **Alois Biermaier** was born in Eggerding, Austria on November 7, 1917. Assigned to the 297th Infantry Division in one of the infantry regiments, he died of his wounds at Gavrilovka on October 15, 1942, in the care of the 2nd Medical Company of the 297th Medical Detachment. His name is listed in the remembrance book at the German Military Cemetery at Rossoschka.

Sources, October 15, 1942: ***Oberkommando des Heeres, Lage Ost: Stand: 15.10.42, Eastern Front Situation Map, National Archives Identifier: 559733, Record Group 242 – National Archives Collection of Foreign Records Seized, 1675-1958, National Archives, College Park, Maryland; Ia, Armeeoberkommando 6, "Morgen Meldung" and assorted reports, Kriegstagebuch 14, 16 October 1942, as found in Microfilm Series, T-312, Records of German Field Commands, Armies, Roll 1453 and 1688, National Archives and Records Service, College Park, Maryland; Korpsarzt, XXXXVIII Panzerkorps, "Meldung über Personelle Verluste," Stand 15.10.42, as found on T-314, Records of German Field Commands, Corps, Roll 1158, National Archives, College Park, Maryland; Florian Freiherr von und zu Aufsess, Die Anlagenbände zu den Kriegstagebüchern der 6. Armee vom 14.09.1942 bis 24.11.1942, Band 1, Schwabach, Germany: Selbstverlag, 2006, 172-179; Antony Beevor, Stalingrad: The Fateful Siege: 1942-1943, London: Penguin Books, 1998, 194-195; David M. Glantz & Jonathan M. House, Armageddon in Stalingrad: September-November 1942, (The Stalingrad Trilogy, Volume 2), Lawrence, Kansas: University Press of Kansas, 2009, 393-400; Adalbert Holl, An Infantryman in Stalingrad, translated by Jason D. Mark and Neill Page, Sydney, Australia: Leaping Horseman Books, 2005, 106; Manfred Kehrig, Stalingrad: Analyse und Dokumentation einer Schlacht, Stuttgart, FRG: Deutsche Verlags-Anstalt, 1976, 38; Jason Mark, Death of the Leaping Horseman: 24. Panzer-Division in Stalingrad, Sydney, Australia: Leaping Horsemen Books, 2003, 278-279; Jason Mark, Island of Fire: The Battle for the Barrikady Gun Factory in Stalingrad, November 1942 – February 1943, Sydney, Australia: Leaping Horsemen Books, 2006, 4, 6; Anton Schimak, Karl Lamprecht & Friedrich Dettmer, Die 44. Infanterie Division: Tagebuch der Hoch- und Deutschmeister, Wien: Verlag Austria Press, 169, 233 and Map: Marschweg der 44. Infanterie Division im Russland.***

October 16, 1942
Weather: changing cloudiness, cool, frost at night
Sunrise: 6:22 a.m.; **Sunset:** 5:12 p.m.
Moon: First Quarter; 50% illumination

Sixth Army – Bombers and dive-bombers from the ***Luftwaffe***'s VIII Air Corps pounded enemy positions at the Barrikady Gun Factory. The army headquarters was located at Golubinskaya. From August 13 to October 16, the army lost 69 officers and 2,438 NCOs/enlisted killed in action; 271 officers and 10,107 NCOs/enlisted were wounded in action; three officers and 298 NCOs/enlisted were reported missing in action.

VIII Corps – The 851st Heavy Artillery Detachment and the 849th Heavy Artillery Detachment were attached to support the corps. The corps suffered the following officer casualties: one killed in action; one wounded in action

76th Infantry Division – The division defended in sector, east of the Don River, north of Nizhne-Gnilovskii, to west of Kotluban' against the 27th Guards Rifle Division and the 298th Rifle Division. To the southeast was the 113th Infantry Division; to the northwest was the 384th Infantry Division. The division lost one NCO/enlisted killed in action; seven NCOs/enlisted were wounded in action.

113th Infantry Division – The division defended in sector southwest of Samofalovka and north of Borodkin against the 258th Rifle Division, the 207th Rifle Division, the 221st Rifle Division, the 273rd Rifle Division and the 173rd Rifle Division. To the northwest was the 76th Infantry Division; to the east was the 60th Infantry Division (Motorized.) The division lost one officer and nine NCOs/enlisted killed in action; 48 NCOs/enlisted were wounded in action.

XI Corps

44th Infantry Division – The division defended in sector Kurchajessowskij-Kamyshinskiy-Hill 171.0-Hill 180.9-Sirotinskaya-Khmelevskoy, against the 40th Guards Rifle Division and the 23rd Rifle Division. The division headquarters was located at Verkhne-Golubaja. To the west was 376th Infantry Division; to the east was the 384th Infantry Division. The division lost two NCOs/enlisted killed in action; six NCOs/enlisted were wounded in action.

376th Infantry Division – The division defended in sector, south of Perekopskaja, near Logowskii and Ossinskij against the 321st Rifle Division and the 23rd Rifle Division. To the east was the 44th Infantry Division; to the west was the Romanian Third Army.

384th Infantry Division – The division defended in sector west of the Don River near Trekhostrovskaia to Podgorskii against the 214th Rifle Division and the 22nd Mechanized Brigade. To the west was the 44th Infantry Division; to the southeast was the 76th Infantry Division. The division lost one NCO/enlisted wounded in action.

XIV *Panzer* Corps – The corps headquarters was located east of Ssadtschi-Kowa. The 631st Heavy Artillery Detachment, the 2nd Battalion of the 46th Artillery Regiment, the 51st ***Werfer*** Regiment and the 177th ***Sturmgeschütz*** Detachment were attached to the corps. The corps suffered the following officer casualties: two wounded in action.

3rd Infantry Division (Motorized) – The division defended in sector, from the Tartar Hill-Hill 111.1-Hill 129.6-Hill 131.2 against the 343rd Rifle Division, the 116th Rifle Division and the 114th Tank Brigade. To the east was the 16th ***Panzer*** Division; to the west was the 60th Infantry Division (Motorized.)

16th Panzer Division – The division defended in sector, from Hill 139.7 to the Volga and from the Volga southwest to Hill 145.1, north of Orlovka against the 299th Rifle Division, the 64th Rifle Division, the 120th Rifle Division and the 99th Rifle Division. To the west was the 3rd Infantry Division (Motorized); to the southwest was the 94th Infantry Division. In its southern sector, the division – reinforced by the 651st Engineer Battalion – attacked at Spartakovka and Rynok, seizing part of the former against the 124th Rifle Brigade, the 149th Rifle Brigade, the 115th Rifle Brigade and the 2nd Motorized Rifle Brigade. The division lost 18 NCOs/enlisted killed in action; 72 NCOs/enlisted were wounded in action; seven men were reported missing in action.

60th Infantry Division (Motorized) – The division defended in sector, from south of Kotluban' Station near Borodkin to Kuz'michi, against the 260th Rifle Division, the 49th Rifle Division and the 231st Rifle Division. To the west was the 113th Infantry Division; to the east was the 3rd Infantry Division (Motorized.) The division lost five NCOs/enlisted wounded in action.

94th Infantry Division – The division attacked in zone, seizing terrain south of Hill 93.2 against the 124th Rifle Brigade, the 149th Rifle Brigade, the 115th Rifle Brigade and the 2nd Motorized Rifle Brigade. To the south was the 389th Infantry Division; to the northeast was the 16th ***Panzer*** Division. The division lost one officer and eight NCOs/enlisted wounded in action.

Battle Group Stahel – The battle group defended in sector, south of Erzovka, from the Volga River west.

LI Corps – The corps headquarters was located at Gumrak. The 855th Heavy Artillery Detachment and the 2nd ***Werfer*** Regiment were assigned to support the corps. The corps suffered the following officer casualties: six killed in action; 16 wounded in action.

14th Panzer Division – The division attacked south in zone along Tramvainaia Street and the railroad line to the front of the 24th ***Panzer*** Division and seized the northern half of the Barrikady Gun Factory against the 95th Rifle Division. To the north was the 389th Infantry Division; to the east was the 305th Infantry Division. The division lost two officers and 21 NCOs/enlisted killed in action; four officers and 121 NCOs/enlisted were wounded in action; two men were reported missing in action.

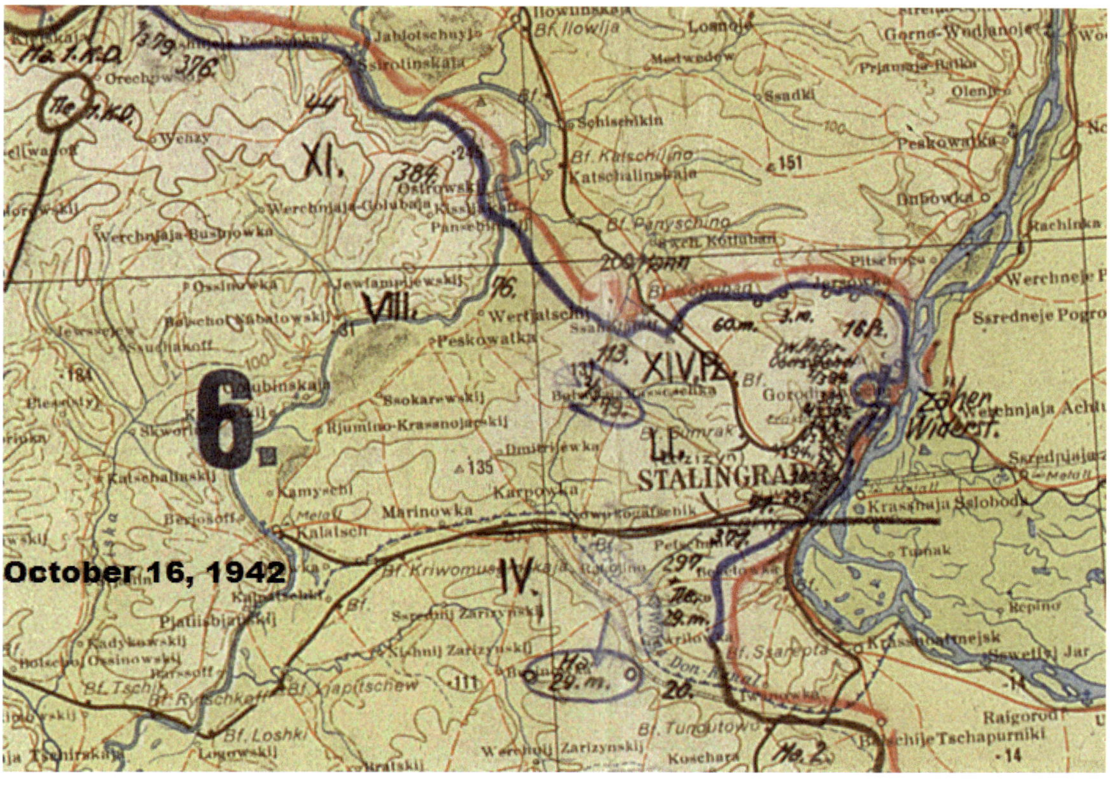

24th Panzer Division – The division conducted a supporting attack against the 308th Rifle Division, to assist the 14th ***Panzer*** Division and the 305th Infantry Division. The division suffered four NCOs/enlisted killed in action; 20 NCOs/enlisted were wounded in action; one of them died of wounds later in the day. To the north was the 14th ***Panzer***; to the south was the 100th ***Jäger*** Division.

71st Infantry Division – The division defended in sector. To the north was the 295th Infantry Division; to the south was the 371st Infantry Division. The division lost four NCOs/enlisted wounded in action.

100th Jäger Division – The division conducted several reconnaissance-in-force operations against the 39th Guards Rifle Division and the 193rd Rifle Division to prevent enemy units from moving north. To the north was the 24th ***Panzer*** Division; to the south was the 295th Infantry Division. The division lost two NCOs/enlisted killed in action; two officers and 34 NCOs/enlisted were wounded in action; five men were reported missing in action.

295th Infantry Division – The division defended in sector against the 284th Rifle Division. To the north was the 100th ***Jäger*** Division; to the south was the 71st Infantry Division. The division lost three NCOs/enlisted killed in action; one officer and 17 NCOs/enlisted were wounded in action.

305th Infantry Division – The division attacked south in zone – along the eastern flank of the 14th ***Panzer*** Division – along Pribaltiiskaia Street and Lenin Prospect and seized the northern half of the Barrikady Gun Factory against the 95th Rifle Division. The division was hit by fire from ***Katyusha*** rocket launchers and lost one officer and 30 NCOs/enlisted killed in action; five officers and 74 NCOs/enlisted were wounded in action; one officer and 13 NCOs/enlisted were reported missing in action. The division was reinforced by the 244th ***Sturmgeschütz*** Detachment and the 245th ***Sturmgeschütz*** Detachment. To the north was the 389th Infantry Division; to the west was the 14th ***Panzer*** Division.

389th Infantry Division – The division attacked in zone to continue to clear enemy forces from the Dzerzhinsky Tractor Factory and the Dzerzhinsky Tractor Factory Workers' Settlement. To the north was the 94th Infantry Division; to the south were the 14th ***Panzer*** Division and the 305th Infantry Division.

Sixth Army Reserve

79th Infantry Division – One-third of the division defended in sector south of the Don River. To the east was the 44th Infantry Division; to the west was the Romanian V Corps of the Romanian Third Army. The rest of the division was at Bol'shaya Rossoschka.

Fourth *Panzer* Army – The army headquarters was located east of Verkhne-Zaryzinskij.

IV Corps

297th Infantry Division – The division defended in sector east of Elkhi and Iagodniki against the 36th Guards Rifle Division and the 29th Rifle Division. To the north was the 371st Infantry Division; to the south was the 29th Infantry Division (Motorized.)

371st Infantry Division – The division defended in sector from Kuporosnoye in the east to northwest of Gornaia Poliana against part of the 422nd Rifle Division. To the north was the 71st Infantry Division; to the south was the 297th Infantry Division.

20th Romanian Infantry Division – The division defended in sector, west of the Tundutovo Rail Station and east of Andreevka against the 204th Rifle Division and the 38th Rifle Division. To the north was the 29th Infantry Division (Motorized); to the south was the 2nd Romanian Infantry Division.

Fourth *Panzer* Army Reserve

29th Infantry Division (Motorized) – The division moved south to a new assembly area, between Businovka and Gavrilovka, to prepare for future operations. Part of the division defended in sector east of the Volga-Don Canal. To the north was the 297th Infantry Division; to the south was the 20th Romanian Infantry Division. The division lost six NCOs/enlisted wounded in action.

1939

Zur frommen Erinnerung
an meinen lieben Gatten, unsern Vater
und Bruder

Johann Böhm

von Dünzlau,
Obergefreiter in einem Inf.-Regt., Teilnehmer
am Frankreich- und Rußland-Feldzug,
geboren am 2. September 1910,
den Heldentod gestorben am 16. Okt. 1942
bei den Kämpfen im Osten.

O liebe Gattin und Kinder mein,
Ich kehre nicht mehr zu Euch Lieben heim,
Mein letzter Gedanke, mein letzter Blick,
Der eilte noch zu Euch zurück.
Als ich starb im Feindesland,
Reichte niemand mir die Hand;
Doch eh' mein Auge war gebrochen,
Sah ich schon den Himmel offen.

DRUCK: L. STADELMEIER, INGOLSTADT

Obergefreiter **Johann Böhm** was born in Dünzlau near Ingolstadt in Bavaria on September 2, 1910. Assigned to an infantry regiment in the 113th Infantry Division, he had previously fought in the 1940 French Campaign. He was killed in action three miles north of Rossoschka on October 16, 1942.

Sources, October 16, 1942: ***Oberkommando des Heeres, Lage Ost: Stand: 16.10.42, Eastern Front Situation Map, National Archives Identifier: 559733, Record Group 242 – National Archives Collection of Foreign Records Seized, 1675-1958, National Archives, College Park, Maryland; Ia, Armeeoberkommando 6, "Morgen Meldung" and assorted reports, Kriegstagebuch 14, 17 October 1942, as found in Microfilm Series, T-312, Records of German Field Commands, Armies, Roll 1453 and 1688, National Archives and Records Service, College Park, Maryland; Korpsarzt, XXXXVIII Panzerkorps, "Meldung über Personelle Verluste," Stand 16.10.42, as found on T-314, Records of German Field Commands, Corps, Roll 1158, National Archives, College Park, Maryland; Florian Freiherr von und zu Aufsess, Die Anlagenbände zu den Kriegstagebüchern der 6. Armee vom 14.09.1942 bis 24.11.1942, Band 1, Schwabach, Germany: Selbstverlag, 2006, 175-180; Antony Beevor, Stalingrad: The Fateful Siege: 1942-1943, London: Penguin Books, 1998, 194-196; David M. Glantz & Jonathan M. House, Armageddon in Stalingrad: September-November 1942, (The Stalingrad Trilogy, Volume 2), Lawrence, Kansas: University Press of Kansas, 2009, 401-412; Manfred Kehrig, Stalingrad: Analyse und Dokumentation einer Schlacht, Stuttgart, FRG: Deutsche Verlags-Anstalt, 1976, 39; Jason Mark, Death of the Leaping Horseman: 24. Panzer-Division in Stalingrad, Sydney, Australia: Leaping Horsemen Books, 2003, 279-282; Jason Mark, Island of Fire: The Battle for the Barrikady Gun Factory in Stalingrad, November 1942 – February 1943, Sydney, Australia: Leaping Horsemen Books, 2006, 6; Kurt Mehner, Die Geheimen Tagesberichte der Deutschen Wehrmachtführung im Zweiten Weltkrieg 1939-1945, Band 5: 1. Juni 1942 – 30. November 1942, Osnabrück, Germany: Biblio Verlag, 1991, 240; Anton Schimak, Karl Lamprecht & Friedrich Dettmer, Die 44. Infanterie Division: Tagebuch der Hoch- und Deutschmeister, Wien: Verlag Austria Press, 169, 233 and Map: Marschweg der 44. Infanterie Division im Russland; Joachim Wieder and Heinrich Graf von Einsiedel, Stalingrad: Memories and Reassessments, translated by Helmut Bogler, London: Arms & Armour, 1993, 20.***

October 17, 1942
Weather: clear, dry, cool, later predominantly cloudy
Sunrise: 6:24 a.m.; **Sunset:** 5:10 p.m.
Moon: Waxing Gibbous; 56% illumination

Sixth Army – Bombers and dive-bombers from the ***Luftwaffe***'s VIII Air Corps pounded enemy positions in the northern half of Stalingrad. The army headquarters was located at Golubinskaya. The OKH informed Hitler that German forces had captured the Dzerzhinsky Tractor Factory on October 15 and the Barrikady Gun Factory on October 16. ***Major*** Gerhard Engel, one of Hitler's Army Adjutants, arrived at the army headquarters to gather personnel observations of the battle.

VIII Corps

76th Infantry Division – The division defended in sector, east of the Don River, north of Nizhne-Gnilovskii, to west of Kotluban', against the 298th Rifle Division. To the southeast was the 113th Infantry Division; to the northwest was the 384th Infantry Division. The division lost three NCOs/enlisted killed in action; seven NCOs/enlisted were wounded in action.

113th Infantry Division – The division defended in sector southwest of Samofalovka and north of Borodkin, against the 27th Guards Rifle Division, the 173rd Rifle Division and the 273rd Rifle Division. To the northwest was the 76th Infantry Division; to the east was the 60th Infantry Division (Motorized.) The division suffered one NCO/enlisted killed in action; seven NCOs/enlisted were wounded in action.

XI Corps

44th Infantry Division – The division defended in sector Kurchajessowskij-Kamyshinskiy-Hill 171.0-Hill 180.9-Sirotinskaya-Khmelevskoy, against the 40th Guards Rifle Division and the 23rd Rifle Division. The division headquarters was located at Verkhne-Golubaja. To the west was the 376th Infantry Division; to the southeast was the 384th Infantry Division. The division lost five NCOs/enlisted wounded in action.

376th Infantry Division – The division defended in sector, south of Perekopskaja, near Logowskii and Ossinskij, against the 321st Rifle Division and the 23rd Rifle Division. To the east was the 44th Infantry Division; to the west was the Romanian Third Army. The division suffered one NCO/enlisted killed in action; four NCOs/enlisted were wounded in action.

384th Infantry Division – The division defended in sector west of the Don River near Trekhostrovskaia to Podgorskii, against the 24th Rifle Division, the 214th Rifle Division and the 22nd Mechanized Brigade. To the northwest was the 44th Infantry Division; to the southeast was the 76th Infantry Division.

XIV *Panzer* Corps – The corps headquarters was located east of Ssadtschi-Kowa. The corps suffered the following officer casualties: three wounded in action;

3rd Infantry Division (Motorized) – The division defended in sector, from the Tartar Hill-Hill 111.1-Hill 129.6-Hill 131.2. To the east was the 16th ***Panzer*** Division; to the west was the 60th Infantry Division (Motorized.)

16th Panzer Division – The division defended in sector, from Hill 139.7 to the Volga and from the Volga southwest to Hill 145.1, north of Orlovka, against the 299th Rifle Division. In its southern sector, the division – reinforced by the 651st Engineer Battalion – attacked north of the Orlovka stream into Spartakovka and cleared the area west of Spartakovka against the 124th Rifle Brigade, the 149th Rifle Brigade, the 115th Rifle Brigade and the 2nd Motorized Rifle Brigade.

60th Infantry Division (Motorized) – The division defended in sector, from south of

Kotluban' Station near Borodkin to Kuz'michi, against the 41st Guards Rifle Division and the 231st Rifle Division. To the west was the 113th Infantry Division; to the east was the 3rd Infantry Division (Motorized.)

94th Infantry Division – The division attacked in zone from the southeast into Spartakovka and cleared the area west of Spartakovka against the 124th Rifle Brigade, the 149th Rifle Brigade, the 115th Rifle Brigade and the 2nd Motorized Rifle Brigade. To the south was the 389th Infantry Division; to the northeast was the 16th ***Panzer*** Division.

Battle Group Stahel – The battle group defended in sector, south of Erzovka, from the Volga River west.

LI Corps – The corps headquarters was located at Gumrak. The corps suffered the following officer casualties: five killed in action; 13 wounded in action.

14th Panzer Division – The division continued the attack south in zone in front of the 24th ***Panzer*** Division to seize more of the Barrikady Gun Factory from the 95th Rifle Division, the 138th Rifle Division and the 308th Rifle Division. To the north was the 389th Infantry Division; to the east was the 305th Infantry Division; to the west was the 24th ***Panzer*** Division. The division lost two officers and 32 NCOs/enlisted killed in action; four officers and 116 NCOs/enlisted were wounded in action; four men were reported missing in action.

24th Panzer Division – The division attacked in zone to seize Skulpturny Park against the 308th Rifle Division in support of an attack by the 14th ***Panzer*** Division and the 305th Infantry Division. To the south was the 100th ***Jäger*** Division; to the east was the 14th ***Panzer*** Division. The division suffered five NCOs/enlisted killed in action; one officer and 17 NCOs/enlisted were wounded in action.

71st Infantry Division – The division defended in sector. To the north was the 295th Infantry Division; to the south was the 371st Infantry Division. The division lost four NCOs/enlisted wounded in action.

79th Infantry Division – One-third of the division defended in sector south of the Don River. To the east was the 376th Infantry Division; to the west was the Romanian V Corps of the Romanian Third Army. The rest of the division moved from Bol'shaya Rossoschka to Gumrak.

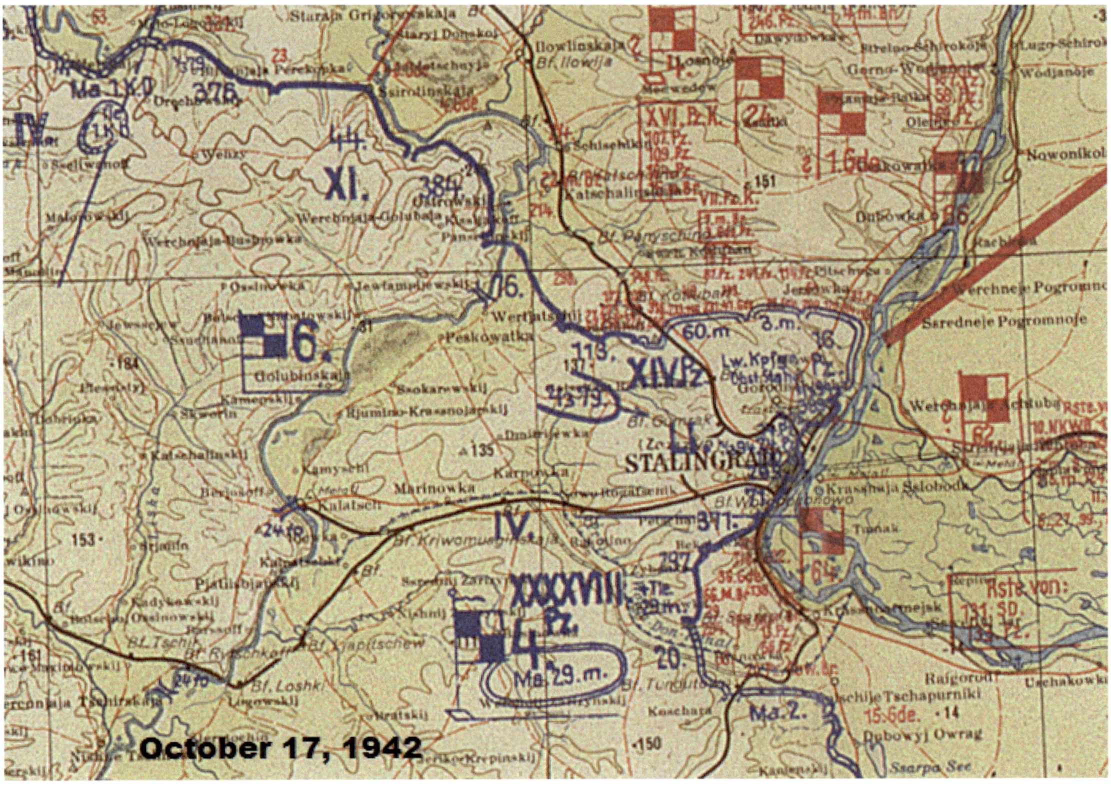

100th Jäger Division – The division conducted limited attacks to the east against the 39th Guards Rifle Division and the 193rd Rifle Division. To the north was the 24th ***Panzer*** Division; to the south was the 295th Infantry Division. The division suffered 22 NCOs/enlisted killed in action; 92 NCOs/enlisted were wounded in action; eight men were reported missing in action.

295th Infantry Division – The division defended in sector against the 284th Rifle Division. To the north was the 100th ***Jäger*** Division; to the south was the 71st Infantry Division. The division lost one NCO/enlisted killed in action; one officer and one NCO/enlisted were wounded in action.

305th Infantry Division – The division attacked south in zone along the eastern flank of the 14th ***Panzer*** Division, seizing more of the Barrikady Gun Factory and the area near the Brick Works from the 95th Rifle Division and the 308th Rifle Division. To the north was the 389th Infantry Division; to its right was the 14th ***Panzer*** Division. The division lost two officers and 29 NCOs/enlisted killed in action; two officers 124 NCOs/enlisted were wounded in action; four men were reported missing in action. The division was reinforced by the 244th ***Sturmgeschütz*** Detachment and the 245th ***Sturmgeschütz*** Detachment.

389th Infantry Division – The division attacked in zone to continue to clear enemy forces from the Dzerzhinsky Tractor Factory and the Dzerzhinsky Tractor Factory Workers' Settlement. To the north was the 94th Infantry Division; to the south were the 14th ***Panzer*** Division and the 305th Infantry Division. The division reported one officer killed in action and 15 NCOs/enlisted wounded in action.

Fourth *Panzer* Army – The army headquarters was located east of Verkhne-Zaryzinskij.

IV Corps

297th Infantry Division – The division defended in sector east of Elkhi and Iagodniki, against the 36th Guards Rifle Division and the 56th Mechanized Brigade. To the north was the 371st Infantry Division; to the south was part of the 29th Infantry Division (Motorized.)

371st Infantry Division – The division defended in sector from Kuporosnoye in the east to northwest of Gornaia Poliana against part of the 422nd Rifle Division. To the north was the 71st Infantry Division; to the south was the 297th Infantry Division.

20th Romanian Infantry Division – The division defended in sector, west of the Tundutovo Rail Station and east of Andreevka, against the 38th Rifle Division and the 294th Rifle Division. To the north was part of the 29th Infantry Division (Motorized); to the south was the 2nd Romanian Infantry Division of the Romanian VI Corps.

Fourth *Panzer* Army Reserve

29th Infantry Division (Motorized) – The division occupied an assembly area, between Businovka and Gavrilovka, to prepare for future operations. Part of the division defended in sector east of the Volga-Don Canal against the 29th Rifle Division. To the north was the 297th Infantry Division; to the south was the 20th Romanian Infantry Division.

Sources, October 17, 1942: *Oberkommando des Heeres, Lage Ost: Stand: 17.10.42, Eastern Front Situation Map, National Archives Identifier: 559733, Record Group 242 – National Archives Collection of Foreign Records Seized, 1675-1958, National Archives, College Park, Maryland; Ia, Armeeoberkommando 6, "Morgen Meldung" and assorted reports, Kriegstagebuch 14, 18 October 1942, as found in Microfilm Series, T-312, Records of German Field Commands, Armies, Roll 1453 and 1688, National Archives and Records Service, College Park, Maryland; Korpsarzt, XXXXVIII Panzerkorps, "Meldung über Personelle Verluste," Stand 17.10.42, as found on T-314, Records of German Field Commands, Corps, Roll 1158, National Archives, College Park, Maryland; Florian Freiherr von und zu Aufsess, Die Anlagenbände zu den Kriegstagebüchern der 6. Armee vom 14.09.1942 bis 24.11.1942, Band 1, Schwabach, Germany: Selbstverlag, 2006, 180-182; Antony Beevor, Stalingrad: The Fateful Siege: 1942-1943, London: Penguin Books, 1998, 194-195; David M. Glantz & Jonathan M. House, Armageddon in Stalingrad: September-November 1942, (The Stalingrad Trilogy, Volume 2), Lawrence, Kansas: University Press of Kansas, 2009, 412-422; Helmuth Greiner, "Greiner Diary Notes, 12 August 1942 – 12 March 1943," MS #C-065a, Heidelberg, Germany: Historical Division, Headquarters, United States Army Europe, 1949, 87; Jason Mark, Death of the Leaping Horseman: 24. Panzer-Division in Stalingrad, Sydney, Australia: Leaping Horsemen Books, 2003, 282-288; Jason Mark, Island of Fire: The Battle for the Barrikady Gun Factory in Stalingrad, November 1942 – February 1943, Sydney, Australia: Leaping Horsemen Books, 2006, 4; Kurt Mehner, Die Geheimen Tagesberichte der Deutschen Wehrmachtführung im Zweiten Weltkrieg 1939-1945, Band 5: 1. Juni 1942 – 30. November 1942, Osnabrück, Germany: Biblio Verlag, 1991, 241; Janusz Piekalkiewicz, Stalingrad: Anatomie einer Schlacht, München, BRD: Wilhelm Heyne Verlag, 1977, 296; Anton Schimak, Karl Lamprecht & Friedrich Dettmer, Die 44. Infanterie Division: Tagebuch der Hoch- und Deutschmeister, Wien: Verlag Austria Press, 169, 233 and Map: Marschweg der 44. Infanterie Division im Russland; Hans J. Wijers, Der Kampf um Stalingrad: Die Kämpfe im Industriegelände – 14. Oktober bis 19. November 1942, Selbstverlag, 51.*

Letter to Next of Kin for a soldier in the 11th Company, 3rd Battalion, 71st Infantry Regiment of the 29th Infantry Division (Motorized.) Dated October 17, 1942, it describes how ***Schütze*** Johann Franz Ziegler went missing in action northwest of Stalingrad, near Gorodishche, on October 14, 1943. Ziegler, who was born in Tiefenbach on September 6, 1923, was never seen again. The company commander, ***Oberleutnant*** Arthur Riedmann, who had been born in Innsbruck, Austria on January 21, 1909, was posted missing in action near Dmitriyevka on January 10, 1943.

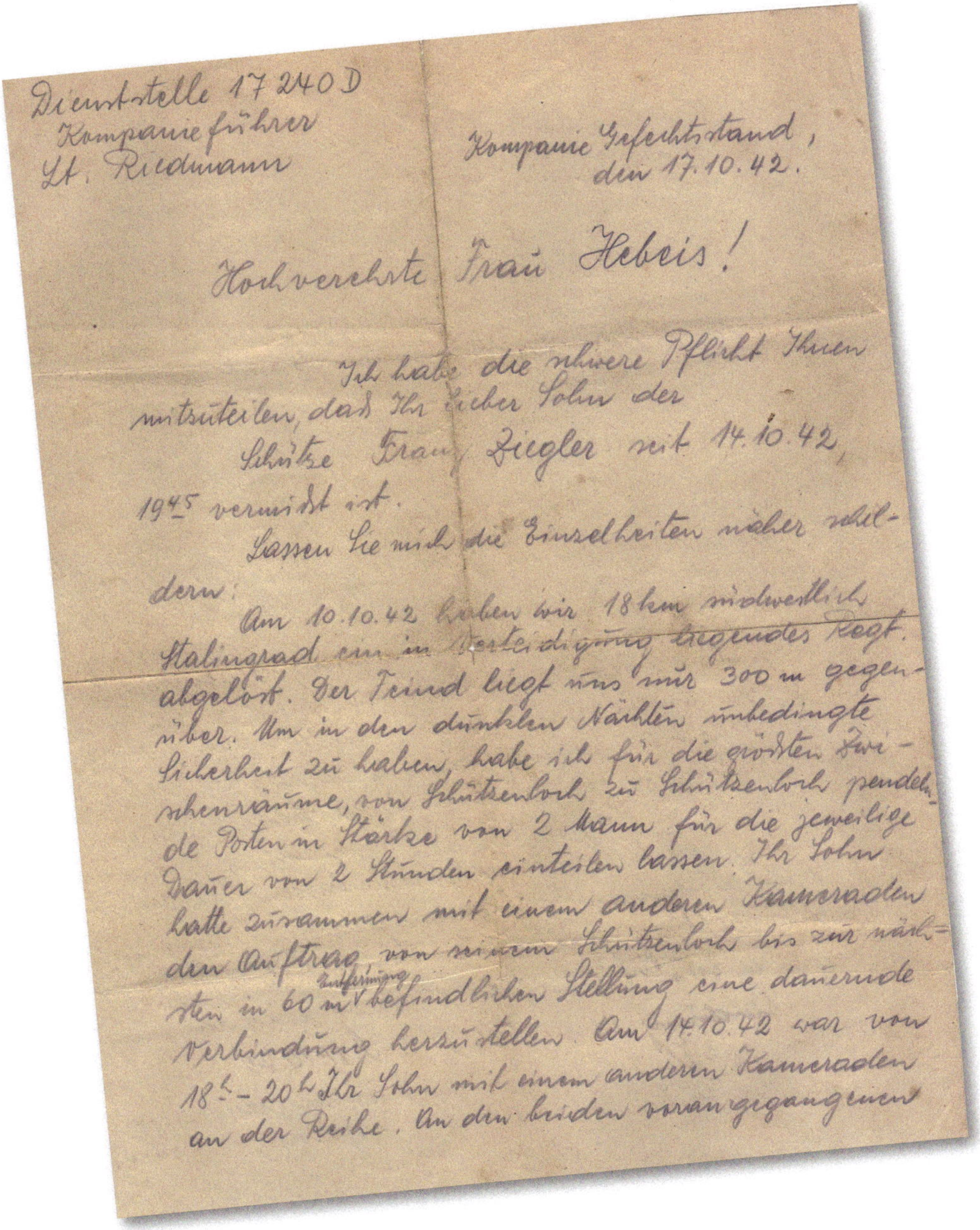

Dienststelle 17 240 D
Kompanieführer
Lt. Riedmann

Kompanie Gefechtsstand,
den 17.10.42.

Hochverehrte Frau Hebeis!

Ich habe die schwere Pflicht Ihnen mitzuteilen, daß Ihr lieber Sohn der Schütze Franz Ziegler seit 14.10.42, 19^{45} vermißt ist.

Lassen Sie mich die Einzelheiten näher schildern:

Am 10.10.42 haben wir 18 km nordwestlich Stalingrad ein in Verteidigung liegendes Regt. abgelöst. Der Feind liegt uns nur 300 m gegenüber. Um in den dunklen Nächten unbedingte Sicherheit zu haben, habe ich für die größten Zwischenräume, von Schützenloch zu Schützenloch pendelnde Posten in Stärke von 2 Mann für die jeweilige Dauer von 2 Stunden einteilen lassen. Ihr Sohn hatte zusammen mit einem anderen Kameraden den Auftrag, von seinem Schützenloch bis zur nächsten in 60 m Entfernung befindlichen Stellung eine dauernde Verbindung herzustellen. Am 14.10.42 war von 18^h - 20^h Ihr Sohn mit einem anderen Kameraden an der Reihe. An den beiden vorangegangenen

October 18, 1942
Weather: completely cloudy, rain, windy, heavy rain at times
Sunrise: 6:25 a.m.; **Sunset:** 5:08 p.m.
Moon: Waxing Gibbous; 67% illumination

Sixth Army – Bombers and dive-bombers from the ***Luftwaffe***'s VIII Air Corps pounded enemy positions in the northern half of Stalingrad. The army headquarters was located at Golubinskaya. The army had suffered 13,343 casualties since September 13, 1942.

VIII Corps

76th Infantry Division – The division defended in sector, east of the Don River, north of Nizhne-Gnilovskii, to west of Kotluban', against the 298th Rifle Division. To the southeast was the 113th Infantry Division; to the northwest was the 384th Infantry Division. The division suffered one NCO/enlisted killed in action.

113th Infantry Division – The division defended in sector southwest of Samofalovka and north of Borodkin, against the 27th Guards Rifle Division, the 173rd Rifle Division and the 273rd Rifle Division. To the northwest was the 76th Infantry Division; to the east was the 60th Infantry Division (Motorized.) The division lost four NCOs/enlisted killed in action; 15 NCOs/enlisted were wounded in action.

XI Corps

44th Infantry Division – The division defended in sector Kurchajessowskij-Kamyshinskiy-Hill 171.0-Hill 180.9-Sirotinskaya-Khmelevskoy, against the 40th Guards Rifle Division and the 23rd Rifle Division. The division headquarters was located at Verkhne-Golubaja. To the west was 376th Infantry Division; to the southeast was the 384th Infantry Division.

376th Infantry Division – The division defended in sector, south of Perekopskaja, near Logowskii and Ossinskij, against the 321st Rifle Division and the 23rd Rifle Division. To the east was the 44th Infantry Division; to the west was the Romanian Third Army. The division lost one NCO/enlisted wounded in action; three NCOs/enlisted were wounded in action.

384th Infantry Division – The division defended in sector west of the Don River near Trekhostrovskaia to Podgorskii, against the 24th Rifle Division, the 214th Rifle Division, the 22nd Mechanized Brigade and the 4th Guards Rifle Division. To the northwest was the 44th Infantry Division; to the southeast was the 76th Infantry Division. The division suffered one NCO/enlisted wounded in action.

XIV *Panzer* Corps – The corps headquarters was located east of Ssadtschi-Kowa.

3rd Infantry Division (Motorized) – The division defended in sector, from the Tartar Hill-Hill 111.1-Hill 129.6-Hill 131.2 against the 299th Rifle Division. To the east was the 16th ***Panzer*** Division; to the west was the 60th Infantry Division (Motorized.) The division lost two NCOs/enlisted killed in action; one officer and two NCOs/enlisted were wounded in action.

16th Panzer Division – The division defended in sector, from Hill 139.7 to the Volga and from the Volga southwest to Hill 145.1, north of Orlovka against the 299th Rifle Division. In its southern sector, the division – reinforced by the 651st Engineer Battalion – attacked into Spartakovka, but failed to make significant gains. The division suffered one NCO/enlisted killed in action; one officer and 17 NCOs/enlisted were wounded in action.

60th Infantry Division (Motorized) – The division defended in sector, from south of Kotluban' Station near Borodkin to Kuz'michi, against the 41st Guards Rifle Division and the 231st Rifle Division. To the west was the 113th Infantry Division; to the east was the 3rd Infantry Division (Motorized.) The division lost 20 NCOs/enlisted wounded in action.

94th Infantry Division – The division attacked in zone from the southeast into Spartakovka, but failed to make progress. To the south was the 389th Infantry Division; to the northeast was the 16th ***Panzer*** Division. The division suffered six NCOs/enlisted killed in action; six NCOs/enlisted were wounded in action.

Battle Group Stahel – The battle group defended in sector, south of Erzovka, from the Volga River west. It received an order that after the fighting in northern Stalingrad was completed, the battle group would be transported to the Caucasus.

LI Corps – The corps re-positioned artillery and rocket launchers to support attacks on the Krasny Oktyabr Steel Factory. The corps headquarters was located at Gumrak. The corps suffered the following officer casualties: one killed in action; ten wounded in action.

14th Panzer Division – The division continued to attack south in zone in front of the 24th ***Panzer*** Division to seize more of the Barrikady Gun Factory against the 95th Rifle Division and the 308th Rifle Division. To the north was the 389th Infantry Division; to the east was the 305th Infantry Division; to the west was the 14th ***Panzer*** Division. The division lost 21 NCOs/enlisted killed in action; two officers and 58 NCOs/enlisted were wounded in action. The division received orders to be prepared to transfer ***Panzer*** elements to Kamensk (near Rostov) for the formation of a new unit.

24th Panzer Division – The division attacked in zone, seized the Brick Works (south of the Dzerzhinsky Tractor Factory) and reached the Volga River against the 95th Rifle Division in support of an attack by the 14th ***Panzer*** Division and the 305th Infantry Division. To the north was the 389th Infantry Division; to the south was now the 305th Infantry Division. The division suffered four NCOs/enlisted killed in action; one officer and 11 NCOs/enlisted were wounded in action; one man died of wounds later that day.

71st Infantry Division – The division defended in sector. To the north was the 295th Infantry Division; to the south was the 371st Infantry Division. The division reported two NCOs/enlisted wounded in action.

79th Infantry Division – The division, minus one regiment with the 376th Infantry Division, was ordered to move into Stalingrad.

100th Jäger Division – The division conducted limited attacks to the east against the 39th Guards Rifle Division and the 193rd Rifle Division. To the north was the 24th ***Panzer*** Division; to the south was the 295th Infantry Division. The division lost seven NCOs/enlisted killed in action; one officer and 38 NCOs/enlisted were wounded in action; one man was reported missing in action.

295th Infantry Division – The division defended in sector against the 284th Rifle Division. To

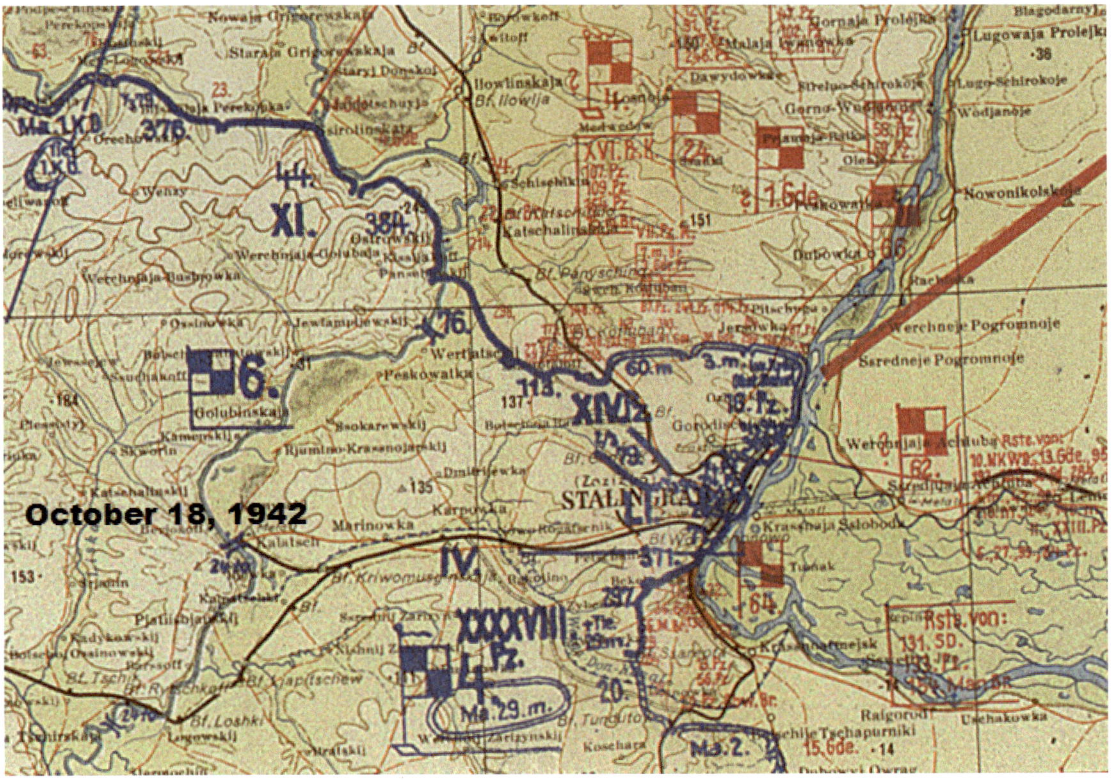

the north was the 100th ***Jäger*** Division; to the south was the 71st Infantry Division.

305th Infantry Division – The division attacked south in zone along the eastern flank of the 14th ***Panzer*** Division into the depths of the Barrikady Gun Factory, reaching the Volga River near the Brick Works against the 95th Rifle Division and the 308th Rifle Division. To the north was the 389th Infantry Division; to the west was the 14th ***Panzer*** Division. The division was reinforced by the 244th ***Sturmgeschütz*** Detachment and the 245th ***Sturmgeschütz*** Detachment. The division lost 17 NCOs/enlisted killed in action; one officer and 38 NCOs/enlisted were wounded in action.

389th Infantry Division – The division attacked in zone to continue to clear enemy forces from the Dzerzhinsky Tractor Factory and the Dzerzhinsky Tractor Factory Workers' Settlement. To the north was the 94th Infantry Division; to the south were the 14th ***Panzer*** Division and the 305th Infantry Division. The division lost six NCOs/enlisted wounded in action.

Fourth *Panzer* Army – The army headquarters was located east of Verkhne-Zaryzinskij.

IV Corps – ***General der Panzertruppe*** Friedrich Paulus relieved ***General der Infanterie*** Viktor von Schwedler of command of the corps for a lack of aggression.

297th Infantry Division – The division defended in sector east of Elkhi and Iagodniki. To the north was the 371st Infantry Division; to the south was the 29th Infantry Division (Motorized.)

371st Infantry Division – The division defended in sector from Kuporosnoye in the east to northwest of Gornaia Poliana against part of the 422nd Infantry Division. To the north was the 71st Infantry Division; to the south was the 297th Infantry Division.

20th Romanian Infantry Division – The division defended in sector, west of the Tundutovo Rail Station and east of Andreevka against the 204th Rifle Division. To the north was the 29th Infantry Division (Motorized); to the south was the 2nd Romanian Infantry Division of the Romanian VI Corps.

Fourth *Panzer* Army Reserve

29th Infantry Division (Motorized) – The division occupied an assembly area, between Businovka and Gavrilovka, to prepare for future operations. Part of the division defended in sector east of the Volga-Don Canal against the 29th Rifle Division. To the north was the 297th Infantry Division; to the south was the 20th Romanian Infantry Division.

Schütze **Georg Schmaus**, a brewer, was born on July 30, 1923 in Irchenrieth near Weiden, in Bavaria. A machine-gunner in an infantry regiment in the 113th Infantry Division, Schmaus was killed in action five miles north of Malaia Rossoschka on October 18, 1942. His name is listed in the remembrance book at the German Military Cemetery at Rossoschka.

Sources, October 18, 1942: ***Oberkommando des Heeres, Lage Ost: Stand: 18.10.42, Eastern Front Situation Map, National Archives Identifier: 559733, Record Group 242 – National Archives Collection of Foreign Records Seized, 1675-1958, National Archives, College Park, Maryland; Ia, Armeeoberkommando 6, "Morgen Meldung" and assorted reports, Kriegstagebuch 14, 19 October 1942, as found in Microfilm Series, T-312, Records of German Field Commands, Armies, Roll 1453 and 1688, National Archives and Records Service, College Park, Maryland; Korpsarzt, XXXXVIII Panzerkorps, "Meldung über Personelle Verluste," Stand 18.10.42, as found on T-314, Records of German Field Commands, Corps, Roll 1158, National Archives, College Park, Maryland; Florian Freiherr von und zu Aufsess, Die Anlagenbände zu den Kriegstagebüchern der 6. Armee vom 14.09.1942 bis 24.11.1942, Band 1, Schwabach, Germany: Selbstverlag, 2006, 181-184; Antony Beevor, Stalingrad: The Fateful Siege: 1942-1943, London: Penguin Books, 1998, 194-195; Paul Carell, Stalingrad: The Defeat of the German Sixth Army, Atglen, Pennsylvania: Schiffer Publishing, 1993, 148; Alan Clark, Barbarossa: The Russian-German Conflict, 1941-45, New York: William Morrow and Company, 1965, 233; David M. Glantz & Jonathan M. House, Armageddon in Stalingrad: September-November 1942, (The Stalingrad Trilogy, Volume 2), Lawrence, Kansas: University Press of Kansas, 2009, 422-428; Rolf Grams, Die 14. Panzer-Division, 1940-1945, Friedberg, FRG: Podzun Pallas Verlag, 1986, 69; Jason Mark, Death of the Leaping Horseman: 24. Panzer-Division in Stalingrad, Sydney, Australia: Leaping Horsemen Books, 2003, 289-294; Anton Schimak, Karl Lamprecht & Friedrich Dettmer, Die 44. Infanterie Division: Tagebuch der Hoch- und Deutschmeister, Wien: Verlag Austria Press, 169, 233 and Map: Marschweg der 44. Infanterie Division im Russland; Wolfgang Werthen, Geschichte der 16. Panzer-Division 1939-1945, Friedberg, FRG: Podzun-Pallas-Verlag, 1958, 115.***

October 19, 1942
Weather: heavy rain, cloudy, windy, snow-showers, bad road conditions (especially for wheeled vehicles)
Sunrise: 6:27 a.m.; **Sunset:** 5:07 p.m.
Moon: Waxing Gibbous; 77% illumination

Sixth Army – Bombers and dive-bombers from the ***Luftwaffe***'s VIII Air Corps pounded enemy positions in the northern half of Stalingrad. The army headquarters was located at Golubinskaya.

VIII Corps

76th Infantry Division – The division defended in sector, east of the Don River, north of Nizhne-Gnilovskii, to west of Kotluban' against the 298th Rifle Division. To the southeast was the 113th Infantry Division; to the northwest was the 384th Infantry Division. The division reported that of its six infantry battalions, one was medium-strong and five were average in combat power; the division rated its combat engineer battalion as average. The division lost three NCOs/enlisted killed in action; three NCOs/enlisted were wounded in action. Ten men were admitted to the hospital due to illness.

113th Infantry Division – The division defended in sector southwest of Samofalovka and north of Borodkin against the 27th Guards Rifle Division, the 173rd Rifle Division, the 292nd Rifle Division, the 207th Rifle Division, the 221st Rifle Division and the 273rd Rifle Division. To the northwest was the 76th Infantry Division; to the east was the 60th Infantry Division (Motorized.) The division reported that of its seven infantry battalions, two were medium-strong and five were average in combat power; the division rated its combat engineer battalion as medium-strong. The division lost two NCOs/enlisted killed in action; one officer and 19 NCOs/enlisted were wounded in action.

XI Corps

44th Infantry Division – The division defended in sector Kurchajessowskij-Kamyshinskiy-Hill 171.0-Hill 180.9-Sirotinskaya-Khmelevskoy, against the 40th Guards Rifle Division and the 23rd Rifle Division. The division headquarters was located at Verkhne-Golubaja. To the west was 376th Infantry Division; to the southeast was the 384th Infantry Division. The division reported that of its seven infantry battalions, five were medium-strong and two were average in combat power; the division rated its combat engineer battalion as average. The division lost one NCO/enlisted killed in action; one NCO/enlisted was wounded in action.

376th Infantry Division – The division defended in sector, south of Perekopskaja, near Logowskii and Ossinskij, against the 321st Rifle Division and the 23rd Rifle Division. To the east was the 44th Infantry Division; to the west was the 1st Romanian Cavalry Division of the Romanian Third Army. The division reported that of its seven infantry battalions, two were medium-strong and three were average in combat power; the division rated its combat engineer battalion as average.

384th Infantry Division – The division defended in sector west of the Don River near Trekhostrovskaia to Podgorskii, against the 24th Rifle Division, the 214th Rifle Division and the 22nd Mechanized Brigade. To the northwest was the 44th Infantry Division; to the southeast was the 76th Infantry Division. The division reported that of its six infantry battalions, one was medium-strong and five were average in combat power; the division rated its combat engineer battalion as average.

XIV *Panzer* Corps – The aim of the corps was to resume offensive operations at Spartakovka. The corps headquarters was located east of Ssadtschi-Kowa. The corps suffered the following officer casualties: two killed in action; seven wounded in action.

3rd Infantry Division (Motorized) – The division defended in sector, from the Tartar Hill-Hill 111.1-Hill 129.6-Hill 131.2. To the east was the 16th ***Panzer*** Division; to the west was the 60th

Infantry Division (Motorized.) The division lost two NCOs/enlisted killed in action; one officer and two NCOs/enlisted were wounded in action. The division reported that of its five motorized infantry battalions, three were medium-strong and two were average in combat power; the division rated its combat engineer battalion as weak.

16th Panzer Division – The division defended in sector, from Hill 139.7 to the Volga and from the Volga southwest to Hill 145.1, north of Orlovka, repelling the attack by the 64th Rifle Division at Hill 141.5 and conducting its own attack against the 84th Rifle Division at Hill 129.6. In its southern sector, the division – reinforced by the 651st Engineer Battalion – conducted limited offensive operations, but soon went into the defensive. The division suffered one NCO/enlisted killed in action; one officer and 17 NCOs/enlisted were wounded in action. The division reported that of its four ***panzer*** grenadier battalions, one was medium-strong, one was average and two were weak in combat power; the division rated its combat engineer battalion as weak.

60th Infantry Division (Motorized) – The division defended in sector, from south of Kotluban' Station near Borodkin to Kuz'michi, against the 49th Rifle Division, the 233rd Rifle Division, the 62nd Rifle Division and the 231st Rifle Division. To the west was the 113th Infantry Division; to the east was the 3rd Infantry Division (Motorized.) The division lost 20 NCOs/enlisted wounded in action. The division reported that of its seven motorized infantry battalions, two were medium-strong, four were average and one was exhausted in combat power; the division rated its combat engineer battalion as weak.

94th Infantry Division – The division attacked at the Barrikady Gun Factory, but quickly went over to the defensive. To the south was the 389th Infantry Division; to the northeast was the 16th ***Panzer*** Division. The division reported seven NCOs/enlisted killed in action and 24 NCOs/enlisted wounded in action. The division reported that of its seven infantry battalions, all seven were exhausted in combat power; the division rated its combat engineer battalion as weak.

Battle Group Stahel – The battle group defended in eight kilometer sector, south of Erzovka, from the Volga River west.

LI Corps – The corps headquarters was located at Gumrak. The 2nd ***Werfer*** Regiment was assigned to support the corps. The corps reported losses of

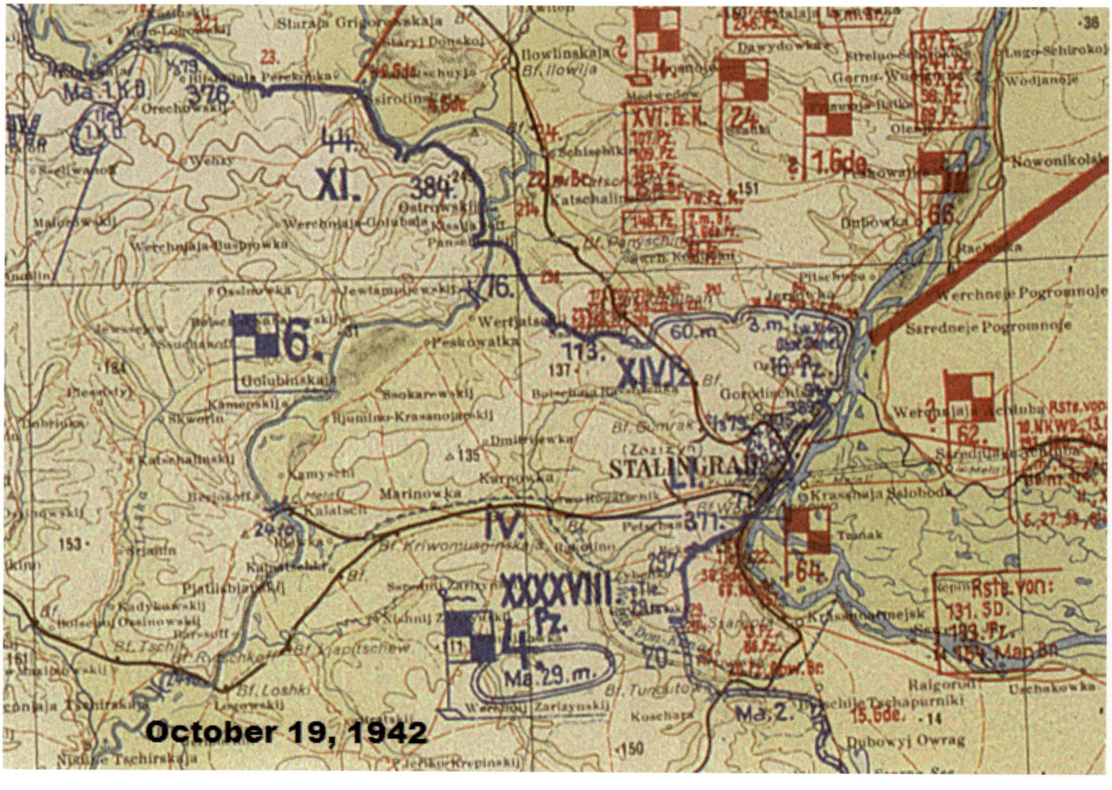

October 19, 1942

34 killed in action, 137 wounded in action and 15 missing in action. The corps suffered the following officer casualties: one killed in action; seven wounded in action.

14th Panzer Division – The division initially attacked toward the Bread Factory against the 138th Rifle Division and the 95th Rifle Division, but this stalled and it went over to the defensive. The division lost ten NCOs/enlisted killed in action; two officers and 58 NCOs/enlisted were wounded in action. The division reported that 22 tanks were damaged for the day out of 33 operational. The division reported that of its four ***panzer*** grenadier battalions, all four were medium-strong in combat power; the division rated its combat engineer battalion as average and its motorcycle battalion as strong. To the north was the 305th Infantry Division; to the south was the 24th ***Panzer*** Division.

24th Panzer Division – The division defended in positions overlooking the Volga River; some positions were on the Volga, while in other certain sectors the enemy held the near shore. Part of the division attacked against the 138th Rifle Division and the 37th Guards Rifle Division. The division suffered three enlisted killed in action; 28 NCOs/enlisted were wounded in action; one man was reported missing in action. The division reported that seven tanks were damaged for the day out of 29 operational. The division reported that of its four ***panzer*** grenadier battalions, one was weak and three were exhausted in combat power; the division rated its combat engineer battalion as exhausted and its motorcycle battalion as weak.

71st Infantry Division – The division defended in sector. To the north was the 295th Infantry Division; to the south was the 371st Infantry Division. The division suffered two NCOs/enlisted wounded in action. The division reported that of its seven infantry battalions, three were weak and four were exhausted in combat power; the division rated its combat engineer battalion as exhausted.

79th Infantry Division – The division was enroute to Stalingrad to assume a sector northwest of the Krasny Oktyabr Steel Factory. The division reported that of its six infantry battalions, three were strong, two were medium-strong and one was average in combat power; the division rated its combat engineer battalion as medium-strong.

100th Jäger Division – The division conducted limited attacks to the east against the 39th Guards Rifle Division and the 193rd Rifle Division, but those stalled and it went over to the defensive. To the north was the 24th ***Panzer*** Division; to the south was the 295th Infantry Division. The division lost five NCOs/enlisted killed in action; one NCO/enlisted was wounded in action; one man was reported missing in action. The division reported that of its four ***jäger*** battalions, one was strong and three were medium-strong in combat power; the Croatian infantry battalion was average; the division rated its combat engineer battalion as medium-strong.

295th Infantry Division – The division defended in sector against the 284th Rifle Division. To the north was the 100th ***Jäger*** Division; to the south was the 71st Infantry Division. The division suffered two NCOs/enlisted killed in action; six NCOs/enlisted were wounded in action. The division reported that of its seven infantry battalions, four were weak and three were exhausted in combat power; the division rated its combat engineer battalion as weak.

305th Infantry Division – The division attacked and initially seized the northern half of the Barrikady Gun Factory against the 138th Rifle Division. However, Soviet counterattacks retook the area later in the day. The division lost one officer and 13 NCOs/enlisted killed in action; two officers and 55 NCOs/enlisted were wounded in action; 13 men were reported missing in action. The division reported that of its nine infantry battalions, all nine were weak in combat power; the division rated its combat engineer battalion as weak. To the north was the 389th Infantry Division; to the west was the 14th ***Panzer*** Division.

389th Infantry Division – The division attempted to conduct offensive operations to continue to clear enemy forces from the Dzerzhinsky Tractor Factory and the Dzerzhinsky Tractor Factory Workers' Settlement against the 138th Rifle Division and the 37th Guards Rifle Division, but the attack stalled and it went over to the defensive. To the north was the 94th Infantry Division; to the south were the 14th ***Panzer*** Division and the 305th Infantry Division. The division suffered one NCO/enlisted killed in action; one officer and two NCOs/enlisted were wounded in action; one man was reported missing in action. The division reported that of its four infantry battalions, one was average, one was weak and two were exhausted in combat power; the division rated its combat engineer battalion as exhausted.

Fourth *Panzer* Army – The army headquarters was located east of Verkhne-Zaryzinskij.

IV Corps

297th Infantry Division – The division defended in sector east of Elkhi and Iagodniki against the 157th Rifle Division. To the north was the 371st Infantry Division; to the south was the 29th Infantry Division (Motorized.)

371st Infantry Division – The division defended in sector from Kuporosnoye in the east to northwest of Gornaia Poliana against part of the 422nd Rifle Division. To the north was the 71st Infantry Division; to the south was the 297th Infantry Division.

20th Romanian Infantry Division – The division defended in sector, west of the Tundutovo Rail Station and east of Andreevka against the 204th Rifle Division. To the north was the 29th Infantry Division (Motorized); to the south was the 2nd Romanian Infantry Division of the Romanian VI Corps.

Fourth *Panzer* Army Reserve

29th Infantry Division (Motorized) – The division occupied an assembly area, between Businovka and Gavrilovka, to prepare for future operations. Part of the division defended in sector east of the Volga-Don Canal, against the 29th Rifle Division. To the north was the 297th Infantry Division; to the south was the 20th Romanian Infantry Division. The division lost six NCOs/enlisted wounded in action.

Zur frommen Erinnerung
im Gebete an
Hans Stütz
Gefr. in einem Grenadier-Regt.
geb. am 20. November 1919 in Unterkochen
gef. am 19. Oktober 1942 in Stalingrad

Du gingst von uns mit frohem Herzen
Und hofftest auf ein Wiederseh'n;
Doch größer sind jetzt unsere Schmerzen
Da dieses kann nicht mehr gescheh'n!
Du warst so gut, du starbst zu früh,
Wer dich gekannt vergißt dich nie.
Du gutes Herz, ruh' still in Frieden
Stets beweint von deinen Lieben!

Vater unser. Ave Maria.
Mein Jesus Barmherzigkeit!
100 Tage Ablaß.

Gefreiter **Hans Stütz** was born on November 20, 1919 in Unterkochen, near Aalen in Baden-Württemberg. Assigned to an infantry regiment, he was killed in action at Stalingrad on October 19, 1942.

Sources, October 19, 1942: *Oberkommando des Heeres, Lage Ost: Stand: 19.10.42, Eastern Front Situation Map, National Archives Identifier: 559733, Record Group 242 – National Archives Collection of Foreign Records Seized, 1675-1958, National Archives, College Park, Maryland; Ia, Armeeoberkommando 6, "Morgen Meldung" and assorted reports, Kriegstagebuch 14, 20 October 1942, as found in Microfilm Series, T-312, Records of German Field Commands, Armies, Roll 1453 and 1688, National Archives and Records Service, College Park, Maryland; Korpsarzt, XXXXVIII Panzerkorps, "Meldung über Personelle Verluste," Stand 19.10.42, as found on T-314, Records of German Field Commands, Corps, Roll 1158, National Archives, College Park, Maryland; Florian Freiherr von und zu Aufsess, Die Anlagenbände zu den Kriegstagebüchern der 6. Armee vom 14.09.1942 bis 24.11.1942, Band 1, Schwabach, Germany: Selbstverlag, 2006, 183-191; Antony Beevor, Stalingrad: The Fateful Siege: 1942-1943, London: Penguin Books, 1998, 194-195; David M. Glantz & Jonathan M. House, Armageddon in Stalingrad: September-November 1942, (The Stalingrad Trilogy, Volume 2), Lawrence, Kansas: University Press of Kansas, 2009, 431-434, 449; Rolf Grams, Die 14. Panzer-Division, 1940-1945, Friedberg, FRG: Podzun Pallas Verlag, 1986, 69; Manfred Kehrig, Stalingrad: Analyse und Dokumentation einer Schlacht, Stuttgart, FRG: Deutsche Verlags-Anstalt, 1976, 40; Jason Mark, Death of the Leaping Horseman: 24. Panzer-Division in Stalingrad, Sydney, Australia: Leaping Horsemen Books, 2003, 294-298; Janusz Piekalkiewicz, Stalingrad: Anatomie einer Schlacht, München, BRD: Wilhelm Heyne Verlag, 1977, 304; Anton Schimak, Karl Lamprecht & Friedrich Dettmer, Die 44. Infanterie Division: Tagebuch der Hoch- und Deutschmeister, Wien: Verlag Austria Press, 169, 233 and Map: Marschweg der 44. Infanterie Division im Russland; Horst Zank, Stalingrad: Kessel und Gefangenschaft, Hamburg, Germany: Verlag E.S. Mittler & Sohn, 1993, 14.*

October 20, 1942
Weather: windy, increasing cloudiness, rain, snow-showers, at times clearing, road conditions drying but still bad for wheeled vehicles
Sunrise: 6:29 a.m.; **Sunset:** 5:05 p.m.
Moon: Waxing Gibbous; 86% illumination

Sixth Army – Bombers and dive-bombers from the ***Luftwaffe***'s VIII Air Corps pounded enemy positions at the Barrikady Gun Factory. The army headquarters was located at Golubinskaya.

VIII Corps

76th Infantry Division – The division defended in sector, east of the Don River, north of Nizhne-Gnilovskii, to west of Kotluban' against the 214th Rifle Division and the 260th Rifle Division. To the southeast was the 113th Infantry Division; to the northwest was the 384th Infantry Division. The division lost one NCO/enlisted killed in action; one NCOI/enlisted was wounded in action.

113th Infantry Division – The division defended in sector southwest of Samofalovka and north of Borodkin, against the 298th Rifle Division, the 258th Rifle Division, the 207th Rifle Division and the 316th Rifle Division. To the west was the 76th Infantry Division; to the east was the 60th Infantry Division (Motorized.) The division lost two NCOs/enlisted killed in action; one NCO/enlisted was wounded in action.

XI Corps

44th Infantry Division – The division defended in sector Kurchajessowskij-Kamyshinskiy-Hill 171.0-Hill 180.9-Sirotinskaya-Khmelevskoy, against the 40th Guards Rifle Division, the 23rd Rifle Division and the 4th Guards Rifle Division. The division headquarters was located at Verkhne-Golubaja. To the west was 376th Infantry Division; to the southeast was the 384th Infantry Division. The division lost three NCOs/enlisted wounded in action.

376th Infantry Division – The division defended in sector, south of Perekopskaja, near Logowskii and Ossinskij, against the 321st Rifle Division and the 23rd Rifle Division. To the east was the 44th Infantry Division; to the west was the 1st Romanian Cavalry Division of the Romanian Third Army. The division lost two NCOs/enlisted wounded in action.

384th Infantry Division – The division defended in sector west of the Don River near Trekhostrovskaia to Podgorskii, against the 24th Rifle Division, the 214th Rifle Division and the 22nd Mechanized Brigade. To the northwest was the 44th Infantry Division; to the southeast was the 76th Infantry Division. The division reported one man missing in action.

XIV *Panzer* Corps – The corps headquarters was located east of Ssadtschi-Kowa. The 177th ***Sturmgeschütz*** Detachment was assigned to the corps. The corps suffered the following officer casualties: one killed in action; two wounded in action.

3rd Infantry Division (Motorized) – The division defended in sector, from the Tartar Hill-Hill 111.1-Hill 129.6-Hill 131.2, destroying an enemy attack at Hill 129.6, but losing Hill 130.7 against the 252nd Rifle Division, the 212th Rifle Division, the 116th Rifle Division, the 299th Rifle Division, the 91st Tank Brigade, the 121st Tank Brigade and the 58th Tank Brigade. To the east was the 16th ***Panzer*** Division; to the west was the 60th Infantry Division (Motorized.) The division lost nine NCOs/enlisted killed in action; 18 NCOs/enlisted were wounded in action.

16th Panzer Division – The division defended in sector, from Hill 139.7 to the Volga and then south to Rynok against the 64th Rifle Division, the 120th Rifle Division, the 84th Rifle Division and the 99th Rifle Division. Part of the division attacked into western Spartakovka and seized a group of houses. To the south was the

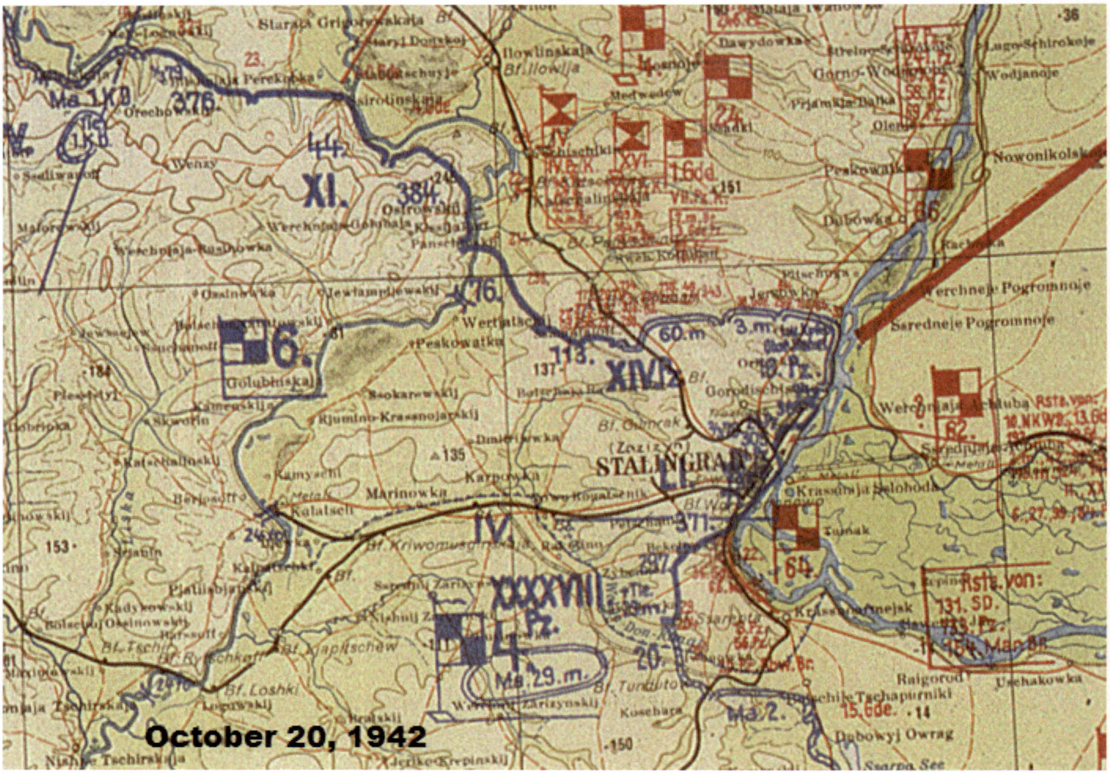

94th Infantry Division; to the west was the 3rd Infantry Division (Motorized.) The division lost one NCO/enlisted killed in action; 15 NCOs/enlisted were wounded in action.

60th Infantry Division (Motorized) – The division defended, from south of Kotluban' Station near Borodkin to Kuz'michi, repelling an attack by the 316th Rifle Division. The attached 9th Machinegun Battalion defeated an attack by the 233rd Rifle Division. The 173rd Rifle Division was able to make a small penetration in the main defensive line near Hill 128.1. To the west was the 113th Infantry Division; to the east was the 3rd Infantry Division (Motorized.) The division lost 30 NCOs/enlisted killed in action; 60 NCOs/enlisted were wounded in action.

94th Infantry Division – The division received the previously detached 276th Infantry Regiment; the division also conducted patrolling and reconnaissance operations near Spartakovka and seized a group of houses in the western part of Spartakovka. To the south was the 389th Infantry Division; to the northeast was the 16th ***Panzer*** Division. The division lost four NCOs/enlisted killed in action; eight NCOs/enlisted were wounded in action.

Battle Group Stahel – The battle group defended in sector, south of Erzovka, from the Volga River west.

LI Corps – The corps headquarters was located at Gumrak. The 245th ***Sturmgeschütz*** Detachment was assigned to the corps. The corps reported 45 killed in action, 95 wounded in action and seven missing in action. The corps suffered the following officer casualties: two wounded in action.

14th Panzer Division – The division conducted reconnaissance and local attacks south in front of the 24th ***Panzer*** Division on their right flank to seize more of the Barrikady Gun Factory. The division lost three NCOs/enlisted killed in action; 16 NCOs/enlisted were wounded in action; one man was reported missing in action. To the north was the 389th Infantry Division; to the south was the 79th Infantry Division.

24th Panzer Division – The division defended in positions along the Volga River. The attached 276th Infantry Regiment returned to its parent unit, the 94th Infantry Division. The division suffered nine NCOs/enlisted killed in action; one officer and 31 NCOs/enlisted were wounded in action. To the south was the 305th Infantry Division.

71st Infantry Division – The division defended in sector. To the north was the 295th Infantry Division; to the south was the 371st Infantry Division. The division lost two NCOs/enlisted wounded in action.

79th Infantry Division – The division relieved the 100th ***Jäger*** Division of the northern half of its defensive sector. To the north was the 14th ***Panzer*** Division; to the south was the 100th ***Jäger*** Division. The division reported ten NCOs/enlisted killed in action; two officers and 38 NCOs/enlisted were wounded in action.

100th Jäger Division – The division was relieved of its northern sector by the 79th Infantry Division and continued to defend in sector; the division also conducted patrolling and reconnaissance operations against the 39th Guards Rifle Division and the 193rd Rifle Division. The division suffered four NCOs/enlisted killed in action; 11 NCOs/enlisted were wounded in action; five men were reported missing in action. To the north was the 79th Infantry Division; to the south was the 295th Infantry Division.

295th Infantry Division – The division defended in sector against the 284th Rifle Division; the division also conducted patrolling and reconnaissance operations. To the north was the 100th ***Jäger*** Division; to the south was the 71st Infantry Division. The division reported one NCO/enlisted killed in action and nine NCOs/enlisted wounded in action.

305th Infantry Division – The division attacked south along the eastern flank of the 14th ***Panzer*** Division, reaching the Volga River near the Brick Works. To the north was the 389th Infantry Division; to its right was the 14th ***Panzer*** Division. The division lost 12 NCOs/enlisted killed in action; one officer and 16 NCOs/enlisted were wounded in action; one man was reported missing in action.

389th Infantry Division – The division attempted to conduct offensive operations to continue to clear enemy forces from the Dzerzhinsky Tractor Factory and the Dzerzhinsky Tractor Factory Workers' Settlement, but the attack stalled and it went over to the defensive. To the north was the 94th Infantry Division; to the south were the 14th ***Panzer*** Division and the 305th Infantry Division.

Fourth *Panzer* Army – The army headquarters was located east of Verkhne-Zaryzinskij.

IV Corps

297th Infantry Division – The division defended in sector east of Elkhi and Iagodniki against the 157th Rifle Division. To the north was the 371st Infantry Division; to the south was the 29th Infantry Division (Motorized.)

371st Infantry Division – The division defended in sector from Kuporosnoye in the east to northwest of Gornaia Poliana against part of the 422nd Rifle Division. To the north was the 71st Infantry Division; to the south was the 297th Infantry Division.

20th Romanian Infantry Division – The division defended in sector, west of the Tundutovo Rail Station and east of Andreevka. To the north was the 29th Infantry Division (Motorized.)

Fourth *Panzer* Army Reserve

29th Infantry Division (Motorized) – The division occupied an assembly area, between Businovka and Gavrilovka, to prepare for future operations. Part of the division defended in sector east of the Volga-Don Canal against the 29th Rifle Division. To the north was the 297th Infantry Division; to the south was the 20th Romanian Infantry Division.

Sources, October 20, 1942: ***Oberkommando des Heeres, Lage Ost: Stand: 20.10.42, Eastern Front Situation Map, National Archives Identifier: 559733, Record Group 242 – National Archives Collection of Foreign Records Seized, 1675-1958, National Archives, College Park, Maryland; Ia, Armeeoberkommando 6, "Morgen Meldung" and assorted reports, Kriegstagebuch 14, 21 October 1942, as found in Microfilm Series, T-312, Records of German Field Commands, Armies, Roll 1453 and 1688, National Archives and Records Service, College Park, Maryland; Korpsarzt, XXXXVIII Panzerkorps, "Meldung über Personelle Verluste," Stand 20.10.42, as found on T-314, Records of German Field Commands, Corps, Roll 1158, National Archives, College Park, Maryland; Florian Freiherr von und zu Aufsess, Die Anlagenbände zu den Kriegstagebüchern der***

6. Armee vom 14.09.1942 bis 24.11.1942, Band 1, Schwabach, Germany: Selbstverlag, 2006, 190-195; David M. Glantz & Jonathan M. House, Armageddon in Stalingrad: September-November 1942, (The Stalingrad Trilogy, Volume 2), Lawrence, Kansas: University Press of Kansas, 2009, 434-437, 449; Rolf Grams, Die 14. Panzer-Division, 1940-1945, Friedberg, FRG: Podzun Pallas Verlag, 1986, 69; Adalbert Holl, An Infantryman in Stalingrad, translated by Jason D. Mark and Neill Page, Sydney, Australia: Leaping Horseman Books, 2005, 131; Jason Mark, Death of the Leaping Horseman: 24. Panzer-Division in Stalingrad, Sydney, Australia: Leaping Horsemen Books, 2003, 299-300; Kurt Mehner, Die Geheimen Tagesberichte der Deutschen Wehrmachtführung im Zweiten Weltkrieg 1939-1945, Band 5: 1. Juni 1942 – 30. November 1942, Osnabrück, Germany: Biblio Verlag, 1991, 244; Hans Sanger, Die 79. Infanterie Division, Friedberg, FRG: Podzun Pallas Verlag, 71; Anton Schimak, Karl Lamprecht & Friedrich Dettmer, Die 44. Infanterie Division: Tagebuch der Hoch- und Deutschmeister, Wien: Verlag Austria Press, 169, 233 and Map: Marschweg der 44. Infanterie Division im Russland.

Zur frommen Erinnerung
im Gebet
an unseren lieben Sohn, Bruder, Schwager und Onkel

Anton Moser

Obergefreiter in einem Gren.-Regt.
Geboren am 25. Januar 1919.
Gefallen am 20. Oktober 1942 in Stalingrad.

Allmächtiger Gott, gütiger Vater, ohne dessen Willen kein Blatt vom Baume fällt, siehe liebreich auf unseren gefallenen Helden, nimm ihn, der nach deinem Willen für das irdische Vaterland gestorben ist, in das bessere himmlische Vaterland auf!

Sohn Gottes, unser lieber Heiland, du hast Blut und Leben für uns geopfert. Rufe den Helden, der im Gehorsam gegen die Obrigkeit und aus Liebe zu unserem Volke sein Leben eingesetzt und sein Blut vergossen hat, zur Zahl deiner Auserwählten!

Gott, Heiliger Geist, laß die Seele des gefallenen Helden, durch die Leiden des Krieges geläutert, und durch das Martyrium des Heldentodes geheiligt, in der Schar der Martyrer und Bekenner an der ewigen Herrlichkeit teilehmen!

Amen!

***Obergefreiter* Anton Moser** was born on January 25, 1919 in Ummendorf, near Biberach, in Baden-Württemberg. Assigned to an infantry regiment, he was killed in action at Stalingrad on October 20, 1942. His name is listed in the remembrance book at the German Military Cemetery at Rossoschka.

October 21, 1942
Weather: windy, changing cloudiness, drying, brighter, ***balkas*** swampy, road traffic impeded
Sunrise: 6:30 a.m.; **Sunset:** 5:03 p.m.
Moon: Waxing Gibbous; 92% illumination

Sixth Army – Bombers and dive-bombers from the ***Luftwaffe***'s VIII Air Corps pounded enemy positions in the northern part of Stalingrad. The army headquarters was located at Golubinskaya.

VIII Corps

76th Infantry Division – The division defended in sector, east of the Don River, north of Nizhne-Gnilovskii, to west of Kotluban' against the 214th Rifle Division and the 260th Rifle Division. To the southeast was the 113th Infantry Division; to the northwest was the 384th Infantry Division. The division suffered one NCO/enlisted wounded in action.

113th Infantry Division – The division defended in sector southwest of Samofalovka and north of Borodkin against the 298th Rifle Division, the 258th Rifle Division, the 207th Rifle Division and the 316th Rifle Division. To the northwest was the 76th Infantry Division; to the east was the 60th Infantry Division (Motorized.) The division lost one officer wounded in action.

384th Infantry Division – The division defended in sector west of the Don River near Trekhostrovskaia to Podgorskii against the 24th Rifle Division, the 214th Rifle Division and the 22nd Mechanized Brigade. To the west was the 44th Infantry Division; to the southeast was the 76th Infantry Division. The division lost two NCOs/enlisted killed in action; one man was reported missing in action.

XI Corps

44th Infantry Division – The division defended in sector Kurchajessowskij-Kamyshinskiy-Hill 171.0-Hill 180.9-Sirotinskaya-Khmelevskoy against the 40th Guards Rifle Division and the 4th Guards Rifle Division. The division headquarters was located at Verkhne-Golubaja. To the west was 376th Infantry Division; to the southeast was the 384th Infantry Division.

376th Infantry Division – The division defended in sector, south of Perekopskaja, near Logowskii and Ossinskij against the 321st Rifle Division and the 23rd Rifle Division. To the east was the 44th Infantry Division; to the west was the 1st Romanian Cavalry Division of the Romanian Third Army.

XIV *Panzer* Corps – The corps headquarters was located east of Ssadtschi-Kowa. The corps suffered the following officer casualties: one wounded in action.

3rd Infantry Division (Motorized) – The division defended in sector, from the Tartar Hill-Hill 111.1-Hill 129.6-Hill 131.2 against the 252nd Rifle Division, the 212th Rifle Division, the 116th Rifle Division, the 299th Rifle Division, the 91st Tank Brigade, the 121st Tank Brigade and the 58th Tank Brigade, destroying an enemy attack at Hill 129.6 and Hill 112.7. To the east was the 16th ***Panzer*** Division; to the west was the 60th Infantry Division (Motorized.) The division lost 19 NCOs/enlisted killed in action; 38 NCOs/enlisted were wounded in action; one man was reported missing in action.

16th Panzer Division – The division defended in sector, from Hill 139.7 to the Volga and then south to Rynok against the 64th Rifle Division, the 120th Rifle Division, the 84th Rifle Division and the 99th Rifle Division. The division suffered three NCOs/enlisted killed in action; one officer and 15 NCOs/enlisted were wounded in action.

60th Infantry Division (Motorized) – The division defended in sector, from south of Kotluban' Station near Borodkin to Kuz'michi against the 316th Rifle Division, the 233rd Rifle Division, the 173rd Rifle Division, the 273rd Rifle

Division, the 49th Rifle Division, the 343rd Rifle Division and the 62nd Rifle Division. To the west was the 113th Infantry Division; to the east was the 3rd Infantry Division (Motorized.) The division lost 30 NCOs/enlisted killed in action; 70 NCOs/enlisted were wounded in action; one man was reported missing in action.

94th Infantry Division – The division conducted limited offensive action. To the south was the 389th Infantry Division; to the northeast was the 16th ***Panzer*** Division. The division lost six NCOs/enlisted killed in action; 14 NCOs/enlisted were wounded in action; one man was reported missing in action.

Battle Group Stahel – The battle group defended in sector, south of Erzovka, from the Volga River west.

LI Corps – The corps headquarters was located at Gumrak. The 101st Heavy Artillery Detachment was assigned to support the corps. The corps suffered the following officer casualties: one killed in action; six wounded in action; and one missing in action.

14th Panzer Division – The division turned toward the Volga River to seize the southwestern part of the Barrikady Gun Factory from the 138th Rifle Division. To the north was the 305th Infantry Division; to the south was the 79th Infantry Division. The division suffered two NCOs/enlisted killed in action; 12 NCOs/enlisted were wounded in action.

24th Panzer Division – The division defended in positions along the Volga River. To the south was the 305th Infantry Division. The division suffered one officer and two NCOs/enlisted killed in action; 33 NCOs/enlisted were wounded in action.

71st Infantry Division – The division defended in sector. To the north was the 295th Infantry Division; to the south was the 371st Infantry Division. The division suffered one NCO/enlisted killed in action; six NCOs/enlisted were wounded in action.

79th Infantry Division – The division, reinforced by the 54th ***Jäger*** Regiment of the 100th ***Jäger*** Division, attacked to seize the remainder of the Barrikady Gun Factory, seizing the Cooking Factory. To the north was the 14th ***Panzer*** Division; to the south was the 100th ***Jäger*** Division. The division lost four NCOs/enlisted killed in action and seven NCOs/

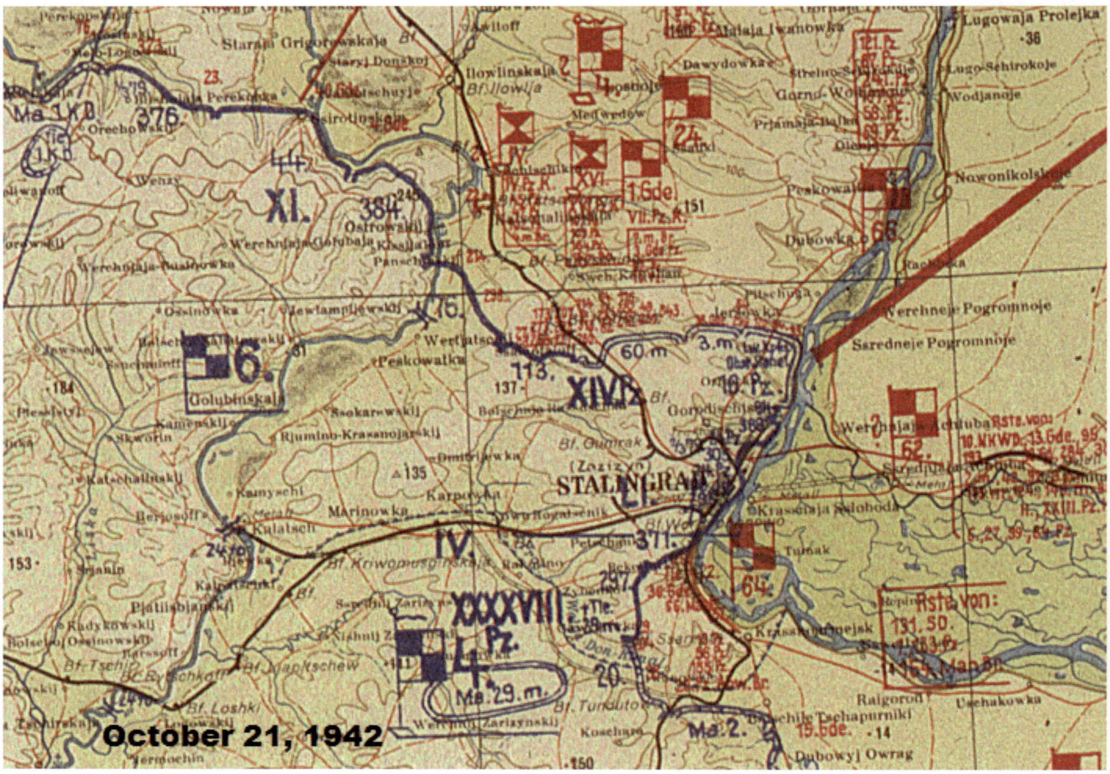

October 21, 1942

enlisted wounded in action. The 54th ***Jäger*** Regiment lost one officer and 19 NCOs/enlisted killed in action; two officers and 129 NCOs/enlisted were wounded in action; eight men were reported missing in action. One infantry regiment, defending with the 376th Infantry Division south of the Don River, began moving toward Stalingrad.

100th Jäger Division – The division defended in sector. To the north was the 79th Infantry Division; to the south was the 295th Infantry Division. The division suffered two NCOs/enlisted killed in action; 15 NCOs/enlisted were wounded in action.

295th Infantry Division – The division defended in sector against the 284th Rifle Division; the division also conducted patrolling and reconnaissance operations. To the north was the 100th ***Jäger*** Division; to the south was the 71st Infantry Division. The division reported one NCO/enlisted killed in action and eight NCOs/enlisted wounded in action.

305th Infantry Division – The division attacked south along the eastern flank of the 14th ***Panzer*** Division against the 138th Rifle Division. The division seized a housing block north of the Barrikady Gun Factory. To the north was the 389th Infantry Division; to the west was the 14th ***Panzer*** Division. The division lost 12 NCOs/enlisted killed in action; 32 NCOs/enlisted were wounded in action.

389th Infantry Division – The division attacked near the Dzerzhinsky Tractor Factory. To the north was the 94th Infantry Division; to the south were the 14th ***Panzer*** Division and the 305th Infantry Division.

Fourth *Panzer* Army – The army headquarters was located east of Verkhne-Zaryzinskij.

IV Corps

297th Infantry Division – The division defended in sector east of Elkhi and Iagodniki against the 36th Guards Rifle Division. To the north was the 371st Infantry Division; to the south was the 29th Infantry Division (Motorized.)

371st Infantry Division – The division defended in sector from Kuporosnoye in the east to northwest of Gornaia Poliana against part of the 422nd Rifle Division. To the north was the 71st Infantry Division; to the south was the 297th Infantry Division.

20th Romanian Infantry Division – The division defended in sector, west of the Tundutovo Rail Station and east of Andreevka against the 204th Rifle Division. To the north was the 29th Infantry Division (Motorized.)

Fourth *Panzer* Army Reserve

29th Infantry Division (Motorized) – The division occupied an assembly area, between Businovka and Gavrilovka, to prepare for future operations. Part of the division defended in sector east of the Volga-Don Canal against the 29th Rifle Division. To the north was the 297th Infantry Division; to the south was the 20th Romanian Infantry Division. The division lost three NCOs/enlisted killed in action.

Sources, October 21, 1942: ***Oberkommando des Heeres, Lage Ost: Stand: 21.10.42, Eastern Front Situation Map, National Archives Identifier: 559733, Record Group 242 – National Archives Collection of Foreign Records Seized, 1675-1958, National Archives, College Park, Maryland; Ia, Armeeoberkommando 6, "Morgen Meldung" and assorted reports, Kriegstagebuch 14, 22 October 1942, as found in Microfilm Series, T-312, Records of German Field Commands, Armies, Roll 1453 and 1688, National Archives and Records Service, College Park, Maryland; Korpsarzt, XXXXVIII Panzerkorps, "Meldung über Personelle Verluste," Stand 21.10.42, as found on T-314, Records of German Field Commands, Corps, Roll 1158, National Archives, College Park, Maryland; Florian Freiherr von und zu Aufsess, Die Anlagenbände zu den Kriegstagebüchern der 6. Armee vom 14.09.1942 bis 24.11.1942, Band 1, Schwabach, Germany: Selbstverlag, 2006, 196-197; David M. Glantz & Jonathan M. House, Armageddon in Stalingrad: September-November 1942, (The Stalingrad Trilogy, Volume 2), Lawrence, Kansas: University Press of Kansas, 2009, 437-439, 450; Adalbert Holl, An Infantryman in Stalingrad, translated by Jason D. Mark and Neill Page, Sydney, Australia: Leaping Horseman Books, 2005, 129; Jason Mark, Death of the Leaping Horseman: 24. Panzer-Division in Stalingrad, Sydney, Australia: Leaping Horsemen Books, 2003, 301-305; Kurt Mehner, Die Geheimen Tagesberichte der Deutschen Wehrmachtführung im Zweiten Weltkrieg 1939-1945, Band 5: 1. Juni 1942 – 30. November 1942, Osnabrück, Germany: Biblio Verlag, 1991, 245; Anton Schimak, Karl Lamprecht & Friedrich Dettmer, Die 44. Infanterie Division: Tagebuch der Hoch- und Deutschmeister, Wien: Verlag Austria Press, 169, 233 and Map: Marschweg der 44. Infanterie Division im Russland.***

Zur frommen Erinnerung im Gebete

an

Heinz Alengs

Sanitätsfeldw. in einem Art.-Rgt.
Teilnehmer an sämtl. Feldzügen
Inh. des Kriegsverdienstkreuzes
mit Schwertern u. Ostmdaille

geb. am 2. Januar 1915
gefallen am 21. Oktober 1942
bei Stalingrad.

Der Tod zerriß das schöne Band,
Das einst die Liebe um uns schlang.
Er nahm das beste Gatten u. Vaterherz
Und bracht uns bitteren Trennungsschmerz
Allzufrüh hast du uns verlassen
Ach wir konntens nicht erfleh'n
Ruhe sanft in Gottes Frieden
Bis wir dich im Himmel wiedersehn.
Nicht wir allein, die um Dich weinen
Nein, wer Dich kannte, liebte Dich,
Der Herr auch kennt u. liebt die Seinen
Drum nahm er frühe Dich zu sich.

Wenn Tränen könnten dich erwecken,
würde fremde Erde dich nicht decken.

Sanitäts-Feldwebel **Heinz Alengs** was born on January 2, 1915. A medical non-commissioned officer assigned to an artillery regiment, he had previously won the War Service Cross with Swords 2nd Class and the Eastern Front Medal. Alengs was killed in action near Stalingrad on October 21, 1942.

Zum Andenken

an Jäger

Franz Minroiter

Hausbesitzerssohn in Holzhäuseln,
Gemeinde Tumeltsham

welcher am 21. Oktober 1942 beim Angriff auf den Nordteil der Stadt Stalingrad schwer verwundet wurde und am gleichen Tage auf dem Hauptverbandsplatz im 19. Lebensjahre für Führer, Volk und Heimat den Heldentod starb.

Eltern, Geschwister und Freunde mein!
So gern schrieb ich aus der Ferne heim,
Doch heut ist's zum letztenmal,
Daß ich Euch grüße tausendmal
Und sage Dank für jede Gab',
Die ich von Euch empfangen hab'.
Richte an Euch die letzte Bitt',
Vergeßt ja im Gebet mich nicht.
Nur keine Träne, keine Klag',
Der liebe Gott, der mir das Leben gab,
Rief mich so früh ins Heldengrab.
Und ich werde in des Himmels Auen
Im Lorbeerkranz Euch wiederschauen.

4239—42

Jäger **Franz Minroiter** was ninteen years old, hailing from Holzhäuseln in the Tumeltsham district near Ried, Austria. He was seriously wounded during an attack in northern Stalingrad on October 21, 1942 and died the same day at a casualty collection point. He was probably assigned to the 100th ***Jäger*** Division.

October 22, 1942
Weather: changing cloudiness, morning rain, windy, after noon clearing, 46° F, poor conditions for aerial reconnaissance
Sunrise: 6:32 a.m.; **Sunset:** 5:01 p.m.
Moon: Waxing Gibbous; 97% illumination

Sixth Army – Bombers and dive-bombers from the ***Luftwaffe***'s VIII Air Corps pounded enemy positions in the northern part of Stalingrad. The army headquarters was located at Golubinskaya.

VIII Corps

76th Infantry Division – The division defended in sector, east of the Don River, north of Nizhne-Gnilovskii, to west of Kotluban' against the 214th Rifle Division and the 298th Rifle Division. To the east was the 113th Infantry Division; to the northwest was the 384th Infantry Division. The division lost one NCO/enlisted killed in action; six NCOs/enlisted were wounded in action.

113th Infantry Division – The division defended in sector southwest of Samofalovka and north of Borodkin against the 298th Rifle Division, the 258th Rifle Division, the 207th Rifle Division and the 316th Rifle Division. To the northwest was the 76th Infantry Division; to the east was the 60th Infantry Division (Motorized.) The division lost three NCOs/enlisted killed in action; nine NCOs/enlisted were wounded in action.

XI Corps

44th Infantry Division – The division defended in sector Kurchajessowskij-Kamyshinskiy-Hill 171.0-Hill 180.9-Sirotinskaya-Khmelevskoy against the 40th Guards Rifle Division, the 4th Guards Rifle Division and the 23rd Rifle Division. The division headquarters was located at Verkhne-Golubaja. To the west was 376th Infantry Division; to the east was the 384th Infantry Division. The division lost five NCOs/enlisted wounded in action.

376th Infantry Division – The division defended in sector, south of Perekopskaja, near Logowskii and Ossinskij against the 321st Rifle Division and the 23rd Rifle Division. The division released the attached regiment of the 79th Infantry Division. To the east was the 44th Infantry Division; to the west was the 1st Romanian Cavalry Division of the Romanian Third Army. The division lost two NCOs/enlisted wounded in action.

384th Infantry Division – The division defended in sector west of the Don River near Trekhostrovskaia to Podgorskii against the 22nd Mechanized Brigade. To the west was the 44th Infantry Division; to the southeast was the 76th Infantry Division.

XIV *Panzer* Corps – The corps headquarters was located east of Ssadtschi-Kowa. The 631st Heavy Artillery Detachment was assigned to support the corps. The corps suffered the following officer casualties: one wounded in action.

3rd Infantry Division (Motorized) – The division defended in sector, from the Tartar Hill-Hill 111.1-Hill 129.6-Hill 131.2 against the 252nd Rifle Division, the 212th Rifle Division, the 116th Rifle Division, the 299th Rifle Division, the 91st Tank Brigade, the 121st Tank Brigade and the 58th Tank Brigade, destroying an enemy attack at Hill 129.6, but losing Hill 112.7. The 252nd Rifle Division captured the area around the Motor Tractor Station. To the east was the 16th ***Panzer*** Division; to the west was the 60th Infantry Division (Motorized.) The division lost 11 NCOs/enlisted killed in action; 40 NCOs/enlisted were wounded in action.

16th Panzer Division – The division defended in sector, from Hill 139.7 to the Volga and then south to Rynok, repelling attacks by the 64th Rifle Division, the 120th Rifle Division, the 84th Rifle Division and the 99th Rifle Division.

To the west was the 3rd Infantry Division (Motorized); to the southwest was the 94th Infantry Division. The division lost five NCOs/enlisted killed in action; eight NCOs/enlisted were wounded in action.

60th Infantry Division (Motorized) – The division defended in sector, from south of Kotluban' Station near Borodkin to Kuz'michi, repelling attacks by the 316th Rifle Division, the 233rd Rifle Division, the 173rd Rifle Division, the 273rd Rifle Division, the 49th Rifle Division, the 343rd Rifle Division and the 62nd Rifle Division. The 62nd Rifle Division captured Hill 112.7. To the west was the 113th Infantry Division; to the east was the 3rd Infantry Division (Motorized.) The division lost one officer and 14 NCOs/enlisted killed in action; 40 NCOs/enlisted were wounded in action.

94th Infantry Division – The division attacked at Spartakovka. To the south was the 389th Infantry Division; to the northeast was the 16th ***Panzer*** Division. The division lost six NCOs/enlisted killed in action; 12 NCOs/enlisted were wounded in action.

Battle Group Stahel – The battle group defended in sector, south of Erzovka, from the Volga River west.

LI Corps – Corps artillery observers identified 35 enemy artillery batteries firing from the east bank of the Volga River. The corps headquarters was located at Gumrak. The corps suffered the following officer casualties: four wounded in action; and one missing in action.

14th Panzer Division – The division continued offensive operations in the Barrikady Gun Factory. To the north was the 305th Infantry Division; to the south was the 79th Infantry Division. The division lost two NCOs/enlisted killed in action; one officer and 26 NCOs/enlisted were wounded in action. The division reported that five heavy and no medium anti-tank guns were operational.

24th Panzer Division – The division defended in positions along the Volga River. To the north was the 389th Infantry Division; to the south was the 305th Infantry Division. The division suffered ten NCOs/enlisted wounded in action.

71st Infantry Division – The division defended in sector. To the north was the 295th Infantry Division; to the south was the 371st Infantry Division. The division suffered one NCO/enlisted killed in action and one NCO/

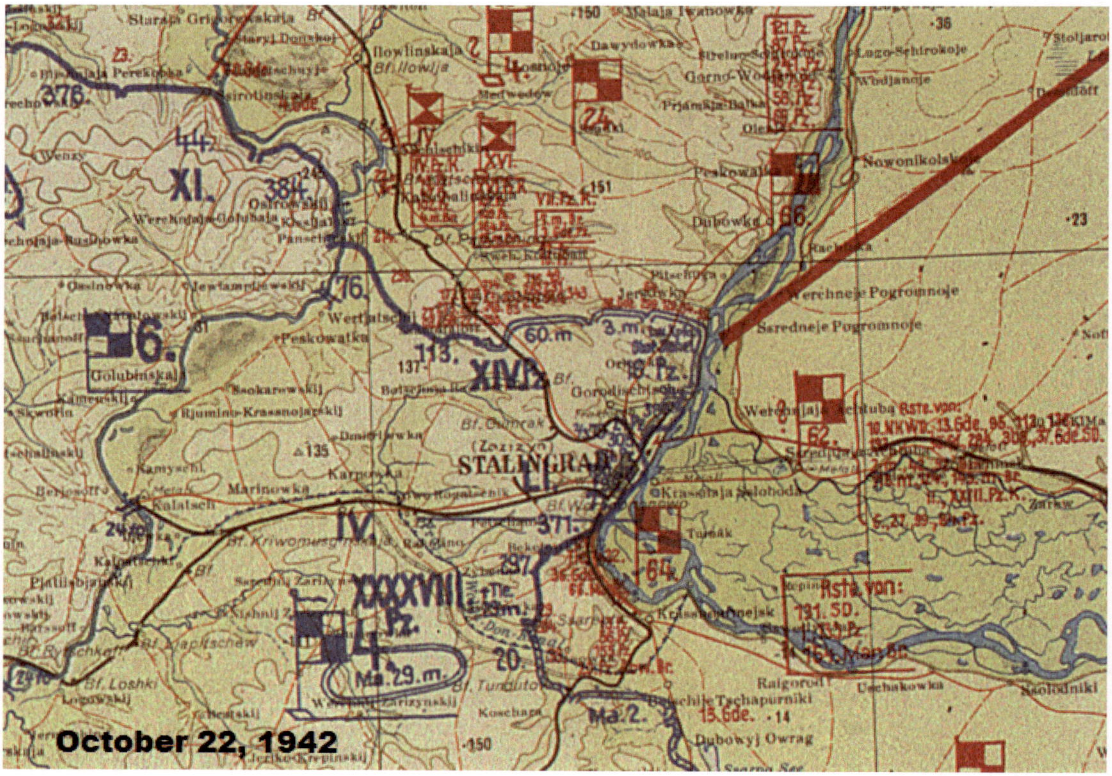

enlisted wounded in action. The division reported that six heavy and no medium anti-tank guns were operational.

79th Infantry Division – The division, reinforced by the 54th ***Jäger*** Regiment of the 100th ***Jäger*** Division, attacked in zone at the Barrikady Gun Factory and north of the factory to the rail line. To the north was the 14th ***Panzer*** Division; to the south was the 100th ***Jäger*** Division. One infantry regiment moved toward Stalingrad, reaching Verkhne-Businovka. The division lost three NCOs/enlisted killed in action; five NCOs/enlisted were wounded in action; six men were reported missing in action. The division reported that 16 heavy and 11 medium anti-tank guns were operational.

100th Jäger Division – The division defended in sector. To the north was the 79th Infantry Division; to the south was the 295th Infantry Division. The division lost five NCOs/enlisted killed in action; 48 NCOs/enlisted were wounded in action; one man was reported missing in action. The division reported that six heavy and ten medium anti-tank guns were operational.

295th Infantry Division – The division defended in sector against the 284th Rifle Division; the division also conducted patrolling and reconnaissance operations. To the north was the 100th ***Jäger*** Division; to the south was the 71st Infantry Division. The division reported two NCOs/enlisted killed in action and one officer and seven NCOs/enlisted wounded in action. The division reported that ten heavy and five medium anti-tank guns were operational.

305th Infantry Division – The division attacked south in zone along the eastern flank of the 14th ***Panzer*** Division against the 138th Rifle Division. To the north was the 24th ***Panzer*** Division; to the west was the 14th ***Panzer*** Division. The division lost six NCOs/enlisted killed in action; two officers and 33 NCOs/enlisted were wounded in action. The division reported that ten heavy and 14 medium anti-tank guns were operational.

389th Infantry Division – The division attacked in zone, cleaning out pockets of resistance near the Dzerzhinsky Tractor Factory. To the north was the 94th Infantry Division; to the south was the 24th ***Panzer*** Division. The division suffered one NCO/enlisted killed in action and one NCO/enlisted wounded in action. The division reported that four heavy and 12 medium anti-tank guns were operational.

Fourth *Panzer* Army – The army headquarters was located east of Verkhne-Zaryzinskij.

IV Corps

297th Infantry Division – The division defended in sector east of Elkhi and Iagodniki against attacking elements of the Soviet 64th Army, including the 36th Guards Rifle Division. To the north was the 371st Infantry Division; to the south was the 29th Infantry Division (Motorized.)

371st Infantry Division – The division defended in sector from Kuporosnoye in the east to northwest of Gornaia Poliana against attacking elements of the Soviet 64th Army, including part of the 422nd Rifle Division. To the north was the 71st Infantry Division; to the south was the 297th Infantry Division.

20th Romanian Infantry Division – The division defended in sector, west of the Tundutovo Rail Station and east of Andreevka against attacking elements of the Soviet 64th Army, to include the 204th Rifle Division. To the north was the 29th Infantry Division (Motorized); to the south was the 2nd Romanian Infantry Division of the Romanian VI Corps.

Fourth *Panzer* Army Reserve

29th Infantry Division (Motorized) – The division occupied an assembly area, between Businovka and Gavrilovka, to prepare for future operations. Part of the division defended in sector east of the Volga-Don Canal against the 29th Rifle Division. To the north was the 297th Infantry Division; to the south was the 20th Romanian Infantry Division. The division lost one NCO/enlisted killed in action; one NCO/enlisted was wounded in action.

Sources, October 22, 1942: *Oberkommando des Heeres, Lage Ost: Stand: 22.10.42, Eastern Front Situation Map, National Archives Identifier: 559733, Record Group 242 – National Archives Collection of Foreign Records Seized, 1675-1958, National Archives, College Park, Maryland; Ia, Armeeoberkommando 6, "Morgen Meldung" and assorted reports, Kriegstagebuch 14, 23 October 1942, as found in Microfilm Series, T-312, Records of German Field Commands, Armies, Roll 1453 and 1688, National Archives and Records Service, College Park, Maryland; Korpsarzt, XXXXVIII Panzerkorps, "Meldung über Personelle Verluste," Stand 22.10.42, as found on T-314, Records of German Field Commands, Corps, Roll 1158, National Archives, College Park, Maryland; Florian Freiherr von und zu Aufsess, Die Anlagenbände zu den Kriegstagebüchern der 6. Armee vom 14.09.1942 bis 24.11.1942, Band 1, Schwabach, Germany: Selbstverlag, 2006, 196-198; John Erickson, The Road to Stalingrad, New York: Harper & Row, 1975, 440, 444; David M. Glantz & Jonathan M. House, Armageddon in Stalingrad: September-November 1942, (The Stalingrad Trilogy, Volume 2), Lawrence, Kansas: University Press of Kansas, 2009, 437-440, 450-451; Adalbert Holl, An Infantryman in Stalingrad, translated by Jason D. Mark and Neill Page, Sydney, Australia: Leaping Horseman Books, 2005, 131; Jason Mark, Death of the Leaping Horseman: 24. Panzer-Division in Stalingrad, Sydney, Australia: Leaping Horsemen Books, 2003, 305-306; Kurt Mehner, Die Geheimen Tagesberichte der Deutschen Wehrmachtführung im Zweiten Weltkrieg 1939-1945, Band 5: 1. Juni 1942 – 30. November 1942, Osnabrück, Germany: Biblio Verlag, 1991, 247; Janusz Piekalkiewicz, Stalingrad: Anatomie einer Schlacht, München, BRD: Wilhelm Heyne Verlag, 1977, 314; Anton Schimak, Karl Lamprecht & Friedrich Dettmer, Die 44. Infanterie Division: Tagebuch der Hoch- und Deutschmeister, Wien: Verlag Austria Press, 169, 233 and Map: Marschweg der 44. Infanterie Division im Russland.*

Chriſtliches Andenken
an unſeren guten, innigſtgeliebten, unvergeßlichen Sohn, bezw. Bruder und Bräutigam

Joſef Benczak

Soldat in einer Nachrichten-Abt.,

geb. am 7. Jänner 1920 in Siegendorf welcher vor Stalingrad am 21. Oktober 1942 ſchwer verwundet wurde und am 22. Oktober 1942 auf dem Verbandsplatz in Nowo-Rogazyk im 23. Lebensjahre ſeinen Verletzungen erlegen iſt.

Weit von Euch Lieben müßt ich ſterben,
In fremder Erd' mein Grab ich fand,
Doch meine Seele zog zur Heimat,
Zum Himmel auf ins Vaterland.
O liebe Eltern, Braut u. Brüder mein,
Ich kehre nicht mehr zu Euch heim,
Der letzte Gedanke, der letzte Blick,
Sie eilten noch zu Euch zurück.
Als ich ſtarb im Feindesland
Reichte niemand mir die Hand,
Troſt ſei euch: nur kurze Zeit wird vergehn,
Bis wir uns alle Wiederſehn.

Du gutes Herz ruhe in Gottes Frieden,
Unvergeßlich bleibſt Du deinen Lieben.

Druck: L. Rödlger, Wien 15, Sechshauserstr. 47

Schütze **Josef Benczak** was born on January 7, 1920 in Siegendorf, near Eisenstadt-Umgebung in Austria. A scheduled bridegroom, he was assigned to a signal detachment and was severely wounded on October 21, 1942. He died of his wounds October 22, 1942. He is buried at the German Military Cemetery in Rossoschka, in Block 26, Row 11 in Grave 435.

October 23, 1942
Weather: bad weather overnight, morning sunny, increasing cloudiness, later dry and sunny, road conditions passable for half-track and fully-tracked vehicles
Sunrise: 6:33 a.m.; **Sunset:** 4:59 p.m.
Moon: Waxing Gibbous; 99% illumination

Sixth Army – Bombers and dive-bombers from the ***Luftwaffe***'s VIII Air Corps pounded enemy positions in the northern part of Stalingrad. The army headquarters was located at Golubinskaya.

VIII Corps

76th Infantry Division – The division defended in sector, east of the Don River, north of Nizhne-Gnilovskii, to west of Kotluban' against the 214th Rifle Division and the 260th Rifle Division. To the southeast was the 113th Infantry Division; to the northwest was the 384th Infantry Division. The division lost one NCO/enlisted killed in action; five NCOs/enlisted were wounded in action.

113th Infantry Division – The division defended in sector southwest of Samofalovka and north of Borodkin against the 298th Rifle Division, the 258th Rifle Division, the 207th Rifle Division and the 316th Rifle Division. To the northwest was the 76th Infantry Division; to the east was the 60th Infantry Division (Motorized.) The division suffered one NCO/enlisted killed in action; seven NCOs/enlisted were wounded in action.

XI Corps

44th Infantry Division – The division defended in sector Kurchajessowskij-Kamyshinskiy-Hill 171.0-Hill 180.9-Sirotinskaya-Khmelevskoy against the 40th Guards Rifle Division. The division headquarters was located at Verkhne-Golubaja. To the west was 376th Infantry Division; to the east was the 384th Infantry Division. The division lost two NCOs/enlisted killed in action; three NCOs/enlisted were wounded in action.

376th Infantry Division – The division defended in sector, south of Perekopskaja, near Logowskii and Ossinskij against the 321st Rifle Division and the 23rd Rifle Division. To the east was the 44th Infantry Division; to the west was the 1st Romanian Cavalry Division of the Romanian Third Army. The division lost two NCOs/enlisted killed in action; one NCO/enlisted was wounded in action.

384th Infantry Division – The division defended in sector west of the Don River near Trekhostrovskaia to Podgorskii against the 4th Guards Rifle Division and the 22nd Mechanized Brigade. To the northwest was the 44th Infantry Division; to the southeast was the 76th Infantry Division. The division lost one NCO/enlisted wounded in action.

XIV *Panzer* Corps – The corps headquarters was located east of Ssadtschi-Kowa. The corps suffered the following officer casualties: five wounded in action.

3rd Infantry Division (Motorized) – The division defended in sector, from the Tartar Hill-Hill 111.1-Hill 129.6-Hill 131.2 against the 252nd Rifle Division, the 212th Rifle Division, the 116th Rifle Division, the 299th Rifle Division, the 91st Tank Brigade, the 121st Tank Brigade and the 58th Tank Brigade. The 252nd Rifle Division captured Hill 137.8, while the 212th Rifle Division advanced one kilometer. To the east was the 16th ***Panzer*** Division; to the west was the 60th Infantry Division (Motorized.) The division lost nine NCOs/enlisted killed in action; 24 NCOs/enlisted were wounded in action; two men were reported missing in action.

16th Panzer Division – The division defended in sector, from Hill 139.7 to the Volga and then south to Rynok against the 64th Rifle Division, the 120th Rifle Division, the 84th Rifle Division and the 99th Rifle Division. To the west was the 3rd Infantry Division (Motorized); to the southwest was the 94th Infantry Division. The division lost eight NCOs/enlisted killed in action; 21 NCOs/enlisted were wounded in action; three men were reported missing in action.

60th Infantry Division (Motorized) – The division defended in sector, from south of

Kotluban' Station near Borodkin to Kuz'michi, repelling attacks by the 316th Rifle Division, the 233rd Rifle Division, the 173rd Rifle Division, the 273rd Rifle Division, the 49th Rifle Division, the 343rd Rifle Division; the 62nd Rifle Division advanced 300 meters. To the west was the 113th Infantry Division; to the east was the 3rd Infantry Division (Motorized.) The division lost 12 NCOs/enlisted killed in action; 30 NCOs/enlisted were wounded in action.

94th Infantry Division – The division defended in sector. To the south was the 389th Infantry Division; to the northeast was the 16th ***Panzer*** Division. The division lost one NCO/enlisted killed in action; three NCOs/enlisted were wounded in action.

Battle Group Stahel – The battle group defended in sector, south of Erzovka, from the Volga River west.

LI Corps – The corps headquarters was located at Gumrak. The 733rd Heavy Artillery Detachment, 430th Heavy Artillery Detachment, 2nd Battalion of the 64th Artillery Regiment, 855th Heavy Artillery Detachment, 616th Heavy Artillery Detachment, 101st Heavy Artillery Detachment and the 2nd Battalion of the 59th Artillery Regiment were attached to the corps for the attack. The corps suffered the following officer casualties: three killed in action; 24 wounded in action; and one missing in action.

14th Panzer Division – The division attacked east toward the Volga River, making limited gains at the Bread Factory against the 308th Rifle Division and the 193rd Rifle Division. To the north was the 305th Infantry Division; to the south was the 79th Infantry Division. The 2nd Battalion of the 53rd ***Werfer*** Regiment and the 2nd Battalion of the 2nd ***Werfer*** Regiment were in support of the division. The division suffered nine NCOs/enlisted killed in action; six officers and 60 NCOs/enlisted were wounded in action. Operational ***panzer*** status in the division was: two Mark II, one Mark III-Short, eight Mark III-Long and one Mark IV-Long tanks. Infantry strength stood at 750 soldiers.

24th Panzer Division – The division defended in positions along the Volga River and north of the Barrikady Gun Factory against the 308th Rifle Division and the 138th Rifle Division. To the north was the 389th Infantry Division; to the south was the 305th Infantry Division. The division suffered four NCOs/enlisted killed in action; five NCOs/enlisted were wounded in action. Operational ***panzer*** status in the division was: one Mark II, three Mark III-Short and seven Mark III-Long tanks.

71st Infantry Division – The division defended in sector. To the north was the 295th Infantry Division; to the south was the 371st Infantry Division. The division lost three NCOs/enlisted wounded in action.

79th Infantry Division – The division, with the 244th ***Sturmgeschütz*** Detachment and the 245th ***Sturmgeschütz*** Detachment in direct support and the 54th ***Jäger*** Regiment attached, attacked east against the 39th Guards Rifle Division and the 193rd Rifle Division and seized a significant portion of the Krasny Oktyabr Steel Factory, including the rail line on the west and Halls 3, 5, 6, 7, 8 and 10. Supporting the division were the 1st Battalion of the 53rd ***Werfer*** Regiment, 1st Battalion of the 2nd ***Werfer*** Regiment and the 3rd Battalion of the 2nd ***Werfer*** Regiment. The division suffered two officers and 76 NCOs/enlisted killed in action; seven officers and 357 NCOs/enlisted were wounded in action; six men were reported missing in action. To the north was the 14th ***Panzer*** Division; to the south was the 100th ***Jäger*** Division. At the end of the day, 244th ***Sturmgeschütz*** Detachment was returned to LI Corps control and the 54th ***Jäger*** Regiment returned to the 100th ***Jäger*** Division, while the 367th Infantry Regiment (Croat) of the 100th ***Jäger*** Division was attached to the 79th.

100th Jäger Division – The division defended in sector. To the north was the 79th Infantry Division; to the south was the 295th Infantry Division. The division lost one officer and three NCOs/enlisted killed in action; one officer and 21 NCOs/enlisted were wounded in action; one man was reported missing in action. At the end of the day, the 54th ***Jäger*** Regiment returned to the 100th ***Jäger*** Division from the 79th Infantry Division, while the 367th Infantry Regiment (Croat) of the 100th ***Jäger*** Division was attached to the 79th Infantry Division.

295th Infantry Division – The division defended in sector against the 284th Rifle Division; the division also conducted patrolling and reconnaissance operations. To the north was the 100th ***Jäger*** Division; to the south was the 71st Infantry Division. The division suffered two

NCOs/enlisted killed in action; 11 NCOs/enlisted were wounded in action.

305th Infantry Division – The division attacked east in the Barrikady Gun Factory against elements of the 308th Rifle Division and the 138th Rifle Division; in mid-morning the Soviets counterattacked and retook Hall 4 of the factory. The division lost 17 NCOs/enlisted killed in action; five officers and 53 NCOs/enlisted were wounded in action; one man was reported missing in action. To the north was the 389th Infantry Division; to the south was the 14th ***Panzer*** Division.

389th Infantry Division – The division conducted limited offensive operations near the Dzerzhinsky Tractor Factory. To the north was the 94th Infantry Division; to the south were the 24th ***Panzer*** Division.

Fourth *Panzer* Army – The army headquarters was located east of Verkhne-Zaryzinskij.

IV Corps

297th Infantry Division – The division defended in sector east of Elkhi and near Staro-Dubovka against the 36th Guards Rifle Division and the 157th Rifle Division. To the north was the 371st Infantry Division; to the south was the 29th Infantry Division (Motorized.)

371st Infantry Division – The division defended in sector from Kuporosnoye in the east to northwest of Gornaia Poliana against the 422nd Rifle Division, the 126th Rifle Division, the 93rd Rifle Brigade and the 97th Rifle Brigade. To the north was the 71st Infantry Division; to the south was the 297th Infantry Division.

20th Romanian Infantry Division – The division defended in sector, west of the Tundutovo Rail Station and east of Andreevka against the 204th Rifle Division. To the north was the 29th Infantry Division (Motorized); to the south was the 2nd Romanian Infantry Division of the Romanian VI Corps.

Fourth *Panzer* Army Reserve

29th Infantry Division (Motorized) – The division occupied an assembly area, between Businovka and Gavrilovka, to prepare for future operations. Part of the division defended in sector east of the Volga-Don Canal against the 29th Rifle Division. To the north was the 297th Infantry Division; to the south was the 20th Romanian Infantry Division.

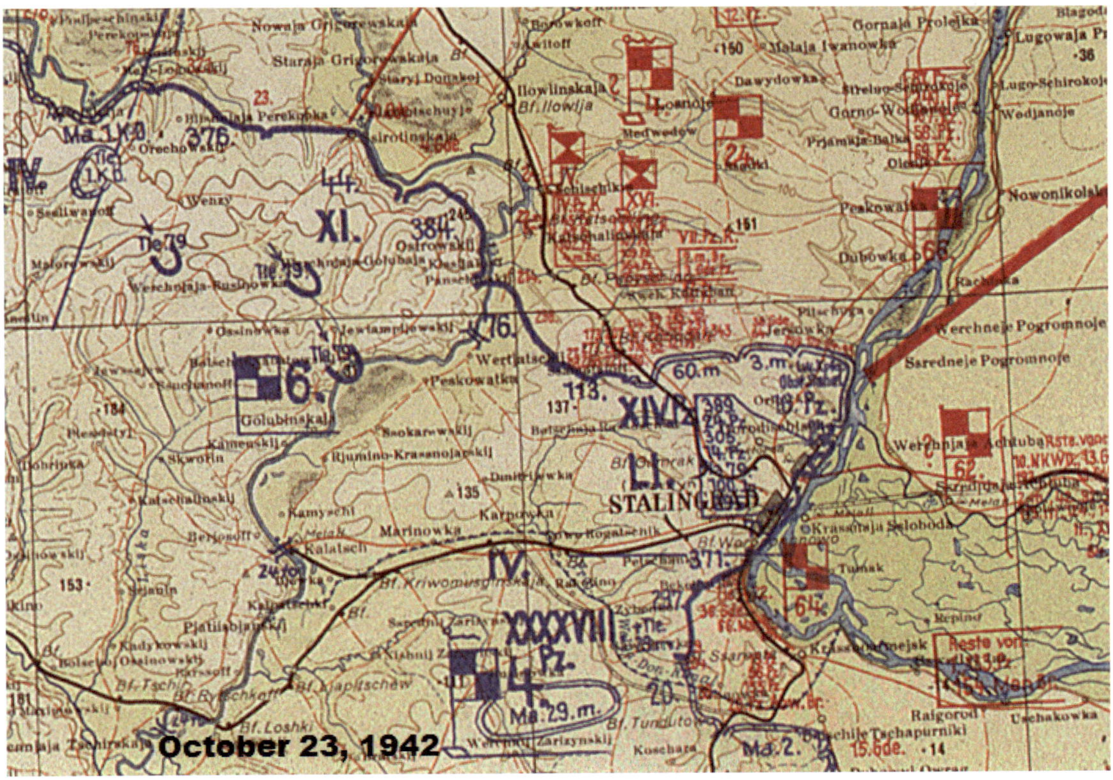

Luftwaffe Unteroffizier **Alois Flieher** was born in Aiging, near Chiemsee, Bavaria on May 11, 1914. Probably assigned to the 9th ***Flak*** Division, he was killed in action northeast of Orlovka on October 23, 1942. He was engaged at the time of his death.

Gefreiter **Sebastian Kaltenberger** was born in Falterhaid near Landau in Bavaria on January 20, 1922. The son of a farmer, Kaltenberger was assigned to an anti-tank company, probably in the 60th Infantry Division (Motorized) that was listed as fighting north of Stalingrad; he was killed six miles north of the Gumrak rail station on October 23, 1942. His name is listed in the remembrance book at the German Military Cemetery at Rossoschka.

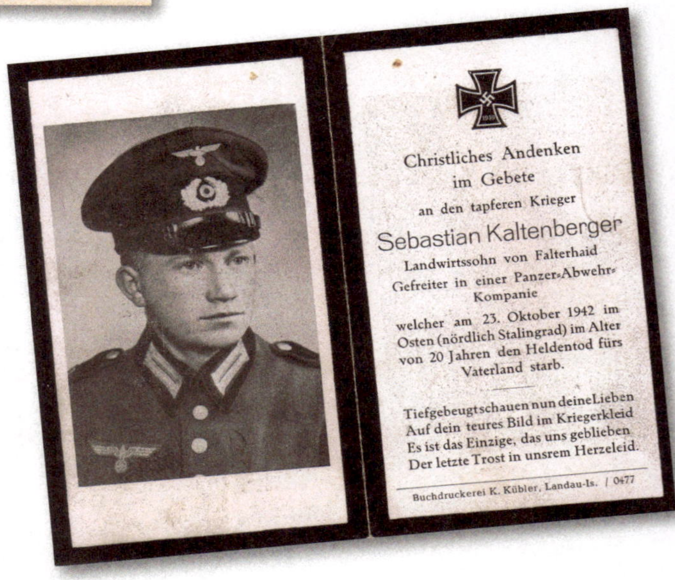

Sources, October 23, 1942: *Oberkommando des Heeres, Lage Ost: Stand: 23.10.42, Eastern Front Situation Map, National Archives Identifier: 559733, Record Group 242 – National Archives Collection of Foreign Records Seized, 1675-1958, National Archives, College Park, Maryland; Ia, Armeeoberkommando 6, "Morgen Meldung" and assorted reports, Kriegstagebuch 14, 24 October 1942, as found in Microfilm Series, T-312, Records of German Field Commands, Armies, Roll 1453 and 1688, National Archives and Records Service, College Park, Maryland; Korpsarzt, XXXXVIII Panzerkorps, "Meldung über Personelle Verluste," Stand 23.10.42, as found on T-314, Records of German Field Commands, Corps, Roll 1158, National Archives, College Park, Maryland; Florian Freiherr von und zu Aufsess, Die Anlagenbände zu den Kriegstagebüchern der 6. Armee vom 14.09.1942 bis 24.11.1942, Band 1, Schwabach, Germany: Selbstverlag, 2006, 198-206; John Erickson, The Road to Stalingrad, New York: Harper & Row, 1975, 440; David M. Glantz & Jonathan M. House, Armageddon in Stalingrad: September-November 1942, (The Stalingrad Trilogy, Volume 2), Lawrence, Kansas: University Press of Kansas, 2009, 451-452, 477-489; Manfred Kehrig, Stalingrad: Analyse und Dokumentation einer Schlacht, Stuttgart, FRG: Deutsche Verlags-Anstalt, 1976, 39; Jason Mark, Death of the Leaping Horseman: 24. Panzer-Division in Stalingrad, Sydney, Australia: Leaping Horsemen Books, 2003, 306-310; Jason Mark, Island of Fire: The Battle for the Barrikady Gun Factory in Stalingrad, November 1942 – February 1943, Sydney, Australia: Leaping Horsemen Books, 2006, 6; Kurt Mehner, Die Geheimen Tagesberichte der Deutschen Wehrmachtführung im Zweiten Weltkrieg 1939-1945, Band 5: 1. Juni 1942 – 30. November 1942, Osnabrück, Germany: Biblio Verlag, 1991, 249; Hans Sanger, Die 79. Infanterie Division, Friedberg, FRG: Podzun Pallas Verlag, 74; Anton Schimak, Karl Lamprecht & Friedrich Dettmer, Die 44. Infanterie Division: Tagebuch der Hoch- und Deutschmeister, Wien: Verlag Austria Press, 440; Hans J. Wijers, Der Kampf um Stalingrad: Die Kämpfe im Industriegelände – 14. Oktober bis 19. November 1942, Selbstverlag, 73-74.*

October 24, 1942
Weather: sunny, bright, dry, mostly cloudless, windy, cool, 36° F, good road conditions
Sunrise: 6:35 a.m.; **Sunset:** 4:57 p.m.
Moon: Full Moon; 100% illumination

Sixth Army – Bombers and dive-bombers from the ***Luftwaffe***'s VIII Air Corps pounded enemy positions in the northern part of Stalingrad. The army headquarters was located at Golubinskaya.

VIII Corps – The corps suffered the following officer casualties: one killed in action;

76th Infantry Division – The division defended in sector, east of the Don River, north of Nizhne-Gnilovskii, to west of Kotluban' against the 214th Rifle Division and the 260th Rifle Division. To the east was the 113th Infantry Division; to the northwest was the 384th Infantry Division. The division reported a ration's strength of 12,125 men, a combat arms' strength of 4,809 men and an infantry strength of 2,702 men. The division lost one NCO/enlisted killed in action; four NCOs/enlisted were wounded in action.

113th Infantry Division – The division defended in sector southwest of Samofalovka and north of Borodkin against the 298th Rifle Division, the 258th Rifle Division, the 207th Rifle Division and the 316th Rifle Division. To the west was the 76th Infantry Division; to the east was the 60th Infantry Division (Motorized.) The division reported a ration's strength of 12,458 men, a combat arms' strength of 5,169 men and an infantry strength of 2,878 men. The division lost one officer and three NCOs/enlisted killed in action; eight NCOs/enlisted were wounded in action.

XI Corps

44th Infantry Division – The division defended in sector Kurchajessowskij-Kamyshinskiy-Hill 171.0-Hill 180.9-Sirotinskaya-Khmelevskoy against the 40th Guards Rifle Division. The division headquarters was located at Verkhne-Golubaja. The division lost three NCOs/enlisted wounded in action. To the west was 376th Infantry Division; to the east was the 384th Infantry Division. The division reported a ration's strength of 15,097 men, a combat arms' strength of 5,906 men and an infantry strength of 3,264 men.

376th Infantry Division – The division defended in sector, south of Perekopskaja, near Logowskii and Ossinskij, repelling a large attack on the western flank. The division lost two NCOs/enlisted killed in action; four NCOs/enlisted were wounded in action. To the east was the 44th Infantry Division; to the west was the 1st Romanian Cavalry Division of the Romanian Third Army. The division reported a ration's strength of 10,817 men, a combat arms' strength of 4,830 men and an infantry strength of 2,567 men.

384th Infantry Division – The division defended in sector west of the Don River near Trekhostrovskaia to Podgorskii. To the west was the 44th Infantry Division; to the east was the 76th Infantry Division. The division reported a ration's strength of 10,774 men, a combat arms' strength of 5,394 men and an infantry strength of 3,119 men.

XIV *Panzer* Corps – The corps seized the western two-thirds of Spartakovka, including the prison. The corps headquarters was located east of Ssadtschi-Kowa. The 651st Pioneer Battalion (Motorized) was assigned to the corps. The corps suffered the following officer casualties: three killed in action; eight wounded in action.

3rd Infantry Division (Motorized) – The division defended in sector, from the Tartar Hill-Hill 111.1-Hill 129.6-Hill 131.2 against the 252nd Rifle Division, the 212th Rifle Division, the 116th Rifle Division, the 299th Rifle Division, the 91st Tank Brigade, the 121st Tank Brigade and the 58th Tank Brigade, losing Hill 139.7. To the east was the 16th ***Panzer*** Division; to the west was the 60th Infantry Division (Motorized.) The division suffered eight

NCOs/enlisted killed in action; 30 NCOs/enlisted were wounded in action. The division reported a ration's strength of 10,442 men, a combat arms' strength of 4,196 men and an infantry strength of 1,707 men.

16th Panzer Division – The division defended in sector, from Hill 139.7 to the Volga and then south to Rynok, repelling attacks by the against the 64th Rifle Division, the 120th Rifle Division, the 84th Rifle Division and the 99th Rifle Division. In the south, the division attacked to eliminate enemy forces in the eastern sector of the Spartakovka Workers' Settlement. To the west was the 3rd Infantry Division (Motorized); to the southwest was the 94th Infantry Division. The division reported a ration's strength of 13,126 men, a combat arms' strength of 5,164 men and an infantry strength of 1,607 men. The division lost six NCOs/enlisted killed in action; 11 NCOs/enlisted were wounded in action; four men were reported missing an action.

60th Infantry Division (Motorized) – The division defended in sector, from south of Kotluban' Station near Borodkin to Kuz'michi, repelling attacks by the 316th Rifle Division, the 233rd Rifle Division, the 173rd Rifle Division, the 273rd Rifle Division, the 49th Rifle Division, the 343rd Rifle Division and the 62nd Rifle Division. The division lost 12 NCOs/enlisted killed in action; one officer and 34 NCOs/enlisted were wounded in action. To the west was the 113th Infantry Division; to the east was the 3rd Infantry Division (Motorized.) The division reported a ration's strength of 10,672 men, a combat arms' strength of 4,552 men and an infantry strength of 1,948 men.

94th Infantry Division – The division attacked to destroy enemy forces around Spartakovka. To the south was the 389th Infantry Division; to the northeast was the 16th ***Panzer*** Division. The division lost two officers and 18 NCOs/enlisted killed in action; four officers and 121 NCOs/enlisted were wounded in action. The division reported a ration's strength of 11,438 men, a combat arms' strength of 3,473 men and an infantry strength of 1,284 men.

Battle Group Stahel – The battle group defended in sector, south of Erzovka, from the Volga River west.

LI Corps – The corps headquarters was located at Gumrak. The corps suffered the following officer casualties: one killed in action; six wounded in action.

14th Panzer Division – The division attacked to seize terrain between the Krasny Oktyabr Steel Factory and the Bread Factory Nr.2 against the 308th Rifle Division and the 193rd Rifle Division, but failed to achieve the objective. The division lost 15 NCOs/enlisted killed in action; one officer and 56 NCOs/enlisted were wounded in action; two men were reported missing in action. To the north was the 305th Infantry Division; to the south was the 79th Infantry Division. The division reported a ration's strength of 12,070 men, a combat arms' strength of 5,462 men and an infantry strength of 1,640 men.

24th Panzer Division – The division defended in positions along the Volga River and north of the Barrikady Gun Factory against the 308th Rifle Division and the 138th Rifle Division. The division suffered four NCOs/enlisted wounded in action. To the north was the 389th Infantry Division; to the south was the 305th Infantry Division. The division reported a ration's strength of 11,785 men, a combat arms' strength of 5,387 men and an infantry strength of 1,437 men.

71st Infantry Division – The division defended in sector. To the north was the 295th Infantry Division; to the south was the 371st Infantry Division. The division lost two NCOs/enlisted killed in action; three NCOs/enlisted were wounded in action. The division reported a ration's strength of 12,277 men, a combat arms' strength of 4,723 men and an infantry strength of 2,235 men.

79th Infantry Division – The division, with the 367th Infantry Regiment (Croat) of the 100th ***Jäger*** Division attached, attacked to seize terrain between the Krasny Oktyabr Steel Factory and the Bread Factory Nr.2, seizing Hall 5, 8 and 8a in the factory from the 39th Guards Rifle Division and the 193rd Rifle Division; an assault group reached the Volga River. Bitter fighting occurred at Hall 1, 3, 4 and 6. To the north was the 14th ***Panzer*** Division; to the south was the 100th ***Jäger*** Division.

100th Jäger Division – The division defended in sector. The division lost five NCOs/enlisted killed in action; 12 NCOs/enlisted were wounded in action; one man was reported missing in action. To the north was the 79th Infantry Division; to the south was the 295th Infantry Division. The division reported a ration's strength of 11,700 men, a combat arms' strength of 5,765 men and an infantry strength of 2,806 men.

295th Infantry Division – The division defended in sector against the 284th Rifle Division; the division also conducted patrolling and reconnaissance operations. The division lost five NCOs/enlisted killed in action; 11 NCOs/enlisted were wounded in action. To the north was the 100th

Jäger Division; to the south was the 71st Infantry Division. The division reported a ration's strength of 10,865 men, a combat arms' strength of 2,887 men and an infantry strength of 1,990 men.

305th Infantry Division – The division attacked east in the Barrikady Gun Factory against elements of the 308th Rifle Division and the 138th Rifle Division and seized Hall 4 and Hall 6 in the factory. To the north was the 389th Infantry Division; to the south was the 14th ***Panzer*** Division. The division reported a ration's strength of 10,578 men, a combat arms' strength of 3,345 men and an infantry strength of 1,231 men. The division commander, ***Generalmajor*** Kurt Oppenländer was relieved of command, when ***Generalleutnant*** Walther von Seydlitz – the corps commander – visited the headquarters and found Oppenländer intoxicated. ***Generalmajor*** Bernhard Steinmetz assumed command.

389th Infantry Division – The division conducted limited offensive operations near the Dzerzhinsky Tractor Factory. To the north was the 94th Infantry Division; to the south were the 24th ***Panzer*** Division. The division reported a ration's strength of 8,604 men, a combat arms' strength of 2,736 men and an infantry strength of 903 men.

Sixth Army Reserve

One infantry regiment of the 79th Infantry Division moved toward Stalingrad, reaching the Don River at Bol'shaya Nabatowskij.

Fourth *Panzer* Army – The army headquarters was located east of Verkhne-Zaryzinskij.

IV Corps

297th Infantry Division – The division defended in sector east of Elkhi and near Staro-Dubovka against the 36th Guards Rifle Division and the 157th Rifle Division. To the north was the 371st Infantry Division; to the south was the 29th Infantry Division (Motorized.)

371st Infantry Division – The division defended in sector from Kuporosnoye in the east to northwest of Gornaia Poliana against the 422nd Rifle Division, the 126th Rifle Division, the 93rd Rifle Brigade and the 97th Rifle Brigade. To the north was the 71st Infantry Division; to the south was the 297th Infantry Division.

20th Romanian Infantry Division – The division defended in sector, west of the Tundutovo Rail Station and east of Andreevka. To the north was the 29th Infantry Division (Motorized); to the south was the 2nd Romanian Infantry Division of the Romanian VI Corps.

Fourth *Panzer* Army Reserve

29th Infantry Division (Motorized) – The division occupied an assembly area, between Businovka and Gavrilovka, to prepare for future operations. Part of the division defended in sector east of the Volga-Don Canal against the 29th Rifle Division. To the north was the 297th Infantry Division; to the south was the 20th Romanian Infantry Division. The division lost one NCO/enlisted killed in action; four NCOs/enlisted were wounded in action.

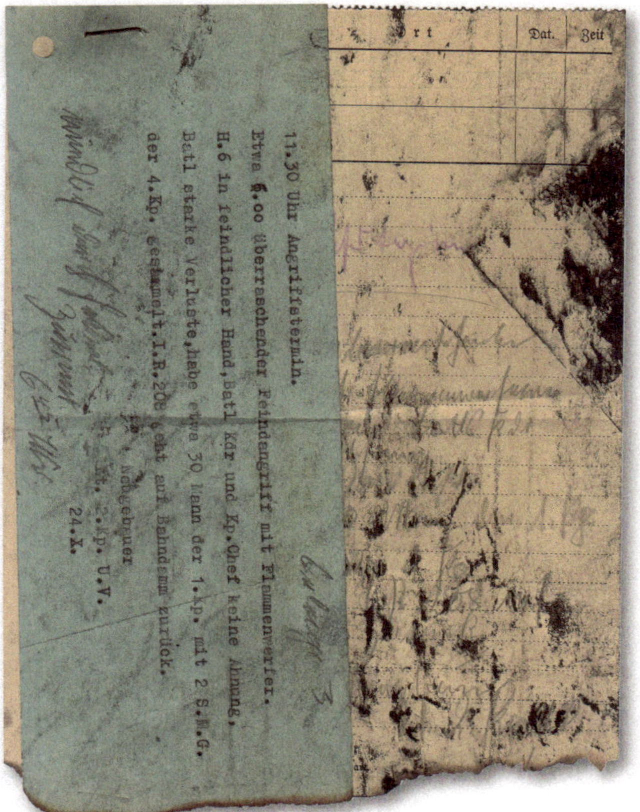

11.30 Uhr Angriffstermin.
Etwa 6.00 überraschender Feindangriff mit Flammenwerfer.
H.6 in feindlicher Hand, Batl Kdr und Kp.Chef keine Ahnung,
Batl starke Verluste, habe etwa 30 Mann der 1.Kp. mit 2 s.M.G.
der 4.Kp. gesammelt. I.R.208 geht auf Bahndamm zurück.
Neugebauer
Lt. 2.Kp. u.V.
24.X.

Battle Report from the 1st Battalion of the 208th Infantry Regiment, in the 79th Infantry Division on October 24, 1942 at the Krasny Oktyabr Steel Factory in Stalingrad. In it, *Leutnant* Neugebauer, assigned to the 2nd Company, reported that at 6:00 a.m. there was a surprise attack by the enemy with a flamethrower. Hall 6 was in enemy hands and there was no idea of the whereabouts of the battalion commander or the company commander. The battalion had heavy losses. Neugebauer collected 30 men of the 1st Company and two heavy machine-guns of the 4th Company, and the regiment retreated to the railroad embankment. The son of a baker from Krefeld in North Rhine-Westphalia, Neugebauer was wounded in action at the Krasny Oktyabr Steel Factory on December 30, 1942. Later flown out of the pocket and back to Germany, he died of his wounds at a military hospital near Arnstadt, Thuringia in March 1943.

Sources, October 24, 1942: ***Oberkommando des Heeres, Lage Ost: Stand: 24.10.42, Eastern Front Situation Map, National Archives Identifier: 559733, Record Group 242 – National Archives Collection of Foreign Records Seized, 1675-1958, National Archives, College Park, Maryland; Ia, Armeeoberkommando 6, "Morgen Meldung" and assorted reports, Kriegstagebuch 14, 25 October 1942, as found in Microfilm Series, T-312, Records of German Field Commands, Armies, Roll 1453 and 1688, National Archives and Records Service, College Park, Maryland; Korpsarzt, XXXXVIII Panzerkorps, "Meldung über Personelle Verluste," Stand 24.10.42, as found on T-314, Records of German Field Commands, Corps, Roll 1158, National Archives, College Park, Maryland; Florian Freiherr von und zu Aufsess, Die Anlagenbände zu den Kriegstagebüchern der 6. Armee vom 14.09.1942 bis 24.11.1942, Band 1, Schwabach, Germany: Selbstverlag, 2006, 199-210; Paul Carell, Stalingrad: The Defeat of the German Sixth Army, Atglen, Pennsylvania: Schiffer Publishing, 1993, 148; David M. Glantz & Jonathan M. House, Armageddon in Stalingrad: September-November 1942, (The Stalingrad Trilogy, Volume 2), Lawrence, Kansas: University Press of Kansas, 2009, 452, 489-497; Rolf Grams, Die 14. Panzer-Division, 1940-1945, Friedberg, FRG: Podzun Pallas Verlag, 1986, 70; Manfred Kehrig, Stalingrad: Analyse und Dokumentation einer Schlacht, Stuttgart, FRG: Deutsche Verlags-Anstalt, 1976, 40; Jason Mark, Death of the Leaping Horseman: 24. Panzer-Division in Stalingrad, Sydney, Australia: Leaping Horsemen Books, 2003, 310-311; Kurt Mehner, Die Geheimen Tagesberichte der Deutschen Wehrmachtführung im Zweiten Weltkrieg 1939-1945, Band 5: 1. Juni 1942 – 30. November 1942, Osnabrück, Germany: Biblio Verlag, 1991, 250; Janusz Piekalkiewicz, Stalingrad: Anatomie einer Schlacht, München, BRD: Wilhelm Heyne Verlag, 1977, 320; Hans Sanger, Die 79. Infanterie Division, Friedberg, FRG: Podzun Pallas Verlag, 74; Anton Schimak, Karl Lamprecht & Friedrich Dettmer, Die 44. Infanterie Division: Tagebuch der Hoch- und Deutschmeister, Wien: Verlag Austria Press, 169, 233 and Map: Marschweg der 44. Infanterie Division im Russland; Hans J. Wijers, Der Kampf um Stalingrad: Die Kämpfe im Industriegelände – 14. Oktober bis 19. November 1942, Selbstverlag, 133.***

Letter from *Gefreiter* Franz Schatten to a friend on October 28, 1942. The soldier was assigned to the 1st Battalion of the 29th Infantry Regiment in the 3rd Infantry Division (Motorized.) In his letter, he writes:

> "A few days ago, we ended up in a new position and another bunker. Imagine 15 of us in a bunker, with all our gear and weapons in a space four meters by five meters. Well, we lost six men so we are left with nine in here, but we do not mind as we are out of the Don River swamp. Tomorrow I will see a front cinema, which is not very entertaining, when you have to walk 12 kilometers to get there and 12 back in pouring rain without a meal. That's what they call entertainment at the front. But it is Sunday morning.
>
> You must be a good leader in the Labor Service camp there, in Königsberg. They send you to many different lessons and schools, all week on the move, but I hope you will pass the test and examinations and maybe when all this is over here, we will all meet in January there. This would be a reunion, believe me. If it comes about, I will pay for the food and you get the schnapps; we will have fried potatoes. I hope you can make them. My new comrades here send me at times to organize some extra food. I swapped cigarettes for bread or barbed wire. I also scrounged a wire-cutter; any goes for cigarettes. I met my old friend Jochen Reuter yesterday, too. He has a nasty cold; they too have a bunker with 12 men to share. I have to wait in line to sit at the table to eat. That shows you what we have to endure around here. But soon it will be dark and I can go to sleep; there is no guard for me tonight. Hope you have a good time in East Prussia."

October 25, 1942
Weather: sunny, bright, clear, good road conditions, 36° F
Sunrise: 6:36 a.m.; **Sunset:** 4:55 p.m.
Moon: Waning Gibbous; 98% illumination

Sixth Army – The army headquarters was located at Golubinskaya. The OKH informed Hitler that German forces had captured the Krasny Oktyabr Steel Factory, with the exception of one building.

VIII Corps

76th Infantry Division – The division defended in sector, east of the Don River, north of Nizhne-Gnilovskii, to west of Kotluban' against the 214th Rifle Division and the 260th Rifle Division. The division lost one NCO/enlisted killed in action; one NCO/enlisted was wounded in action; five men were admitted to a hospital with illness. To the southeast was the 113th Infantry Division; to the northwest was the 384th Infantry Division.

113th Infantry Division – The division defended in sector southwest of Samofalovka and north of Borodkin against the 298th Rifle Division, the 258th Rifle Division, the 207th Rifle Division and the 316th Rifle Division. The division lost two NCOs/enlisted killed in action; two NCOs/enlisted were wounded in action; one man was reported missing in action. To the northwest was the 76th Infantry Division; to the east was the 60th Infantry Division (Motorized.)

XI Corps

44th Infantry Division – The division defended in sector Kurchajessowskij-Kamyshinskiy-Hill 171.0-Hill 180.9-Sirotinskaya-Khmelevskoy against the 40th Guards Rifle Division. The division lost one NCO/enlisted wounded in action. The division headquarters was located at Verkhne-Golubaja. To the west was 376th Infantry Division; to the east was the 384th Infantry Division.

376th Infantry Division – The division defended in sector, south of Perekopskaja, near Logowskii and Ossinskij against the 23rd Rifle Division. The division lost one NCO/enlisted wounded in action. To the east was the 44th Infantry Division; to the west was the 1st Romanian Cavalry Division of the Romanian Third Army.

384th Infantry Division – The division defended in sector west of the Don River near Trekhostrovskaia to Podgorskii, against the 4th Guards Rifle Division. To the west was the 44th Infantry Division; to the southeast was the 76th Infantry Division.

XIV *Panzer* Corps – The corps headquarters was located east of Ssadtschi-Kowa. The corps suffered the following officer casualties: two killed in action; three wounded in action.

3rd Infantry Division (Motorized) – The division defended in sector, from the Tartar Hill-Hill 111.1-Hill 129.6-Hill 131.2, repelling attacks by the 252nd Rifle Division, the 212th Rifle Division, the 116th Rifle Division, the 299th Rifle Division, the 91st Tank Brigade, the 121st Tank Brigade and the 58th Tank Brigade. The division lost eight NCOs/enlisted killed in action; 30 NCOs/enlisted were wounded in action. To the east was the 16th ***Panzer*** Division; to the west was the 60th Infantry Division (Motorized.)

16th Panzer Division – The division defended in sector, from Hill 139.7 to the Volga and then south to Rynok, repelling attacks by the 64th Rifle Division, the 120th Rifle Division, the 84th Rifle Division and the 99th Rifle Division. The division lost two NCOs/enlisted killed in action; one officer and 17 NCOs/enlisted were wounded in action; one man was reported missing in action. In the south, the division attacked to eliminate enemy forces in Spartakovka.

60th Infantry Division (Motorized) – The division defended in sector, from south of Kotluban' Station near Borodkin to Kuz'michi, repelling attacks by the 316th Rifle Division, the 233rd Rifle Division, the 173rd Rifle Division, the 273rd Rifle

Division, the 49th Rifle Division, the 343rd Rifle Division and the 62nd Rifle Division. The division lost one officer and nine NCOs/enlisted killed in action; 35 NCOs/enlisted were wounded in action. To the west was the 113th Infantry Division; to the east was the 3rd Infantry Division (Motorized.)

94th Infantry Division – The division attacked eastward along the northern bank of the Mokraia Mechetka River to destroy enemy forces around Spartakovka, seizing buildings in the eastern outskirts of Spartakovka. The division lost one officer and five NCOs/enlisted killed in action; two officers and 30 NCOs/enlisted were wounded in action; 19 men were reported missing in action. To the south was the 389th Infantry Division; to the northeast was the 16th ***Panzer*** Division.

Battle Group Stahel – The battle group defended in sector, south of Erzovka, from the Volga River west.

LI Corps – The corps headquarters was located at Gumrak. The corps suffered the following officer casualties: two killed in action; five wounded in action.

14th Panzer Division – The division attacked east and seized Bread Factory Nr.2 against the 308th Rifle Division and the 193rd Rifle Division. The division lost 13 NCOs/enlisted killed in action; three officers and 74 NCOs/enlisted were wounded in action; two NCOs/enlisted were missing in action. To the north was the 305th Infantry Division; to the south was the 79th Infantry Division.

24th Panzer Division – The division defended in positions along the Volga River and north of the Barrikady Gun Factory against the 308th Rifle Division and the 138th Rifle Division. The division suffered five NCOs/enlisted killed in action; five NCOs/enlisted were wounded in action. To the north was the 389th Infantry Division; to the south was the 305th Infantry Division.

71st Infantry Division – The division defended in sector. To the north was the 295th Infantry Division; to the south was the 371st Infantry Division. The division lost one NCO/enlisted killed in action; 11 NCOs/enlisted were wounded in action; one man was reported missing in action.

79th Infantry Division – The division attacked east attempting to seize the remainder of the Krasny Oktyabr Steel Factory, but failed against the 39th Guards Rifle Division and the 193rd Rifle Division. Bitter fighting occurred at Halls 1, 5 and 8. The division suffered 13 NCOs/enlisted killed in action; one officer and 54 NCOs/enlisted were wounded in action. To the north was the 14th ***Panzer*** Division; to the south was the 100th ***Jäger*** Division.

100th Jäger Division – The division defended in sector. The division lost four NCOs/enlisted killed in action; 36 NCOs/enlisted were wounded in action; one man was reported missing in action. To the north was the 79th Infantry Division; to the south was the 295th Infantry Division.

295th Infantry Division – The division defended in sector against the 284th Rifle Division. The division suffered one NCO/enlisted killed in action; eight NCOs/enlisted were wounded in action. To the north was the 100th ***Jäger*** Division; to the south was the 71st Infantry Division.

305th Infantry Division – The division attacked east in the Barrikady Gun Factory against elements of the 308th Rifle Division and the 138th Rifle Division, seizing all but the northeastern corner of the factory. The division lost two officers and ten NCOs/enlisted killed in action; one officer and 37 NCOs/enlisted were wounded in action. To the north was the 389th Infantry Division; to the south was the 14th ***Panzer*** Division.

389th Infantry Division – The division conducted limited offensive operations near the Dzerzhinsky Tractor Factory. The division suffered three NCOs/enlisted wounded in action. To the north was the 94th Infantry Division; to the south was the 24th ***Panzer*** Division.

Sixth Army Reserve

One infantry regiment of the 79th Infantry Division occupied an assembly area at the Don River at Bol'shaya Nabatowskij.

Fourth *Panzer* Army – The army headquarters was located east of Verkhne-Zaryzinskij.

IV Corps

297th Infantry Division – The division defended in sector east of Elkhi and near Staro-Dubovka against the 36th Guards Rifle Division and the 157th Rifle Division. To the north was the 371st Infantry Division; to the south was the 29th Infantry Division (Motorized.)

371st Infantry Division – The division defended in sector from Kuporosnoye in the east to northwest of Gornaia Poliana against heavy enemy attacks with 30-40 tanks, heavy artillery and ground-attack aircraft of the 7th Rifle Corps and against the 422nd Rifle Division, the 126th Rifle Division, the 93rd Rifle Brigade and the 97th Rifle Brigade. To the north was the 71st Infantry Division; to the south was the 297th Infantry Division.

20th Romanian Infantry Division – The division defended in sector, west of the Tundutovo Rail Station and east of Andreevka against the 204th Rifle Division. To the north was the 29th Infantry Division (Motorized); to the south was the 2nd Romanian Infantry Division of the Romanian VI Corps.

Fourth *Panzer* Army Reserve

29th Infantry Division (Motorized) – The division occupied an assembly area, between Businovka and Gavrilovka, to prepare for future operations. Part of the division defended in sector east of the Volga-Don Canal against the 29th Rifle Division. To the north was the 297th Infantry Division; to the south was the 20th Romanian Infantry Division. The division lost 11 NCOs/enlisted killed in action; ten NCOs/enlisted were wounded in action.

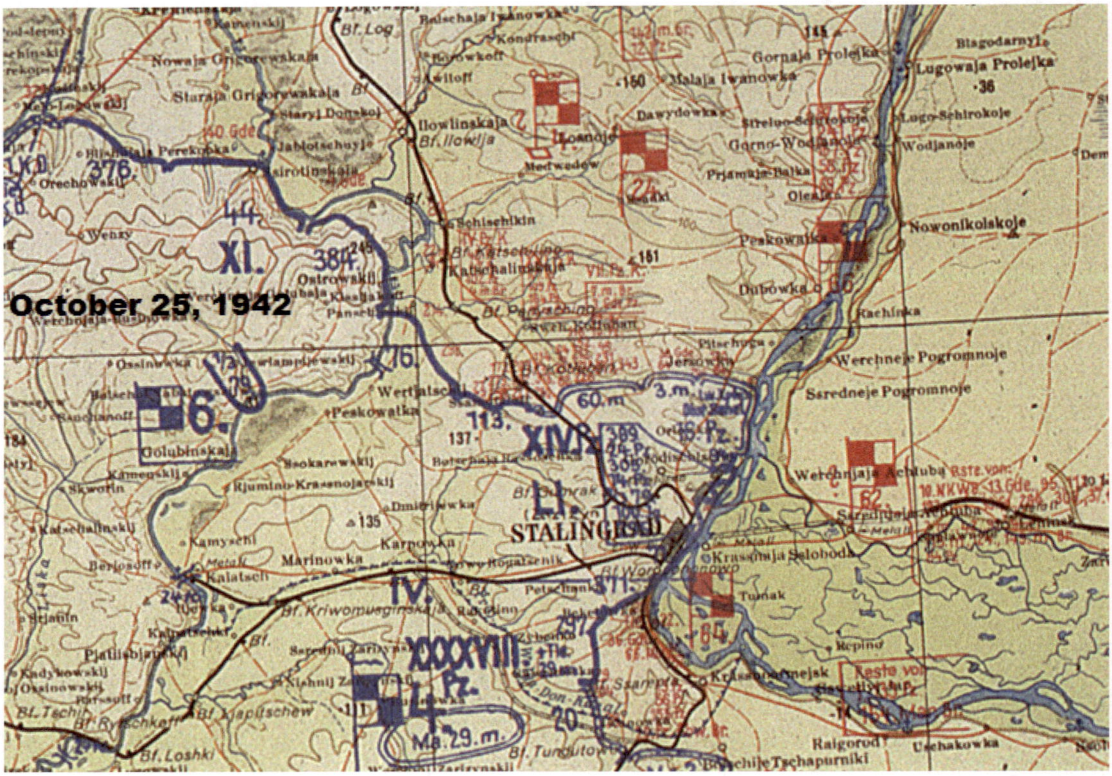

Sources, October 25, 1942: *Oberkommando des Heeres, Lage Ost: Stand: 25.10.42, Eastern Front Situation Map, National Archives Identifier: 559733, Record Group 242 – National Archives Collection of Foreign Records Seized, 1675-1958, National Archives, College Park, Maryland; Ia, Armeeoberkommando 6, "Morgen Meldung" and assorted reports, Kriegstagebuch 14, 26 October 1942, as found in Microfilm Series, T-312, Records of German Field Commands, Armies, Roll 1453 and 1688, National Archives and Records Service, College Park, Maryland; Korpsarzt, XXXXVIII Panzerkorps, "Meldung über Personelle Verluste," Stand 25.10.42, as found on T-314, Records of German Field Commands, Corps, Roll 1158, National Archives, College Park, Maryland; Florian Freiherr von und zu Aufsess, Die Anlagenbände zu den Kriegstagebüchern der 6. Armee vom 14.09.1942 bis 24.11.1942, Band 1, Schwabach, Germany: Selbstverlag, 2006, 211-212; David M. Glantz & Jonathan M. House, Armageddon in Stalingrad: September-November 1942, (The Stalingrad Trilogy, Volume 2), Lawrence, Kansas: University Press of Kansas, 2009, 452, 497-501; Rolf Grams, Die 14. Panzer-Division, 1940-1945, Friedberg, FRG: Podzun Pallas Verlag, 1986, 70; Helmuth Greiner, "Greiner Diary Notes, 12 August 1942 – 12 March 1943," MS #C-065a, Heidelberg, Germany: Historical Division, Headquarters, United States Army Europe, 1949, 93; Jason Mark, Death of the Leaping Horseman: 24. Panzer-Division in Stalingrad, Sydney, Australia: Leaping Horsemen Books, 2003, 311-313; Kurt Mehner, Die Geheimen Tagesberichte der Deutschen Wehrmachtführung im Zweiten Weltkrieg 1939-1945, Band 5: 1. Juni 1942 – 30. November 1942, Osnabrück, Germany: Biblio Verlag, 1991, 252; Janusz Piekalkiewicz, Stalingrad: Anatomie einer Schlacht, München, BRD: Wilhelm Heyne Verlag, 1977, 320; Hans Sanger, Die 79. Infanterie Division, Friedberg, FRG: Podzun Pallas Verlag, 75; Anton Schimak, Karl Lamprecht & Friedrich Dettmer, Die 44. Infanterie Division: Tagebuch der Hoch- und Deutschmeister, Wien: Verlag Austria Press, 169, 233 and Map: Marschweg der 44. Infanterie Division im Russland; Wolfgang Werthen, Geschichte der 16. Panzer-Division 1939-1945, Friedberg, FRG: Podzun-Pallas-Verlag, 1958, 115.*

Luftwaffe Unteroffizier **Georg Dobmeier** was born on March 2, 1917 at Bodenwöhr near Schwandorf, Bavaria. Probably assigned to the 9th ***Flak*** Division, he died of his wounds near Stalingrad on October 25, 1942. His name is listed in the remembrance book at the German Military Cemetery at Rossoschka.

Reverse of death card for *Luftwaffe Unteroffizier* Georg Dobmeier. Note that the drawing of his grave shows he died near Stalingrad. Often families knew nothing more.

October 26, 1942
Weather: cool, changing cloudiness, at times overcast
Sunrise: 6:38 a.m.; **Sunset:** 4:54 p.m.
Moon: Waning Gibbous; 94% illumination

Sixth Army – The army headquarters was located at Golubinskaya.

VIII Corps

76th Infantry Division – The division defended in sector, east of the Don River, north of Nizhne-Gnilovskii, to west of Kotluban' against the 214th Rifle Division and the 260th Rifle Division. The division lost four NCOs/enlisted wounded in action. To the southeast was the 113th Infantry Division; to the northwest was the 384th Infantry Division. The division reported that of its six infantry battalions, one was medium-strong and five were average in combat power; the division rated its combat engineer battalion as average.

113th Infantry Division – The division defended in sector southwest of Samofalovka and north of Borodkin against the 298th Rifle Division, the 258th Rifle Division, the 207th Rifle Division and the 316th Rifle Division. The division lost five NCOs/enlisted killed in action. To the west was the 76th Infantry Division; to the east was the 60th Infantry Division (Motorized.) The division reported that of its six infantry battalions, four were medium-strong and two were average in combat power; the division rated its combat engineer battalion as medium-strong.

XI Corps

44th Infantry Division – The division defended in sector Kurchajessowskij-Kamyshinskiy -Hill 171.0-Hill 180.9-Sirotinskaya-Khmelevskoy, against the 40th Guards Rifle Division. The division lost three NCOs/enlisted killed in action; two NCOs/enlisted were wounded in action. The division headquarters was located at Verkhne-Golubaja. To the west was 376th Infantry Division; to the east was the 384th Infantry Division. The division reported that of its seven infantry battalions, five were medium-strong and two were average in combat power; the division rated its combat engineer battalion as average.

376th Infantry Division – The division defended in sector, south of Perekopskaja, near Logowskii and Ossinskij against the 23rd Rifle Division. The division lost one NCO/enlisted wounded in action. To the east was the 44th Infantry Division; to the west was the 1st Romanian Cavalry Division of the Romanian Third Army. The division reported that of its seven infantry battalions, two were medium-strong and three were average in combat power; the division rated its combat engineer battalion as average. (The 376th had a habitual problem with report numbers not adding up.)

384th Infantry Division – The division defended in sector west of the Don River near Trekhostrovskaia to Podgorskii, against the 4th Guards Rifle Division. The division lost three NCOs/enlisted killed in action; two NCOs/enlisted were wounded in action. To the west was the 44th Infantry Division; to the east was the 76th Infantry Division. The division reported that of its six infantry battalions, one was medium-strong and five were average in combat power; the division rated its combat engineer battalion as average.

XIV *Panzer* Corps – The corps seized most of Spartakovka. The corps headquarters was located east of Ssadtschi-Kowa. The corps suffered the following officer casualties: two killed in action; three wounded in action.

3rd Infantry Division (Motorized) – The division defended in sector, from the Tartar Hill-Hill 111.1-Hill 129.6-Hill 131.2, repelling attacks by the 252nd Rifle Division, the 212th Rifle Division, the 116th Rifle Division, the 299th Rifle Division, the 91st Tank Brigade, the 121st Tank Brigade and the 58th Tank Brigade. The division lost eight NCOs/enlisted killed in action; 20 NCOs/enlisted were wounded in action; one man was reported missing in action. To the east was the 16th ***Panzer*** Division; to the west was the 60th Infantry Division (Motorized.) The division reported that of its four motorized infantry battalions, all four were medium-strong in combat power; the division rated its combat engineer battalion as weak.

16th Panzer Division – The division defended in sector, from Hill 139.7 to the Volga and south to Rynok, repelling attacks by the 64th Rifle Division, the 120th Rifle Division, the 84th Rifle Division and the 99th Rifle Division. In the south, the division attacked to eliminate enemy forces in Spartakovka. The division lost six NCOs/enlisted killed in action; 12 NCOs/enlisted were wounded in action. To the west was the 3rd Infantry Division (Motorized); to the southwest was the 94th Infantry Division. The division reported that of its four ***panzer*** grenadier battalions, one was medium-strong, one was average and two were weak in combat power; the division rated its combat engineer battalion as weak.

60th Infantry Division (Motorized) – The division defended in sector, from south of Kotluban' Station near Borodkin to Kuz'michi, repelling attacks by the 316th Rifle Division, the 233rd Rifle Division, the 173rd Rifle Division, the 273rd Rifle Division, the 49th Rifle Division, the 343rd Rifle Division and the 62nd Rifle Division. The division lost eight NCOs/enlisted killed in action; 25 NCOs/enlisted were wounded in action. To the west was the 113th Infantry Division; to the east was the 3rd Infantry Division (Motorized.) The division reported that of its seven motorized infantry battalions, two were medium-strong, one was average, three were weak and one was exhausted in combat power; the division rated its combat engineer battalion as weak.

94th Infantry Division – The division attacked at Spartakovka, defeating the 124th Rifle Brigade and the 149th Rifle Brigade and seizing additional houses on the eastern edge of the village. The division lost six NCOs/enlisted killed in action; two officers and 44 NCOs/enlisted were wounded in action; two men were reported missing in action. To the south was the 389th Infantry Division; to the northeast was the 16th ***Panzer*** Division. The division reported that of its seven infantry battalions, all seven were weak in combat power; the division rated its combat engineer battalion as average.

Battle Group Stahel – The battle group defended in sector, south of Erzovka, from the Volga River west.

LI Corps – The corps headquarters was located at Gumrak. The corps suffered the following officer casualties: two killed in action; 14 wounded in action.

14th Panzer Division – The division conducted limited offensive operations east and seized outlying buildings of Bread Factory Nr.2 against the 308th Rifle Division and the 193rd Rifle Division. The division lost ten NCOs/enlisted killed in action; seven officers and 17 NCOs/enlisted men were wounded in action. To the north was the 305th Infantry Division; to the south was the 79th Infantry Division. The division reported that of its four ***panzer*** grenadier battalions, all four were weak in combat power; the division rated its combat engineer battalion as average and its motorcycle battalion as strong.

24th Panzer Division – The division defended in positions along the Volga River and north of the Barrikady Gun Factory against the 308th Rifle Division and the 138th Rifle Division. Late in the day, a Soviet counter-attack seized part of the Barrikady Gun Factory. The division suffered nine NCOs/enlisted killed in action; five NCOs/enlisted were wounded in action. To the north was the 389th Infantry Division; to the south was the 305th Infantry Division. The division reported that of its four ***panzer*** grenadier battalions, one was weak and three were exhausted in combat power; the division rated its combat engineer battalion as exhausted and its motorcycle battalion as weak.

71st Infantry Division – The division defended in sector. To the north was the 295th Infantry Division; to the south was the 371st Infantry Division. The division lost two NCOs/enlisted killed in action; one officer and seven NCOs/enlisted were wounded in action. The division reported that of its seven infantry battalions, two were average and five were weak in combat power; the division rated its combat engineer battalion as weak.

79th Infantry Division – The division continued to attack at the Krasny Oktyabr Steel Factory against the 39th Guards Rifle Division and the 193rd Rifle Division. Bitter fighting occurred at Halls 2, 3, 4 and 7. The division lost one officer and 16 NCOs/enlisted killed in action; three officers and 48 NCOs/enlisted were wounded in action. To the north was the 14th ***Panzer*** Division; to the south was the 100th ***Jäger*** Division. The division reported that of its six infantry battalions, three were average and two were weak in combat power; the division rated its combat engineer battalion as average.

100th Jäger Division – The division attacked, with several small elements reaching the

Volga River. To the north was the 79th Infantry Division; to the south was the 295th Infantry Division. The division lost four NCOs/enlisted killed in action; 25 NCOs/enlisted were wounded in action. The division reported that of its four ***jäger*** battalions, one was strong, one was medium-strong and two were average in combat power; the division rated its Croatian infantry battalion as weak; the division rated its combat engineer battalion as average.

295th Infantry Division – The division attacked at the Lazur Chemical Factory at the "Tennis Racquet" against the 284th Rifle Division. To the north was the 100th ***Jäger*** Division; to the south was the 71st Infantry Division. The division lost two NCOs/enlisted killed in action; one officer and 19 NCOs/enlisted were wounded in action. The division reported that of its seven infantry battalions, one was average, four were weak and two were exhausted in combat power; the division rated its combat engineer battalion as weak.

305th Infantry Division – The division attacked east in the Barrikady Gun Factory against elements of the 308th Rifle Division and the 138th Rifle Division. The division lost four NCOs/enlisted killed in action; 27 NCOs/enlisted were wounded in action. To the north was the 389th Infantry Division; to the south was the 14th ***Panzer*** Division. The division reported that of its nine infantry battalions, five were weak and four were exhausted in combat power; the division rated its combat engineer battalion as exhausted.

389th Infantry Division – The division conducted limited offensive operations near the Dzerzhinsky Tractor Factory. The division lost two officers wounded in action. To the north was the 94th Infantry Division; to the south were the 24th ***Panzer*** Division. The division reported that of its seven infantry battalions, three were average, two were weak and two were exhausted in combat power; the division rated its combat engineer battalion as exhausted.

Sixth Army Reserve

One infantry regiment of the 79th Infantry Division moved from an assembly area at the Don River at Bol'shaya Nabatowskij to Dmitriyevka.

Fourth *Panzer* Army – The army headquarters was located east of Verkhne-Zaryzinskij.

IV Corps

297th Infantry Division – The division defended in sector east of Elkhi and near Staro-

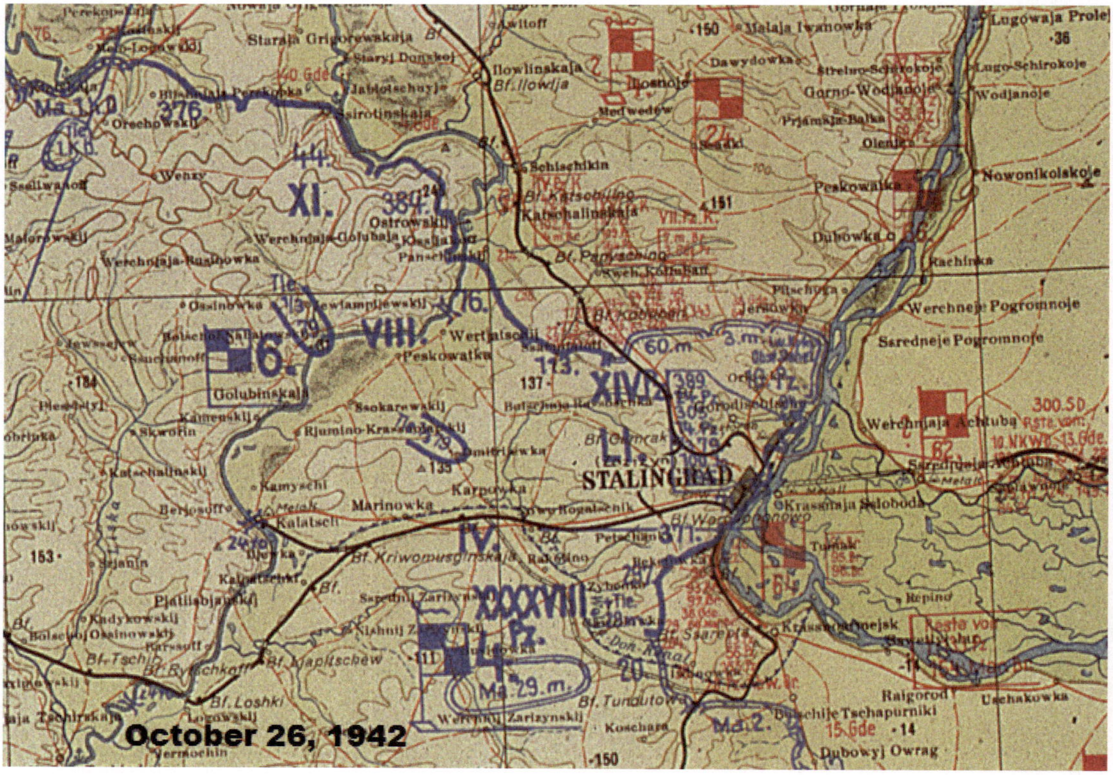

Dubovka against the 36th Guards Rifle Division and the 157th Rifle Division. To the north was the 371st Infantry Division; to the south was the 29th Infantry Division (Motorized.)

371st Infantry Division – The division defended in sector from Kuporosnoye in the east to northwest of Gornaia Poliana. While the division lost several hundred yards of terrain in downtown Kuporosnoye, it repelled attacks by the 422nd Rifle Division, the 126th Rifle Division, the 93rd Rifle Brigade and the 97th Rifle Brigade. To the north was the 71st Infantry Division; to the south was the 297th Infantry Division.

20th Romanian Infantry Division – The division defended in sector, west of the Tundutovo Rail Station and east of Andreevka against the 204th Rifle Division. To the north was the 29th Infantry Division (Motorized); to the south was the 2nd Romanian Infantry Division of the Romanian VI Corps.

Fourth *Panzer* Army Reserve

29th Infantry Division (Motorized) – The division occupied an assembly area, between Businovka and Gavrilovka, to prepare for future operations. Part of the division defended in sector east of the Volga-Don Canal against the 29th Rifle Division. To the north was the 297th Infantry Division; to the south was the 20th Romanian Infantry Division. The division lost four NCOs/enlisted wounded in action.

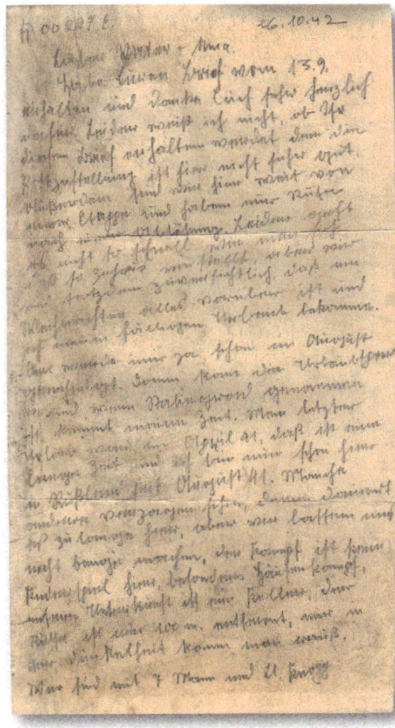

Letter from "Mathias" to his father and grandmother on October 26, 1942. He was assigned to the 4th Company, in the 1st Battalion of the 54th Infantry Regiment in the 100th ***Jäger*** Division. In his letter, he writes:

> "I did receive your letter from September 13 and thank you very much. Unfortunately, I do not know if this letter will reach you; the mail service here is not good, besides that, we are far away from a rest area and the only relief we have is in a rear area. Things are not going as fast as you might think at home, but we are confident that by Christmas, this battle will be over and I can take my promised home leave. Leave was granted to me way back in August; then a stop came to all leave, but now if we take Stalingrad, my time will come. My last home leave was in April 1941; a long time has gone by since; and I have been here in Russia since August 1941. Some men here are in despair; they think it will never end, but then we must not let ourselves down. The fighting is no child's play, especially in the built-up areas; our shelter is a solid cellar and the enemy is only 100 meters from us. We can only move out in darkness; we are seven men and a Lieutenant Knopp here; an advanced post this is, and food only gets through at night. We had a relief operation two nights ago and we lost four men; one dead and four wounded; among them was my old comrade Horst Esser, who was from Vörde. He is the one who brought you my letter last winter. He is in a first aid shelter; he lost a hand and hopefully gets to a base hospital soon. Today it is a bit quieter; the main fighting is near the river. Our relief will be in two days; I will have more time to write. Just now we have a few artillery shells falling near here so I have to end."

Sources, October 26, 1942: ***Oberkommando des Heeres, Lage Ost: Stand: 26.10.42, Eastern Front Situation Map, National Archives Identifier: 559733, Record Group 242 – National Archives Collection of Foreign Records Seized, 1675-1958, National Archives, College Park, Maryland; Ia, Armeeoberkommando 6, "Morgen Meldung" and assorted reports, Kriegstagebuch 14, 27 October 1942, as found in Microfilm Series, T-312, Records of German Field Commands, Armies, Roll 1453 and 1688, National Archives and Records Service, College Park, Maryland; Korpsarzt, XXXXVIII Panzerkorps, "Meldung über Personelle Verluste," Stand 26.10.42, as found on T-314, Records of German Field Commands, Corps, Roll 1158, National Archives, College Park, Maryland; Florian Freiherr von und zu Aufsess, Die Anlagenbände zu den Kriegstagebüchern der 6. Armee vom 14.09.1942 bis 24.11.1942, Band 1, Schwabach, Germany: Selbstverlag, 2006, 211-218; Paul Carell, Stalingrad: The Defeat of the German Sixth Army, Atglen, Pennsylvania: Schiffer Publishing, 1993, 150; William Craig, Enemy at the Gates: The Battle for Stalingrad, New York: Readers' Digest Press, 1973, 143; David M. Glantz & Jonathan M. House, Armageddon in Stalingrad: September-November 1942, (The Stalingrad Trilogy, Volume 2), Lawrence, Kansas: University Press of Kansas, 2009, 453, 505-512; Rolf Grams, Die 14. Panzer-Division, 1940-1945, Friedberg, FRG: Podzun Pallas Verlag, 1986, 70; Manfred Kehrig, Stalingrad: Analyse und Dokumentation einer Schlacht, Stuttgart, FRG: Deutsche Verlags-Anstalt, 1976, 40; Jason Mark, Death of the Leaping Horseman: 24. Panzer-Division in Stalingrad, Sydney, Australia: Leaping Horsemen Books, 2003, 312-313; Hans Sanger, Die 79. Infanterie Division, Friedberg, FRG: Podzun Pallas Verlag, 75; Anton Schimak, Karl Lamprecht & Friedrich Dettmer, Die 44. Infanterie Division: Tagebuch der Hoch- und Deutschmeister, Wien: Verlag Austria Press, 169, 233 and Map: Marschweg der 44. Infanterie Division im Russland.***

October 27, 1942
Weather: clear, very cool, dry, bright, sunny
Sunrise: 6:39 a.m.; **Sunset:** 4:52 p.m.
Moon: Waning Gibbous; 89% illumination

Sixth Army – The army headquarters was located at Golubinskaya.

VIII Corps

76th Infantry Division – The division defended in sector, east of the Don River, north of Nizhne-Gnilovskii, to west of Kotluban' against the 214th Rifle Division and the 298th Rifle Division. The division suffered six NCOs/enlisted wounded in action. To the southeast was the 113th Infantry Division; to the northwest was the 384th Infantry Division.

113th Infantry Division – The division defended in sector southwest of Samofalovka and north of Borodkin against the 173rd Rifle Division and the 273rd Rifle Division. The division lost six NCOs/enlisted wounded in action. To the northwest was the 76th Infantry Division; to the east was the 60th Infantry Division (Motorized.)

XI Corps

44th Infantry Division – The division defended in sector Kurchajessowskij-Kamyshinskiy-Hill 171.0-Hill 180.9-Sirotinskaya-Khmelevskoy against the 40th Guards Rifle Division and the 4th Guards Rifle Division. The division lost one NCO/enlisted wounded in action. The division headquarters was located at Verkhne-Golubaja. To the west was 376th Infantry Division; to the southeast was the 384th Infantry Division.

376th Infantry Division – The division defended in sector, south of Perekopskaja, near Logowskii and Ossinskij. The division suffered one NCO/enlisted killed in action. To the east was the 44th Infantry Division; to the west was the 1st Romanian Cavalry Division of the Romanian Third Army.

384th Infantry Division – The division defended in sector west of the Don River near Trekhostrovskaia to Podgorskii against the 22nd Mechanized Brigade. The division lost three NCOs/enlisted wounded in action. To the northwest was the 44th Infantry Division; to the southeast was the 76th Infantry Division.

XIV *Panzer* Corps – The corps headquarters was located east of Ssadtschi-Kowa. The corps suffered the following officer casualties: two wounded in action.

3rd Infantry Division (Motorized) – The division defended in sector, from the Tartar Hill-Hill 111.1-Hill 129.6-Hill 131.2, against the 64th Rifle Division and the 38th Guards Rifle Division. The division suffered four NCOs/enlisted killed in action; 15 NCOs/enlisted were wounded in action. To the east was the 16th ***Panzer*** Division; to the west was the 60th Infantry Division (Motorized.)

16th Panzer Division – The division defended in sector, from Hill 139.7 to the Volga and south to Rynok against the 99th Rifle Division. The division lost ten NCOs/enlisted wounded in action. To the west was the 3rd Infantry Division (Motorized); to the southwest was the 94th Infantry Division.

60th Infantry Division (Motorized) – The division defended in sector, from south of Kotluban' Station near Borodkin to Kuz'michi against the 49th Rifle Division, the 343rd Rifle Division and the 231st Rifle Division. The division lost five NCOs/enlisted killed in action; 15 NCOs/enlisted were wounded in action. To the west was the 113th Infantry Division; to the east was the 3rd Infantry Division (Motorized.)

94th Infantry Division – The division attacked in the Spartakovka Workers' Settlement and seized another block of buildings. The division suffered one officer and 11 NCOs/enlisted killed in action; one officer and 52 NCOs/enlisted were wounded in action; two men were reported missing in action. To the south was the 389th Infantry Division; to the northeast was the 16th ***Panzer*** Division.

Battle Group Stahel – The battle group defended in sector, south of Erzovka, from the Volga River west.

LI Corps – The corps headquarters was located at Gumrak. The corps suffered the following officer casualties: three killed in action; five wounded in action.

14th Panzer Division – The division attacked east through the Khost Ravine, reaching the ferry crossing site on the Volga River against the 308th Rifle Division and the 193rd Rifle Division. The division suffered one officer and 21 NCOs/enlisted killed in action; three officers and 103 NCOs/enlisted were wounded in action; seven men were reported missing in action. To the north was the 305th Infantry Division; to the south was the 79th Infantry Division.

24th Panzer Division – The division defended in positions along the Volga River and north of the Barrikady Gun Factory against the 308th Rifle Division and the 138th Rifle Division. Late in the day, elements of the 389th Infantry Division relieved the division of its positions in the Brick Works. The division suffered no casualties. To the south was the 305th Infantry Division.

71st Infantry Division – The division defended in sector. The division lost eight NCOs/enlisted killed in action; 13 NCOs/enlisted were wounded in action. To the north was the 295th Infantry Division; to the south was the 371st Infantry Division.

79th Infantry Division – The division continued to attack in zone, seizing much of the Krasny Oktyabr Steel Factory to include Hall 1 and 2 from the 39th Guards Rifle Division. Bitter fighting also occurred at Halls 3 and 9. The division lost 23 NCOs/enlisted killed in action; two officers and 67 NCOs/enlisted were killed in action; one man was reported missing in action. To the north was the 14th ***Panzer*** Division; to the south was the 100th ***Jäger*** Division.

100th Jäger Division – The division defended in sector. The division suffered eight NCOs/enlisted killed in action; 49 NCOs/enlisted were wounded in action. To the north was the 79th Infantry Division; to the south was the 295th Infantry Division.

295th Infantry Division – The division attacked in zone at the Lazur Chemical Factory and the "Tennis Racquet" against the 284th Rifle Division. The division lost one NCO/enlisted killed in action and nine NCOs/enlisted wounded in action. To the north was the 100th ***Jäger*** Division; to the south was the 71st Infantry Division.

305th Infantry Division – The division attacked east in the Barrikady Gun Factory against elements of the 308th Rifle Division and the 138th Rifle Division. The division suffered one officer and 12 NCOs/enlisted killed in action; 70 NCOs/enlisted were wounded in action. To the north was the 389th Infantry Division; to the south was the 14th ***Panzer*** Division.

389th Infantry Division – The division defended at the Brick Works, after relieving the 24th ***Panzer*** Division. The division suffered one NCO/enlisted killed in action and five NCOs/enlisted wounded in action. To the north was the 94th Infantry Division; to the south was the 305th Infantry Division.

Sixth Army Reserve

One infantry regiment of the 79th Infantry Division moved toward Stalingrad, reaching Bol'shaya Rossoschka.

Fourth *Panzer* Army – The army headquarters was located east of Verkhne-Zaryzinskij.

IV Corps

297th Infantry Division – The division defended in sector east of Elkhi and near Staro-Dubovka against the 36th Guards Rifle Division and the 157th Rifle Division. To the north was the 371st Infantry Division; to the south was the 29th Infantry Division (Motorized.)

371st Infantry Division – The division defended in sector from Kuporosnoye in the east to northwest of Gornaia Poliana, repelling the 422nd Rifle Division; heavy fighting occurred at Hill 145.5 against the 126th Rifle Division, the 93rd Rifle Brigade and the 97th Rifle Brigade. To the north was the 71st Infantry Division; to the south was the 297th Infantry Division.

20th Romanian Infantry Division – The division defended in sector, west of the

Tundutovo Rail Station and east of Andreevka against the 204th Rifle Division. To the north was the 29th Infantry Division (Motorized); to the south was the 2nd Romanian Infantry Division of the Romanian VI Corps.

Fourth *Panzer* Army Reserve

29th Infantry Division (Motorized) – The division occupied an assembly area, between Businovka and Gavrilovka, to prepare for future operations. Part of the division defended in sector east of the Volga-Don Canal against the 29th Rifle Division. The division lost one officer and two NCOs/enlisted killed in action; one officer and five NCOs/enlisted were wounded in action. To the north was the 297th Infantry Division; to the south was the 20th Romanian Infantry Division.

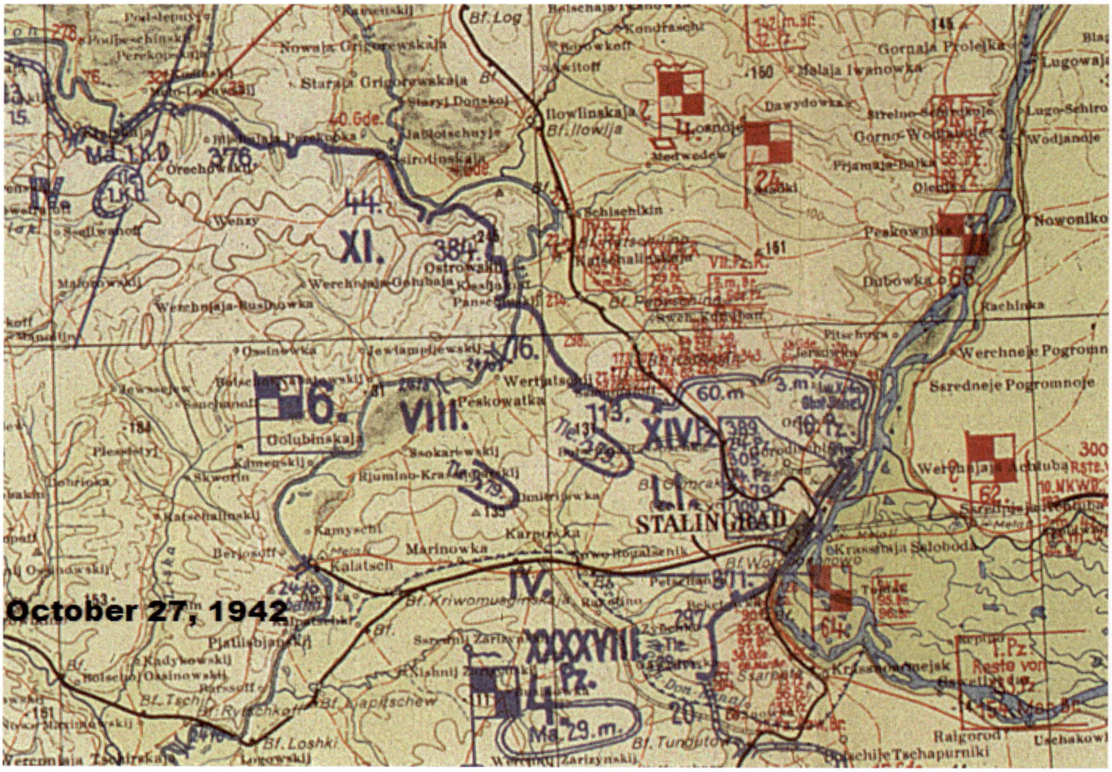

Sources, October 27, 1942: *Oberkommando des Heeres, Lage Ost: Stand: 27.10.42, Eastern Front Situation Map, National Archives Identifier: 559733, Record Group 242 – National Archives Collection of Foreign Records Seized, 1675-1958, National Archives, College Park, Maryland; Ia, Armeeoberkommando 6, "Morgen Meldung" and assorted reports, Kriegstagebuch 14, 28 October 1942, as found in Microfilm Series, T-312, Records of German Field Commands, Armies, Roll 1453 and 1688, National Archives and Records Service, College Park, Maryland; Korpsarzt, XXXXVIII Panzerkorps, "Meldung über Personelle Verluste," Stand 27.10.42, as found on T-314, Records of German Field Commands, Corps, Roll 1158, National Archives, College Park, Maryland; Florian Freiherr von und zu Aufsess, Die Anlagenbände zu den Kriegstagebüchern der 6. Armee vom 14.09.1942 bis 24.11.1942, Band 1, Schwabach, Germany: Selbstverlag, 2006, 218-221; David M. Glantz & Jonathan M. House, Armageddon in Stalingrad: September-November 1942, (The Stalingrad Trilogy, Volume 2), Lawrence, Kansas: University Press of Kansas, 2009, 509-512, 517, 519, 538; Jason Mark, Death of the Leaping Horseman: 24. Panzer-Division in Stalingrad, Sydney, Australia: Leaping Horsemen Books, 2003, 313; Jason Mark, Island of Fire: The Battle for the Barrikady Gun Factory in Stalingrad, November 1942 – February 1943, Sydney, Australia: Leaping Horsemen Books, 2006, 10; Hans Sanger, Die 79. Infanterie Division, Friedberg, FRG: Podzun Pallas Verlag, 76; Anton Schimak, Karl Lamprecht & Friedrich Dettmer, Die 44. Infanterie Division: Tagebuch der Hoch- und Deutschmeister, Wien: Verlag Austria Press, 169, 233 and Map: Marschweg der 44. Infanterie Division im Russland.*

Gebets-
andenken
an unsern lb. guten Gatten
und Vater, Herrn
Hans Waldherr
Soldat b. einem Inft. Regt.
Inhaber d. Inf. Sturm- u. d. Verwund. Abz.
welcher am 27. Oktober 1942 bei den Kämpfen bei Stalingrad im Alter von 42 Jahren, den Heldentod fand.

Ach, es ist ja kaum zu fassen,
Daß Du nicht mehr kehrst zurück,
So bald mußt Du Dein Leben lassen,
Zerstört ist unser ganzes Glück.
Du warst so gut, Du starbst so früh,
Wer Dich gekannt, vergißt Dich nie.

O Herr gib ihm und allen gefallenen Kriegern die ewige Ruhe!

Fritz Keerls Ww. Laufen

Soldat **Hans Waldherr** was 42 years old when he was killed in action on October 27, 1942 at Stalingrad. A winner of the Infantry Assault badge and the Black Wound Badge, Waldherr was married and a father.

Obergefreiter in einem Grenadier-Rgmt.
Franz Barth
aus Eck, Gemeinde Natternbach
gefallen im Kampfe gegen Sowjetrußland
am 9. August 1942 im 24. Lebensjahre.

Obergefreiter in einem Grenadier-Regmt.
Johann Barth
aus Eck, Gemeinde Natternbach
gefallen im Kampfe gegen Sowjetrußland
am 27. Oktober 1942 im 28. Lebensjahre.

***Obergefreiter* Johann Barth** was born in Natternbach, near Grieskirchen, in Upper Austria on December 23, 1914. He was killed in action at Kuporosnoye on October 27, 1942, probably assigned to the 371st Infantry Division. His name is listed in the remembrance book at the German Military Cemetery at Rossoschka. His younger brother Franz, shown at left, died of his wounds at the 2nd Company, 44th Medical Battalion casualty collection area, of the 44th Infantry Division, near Nizhne-Ossinowskij on August 9, 1942.

October 28, 1942
Weather: clear, cool, sunny, dry
Sunrise: 6:41 a.m.; **Sunset:** 4:50 p.m.
Moon: Waning Gibbous; 83% illumination

Sixth Army – Bombers and dive-bombers from the ***Luftwaffe***'s VIII Air Corps pounded enemy positions near the Krasny Oktyabr Steel Factory and the Barrikady Gun Factory. The army headquarters was located at Golubinskaya.

VIII Corps

76th Infantry Division – The division defended in sector, east of the Don River, north of Nizhne-Gnilovskii, to west of Kotluban' against the 214th Rifle Division. The division lost four NCOs/enlisted wounded in action; one man was reported missing in action. To the southeast was the 113th Infantry Division; to the northwest was the 384th Infantry Division.

113th Infantry Division – The division defended in sector southwest of Samofalovka and north of Borodkin against the 173rd Rifle Division and the 273rd Rifle Division. The division lost one NCO/enlisted killed in action; ten NCOs/enlisted were wounded in action; one man was reported missing in action. To the northwest was the 76th Infantry Division; to the east was the 60th Infantry Division (Motorized.)

XI Corps

44th Infantry Division – The division defended in sector Kurchajessowskij-Kamyshinskiy-Hill 171.0-Hill 180.9-Sirotinskaya-Khmelevskoy against the 40th Guards Rifle Division. The division headquarters was located at Verkhne-Golubaja. To the west was 376th Infantry Division; to the southeast was the 384th Infantry Division.

376th Infantry Division – The division defended in sector, south of Perekopskaja, near Logowskii and Ossinskij against the 23rd Rifle Division. The division suffered two NCOs/enlisted killed in action; three NCOs/enlisted were wounded in action. To the east was the 44th Infantry Division; to the west was the1st Romanian Cavalry Division of the Romanian Third Army.

384th Infantry Division – The division defended in sector west of the Don River near Trekhostrovskaia to Podgorskii against the 4th Guards Rifle Division and the 22nd Mechanized Brigade. To the northwest was the 44th Infantry Division; to the southeast was the 76th Infantry Division. The division lost one NCO/enlisted killed in action; one NCO/enlisted was wounded in action.

XIV *Panzer* Corps – The corps headquarters was located east of Ssadtschi-Kowa. The corps suffered the following officer casualties: one killed in action; one wounded in action.

3rd Infantry Division (Motorized) – The division defended in sector, from the Tartar Hill-Hill 111.1-Hill 129.6-Hill 131.2 against the 38th Guards Rifle Division and the 64th Rifle Division. The division suffered four NCOs/enlisted killed in action; two officers and 11 NCOs/enlisted were wounded in action. To the east was the 16th ***Panzer*** Division; to the west was the 60th Infantry Division (Motorized.)

16th Panzer Division – The division defended in sector, from Hill 139.7 to the Volga and south to Rynok against the 99th Rifle Division. The division attacked in the Spartakovka area. The division lost ten NCOs/enlisted wounded in action.

60th Infantry Division (Motorized) – The division defended in sector, from south of Kotluban' Station near Borodkin to Kuz'michi against the 343rd Rifle Division and the 116th Rifle Division. The division lost five NCOs/enlisted killed in action; 15 NCOs/enlisted were wounded in action. To the west was the 113th Infantry Division; to the east was the 3rd Infantry Division (Motorized.)

94th Infantry Division – The division attacked in the Spartakovka Workers' Settlement and seized another block of buildings. The division suffered two officers and 11 NCOs/enlisted killed in action; 59 NCOs/enlisted were wounded in action; four men were reported missing in action. To the south was the 389th Infantry Division; to the northeast was the 16th ***Panzer*** Division. From October 19 through October 28, 1942, the division suffered 565 casualties.

Battle Group Stahel – The battle group defended in sector, south of Erzovka, from the Volga River west.

LI Corps – The corps headquarters was located at Gumrak. The corps suffered the following officer casualties: two killed in action; nine wounded in action.

14th Panzer Division – The division attacked consolidated along the line of Mashinnaia Street, against the 193rd Rifle Division, between the two factories. The division lost 22 NCOs/enlisted killed in action; four officers and 102 NCOs/enlisted were wounded in action; ten men were reported missing in action. To the north was the 305th Infantry Division; to the south was the 79th Infantry Division. The 245th ***Sturmgeschütz*** Detachment was placed in support of the division.

24th Panzer Division – The division defended in positions along the Volga River against the 308th Rifle Division and the 138th Rifle Division. The division suffered three NCOs/enlisted killed in action; four NCOs/enlisted were wounded in action; one man was reported missing in action. To the north was the 389th Infantry Division; to the south was the 305th Infantry Division.

71st Infantry Division – The division defended in sector. To the north was the 295th Infantry Division; to the south was the 371st Infantry Division. The division suffered two officers and two NCOs/enlisted killed in action; 12 NCOs/enlisted were wounded in action.

79th Infantry Division – The division continued to attack in the central and southern portions of the Krasny Oktyabr Steel Factory against the 39th Guards Rifle Division and seized Halls 1 and 2. Bitter fighting also occurred at Halls 4 and 8. The division lost 12 NCOs/enlisted killed in action; 51 NCOs/enlisted were wounded in action; two men were reported missing in action. To the north was the 14th ***Panzer*** Division; to the south was the 100th ***Jäger*** Division.

100th Jäger Division – The division defended in sector. The division lost five NCOs/enlisted wounded in action; ten men were reported missing in action. To the north was the 79th Infantry Division; to the south was the 295th Infantry Division.

295th Infantry Division – The division attacked at the Lazur Chemical Factory at the "Tennis Racquet" against the 284th Rifle Division. The division reported one NCO/enlisted killed in action; 12 NCOs/enlisted were wounded in action. To the north was the 100th ***Jäger*** Division; to the south was the 71st Infantry Division.

305th Infantry Division – The division attacked east through the Mezensk Ravine, reaching 100 meters from the Volga River in bitter fighting against elements of the 308th Rifle Division and the 138th Rifle Division. The division suffered one officer and 26 NCOs/enlisted killed in action; one officer and 84 NCOs/enlisted were wounded in action; one officer and 13 NCOs/enlisted were reported missing in action. To the north was the 24th ***Panzer*** Division; to the south was the 14th ***Panzer*** Division.

389th Infantry Division – The division defended at the Brick Works. The division lost one NCO/enlisted wounded in action. To the north was the 94th Infantry Division; to the south was the 24th ***Panzer*** Division.

Sixth Army Reserve

One infantry regiment of the 79th Infantry Division moved toward Stalingrad, reaching Gumrak.

Fourth *Panzer* Army – The army headquarters was located east of Verkhne-Zaryzinskij.

IV Corps

297th Infantry Division – The division defended in sector east of Elkhi and near Staro-Dubovka against the 36th Guards Rifle Division and the 157th Rifle Division, repelling an attack by the 36th Guards Rifle Division toward Hill 145.5. To the north was the 371st Infantry Division; to the south was the 29th Infantry Division (Motorized.)

371st Infantry Division – The division defended in sector from Kuporosnoye in the east to northwest of Gornaia Poliana and conducted several counter-attacks that seized Kuporosnoye Balka, Topor Grove and Kvadratnaia Grove just west of Kuporosnoye against the 422nd Rifle Division, the 126th Rifle Division, the 93rd Rifle Brigade and the 97th Rifle Brigade. To the north was the 71st Infantry Division; to the south was the 297th Infantry Division.

20th Romanian Infantry Division – The division defended in sector, west of the Tundutovo Rail Station and east of Andreevka against the 204th Rifle Division. To the north was the 29th Infantry Division (Motorized); to the south was the 2nd Romanian Infantry Division.

Fourth *Panzer* Army Reserve

29th Infantry Division (Motorized) – The division occupied an assembly area, between Businovka and Gavrilovka, to prepare for future operations. Part of the division defended in sector east of the Volga-Don Canal against the 29th Rifle Division. The division lost one NCO/enlisted killed in action. To the north was the 297th Infantry Division; to the south was the 20th Romanian Infantry Division.

Den Heldentod fürs Vaterland starb
Obergefr. Josef Ketterl
Musiker von Chammünster, Teilnehmer an den Feldzügen in Polen, Frankr., Balkan u. Osten, geboren am 18. Januar 1910, gestorben am 28. Oktober 1942 im Osten.
N/0576

A musician by trade, ***Obergefreiter*** **Josef Ketterl** was born on January 18, 1910 in Chammünster, in Bavaria. Earlier Josef participated in the Polish, French, and Balkan campaigns, before he was killed in action at Kalach on October 28, 1942. He is buried at the German Military Cemetery at Rossoschka in Block 30, Row 9, in Grave 244.

Sources, October 28, 1942: *Oberkommando des Heeres, Lage Ost: Stand: 28.10.42, Eastern Front Situation Map, National Archives Identifier: 559733, Record Group 242 – National Archives Collection of Foreign Records Seized, 1675-1958, National Archives, College Park, Maryland; Ia, Armeeoberkommando 6, "Morgen Meldung" and assorted reports, Kriegstagebuch 14, 29 October 1942, as found in Microfilm Series, T-312, Records of German Field Commands, Armies, Roll 1453 and 1688, National Archives and Records Service, College Park, Maryland; Korpsarzt, XXXXVIII Panzerkorps, "Meldung über Personelle Verluste," Stand 28.10.42, as found on T-314, Records of German Field Commands, Corps, Roll 1158, National Archives, College Park, Maryland; Florian Freiherr von und zu Aufsess, Die Anlagenbände zu den Kriegstagebüchern der 6. Armee vom 14.09.1942 bis 24.11.1942, Band 1, Schwabach, Germany: Selbstverlag, 2006, 228-229; David M. Glantz & Jonathan M. House, Armageddon in Stalingrad: September-November 1942, (The Stalingrad Trilogy, Volume 2), Lawrence, Kansas: University Press of Kansas, 2009, 512-517, 519, 538-539; Adalbert Holl, An Infantryman in Stalingrad, translated by Jason D. Mark and Neill Page, Sydney, Australia: Leaping Horseman Books, 2005, 131; Jason Mark, Death of the Leaping Horseman: 24. Panzer-Division in Stalingrad, Sydney, Australia: Leaping Horsemen Books, 2003, 314; Jason Mark, Island of Fire: The Battle for the Barrikady Gun Factory in Stalingrad, November 1942 – February 1943, Sydney, Australia: Leaping Horsemen Books, 2006, 10; Kurt Mehner, Die Geheimen Tagesberichte der Deutschen Wehrmachtführung im Zweiten Weltkrieg 1939-1945, Band 5: 1. Juni 1942 – 30. November 1942, Osnabrück, Germany: Biblio Verlag, 1991, 255; Janusz Piekalkiewicz, Stalingrad: Anatomie einer Schlacht, München, BRD: Wilhelm Heyne Verlag, 1977, 330; Hans Sanger, Die 79. Infanterie Division, Friedberg, FRG: Podzun Pallas Verlag, 76-77; Anton Schimak, Karl Lamprecht & Friedrich Dettmer, Die 44. Infanterie Division: Tagebuch der Hoch- und Deutschmeister, Wien: Verlag Austria Press, 169, 233 and Map: Marschweg der 44. Infanterie Division im Russland.*

October 29, 1942
Weather: clear, mild, dry, light clouds
Sunrise: 6:43 a.m.; **Sunset:** 4:48 p.m.
Moon: Waning Gibbous; 75% illumination

Sixth Army – The army headquarters was located at Golubinskaya.

VIII Corps – The corps suffered the following officer casualties: one wounded in action.

76th Infantry Division – The division defended in sector, east of the Don River, north of Nizhne-Gnilovskii, to west of Kotluban' against the 214th Rifle Division. The division lost four NCOs/enlisted killed in action; one officer and six NCOs/enlisted were wounded in action. To the southeast was the 113th Infantry Division; to the northwest was the 384th Infantry Division.

113th Infantry Division – The division defended in sector southwest of Samofalovka and north of Borodkin against the 173rd Rifle Division and the 273rd Rifle Division. The division suffered three NCOs/enlisted killed in action; three NCOs/enlisted were wounded in action; two men were reported missing in action. To the northwest was the 76th Infantry Division; to the east was the 60th Infantry Division (Motorized.)

XI Corps

44th Infantry Division – The division defended in sector Kurchajessowskij-Kamyshinskiy-Hill 171.0-Hill 180.9-Sirotinskaya-Khmelevskoy against the 40th Guards Rifle Division. The division headquarters was located at Verkhne-Golubaja. The division lost two NCOs/enlisted killed in action; three NCOs/enlisted were wounded in action. To the west was the 376th Infantry Division; to the southeast was the 384th Infantry Division.

376th Infantry Division – The division defended in sector, south of Perekopskaja, near Logowskii and Ossinskij against the 23rd Rifle Division. The division suffered two NCOs/enlisted wounded in action. To the east was the 44th Infantry Division; to the west was the 1st Romanian Cavalry Division of the Romanian Third Army.

384th Infantry Division – The division defended in sector west of the Don River near Trekhostrovskaia to Podgorskii against the 4th Guards Rifle Division. The division lost one NCO/enlisted killed in action and four NCOs/enlisted wounded in action. To the west was the 44th Infantry Division; to the southeast was the 76th Infantry Division.

XIV *Panzer* Corps – The corps headquarters was located east of Ssadtschi-Kowa. The corps suffered the following officer casualties: two wounded in action.

3rd Infantry Division (Motorized) – The division defended in sector, from the Tartar Hill-Hill 111.1-Hill 129.6-Hill 131.2 against the 38th Guards Rifle Division and the 64th Rifle Division. The division lost three NCOs/enlisted killed in action; 12 NCOs/enlisted were wounded in action; one man was reported missing in action. To the east was the 16th ***Panzer*** Division; to the west was the 60th Infantry Division (Motorized.) Operational ***panzer*** status in the division was: three Mark II, 24 Mark III-Long, four Mark IV-Short and six Mark IV-Long tanks.

16th Panzer Division – The division defended in sector, from Hill 139.7 to the Volga and then south to Rynok against the 99th Rifle Division. The division attacked in the Spartakovka area. The division lost two NCOs/enlisted killed in action; six NCOs/enlisted were wounded in action. To the west was the 3rd Infantry Division (Motorized); to the southwest was the 94th Infantry Division. Operational

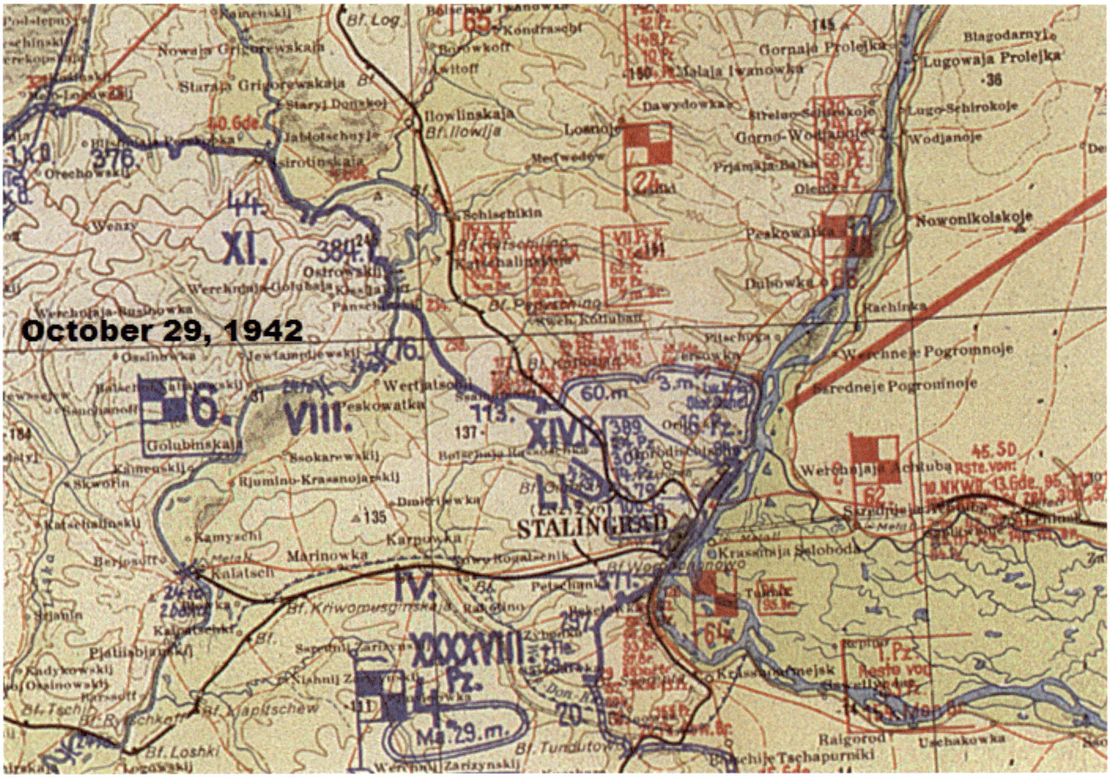

panzer status in the division was: 38 Mark III-Long, three Mark IV-Short and 12 Mark IV-Long tanks.

60th Infantry Division (Motorized) – The division defended in sector, from south of Kotluban' Station near Borodkin to Kuz'michi against the 343rd Rifle Division, the 49th Rifle Division, the 231st Rifle Division and the 116th Rifle Division. The division lost three NCOs/enlisted killed in action; one officer and nine NCOs/enlisted were wounded in action. To the west was the 113th Infantry Division; to the east was the 3rd Infantry Division (Motorized.)

94th Infantry Division – The division attacked in the Spartakovka area. The division lost ten NCOs/enlisted killed in action; 17 NCOs/enlisted were wounded in action. To the south was the 389th Infantry Division; to the northeast was the 16th ***Panzer*** Division.

Battle Group Stahel – The battle group defended in sector, south of Erzovka, from the Volga River west.

LI Corps – The corps headquarters was located at the Gumrak Rail Station. The corps suffered the following officer casualties: two killed in action; one wounded in action

14th Panzer Division – The division attacked in the vicinity of the ferry crossing site on the Volga River against the 193rd Rifle Division and the 84th Tank Battalion. The division lost 17 NCOs/enlisted killed in action; one officer and 77 NCOs/enlisted were wounded in action; 12 men were reported missing in action. To the north was the 305th Infantry Division; to the south was the 79th Infantry Division. Operational ***panzer*** status in the division was: one Mark II, one Mark III-Short, five Mark III-Long and two Mark IV-Long tanks.

24th Panzer Division – The division defended in positions along the Volga River against the 308th Rifle Division and the 138th Rifle Division. The division suffered three NCOs/enlisted killed in action; five NCOs/enlisted were wounded in action. To the south was the 305th Infantry Division. Operational ***panzer*** status in the division was: two Mark II, two Mark III-Short, five Mark III-Long and one Mark IV-Long tanks.

71st Infantry Division – The division defended in sector. The division lost one NCO/enlisted killed in action; eight NCOs/enlisted were wounded in action. To the north was the 295th Infantry Division; to the south was the 371st Infantry Division.

79th Infantry Division – The division continued to attack in the central and southern portions of the Krasny Oktyabr Steel Factory against the 39th Guards Rifle Division. Bitter fighting occurred at Hall 4 and 5. The division suffered 19 NCOs/enlisted killed in action; 96 NCOs/enlisted were wounded in action; four men were reported missing in action. To the north was the 14th ***Panzer*** Division; to the south was the 100th ***Jäger*** Division.

100th Jäger Division – The division defended in sector. The division lost five NCOs/enlisted killed in action; 13 officers and 40 NCOs/enlisted were wounded in action. To the north was the 79th Infantry Division; to the south was the 295th Infantry Division.

295th Infantry Division – The division attacked at the Lazur Chemical Factory at the "Tennis Racquet" against the 284th Rifle Division. The division suffered one NCO/enlisted killed in action and eight NCOs/enlisted wounded in action. To the north was the 100th ***Jäger*** Division; to the south was the 71st Infantry Division.

305th Infantry Division – The division attacked east in the Barrikady Gun Factory against elements of the 308th Rifle Division and the 138th Rifle Division, pushing those units toward the Volga River. The division also repelled enemy attacks from the fuel installation, east of the factory. The division lost one officer and 37 NCOs/enlisted killed in action; two officers and 93 NCOs/enlisted were wounded in action; five men were reported missing in action. To the north was the 389th Infantry Division; to the south was the 14th ***Panzer*** Division.

389th Infantry Division – The division defended at the Brick Works. The division reported one NCO/enlisted killed in action and one NCO/enlisted wounded in action. To the north was the 94th Infantry Division; to the south was the 305th Infantry Division.

Sixth Army Reserve

One infantry regiment of the 79th Infantry Division moved toward Stalingrad, reaching the Razgulyayevka Rail Station.

Fourth *Panzer* Army – The army headquarters was located east of Verkhne-Zaryzinskij.

IV Corps

297th Infantry Division – The division defended in sector east of Elkhi and near Staro-Dubovka against the 36th Guards Rifle Division and the 157th Rifle Division. To the north was the 371st Infantry Division; to the south was the 29th Infantry Division (Motorized.)

371st Infantry Division – The division defended in sector from Kuporosnoye in the east to northwest of Gornaia Poliana and conducted several counter-attacks that seized some terrain in Kuporosnoye against the 422nd Rifle Division, the 126th Rifle Division, the 93rd Rifle Brigade and the 97th Rifle Brigade. To the north was the 71st Infantry Division; to the south was the 297th Infantry Division.

20th Romanian Infantry Division – The division defended in sector, west of the Tundutovo Rail Station and east of Andreevka. To the north was the 29th Infantry Division (Motorized); to the south was the 2nd Romanian Infantry Division of the Romanian VI Corps.

Fourth *Panzer* Army Reserve

29th Infantry Division (Motorized) – The division occupied an assembly area, between Businovka and Gavrilovka, to prepare for future operations. Part of the division defended in sector east of the Volga-Don Canal against the 29th Rifle Division. To the north was the 297th Infantry Division; to the south was the 20th Romanian Infantry Division.

Sources, October 29, 1942: *Oberkommando des Heeres, Lage Ost: Stand: 29.10.42, Eastern Front Situation Map, National Archives Identifier: 559733, Record Group 242 – National Archives Collection of Foreign Records Seized, 1675-1958, National Archives, College Park, Maryland; Ia, Armeeoberkommando 6, "Morgen Meldung" and assorted reports, Kriegstagebuch 14, 30 October 1942, as found in Microfilm Series, T-312, Records of German Field Commands, Armies, Roll 1453 and 1688, National Archives and Records Service, College Park, Maryland; Korpsarzt, XXXXVIII Panzerkorps, "Meldung über Personelle Verluste," Stand 29.10.42, as found on T-314, Records of German Field Commands, Corps, Roll 1158, National Archives, College Park, Maryland; Florian Freiherr von und zu Aufsess, Die Anlagenbände zu den Kriegstagebüchern der 6. Armee vom 14.09.1942 bis 24.11.1942, Band 1, Schwabach, Germany: Selbstverlag, 2006, 230-233; David M. Glantz & Jonathan M. House, Armageddon in Stalingrad: September-November 1942, (The Stalingrad Trilogy, Volume 2), Lawrence, Kansas: University Press of Kansas, 2009, 515-517, 519; Jason Mark, Death of the Leaping Horseman: 24. Panzer-Division in Stalingrad, Sydney, Australia: Leaping Horsemen Books, 2003, 315-317; Jason Mark, Island of Fire: The Battle for the Barrikady Gun Factory in Stalingrad, November 1942 – February 1943, Sydney, Australia: Leaping Horsemen Books, 2006, 10; Hans Sanger, Die 79. Infanterie Division, Friedberg, FRG: Podzun Pallas Verlag, 77; Anton Schimak, Karl Lamprecht & Friedrich Dettmer, Die 44. Infanterie Division: Tagebuch der Hoch- und Deutschmeister, Wien: Verlag Austria Press, 169, 233 and Map: Marschweg der 44. Infanterie Division im Russland.*

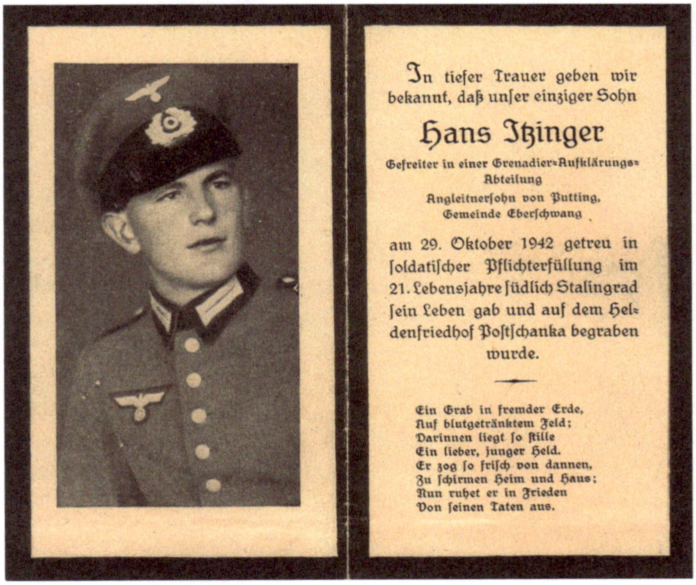

In tiefer Trauer geben wir bekannt, daß unser einziger Sohn

Hans Itzinger

Gefreiter in einer Grenadier-Aufklärungs-Abteilung

Angleitnersohn von Putting, Gemeinde Eberschwang

am 29. Oktober 1942 getreu in soldatischer Pflichterfüllung im 21. Lebensjahre südlich Stalingrad sein Leben gab und auf dem Heldenfriedhof Postschanka begraben wurde.

Ein Grab in fremder Erde,
Auf blutgetränktem Feld;
Darinnen liegt so stille
Ein lieber, junger Held.
Er zog so frisch von dannen,
Zu schirmen Heim und Haus;
Nun ruhet er in Frieden
Von seinen Taten aus.

Johannes "Hans" Itzinger was born on December 18, 1921 at the village of Putting near Eberschwang in Austria. Itzinger was killed in action at Kuporosnoye on October 29, 1942, probably while assigned to the reconnaissance battalion of the 29th Infantry Division (Motorized). His name is listed in the remembrance book at the German Military Cemetery at Rossoschka.

Zum Gedenken im Gebete
an unseren lieben, unvergeßlichen Sohn, Bruder, Schwager und Onkel

Josef Ries

von Tirschenreuth
Unteroffizier in einem Infanterie-Regt.
Inhaber des EK. II.
Geboren am 21. August 1912, gefallen am 29. Oktober 1942 vor Stalingrad.

Jäh hat Dich der Tod von uns gerissen,
Du ruhst in einem fremden Grab so weit.
Der einzige Trost ist, daß wir wissen,
Wir sehn uns wieder in der Ewigkeit.
Dein junges, hoffnungsvolles Leben
Gabst Du für uns im Kampfe heiß;
Dafür wird aber Gott Dir geben
Den ewigen Frieden nun als Preis.

Vater unser. Gegrüßt seist Du, Maria.
O Herr, gib ihm die ewige Ruhe . . . .

Unteroffizier **Josef Ries** was born in Tirschenreuth, Bavaria on August 21, 1912. Assigned to an infantry regiment, probably in the 113th Infantry Division, he was killed in action near Rossoschka on October 29, 1942. He is probably buried at the German Military Cemetery at Rossoschka.

October 30, 1942
Weather: overcast, light afternoon rain, overall conditions beginning to change
Sunrise: 6:44 a.m.; **Sunset:** 4:47 p.m.
Moon: Waning Gibbous; 66% illumination

Sixth Army – Army headquarters was located at Golubinskaya.

VIII Corps – The corps suffered the following officer casualties: one wounded in action.

76th Infantry Division – The division defended in sector, east of the Don River, north of Nizhne-Gnilovskii, to west of Kotluban' against the 214th Rifle Division. The division lost two NCOs/enlisted killed in action; one officer and two NCOs/enlisted were wounded in action. To the east was the 113th Infantry Division; to the northwest was the 384th Infantry Division.

113th Infantry Division – The division defended in sector southwest of Samofalovka and north of Borodkin against the 173rd Rifle Division and the 273rd Rifle Division. The division lost three NCOs/enlisted killed in action; eight NCOs/enlisted were wounded in action. To the northwest was the 76th Infantry Division; to the east was the 60th Infantry Division (Motorized.)

XI Corps

44th Infantry Division – The division defended in sector Kurchajessowskij-Kamyshinskiy-Hill 171.0-Hill 180.9-Sirotinskaya-Khmelevskoy against the 40th Guards Rifle Division. The division lost one NCO/enlisted wounded in action. The division headquarters was located at Verkhne-Golubaja. To the west was 376th Infantry Division; to the southeast was the 384th Infantry Division.

376th Infantry Division – The division defended in sector, south of Perekopskaja, near Logowskii and Ossinskij against the 23rd Rifle Division. The division lost four NCOs/enlisted wounded in action. To the east was the 44th Infantry Division; to the west was the 1st Romanian Cavalry Division of the Romanian Third Army.

384th Infantry Division – The division defended in sector west of the Don River near Trekhostrovskaia to Podgorskii against the 4th Guards Rifle Division. The division lost one NCO/enlisted wounded in action. To the west was the 44th Infantry Division; to the southeast was the 76th Infantry Division.

XIV *Panzer* Corps – The corps headquarters was located east of Ssadtschi-Kowa. The corps suffered the following officer casualties: three wounded in action.

3rd Infantry Division (Motorized) – The division defended in sector, from the Tartar Hill-Hill 111.1-Hill 129.6-Hill 131.2 against the 62nd Rifle Division, the 226th Rifle Division, the 212th Rifle Division, the 116th Rifle Division, the 299th Rifle Division and the 64th Rifle Division. The division lost one officer and three NCOs/enlisted killed in action; 21 NCOs/enlisted were wounded in action. To the east was the 16th ***Panzer*** Division; to the west was the 60th Infantry Division (Motorized.)

16th Panzer Division – The division defended in sector, from Hill 139.7 to the Volga and south to Rynok against the 84th Rifle Division and the 99th Rifle Division. The division attacked in the Spartakovka area. The division suffered three NCOs/enlisted killed in action; one officer and 11 NCOs/enlisted were wounded in action. To the west was the 3rd Infantry Division (Motorized); to the southwest was the 94th Infantry Division.

60th Infantry Division (Motorized) – The division defended in sector, from south of Kotluban' Station near Borodkin to Kuz'michi against the 49th Rifle Division, the 343rd Rifle

Division, the 231st Rifle Division, the 62nd Rifle Division and the 226th Rifle Division. To the west was the 113th Infantry Division; to the east was the 3rd Infantry Division (Motorized.) The division lost eight NCOs/enlisted killed in action; 21 NCOs/enlisted were wounded in action.

94th Infantry Division – The division attacked in the Spartakovka area. To the south was the 389th Infantry Division; to the northeast was the 16th ***Panzer*** Division. The division suffered one NCO/enlisted killed in action; ten NCOs/enlisted were wounded in action.

Battle Group Stahel – The battle group defended in sector, south of Erzovka, from the Volga River west.

LI Corps – The corps headquarters was located at Gumrak. The corps suffered the following officer casualties: one killed in action; four wounded in action. The corps reported that the attached 244th ***Sturmgeschütz*** Detachment had four Mark III-Short and two Mark III-Long operational assault guns and the 245th ***Sturmgeschütz*** Detachment had one Mark III-Long operational assault gun.

14th Panzer Division – The division attacked in the vicinity of the ferry crossing site on the Volga River against the 193rd Rifle Division. The division lost six NCOs/enlisted killed in action; one officer and 25 NCOs/enlisted were wounded in action; one man was reported missing in action. To the north was the 305th Infantry Division; to the south was the 79th Infantry Division.

24th Panzer Division – The division defended in positions along the Volga River against the 308th Rifle Division and the 138th Rifle Division. The 389th Infantry Division began to relieve the 24th ***Panzer*** Division from its positions. The division suffered one NCO/enlisted killed in action; four NCOs/enlisted were wounded in action; one man died of his wounds the following day. To the south was the 305th Infantry Division.

71st Infantry Division – The division defended in sector. The division lost two NCOs/enlisted wounded in action. To the north was the 295th Infantry Division; to the south was the 371st Infantry Division.

79th Infantry Division – The division continued to attack at the Krasny Oktyabr Steel

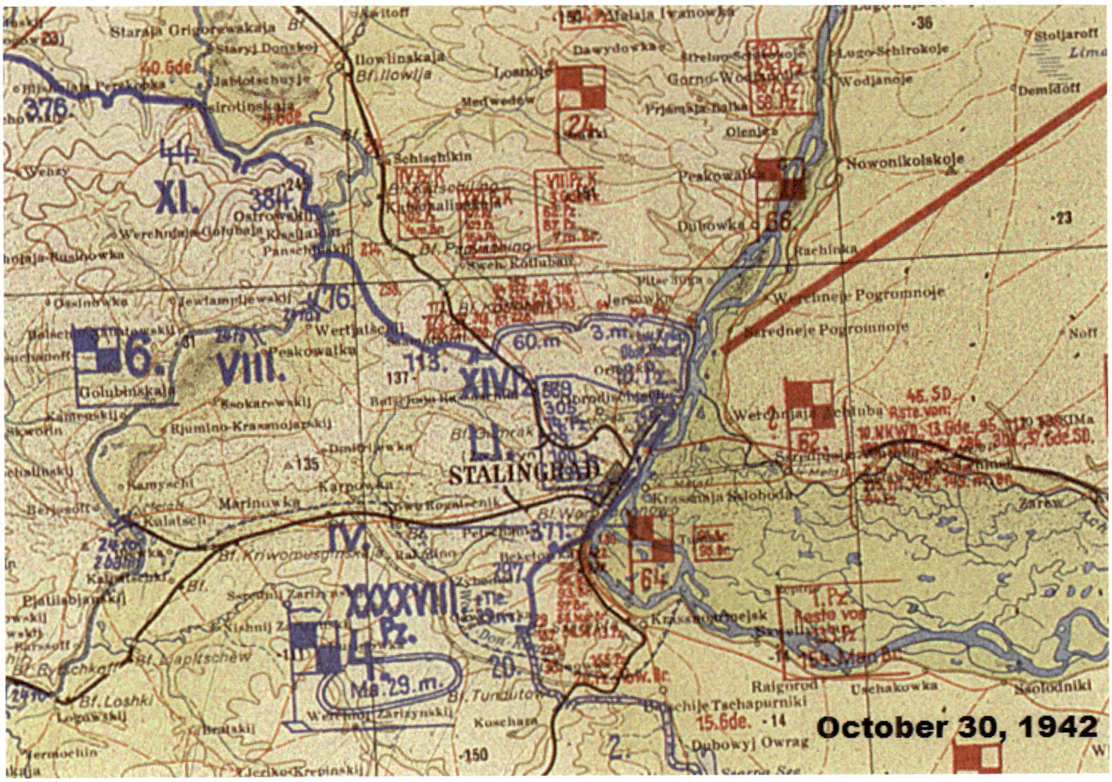

Factory, but progress against the 39th Guards Rifle Division was limited. Bitter fighting occurred at Hall 10. The division suffered two NCOs/enlisted killed in action; one officer and 28 NCOs/enlisted were wounded in action; four men were reported missing in action. To the north was the 14th ***Panzer*** Division; to the south was the 100th ***Jäger*** Division. The last infantry regiment arrived at the division from the Sixth Army Reserve.

100th Jäger Division – The division defended in sector. The division lost five NCOs/enlisted killed in action; 22 NCOs/enlisted were wounded in action. To the north was the 79th Infantry Division; to the south was the 295th Infantry Division.

295th Infantry Division – The division attacked along Artilleriiskaia Street against the 284th Rifle Division. The division reported one officer and one NCO/enlisted killed in action, eight NCOs/enlisted wounded in action and one man missing in action. To the north was the 100th ***Jäger*** Division; to the south was the 71st Infantry Division.

305th Infantry Division – The division attacked east in the Barrikady Gun Factory against elements of the 308th Rifle Division and the 138th Rifle Division. The division suffered three NCOs/enlisted killed in action; 25 NCOs/enlisted were wounded in action; five men were reported missing in action. To the north was the 389th Infantry Division; to the south was the 14th ***Panzer*** Division.

389th Infantry Division – The division defended in sector. The division began to relieve the 24th ***Panzer*** Division from its defensive positions. To the north was the 94th Infantry Division; to the south was the 305th Infantry Division.

Fourth *Panzer* Army – The army headquarters was located east of Verkhne-Zaryzinskij.

IV Corps

297th Infantry Division – The division defended in sector east of Elkhi and near Staro-Dubovka against the 36th Guards Rifle Division and the 157th Rifle Division. To the north was the 371st Infantry Division; to the south was the 29th Infantry Division (Motorized.)

371st Infantry Division – The division defended in sector from Kuporosnoye in the east to northwest of Gornaia Poliana, repulsing several attacks, and conducted several counter-attacks at the Kuporosnoye Balka against the 422nd Rifle Division, the 126th Rifle Division, the 93rd Rifle Brigade and the 97th Rifle Brigade. To the north was the 71st Infantry Division; to the south was the 297th Infantry Division.

20th Romanian Infantry Division – The division defended in sector, west of the Tundutovo Rail Station and east of Andreevka. To the north was the 29th Infantry Division (Motorized); to the south was the 2nd Romanian Infantry Division of the Romanian VI Corps.

Fourth *Panzer* Army Reserve

29th Infantry Division (Motorized) – The division occupied an assembly area, between Businovka and Gavrilovka, to prepare for future operations. Part of the division defended in sector east of the Volga-Don Canal against the 29th Rifle Division. To the north was the 297th Infantry Division; to the south was the 20th Romanian Infantry Division. The division lost three NCOs/enlisted wounded in action.

Sources, October 30, 1942: ***Oberkommando des Heeres, Lage Ost: Stand: 30.10.42, Eastern Front Situation Map, National Archives Identifier: 559733, Record Group 242 – National Archives Collection of Foreign Records Seized, 1675-1958, National Archives, College Park, Maryland; Ia, Armeeoberkommando 6, "Morgen Meldung" and assorted reports, Kriegstagebuch 14, 31 October 1942, as found in Microfilm Series, T-312, Records of German Field Commands, Armies, Roll 1453 and 1688, National Archives and Records Service, College Park, Maryland; Korpsarzt, XXXXVIII Panzerkorps, "Meldung über Personelle Verluste," Stand 30.10.42, as found on T-314, Records of German Field Commands, Corps, Roll 1158, National Archives, College Park, Maryland; Florian Freiherr von und zu Aufsess, Die Anlagenbände zu den Kriegstagebüchern der 6. Armee vom 14.09.1942 bis 24.11.1942, Band 1, Schwabach, Germany: Selbstverlag, 2006, 231-235; David M. Glantz & Jonathan M. House, Armageddon in Stalingrad: September-November 1942, (The Stalingrad Trilogy, Volume 2), Lawrence, Kansas: University Press of Kansas, 2009, 519, 539; Jason Mark, Death of the Leaping Horseman: 24. Panzer-Division in Stalingrad, Sydney, Australia: Leaping Horsemen Books, 2003, 317-318; Kurt Mehner, Die Geheimen Tagesberichte der Deutschen Wehrmachtführung im Zweiten Weltkrieg 1939-1945, Band 5: 1. Juni 1942 – 30. November 1942, Osnabrück, Germany: Biblio Verlag, 1991, 259; Hans Sanger, Die 79. Infanterie Division, Friedberg, FRG: Podzun Pallas Verlag, 77; Anton Schimak, Karl Lamprecht & Friedrich Dettmer, Die 44. Infanterie Division: Tagebuch der Hoch- und Deutschmeister, Wien: Verlag Austria Press, 169, 233 and Map: Marschweg der 44. Infanterie Division im Russland.***

GEBETSANDENKEN

an den tugendsamen Jüngling

Herrn Josef Hurzlmeier

Bauerssohn von Upfkofen

Soldat in einem Infanterie-Regt.

gefallen am 30. Oktober 1942 bei den schweren Kämpfen um Stalingrad im Alter von 33 Jahren 11 Mon.

O, liebste Mutter und Geschwister mein,
Ich kehre nicht mehr zu euch heim,
Der letzte Gedanke, der letzte Blick
Sie eilen noch zu euch zurück.
Als ich starb im Feindesland
Reichte niemand mir die Hand
Doch eh' mein Auge war gebrochen
Sah den Himmel ich schon offen.
Ihr Lieben mein
Schließt ins Gebet mich ein
Vergeßt Euern lieben Josef nicht
Der im Feindesland begraben liegt.

Jesus, Maria und Josef, euch schenke ich mein Herz und meine Seele!

Süßes Herz Jesu, sei meine Rettung!

R. I. P.

Buchdruckerei des „Laber-Bote", Geiselhöring

Soldat **Josef Hurzlmeier**, a farmer's son from Upfkofen, a village southeast of Regensburg in Bavaria, was assigned to an infantry regiment. He was killed in action on October 30, 1942 at Stalingrad. Hurzlmeier was just shy of 34 when he died.

October 31, 1942
Weather: overcast, rainy, later cooler and dryer, roads still passable
Sunrise: 6:46 a.m.; **Sunset:** 4:45 p.m.
Moon: Waning Gibbous; 57% illumination

Sixth Army – The army headquarters was located at Golubinskaya.

VIII Corps

76th Infantry Division – The division defended in sector, east of the Don River, north of Nizhne-Gnilovskii, to west of Kotluban' against the 214th Rifle Division and the 298th Rifle Division. The division lost six NCOs/enlisted wounded in action. To the southeast was the 113th Infantry Division; to the northwest was the 384th Infantry Division. During the period October 3, 1942 through October 31, 1942, the division suffered 226 overall casualties.

113th Infantry Division – The division defended in sector southwest of Samofalovka and north of Borodkin against the 173rd Rifle Division and the 273rd Rifle Division. The division lost one NCO/enlisted killed in action; five NCOs/enlisted were wounded in action. To the northwest was the 76th Infantry Division; to the east was the 60th Infantry Division (Motorized.) During the period October 3, 1942 through October 31, 1942, the division suffered 1,259 overall casualties.

XI Corps

44th Infantry Division – The division defended in sector Kurchajessowskij-Kamyshinskiy-Hill 171.0-Hill 180.9-Sirotinskaya-Khmelevskoy against the 40th Guards Rifle Division. The division lost two NCOs/enlisted killed in action; six NCOs/enlisted were wounded in action. The division headquarters was located at Verkhne-Golubaja. To the west was the 376th Infantry Division; to the southeast was the 384th Infantry Division. During the period October 3, 1942 through October 31, 1942, the division suffered 185 overall casualties.

376th Infantry Division – The division defended in sector, south of Perekopskaja, near Logowskii and Ossinskij against the 23rd Rifle Division. The division lost three NCOs/enlisted wounded in action. To the east was the 44th Infantry Division; to the west was the 1st Romanian Cavalry Division of the Romanian Third Army. During the period October 3, 1942 through October 31, 1942, the division suffered 158 overall casualties.

384th Infantry Division – The division defended in sector west of the Don River near Trekhostrovskaia to Podgorskii. The division lost one NCO/enlisted killed in action; three NCOs/enlisted were wounded in action. To the west was the 44th Infantry Division; to the southeast was the 76th Infantry Division. During the period October 3, 1942 through October 31, 1942, the division suffered 72 overall casualties.

XIV *Panzer* Corps – The corps headquarters was located east of Ssadtschi-Kowa. The corps suffered the following officer casualties: two wounded in action.

3rd Infantry Division (Motorized) – The division defended in sector, from the Tartar Hill-Hill 111.1-Hill 129.6-Hill 131.2 against the 62nd Rifle Division, the 226th Rifle Division, the 212th Rifle Division, the 116th Rifle Division, the 299th Rifle Division and the 64th Rifle Division,. The division lost one officer and three NCOs/enlisted killed in action; 21 NCOs/enlisted were wounded in action. To the east was the 16th ***Panzer*** Division; to the west was the 60th Infantry Division (Motorized.)

16th Panzer Division – The division defended in sector, from Hill 139.7 to the Volga and south to Rynok against the 84th Rifle Division and the 99th Rifle Division.

The division attacked in the Spartakovka and Lataschanka areas against the 300th Rifle Division, after elements of that unit conducted an amphibious landing from the Volga. The division suffered three NCOs/enlisted killed in action; one officer and 11 NCOs/enlisted were wounded in action. To the west was the 3rd Infantry Division (Motorized); to the southwest was the 94th Infantry Division.

60th Infantry Division (Motorized) – The division defended in sector, from south of Kotluban' Station near Borodkin to Kuz'michi against the 49th Rifle Division, the 343rd Rifle Division, the 231st Rifle Division, the 62nd Rifle Division and the 226th Rifle Division. The division lost two NCOs/enlisted killed in action; eight NCOs/enlisted were wounded in action. To the west was the 113th Infantry Division; to the east was the 3rd Infantry Division (Motorized.)

94th Infantry Division – The division attacked in the Spartakovka area. To the south was the 389th Infantry Division; to the northeast was the 16th ***Panzer*** Division. The division suffered one NCO/enlisted killed in action; ten NCO/enlisted were wounded in action. During the period October 3, 1942 through October 31, 1942. the division suffered 1,233 overall casualties.

Battle Group Stahel – The battle group defended in sector, south of Erzovka, from the Volga River west.

LI Corps – The corps headquarters was located at Gumrak. The corps suffered the following officer casualties: one killed in action; ten wounded in action.

14th Panzer Division – The division attacked near the ferry crossing site on the Volga River against the 193rd Rifle Division, but was repelled. The division lost 13 NCOs/enlisted killed in action; five officers and 58 NCOs/enlisted were wounded in action. To the north was the 305th Infantry Division; to the south was the 79th Infantry Division. ***Generalleutnant*** Ferdinand Heim, the division commander, was selected to command the XXXXVIII ***Panzer*** Corps. He was replaced by ***Generalmajor*** Hans ***Freiherr*** von Falkenstein.

24th Panzer Division – The division was relieved in place by the 389th Infantry Division and moved west near Gumrak to an assembly area to conduct refit and recovery

operations. The division suffered one NCO/enlisted killed in action; three NCOs/enlisted were wounded in action. The division reported a combat strength of 960 infantrymen.

71st Infantry Division – The division defended in sector. The division lost three NCOs/enlisted killed in action; one NCO/enlisted was wounded in action. To the north was the 295th Infantry Division; to the south was the 371st Infantry Division. During the period October 3, 1942 through October 31, 1942, the division suffered 274 overall casualties.

79th Infantry Division – The division defended at the Krasny Oktyabr Steel Factory against elements of the 39th Guards Rifle Division and the 45th Rifle Division, losing Hall 4. The division lost two NCOs/enlisted killed in action; 28 NCOs/enlisted were wounded in action. To the north was the 14th ***Panzer*** Division; to the south was the 100th ***Jäger*** Division. During the period October 3, 1942 through October 31, 1942, the division suffered 1,970 overall casualties.

100th Jäger Division – The division defended in sector. The division lost two NCOs/enlisted killed in action; seven NCOs/enlisted were wounded in action. To the north was the 79th Infantry Division; to the south was the 295th Infantry Division. During the period October 3, 1942 through October 31, 1942, the division suffered 2,034 overall casualties.

295th Infantry Division – The division defended in sector against the 284th Rifle Division. The division lost two NCOs/enlisted killed in action; nine NCOs/enlisted were wounded in action. To the north was the 100th ***Jäger*** Division; to the south was the 71st Infantry Division. During the period October 3, 1942 through October 31, 1942, the division suffered 724 overall casualties.

305th Infantry Division – The division attacked east against elements of the 308th Rifle Division and the 138th Rifle Division, but was repulsed. The division lost 15 NCOs/enlisted killed in action; one officer and 36 NCOs/enlisted were wounded in action; three men were reported missing in action. To the north was the 389th Infantry Division; to the south was the 14th ***Panzer*** Division. During the period October 3, 1942 through October 31, 1942, the division suffered 2,876 overall casualties.

389th Infantry Division – The division completed its relief in place operation of the 24th ***Panzer*** Division and assumed defensive positions near the Brick Works. The division lost 11 NCOs/enlisted killed in action; seven NCOs/enlisted were wounded in action. To the north was the 94th Infantry Division; to the south was the 305th Infantry Division. During the period October 3, 1942 through October 31, 1942, the division suffered 1,296 overall casualties.

Fourth *Panzer* Army – The army headquarters was located east of Verkhne-Zaryzinskij.

IV Corps

297th Infantry Division – The division defended in sector east of Elkhi and Iagodniki against the 36th Guards Rifle Division. To the north was the 371st Infantry Division; to the south was the 29th Infantry Division (Motorized.)

371st Infantry Division – The division defended in sector from Kuporosnoye in the east to northwest of Gornaia Poliana, repulsing attacks by the 36th Guards Rifle Division, the 422nd Rifle Division, the 126th Rifle Division, the 93rd Rifle Brigade and the 97th Rifle Brigade. To the north was the 71st Infantry Division; to the south was the 297th Infantry Division.

20th Romanian Infantry Division – The division defended in sector, west of the Tundutovo Rail Station and east of Andreevka against the 38th Rifle Division. To the north was the 29th Infantry Division (Motorized); to the south was the 2nd Romanian Infantry Division of the Romanian VI Corps.

Fourth *Panzer* Army Reserve

29th Infantry Division (Motorized) – The division occupied an assembly area, between Businovka and Gavrilovka, to prepare for future operations. Part of the division defended in sector east of the Volga-Don Canal against the 29th Rifle Division. The division lost three NCOs/enlisted wounded in action. To the north was the 297th Infantry Division; to the south was the 20th Romanian Infantry Division.

Sources, October 31, 1942: *Oberkommando des Heeres, Lage Ost: Stand: 31.10.42, Eastern Front Situation Map, National Archives Identifier: 559733, Record Group 242 – National Archives Collection of Foreign Records Seized, 1675-1958, National Archives, College Park, Maryland; Ia, Armeeoberkommando 6, "Morgen Meldung" and assorted reports, Kriegstagebuch 14, 1 November 1942, as found in Microfilm Series, T-312, Records of German Field Commands, Armies, Roll 1453 and 1688, National Archives and Records Service, College Park, Maryland; Korpsarzt, XXXXVIII Panzerkorps, "Meldung über Personelle Verluste," Stand 31.10.42, as found on T-314, Records of German Field Commands, Corps, Roll 1158, National Archives, College Park, Maryland; Florian Freiherr von und zu Aufsess, Die Anlagenbände zu den Kriegstagebüchern der 6. Armee vom 14.09.1942 bis 24.11.1942, Band 1, Schwabach, Germany: Selbstverlag, 2006, 271; David M. Glantz & Jonathan M. House, Armageddon in Stalingrad: September-November 1942, (The Stalingrad Trilogy, Volume 2), Lawrence, Kansas: University Press of Kansas, 2009, 519-524, 539; Rolf Grams, Die 14. Panzer-Division, 1940-1945, Friedberg, FRG: Podzun Pallas Verlag, 1986, 55; Jason Mark, Death of the Leaping Horseman: 24. Panzer-Division in Stalingrad, Sydney, Australia: Leaping Horsemen Books, 2003, 318-322; Kurt Mehner, Die Geheimen Tagesberichte der Deutschen Wehrmachtführung im Zweiten Weltkrieg 1939-1945, Band 5: 1. Juni 1942 – 30. November 1942, Osnabrück, Germany: Biblio Verlag, 1991, 259 and 261; Anton Schimak, Karl Lamprecht & Friedrich Dettmer, Die 44. Infanterie Division: Tagebuch der Hoch- und Deutschmeister, Wien: Verlag Austria Press, 169, 233 and Map: Marschweg der 44. Infanterie Division im Russland; Wolfgang Werthen, Geschichte der 16. Panzer-Division 1939-1945, Friedberg, FRG: Podzun-Pallas-Verlag, 1958, 115.*

Zur frommen Erinnerung
im Gebete
an unsern lieben Sohn und Bruder

Matthias Sommer

Unteroffizier in einem Art.-Regt.

geboren am 3. Mai 1913
gefallen am 31. Oktober 1942
in Stalingrad (Rußland)

O ihr Eltern und Geschwister mein,
Ich kehre nicht mehr zu Euch heim.
Mein letzter Gedanke, letzter Blick,
Der eilte noch zu Euch zurück.

Als ich starb fürs Vaterland,
Reichte niemand mir die Hand.
Doch eh mein Auge war gebrochen
Sah ich schon den Himmel offen.

Gebet.

Vater der Barmherzigkeit und Gott alles Trostes, erbarme Dich dieses im Kampf gefallenen Soldaten Matthias. Fern der Heimat liegt er nun begraben. Doch Du, o Vater, sei ihm nahe durch Deine Liebe. Vergib ihm die Vergehungen, laß ihm alle zeitlichen Strafen nach, lohne ihm seinen Tod, den er für das Vaterland erduldet hat, mit dem ewigen Leben. Schmücke ihn mit dem Siegeskranz des treuen Soldaten und gib uns allen die Freude des Wiedersehens im Himmel. Durch Christus unsern Herrn. Amen.

Vater unser . . .

Barmherziger Jesus, gib ihm die ewige Ruhe.

Unteroffizier **Matthias Sommer** was born on May 3, 1913 at Oberdischingen, near Ehingen on the Donau River, in Baden-Württemberg. Assigned to an artillery regiment, he was killed in action on Hill 107.5 at Stalingrad on October 31, 1942. His name is listed in the remembrance book at the German Military Cemetery at Rossoschka.

German assault infantry squad (*Stosstrup*) outside of Stalingrad in October 1942.

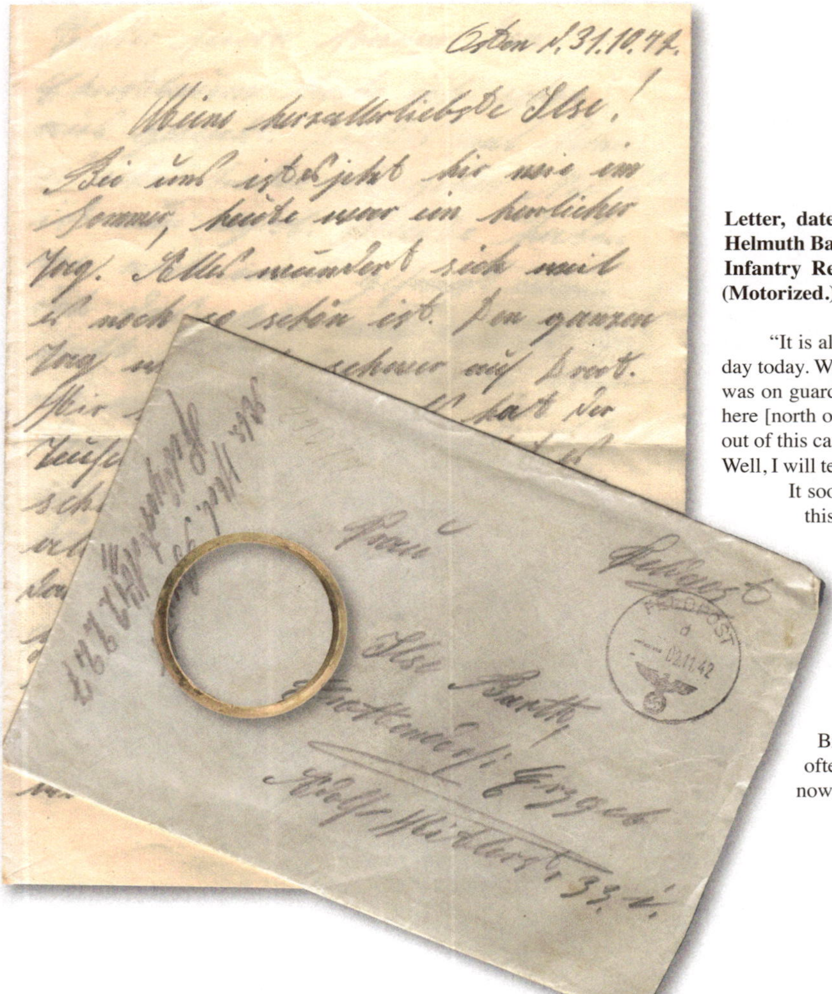

Letter, dated October 31, 1942, from *Gefreiter* Helmuth Barth in the Heavy Company of the 29th Infantry Regiment in the 3rd Infantry Division (Motorized.) The letter is to his wife; he writes:

"It is almost like summer here and it is a lovely day today. We are all wondering about it, but all day I was on guard duty. The ground looks terrible around here [north of Stalingrad.] I wonder how the men got out of this cauldron. They must have been very lucky. Well, I will tell you more about it in my next furlough.

It soon will be Christmas and I will celebrate this holy day here in my bunker. I have already found a small tree. But this time around, Christmas will not be a nice one.

Well, it does not matter much. I was asked when my last furlough was and I was told that it would now be a long time until I go.

Dear Ilse, have you heard from Bremen? I am glad to be out of there. I often worry about it anyway. I must close now and say good night."